American Public Policy

An Introduction

ELEVENTH EDITION

CLARKE E. COCHRAN
Texas Tech University (Emeritus)

LAWRENCE C. MAYER
Texas Tech University

T.R. CARR
Southern Illinois University at Edwardsville

N. JOSEPH CAYER
Arizona State University (Emeritus)

MARK J. McKENZIE
Texas Tech University

LAURA R. PECK
Abt Associates Inc.
Social and Economic Policy Division

CENGAGE
Learning·

Australia • Brazil • Japan • Korea • Mexico • Singapore • Spain • United Kingdom • United States

CENGAGE
Learning®

American Public Policy: An Introduction, Eleventh Edition
Clarke E. Cochran, Lawrence C. Mayer, T.R. Carr, N. Joseph Cayer, Mark J. McKenzie, and Laura R. Peck

Product Manager: Carolyn Merrill

Content Developer: Lauren Athmer, LEAP Publishing

Associate Content Developer: Jessica Wang

Product Assistant: Abigail Hess

Media Developer: Laura Hildebrand

IP Analyst: Alexandra Ricciardi

IP Project Manager: Sarah Shainwald

Manufacturing Planner: Fola Orekoya

Art and Design Direction, Production Management, and Composition: MPS Limited

Cover Designer: Lisa Buckley

Cover Image: Top: Justin Sullivan/ Staff/Getty Images News/Getty Images; Middle: JOHN GRESS/ Reuters/Corbis; Bottom: Tetra Images/Corbis

For product information and technology assistance, contact us at **Cengage Learning Customer & Sales Support, 1-800-354-9706.**

For permission to use material from this text or product, submit all requests online at **www.cengage.com/permissions**.

Further permissions questions can be e-mailed to **permissionrequest@cengage.com.**

Library of Congress Control Number: 2014946137

Student Edition:
ISBN: 978-1-285-86977-3

Cengage Learning
20 Channel Center Street
Boston, MA 02210
USA

Cengage Learning is a leading provider of customized learning solutions with office locations around the globe, including Singapore, the United Kingdom, Australia, Mexico, Brazil, and Japan. Locate your local office at **www.cengage.com/global**.

Cengage Learning products are represented in Canada by Nelson Education, Ltd.

To learn more about Cengage Learning Solutions, visit **www.cengage.com**.

Purchase any of our products at your local college store or at our preferred online store **www.cengagebrain.com**.

Instructors: Please visit **login.cengage.com** and log in to access instructor-specific resources.

Printed in the United States of America
Print Number: 01   Print Year: 2015

To
Anne
Etta
Lucy
Matt
Bob, Gret, Robbie, and Scarlett
Brad

JOHN GRESS/Reuters/Co

Brief Contents

Contents

Preface

American Public Policy is an introductory undergraduate text that focuses on the substantive issues of public policy. Most texts stress methods of policy analysis, models of policy, or the policymaking process. Although these topics are important, their dominance at the introductory level often makes the subject too abstract to engage students' imaginations. In our own teaching, we have found that an interest in more rigorous analysis grows most naturally out of a lively classroom discussion of specific policy debates—for example, welfare, abortion, tax reform, immigration, or crime control. *American Public Policy* is unique in its emphasis on such issues, combining history and description with presentation of alternative solutions.

This text is intended for the first undergraduate course in public policy, either a one-semester course or part of a two-semester sequence that includes both political institutions and public policy. We do not assume any prior knowledge of public policy on the student's part, although we do presume an understanding of the structure of American government. Therefore, we present the policy material step by step, building a picture of existing policy that students can use to evaluate alternatives.

APPROACHES TAKEN BY THIS BOOK

This text covers areas that are of permanent major interest and controversy. Though other issues occasionally rise to prominence, the issues we discuss— welfare, health, education, economic regulation, crime, immigration, foreign and defense policy—are issues of long-range interest and controversy.

Chapter Plan

The chapters that follow present the major policy issues in American politics. Each chapter (except Chapters 2 and 13) follows a similar pattern. This pattern assumes that students need to know the history of policies and the most fundamental facts about them before evaluation is possible. Also vital is an understanding of the ways the policies work (or do not work). Then it is possible to speculate intelligently about possible modifications that the future will present.

Issue Background. Each chapter discusses the basic issue, problem, or dilemma toward which public policy is directed, that is, the general background. Policies do not arise in a vacuum, as we have already noted, but, rather, grow in response to developments that the public, or some part of it, perceives as requiring government action.

Contemporary Policy. Each chapter describes the evolution of present public policies in their areas of concern. They sketch the major features of substantive public policies, as adopted and implemented. The principal goals and target populations intended by the policymakers are also outlined, and some of the political factors surrounding adoption are described. Although absolute neutrality and objectivity are impossible, we have tried to be as unbiased as possible.

Policy Evaluation. The third section of each chapter evaluates policy outputs and impacts empirically and normatively. Here our concern centers on the major successes and failures of policy in responding to the dilemmas specified. We focus on the ability of existing policies to reach their goals and to have maximum effect, and we discuss the main differences of opinion on the good and bad effects of the policies. Our level of analysis is the general shape of the policy and its alternatives, not the detailed cost–benefit or other evaluation analysis discussed previously.

Continuing Debates. Each chapter lists the major policy alternatives and their supporting arguments. Here again, we present different values, different definitions of the issue, and different predictions for policy options. The authors do not put forth their own proposals but, rather, attempt to help the reader make sense of the welter of policy proposals, statistics, and competing values. The arguments of conservatives, radicals, and liberals, as well as a variety of other interested parties, find their way into the following pages in order to illustrate the range of alternatives from which policy selections may be made.

Policy Dilemmas. This new feature is designed to offer students a chance to exercise their critical thinking skills. It provides a current event or recent policy action and asks students to analyze the benefits or concerns brought about by the issue at hand.

Summary. Each chapter discussion concludes with a brief summary of the most important topics that are addressed. This is designed to provide students with a concise recap and an understanding of underlying issues.

Resources. Finally, each chapter ends with a list of websites to assist study and reflection. To facilitate study and reference, a glossary of major terms and concepts from each chapter appears at the end of the book.

National Focus

Although the chapters on education and the section on intergovernmental relations discuss state and local government activity extensively, our attention is on the national arena, for the issues at stake on the state and local level, given the tremendous variation in their social, political, and economic climates, are less clear and less easily presented than those at the national level. Therefore, although state and local policies are obviously important, here they are discussed as they relate to national policies.

Comparative Information

Many chapters discuss comparable policies in other modern industrial nations. Noting international trends is essential to evaluate U.S. public policy properly.★ To discuss American health care policies as though they were the best possible policies would be like discussing American wine as though France and Germany grew no grapes. Moreover, issues of crime, employment, economic stagnation, immigration, social welfare spending, and cultural change have begun to affect other advanced nations in ways similar to those occurring in the American context. But the focus of this book is on *American* public policy.

We have made a variety of changes for the eleventh edition of *American Public Policy*. Having completed this edition in April 2014, we have tried to keep our text current with the issues most prominent in the political debate, particularly the dynamics leading up to the 2014 midterm election, without simply focusing on "current events." Some issues, such as the outcome of the challenge of the Iranian, Syrian, and Ukrainian crises, tax reform, immigration reform, and increased attention on global climate change, were not clear in their full effects at the time of writing. The chapter on crime considers the continued decline in crime rates and the reasons for them. Chapter 8 covers the major changes in health policy, especially the implementation of the 2010 Patient Protection and Affordable Care Act (PPACA). Immigration remains a topic of intense passions, which are covered in Chapter 11. Each chapter highlights, in **bold**, terms that appear in the Glossary.

We have also reduced the detail in the historical background of issues, thus shortening each chapter and leaving more room for current debates on issues. We hope these changes improve the readability of the book.

Chapter 1 introduces the study of public policy. Major policy concepts are defined, illustrated, and explained. Chapter 2 focuses on the contexts in which contemporary public policy operates—institutional, economic, demographic, cultural, and ideological. This chapter continues the structural introduction of Chapter 1. Each succeeding chapter examines an individual policy arena.

★See Richard Rose, *Lesson-Drawing in Public Policy: A Guide to Learning across Time and Space* (Chatham, NJ: Chatham House, 1993); and Arnold J. Heidenheimer, Hugh Heclo, and Carolyn Teich Adams, *Comparative Public Policy,* 3rd ed. (New York: St. Martin's Press, 1990).

Chapter 3 gives attention to economic theory, economic regulation, changes in the economy, and international competition, leaving the entirety of Chapter 4 for macroeconomic policy, including the federal budget, taxes, and spending. Chapter 5 deals with environmental and energy policy, highlighting the important interaction between these two policy areas.

Chapter 6 considers fluctuation in rates of crime, including speculation about the causes of crime. This chapter evaluates the impact of policies specifying an individual's constitutional rights: confessions and the right to counsel, the exclusionary rule and search and seizure, and capital punishment. It considers alternative methods of responding to crime, including gun control, capital punishment, and sentencing reform.

Chapter 7 looks at the bifurcated nature of social welfare policy by considering the definition of poverty and the evolution of the U.S. welfare state. This chapter examines the distinction between social insurance and social assistance and describes the various programs and policies that make up the U.S. system, concluding with an assessment of effectiveness and shortcomings.

Chapter 8 describes the nation's health care system at a crossroads. The rising cost of health care has been on an unsustainable trajectory. Access to care and the quality of care delivered have major gaps. The Affordable Care Act aimed to address these shortcomings, but became the subject of intense political controversy. This chapter addresses the Act and whether it will transform health care or whether the system will remain in crisis.

Chapter 9 shows the tradition of free public education in the United States to be in jeopardy. This chapter considers such problems as poor student achievement, teacher competence, inequities resulting from the system of local control, and the role of the federal government in education. The idea of equality, both legal and social, is discussed in Chapter 10. Programs of the 1960s and 1970s—those aimed at achieving equality in the schools and in employment—are now questioned seriously. Chapter 11 is then devoted to the issue of immigration and the challenges that the American government continues to face on the issue. Chapter 12 describes the challenges to American foreign policy. Chapter 13 focuses on issues involving strong moral content—abortion, freedom of speech and censorship, the right to die, the role of religion in society and politics, and feminism and family values.

American Public Policy may be used in a variety of ways. Instructors may choose to consider all of the policy areas presented or to select a group of them for special emphasis. Chapters 1 and 2 should be read first, but the rest of the chapters can be assigned in any sequence the instructor prefers. Supplementary readings focusing on particular issues may be conveniently added, or the text may be used in conjunction with other texts focusing on political institutions or the policy process. Cengage Learning also offers an Instructor's Manual with Test Bank (ISBN-13: 9781285869797) that provides suggestions for critical thinking questions, lecture launchers, in-class activities, and exam questions to make course preparation easier. Access the Instructor's Manual with Test Bank on the companion website at cengage.com/login.

We would like to thank the following reviewers for their helpful feedback on this edition: John Barkdull, Texas Tech University; William E. Carroll, Sam Houston State University; Patricia Freeman, University of Tennessee; and Mordu Serry-Kamal, Winston-Salem State University. Our thanks also go to the following instructors who reviewed earlier editions: Justin Halpern, Northeastern State University; Rebecca C. Hams, Washington and Lee University; Gary Klass, Illinois State University; John Lofton, Arkansas State University; Pachard Paley, Baylor University; Christine H. Rossell, Boston University; Timothy Sherratt, Gordon College; and Kim Spiezio, Cedar Crest College.

Matthew Young provided help on tables and figures. Carolyn Merrill of Cengage Learning provided invaluable editorial assistance and Lauren Athmer of LEAP Publishing Services, Inc. demonstrated immense patience and professionalism in working with our draft chapters, helping us to mold them into the finished products. Preeti Longia Sinha handled the copyediting efficiently. Romona Saunders of Arizona State University expertly authored this edition's Instructor's Manual with Test Bank. Our thanks to all of them.

We want to express particular appreciation to colleagues in the Political Science Department at Texas Tech who use the book and have been forthcoming with helpful comments that have helped us to improve the text. In particular, we thank John Barkdull, chair of the Undergraduate Committee and Greg R. Murray, a member of the committee. We also thank Dennis Patterson, department chair and Frank Thames, associate chair of the department. Kristina Mitchell, Lecturer, helped in the construction of the online course using the book.

Clarke E. Cochran
Lawrence C. Mayer
T.R. Carr
N. Joseph Cayer
Mark J. McKenzie
Laura R. Peck

About the Authors

Clarke E. Cochran retired as Vice-President of Mission Integration at Covenant Health System in Lubbock, Texas, in 2013. He is also Professor Emeritus of Political Science at Texas Tech University, where he specialized in religion and politics, political philosophy, and health care policy. Dr. Cochran received his Ph.D. from Duke University in 1971 and taught at Texas Tech from 1970 to 2007. He is the author of four books and numerous journal articles. Dr. Cochran held the position of Research Fellow in the Erasmus Institute at the University of Notre Dame (1998–1999) and the Shannon Chair in Catholic Studies at Nazareth College (Spring 2001). His research interests include religious institutions and health care policy, Catholic social theory and health care reform, and church and state controversies.

Lawrence C. Mayer is Professor of Political Science at Texas Tech University specializing in Comparative Politics and the Politics of Advanced Western Democracy. In addition to *American Public Policy: An Introduction,* he is the author of *Comparative Political Inquiry, The Politics of Industrial Societies, Redefining Comparative Politics: Promise versus Performance, Comparative Politics: Nations and Theories in a Changing World, Comparative Politics: The Quest for Theory and Explanation, Conflicting Perspectives in Comparative Politics: A Reader, Identity Politics: The Emergence of Neo Volkism in Advanced Western Societies,* and *The Changing Basis of Political Conflict in Advanced Western Democracy.* His current research is on the determinants of tolerance in Western societies.

T.R. Carr is Professor of Public Administration and Policy Analysis and Senior Research Fellow in the Institute for Urban Research at Southern Illinois University Edwardsville. He teaches primarily in the area of quantitative methods and policy analysis. In addition to *American Public Policy,* he has published chapters and articles focusing on public management issues. He is active in academic and professional associations and has served in numerous offices in state and local chapters of the American Society for Public Administration. He serves as a Police Commissioner for St. Louis County, Missouri, and has served as the Mayor of Hazelwood, Missouri.

N. Joseph Cayer is Professor Emeritus of Public Administration at Arizona State University. He received his Ph.D. from the University of Massachusetts, Amherst, and a B.A. and M.P.A. from the University of Colorado, Boulder. He also has taught at Lamar University, the University of Maine, Orono, and Texas Tech University. He is the author or coauthor of seven books and numerous chapters and articles on public management and policy, with an emphasis on issues of human resources management in the public sector. Books he has authored or coauthored include *Public Administration: Social Change and Adaptive Management, American Public Policy: An Introduction, Managing Human Resources, Handbook of Training and Development for the Public Sector,* and *Supervision for Success in Government.*

Mark J. McKenzie is an Associate Professor of Political Science at Texas Tech University. He specializes in judicial decision making (particularly in the areas of national security, crime, redistricting and electoral law), judicial campaigns and elections, and public opinion and the courts. Dr. McKenzie received his Ph.D. in government from the University of Texas at Austin in 2007 and a Doctor of Jurisprudence from the University of Texas School of Law in 1998. Between 1998 and 2001, he practiced general litigation in Texas at the law firm of Ross & Matthews He has published articles in such journals as Political Research Quarterly, Judicature, Justice System Journal, Politics & Policy, and American Politics Research.

Laura R. Peck is a Principal Scientist at Abt Associates and has over eighteen years of experience evaluating social welfare and employment policies and programs, both in research and academic settings. Prior to joining Abt in 2011, Dr. Peck had been a tenured Associate Professor at the Arizona State University School of Public Affairs, where she taught public policy analysis, program evaluation, and research methods; and served as Associate Dean for Barrett, The Honors College. At Abt Associates, Dr. Peck is the Principal Investigator, Co-PI and Director of Analysis for several major national evaluations for the U.S. Departments of Health and Human Services, Labor, Agriculture, and Housing and Urban Development. Dr. Peck is well published (and cited) on program evaluation topics in respected journals such as *Evaluation Review,* the *Journal of Policy Analysis and Management,* the *Policy Studies Journal,* and the *Journal of Poverty.* Dr. Peck was elected to the Policy Council (2012–2015 term) for the Association for Public Policy Analysis and Management (APPAM); and recently completed her term as Associate Editor (2009–2013) for the *American Journal of Evaluation.*

Chapter 1

Public Policy: An Introduction

Public policy affects each citizen in hundreds of ways, some of them familiar and some unsuspected. Citizens directly confront public policy when they are arrested for speeding, but they seldom remember that the advertising on the television shows that they watch is regulated by the Federal Communications Commission (FCC) and the Federal Trade Commission (FTC). Many citizens who complain loudly at tax time about government bureaucracy and overregulation have forgotten about the fire and police protection or the paved streets that those revenues provide. Indeed, public policy in America affects a vast range of activities, from nuclear warheads to bathroom plumbing, from arresting lawbreakers to providing medical care for the elderly. Indeed, the expanding reach of government and the threatened dominance of the public sector over the private sector with accompanying record budget deficits for the national government constituted a major political issue toward the end of the first year of the Obama administration. By the middle of President Obama's second term, America's debt totaled over $17 trillion. This book aims to clarify key dimensions of this ubiquitous influence on American life and to introduce the debates swirling around its major controversies. It takes an *issue-oriented approach* to the beginning study of public policy.

STUDYING PUBLIC POLICY

What Constitutes Public Policy?

Even though examples of public policy come readily to mind, defining public policy in clear and unambiguous terms is not easy. Political scientists have devoted considerable attention to the problem without reaching a consensus.[1] In this text, the term **public policy** refers to a set of actions taken by the government that includes, but is not limited to, making laws and is defined in terms of a common goal or purpose. For example, a policy to stimulate economic growth in a time of economic stagnation may include tax cuts for businesses, increased spending to put money into the economy, or actions by the Federal Reserve System to increase the money supply. A policy to secure the country from possible terrorist attacks may include a law, such as the USA Patriot Act, which enables the government to listen to the phone conversations of potential terrorists; an invasion of putative terrorist strongholds in Iraq and Afghanistan; encouraging dissidents in Iran to effect regime change; searching prospective passengers boarding airplanes; or assassinating known terrorist leaders with "drone strikes." Making policy requires choosing among goals and alternatives, and choice always involves intention. The federal government under President Obama, for example, chose to pursue a wholesale restructuring of our system of delivering health care. The intention was to have everyone insured, including the 15 percent or so who were not already, or chose not to be, insured. Policy is not a single action, but is a set of actions coordinated to achieve a goal. Such an action may be manifested in laws, public statements, official regulations, or widely accepted and publicly visible patterns of behavior, such as the vigorous implementation of existing laws to control and deter crime, or having the Environmental Protection Agency (EPA) issue bureaucratic regulations. Public policy, however, is ultimately rooted in law and in the authority and coercion associated with law. (The terms *public policy* and *policy* will be used interchangeably.)

Three qualifications are necessary, however, for this definition of public policy. First, the idea of an intentional course of action also includes decisions made *not* to take a certain action. In 2013, for example, some leading members of the Republican Party sought unsuccessfully to stop Congress from funding the Affordable Care Act (ACA). Second, the requirement that official actions be sanctioned by law or accepted custom is necessary because public officials often take courses of action that step outside of public policy—for example, they sometimes take bribes or exceed their legal authority. Such deeds should not be considered public policy—that is, unless they are openly tolerated in a particular political system. Third, laws or official regulations should not be mistaken for the whole realm of policy; nor does policy always meet intended goals. Lawmaking is not enough to establish a policy; the **implementation**, interpretation, enforcement, and impact of policies are also part of the policymaking process. Moreover, as we shall see later in this chapter, quite often there are **unintended impacts** to public policies. What actually happens when policy is put into effect (or *implemented*) is called policy impact. Although some political scientists argue that these unintended impacts are part of the policy, we believe that it is conceptually clearer to consider policy and its impacts separately. For example, a major issue erupted in November 2013 when millions of Americans lost the health plans that they could afford and that served their needs because the Obama administration sought to impose higher standards for what should be covered in health insurance plans. This issue raised the question of whether the government was over-reaching the limits of what could be effectively shaped through public policy. Next, we shall consider the strategies and factors that make it more or less likely that the impact of a policy will be what the policymakers intended.

Why Study Public Policy?

Students of political science and public administration have several reasons for studying public policy. The first is *theoretical*: Political scientists seek to understand and explain the world of politics—that is, they attempt to develop and test explanatory generalizations about the political behavior of individuals and institutions. Because public policy is a part of politics, political scientists are concerned with how it is related to such things as political party structure, interest groups, interparty competition, electoral systems, and executive-legislative relations. Political scientists who seek explanation call for the discipline to develop and test explanatory theory.[2]

A second reason for studying public policy is *practical*. Political scientists and students of policy apply knowledge to solve practical problems. Public policy has become increasingly pervasive over time as measured by such data as the percent of the **gross domestic product (GDP)**, which is the value of all the goods and services produced in the United States in a year and spent by the federal government. This figure has risen from about five percent at the turn of the century to about a quarter of the GDP in 2010. With the heavy indebtedness and an expensive health care bill passed at the end of the first year of the Obama administration, the percent of the gross domestic product in the public sector reached 40 percent by 2012 as government assumed the responsibility and power to "transform" much of the American political and economic system; hence, citizens are continually confronted with impact of public policy on their lives and well-being.

A third reason for studying public policy, related to the second, is *political*. Debate and controversy over public policy in America are not new, but today the range of issues over which serious disagreement occurs is far greater than in the past. This is due in large part to the spread of education, which is strongly related to political involvement and to the mobilization of the population through the mass media. Participation in, and awareness of, government and its policies are greater than any time in our history. The **Tea Party** movement of 2010 exemplifies the extent to which more people are involved with politics and policy than ever before. It makes sense to channel this new mobilization of the population into paths guided by understanding and information.

The emphasis of this book is on the second and third reasons for studying policy—the practical and political—but it draws on the first as well, for intelligent policy selection depends on the analysis and understanding developed by the theoretical findings of political science.

Reasons for the Growing Pervasiveness of Public Policy

The growing pervasiveness of public policy is primarily a consequence of modernization. Modernization entails the development of technology and knowledge and the consequent role specialization and division of labor. This makes us all interdependent. The pioneer could erect a log cabin without outside assistance, but the erection of a modern dwelling requires the expertise of a cement contractor, a carpenter, an electrician, a plumber, a bricklayer, a roofer, etc. We can rely on the competence and performance of these tradespeople, whose work we are not qualified to judge, because they are given their credentials by an agency of the state. We are usually even more unqualified to independently judge the work of professionals such as physicians or attorneys. Whenever new technology is developed, we need a new agency to regulate it.

Modernization requires the concentration of a workforce that was not needed in an agrarian society. This means an urbanization of modern society, with its concomitant issues of traffic, public health and sanitation, sewage and garbage disposal, crime, and the myriad ways in which the choices that people make affect others in patterns of close interaction.

This expansion of the role of public policy is frustrating to many because each new regulation emanating from a government agency circumscribes our freedom to some extent. The needs and desires of each person must be balanced against the needs and desires of others with whom one interacts. Hence, government treats people according to impersonal principles and rules that may offend one's sense of justice for one particular case.

Because of this frustration with an expanding public sector, many people feel that government has become too big and too intrusive. The Tea Party movement mobilizing large numbers of ordinary people in demonstrations against big government (which they saw as allegedly out of touch with ordinary folk) exemplifies this frustration. Some people yearn for a return to the seemingly simpler times of the good old days. Yet, in many ways "the good old days" were not so good. Life tended to be shorter and less comfortable and convenient. Opportunities for travel and communication were significantly fewer. To return to an era of a much smaller public sector, we would have to "un-invent" much of the technology that has made life longer and more enjoyable.

Policy Impact: The Frequent Failure
of Public Policies to Achieve Their Goals

Americans are by and large an optimistic people who tend to believe that for every identified problem there must be a solution if we simply have the will to find it. Yet despite the growing pervasiveness and expansion of government, the actual impact of policies is all too frequently not what those who formulated the policy intended. This frequent failure of policies to achieve their intended impact is due to the following factors.

First, there is disagreement about the issues of society and what constitutes a social or political problem that must be addressed by policymakers. One of the core issues dividing the social and political Left from the Right regards the imperatives of social justice. In December 2013, President Obama proclaimed that income inequality was the defining issue of our time. Does the fact that some people have a great deal more than others, either through inheritance, hard work, creativity, or just luck, constitute a problem that must be rectified? What are one's entitlements in one's society? The subprime lending crisis of 2009–2010 was a result of elevating home ownership to an entitlement. Does social justice require that we "spread the wealth" around?

Second, for some issues there is no plausible scenario on which the contending parties conceivably agree. For example, the attempts to engineer a two-state solution to the tensions in the Middle East between the Israelis and the Palestinian Arabs have resulted in failure despite continued efforts for over sixty years. The conflict is not about borders or what lands will be set aside for Palestinian statehood. The Arab leaders were formally offered such a state on five separate occasions (see Chapter 12 for details) and they eschewed the offer each time. Clearly, their ultimate goal is not just statehood. Many Arab leaders have reiterated over and over that they will never accept the existence of Israel as a Jewish state. Obviously, one's extermination is not a scenario to which one will ever agree as a result of negotiation. Hence, no plausible resolution to the conflict exists to which both parties might possibly agree. Similarly, the odds seem strongly against the achievement of an agreement with Iran in the 2013–2014 global discussions regarding the nation's nuclear ambitions. Critics suggest that one would have to stretch beyond the limits of credulity to believe that Iran would settle for less than a deliverable nuclear warhead, an outcome that the Saudis and Israelis would never accept.

Third, a solution that is socially acceptable may simply not exist for a problem. Assume, for example, that society agrees that greater socioeconomic equality must be engineered. One should then address the causes of such inequality. The strongest predictor of one's ultimate socioeconomic well-being is academic achievement. Each step up the academic ladder brings significantly greater lifetime earnings, regardless of one's academic specialty. One should therefore engineer greater equality of academic achievement, as with President George W. Bush's policy of "no child left behind." This policy assumes that everyone is educable. President Obama's "Race to the Top" initiative offers incentives to states willing to spur systemic reform to improve teaching and learning in America's schools. An important massive study of the causes of educational achievement, the *Coleman Report*, found that the best single predictor of educational achievement is the academic achievement level of one's parents.[3] Thus, to best engineer equality of educational achievement, the state would have to specify that only educated people would be allowed to reproduce. Obviously, no reasonably free society is going to specify who can or cannot have children. Hence, the solution to our hypothetical problem may theoretically exist, but would be socially unacceptable.

Fourth, fall 2013 brought another lesson on the limits of government's ability to effectively regulate and control large segments of a complex modern society with the attempt to implement President Obama's signature health care system, the ACA. (See Chapter 8 for a more detailed discussion.) While at the time of this writing the final outcome of the Act has yet to be observed, some serious problems in the projected structure and operation of the system have already appeared. Despite the individual mandate backed by a fine, there is a shortfall in the number of young and healthy people joining and paying into the system, which is needed in order to meet the greater health care needs of the older generation. Because of the extensive requirements for coverage, many existing health care policies were deemed unacceptable to the ACA, causing millions of existing policies that served the needs of their beneficiaries to be canceled, which forced these people to try to purchase more extensive policies that they could not afford. Third, there was a failure to clearly calculate the amount of the subsidies to be paid to insurance companies for insuring low-income citizens trying to become insured. This left the insurance companies with the task of determining their own compensation. These structural problems, combined with failures in setting up functioning websites, have caused great concern and hesitation among citizens and officials alike. The authors of the ACA did not take into account the diminishing supply of health care providers in the face of increasing demands for health care. The problems facing the ACA demonstrate the limited capacity of the government. It is unable to take account of, and to predict, the myriad of factors, as well as the interaction among those factors, that make up the complex American health care system. In an attempt to regulate such a large and complex segment of our economy, it must be assumed that a large number of factors will operate according to plan. The failure of any one of these factors will prevent the realization of the desired outcome. The struggle to implement the ACA epitomizes the principle that unnecessary complexity in the implementation of policy increases the likelihood of the failure of the policy.

Fifth, policies are usually ambiguous enough to permit various interpretations of them. The more actors involved in the process of implementation, the more that the original intended meaning of the law or policy will be distorted. In this technologically advanced society, lawmakers are frequently generalists. As an example, consider the lawyers or business people who lack the technical expertise to determine how much of which emissions could be allowed to protect air quality. They set up the EPA to make those rules. Appointed bureaucrats, selected according to the standard of specialization and division of labor, are more likely to have such expertise. Accordingly, the politically accountable parts of the government—Congress and the presidency—pass general authorizations to some agencies to actually make the specific decisions about who gets how much of what, where, and why.

The attributes of the administrative sector that make it effective in implementing policy are undesirable attributes for policymaking. The attributes of the civil service or public bureaucracy are a hierarchical structure; specialization and the division of labor; an elaborate set of impersonal rules, which enhance predictability but stifle creativity and adaptability; and tenure of office, which insulates the bureaucrats from the public. Moreover, the discretion that bureaucrats inevitably have in interpreting the law means that the intent of the original policymakers will likely be changed in the implementation process.

POLICY DILEMMAS   The Ongoing Issue of the Role of Government

---

Throughout the second term of the Obama presidency, the approval ratings for both the president and Congress plummeted to almost historic lows, indicating a growing impatience with these institutions on the part of the citizenry. This impatience grows from a perception of failure to resolve major issues that have been plaguing the United States for years—issues that include long drawn-out wars, a persisting stagnant economy, a massive national debt, soaring costs for health care and insurance despite a new health care bill, and the perception of government cover-ups of serious malfeasance. The public does not appreciate the complexity of these kinds of issues and the array of factors that must be taken into account in addressing them.

The difficulty in constructing solutions to these issues is compounded by the fact that we live in a free society in which many of the factors affecting these issues are beyond the reach of government. This book will address this complexity and the extent to which government should be held responsible for finding solutions to these issues.

1. What can government do to increase the chances for a policy to reach its objectives?

2. What principles can help government to decide what issues ought to be addressed at what level in the public sector and what issues should best be left to the private sector?

DEFINING MAJOR CONCEPTS

People acquire interests out of the roles that they play in the social and economic system. These interests often come into conflict. For example, what is good for the blue-collar working class may not be good for the entrepreneurs who employ them. The interests of people who live in one geographical setting may conflict with the interests of people in another setting. The point is that the distinction between "the special interests" and the good of "the people" is a false one. All interests are special because no one can rise completely above his or her socioeconomic role to promote the "general interests."

Because interests conflict, policies that benefit some will harm or impede others. This idea that because the resources of society are finite, that one cannot allocate values to some groups without taking them from others, is known as a **zero–sum society**. Hence, it seems laudable to place members of underrepresented groups in desired roles that they otherwise would not have attained, such as admission to medical school or a place in corporate management. For each individual so placed, however, another individual who otherwise would have attained the coveted role is excluded. Thus, in a zero–sum society, the allocation of values to members of one underrepresented group requires that members of other groups will have to pay the costs. This of course increases the intensity of partisanship.

Some values, such as clean, unpolluted air, are at first glance good for everyone. These are known as **public goods**. These are values that are shared by everyone concerned. They cannot be allocated according to some criterion of merit or justice. But the costs of such values are not equally shared. The owner of a factory who cleans up the factory's emissions at a considerable cost has paid a disproportionate share of the costs of the clean air. He or she does not, however, get a disproportionate amount of that air to breathe. It would therefore be rational for that factory owner to not clean up the emissions.

Private rationality, when pursued by all the members of a collectivity, can lead to disaster for that collectivity. California, for example, requires that each motor vehicle have a catalytic converter attached to the exhaust system. When most people began to obey that requirement, the air quality over the state's cities greatly improved. The converter lowers the performance of the vehicle, however, and increases its fuel consumption. It would therefore be rational for any one motorist to have the device removed. If everyone did that, however, the cities would again be enveloped in smog. This is a case when private rationality conflicts with public necessity. In such cases, government may step in to coerce people to violate private rationality for the public good.

Private goods are the opposite. These are goods that can be divided and given to some persons, but not others. Most distribution and redistribution policies fall into this classification. Some persons qualify for food stamps while others do not. Some students qualify for admission to a selective state university while others may be admitted to second-tier colleges or to junior colleges. Liberals, conservatives, and other ideological groups strongly disagree about the range of private goods that is appropriate for government to distribute.

Models of the Policy Process

Making public policy is extraordinarily complex. It involves public opinion, media attitudes, expert ideas, active citizens, business and labor leaders, elected representatives, presidents and governors, judges, and bureaucrats. Policymaking calls on political resources, economic conditions, popular cultural attitudes, and international conditions. When political scientists do research in an attempt to understand public policy, they try to reduce the complexity of the policymaking process to a manageable degree by creating **models of policymaking** that summarize the primary forces at work. None of these models is complete and none captures all of the relationships that are important. It is indeed the purpose of such models to simplify aspects of the reality they represent. No one model best describes the features of policymaking in every area. Although the chapters that follow do not adhere strictly to any of these models, they draw upon the primary qualities of some political science models.

Features of the **institutional model** appear in the description of the institutional context of public policy in Chapter 2. This model stresses the opportunities and constraints on policy that are part of the very structure of the American constitutional order: judiciary, bureaucracy, executives, legislatures, separation of powers, federalism, and so forth. A variant of the institutional model is **historical institutionalism**, which combines the institutional focus with the effect of long-term patterns of development. Here there is recognition that early policy decisions carry large effects through time, so that policies become **path dependent**. The cost of changing policy direction increases over time. Once, for example, a state legislature takes a get-tough approach to crime by building more prisons, these very prisons become institutional forces that prevent different approaches in the future. What would the state do with empty prisons if it decided on a different approach?[4]

The **elite model** focuses on the influence over policy exercised by powerful individuals or groups to maximize their own interests at the expense of competing groups. Scholars who claim this model describes American society paint a scenario in which the country is controlled by a single coherent elite sharing a distinct set of values.[5] Members of this elite possess similar attributes (white, male, and mostly Protestant), come from the same background (prestigious prep school, Ivy League university), and move from one leadership role to another (from corporate boards of directors, to academia at our most prestigious universities, to the highest ranks in the military).

This model contrasts with the **pluralist model**, which stresses that many elites with competing interests bargain with one another to affect policy. Generally no one group gets all of what it wants. Hence, policy is an impersonal outcome of the bargaining process. Each of these group's interests and ideas must be taken into account. Both of these models picture these individuals and groups being active and influential across many policy areas. The **group** or **subgovernment model** recognizes that different policy areas, such as crime, must be treated differently than social or economic policy. Legislators, bureaucrats, experts, and interest groups that are active in one area are often quite different from those active in a different policy arena. These groups form advocacy coalitions that are active in particular policy areas, but not in others. Under these conditions, policy networks develop webs of lobbyists, committee staff members, and policy administrators all deeply involved in a particular policy domain, but not active in other policy areas.

Some political scientists model policy as a rational process. Policymakers in the **rational-comprehensive model** take account of all information about the policy problems and of all policy options, then select the options that best fulfill the policymaker's goals. This model assumes rationality and perfect information about choices available and their impact. The **public choice model** thinks of those active in policymaking as actors attempting to choose options that maximize their self-interest. They select policy options that help them realize their interests. Game models are a variation of this idea, focused on situations of policy choice with options that cannot be compromised.[6]

Policy Analysis

Policy analysis is principally concerned with describing and investigating how and why particular policies are proposed, adopted, and implemented. This is the theoretical side of policy studies. A policy option must be evaluated in light of what policy analysis reveals about its chances of being adopted, the probable effectiveness or impact of the option, and the difficulties of implementation.

A proposal for increased spending for high school education, for example, would need to be tested against data from the *Coleman Report*, which concluded that increased spending had no significant impact on student achievement levels.

Policy analysis is not, however, value neutral. Policy analysts want to discover which policy proposals best fulfill important public values.[7] Thus, policy analysis invokes such principles as freedom, equality, justice, decency, and peace. Indeed, politics often concerns debates about the very meaning of these terms. Those who would sharply separate policy analysis from fundamental social values make a grave mistake. Policy analysis without awareness of ethical perspectives is incomplete. This is particularly true when evaluating the impact of policy. Ethical principles must be brought to bear on the discovery of the good and bad effects of policy. Such principles not only measure success and failure. They also provide insight into consequences that otherwise would not be revealed.

Policy analysis carried out by political scientists can be distinguished from **policy advocacy** by politicians, partisans, or interest groups. Advocacy differs from analysis, because advocacy begins with a commitment to economic interests or to principles as interpreted by specific ideological systems, such as liberalism, conservatism, and environmentalism. Analysis should better equip policymakers to make policy choices while advocacy attempts to impose such choices on others. Nevertheless, both advocacy and analysis draw upon similar principles and goals, and the two intertwine in the real world of politics. Although ideological commitments can bring important overlooked values to policy analysis, policy advocates are more concerned to advance their ideology than to understand the policy process, which is the goal of policy analysis. The following chapters will discuss different ideological perspectives on policy at some length because the policy debates are often framed by ideology.

Stages of Policy Development

Political scientists often use a model of the policymaking process that focuses on the stages through which ideas and proposals move before becoming public policy. Some political scientists criticize these models as overly rigid. They argue that politics does not follow the clear lines and divisions of the stages model. Windows of opportunity for policy creativity open many times in unexpected ways, so that policy entrepreneurs have to be ready at any time to jump or to move through stages of the process rapidly. Multiple streams of policy proposals and political forces can converge and overwhelm careful policy deliberation.[8] Moreover, these models have not generated important theoretical insights into policymaking.[9] Despite the importance of such criticisms, the stages model is a suggestive tool. It isolates various aspects of public policy and helps to focus attention on them. Some of these aspects are widely recognized and need to be part of any introduction to public policy.[10] Different scholars label the stages differently and place different emphasis on them, but the terms in Figure 1.1 are common.

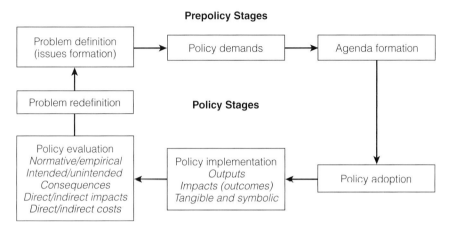

FIGURE 1.1 Stages of the Policy Process

SOURCE: American Public Policy: An Introduction 9e; Cengage Learning © 2009.

The development of a public policy begins with a public belief that a problem exists. The three prepolicy stages are (1) problem definition or issues formation, (2) policy demands, and (3) agenda formation. Before a policy issue is defined or adopted, a problem of public concern must be perceived. For example, in the health care debate that dominated politics in the fall of 2013, one of the points at issue was whether it was a violation of social justice that 15 percent of our population of some 300 million did not have health insurance. The economic crisis of 2008 was brought about in part by elevating home ownership to an entitlement under the imperatives of social justice. Reasonable people disagreed on these questions. Thus, ethical and ideological perspectives play an important role during this problem perception stage because different perspectives will see and define problems differently. Due to the contrasting opinions of different groups, different formulations of the issue will result. Similarly, people with different values disagree as to whether socioeconomic inequality violates the concept of social justice and is therefore a problem that must be rectified.

Thus, the issues formation stage leads to the next stage: policy demands. Opposing demands are now made for government action. Gradually, a social give-and-take may coalesce into a perception that policymakers must deal with a given problem, and it competes with other problems for the attention of policymakers. Some problems fail to sustain attention in this competition while others rise to prominence. Various demands and perspectives create an agenda of alternative proposals for dealing with an issue. Some proposals and demands never make it to the agenda, while others are put on the agenda in altered form.

Agenda setting is always a political process—groups struggle for power to control the agenda. Because all legislative and executive bodies are limited in the issues that they can address at any given time, the power to have attention paid to "your" issue on the agenda is invaluable. Therefore, ideological and interest groups compete to broaden the agenda to include their issues or to narrow it by excluding issues that they do not want considered. Such groups may be elected officials, bureaucrats responsible for policy administration, public interest groups, or groups directly affected by particular policies. The following chapters call attention to groups active in the problem definition, policy demand, and agenda formation stages.

Following the prepolicy stages, the next major stage in the development of a public policy is deliberation and **policy adoption**. From the policy agenda, decision makers, with the input of interest groups, policy experts, and constituents, debate and bargain over alternative policy formulations, settling on an alternative or a combination of alternatives to respond to the problem. Decisions are made, policies are formulated, and policy statements are issued, taking such forms as orders, regulations, or laws. Clearly, the same kinds of considerations of power as in the policy agenda stage are relevant here. Also important is the constitutional and statutory structure of the institution that makes the policy decision. Structure often determines which outcomes have a greater chance of success in the political struggle.

Policy statements and lawmaking are not the whole of policymaking. Policy decisions must be implemented—a concept defined earlier in the chapter as putting the policy into effect. Policy implementation means money spent, laws enforced, employees hired, and plans of action formulated. A law against theft would hardly be a policy if no public resources were devoted to preventing thefts and apprehending thieves. In implementation, the intent of the policymakers is often distorted. Even programs involving little conflict can be difficult to implement if there are numerous participants with differing perspectives and if many particular decisions have to be made before the policy is fully implemented.[11] As noted previously, the more complex the implementation process, the more likely that the intent of the policy will become distorted or lost. With increased complexity there are more actors who may not necessarily share the original goals. Successful achievement of policy goals depends upon the tractability of the problem being addressed by the policy; that is, how possible it really is to make a change. Implementation also depends on the clarity of the law, the talents and financial resources available to those administering it, and a variety of political factors, such as public support, media attention, socioeconomic conditions, and the attitudes and resources of groups affected by the policy.[12]

Policy implementation produces impact. Policy impact, it will be recalled, refers to what actually happens when the policy is implemented. The impact of a policy may be unforeseen, as in the case of busing for racially balanced schools. Whites were usually able to avoid having their children being bused with blacks by moving to the suburbs, which often meant a different school district. This "white flight" left the cities and their schools more racially unbalanced than before busing.

Policy impact is a major component of the evaluation of public policy, which is an important focus of this text. Policy evaluation focuses principally on the impact of policy, because it is largely from the performance and consequences of policy that we assess its success or failure. This is the question of impact. Evaluation attempts to assess the outcomes of policies (the effects on society) in order to compare the outcomes with the policies' intended goals while balancing the actual benefits of a policy with its cost. It asks whether the goals have or have not been met, with what costs, and with what unintended consequences. For example, policy evaluation asks whether the welfare reforms legislated in 1996 did in fact reduce poverty, increase work, or improve the lives of low-income persons. With regard to the war in Iraq, it was not enough to show that we would be better off with a pro-Western government in that country. The question was whether that benefit was worth the cost of life and money that it would require to achieve it. A policy can be evaluated only after those benefits and costs are known. Moreover, evaluation leads back to issue formation and policy deliberation in a (nearly) endless loop. Evaluations of policy inevitably produce advocates for change and other advocates for maintaining the policy as has clearly been the case of implementing the ACA in 2013. The social problems that stimulate policy responses can seldom be completely fixed. "Policy is more like an endless game of Monopoly than a bicycle repair."[13]

Aspects of Policy Evaluation

Policy evaluation involves collecting and analyzing information about the efficiency and effectiveness of policies. The purpose is to determine whether goals of policy have been achieved and to improve policy performance. Evaluating policy has both normative and empirical dimensions. The **normative dimension** refers to values, beliefs, and attitudes of society as a whole, of particular groups and individuals in society, and of the policy evaluators themselves. Persons of different values and ideologies use different normative concepts to evaluate policy. For example, if one can assume that the right to produce and publish material with strong sexual content leads to greater sexual promiscuity, then that would be a cost for social conservatives. It may be less of a problem, however, for social liberals. Evaluation, therefore, is always political. Progressives, conservatives, socialists, feminists, and anarchists differ fundamentally in their understanding of such concepts and in their ranking of them. Conservatives, for example, believe that free competition and protection of private property are fundamental values to be pursued by economic policy. Socialists, however, see just distribution of the social product as the principal value. Different policy evaluators and different political groups will evaluate public policy differently. Normative perspectives come into play, not only in assessing the goals of policy but also in analyzing how well policy accomplishes the desired goals.

Normative evaluation, however, is not enough. The **empirical dimension**—that is, understanding the facts—must precede judgment. Before praising or damning the Supreme Court's freedom-of-the-press decisions, one must examine the actual decisions and attempt to assess what difference, if any, they have made or are likely to make in the day-to-day operations of the press. And before criticizing welfare fraud, one should obtain the most accurate statistics available on money lost through fraudulent claims. Policy evaluation without empirical analysis of policy content, output, and impact is like voting for a baseball all-star team without information on players' batting, earned-run, or fielding averages.

Specifically, policy evaluation is used to:

1. determine which goals are being met and to what degree (including unintended consequences).
2. identify reasons for success and failure.
3. allocate (or reallocate) resources.
4. make changes to improve policies or decide to end policies that are not working.

Through these efforts, policymakers can make sure that policies accomplish what they are intended to and are responsive to the public and elected leaders. Table 1.1 suggests the multiple factors involved in a public policy. Complex social problems, such as crime, the economy, health care, and foreign policy, have multiple dimensions requiring multiple approaches. The various dimensions and the many policy initiatives required to address them mean that major public problems will never have single policy solutions. There is no "one policy fits all" for responding to terrorism, for example. Border security, electronic and human intelligence, military action, disaster preparedness, and many other initiatives are required. This also means that any major policy issue requires choices and trade-offs. There are limited resources of time, money, and attention. Spending more on border security may leave less money for intelligence gathering, not to mention less for education or crime policy. Profiling more likely perpetrators of terrorist activities may more efficiently allocate antiterrorist resources, at the cost of offending innocent members of the profiled group. As suggested by the concept of the zero-sum society discussed above, scarce resources demand, in turn, careful policy evaluation to make sure that assets are being used most effectively.

Policy evaluation may be required by the legislation creating the policy or by more general legislation, such as **sunset laws**. These are statutes that require each program to be terminated at some specific time (five or ten years, for example), unless an evaluation leads to a decision to continue it. Administrative rules or executive orders also may require evaluation. Most grant-in-aid programs also include a requirement that the program being funded be evaluated. The evaluation determines whether the program should continue or what improvements should be made in it. Public administrators are responsible for **performance management**, the ongoing review of accomplishments and problems. Evaluation goes beyond performance management reviews and involves a systematic process of data collection and analysis of a program's goal achievement over a particular period of time. This text cannot accomplish the detailed **program evaluation** described here for the policies it discusses. Its evaluation is at a higher level of generality. The same considerations and concepts, however, apply to this evaluation of general policies (such as Medicare or criminal justice policy) as to specific programs.

Evaluations may be process (often called formative) or outcome (often called summative) evaluations. **Process evaluation** assesses the activities and structures

T A B L E 1.1   Concepts in Policy Analysis

Concept	Definition	Illustration
Implementation	Steps taken to put a policy into practice	Hiring police; building prisons
Outputs	Measurable results of policy adoption and implementation	Numbers of police; conviction rates
Impacts (outcomes)	Actual effects that policy outputs have on society	Crime rates; feelings of safety and security
Direct	A policy's impact on its intended population	Impact on criminals or potential criminals
Indirect (externalities)	Policy's impact on individuals and groups other than intended population	Impact on families of persons in prison
Intended	Consequences anticipated by a policy or program	Higher arrest and conviction rates
Unintended	Consequences not anticipated by a policy or program	Greater public assistance usage by prisoners' families
Short-term	Outcomes evaluated shortly after policy is implemented	Changes in crime rate during the year after a policy change
Long-term	Outcomes evaluated after policy has been in place for a longer time	Changes in crime rate over 10 years
Policy evaluation	Process of assessing impacts of a policy	Assessment of effectiveness of a program intended to reduce crime rate
Empirical dimension	Evaluation by policy's measurable outputs and outcomes	Crime statistics; prison statistics; conviction rates
Normative dimension	Evaluation by policy's effect on values, beliefs, and attitudes	Effect of policy on freedom, justice, security, and family stability
Cost–benefit analysis	Compares benefits of a program with costs of implementing it	Money spent; crime rate reduction
Direct	Costs and benefits from allocation of resources and impact on other than intended population	Prison costs; recidivism rate of persons released from prison
Indirect (externalities)	Costs and benefits from allocation of resources and impact on other than intended population	Economic prosperity in communities housing new prisons; public assistance costs

of the policy implementation. The processes may include, for example, whether a community policing program follows procedure, how many police are assigned to the program, or what kind of patrol is practiced. **Outcome evaluations** focus on the impact of the policy or program. Thus, outcome evaluation of a community policing policy would examine whether there was an impact on crime in the neighborhood, such as reduction in burglaries or muggings. Both forms of evaluation are necessary for a complete assessment of the policy.[14] It would not make much sense, for example, to know that community policing was not working, but not know why. Thus, it would be important to know that it is not working (outcome) and what processes led to the failure so that the processes can be corrected.

In order to conduct an evaluation, it is necessary to plan ahead. As in writing a research paper, it goes much smoother if a plan is developed in advance. It is therefore necessary to decide what purpose the evaluation serves. Is it to focus on process or outcome? What is the goal of the policy or program? What does the evaluation need to determine? What assumptions are being used? How much money, time, and people resources are available for the evaluation? What indicators or measures are going to be used? How will the information be collected? How will unexpected circumstances be handled? What is the schedule for completion? What use will be made of the results? These essential questions need to be thought through before beginning the evaluation. Once they have been addressed, the evaluator needs to decide on the evaluation method or tool to use.

Cost-benefit analysis compares the benefits or outcomes of the program with the costs of implementing it. The benefits and costs may be stated in dollar terms, allowing for determining how much the outcomes cost. While on the surface, it may seem easy to determine costs and benefits, it is much more complicated. **Direct costs and benefits** may be easy to determine. **Indirect costs and benefits**, however, are another matter.

Direct costs and benefits relate to the specific allocation of resources and the impact on the intended population. A plan to develop a light rail system in an urban area presumably would be designed to improve commuting. It might also have the goals of reducing pollution and decreasing the need for roads and highways. The amount of money spent on the system and the disruption caused to residents and businesses along the route are direct costs. Indirect costs might include the loss of business to areas not served by the light rail line and the increase in time needed for delivery of goods to businesses along the lines because of more limited access. The increase in the value of property along the route may be an indirect benefit to owners of the property but a negative, indirect impact on those who rent the property. These indirect costs and benefits are also called **externalities**, or spillover effects. So, in evaluating a program or policy, it is necessary to consider all the costs and benefits, not just the obvious direct costs and benefits.

Policies also have long-term effects and short-term impacts. Both need to be considered in evaluation. Similarly, some policies have symbolic importance. The decision to build a new football stadium for a professional team may have great symbolic importance to the residents of a city. The stadium project may have been justified in part on the basis of making a world-class city and would be an intended **symbolic benefit**. Unintended and long-term costs can be illustrated by the Iraq War. With one out of six soldiers who served in Iraq suffering some degree of post-traumatic stress disorder or major health problem, likely long-term increases in health care costs, drug abuse, family violence, suicide, mental illness, and crime must be considered long-term costs.

Costs and benefits of some programs are difficult to measure. How do we measure the benefit of public goods, such as clean air? Businesses may want to measure it in one way: the cost to them. This would include such things as the cost of clean-burning fuel, such as natural gas instead of coal. Clean air advocates, however, may want to measure it in terms of the incidence of medical problems in the communities affected by the quality of the air near a manufacturing plant. Still others may focus on the aesthetics of the community and the presence or absence of a brown cloud over the area. The Obama administration has been strongly influenced by public sector unions. The powerful environmental lobby has been influential in keeping President Obama from authorizing the construction of the Keystone oil pipeline from Canada to Gulf refineries despite the likely creation of thousands of private sector jobs. Similarly, debates over whether to facilitate embryonic stem cell research or to make a morning-after birth control pill available over the counter illustrate the interweaving of political reasons with scientific data in the adoption and evaluation of policies.

Program evaluation is conducted by various agencies or officials. At the national level, the Government Accountability Office (GAO) conducts evaluation of federal government programs, usually at the request of members of Congress, as it is an agency of Congress. GAO may initiate evaluations on its own, and many of the evaluations required in the legislation setting up programs are its responsibility. The Congressional Budget Office (CBO) and Congressional Research Office (CRO) also conduct many evaluations. Most states have an auditing agency responsible for evaluation, or have legislative committees with such responsibilities. Local governments use a variety of similar agencies. Governments often also contract with independent contractors to conduct evaluations. The result of all of them is the evaluation report. It then is the responsibility of managers and policymakers to make effective use of the evaluations. Politics affects how they do so.

Policies do not go on forever (though some appear to). Policies change over time. For example, welfare policy changed fundamentally in the 1990s. Policies sometimes are terminated. Their reason for being passes, and legislatures end them, although it is far easier to create or adopt policies than to end them. More interests clearly benefit from a policy than are directly harmed by it, as the costs of a policy are usually spread over a number of segments of society. It is easier to grant benefits than to remove them; hence, the inexorable growth in the size and scope of government continues. The processes involved in changing and terminating policies are the same as those involved in policymaking.

SUMMARY

Public policy refers to a specific intentional act of government to do something and includes the decision to *not* do something. Scholars study public policy to understand how it is created and implemented as well as to understand what effect policy has. To do so, scholars have developed various models of the policy process. These models emphasize different aspects of policy, but most include some form of stages or steps in the policy process. Evaluation of policy is used to determine whether or not it is working and to help in deciding how to improve or end the policy.

 # RESOURCES

Association for Public Policy Analysis and Management: **www.appam.org**

Congressional Budget Office: **www.cbo.gov**

FedStats (Government Statistics): **www.fedstats.gov/index.html**

Project Vote Smart: **www.vote–smart.org**

Public Agenda: **www.publicagenda.org**

Statistical Abstract of the United States: **www.census.gov/compendia/statab/**

U.S. Government Accountability Office (GAO): **www.gao.gov**

Chapter 2

Contexts of Public Policy

Public policymaking takes place within the general social, political, and economic environment of the nation. It takes place as well within contexts specific to each policy area. Substantive chapters will outline these specialized influences, but first we examine some general factors that influence all policies. This chapter describes those trends in U.S politics, culture, and society that determine the framework for policy debates in a wide variety of issue areas. Five contexts are particularly important: institutional (especially intergovernmental relations), economic, demographic, ideological, and cultural.

THE INSTITUTIONAL CONTEXT

The unique features of the American political system, its basic structures—federalism, the party system, the power of the presidency, and the system of checks and balances—shape policy. Policy in the area of civil rights, for example, continues to be determined substantially by the federal courts because of the constitutional system of government and the courts' power of judicial review.

In addition to lasting features of the American political system, however, a serious distrust of institutions, particularly political ones, is now endemic in the American electorate. This is not the simple distrust of government that is a constant in American history, but a deep cynicism and anger about government, politics, and politicians, even to the point of violence (most shockingly in the Oklahoma City Federal Building bombing in April 1995, but also in the attacks on members of Congress and their offices in the wake of their votes on health care reform in 2010). The statistics illustrate the American public's lackluster response to the political process: The percentage of the eligible population voting in presidential and congressional elections declined substantially after 1960, with barely half of voting-age Americans now voting for president, little more than one-third for Congress in nonpresidential years, and far fewer voting for state and local offices. Polls on confidence in leadership reveal substantial decline in the trust the public holds for leadership in all areas of life. The popularity of politician and incumbent bashing on talk radio testifies to distrust of politics and politicians generally.

The trend among young Americans is uneven. In the early 1970s, about half of eighteen- to twenty-nine-year-olds voted in presidential elections. Rates reached a low of 39.6 percent in 1996, rose to 51.1 percent in 2008, and dipped to 45 percent in 2012. While many lament that young people are more and more disengaged from the civic and political life of society, and that their knowledge of politics and world events is substantially lower than that of their elders, they often participate at about the same rate as their elders.[1]

We need not go far to seek the sources for the decline in trust of government.[2] The Vietnam War, the protests and social divisions it spawned, and its tragic impact on many veterans, put American foreign policy leadership under a cloud; the leadership had only partially emerged from this cloud before the Iraq War began creating similar scenarios that have been perpetuated by the war in Afghanistan. Findings of corruption and illegality at the highest levels of government have fed distrust. Such revelations have included the Watergate conspiracy during the Nixon administration, criminal investigations of major Reagan administration officials, and the revelation of corruption at the highest levels of the CIA and FBI in the Aldrich Ames and Robert Hanssen cases in the mid-1990s. "Monicagate" and the impeachment trial of President Clinton kept the scandal pot at boiling point in the 1990s. In the 2000s, the major scandal involved lobbyist Jack Abramoff, with a number of congresspersons indicted and convicted of bribery and abuses of office. Discovery of corruption and lawlessness in politics is nothing new, but these abuses were so serious and widespread and occurred in such rapid sequence that public trust in the ability and willingness of public officials to produce policy in the public interest eroded. The inept response to Hurricane Katrina in 2005 and the troubled rollout of the Affordable Care Act in 2013 only added to the lack of confidence in government. Gridlock within Congress since 2007 further eroded people's trust and confidence in government. In October 2013, only 19 percent of people said that they trusted "government in Washington to do what is right."[3]

The distrust of government is reflected in the strong partisanship and resistance to compromise found in Congress since the 1990s and 2000s. The health care reform debate of 2010 demonstrates the strong partisan divisions that now make it difficult to pass legislation addressing major national issues such as immigration reform and tax reform.

At the same time that public distrust has grown, the presence of the federal government in economic, cultural, and social life has expanded as a product of modernization and technology. Federal regulations and federal spending increase each year. Suspicion that such growth is inevitable no matter which party is in power, that neither party has an interest in halting it, and that such growth produces no noticeable or dramatic improvement in the quality of life contributes to distrust in government. It also contributes to substantial resistance to new policy initiatives in health, education, and consumer protection, to cite only a few cases. Suspicion is growing among the public that the national government has been captured by corporate and other interest groups who use it for private benefit rather than for public good. In the technocratic age, leadership, responsibility, and accountability seem divorced from ordinary citizens. At the same time, as Americans become more cynical, they become less interested in, and less informed about, politics and policy.[4] Some speculated that the war on terror and revived patriotic fervor would check the spread of government distrust and restore some measure of legitimacy to an active federal government. Public anger at the outcome of the war in Iraq, the financial bailout of Wall Street and automobile companies, the inept response to Hurricane Katrina, a perceived lack of urgency in response to the 2010 *Deepwater Horizon* oil spill in the Gulf of Mexico, the 2013 federal government shutdown, and the problematic 2013 Affordable Care Act rollout suggest the opposite result.

Intergovernmental Relations

The U.S. political system is based in part on a separation of responsibilities among different units of government. Problems that must be addressed by government, however, do not respect jurisdictional boundaries. **Intergovernmental relations** refer to the links between the national government, the states, and local governments, as well as the interactions between and among states and local governments. Because approaches to contemporary policy issues often involve controversies about which level or levels of government are most appropriate to address them, we devote considerable attention in the present chapter to this particular context of public policy.

Because most intergovernmental relations are vertical, with the federal government above and state and local governments below, most discussions in this text involve vertical relations. Some forms of intergovernmental relations are referred to as horizontal intergovernmental relations because they involve relationships between or among units at the same level. **Interstate compacts** are examples of horizontal intergovernmental relations. States enter into formal agreements to deal with issues that cross state lines and cannot be dealt with effectively by individual states. The Education Commission of the States, the New York and New Jersey Port Authority, the Delaware River Basin Compact, and the Colorado River Authority are examples of interstate compacts that deal with specific issues of mutual concern. Local governments also often enter into agreements to deal with common concerns. Mass transit authorities in metropolitan areas are results of interlocal government agreements. Such agreements also deal with air and water pollution, airports, community colleges, and public safety services. Compacts between states and tribal governments regarding casino gambling are examples of special intergovernmental compacts.

Issues in a Federal System.   The federal system established by the U.S. Constitution ensured both the need for interaction among governmental units as well as flexibility and tension in those interactions. The principal issue in federalism is what role each level of government should assume. The authors of the Constitution were wary of a central government that was too strong and cognizant of the problems of one too weak. They felt that it was necessary to have a national government that could reasonably coordinate the actions of the states, but they also wanted to give the states the autonomy to deal with their own concerns. Generally, the states were relatively strong from the beginning of the Republic until the 1930s. After the 1930s, the national government assumed greater and greater responsibility until 1980. President Ronald Reagan strove to reduce the influence of the national government, an effort that most national leaders continue to espouse. It is now a settled issue that, by virtue of the **supremacy clause** in Article VI of the Constitution, the powers of the national government are not limited by any specific state power. Since 1992, however, the Supreme Court has been limiting national power relative to state autonomy, thus restricting the reach of the national government. After passage of health care reform in 2010, several states joined to sue over federal mandates such as requiring people to buy insurance and some states passed legislation to opt out of the law. On June 28, 2012, the Supreme Court upheld the constitutionality of the Affordable Care Act, except for the provision requiring states to expand Medicaid.[5]

Intergovernmental relations raise numerous questions. Should governmental units work together on common problems? Should the national government deal through the states to work with local units of government? Questions also arise as to whether the national government should only help other levels of government deal with their problems or whether it should also implement its own programs at the state and local levels.

Yet another concern is who should control program implementation. If the national government's money is used in programs, it is not surprising that the national government wants control over how the money is spent. Without such control, the national government would take the blame for raising tax revenue but would have no say in how it is spent. Those responsible for raising money usually are not willing to give up that say. On the other hand, state and local officials wish to retain as much discretion as possible and do not want to be told by federal bureaucrats how to conduct their business, because they believe they can better address their own differing needs and situations.

Opponents of the national government effort usually argue that state and local governments can deliver needed programs more efficiently. On the other hand, many programs may be developed on the national level that would not get off the ground if left to the lower levels, such as those that require tremendous capital and other resources available only to the national government or that require consistent application throughout the nation.

Many national government programs are created to stimulate states or local units to take action in areas in which they have been reluctant to do so. They also may be applied where there are great inequities among the states or localities. For example, intergovernmental programs may be created to eliminate inequity in education, health, or welfare programs. Other programs may stimulate states to improve transportation, the environment, or work safety when they would not be so inclined without federal government prodding. Of course, critics argue that federal programs reduce the initiative and creativity of local or state units. If left to themselves, without the carrot of federal monies, they might

---

POLICY DILEMMAS   Marijuana and Federal/State Relations

The states of Colorado and Washington allow the sale of marijuana for recreational use. Several others allow its sale for medical purposes. All states strictly regulate the sale and use of it. Colorado has seen a great increase in sales tax revenue since the start of marijuana sales and Washington anticipates the same result. Many other states are looking at the possibility of allowing recreational use of the drug. Colorado does not allow people who buy marijuana to take it out of state—it must be used in Colorado.

The national government prohibits the sale and use of marijuana. Nonetheless, President Obama has assured citizens that the federal government will not prosecute people for the lawful sale and use of it under state law where it is legal.

Proprietors of marijuana dispensaries have found that banks are unwilling to allow them to have accounts to deposit their profits and conduct normal banking functions with the money because of federal law.

1. What institutional and political forces are at work in this scenario? What level of government should control the sale and use of marijuana? Why?

2. Do you think marijuana should be legal for medical use? For recreational use? Why or why not? What are the risks for users and proprietors?

---

experiment more and develop innovative approaches to solving problems. Innovative approaches often have difficulty getting by the federal bureaucracy. On the other hand, various groups believe that state experimentation can take the nation in the wrong direction. Controversies discussed in subsequent chapters over marijuana legalization, same-sex marriage, crime, public assistance, immigration, and health care illustrate these conflicting viewpoints.

Forms of Funding.   Most federal funding has been in the form of **categorical grants** in which money is provided for a specific project with stipulations on exactly how the money can be used. A grant to develop a program for gifted children is an example.

Advocates of fewer restrictions support **block grants**, which give money to state or local units for general purposes instead of a specific project. For example, instead of grants for a program for gifted students, a state may receive an education block grant. The state then determines how best to use the education funds.

General revenue sharing, which refers to the transfer of money from one level of government to another with little or no restriction on its use, was another popular form of national intergovernmental policy in the 1970s. A formula is used to determine how much money each jurisdiction is entitled to receive.

Unfunded mandates of the national government have become common and are the source of much complaint by state and local officials. Unfunded mandates are requirements imposed on state and local governments with no national government funding to implement them. For example, national government requirements on reducing air pollution or attaining a certain standard in drinking water system quality are mandates without funding that must be paid for by the state or local governments. State and local governments become especially upset with the fact that they are under pressure to operate with less revenue and, at the same time, the federal government develops policies requiring them to engage in new initiatives without providing money for those activities. States have even gone to court to attempt to reverse some of the mandates or to require the federal government to provide resources, but such efforts so far have been unsuccessful.

Participants in Intergovernmental Relations

Numerous groups or special interests affect intergovernmental policies. Congress is the main actor in that it passes the legislation that fosters intergovernmental activities. Congress also tends to want to impose conditions on programs it funds and is the focal point for broad national policy development, which often results in particular mandates on state and local government.

The executive branch, particularly the president, often takes the lead in pushing particular policy agendas. Many of those agendas have intergovernmental implications. In addition to the executive leadership, the bureaucracy is part of the executive branch and has the responsibility for implementing policies developed by Congress and the president. In the implementation process, the administrative agencies often impose their own restrictions and conditions, particularly regarding how the policy is to be administered. Much of the federal government red tape complained about is the result of agency action. Administrators who make their concerns about policies known also influence Congress and the president; thus, they also are involved in policymaking processes.

The courts have become significant actors in intergovernmental relations as well.[6] Since the 1960s, courts have mandated state and local governments to take particular actions, especially in school desegregation, school funding, and management of corrections. They even have required local governments to impose taxes. Some courts have assumed administrative responsibility for schools and prison systems. Since the 1990s, the courts have sided more with the states, but their intrusion into state activities remains significant.[7]

The national government's actions are affected by the concerns of state and local governmental officials. The mayors and governors, through their conferences and organizations, make pronouncements on those national government policies that affect them. Within their own parties, they also attempt to influence the direction of national leaders on relevant issues.

The recipients of services under intergovernmental programs often voice their feelings. For example, when aid to education is slated for change or reduction, teachers and school administrators are likely to make entreaties to Congress and the president. Similarly, changes in welfare programs bring reactions from welfare advocates. Other groups that might not benefit directly from a program may also participate in intergovernmental policy development; a program to develop a recreational lake is likely to stimulate environmental or chamber of commerce groups to take a stand on the issue. Of course, the taxpayer is another interested party, to whom political candidates often appeal in their efforts to reduce federal government spending. The main contention is that federal government involvement creates unnecessary administrative expenses that taxpayers have to absorb.

Contemporary Intergovernmental Realities

During its first century and a half, the U.S. federal system changed gradually. Because the nation was essentially rural and society was relatively uncomplicated, the responsibilities of the national government and the states were easy to define. Although there were major controversies, as illustrated by states' rights conflicts, for the most part the powers of the national government were interpreted to be rather narrowly defined. Citizens dealt primarily with state and local jurisdictions. Overriding the separation-of-powers concept was the general philosophy that government at all levels should be restricted in scope.

In the late nineteenth century, intergovernmental relationships began to develop more formally. In 1862, for example, the Morrill Act provided federal land grants for agricultural education programs; the land grant universities are the result of this program. Hatch Act grants for establishing agricultural experiment stations beginning in 1887 were the first actual cash transfers from the national government to the states for specific program development. Still, intergovernmental activities grew gradually until the 1930s. Thereafter, changes occurred much more rapidly.

Forms of Intergovernmental Interaction

Because money provided by the national government is a major source of funding for intergovernmental activity, the emphasis in intergovernmental relations is often on fiscal relationships, but there are other forms of interaction as well, such as regulations and voluntary cooperative efforts.

In 1984, the then Advisory Commission on Intergovernmental Relations identified four types of *regulations* that are part of intergovernmental relations: direct orders, cross-cutting requirements, crossover sanctions, and partial preemption.[8] **Direct orders** either prohibit or mandate state and local government actions. For example, equal employment opportunity legislation prohibits discrimination in employment by state and local government. The Safe Drinking Water Act requires water providers to reach and maintain certain standards in the drinking water they supply. **Preemption** is a form of direct order that has concerned many state and local officials, especially as they have become more prevalent, partly in response to the terrorist attacks of September 11, 2001.[9] Immigration became the subject of the preemption discussion as several states adopted strict laws against undocumented immigrants in 2010–2014. It was argued that the federal government was not living up to its responsibility. The courts have generally agreed that it is a federal responsibility and that states cannot impose their own limits (see Chapter 11).

Cross-cutting requirements are those in which a condition in one law is applied to all programs using federal funds. Thus, the Civil Rights Act of 1964 requires that jurisdictions not discriminate against people on the basis of race, color, national origin, gender, or disability status where federal funds are used. The Drug Free Workplace Act of 1988 and the Cash Management Improvement Act of 1990 are other examples. **Crossover sanctions** are sanctions applied to one area or activity for failure to comply with certain conditions in another area. For example, federal highway funds can be withheld from states that fail to enforce air quality standards.

Partial preemption refers to situations in which the national government requires or permits states to administer policies as long as the states meet federal criteria for the program. If the states do not meet the federal criteria, the federal government may administer the program directly. Examples include the Clean Air Act Amendments of 1990, Hazardous and Solid Waste Amendments of 1984, and the provisions of the Affordable Care Act of 2010 on Medicaid.

These regulatory processes engender much criticism from state and local government officials. Generally, the policies reflected in these regulations are in response to the desire by some elements of society to further their vision of the public good. Imposing requirements without having to provide funding for implementation (unfunded mandates) allows Congress to respond to strong interests without having to raise the revenue to fund them. Of course, state and local governments then have to find the revenue, thus raising the ire of officials at those levels. The Unfunded Mandates Reform Act of 1995 requires federal funding for mandates costing more than $50 million and requires federal agencies to assess impacts of their new rules and regulations on state and local governments. In every session of Congress, bills are introduced, but not passed, to require reimbursement by the national government of any direct cost to state and local governments resulting from federal mandates.

Changing Intergovernmental Relations

Complaints about the intergovernmental system usually focus on the growth of the national government at the expense of state and local autonomy. We shall encounter these arguments in later chapters, particularly with respect to economic regulation, education, and public assistance. State and local governments also have grown as the national government has expanded its involvement in domestic policy issues. The result has been more and more intergovernmental activities and a more complex web of relations. Of course, the intention of most advocates of reform of the system is to reverse that complexity and lighten the hand of the national government in the affairs of state and local governments.

Administrative Problems.   One of the most common complaints about the federal government is that it imposes too much red tape on the state and local recipients of aid. State and local administrators complain about the amount of paperwork in applying for and administering grants. The paperwork increases the costs to the recipients and delays the project's completion. Disputes in interpreting program criteria and rules and regulations take a long time to resolve, and conflicting rules and regulations and duplication of effort only compound the problem.

Even more difficult for the state and local agencies is the need for clearance from numerous agencies from local officials on up to federal agency managers.

These requirements lead to inflexibility in the categorical programs. Local officials feel that their needs cannot be met; rather, the program requirements appear to be oriented more to the needs of the federal agency. Additionally, many of the categorical programs are so narrowly defined that it becomes difficult to fit them to the particular needs of the state and local governments.

Block grants and general revenue sharing were supposed to eliminate some of the administrative problems previously noted. Giving state and local officials more discretion in the structure of their programs would subject the money to fewer restrictions. Although block grants generally begin with such aspirations, state program administrators seem to recategorize them as part of their actual implementation. Conflicts develop within the state block grant administrative agencies. Program specialists fight for funds for their programs, and the funds end up being allocated on a program basis. The result is that after they reach the state level, the block grants often begin to look again like categorical grants. Additionally, national government policy seems to reimpose conditions. For example, general revenue sharing was found to contain the compliance requirements of fifteen different federal agencies just four years after its adoption as federal aid without strings.[10]

Related to administrative problems is monitoring by federal agencies. In granting money to other units of government, the national government tries to see that the money is used properly and for beneficial programs. Federal agencies and many state and local governments recognize the need for coordination. Typically, a regional council of governments or a regional planning commission is responsible for reviewing and commenting on grant applications. Additionally, the request usually faces review by some statewide agency before going to the federal agency. These requirements should reduce overlapping projects and ensure that one project does not work at cross-purposes to another. The end result should be cost savings to the taxpayer and more efficient use of grant monies, but there is no hard evidence that such objectives are met.

Granting agencies also monitor recipients of a grant. Most federal agencies have so many programs and grants to monitor that it is impossible to do a complete job of monitoring, so recipient governments may find ways to get around or ignore compliance with impunity. And when an agency decides to take action against a unit, the affected government has many options at its command to lessen the agency's ability to do so. Because the agencies rely on congressional support to continue their activities, the affected government can turn to members of Congress to put pressure on the granting agency. The agency also depends on its clientele, the recipient units of government, to ensure support for its programs. Thus, agency administrators usually see the advantage of working things out with the state or local units rather than fighting with them.

Finances.   The financial relationships between governmental units are among the most significant interactions. The national government increased the numbers of funded programs during the mid-twentieth century; thus, intergovernmental transfers of funds became significant (see Figure 2.1). The problem with

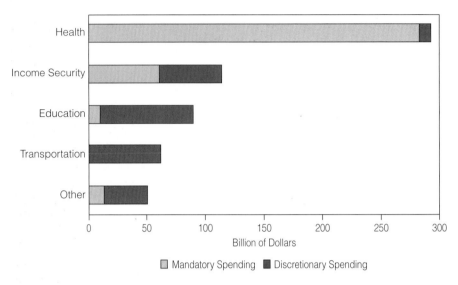

FIGURE 2.1 Federal Grants to State and Local Governments (outlays)

Notes: For the purposes of organizing the budget, federal resources are grouped into 20 general-subject categories—referred to as budget functions—so that all budget authority and outlays can be presented according to the national interests being addressed.

"Other" includes the following budget functions: national defense, international affairs, energy, natural resources and environment, agriculture, commerce and housing credit, community and regional development, Social Security, veterans benefits and services, administration of justice, and general government.

SOURCE: http://www.cbo.gov/sites/default/files/cbofiles/attachments/03-05-13FederalGrants_onecol.pdf, accessed February 14, 2014.

providing federal funds lies in who controls the use of those funds. With categorical grants, the national government clearly establishes criteria for using the money. With block grants and general revenue sharing, the expectation was that the national government would loosen its control. Recent domestic policy has focused on loosening restrictions and cutting domestic spending. The Personal Responsibility and Work Opportunity Reconciliation Act of 1996, which reformed the welfare system (see Chapter 7), is a good example of devolving responsibility to the states and, in the process, controversy about levels of financial support for the program.

With grants, state and local levels are never certain what amount of money is going to be available from year to year. This uncertainty in the level of funding makes it more difficult for them to plan their own activities and budgets. Another irritating aspect of most federal grants for the recipient units is the **maintenance of effort** requirement, which means that state and local governments cannot use federal money to replace their own spending on the affected program. The receiving governments are locked into spending patterns if they wish to receive the grants with such requirements. For example, Community Development Block Grants cannot be used to reduce the amount of money that the local government spends on redevelopment. Instead, the program requires a government to continue to spend at previous levels or it cannot continue to receive Community Development funds.

Whither Federalism?

Issues in the debate revolve around which levels of government have particular powers and how those powers are exercised. The argument about which level has what powers arises as the national government adopts policies or implements decisions on any number of issues. The trend in the courts until the 1990s had been a centralizing one in which national government authority expanded. Since the 1990s, however, the U.S. Supreme Court has reversed the trend. While some argue that it has favored the states over the national government, others argue that it just has slowed the trend. Analysis of the Court's decisions suggests that the Court sees itself as setting a balance. It slowed federal expansion of power in some cases, but sanctioned it in others.[11]

The National Governors Association, the Conference of State Legislatures, and the American Council on Intergovernmental Relations believe that the roles of the national government and states can be better defined. The problem is in determining exactly which functions should be the responsibility of the national government and what should be the responsibility of state and local units. Commonly, suggestions are made that the national government assume all responsibility for health and income support programs and shift the responsibility for all other social programs to the states. Governors occasionally call upon the national government to assume all responsibility for funding welfare programs, in return for the states picking up other programs, such as education and transportation. Again, the primary emphasis is on turning over many functions to the state and local governments while reducing federal involvement, but there is little agreement on exactly how the division should be made. For example, in 1995 and 1996, many governors suggested devolving Medicaid more fully to the states. By 2004, many governors wanted responsibility for the program to remain national, as many states were overwhelmed by the financial demands of the Medicaid system. Governors keep asking the federal government to provide more funding. Nonetheless, under the Affordable Care Act of 2010, many governors declined to expand Medicaid, although the federal government agreed to pick up 100 percent of the cost in the first three years.

The process of dividing responsibility suggests a view of federalism in which functions can be neatly separated. But history has suggested that such neat divisions are unrealistic. Because most policy activities affect more governments than one, it is unrealistic to leave such activities exclusively under the control of any one government. Therefore, it is improbable that any system could be devised that abolished sharing and cooperation. Nonetheless, proponents of this view continue to expound these objectives.

Opponents of the shift of responsibility to the states argue that states are not able to assume that responsibility. States are not likely to have the resources to fund the programs adequately. As noted, states may not always be inclined to continue such programs. Opponents of these proposals see the administrative complexity of fifty states administering programs, such as under block grants, as inefficient and burdensome. There are also concerns that some states will be less sensitive to issues such as equity, fairness, and civil rights in developing and implementing programs. Concerns also arise over which groups have access to decision makers with many arguing that the poor and powerless bear the greatest burden of these reforms.

THE ECONOMIC CONTEXT

The Great Recession lasted from December 2007 to June 2009. The housing bubble reached its peak in 2008 but burst, causing homeowners to lose value in their homes and a mortgage crisis to ensue. Large banks and other financial institutions lost money and some collapsed entirely. Unemployment and productivity declines followed. While the recession technically ended in June 2009, the economy has recovered very slowly—confidence in the economy has not yet fully recovered. Early 2014 brought signs that recovery is progressing, but it is at a slow pace. While the stock market rallied during the last half of 2013 and early 2014, family median income peaked in 2007 ($57,000) and has been falling ever since ($51,371 in 2013). The wealthiest Americans have been doing very well, while the middle class and poor have seen their relative incomes drop, resulting in a widening gap between the rich and the poor. The widening gap has brought about calls for different approaches by Democrats and Republicans for policies to address it. Disparities in income by race and gender have also led to differing policy proposals.

Later chapters more fully discuss these matters, especially economic policy (Chapters 3 and 4) and income maintenance (Chapter 7), but it is important to recognize here that these economic trends have an impact well beyond strictly economic issues. Budget deficits, fear of sending jobs overseas if too much regulation affects corporations, and changing job requirements have influenced education, health policy, and foreign policy, for example. New spending initiatives for programs other than defense and homeland security have had great difficulty in Congress. Economically challenging times also have exacerbated racial tensions and affected the controversies over equality issues and immigration considered in Chapters 10 and 11.

THE DEMOGRAPHIC CONTEXT

The generational, racial, and residential characteristics of a nation's population change constantly, reflecting new trends in birthrates, life expectancy, job opportunities, and migration patterns. Some of these trends directly affect policymaking.

The children born during the baby boom after World War II began reaching Social Security retirement age in 2012, placing great pressure on social insurance policies. The proportion of the population under age twenty-five, which rose until the mid-1970s, declined until the mid-1990s, when it leveled off and has since held steady. Such changes in the number of young people not only seriously affect education policy, but other areas as well. For example, persons between the ages of fourteen and twenty-five commit a highly disproportionate number of violent crimes (see Chapter 6). Economic performance from 1960 to 1985 was substantially affected by the need to absorb millions of new, young workers.[12] The aging of the population raises the question of where to find younger workers to sustain a productive economy.

The proportion of the population sixty-five and older, now about 13.2 percent, is increasing at twice the national population rate and is likely to be 20.3 percent by 2030 (see Figure 2.2). Those over age eighty-five will reach 4.5 percent of the population by 2050. Because only a small proportion of persons in this age group work full-time and because their health care requirements exceed those of the rest of the population, pressure on Social Security and Medicare will be intense. Moreover, because life expectancy for women is significantly higher than for men, many of those over sixty-five are widowed women, living alone or in a nursing home, retirement home, or assisted living. It is possible that the working population will come to resent supporting such a large number of retired persons. On the other hand, because the elderly vote more regularly than the young do, the aged themselves have become a large

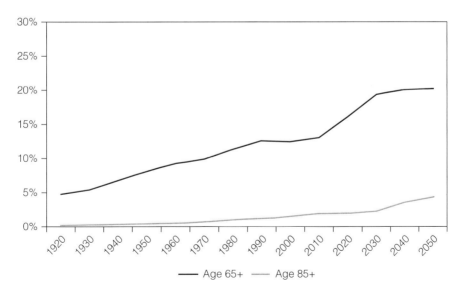

FIGURE 2.2 Population Aging as Percent of Population

Note: 2020 to 2050 are projections.

SOURCE: http://www.aoa.gov/AoARoot/Aging_Statistics/index.aspx, accessed February 14, 2014.

and powerful political force for the protection of their own interests. These generational considerations are much in evidence in continuing debates over Social Security reform (see Chapter 7) as they were in the 2010 health care reform (see Chapter 8).

Immigration continues to change the shape of the American population and present challenges to federal and state policy. Legal immigration set a record of more than 1.8 million persons in 1991 and then dropped gradually so that about 1 million are currently admitted annually. Immigration now accounts for more than half of U.S. population growth. These immigrants, primarily of Asian and Hispanic descent, present both opportunities for dynamic expansion of the economy and challenges for services in housing, schools, jobs, and health care. Moreover, the impact of immigration is not spread evenly across the country. Approximately 60 percent of the new residents settle in California, Florida, New Jersey, New York, and Texas, placing a critical assimilative burden on these states (see Chapter 11).

Public policy in a number of areas will also have to respond to changes in the racial mix of the population. Non-Hispanic whites made up 90 percent of the population in 1955. By 2012, the proportion had declined to just 63 percent. Because of illegal immigration and the younger average age of the Spanish-surname population, the Hispanic proportion of the population has increased rapidly, surpassing the African American proportion. By 2012, Hispanic Americans constituted about 16.9 percent of the population; they accounted for 6 percent in 1980. By 2060, nearly one-third of Americans will be of Hispanic background, and the white percentage will be about half (see Figure 2.3). Though they share

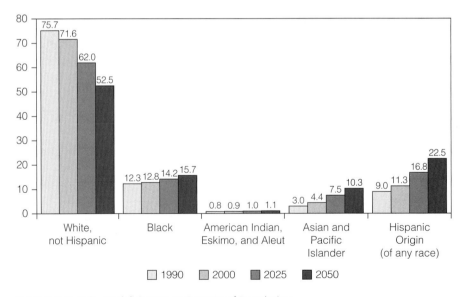

F I G U R E 2.3 Racial Groups as Percent of Population

SOURCE: http://www.census.gov/prod/1/pop/p25-1130.pdf, accessed February 14, 2014.

many problems with African Americans, poverty and racial discrimination being the most important, Hispanics also bring with them a different language and culture. Historically, combinations of simultaneous racial change and economic uncertainty have been volatile. The Great Recession combined with high levels of immigration, especially illegal immigration, led to heated debate but no action on immigration reform. Lack of national government action on immigration frustrated many states, especially those along the border with Mexico. This resulted in state legislation such as Arizona's SB1070 placing state penalties on immigrants being in the state illegally. Thus, the issue became contentious in the 2010, 2012, and 2014 elections once more. In 2014, it appeared that chances for immigration reform were slim until after midterm elections and possibly until after the presidential election in 2016.

Changes in marriage and family life have had a major impact on policy, as shown by the increasing percentages of working women, the high divorce rate, and the high rates of illegitimate births and of single-parent families that affect labor policy, welfare expenditures, child care, schools, and gender equality policies. Moreover, married households with children now constitute less than a quarter of all households. Marriage and family life are increasingly chosen by the college-educated and affluent, with lower-income working families choosing to live together and have children out of wedlock.

Finally, the declining population of large urban centers such as New York, Baltimore, Chicago, and Cleveland and the rising population of rural, suburban, and small urban areas, especially in the South and Southwest, continue to influence a broad range of policies. Controversies rage over how the federal government should allocate its grant-in-aid money for urban rehabilitation, jobs, housing, education, unemployment assistance, water and sewer projects, and many other needs. Between 1980 and 2010, the North and Northeast lost and the South and West gained fifty seats, or more than one-tenth of Congress. The division between "red states" and "blue states" in their partisan loyalties and voting patterns partly reflects these demographic changes.

THE IDEOLOGICAL CONTEXT

Public policy is a field of debate over the meaning of basic values and principles. Defining policy problems is fundamentally about the conceptual and symbolic terms that we use to describe them. The numbers, symbols, and discussions of causality in the following chapters occur in the context of ideological debate over their meaning and significance. Conservatives, feminists, liberals, and socialists fight over the very goals of public policy, such as equity, efficiency, security, and liberty.[13]

Ideological perspectives on American public policy have always ranged along a spectrum—including extreme positions at either end, such as communists on the Left and militia groups on the Right. Historically, however, **conservatism** and liberalism have dominated policymaking and evaluation in America. The majority of Americans, including policymakers, are some variety of liberal or conservative, despite small and periodically powerful numbers of adherents to other ideologies. Although liberals and conservatives in America share a great many commitments to abstract ideals, such as freedom, democracy, the market system, and individualism, they disagree on the principles to be used in making and evaluating policy. First, they disagree over the meaning of freedom and its limits: Conservatives tend to value civil and personal freedoms less and are more willing to limit them. They often favor censorship of sexually explicit materials, for example. Liberals are more ready to limit economic freedom, for example, by placing restrictions on advertisers. Liberals have a deeper commitment to equality than do conservatives. Conservatives are committed to tradition and authority, which is balanced by liberal commitment to change and individual choice in moral and social behavior. Liberals tend to have faith in the power of government to make the world better; conservatives are more pessimistic about such a prospect. These disagreements affect policy debates in all areas, because government itself and the extent to which market forces may be relied on for economic and social health are central issues.

Traditional conservatism and liberalism have fragmented in recent years, with new ideological viewpoints surfacing from the two mainstream movements. Neoconservatives and the *New Right* have competed for influence within the Republican Party. In domestic policy, neoconservatives are critical of the government's regulation of business enterprise and suspicious of government action to correct past injustices, such as affirmative action, when there is basic disagreement about the goals of such policies. They are not, however, as opposed to government economic action as traditional conservatives or libertarians, who also form part of the Right end of the ideological spectrum. The New Right, on the other hand, directs most of its attention to social issues. It opposes abortion, same-sex marriage, feminism, pornography, and what it sees as government interference in religious expression. Included in the New Right are the evangelical religious groups, such as the Christian Coalition, that became a prominent part of electoral politics in the early 1980s. The **Tea Party** movement beginning in 2009 and continuing into 2014 is also associated with conservatives. Since 2008, the newer groups on the Right have created rifts within the Republican Party, making it difficult for Republicans in Congress to agree on issues. Similarly, they push issues in state legislatures that embarrass the more moderate wing of the party.

Movements on the Left of the spectrum are harder to define and classify, as they are more fragmented and less prominent than the Right in recent decades. Communists and socialists stress fundamental change in the social and economic system, government control of the basic means of production, and equal distribution of most income. Such groups have lost virtually all influence in American politics. Other groups on the Left that take a predominantly economic approach to policy stress democratic control of the means of production through worker self-management and local, direct democracy.

Because the term *liberal* has declined in popularity, often being used as a term of disparagement in political campaigns, many on the Left call themselves **progressives**. This term is meant to suggest willingness to improve society and to discard old restrictive attitudes and rules. The remaining chapters employ both the older "liberal" and the newer "progressive" to designate this part of the ideological spectrum. Other groups often classified on the Left focus primarily on social or environmental issues. Moreover, they contain within themselves more and less extreme varieties. The less extreme ones make up an important part of contemporary liberalism and of the Democratic Party politically. These are groups defined by feminism, environmental protection, or gay equality. These movements view public policy primarily through a particular lens. Feminists evaluate policy according to its impact on women. Liberal feminists strive to make sure that men and women are treated equally and that women have the opportunity to achieve success in all areas of political, economic, and social life. More radical variants of feminism seek to challenge the traditional structures of society. Similarly, more liberal elements of the LGBT (lesbian, gay, bisexual, and transgender) community seek to integrate homosexual persons into the fabric of society by guaranteeing the same rights and responsibilities (job access, same-sex marriage, and military service, for example) as heterosexuals. These splits within newer ideological movements and their uneasy relationship with more traditional progressives have made the Left and the Democratic Party highly fractious in recent decades.

Still other groups are more difficult to classify. Although environmentalists are most often counted as part of the liberal coalition, there are many traditional conservatives who value and participate in environmental groups that stress conservation of natural resources and respect for the physical environment. This fact gives some environmental policy issues broad political support. Libertarians combine a conservative economic agenda with a liberal social agenda. Although usually classified on the Right, libertarians support abortion rights, oppose restrictions on sexually explicit speech, and favor keeping government out of the bedroom as well as out of the boardroom.

In the late twentieth century, a movement known as *communitarianism* received national attention. Prominent communitarians, such as political scientist William Galston, have held important positions in the Clinton and second Bush administrations. Communitarians focus on the interconnection between rights and responsibilities. Their policy attention concentrates on revitalizing local neighborhood and city institutions, on community policing, family restoration, character formation, and education reform.

Issue definition is not a neutral, apolitical process. The ideological perspectives just described affect how issues appear on the policy agenda. The definition of a policy problem is always a matter for disagreement among people of competing beliefs and principles. Poverty, for example, was not seen as a problem to be solved until the 1930s. Before that, it was held to be an inevitable social condition. Conservatives still tend to view it, at least partially, in this way. Radicals, on the other hand, view poverty as a requirement of capitalist society; from this standpoint, public assistance policy becomes simply a device used by capitalism to maintain itself, not a response to a neutral problem. Even the statistics used to illustrate the dimensions of an issue will frequently vary depending on the perspective from which the issue is being defined. For example, as we shall see in

Chapter 7, liberals and conservatives cite the same poverty statistics but draw opposite conclusions from them. Care must be exercised in using and interpreting statistics—even those presented in this book!

Particularly significant in the ideological context is the continuing growth of support for conservatism, the New Right, and the Republican Party. Republican dominance of the presidency and Congress in the early 2000s produced policy changes more favorable to free markets, to social conservatism, and to reduction of economic regulations. The unpopularity of the war in Iraq, however, combined with the continuing public strength of progressive attitudes, produced strong Democratic victories in 2006 and 2008 and attempts to roll back some of these conservative gains. Republicans took back the House of Representatives in 2010, thus splitting control of Congress and making it difficult for President Obama to achieve his administration's policy agenda. Voters continue to suspect both Democratic and Republican politicians of self-interest, and they do not trust most interest and ideological groups. Many citizens certainly perceive a failure in domestic policy programs, and this perception tends to support conservative politics. Yet, at the same time, Americans value the benefits that government programs bring them, their cities, and their employers. This commitment points toward more liberal policies. Moreover, **ideology** is very much involved in the cultural changes sweeping American society. The meaning of our connections with each other, the definition of the family and its responsibilities, and acceptable forms of sexual expression all create considerable turmoil within and among ideological groups, making it hard to achieve policy consensus.

THE CULTURAL CONTEXT

During the 1980s, it became increasingly clear that many policy issues were caught up not only in passionate ideological disputes but also in a cultural conflict of increasing dimensions. **Culture** refers to the patterns of fundamental beliefs, principles, traditions, and social assumptions that characterize a society. There is frequently a dominant culture and one or more subcultures. Political conflict challenges which fundamental values dominate American life.

Demographic changes discussed earlier, particularly those affecting the family, directly affect culture. As family life changes, other parts of culture come into question. The family is one of the primary ways of passing on moral understandings, but clearly standards of morality with respect to sexuality, competition, money, material goods, and work, to name just a few, are hotly debated.

Ideology is inextricably bound to attitudes toward culture. Among many, especially conservatives, there is a perception that something is wrong with the fabric of national life, starting with the family, but also reflected in crime, economic noncompetitiveness, political and social corruption, and greed. Communitarians also articulate these themes. According to conservatives, television and movies portray and advocate ways of life at odds with traditional American values. Abortion, pornography, and sexual promiscuity are increasingly acceptable. Public schools do not permit prayer, and the educational system fails hundreds of thousands of young people. The role of women in the workplace and in public life also raises questions about the meaning of traditional cultural values, as does recognition and acceptance of homosexual behavior. Moral crusades have always been part of American history, though their targets and political consequences vary substantially.[14]

Progressives, no less than conservatives, recognize fundamental changes in gender, sexual, and cultural roles of all kinds. Rather than fearing these changes, liberals tend to accept most. They support legislation protecting the right to abortion. They want fundamental political, social, and economic rights available to all persons, regardless of gender or sexual orientation. To the extent that traditional family life oppresses women and children, liberals accept necessary change in family structures.[15] Because these controversies often pertain to the role of religion in public life and the strong divide between religiously observant and secular voters, the Constitution's First Amendment receives a great deal of attention.

Cultural conflict thus runs through many of the policy issues that appear in the following chapters. Chapter 13 directly addresses this conflict. Cultural issues were significant in each of the presidential elections since 1980.

SUMMARY

Public policy is adopted and implemented within the constitutional system of government (which includes a federal system), with a need for intergovernmental interactions. Economic and social forces also affect the development and execution of policy. Similarly, demographic and cultural changes in society raise new concerns about what government should and can do. As a result, public policy-making is a dynamic process affected by numerous forces on a continuous basis.

 **RESOURCES**

American Council on Intergovernmental Relations: **govinfo.library.unt.edu/amcouncil/index.html**

Council of State Governments: **www.csg.org**

Family Facts: **www.familyfacts.org**

The Institute for Communitarian Policy Studies: **icps.gwu.edu**

National Association of Counties: **www.naco.org**

National League of Cities: **www.nlc.org**

The Pew Forum on Religion & Public Life: **www.pewforum.org**

Public Agenda: **www.publicagenda.org**

Urban Institute: **www.urban.org**

Chapter 3

The Economy: Changing Government–Business Relationships

A merican government has always been preoccupied with economic activities. During its first century, the country's main concern was preserving the property of citizens. Although property rights still hold a high place in American values, other economic concerns—such as economic growth, level of employment, international competition, and the scarcity of natural resources—gradually replaced preservation of property rights as a major focus of government. Yet, one factor has remained constant over the years: Government and economic activity are inextricably intertwined; therefore, activity in one sector automatically has major consequences for the other. At the same time, quality of life and the relationship of economic development to the environment and to social issues represent current concerns for economic policy.

ISSUE BACKGROUND: KEY CONCEPTS IN ECONOMICS

Economic systems produce and distribute wealth among people in the form of goods and services. Different systems perform these functions in different ways. In theory, a market system operates according to the concept of supply and demand—that is, it responds to people's demands by supplying what they want, for a profit. The key to understanding the market system is that both prices and the allocation of goods and services are determined impersonally. That is, they are not set by any actor or institution according to some rational criterion, but rather are produced by the interaction of the impersonal forces of supply and demand. This simplified view of economic systems assumes that there will be a balance between supply and demand and that the economic actors have essentially equal ability to bargain with one another. In reality, however, people vary in the economic power they have, and other factors affect the supply–demand relationship. As economist John Kenneth Galbraith noted, people band together in organizations to acquire power.[1] These organizations often serve their own economic self-interest, not that of society. Because some individuals and organizations have more money, property, or political access than others, imbalances in the distribution of wealth develop. Governments often intervene to protect the interests of those with power or to rebalance the system; economic policy deals with these governmental efforts.

The Free-Enterprise System

Industrialized nations are characterized by a variety of economic systems. They can, however, be divided roughly between two extreme alternatives of economic organization: **market capitalism** (or **free enterprise**) and **socialism** (or public ownership). Although each existing economy more closely approximates one of these two extremes, most combine elements of free enterprise and government control. One may actually conceptualize three types of economic systems. *Free-enterprise capitalism* implies both the market system and the private ownership of the major means of production, distribution, and exchange, with these means run for the profit of their owners. *Socialism* involves the public or governmental ownership and control of these major means of production, distribution, and exchange, run for the public interest. In this system, prices and the allocation of goods and services are planned by government agents according to rational considerations. Between these polar opposites is the system practiced in most industrial democracies, a type called **welfare–state capitalism**. In this system, the allocation of goods and services and frequently prices are to a large extent planned, but the major means of production are still in private hands and run for profit.

The major systems champion economic development and industrialization, but they favor different methods for achieving them. Proponents of free-market capitalism justify it on the grounds that the private ownership of firms provides incentives for production. They believe the state should refrain as much as possible from interfering with the conduct of economic activity. In the socialist approach, on the other hand, the political system plays a major role in the conduct of economic activity. Such a system is based on the assumption that economic wealth should be fairly equally distributed among the population and that such distribution improves social welfare. Socialists reject the assumptions that underlie the market system. From the socialist perspective, capitalist societies are dominated by a few wealthy owners and managers of private enterprise, policymakers who are neither chosen by, nor responsible to, the people as a whole. Proponents of capitalism see the same problems in a socialist economy, namely, that government officials concentrate economic power along with political and social power in their own hands, but capitalists view this as a threat to individual liberty.

In socialist economies, such as those in the pre-1989 Soviet Union, the formerly communist countries of Eastern Europe, and China, government ownership predominated. Thus, government controlled economic activity through its normal decision-making processes. Even within such societies, however, there were variations, and some had more mixed economies than others. Eastern European nations, in particular, permitted private enterprise, particularly in agriculture, to coexist with the state-owned economic entities. During the official dissolution of the Soviet Union in 1991, the former Soviet Republics became independent nations and began a gradual transition to market economies. Even in China, where communism still exists, a market economy constantly grows.

With the failure of communism in 1989 and the dissolution of the Soviet Union and its control over Eastern Europe, these socialist, or command, economies collapsed. As a result, the development of the free-market system accelerated. Although they face immense challenges, these countries are developing mixed economies reflecting elements of command and free-market systems.

In most industrialized nations—such as the United States, France, Germany, Italy, Sweden, and Japan—a capitalist approach dominates, but it is inevitably a mixture of private ownership and public control that characterizes such systems.[2] Government monopolies invariably run postal services and, in many nations, other economic activities, such as telephone and telegraph services and transportation. These activities (sometimes called **natural monopolies**) often are viewed as being so basic to the maintenance of society that government monopoly is justified.

What differentiates capitalist and socialist economies for purposes of government-economic interaction is that socialist states, as we have seen, have built-in controls through public ownership and operation of economic enterprise. Capitalist economies, on the other hand, utilize other kinds of intervention as a means of supporting, guiding, or controlling the activities of the private sector. Socialist states do not need the regulation or economic stimulation common in capitalist states as they exercise direct control; capitalist economies, on the other hand, use numerous methods to influence economic enterprise.

Among the industrial nations, the United States is one of the most purely capitalist in the way its economic activity is organized. It is especially distinguished by the extent to which it still relies on market forces. The majority of economic enterprise is privately operated, and few activities are totally publicly owned. Nonetheless, although economic activity is primarily privately owned, the United States does intervene in economic activity to a great extent. Thus, people in the United States, who pride themselves on having a nearly pure form of free-market capitalism, actually function within a regulated economy.

Economist Milton Friedman, probably the preeminent twentieth-century defender of the free-market system, suggested that a pure free-enterprise economy would be based on:

- A self-adjusting free market independent of any government intervention.
- Human beings who seek to maximize their own economic self-interest.

- Competition, stimulated by individual self-interest, that produces maximum benefits for all.

- Private ownership of the means of production and distribution, which leads to competition, which results in the best quality of product at the lowest price.[3]

Critics of Friedman's position argue that the free-market approach is based on several assumptions that simply are not valid, at least as the so-called free market is known in the United States. Free-market theory rests on the imperfect assumptions that:

- Human beings are motivated essentially by economic wants.

- People have perfect information on which to make rational economic choices.

- Demand is elastic (adjusts to changing prices).

- Production and price are elastic (producers can respond easily to shifts in demand).

- There is perfect competition.[4]

These assumptions frequently do not reflect real-life economics. The market often fails because human beings act on bases other than economic rationality. Producers, for example, often create demand through advertising—that is, they create artificial needs in people purely through the power of persuasive advertising and then fill these new needs at a profit to themselves.[5] Furthermore, people often do things because they enjoy doing them, even though there may be negative economic consequences. People do not have perfect information about goods and services and would probably not be able to assimilate and analyze all the information even if it were available. Time is limited, and choices must be made.

Nor is there perfect competition in the market. Instead, the economy is characterized by unevenness in the resources among producers. Some students of economic systems suggest that our economy actually is made up of two different groups of economic entities.[6] On one side are the large, powerful firms that are few in number but have the resources to persist and to influence other actors in the economy. Then there are many very small firms that find it difficult to compete because they lack the resources to keep up with technological innovations. They often are absorbed by the large firms or are forced out of existence because they are not competitive. Consumers, by the same token, have little ability to influence the powerful producers. The result is that little effective competition takes place in the economy, and therefore prices do not follow the supply-and-demand curve. What happens is that those with resources end up dominating the market, taking advantage of their power to further their own interests.

Finally, consumers' choices within the market may be limited. Even though the cost of gasoline may be very high, some people have no other way to get to work than by automobile and thus are limited in how much they can reduce consumption. Similarly, regardless of cost, a sick or injured person needs medical assistance.

Because of the failure of the free-market system to operate perfectly (**market failure**), many governments intervene to guide and control the economic system. Much government policy is based on the intent to protect citizens and consumers against fraud and abuse, to control monopolies (and thus help make the market truly free), and to protect against inequities and inefficiencies. On the other hand, if those with economic power also have political power, government policy also may be oriented toward protecting their interests. Still other goals of economic planners have been to keep the economy operating on a stable basis and to avoid constant sharp fluctuations between **inflation** with full employment and **recession** with unemployment. Such often-conflicting objectives are difficult to pursue, and economic policy often results in numerous unintended consequences and indirect impacts.

History of Government's Role

Many critics of government policies seem to mistakenly believe that the United States began with economic enterprise flourishing, free from intervention by the political system. Policies to influence economic activity have always been a part of the American political landscape. The American Revolution resulted, in part, from financial grievances of the colonists, who felt the British monarchy was unfairly impeding colonial development through its taxation policies. After the Revolution, policies affecting economic well-being continued to be a major concern. Witness the controversy surrounding the establishment of a national bank and its relationship to the national debt during George Washington's administration.

In its early history, the United States government stimulated the economy through public investment or attempts to create an environment in which the economy could prosper. The national government subsidized development through land grant programs to the railroad industry and to states to establish educational institutions that would, in turn, focus on supporting the agricultural economy. State governments set many precedents during this time in their attempts to spur economic growth. Roads and canals also were built with **government subsidy**, further illustrating government's efforts to stimulate development.

Although citizens became accustomed to government playing a supportive role in economic activity, they did not appear willing to accept government interference beyond that role. During the latter part of the nineteenth century, a very strong antigovernment sentiment developed. The national government had begun to develop regulatory policies aimed at curbing some of the abuses of large corporate enterprises. Industry, however, was influential politically and was successful in convincing the political leadership to take a **laissez-faire** approach to economic activities.[7] It was not until the 1930s that government returned to an interventionist approach. The severe economic **depression** following the stock market crash of 1929 led people to accept a greater government role, but even then there was a great deal of hesitation about permitting government to become too deeply involved in private enterprise.

When the Great Depression first hit, the immediate response of President Herbert Hoover's administration was to raise taxes and try to balance the budget. Unfortunately, these actions exacerbated the problem. The nation, in no mood for half-measures, sought a new leader in Franklin D. Roosevelt, who quickly took another approach. He convinced Congress to create several new agencies and programs to address the extraordinary problems of unemployment and the slump in production. The Roosevelt administration brought economic regulation, public works programs, welfare programs, and agricultural support programs to stabilize and stimulate the economy.

An era had begun in which governmental intervention in economic matters would grow immensely. It is important to note, however, that these programs maintained the tradition of government support for economic prosperity and that intervention was limited to rebuilding the economy through aid to particular enterprises. Later came government efforts to influence the private sector to perform in a particular way, sometimes against its will. These programs helped in curing the ills of the Depression, but they did not lead to complete prosperity for the economic system.

During the late 1930s, many leaders, including Roosevelt, became convinced that the free-market system could not regulate itself satisfactorily. The Depression had shown that some of the assumptions of free-market theory, discussed earlier, were not valid. Now it was recognized that, for a variety of reasons, sometimes severe fluctuations in the market economy were inevitable without government intervention. Influenced by the ideas of John Maynard Keynes, whose *General Theory of Employment, Interest, and Money* suggested new approaches to the relationship between government and the economy, Roosevelt and his administration began to modify public policy.[8] Not until the economic impact of World War II became apparent, however, was the immense power of the political system in influencing the economy recognized. Active government intervention began in virtually every aspect of the economy.

The wartime economy of the early 1940s, dictated in large part by the government, had clearly stimulated employment and economic growth. Recognition that government spending could create such dramatic effects created the foundation for sustained government action to influence desirable economic activity and to correct problems in the economy. It was, then, during the late 1940s that maintenance of prosperity became a major public issue. Today, this recognition remains one of the most, if not *the* most, important concerns of any national administration. The American people now expect the government to take action to resolve problems in the economy, but there are major differences of opinion on just what action will produce the desired results. The contrasts between the philosophies of Friedman and Galbraith outlined at the beginning of this chapter are examples of opposing perspectives on what the role of government should be.

Today, few argue that government has no appropriate role in the economic sector. Instead, controversy exists over where government should intervene, and for whom. We already have reviewed most of the areas of responsibility. Traditionally, one purpose of government economic policy has been to stimulate economic growth. Since the 1970s, however, many economic policies also had to address problems of scarcity, particularly in energy and food. Another purpose of economic programs is protecting and supporting the private enterprise system through promoting full employment, protecting the well-being of citizens, and controlling the pressures of inflation and recession. Ultimately, economic policies also result in redistributing resources among the various groups in society. Government involvement in the economy supports both the prosperity goal and meeting the needs of people purposes of government.

Inflation and Recession

Inflation is a rise in price of goods and services, even though the actual value of those goods and services does not increase. Thus, although prices increase, production does not keep pace, resulting in a decline in the purchasing power of money—that is, each dollar purchases less than it did in the past.

Inflation may occur when the demand for goods and services grows at a faster rate than available supplies. Competing consumers drive up the prices for such goods. This type of inflation is known as **demand-pull inflation**. Another type, **cost-push inflation**, refers to an increase in the cost of a product, even though demand remains constant or drops. It occurs when prices are regulated in some way rather than impersonally set by supply and demand. A rise in oil prices, for example, can cause cost-push inflation, as do increases in wage rates without a corresponding rise in productivity. Normally during periods of demand-pull inflation, employment goes up, although this may not be true during times of cost-push inflation. We shall see in Chapter 4 why different remedies are appropriate to these different inflation forms.

Recessions are periods in which there is a decline in economic activity arising from a slump in effective demand for goods and services. An oversupply of goods and services may cause a drop in production, leading to increased unemployment. Unemployed people are able to purchase less, thus further nourishing the recession. Most recently, recessions hit the United States from 1981 to 1982, 1991, in 2001–2002, and in 2007–2009. The 2007–2009 recession began as foreclosures on mortgages surged and the economy lost many jobs. Prolonged recessions are called depressions.

Microeconomic Approaches

Government concerns about the economy fall into two groups, *microeconomic* and *macroeconomic policy*. Generally, microeconomic policy refers to government activities regarding particular firms and businesses, and macroeconomic policy refers to the overall management of the economy. Examples of microeconomic policy are regulation and subsidy programs. Macroeconomic policy includes monetary and fiscal policies. Microeconomic approaches are the primary subject of the rest of this chapter; macroeconomic approaches are examined in the next chapter.

Government intervention now extends to almost every aspect of our lives in efforts to protect the health, safety, welfare, and environment and to promote economic and social justice. The emphasis in this chapter, however, is on intervention that directly affects economic activity. Other chapters address government activities as they relate to other substantive areas, such as the environment, health, education, and equality of opportunity.

As noted earlier, the U.S. government has always intervened in economic activities. Early on, those activities were supportive and eventually gave way to a more regulatory approach. Today, we have a combination of the two. Regulation may be characterized as old style (economic) regulation or new style (social) regulation. Each has an impact on economic activity and the viability of economic enterprises.

Economic Regulation.   Old style, or economic, regulation, in the form of early antitrust laws, began as a way of controlling concentrations of wealth and power in large private-sector economic enterprises; the purpose was to ensure that private economic gain did not hurt the public interest. Guarding the public interest generally meant protection against economic abuse of citizens by prohibiting such practices as charging unreasonable prices, engaging in anticompetitive activities, or selling products hazardous to the health and safety of the public. Basically, the regulators are meant to be watchdogs for the public. In addition to protecting the public interest, economic regulation had the objective of preserving competition and controlling natural monopolies.

Regulatory agencies normally have a fair degree of independence from other governmental institutions. In establishing regulatory agencies, legislative bodies delegate certain of their policymaking powers to them and try to protect them as much as possible against interference from the executive branch. An **independent regulatory commission**, such as the Federal Trade Commission (FTC), for example, is created by legislative action. The mandate that Congress gave to the FTC is somewhat vague: to regulate in the interest of ensuring competition and to prevent deceptive advertising by industry. Five commissioners serve staggered seven-year terms on this commission, with the provision that no more than three may be from the same political party. The president designates one member as chairperson. Once appointed by the president and confirmed by the Senate, a commissioner may not be removed by the president except under unusual circumstances. Other regulatory agencies are similarly created and members similarly appointed, although the number of commissioners varies from agency to agency. Much regulating also is carried out by units within regular operating departments of the executive branch that are, therefore, less independent of the president. One example is the Food and Drug Administration (FDA) in the Department of Health and Human Services. The Department of Justice also regulates activities through its prosecution of parties for violation of laws and rules.

Congress often gives regulatory agencies relative independence from the president because partisan politics should have no place in regulation, and it does not want to surrender its powers to the executive branch. Another reason Congress delegates its powers is simply that it does not have the time, expertise, or other resources to carry out the specialized activities for which regulatory agencies are created. Ideally, the application of expertise and technical judgment is supposed to be free of politics. Though insulated from partisan political forces to the extent that board or commission members have fixed terms and ordinarily cannot be removed by the president, regulatory agencies have not escaped politics entirely. Rather, they are subject to many political pressures from interest groups, legislative committees, and the White House. For example, the Federal Communications Commission (FCC) became much more concerned with indecency on television after George W. Bush was elected in 2000 as he appointed a chair of the FCC who was concerned with the issue. After the infamous 2004 Super Bowl halftime wardrobe malfunction, in which Justin Timberlake exposed the breast of Janet Jackson as they were performing, television viewers and politicians brought pressure on the Commission to do something about it. The FCC eventually fined CBS $550,000 ($27,500 for each of the twenty CBS-owned stations). With the appointment of new commissioners by President Obama, the attention to indecency issues seems to have abated somewhat. Nonetheless, Congress and the president have much to say about the budgets and, indeed, the very existence of regulatory agencies; thus, the agencies pay attention to opinions from those sources.

In applying their expertise to problems, regulatory agencies give meaning to the general policies developed by legislative bodies. To do so, regulatory agencies adopt rules and regulations that have the force of law. Unlike legislative policymakers, however, regulatory agencies also enforce and serve as judges regarding policy. Thus, once they draw up a rule or regulation, they have the responsibility to see that the regulated party abides by the rules. They also decide whether a rule has been violated by an individual party and fashion a punishment appropriate for the violation.

Of course, a commission itself cannot do all the work of a regulatory agency and usually performs only the policymaking and judging functions. Commission policy is executed by its staff, although the staff also creates policy and does the major work in investigating and hearing evidence on cases in which violation of policy is charged. Once a hearing examiner (now called administrative law judge) has heard and evaluated the evidence, the examiner makes a recommendation on how the case should be decided. Normally, the commission accepts the examiner's recommendation, although changes may be made by the commission.

Social Regulation.   New style, or social, regulation attempts to correct problems in society through incentives or regulation to encourage or control various behaviors involving health, safety, welfare, and working conditions. Economic enterprises often are the vehicles for achieving social policy goals and thus are the objects of government intervention. Social regulation may be in the form of financial penalties, such as in emissions fees or fines for emitting pollutants into the air. Presumably, private enterprise will reduce emissions to avoid the financial penalties. An alternative approach is to encourage action by providing financial subsidies for conversion of polluting plants or bonuses for early

---

POLICY DILEMMAS   Emerging Use of Drones

The use of unmanned aerial vehicles (drones) by the U.S. military and Central Intelligence Agency (CIA), especially in Pakistan and Afghanistan, has stirred controversy. Drones were first used during the Bush administration and have increased in use under President Obama, but the government denied the existence of the program until 2013. The drones are used to kill enemy targets but have killed many civilians as well.

Because of the publicity surrounding the military and CIA use of drones, there is now much more information being released about their use in other ways. They are used for such things as crop spraying, surveying, firefighting, film making, and police work. Some enterprising companies are also developing new uses. For example, Amazon noted that it is working on plans for delivering packages by drones. Some television stations send drones to automobile accidents to obtain details for their news coverage. One company in Minnesota has used drones to deliver beer to ice fishers and another person flew a drone over the University of Virginia campus as part of a film promoting the medical school.

These uses of drones raise questions of safety and privacy of the public and other aircraft. Potential interference with other aircraft, as well as with one another, could lead to accidents and danger for people on the ground. Extensive use of drones could also lead to unwanted and unexpected voyeurism. These situations have led to Congress ordering the Federal Aviation Administration (FAA) to develop strict guidelines on the use of drones.

1. Do you think drone use should be regulated? Why or why not?
2. Should law enforcement have to obtain a warrant to use drones for surveillance?

---

compliance. Another alternative is to allocate permits for a specific level of emissions. By reducing emissions below its permitted level, a company could sell portions of its permit to others (**cap and trade**). Presumably, such a system would serve as an incentive to modernize equipment and reduce pollution or at least stop addition of more pollution. Policies that require contractors with the government to subcontract a certain portion of the contract with businesses owned by minorities or females represent another alternative for achieving a social goal.

Typically, social regulation occurs through already established executive departments, although there are exceptions as with the Equal Employment Opportunity Commission, which operates like the typical economic independent regulatory commission. Many social policies are implemented through contract compliance activities or through such departments as Labor and Commerce, although all departments have some role in such activities. State governments mirror many of the national regulatory activities and have many of their own regulatory agencies.[9]

Regulation of economic activity is an attempt to stabilize the economy and protect the interests of the general public. We already have looked at the most common form of regulation in the United States, agencies that create specific rules and regulations to control the behavior of economic enterprises or that provide incentives or penalties to encourage particular actions. Control of activities also is accomplished in several other ways. These methods include government ownership and the creation of government corporations. Ownership of public lands by the Department of the Interior is intended to control how the land is used. The U.S. Postal Service and the Federal Deposit Insurance Corporation are government-owned corporations that regulate and control many postal and banking activities. In addition, there are many programs and policies to protect particular economic interests. In agriculture, for example, many of the programs and policies subsidize particular economic entities and interfere with the free market.

CONTEMPORARY POLICY: PURPOSES AND TOOLS OF ECONOMIC INTERVENTION

In the following section, we examine how different forms of microeconomic intervention have been used in influencing the economy. Virtually every aspect of the economy is subject to some intervention by government, but to inventory them all here would be impossible. As Graham Wilson notes, government intervenes in the economy for multiple purposes.[10] It is there to protect citizens/consumers, to maintain a sound economy, and to stimulate and sustain economic activity. We use examples to illustrate pertinent approaches to today's economic policy.

Protecting Citizens and Consumers

Regulation provides the primary method for protecting citizens and consumers. As noted previously, regulation can be economic or social in nature. Traditional economic regulation took root in the late nineteenth and early twentieth centuries and has grown ever since. Government created economic regulation because some entrepreneurs abused their economic power through monopolies and hurt their employees and consumers in the process.

Economic Regulation. In the late nineteenth and early twentieth centuries, entrepreneurs managed to acquire near monopolies on many American industries, including steel and the railroads. These concentrations of power in a few hands were accompanied by many abuses. Consumers were charged exorbitant prices, small companies were bullied into selling out or were ruined by the large firms, and local governments were pressured into making concessions. Workers in such monopolies, with almost no bargaining power, were exploited at will by ruthless employers. All of these factors led to the reaction, by the public and politicians alike, that concentration of economic power in a small number of enterprises was not in the public interest. A movement grew in the United States to regulate industry. Early efforts focused on prohibiting monopolies that restrained trade. In time, a series of laws was enacted that forms the framework of today's government controls over such economic concentration. Policies eventually included other types of protection of the general public and to support corporate entities as well.

Antitrust policy is aimed at preventing one or a small number of firms from directly dominating all or most of a particular market. It also attempts to prevent private firms from agreeing among themselves to restrict competition. Thus, antitrust policy prohibits monopolies, as well as practices and agreements that fix prices, divide markets, or collude on bidding. To control monopolies and to dissolve those that had already come into being, Congress passed the Sherman Antitrust Act in 1890. The FTC Act of 1914 went further by creating the FTC to stem the development of monopolies and prevent practices that would lead to unfair competition. Because these laws were only partially successful, the policy was strengthened in 1950 with the Anti-Merger Act, which gave enforcement powers to administrative agencies. As part of its activities, the FTC has the responsibility to control anticompetitive and unfair trade practices and to protect consumers from unfair advertising.

Taken together, the antitrust laws give government a number of enforcement tools. The Sherman Act and subsequent legislation make illegal any action in restraint of interstate commerce. Government attorneys, currently the Antitrust Division of the Justice Department, can initiate criminal prosecution against companies charged with this violation. Additionally—and with greater effect—the Antitrust Division may initiate civil suits to obtain court orders requiring firms to cease practices that are found to be in restraint of trade. A similar proceeding may require a firm to break up into several units; the Standard Oil Corporation, for example, was divided into a number of companies in this way during the early part of the twentieth century. AT&T, which controlled 83 percent of the telephone market, was the object of antitrust litigation. Because the government's case was so strong, the company settled out of court in 1982 and agreed to dissolve, resulting in the current decentralized telephone service structure. Starting in 1995, the Antitrust Division charged Microsoft with anticompetitive practices and by 1997 sought orders to break up the company and to require it to desist from some practices. While Microsoft lost the case, it still has been slow to change its practices. Complaints about its software bundling practices, which force purchasers of Microsoft's operating system to buy other Microsoft software, continue to arise. In 2014, for example, Microsoft still owned approximately 90 percent of the market in PC operating systems, but smart phones are shifting market share of computing devices overall away from Microsoft.

The Antitrust Division also has the authority to approve or disapprove *mergers*. In the 1980s, the Justice Department took essentially a hands-off approach leading to virtually uncontrolled mergers. The Clinton administration approach was mixed in that it looked more carefully at mergers, but most of the effort was in adjusting terms of the mergers to assure market competition rather than disallowing them. The Bush administration took a hands-off approach to mergers.[11] The Obama administration signaled "reinvigorated antitrust enforcement," and began review of guidelines on mergers in 2009 and 2010 after being very critical of the hands-off approach of the Bush administration. Nonetheless, mergers continue with little interference, although the Justice Department did oppose the merger of American Airlines and U.S. Air in 2013. The courts approved the merger.

Another weapon that can be used is a suit by an individual who has been hurt by an antitrust violation. Current law permits court awards of triple the amount of damages suffered. But relying on such suits is not a very effective method of enforcing regulations: Both lack of interest and the large amount of time required of the litigants and courts in such procedures discourage victims from suing. It is not an efficient method of controlling behavior unless all the parties affected join in a class action suit. Nonetheless, the Recording Industry Association of America (RIAA) uses suits against those who download copyrighted music from the Internet to discourage the practice. RIAA first subpoenas the Internet Service Provider (ISP) for names and addresses of peer-to-peer file sharers and then selectively sues the users. RIAA hopes the threat of suit causes people to stop the sharing. Many universities have cooperated with RIAA to take away Internet access to anyone who is found to be illegally sharing files.

Class action suits are those in which an individual or individuals sue on behalf of all people who are in a similar situation. Thus, a woman who suffered injury from a breast implant successfully sued the manufacturer on behalf of all women who had that breast implant. Those women would be part of the class on whose behalf litigation is initiated. Because of the large number of people who may be affected in such cases, and because courts usually have required litigants to demonstrate personal injury in order to be a party to a court action, class action suits have been difficult to pursue. Also, courts often require the litigants to identify and notify all members of the class. This requirement can be difficult to meet because the people are hard to locate, and many may be too indifferent to respond. As a result, class action suits are not a major means of accomplishing regulation, although they are used on occasion.[12] Critics of class action lawsuits claim that lawyers shop around for states where the courts are most amenable to such suits. As a result, President Bush in 2005 pushed reform through Congress requiring most class action suits to be filed in federal courts, resulting in a decline in state courts and an increase in federal courts.

The FTC and the courts have been less hostile to mergers in recent years. In the past, market share was a very important consideration in decisions on mergers. The FTC and the courts were likely to disallow any merger that increased market share of a corporation by even as much as 10 percent. In recent years, mergers have been allowed wherein market share was increased as much as 40 percent or, as in the case of Boeing and McDonnell Douglas aircraft manufacturers, 100 percent of domestic production. The courts have sanctioned such mergers even when the FTC has been opposed.

Weaknesses in U.S. antitrust policy are the result of many factors. One is a lack of clarity about goals. Given the responsibility to restore competition and prevent deceptive advertising, the FTC and the Justice Department would seem to have easily understood objectives. However, these are rather ambiguous goals in terms of the precise actions that might be taken to achieve them.

Another factor also explains sometimes erratic performance: The commission and the Justice Department have discretion as to which of these objectives they emphasize. As different presidents influence these regulators through their appointments, the perspectives of the agencies vary. Thus, uneven attention is given to enforcement of rules and regulations. Ambivalence about how strongly antitrust policy should be pursued also provides regulated industries with opportunities to articulate their positions. Industries have the resources and contacts to make their concerns known to regulators, who are often sympathetic in the first place. They are usually effective in mobilizing political forces to reduce the intensity of the enforcement efforts. With the increasingly globally competitive environment, there also are pressures to be more flexible with domestic corporations so that they can compete with foreign corporations.

Global Approaches to Antitrust.   Industrialized nations generally favor some form of control over **monopoly** and restraint of trade, although some nations, such as Italy, have virtually no antitrust or antimonopoly laws. Reflecting a different perspective, most Western European nations identify their policies as **competition policies** as opposed to antitrust policies, as they are named in the United States. Although many of the Western European nations use approaches similar to that of the United States, there are variations. Some countries have weaker policies. For example, in Great Britain the approval of Parliament is required before the Monopolies Commission can prevent mergers. This provision opens regulation much more directly to political pressures and thus lessens its effectiveness. So long as mergers are not found to be contrary to the public interest, they are not prohibited. Very seldom does British government find them to be harmful.

Germany represents the opposite end of the spectrum. There, government approval is required before mergers of large corporations can occur. More significantly, the German Cartel Office also has the authority to dissolve a corporation brought about by merger. Most European nations employ an approach somewhere between these two extremes.

Japan appears less enthusiastic about controlling competition. Nonetheless, after World War II, policy to break up monopolies was imposed upon Japan. Although enforcement has been weak, the law was strengthened in 1977, and efforts have been made to limit price fixing and protect consumers through communication about abuses.[13]

Globalization of the economy poses particular challenges for businesses and regulation. The merger of AT&T and BellSouth required approval of the FTC and three other countries because of its global implications. In 2007, Microsoft lost an appeal to the European Union's Court of First Instance, which upheld a 2004 European Commission antitrust decision against Microsoft. As a result, Microsoft has to sell an unbundled version of Windows and share information about its operating system with competitors so that they can interface with Windows. The European Commission continued to focus on Microsoft's business practices and in 2013 fined Microsoft for failing to comply with its earlier orders, illustrating that regulation is complicated by global policy and trade.

Social Regulation.   While social regulation is not directly economic, it has economic impacts for those regulated. For example, consumer regulation has become very much a part of U.S. policies since the 1970s. The FDA is responsible for insuring the safety of our food supply and the medicine we use. The Consumer Product Safety Commission created by the Consumer Product Protection Act of 1972 produces rules and regulations for virtually any product sold commercially. The warning labels regarding proper use found on products from lawn mowers to washing machines result from the Commission's rules. It costs producers to make products to the standards required by the Commission and to provide the appropriate warning information. Of course, producers then pass the cost on to consumers.

Other social regulation involves such things as nondiscrimination policies, worker safety, and wages and hours policy. All government agencies are responsible for making sure that their activities comply with policies in these areas. They also usually have to make sure that those they contract with or serve also meet these social regulations. Businesses often complain that these regulations cost them money and time. In 2014, there was a major debate over whether the minimum wage should be raised, as pushed by President Obama. Supporters claim that raising the minimum wage would stimulate the economy by putting more money in the pockets of those who are most likely to spend it. Opponents argue that raising the minimum wage will only hurt businesses and further depress the economy because businesses would be able to hire fewer workers, thus also hurting the potential workers themselves.

Maintaining a Sound Economy

Government efforts to maintain a sound economy are covered primarily in Chapter 4 with its discussion of macroeconomic policies. It should be noted here though that business depends on stability in the economy. During the slow economic recovery and slow growth in employment in 2009, many business leaders and critics of the Obama administration argued that business would not invest in the economy because of uncertainty. They blamed the administration for the uncertainty, but many others noted that Congress was just as responsible with its inability to act on many important issues, especially regarding the national debt and adopting a budget.

Sustaining Economic Activity

Supporting Business.   There are many ways in which government provides support to economic enterprises. **Subsidies** represent one of the oldest forms of support. They are particularly important to agriculture and help provide stability to farm production by mitigating the effects of the vagaries of weather and other aspects of the economy on crops. Beginning in the 1930s, farmers have been paid to not grow certain crops to keep prices from falling too low. The government also subsidizes some commodities by purchasing excess crops or provides a price support to keep farmers in business. During 2014, U.S. farmers received over $14 billion in subsidies. While the justification for such subsidies is normally focused on saving the family farm, the reality is that the vast majority of the money goes to large agri-business corporations. While agricultural subsidies are the most common, there are many others.

Passenger railroads and airlines have been subsidized to promote those businesses, especially in less populated areas. Tax breaks for installing antipollution equipment or other such purposes represent another form of subsidy. Low interest loans and depreciation write-offs on taxes are also important forms of subsidy to encourage business to invest in new technology or hire people. The Affordable Care Act (ACA) provides subsidies to people below a certain income level to purchase insurance on the exchanges set up in 2013. That subsidy helped the purchaser, but it was also an important incentive to insurance companies to support passage of the act because it helped ensure that they would have more customers. There are many varied purposes for which government will provide incentives for people and businesses to behave in a given way.

Controlling who can enter the market is another form of subsidy to business, providing protection to those already established. In order to enter some markets, a business needs a license or certificate to operate. Taxi or limousine companies are examples at the local level. At the national level, airlines need certificates to operate and need to satisfy requirements of the Federal Aviation Administration (FAA) before they can be certified to carry passengers. Many businesses favor such regulation because it gives certainty to its business opportunities. Of course, there are many other considerations requiring regulation, but maintaining a stable, profitable business environment is one of the important considerations.

Economic Development.   All levels of government face rapidly changing economic conditions and technology, thus requiring governments to engage in economic development. Economically depressed areas are fraught with many social problems, such as unemployment, crime, deteriorated housing, and limited tax bases. During the 1980s, the concept of **enterprise zones** was imported from Great Britain and implemented in many states.[14] The national government adopted the idea when the Clinton administration made enterprise zones a major part of its urban policy, naming them empowerment zones. The designations carry various names, including Renewal Communities, Brownfield Communities, Empowerment Communities, Enterprise Communities, and Enterprise Zones. The Obama administration proposed new funding in 2014 for the program under the title, "**Promise Zones**."[15]

The zones target economic development geographically. They are partnerships in which government and the private and nonprofit sectors work together to attempt to stimulate economic development and to solve some of the social problems associated with economically depressed areas. The zones help business through such benefits as reduced taxes, tax credits, technical assistance, and reduction or elimination of regulations so that private-sector entities can develop innovative economic activities while also helping depressed neighborhoods and communities.

In addition to the economic incentives and push for economic development, these zones focus intensive governmental agency attention to such social problems as crime, lack of good housing, and high unemployment in the zones. As economic development occurs, many of the social problems are expected to recede in severity, but not all can be cured by economic development alone. Thus, federal agencies, in cooperation with state and local units as well as private and nonprofit organizations, work together to apply resources to address social problems.

The experience so far suggests that the zones can have beneficial effects, although it is difficult to measure just how much improvement can be attributed to the zones themselves.[16] States usually provide income tax credits and some allow property tax abatements as well as waivers of sales taxes in the zone. Businesses building in some zones also receive discounts on utility bills. Encompassing broader purposes, some enterprise zones have reinvested the tax revenues generated in the zones in the infrastructure of the zones to improve conditions even more. Job training programs have been developed for zone residents in some cases.

As economic development tools, these initiatives represent a politically popular notion. Given a political climate supportive of less government and letting the private sector operate with fewer restrictions, the enterprise zone provides one avenue for doing so. Theoretically, innovative approaches will flow from the decreased taxation and regulation. Government is a facilitator, not the owner, of the process. Business benefits and, in the process, so do residents of the zone as well as the general public, who presumably bear less expense resulting from crime and other social problems.

These efforts, however, may cause dislocation of residents with the attendant breakdown of a sense of community. Finding new housing for displaced residents is not easy, either. Sometimes the social problems only move to a new area that becomes overpopulated with the press of residents who have been displaced. Critics of these approaches also note that economic development activity is attracted from other areas that might become economically depressed, thus just moving the problem. The loss in tax revenue caused by the tax abatements and waivers also concerns some people.

As noted earlier, government always has provided support to private enterprise, and these revitalization programs represent one facet of such support. Critics, however, often suggest that government goes too far in supporting economic enterprises. In the debate over government spending, conservatives in Congress target personal welfare and liberals challenge them to look at corporate welfare.

International Trade

International trade represents another aspect of the current economic environment. Most administrations in recent history have supported free trade in theory. In reality, the United States often fosters barriers like tariffs, import quotas, or subsidies to industries that give them advantages over others. Other nations do the same thing.

NAFTA. The *North American Free Trade Agreement* (*NAFTA*), enacted by Congress in November 1993, created a free trade area among the United States, Canada, and Mexico. Theoretically, NAFTA would result in the United States being better able to sell goods in the Mexican market and stimulate economic development in Mexico as well. Immigration pressures on the United States presumably would be lessened as better economic opportunities developed for Mexican citizens. Critics of the agreement feared the migration of U.S. jobs to Mexico and the lessening of health, safety, and environmental standards.[17] NAFTA built upon the United States–Canada Free Trade Agreement of 1988 which provides virtually free trade between the two countries. Most experts suggest that NAFTA has been a success, boosting trade among the three countries, increasing employment, and improving productivity. Nonetheless, there are critics who note that many jobs in specific sectors were lost in the United States, suggesting that NAFTA has weakened unions and contributed to the U.S. trade deficit. Business generally supports free trade while unions do not. Thus, Republicans in Congress are usually supporters while many of the Democrats are suspicious because of the union issue. President Obama pushed for broader authority to negotiate free trade agreements with nations in the Trans-Pacific and the European Union, but has run into opposition from his own party in Congress.

The Omnibus Trade Act of 1988 provides for the United States to impose such restrictions as tariffs or import quotas on any trading partner that imposed barriers on American access to their markets. The trade act was a product of rising concern over the nation's growing trade deficit, particularly the trade imbalance with Japan. The act required the president to identify those nations with unfair trade practices and a large American trade surplus as targets for trade negotiations. If the negotiation process failed, American trade restrictions would follow as retaliation. It also created a training program for American workers adversely affected by international trade practices. Promotion of American exports and training for American industry to enhance the likelihood of success internationally also were parts of the act. The act has been used against even Canada over importation of Canadian lumber into the United States. Similarly, the United States has attempted to limit importation of clothing from China using the law.

GATT. A major debate in Congress in 1994 involved ratification of agreements under the *General Agreement on Tariffs and Trade* (*GATT*). GATT, established after World War II, was designed to reduce national tariff barriers to international trade. It took almost a decade to negotiate the agreement, and it stirred emotions within the political establishment. The agreement reduced tariffs on manufactured goods an average of nearly 40 percent. Presumably, that would translate into lower prices for consumers. Opponents say that reduced U.S. collection of tariffs adds to the federal deficit. The debate for and against GATT was similar to that about NAFTA.

Perhaps the most controversial part of the GATT agreement was the creation of the *World Trade Organization* (*WTO*). WTO is the successor to GATT. It attempts to settle disputes and monitor and crack down on unfair trade practices. While advocates applaud the provision as bringing pressure on others to comply with fair trade practices, opponents suggest that it weakens health, safety, and labor laws in the United States. Further, they argue that it makes state and local governments conform to WTO policies and standards. Any suggestion of a world organization impinging on U.S. sovereignty arouses heated debate. Although political posturing during the 1994 election and after was intense, Congress did ratify the agreement in December of 1994. The United States joined 123 other nations in an effort to eliminate trade barriers on many items. Opponents of WTO argue that it has the power to override federal and state laws on labor and environmental standards among others. WTO decisions have affected many U.S. industries from food to steel. Many countries target U.S. subsidies of farm exports, and their complaints to WTO have been sustained. As a consequence, the level of subsidies is being reduced. An interesting case in 2005 involved Internet gambling. Antigua and Barbuda complained that U.S. restrictions on Internet gambling were illegal. WTO ruled that the United States could restrict such activity under its Wire Communications Act of 1961, based on protecting public morals or maintaining public order. At the same time, WTO said that the United States must apply its Interstate Horseracing Act equally to domestic and foreign betting services. Thus, online betting must be open to international outlets, a position the United States opposed. In 2007, WTO affirmed its earlier decision while criticizing the United States for ignoring the earlier ruling. Thus, WTO has both positive and negative consequences for the United States.

European Union.   Another issue related to trade and the economy is the move by the European Economic Community (EEC) to develop an integrated economy. In 1985, member nations of the EEC developed a detailed plan to achieve a unified economic system by the end of 1992. Restrictions on trade, services, flow of capital, and labor supply would be eliminated. The goal of this plan is to create an environment that stimulates economic growth in member nations. The EEC along with other European organizations became the *European Union* (*EU*) in 1993. With twenty-eight nations in 2014, growth in numbers continues. Iceland, Macedonia, Montenegro, Serbia, and Turkey have applied to join. Former members of the Soviet bloc make up many of the recently added members. In 2002, the EU substituted the Euro for national currencies in all but Denmark, Great Britain, Norway, and Sweden. By 2005, the Euro was competing heavily with the U.S. dollar for world currency domination; however, since 2010, concern over whether the Euro would survive surfaced because of economic and monetary crises in several EU nations including Ireland, Greece, and Portugal.

Successful implementation of the EU economic system provides major economic competition for the United States in the global economy. The EU represents a potential market of over five hundred million consumers with a significant commercial and industrial base. The United States has yet to develop a comprehensive economic policy to address the impact of this change in Europe.

POLICY EVALUATION: ENCOURAGING COMPETITION OR DISCOURAGING INNOVATION?

Deregulation

Deregulation of industries that were previously heavily regulated has been popular since the 1970s. The Carter administration began the process gradually by examining individual regulatory agencies and the industries they regulated. The Reagan and first Bush administrations took a more sweeping approach to deregulation, reflecting a strong commitment to a market economy free of governmental constraints. Ideologically, conservatives have been strong supporters of deregulation. While less enthusiastic about deregulation, the Clinton and Obama administrations have supported some deregulation while insisting that many regulations are essential to the health and safety of the public and to a healthy economy.

Deregulation is promoted as a consumer-oriented policy that will result in more competition and lower prices. In the rush to deregulate in the late 1970s and early 1980s, there was little consideration of the social benefits of regulation. With deregulation came many benefits to consumers and some parts of industry. Some businesses also suffered economic reversals. In the airline industry, for example, consumers benefited from increased competition as airfares declined. In the long run, airfares increased again, but competition sustained many bargain fares. Service to smaller communities suffered on occasion, and bunching of departure times around peak travel hours has led to complaints of delays and inconvenience. The public, however, seems to prefer the bargain fares over matters of scheduling and service. The terrorist attacks of September 11, 2001, resulted in more support for regulations to improve safety.

The financial crisis of 2007–2008 saw the collapse of the housing market, leading some financial institutions to voice strong support for regulation of the financial sector. The U.S. government bailed out numerous firms and banks as a result of high-risk investment schemes, and the housing market collapsed due to mortgage fraud and risky loans. Congress passed the Dodd-Frank Wall Street Reform and Consumer Protection Act of 2010, which imposed new regulations on the financial sector. It created a Financial Services Oversight Panel (FSOP) to identify risks to the financial markets and a new Consumer Financial Protection Bureau. It also allowed these organizations to develop new rules and regulations to ensure financial stability and protection of consumers. Implementation was slowed by controversies over funding and appointments to them. Nonetheless, they are developing the rules and regulations as of 2014.

The benefits of regulation in protecting consumers from capricious action, ensuring a reasonable distribution of important services at a fair cost, and protecting the health and safety of the community are now reemerging concerns as the effects of deregulation are assessed. As with any policy, deregulation has resulted in both positive and negative consequences.

The relaxation of regulation has had broader implications. Republican administrations in the 1980s and from 2000–2008 deemphasized implementation of such policies as antitrust, equal employment opportunity, and labor relations. The business sector found the administrators of these programs willing to interpret policies in ways more sympathetic to business. Thus, the National Labor Relations Board and the federal courts changed the direction of much of labor law. They permitted the use of bankruptcy laws, for example, to release corporations from contract obligations under collective bargaining agreements, as happened with Continental Airlines and the Manville Corporation. One effect is that labor unions found it necessary to accept bargaining agreements that scaled back their earnings and benefits. Corporations thus clearly have a stronger hand in controlling their own destiny. While the Clinton administration generally was more supportive of labor and consumers, its tendency was cautious in reinstituting regulation, especially in light of the public complaints about the overregulated society. The George W. Bush administration emphasized the interests of business in removing as much regulation as possible. Businesses continued to get approval for relaxing rules on such things as labor agreements and pension obligations when they sought bankruptcy protection. Delta, United Airlines, and U.S. Airways, for example, won many such concessions in courts. While the Obama administration is more sympathetic to labor, Congress has refused to confirm his appointments to the National Labor Review Board; so, it has been unable to perform its work because it does not have a quorum required to function.

Similarly, antitrust policy became more flexible since the early 1980s. The FTC seemed less interested than ever in prohibiting mergers based on the size of the market controlled. Merger mania began in the late 1970s and accelerated in the 1980s as the Reagan administration relaxed rules. Many of these mergers were hostile takeovers in which entrepreneurs took over undervalued corporations. The managers of the takeover targets usually are the most resistant to takeovers, although many stockholders also question the long-term wisdom of such actions. Mergers continued at a high rate until the 2001 recession; by 2014, they were trending up again (see Figure 3.1).[18]

Free Trade

The NAFTA (1993) and GATT (1994) treaties were the last major free trade agreements as free trade has been difficult to get through Congress. Congress has refused to approve renewal of the president's **fast track authority** (meaning that Congress has to vote up or down on a treaty with no opportunity to change it) in negotiating agreements despite requests from every president for such authority (also called **trade promotion authority**). Other nations do not want to negotiate a treaty if every member of Congress can try to make a change in it.

Assistance to Business

The efforts to support economic enterprise reflect some reaction to the increasing criticism of government intervention as a regulator of business activity. Thus, instead of being seen as an inhibitor of economic innovation, the effort is to support new approaches. Government provides the support and facilitation of

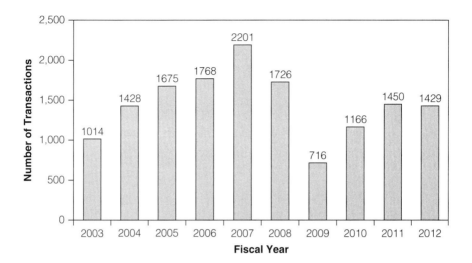

F I G U R E 3.1   Merger Transactions, Fiscal Years 2003–2012

SOURCE: www.ftc.gov.sites/default/files/documents/reports_annual/35th-report-fy2012/130430hsrreport_0.pdf, accessed March 20, 2014.

efforts, but is not the controller of those activities. In the states that have used enterprise zones in the past, supporters usually point to impressive numbers, especially in job creation. Critics note that many of those jobs, however, would have been created in the absence of enterprise zones or other support. While development and job creation may not have occurred in the particular locales, they probably would have happened in other places. Evaluation of the programs then needs to take into account program objectives other than just economic development. For example, do they actually help solve social problems? Debate over their effectiveness and partisanship have caused President Obama's efforts on Promise Zones to languish in Congress.

The use of **risk subsidies** is yet another way government supports economic enterprise. The use of subsidies in agriculture is well known. While normally couched in terms of helping the family farm, such subsidies usually protect corporate farms from risks of the market and ensure profits. The subsidies to sugar producers and tariffs on sugar imports protect the producers from the realities of the marketplace. In the ACA, subsidies to lower- and middle-income people help them to buy health insurance. Similarly, the increase in public deposit insurance guarantees in the 1980s led some financial institutions into high-risk investments that ultimately resulted in the savings and loan crisis and huge costs to the national government to pay off depositors and investors. In 2009, the bailout programs for financial institutions and insurance and auto industry giants represented a form of subsidy for private corporations.

All of these elements of policy are sympathetic to the business community. The theoretical effects of government intervention in the economy were examined at the beginning of this chapter, but actual outcomes do not always match the expected results. Critics of regulation note that although much regulation is justified as a means of promoting competition, it often actually tends to stifle that competition. By making entry into a market very difficult, for example, regulation often restricts competition. Competition also is reduced by price controls, as was true in the airline industry until the 1980s. Ironically, for this same reason many industries also defend regulation. Assured of a comfortable environment in which to do business, industry can count on a certain profit margin. Complete competition would make its situation less predictable. Consumers, or consumer advocates, object to this arrangement because it results in higher prices.

Effects of Regulation

One impact that industry often complains of is that government regulation interferes with its capacity to operate efficiently in a free society. According to this charge, regulatory agencies have become pervasive in all economic areas, and their red tape and complex regulations make compliance almost impossible. Many agencies make conflicting demands on industry, and paperwork has increased to the point that industry must employ people solely to deal with government regulation. Confusion abounds: Industries are firmly instructed not to consider race, sex, age, or religion in personnel decisions and, at the same time, are required to submit data on their workforce according to the same taboo categories. Moreover, many critics wonder whether regulations are developed to benefit society or simply to keep the wheels spinning so the agency will have something to do.

Regulation also may have unintended consequences in terms of its effects on innovation. Generally, regulated industries appear to be less inclined to adopt new technology and improve their methods of doing business than are nonregulated industries.[19] As a result, regulated industry is likely to be outmoded and less efficient. This is especially true when regulation guarantees a profit. The losers are consumers. Many critics raised this issue regarding British Petroleum's (BP) close relationship with the U.S. Minerals Management Service (MMS) after the *Deepwater Horizon* oil spill in 2010. Evidence indicated that MMS allowed BP virtually regulation-free rein to operate. The same seems to have happened with Freedom Industries whose tanks spilled chemicals into the Elk River leading to residents of the City of Charleston, West Virginia, being unable to use the municipal water supply for several days in 2014.

Regulation also is criticized for contributing to the cost of doing business. Estimates in 2013 indicated $236 billion in costs to businesses.[20] Putting that kind of money into nonproductive efforts diverts it from productive ones. Critics, however, are also anxious that deregulation not go too far, that is, to the point of eliminating legitimate controls, though they usually agree that regulation has become excessive.

A common complaint of consumer-oriented critics is that regulation is dominated by the regulated industries themselves, which have the money and other resources to keep abreast of policy. Consumers, especially individuals, find access to regulatory agencies difficult because they lack knowledge of procedures and because of the costs associated with input into decision making. Due to the fact that regulators constantly deal with people from the regulated industries, they develop strong rapport with them. It is only natural that the regulators should consider their interests when making decisions. After all, the regulators would have no one to regulate if they did not help promote their survival. This close relationship often results in strong industry influence and sometimes control over regulators. The interests of consumers may be ignored.

Closely related to the access issue is the complaint that regulatory agencies are outside normal political activities and therefore are not answerable to anyone but themselves and the industries they regulate. It is unreasonable to expect agencies to respond to the major concerns of society if they do not have to answer to the political leadership produced by that society. Of course, regulatory agencies were created to be independent of direct political pressure so that they could consider a wider public interest. This criticism goes to the heart of the original reason for creating independent regulatory agencies in the first place. Independence has both benefits and costs.

It sometimes is argued that government is too involved in too many aspects of everyday life. Government seems to take the position that people need guidance in everything they do, and so virtually no activity is free of government intervention. The duplication of effort, red tape, and examples of bureaucratic bungling, which are constantly given coverage in the news media, reinforce negative images of regulation. Tax revolts and a rejection of governmental paternalism have led to serious questioning of regulatory efforts. As antigovernment feelings seem to grow, regulatory agencies face major challenges to their activities.

A new twist to these regulatory processes is the effort of the FTC to keep state and local governments from interfering with competition in the marketplace. Most notable have been those cases in which the FTC has successfully sued municipalities to force deregulation of taxicab companies and their fares as a restraint of trade. This emphasis is a new use of antitrust law consistent with the probusiness, free trade stance that national elections in the mid- and late 1990s and early 2000s seemed to support. After the disclosures of business practices of banks and financial firms and their contribution to the economic crisis of 2008–2010 and the impact of lax regulation in the Gulf of Mexico oil spill in 2010 and the Charleston, West Virginia, water contamination in 2014, people once again debated the merits of regulation versus deregulation.

Changes in Regulation

Changes in economic regulation have been many, and the effects have varied greatly. For example, the effects of de-emphasis of antitrust policy are very difficult to assess. While the business world generally applauds the reduction of control over its activities, consumers are not so sure of the benefits. The rash of mergers and leveraged buyouts create impressive profits for many opportunists, but there are usually losers as well. Many employees, especially white-collar employees, lose their jobs and pensions (e.g., Sears and Kmart in 2005) as a result of the inevitable restructuring of the corporations that are merged. New and reorganized companies often pay lower wages and provide fewer benefits. For the consumer, of course, mergers can lead to less competition and eventually higher prices. Stockholders also are potential losers as total corporate debt increases, exceeding total corporate assets.

Much deregulation in the business sector reduced sensitivity to safety concerns that affect employees. Thus, the effect on employees has been negative. The 2014 Freedom Industries chemical spill in Elk Creek near Charleston, West Virginia, that contaminated water for as many as three hundred thousand people and the 2010 West Virginia Massey Energy Company coal mine disaster that left twenty-nine miners dead illustrate the impact of lax regulation. Similarly, the elimination of regulations on product safety can benefit producers in the short run and hurt consumers. In the long run, producers may also be hurt as lawsuits over liability for death and injury create major financial setbacks.

Mergers themselves do not always work out well. Many of them are undone through divestiture or spinning off parts of the acquired companies. For example, Daimler-Benz and Chrysler merged in 1998; by 2007, the merged company, DaimlerChrysler, agreed to dissolve. Daimler-Benz paid $36 billion for Chrysler in 1998 and the merged company never was a success. So, in 2007, the company sold 80 percent of its assets for $8.9 billion, losing a lot of money. Bank of America bought Countrywide Bank for $2.5 billion in 2008, and it ended up costing $40 billion because of Countrywide's involvement in the mortgage loan scandals. Arby's and Wendy's merged in 2008 but broke up in 2011 over poor revenue. Some estimate that over 70 percent of mergers end in failure.[21]

Government economic intervention in the form of subsidies and supports for enterprise has raised serious questions as well. The federal government's efforts to stimulate and stabilize financial institutions through loans and loan guarantees, for example, have made them safe places for investors to place their money, but these supports have, at the same time, encouraged risky investments leading to bank and savings and loan failures. Similarly, the federal government provides loans and loan guarantees to homeowners, college students, farmers, and others; moreover, it guarantees other financial instruments, such as pensions. In 2007, many worried about the mortgage industry and government guarantees of credit in it as a possible source of more liability for government, only to see the collapse of the housing industry in 2009 because of mortgage credit abuses. Congress passed, and President Obama signed, financial regulatory reform legislation in 2010 in an effort to ensure that more such liabilities do not develop.

Even though there are questions about support for private enterprise, it always has been a part of American economic policy. Experiments utilizing the concept of enterprise zones are attempting to integrate economic and social issues in a comprehensive program focused on particular geographic areas, but experience is mixed. Many of the successes claimed in jobs created, industries enticed to open in the zones, and improvements in services in the area may have occurred without the enterprise zones. Nonetheless, the zones offer support in the form of subsidies, tax breaks, and technical assistance to business.

The globalization of the world economy and the emergence of the EU have created a new environment for the private sector as well, resulting in efforts by the national government to negotiate trade agreements whose primary emphasis is reducing the barriers to free trade as in NAFTA. Produce farmers claim that they have been hurt by lower production costs in Mexico and thus lower prices for their produce. The movement of industry to Mexico to take advantage of cheap labor has not increased to the extent the opponents of NAFTA had claimed. GATT and WTO represent another effort to reduce trade barriers, and some industries are certain to be hurt. The textile industry, in particular, has been hurt because of the inexpensive labor in those industries in many countries, while high-tech and construction industries benefit. Regulators struggle to keep up with changing technology. Copyright enforcement faces challenges with Internet access to all forms of copyrighted material. The laws creating regulation did not anticipate the change that occurred in all areas of communication technology.

CONTINUING DEBATES

There are many suggestions for reform in government's relationship to the economy. As indicated earlier, many of the recommendations deal with eliminating government's intervention in economic activity. Thus, creation of a free-market economy independent of government influence is seen as a means to stimulate economic enterprise toward more productivity and to restore the economy to a strong position. However, given the long history of government involvement, it is highly unlikely that such action is possible. As critics of Milton Friedman's ideas (noted earlier) suggest, a true free market is likely to produce a situation in which those groups with power dominate the system. There would not be freedom for all participants to compete equally.

Perhaps the most drastic reform proposal is that regulatory agencies be abolished.[22] Legislative bodies create regulatory agencies because of their own inability to regulate. Regulatory agencies became little legislatures of their own, enjoying independence from normal political controls. Advocates of reform want a return to citizen control through elected political leaders and believe that redistributing control over economic activities among the three branches of government would permit the public to influence the regulators' activity more effectively. A variation on this theme is that because much regulatory activity ends up in the slow-moving courts, regulatory agencies could be abolished and the courts could be assigned the responsibility in the first place. Although courts usually are viewed as inappropriate for regulation because of their slowness and lack of expertise, the increasing slowness of regulatory agencies tends to undermine the argument. Nonetheless, courts may only respond to cases brought to them, and they lack the ability to oversee constantly a particular economic activity.

Abolition of the regulatory agencies may appeal to many, but given the tendency of Congress to create more and more regulatory policies and the agencies to enforce them, it is unlikely that such proposals will enjoy much success. First, there are too many interests that oppose abolition, including the regulatory agencies themselves, their clientele, and the beneficiaries of agency regulation. Consider, for example, the obstacles faced by the Reagan administration in its first year as it whittled away at various regulators' powers but failed to dismantle completely all but a few. Second, another factor in opposing abolition is that regulatory policy is likely to have less visibility if placed in a regular administrative department. A particular regulatory policy then may have to compete with other agency priorities and—especially if controversial—may be buried by the agency's politics. Robbed of its independent status, the regulatory unit is likely to be less effective. Hence, for both political and practical reasons, completely abolishing regulatory agencies seems improbable.

Alternative Approaches

Incentives.   A number of new ideas come from industries that would like to put some controls on what they see as overregulation. One alternative proposed by some is that regulatory policy should focus on results rather than on punishment for violations. If the intent of a policy is to improve safety for employees, for example, the most effective method of accomplishing such an objective might be to reward industries for good safety records.

Another idea is that new rules and regulations should include assessing their economic impact. Congress already considers the economic impacts of its policies. Regulators now are required to make such assessments. Congress appears to be strongly in support of identifying the costs up front.

Sunset Laws.   *Sunset laws* are yet another favored means of preventing excessive regulation. Sunset legislation requires that agencies and their programs be given specific periods of existence and be reviewed at the end of the time allotted. Thus, five years might be a common life span for an agency; at the end of that time it would have to justify its existence. The idea is that the regulatory agency would of necessity eliminate unneeded and nonconstructive activities in order to pass this five-year review. Similar state sunset laws exist. This evaluation can lead to better performance and to a careful consideration by the legislature of whether to continue a regulatory activity.

Nationalization.   At the polar opposite of deregulation and regulatory abolition lies *nationalization*. Nationalization of industry would involve government bureaucracy in operating the economic enterprise directly. The criticisms often made of British railroads or the national health service—both nationalized institutions—generate serious opposition to this idea. Some members of Congress and the public advocated a single payer system for the ACA which would have essentially nationalized health care, but it was never seriously considered. Neither the American public nor its political leaders appear to feel that nationalization would lead to anything but more red tape and even less efficiency than regulation involves. Therefore, nationalization does not appear to be a viable alternative. With the move to get government out of business activities and the privatization of many government activities, the trend is clearly in the opposite direction. The opposition is reinforced by the fact that the British government has gradually denationalized some industry. One exception is the safety screening at airports. After the September 11, 2001, terrorist attacks, Congress made airport passenger screening a national function within the Homeland Security Department.

Consumer Oversight.   Another controversial suggestion is to create consumer committees to evaluate economic activities and then make suggestions for change. This is known as direct consumer oversight. Industry tends to be hostile to this innovation, feeling that consumer groups often focus on one specific issue to the exclusion of the industry's general health. As a result, this proposal has not been accorded serious consideration.

Dramatic new economic proposals are often popular, but the realities of the political process must be faced. The parties with the resources to influence policy usually also have access to the regulatory and economic policymaking system. Thus, reform must confront them as well. The likelihood is that influential interests will prevail, and reform, if any, will continue to be gradual.

Community Revitalization.   The experiments with community revitalization, such as enterprise and promise zones, will be watched carefully to determine whether they produce economic development. Enterprise and empowerment zones are likely to be given credit for any success there is in economic development in the targeted areas. Assessing the evidence will be the difficult part. Especially if they are viewed as helping to solve social problems, they are likely to spread.

Trade/Globalization.   Trade has accelerated the connectedness of the world in all aspects of society, meaning that globalization is a contemporary reality. Globalization refers to the international flow of trade, capital, technology, and information. With the constantly increasing strides in technology, transmission and accumulation of information affects all other aspects of society. Although some believe that globalization is an intentional effort of some powerful interests to enhance their own power and wealth, most people understand that it is an inevitable consequence of advances in technology and interchange in world society. Clearly, globalization provides many benefits to society such as enhancing economic output, increasing competition, and enhancing efficiency of economic systems; it also can have negative consequences for particular individuals and groups within a given society.

In American society, supporters of globalization point to the economic gains it creates for the American economy, estimated to be more than $1 trillion every year.[23] Opponents point to the increasing competition and its costs to workers and business owners in declining industries that are hurt. They also point to declining wages brought about by lower paid workers in other countries. Many perceptions lead to opposition, including the belief that foreign nations benefit from unfair trade practices and that globalization benefits only a select few, especially big businesses.[24] United States' policy alternates between promoting global opportunities for business and attempting to mitigate the negative effects. Initiatives for free trade usually favor economic enterprises and have been a staple of recent administrations. It is likely that free trade will continue to be controversial.

Some policies have focused on helping those within American society who are disadvantaged in the short run by globalization. Thus, programs for assistance for people dislocated by international competition include income support, job training, job search assistance, and relocation services. Wage insurance for older workers and tax credits for health insurance also are part of a program known as Trade Adjustment Assistance. There is much support for expanding this program, which is popular with Democrats, but is unlikely to get the support of the 2014 Republican majority in the House of Representatives.

Other policies include education assistance such as job training for skills needed in the new economy. Tax policy is advocated to address income distribution as a way to reduce resistance to globalization. Thus, earned income tax credits and tax credits for employer-sponsored health care benefits and other incentives have some advocates. Creation of high-wage jobs in the United States is also a common theme in discussions of how to deal with globalization. How to do so is a matter of debate. Of course, trade policy itself is addressed directly by many proposals. Many issues are addressed in trade negotiations with enforceable labor standards, working conditions, and collective bargaining being among them. The United States also focuses on unfair trade policies such as subsidies and predatory pricing of other nations in actions before the WTO. As we have seen, other nations accuse the United States of similar practices. Clearly, U.S. policy on globalization is grounded in serving the interests of the U.S. economy.

There are inevitably conflicting goals in public policy, and intervention in the economy is no exception. Agencies have to be concerned with protecting the general public, but they also have to be concerned with the health of the economic sectors with which they work. Therefore, they often get caught in the middle between advocates of their industries and consumer advocates. It is left to the elected policymakers to mediate these conflicts and to determine what is best for everyone.

Clearly, debates on government involvement in the economy will continue as ideology dictates how to approach policy. Those who think the government intrudes too much into the economy want to roll back such efforts. Those who believe that the market economy cannot provide equal access to all want government to play a central role in protecting everyone. Conservatives tend to support the first approach and liberals and progressives generally tend to support the second.

SUMMARY

Government and the economy are intertwined and always have been. Over time, the role of government has changed—and it will continue to do so. Early in U.S. history, government was expected to be supportive of business, and private property rights were used to keep government from otherwise interfering. As the country grew and industrialized, private industry became concentrated and many businesses engaged in processes that hurt people such as corruption and monopoly. In the late nineteenth and early twentieth centuries, government began to be much more proactive in protecting against big business and developed many economic regulations. By the mid-twentieth century, government moved into social regulation. Today, government regulates business, supports its efforts, and also protects citizens and consumers. Conservatives and liberals/progressives differ on how far government should go on either of these issues.

 **RESOURCES**

American Enterprise Institute—Brookings Joint Center for Regulatory Studies:
  www.aei.org

Brookings Institution: **www.brookings.edu**

European Union: **www.eurunion.org**

Federal Communications Commission: **www.fcc.gov**

Federal Trade Commission: **www.ftc.gov**

Heritage Foundation: **www.heritage.org**

U.S. Department of Housing and Urban Development:
  **portal.hud.gov/portal/page/portal/HUD/program_offices/
  comm_planning**

U.S. Department of Justice: **www.usdoj.gov**

U.S. Securities and Exchange Commission: **www.sec.gov**

Chapter 4

Economic Issues: Taxing, Spending, and Budgeting

The role of the federal government in economic policy in the twenty-first century is far greater than it was a hundred years ago. Intense policy conflict continues to characterize the debate over economic policy options arising from external and internal forces. External forces, such as World War II, resulted in federal government control over wages, prices, and private-sector production levels in order to support the war effort. Internal forces arising from the crisis of the Great Depression in the 1930s created public demand for an expanded federal role in the economy. One result of these demands was the New Deal of President Roosevelt. The economic recovery of the United States after the Great Depression provided a foundation of public support for continued economic intervention by the federal government.

The American global diplomatic and military posture is characterized by a domestic economy increasingly dependent on global trade. Liberals/progressives and conservatives alike accept the legitimacy of governmental involvement in economic policy, a marked change from pre-Depression era America. These ideological groups, however, disagree on the nature of governmental economic intervention. Liberals/progressives tend to favor a managed economy, whereas conservatives tend to favor a limited governmental role with an emphasis on policies that promote private-sector initiative.

ISSUE BACKGROUND: CONCEPTS AND ISSUES

America has a mixed economy, with public expectations that government should actively promote economic growth and maintain employment (Chapter 3). The social and political values that guide the nature of government's role are dynamic and involve significant policy conflict. Each value involves questions answerable only in the context of subjective policy preferences. These values establish the boundaries of government activity and provide policy direction for public officials.

One value relates to inflation and interest rates.[1] How much inflation is acceptable in order to sustain economic growth? Interest rates tend to mirror and climb with inflation. What is an acceptable and desirable interest rate that will promote economic growth yet control inflation? How extensive should the role of the federal government be in seeking to control inflation and interest rates?

A second value relates to employment and unemployment. Total employment may not be possible to achieve. What, then, is an acceptable unemployment rate? Economists and the two major political parties have historically accepted 4 to 5 percent unemployment as the appropriate definition of "full employment." Since 2009, the nation's unemployment level has hovered between 7 and 10 percent. What should the role of the federal government be in achieving a lower unemployment rate?

Employment, inflation, and interest rates are also linked. One effective tool to drive down inflation is to raise interest rates. This acts to cut demand (by increasing the cost of consumer borrowing) and exerts a downward pressure on prices. Unfortunately, a reduction in demand for goods also drives up unemployment as producers cut their workforce in response to reduced demand. What is an acceptable rate of inflation in order to maintain full employment? Which presents the greater threat to the economic system: inflation or unemployment?

A third value relates to economic growth.[2] The **gross domestic product (GDP)** represents the total value of all goods and services produced by the economy. What is the desired rate of growth of the GDP? What roles should the federal government play in promoting GDP expansion? What roles should state governments play in economic growth? What level of growth (as measured by GDP) should the federal government actively pursue?[3]

A fourth value relates to equality. What role should the federal government play in promoting economic equality? Is equality of economic opportunity sufficient, or should government actively pursue policies that seek redistribution of economic wealth and benefits in order to achieve some specified level of economic equality either for social groups or for geographic regions?

A fifth value relates to ideology.[4] What should the nature and level of government involvement be in economic policy? How much governmental involvement is consistent with the free-enterprise economic system? At what level of involvement does governmental action cease to be productive and become a counterproductive restriction on the economic system? This value involves significant social and political conflict over the appropriate role of government in a free-enterprise system.

In the absence of universal agreement concerning these values, economic policy becomes the product of either political compromises or the exercise of power by a political party.[5] Government creates and executes economic policy in an environment of political conflict. Compromise limits ideological consistency in economic policy. The exercise of power enhances ideological consistency but may create long-term conflict. Historically, economic policy in the

United States has been neither completely liberal/progressive nor conservative, but has contained a contradictory combination of values.

Macroeconomic Approaches

Traditionally, the free-market system was expected to be self-adjusting without sharp swings in the business cycle. As we have seen in Chapter 3, however, because the free-market system sometimes failed in self-regulation, government intervention served to reduce the impact of downward economic cycles. The Employment Act of 1946 formally assigned responsibility for economic growth to the federal government. This legislation stated that the federal government should "use all practicable means (to achieve) maximum employment, production, and purchasing power." The act did not specify the means that the federal government should use to achieve full employment. The act created the Council of Economic Advisors (CEA) within the Executive Office of the President to provide the president with economic policy advice to meet this responsibility.

The federal government uses two primary instruments, monetary policy and fiscal policy, to accomplish economic goals and achieve stabilization of the economy.

Monetary Policy.   **Monetary policy** refers to the efforts of government to control the supply and flow of money in the economy. Money includes not only cash but also available credit and collateral used for credit or security. The Federal Reserve Act of 1913 created the **Federal Reserve Board**, commonly known as the Fed, with powers to expand or contract the amount of money in circulation.

The Fed serves as the central bank of the United States and works to stabilize the economy through regulations developed by a seven-member board. The president, with Senate confirmation, appoints the chairperson to a four-year term and board members to fourteen-year terms. Board members may *not* be removed over disagreements about economic policy options with either the president or Congress. The Fed is an independent and powerful force in economic policy that is free to pursue monetary policies that may conflict with those of either the president or Congress.

A primary tool of the Fed to regulate the economy is through control over the **money supply**.[6] The Fed uses **open market operations** to either purchase or sell government bonds. Purchasing such bonds places money directly in the hands of potential spenders. Selling bonds, on the other hand, takes money out of circulation. Increasing the supply of money in circulation serves to stimulate demand and economic expansion (with the risk of inflation). Decreasing the supply of money serves to reduce demand and cool the economy down (with the risk of higher unemployment rates).

The currency in circulation today does not represent reserves of gold or silver held by the U.S. Treasury Department. The words "Federal Reserve Note" on paper currency reflect departure from a reliance on these metals, a change from the "Silver Certificate" of years past. The value of American currency is determined by the supply in circulation and the level of confidence in the American economy by both citizens and international bankers and investors.

The Federal Reserve Board oversees the operation of banks participating in the Federal Reserve System and assists them by serving as a clearinghouse for banking transactions and by lending them money. A major tool to control the money supply is the power of the Federal Reserve Board to control the amount of money a bank must keep on reserve, the **reserve requirement**. As the amount required increases, banks have less to lend to customers; as the reserve decreases, banks have more to lend.

Banks also borrow from the Federal Reserve System, and the rate of interest charged by the Fed on such loans, the **discount rate**, affects the costs to banks to lend money to others. The discount rate is a powerful tool available to the Fed for stimulating or cooling off the economy. When the economy is in recession, monetary policy usually aims at encouraging people to spend money. Lower interest rates and increased availability of money are efforts to accomplish this goal. During inflationary periods the opposite is true: Fed policy raises interest rates, making it less attractive for people to spend as it becomes more costly to borrow and encouraging savings by making it more profitable for people to save.

Monetary policy, though highly flexible, often proves difficult and complex for the administration to control. Although the president may attempt to move in a particular direction, others, especially the Federal Reserve Board, are free to follow independent approaches.

Fiscal Policy. **Fiscal policy**—which encompasses tax policy, government spending, and debt management—is the other major way in which government attempts to influence economic activity. Government stimulates or discourages economic activity through its power to impose or reduce taxes. Tax incentives, a form of tax reduction, can encourage corporations to invest in business expansion. Business expansion ordinarily increases employment and stimulates economic growth. The same is true for tax cuts: The demand for goods and services usually increases when taxes take less money from people. Some of the money freed through tax reductions may be saved, however, instead of spent. Thus, when government changes tax rates for reasons of fiscal planning, it pays attention to what the recipients of tax benefits are likely to do with their money. During times of inflation, there is some logic for increasing taxes to reduce the amount of money in circulation.

Managing the national debt is another fiscal policy activity often subject to controversy. A deficit occurs when the federal government spends more in a certain year than it collects in taxes (a surplus is the opposite). The **national debt** is the accumulation over time of annual deficits. **Deficit spending** stimulates demand in times of recession and unemployment. Nevertheless, it may also add to the money supply without adding to production; hence, critics of deficit spending suggest that increases in the national debt contribute to inflation.[7] Deficit spending can contribute to inflation if the government artificially expands the supply of money by printing ever-higher quantities of paper currency to pay for government spending. This type of expanded money supply decreases the value of the dollar with a resultant rise in inflation.

Government borrowing makes it possible to practice deficit spending without fueling inflation, at least in the short run. This approach has been used by all recent presidents (Ronald Reagan, George H. W. Bush, Bill Clinton, George W. Bush, and Barack Obama) to finance budget deficits with minimal inflationary pressure. The result of this approach in the 1980s, and again in the period since 2002, is a dramatic increase in the annual budget deficit and in the national debt. Interest payments on the debt consume a significant percentage of the federal budget. Currently, interest payments absorb about 7 percent of the federal budget. These tools of monetary and fiscal policy are complex approaches to stabilizing the economy. There are those who think that government should act directly to increase the amount of money in the hands of consumers in hopes that they will spend it and thus stimulate economic activity. Others argue that government should make more money available to business in the hope that it will expand activities, increasing employment and putting more money in the hands of employees and therefore of consumers. The first approach, favored by liberals/progressives, is referred to as the percolate-up theory; the latter, championed by conservatives, is known as the trickle-down theory.

CONTEMPORARY POLICY: APPROACHES TO MANAGING THE ECONOMY

Although there are controversies concerning exactly how government should approach economic problems, government intervention is widely accepted. The following section examines approaches to managing the economy, including monetary, fiscal, deficit, and tax policies as part of current macroeconomic policy.

Traditional Economic Theory

With the exception of supply-side economics, fiscal and monetary policy tools reflect the **demand-side theory** of John Maynard Keynes. Keynesian economics holds that demand for goods and services drives the economy. A downward economic cycle occurs when business production and the workforce are downsized in response to reduced demand. This, in turn, reduces demand further, resulting in more downsizing. Unless this cycle is interrupted, an economic recession or depression results. The federal government can create demand by purchasing goods and services through increased spending. Keynes argued that government deficit spending (spending in excess of tax receipts) can stimulate a sluggish economy and prevent recessions. During periods of prosperity, when inflation is a threat, government can reduce demand by adopting politically unpopular measures such as increasing taxes, reducing spending, and balancing the budget.

Supply-Side Economics

An alternative economic approach to Keynesian economics is **supply-side economics**. Supply-siders believe that the best method to achieve economic growth is to allow the market system to operate with minimal governmental interference. One basic tenet of the supply-side theory is that the price of any good, service, or activity determines consumer behavior. If the market operates freely, private demand forces will be sufficient to sustain the economy. Government interference in stimulating demand disrupts the system and has, at best, only a temporary effect on economic growth. Supply-siders believe that government taxes, regulation, and spending interfere with natural economic activity and that government should support free-market operations.

Supply-side economic policy favors low tax rates in order to stimulate production in the economy. The theory is that as tax rates rise above a critical level, they so discourage economic activity that total tax revenue falls. Most supply-side tax cuts focus on upper-income levels, especially corporate profits and capital gains, because they are the most likely sources of significant investment. Accordingly, lowering tax rates for businesses and individuals with higher income should lead to business investment. Investment leads to economic growth, with the bonus of higher levels of employment, a classic trickle-down argument. Supporters of supply-side economics believe that tax cuts pay for themselves through economic growth, because growth creates a greater number of prosperous taxpayers to replace the tax money eliminated in the tax cut. Hence, a tax cut can actually raise tax revenue and reduce deficits by stimulating economic expansion. A fundamental tenet of supply-side economics is that the willingness to invest is a direct function of the tax rate on such risk-taking economic activity. Supply-side economic theory was a guiding value in federal economic policy during the Reagan administration of the early 1980s.[8]

Impact.   Advocates of supply-side economics argue that the economic expansion of the 1990s and the budget surplus created by the turn of the twenty-first century were results of implementing supply-side tax cuts in the 1980s. This supply-side argument was the foundation for President George W. Bush's successful push for major tax cuts in 2001–2003. Supply-side economic theory continues to be debated in economic policy today.

Budget Deficits

Budget deficits have increased dramatically, as shown in Figure 4.1. The annual budget deficits were the result of a combination of factors: tax cuts in 1981–1983; increased levels of defense spending during the 1980s; the Persian Gulf War of 1991; a federally funded bailout of savings and loan institutions; and continued growth in federal spending for Medicare, Social Security, and other **entitlement** programs.

Annual interest payments on the national debt exceed the annual cost of military operations in Iraq and Afghanistan combined, and consumed about 6 percent of the federal budget in 2012. Annual interest payments servicing a national debt of about $13 trillion in 2014 will continue to consume some $230 billion per year and increase to some $400 billion by 2017, when the national debt is projected to reach almost $15 trillion (see Figure 4.2). It is important to

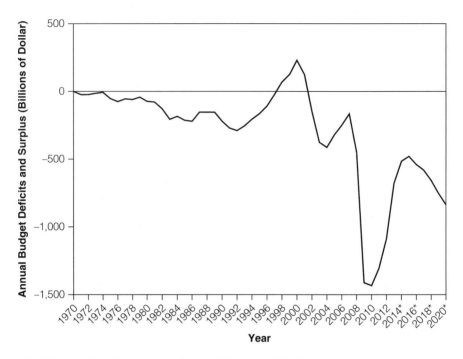

FIGURE 4.1 U.S. Budget Deficits and Surplus, 1970–2020*

*2014–2020 projected by CBO.

SOURCE: Congressional Budget Office, *Budget Outlook, 2014–2024*, Chapter 1: The Budget Outlook, http://www.cbo
.gov/publication/45010, accessed February 2014; Congressional Budget Office, Historical Budget Data and *The Budget
and Economic Outlook: An Update; August 2007*, http://www.cbo.gov/budget/budproj.pdf and http://www.cbo.gov/
budget/historical.shtml, accessed September 2007.

understand that interest payments do not pay for any new public services. They
are simply a payment of interest on money borrowed in previous years to pay for
public services provided during that time. Opponents of deficit spending argue
that inflation in the economy is an unavoidable consequence of such a fiscal
policy.

   The budget deficits seem to have stimulated the economy. During the period
between 2008 and 2014, inflation has not increased dramatically as the deficit and
national debt increased. The reasons are somewhat complex and are tied to the
open market operations of the Fed. Beginning in 2008, the Fed significantly
increased purchases of securities and at the same time announced that it targeted
short-term discount rates between 0 percent and 1.5 percent in order to both
reduce inflationary pressures and stimulate the economy. The Fed also continued
to signal that it would follow this policy for the foreseeable future until unemployment dropped below the 6 percent range. One result is that long-term inflation is projected to remain low, in the 1.5 to 2 percent range. This approach to
monetary policy by the Fed served to reduce the supply of money in circulation,
keep inflation low, and avoid the inflationary spiral traditionally associated with
deficit spending.

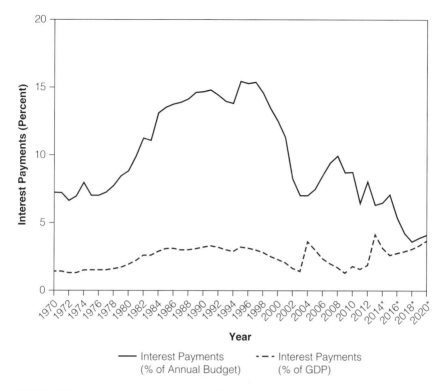

FIGURE 4.2 Interest Payments as Percentage of Annual Budget and Percentage of Gross Domestic Product*

*2014–2020 projected by CBO.

SOURCE: Congressional Budget Office, *Budget Outlook, 2014–2024*, Chapter 3: The Spending Outlook, http://www .cbo.gov/publication/45010, accessed February 2014; Congressional Budget Office, *Current Budget Projections, 2004*; Congressional Budget Office, *The Budget and Economic Outlook Fiscal Years 2004–2014*, accessed March 2005; Congressional Budge Office, *Historical Budget Data*, http://www.cbo.gov/budget/historical.shtml, accessed September 2007; Office of Management and Budget, *Budget of the United States Government Fiscal Year 2008*, http://www .whitehouse.gov/omb/budget/fy2008/, accessed September 2007.

Tax Reform

Tax reform efforts continue to be an integral component of the economic policy agenda under the Obama administration. The Tax Relief Act of 2010 was a major fiscal policy initiative by the Obama administration. After much debate in Congress, the Act was adopted in December 2010 with a series of temporary elements. A major provision of this Act was the Payroll Tax Holiday in which the Social Security payroll tax was reduced by 2 percent, from 6.2 percent to 4.2 percent. The Act also retained the tax cuts implemented during the Bush administration that had reduced personal income tax rates from a range of 15–39.6 percent to a range of 10–35 percent. Unemployment benefits were extended and no changes were made in the capital gains tax rates. The Act was "temporary" with its provisions expiring after two years in 2012.

The American Taxpayer Relief Act of 2012 (ATRA), signed into law in January 2013, allowed the Payroll Tax Holiday to expire, but contained some policy options favored by the president. This Act retained the reduced Bush era tax cuts for individuals earning less than $400,000 (couples less than $450,000) but increased tax rates for those with higher incomes. The Act did increase taxes by reducing tax deductions for individuals earning over $200,000 (couples over $250,000). These tax increases are consistent with the president's belief that wealthier individuals should pay more taxes. The Act addressed the issue of the Alternative Minimum Income Tax by permanently linking it to the inflation rate to protect middle-income taxpayers.

The issues of **tax fairness** and **tax efficiency** are continuing issues for tax policy. Fairness involves questions of assigning tax burden to differing income levels and increasing public confidence in the tax system. Efficiency relates to expanding the tax base by reducing the impact of tax laws (depreciation, loopholes) on business decision making which is counter to economic growth.

Economic Policy Obstacles

Economic policy is created in a climate of conflict in a complex political environment. Consequently, a number of obstacles exist in developing an effective, consistent mix of economic policy options.

Fragmentation of governmental responsibility between the federal and state governments is a major obstacle in developing economic policy. In the American system of **federalism**, state governments share power and responsibilities with the national government, including economic policy options. Given the diversity of the fifty states, they often pursue divergent economic policies. The economic interests of agricultural states, such as Iowa or Nebraska, are not necessarily consistent with those of heavily industrialized states, such as New York. The federal system is an environment in which state governments and the federal government often pursue conflicting economic goals.

Fragmentation of responsibility for economic policy also exists within the national government. The president, representing a national constituency, shares responsibility with Congress for formulating economic policy options. This shared responsibility expands the number of actors legitimately participating in establishing economic policy. This means that every member of the U.S. Senate and the U.S. House of Representatives has the right to exercise a voice in economic policy. Members of Congress tend to represent the economic interests of their state or district with greater zeal than they do the economic interests of the nation as a whole. Conflict between the executive and legislative branches of government over economic policy is a legitimate characteristic of the American political system. The level of conflict between the president and Congress often becomes more intense when one party controls the White House, and the opposing party controls one (or both) chambers of Congress.

Fragmentation within the executive branch of government is another obstacle to developing economic policy. A number of cabinet-level departments share this responsibility, notably the Commerce Department, the Treasury Department, and the Labor Department. This fragmentation of responsibility within the executive branch is extensive. Various agencies below cabinet level also exercise economic policy responsibility. The **Office of Management and Budget (OMB)**, the **Council of Economic Advisers (CEA)**, and the independent Federal Reserve Board (Fed) are just three of a larger number of agencies that exercise an extensive economic policy role.

On the negative side, this extensive structural fragmentation reduces centralized control and coordination over American economic policy. Ineffective policy responses to economic problems may be the product of a lack of policy coordination. On the positive side, fragmentation allows significant private-sector freedom in economic policy, which is consistent with the values of the free-enterprise system.

A second obstacle involves linkages between economic policy options. This is an issue because of significant conflict between economic goals. For example, the pursuit of full employment tends to fuel inflation. Policies designed to reduce inflation often produce higher unemployment. Similarly, a decision to expand domestic spending may exert budgetary pressures for a reduction in military spending levels. This means that economic policies often conflict because they are the product of political compromise to resolve conflicting goals.

A third obstacle to effective economic policy involves uncertainty in predicting policy outcomes. Even when political consensus allows adoption of a specific economic strategy, no guarantee exists that the desired result will follow. For example, only after implementing a tax-rate change can analysts assess the actual impact of a tax-rate reduction on economic expansion and tax revenues. Economic forecasts rest on uncertain political and financial assumptions used to make predictions. The conflict generated by this debate in an environment of uncertainty becomes an obstacle to the development of economic policy.

A fourth obstacle involves the impact of entitlement programs such as Social Security, Medicare, and Medicaid on the federal budget and on the economy. Entitlement programs are redistributive in nature and involve the transfer of wealth from one group to another in order to provide some type of benefit. These programs are created by specific legislation that mandates spending that is independent of the normal budgetary appropriations process. By 2030, the costs for these programs will be more than double that of their level in 2000. Both political parties find it difficult to address the growth of entitlement programs because the American public now views these programs as a moral responsibility of government. The uncontrolled nature of entitlement programs remains a significant issue in formulating economic, taxing, and spending policy.

POLICY EVALUATION: SUCCESS OR FAILURE?

In any policy evaluation effort, the perspective of the analyst has an impact on the conclusions. Economist John K. Galbraith argued that the economic planning system, well developed and representing the people with money, does not help those who need help the most.[9] Business and financial interests capture monetary and fiscal policy; therefore, consumers, workers, and the poor would not receive sufficient consideration. In an alternative view, Milton Friedman suggested that government controls stifle economic activity because they make business too costly to operate profitably.[10] Regardless of perspective, many critics of economic policies agree that these solutions tend to distort economic development and lead to the maldistribution of resources in the society. How that maldistribution is explained depends on the critic's point of view.

Inflation and Growth

The economic recession of 2007–2010 produced high unemployment (10 percent), low economic growth, and a drop in the rate of inflation, as reflected in Figure 4.3. This low rate of inflation was a foundation for economic recovery following the recession period which began in 2008.

Economic growth in the United States remained at about 5 percent of GDP until 2009, when the nation experienced negative economic growth, as reflected in Figure 4.4. Economic growth had recovered to the 3.5 percent range by 2013 and is projected to remain in the 3 percent range for the near future. Economic recovery and expansion would involve an economic growth rate in the 4–5 percent range.

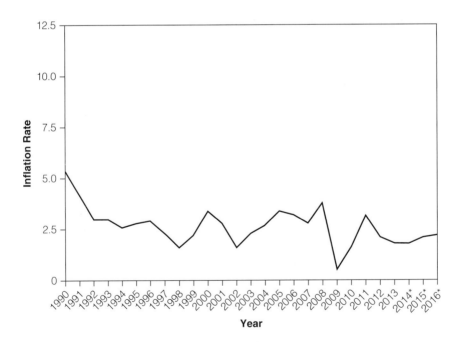

F I G U R E 4.3 Inflation Rates, 2000–2016*

*Projected by CBO.

SOURCE: Congressional Budget Office, *Budget Outlook, 2014–2024,* Chapter 2: The Revenue Outlook, http://www .cbo.gov/publication/45010, accessed February 2014; U.S. Department of Labor, Bureau of Labor Statistics, Consumer Price Indexes, 2007, www.bls.gov/cpi/#data, accessed September 2007.

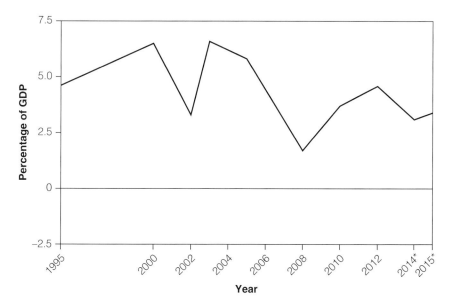

FIGURE 4.4 Economic Growth Rate, 1995–2015

*Projected by CBO.

SOURCE: Congressional *Budget Office, Budget Outlook, 2014–2024*, Chapter 2: The Economic Outlook, http://www
.cbo.gov/publication/45010, accessed February 2014; Congressional Budget Office, *The Budget and Economic Outlook,
An Update*, August 2007, www.cbo.gov/ftpdocs/85xx/doc8565/08-23-Update07.pdf; accessed September 2007.

Fiscal Policy

Supply-side economists took pride in the fiscal and monetary policies that they
claimed fueled the economic recovery and expansion between 1980 and 2001.
Tax reductions pumped money into the economy, resulting in an economic
investment boom.

Critics of supply-side fiscal policies focus on two issues. The first is the fairness
issue related to the equity of tax and spending reductions. A consistent theme of
opponents to tax cuts, including President Obama, are that those policies favor the
rich and hurt the poor, that the impact of domestic budget cuts increase the real
income of those in the highest income categories, and that the majority of taxpayers would experience either no increase in income or a decline. (Chapter 7
discusses the growth of economic inequality during the last two decades.)

A second issue involves the expansion of the national debt and the budget
deficit, whose long-range consequences are subject to debate. Figure 4.5 shows
the growth of the national debt, which temporarily peaked in 1997–1998 and then
decreased only slightly with the advent of budget surpluses (see Figure 4.1). The
upward trend of the national debt has resumed significantly. The U.S. economy
now carries over $13 trillion in debt, which is projected to continue to increase
annually over the next several years.

The size of the debt presents long-term issues for the federal budget. Even if
the annual deficit were to be eliminated, interest payments will continue to

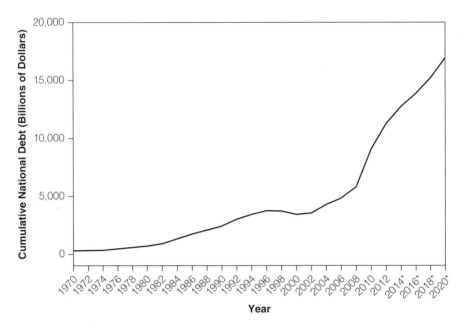

FIGURE 4.5 Cumulative National Debt

*2014–2020 projected by CBO.

SOURCE: Congressional Budget Office, *Budget Outlook, 2014–2024*, Chapter 4: The Revenue Outlook, http://www
.cbo.gov/publication/45010, accessed February 2014; Office of Management and Budget, *The Budget for Fiscal
Year 2007*, Historical Tables, Table 7.1; www.whitehouse.gove/omb/budget/fy2007, accessed September 2007.

consume a significant percentage of the federal budget. Stated another way,
interest payments in 2014 absorbed over $220 billion of federal spending. This
is spending that must be diverted from productive uses.

Budget Deficit Control Efforts.   In its attempt to reduce the deficit and
reduce the national debt by imposing spending limitations, Congress passed the
Balanced Budget and Emergency Deficit Control Act of 1985, known as the
Gramm-Rudman Act. This Act specified target deficit levels for fiscal years
1986 through 1991 that both Congress and the president were required to
follow. Automatic spending cuts across the board were to be imposed if spending
exceeded the targeted budget deficit levels. This process of automatic spending
cuts is known as **sequestration**.

   Gramm-Rudman proved ineffective in reducing the federal budget deficit
because deficit targets had to be met at the beginning of a fiscal year based on
revenue and spending projections. Compliance could be achieved on paper
based on projected, not actual, revenue receipts and spending levels.

The National Commission on Fiscal Responsibility and Reform.   Created
by President Obama by executive order in 2010, the commission consisted of
eighteen members (six Democratic and six Republican members of Congress)
charged with developing a deficit reduction strategy for submission to Congress.

The requirement that fourteen of the eighteen members agree before any recommendation could be forwarded to Congress was not achieved and the Commission did not provide recommendations for Congressional review and action. The creation of the Commission reflected the continuing importance of annual budget deficits and the national debt as major economic issues.

The Budget Control Act of 2011 raised the national debt limit. It also contained a provision that reintroduced the sequestration process of across the board spending cuts. These cuts would be automatically imposed if Congress and the president could not agree by 2013 on a spending package that would reduce the national deficit by $1.2 trillion over the following ten years. Mandatory annual spending cuts in the $109 billion range would be imposed through 2021 to reach $1.2 trillion in cuts. Half of the cuts would be in domestic spending and half from defense spending. Agreement was not reached and sequestration began in March of 2013 with cuts in domestic and military spending. The president closed the White House to public visits and some Washington, DC, monuments were temporarily closed as a symbol to the public of the spending cuts.

Sequestration for 2014 and 2015 was avoided by the approval of an increase in the national debt ceiling through March of 2015. The level of sequestration specified in the 2011 legislation would only be partially effective in reducing the national debt. The Congressional Budget Office examined areas of nondiscretionary spending by the federal government and found that even with sequestration, annual spending would still increase in the $250 to $300 billion range through 2021.

The issue of budget deficits and the national debt will remain on the policy agenda. This debate will intensify if the Fed changes its policy of purchasing government bonds and interest rates and inflation increases.

Federal Revenues and Spending

In order to understand the possibilities and limits of fiscal policy, and the obstacles to deficit reduction faced by Congress and presidents, one must grasp the nature of federal income and expenditures. Figures 4.6 and 4.7 provide a visual display

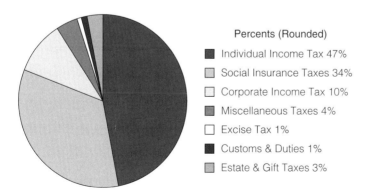

Percents (Rounded)

- Individual Income Tax 47%
- Social Insurance Taxes 34%
- Corporate Income Tax 10%
- Miscellaneous Taxes 4%
- Excise Tax 1%
- Customs & Duties 1%
- Estate & Gift Taxes 3%

FIGURE 4.6   Federal Revenue by Source, 2012

SOURCE: Congressional Budget Office, *Budget Outlook, 2014–2024*, Chapter 4: The Revenue Outlook, http://www.cbo .gov/publication/45010, accessed February 2014.

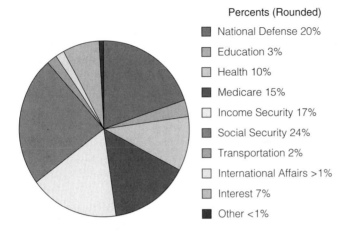

Percents (Rounded)

■ National Defense 20%

■ Education 3%

□ Health 10%

■ Medicare 15%

□ Income Security 17%

■ Social Security 24%

■ Transportation 2%

□ International Affairs >1%

■ Interest 7%

■ Other <1%

FIGURE 4.7 Federal Spending by Category, 2012

SOURCE: Congressional Budget Office, *Budget Outlook 2014–2024*, Chapter 3: The Spending Outlook, http://www.cbo
.gov/publication/45010, accessed February 2014.

of spending and revenues in 2013. As indicated in Figure 4.6, when deficit borrowing is excluded, individual income taxes and social insurance taxes account for 81 percent of federal revenues. Corporate income taxes cover almost 10 percent of federal revenues. Figure 4.7 indicates that federal spending on interest on the national debt amounts to about 7 percent of spending.

Defense spending is projected to decrease as a percent of the federal budget from 18.1 percent in 2012 to about 14 percent by 2017 (see Table 4.1).

Fiscal Policy Evaluation

Some analysts argue that the deficit is a relatively minor economic issue. The annual budget deficit remains between 2 and 3 percent of GDP. They argue that this low percentage places only minor pressure on the nation's economy.

TABLE 4.1   **Defense Spending, Selected Years 2000–2017
(in billions of dollars)**

	2000	2004	2008	2010	2012	2014*	2016*
Dollars	295	452	616	719	625	604	611
Percent of budget	16.0	18.8	20.7	19.0	18.1	17.0	15.1

*Estimated.

SOURCE: Congressional Budget Office, *Budget Outlook, 2014–2024*, Chapter 3: The Spending Outlook and Appendix H, Historical Budget Data, http://www.cbo.gov/publication/45010, accessed February 2014; Office of Management and Budget, *The Budget for Fiscal Year 2011*, Historical Tables, Table 3.1 Outlays by Superfunction and Function, 1940–2015, http://www.whitehouse.gov/omb/budget/Historicals/, accessed May 2010.

Other analysts argue just the opposite. They emphasize the size of the total debt, not the annual deficit. The difference is that the total debt is approximately 50 percent of GDP and is projected to increase to 80 percent of GDP by 2020. The issue concerning how much debt the American economy can support remains unresolved.

Defense Spending

Defense spending places a somewhat consistent pressure on the budget. As indicated in Table 4.1, defense spending increased to $625 billion in 2012. Projected spending in future years includes reductions in appropriations as military operations in Iraq and Afghanistan end. President Obama targeted the end of 2014 for withdrawal of most American troops in Afghanistan with only a small contingent remaining in the future. A continued American presence depends on President Karzai signing the Status of Forces Agreement with the United States. Defense spending levels may reflect the impact of American responses to international terrorism. These threats do have the potential to increase defense spending in response to future attacks and significantly alter budgetary policy. Any change in relationships with China and Russia also has the potential to impact defense spending.

The new patterns of defense spending have potentially significant impacts on military preparedness. Deployment of the American military now requires cooperation and extensive support from allies if any type of long-term, theater-wide action is anticipated. One result has been the significant pressure placed on the United States to secure the cooperation of allied nations. This cooperation is needed to effectively pursue both military and diplomatic goals. The Iraq and Afghanistan Wars strained the military forces, requiring extensive and expensive mobilization of National Guard and Reserve units plus increased pay, benefits, and recruitment spending. Replacement of equipment destroyed in these conflicts will also be very expensive.

CONTINUING DEBATES: SPENDING, TAXES, THE DEFICIT, AND ECONOMIC STIMULUS PROGRAMS

Ideological value differences produce conflict in the debate over economic policy. The issue of governmental involvement in the economy is complex and reflects basic ideological values. Conservatives generally desire to reduce the role of government in the economy. Traditionally, conservatives tend to be stronger advocates of balanced budgets and believe that inflation is more dangerous than rising unemployment.

The progressive wing of the Democratic Party, with its egalitarian values, argues that more, not less, government intervention is necessary to stabilize the economy. Their proposals include such items as industrial policy, plant closure

---

POLICY DILEMMAS   Deficit and Debt

In order to stimulate the economy, the federal government has adopted a program of spending with annual budget deficits far exceeding those of the past. Interest payments on the national debt are projected to remain relatively constant over the next several years, but the debt will increase to some 75 percent of the gross domestic product. The impact of this level of debt on the health of the American economy is unknown. The Fed has utilized monetary policy to minimize the impact of annual deficits on inflation. An unanswered question is when, or if, the level of debt will reach a tipping point such that the economy can no longer support that level of debt. Several European nations have reached their tipping point in 2009 with resulting economic crisis linked to social and political unrest.

Greece, Ireland, and Portugal were the first nations to experience a financial crisis when their cumulative national debt exceeded their annual gross domestic product. High public debt levels in other European nations including Spain, Italy, and Cyprus contributed to the development of the Eurozone Crisis. High levels of public debt were accompanied with high levels of private debt in which banks had loaned more euros to customers than the borrowers resources could repay. A strategy for resolving the crisis involved implementing a combination of extensive cuts in domestic program spending, tax increases, and the infusion of euros by the European Central Bank in the form of loans to stabilize the economy. Progress has been made toward a remedy because (1) some of the nations with the most severe problems were those with the smallest GDP in Europe, and (2) the existence of the European Central Bank could serve as a mechanism for providing bailout funding in the form of loans to impacted nations. The Eurozone Crisis has not yet been completely resolved and it can serve as a potential example of the impact of a large government debt structure on a nation's economy.

1. Given the success of the Fed in using monetary policy to minimize the impact of deficit spending on the economy, what are the risks to the economy of following this policy for the next several years?

2. The national debt has reached levels that will equate to some 75 percent of gross domestic product within the next three or four years. Economists disagree about whether this level of debt is a threat to the economic stability of the nation. Within this context of disagreement, what are the viable fiscal and budgetary policies that the nations should follow during the next 3 to 5 years?

---

warnings, and increases in the national minimum wage. Such policies would increase centralization of economic policy. In fiscal and monetary policy, liberals favor attention to mediating unemployment and other symptoms of economic stagnation. They prefer stimulus of the economy even at the cost of some inflation and support deficit spending.

The Democratic takeover of Congress in 2006 put renewed vigor into Republican attempts to hold the line on spending, setting up major battles over the budget in following years. With Republicans gaining control over the U.S. House in 2010 and retaining control in 2012, conflict over spending and tax policy intensified between the House and the Senate. Tax policy and responses to the deficit and economic uncertainty will drive the agenda of future presidents and Congresses.

Policy Conflict over the Federal Spending to Stimulate the Economy: TARP and ARRA

The Emergency Economic Stabilization Act of 2008 created the Trouble Asset Relief Program (TARP), which expanded the role of the federal government in regulating and controlling the American financial system.[11] Lending institutions had allowed individuals to borrow money for homes through the use of subprime mortgages well beyond their ability to repay. As individuals were unable to meet payments, the rate of mortgage defaults escalated and created a significant economic crisis.[12] Major financial institutions (such as Lehman Brothers, Fannie Mae, Freddie Mac, and the American International Group, AIG) were failing, and the American economy was facing a financial crisis with the prospect of widespread failure of multiple banks and financial institutions. TARP initially provided that the U.S. Treasury could spend up to $700 billion to purchase troubled assets from banks and financial institutions, such as home mortgages, and to provide funds to auto industry companies in risk of default, such as General Motors and Chrysler, to prevent their collapse. That amount was reduced to $478 billion by Congress in 2012. TARP also contained provisions that allowed the federal government to control some of the salaries paid to executives in institutions participating in the program. As of January 2014, the program had generated some $13 billion more in receipts for the government than in expenditures as the program continues to slowly move toward elimination.

Policy issues are reflected in adoption of the American Recovery and Reinvestment Act of 2009 (ARRA) that provided increased federal spending of some $787 billion.[13] This spending bill was intended to stimulate the American economy and to create jobs in order to reduce unemployment from the 10 percent level through the infusion of increased federal spending. Analysis by the CBO indicated that ARRA will add $830 billion to the national debt by 2019, with some 90 percent of the spending having been completed at the end of 2012.

Republicans did not vote for passage. This reflects the depth of policy disagreements over the role of the federal government in economic policy. Liberals/progressives tend to favor the Keynesian approach of significant deficit spending to stimulate economic growth. Conservatives tend to reject this philosophy and rely on market forces to provide economic growth. ARRA is another indication of policy conflict over the role of government in the economy. The Obama administration continues to favor an expanded federal role and the Republican Party continues to oppose federal spending as a fiscal policy of increased spending to stimulate the nation's economy.

Taxes

Taxation can serve to generate revenue to pay for government activities or serve as a mechanism to promote social policy. Social policy goals include items such as educational expense deductions, home mortgage interest deductions, and energy tax. Legislators regularly propose tax reforms. Tax cuts are often confused with tax reform, though the two are not the same. **Tax reforms** change the basic type and incidence (who pays) of taxation; **tax cuts** merely reduce the rate of taxation.

Conservatives argue that the tax system is unfair because in 2013, some 43 percent of Americans did not pay any federal income tax and avoided paying their "fair share" of the tax burden. The 43 percent figure is correct, but explanations for this figure do exist. About 50 percent of those individuals do work and paid payroll tax deductions for Social Security and Medicare. Approximately 20 percent are elderly social security recipients with incomes below the $25,000 level and are exempt from income taxes. A significant number in the remaining group have very low incomes and qualify for a range of tax credits and deductions that remove their total tax liability. One such credit is the earned income tax credit (EITC). Enacted in 1975, the EITC has expanded over the past thirty-five years to the point that in 2012, some 27 million taxpayers received EITC.[14] EITC has resulted in low-income taxpayers not only avoiding paying federal income taxes but receiving payments from the federal government. The result is that some low-income taxpayers receive additional income from the federal government as tax revenue is *redistributed* directly to them from wealthier taxpayers. The EITC has become a negative income tax as its benefits have expanded over time.

Supporters of this policy argue that tax laws allow wealthier income groups to use deductions and tax shelters to reduce their tax burden. Supporters also observe that corporations may be able to avoid paying income taxes as a result of deductions, credits, and exemptions available to support business retention and encourage business expansion. Defenders of the system of deductions, shelters, and incentives argue that investment by wealthier individuals and businesses create jobs and expand the economy which, in turn, provides increased wealth for all segments of society. They continue to question the fairness of tax policy when only 57 percent of Americans actually pay income taxes. All indications are that the debate over tax incidence and tax fairness will continue as economic agenda items.

Fiscal Cliff

In 2012, the nation faced a major economic challenge known as the "**fiscal cliff.**" The central economic issue involved the inability of Congress and the president to agree on balanced tax and spending policies. Under the provisions of the Budget Control Act (BCA) of 2011, mandatory across the board spending cuts would be made in domestic and defense programs unless Congress and the president could reach an agreement that would reduce the national deficit by some $1.2 trillion over a ten-year period by December 2012. These spending cuts would be accompanied by automatic tax increases. Analysts stated that the combination of tax increases and spending cuts would move the nation back into an economic recession. An agreement was not reached and sequestration was implemented in March 2013, with significant debate between the two political parties. Congress was successful in mediating some of the cuts through the passage of a continuing resolution to authorize federal spending and avoid governmental shutdowns. In December 2013, Congress passed the ATRA that retained the Bush era tax cuts, raised the debt limit, and adopted some spending cuts and some tax increases. In February 2014, Congress passed (and the president signed) legislation that raised the national debt limit through March 2015. The issue of tax rates, spending levels, and the national debt remain contentious issues on the policy agenda.

Alternative tax proposals periodically enter the policy debate. One option includes the flat-tax proposal. The flat-tax approach would eliminate many deductions and reduce the number of tax brackets.[15] Additionally, the proposals call for lowering the maximum rate that everyone would pay. Although a true flat tax is unlikely because of the many special interests supporting deductions, it is almost certain that this alternative, along with others, will continue to be debated.

A major conflict is how and where to generate tax revenues in a fair and efficient manner. Another tax reform proposal is a value-added tax (VAT) to supplement income taxes. The VAT is like a national sales tax on goods as they pass through each phase of the economic system. As economic activity adds value to each natural resource or good, a tax is paid on the increase in value. European nations frequently employ a VAT.

Budget Deficit and National Debt

Unanswered questions relate to the impact of continued budget deficits on the American economy. As indicated in Figure 4.1, the annual budget deficit was roughly $1.3 trillion between 2010 and 2012. The annual deficit is projected to remain between $500 and $600 billion dollars through 2018. Budget deficits have not been at this level in the past, and budget surpluses were last present between 2000 and 2001. Proponents of deficit spending argue that this fiscal policy stimulates the economy while critics argue that deficits of this size actually slow economic growth.

Related to the annual budget deficit is the unknown impact of an ever-increasing national debt that is projected to increase to $17 trillion by 2020. The unknown element is the impact of the size of the national debt as compared to the GDP. Figure 4.5 presents the level of national debt as a percent of GDP. The debt is projected to remain above 70 percent for the next decade. The tipping point for economic crisis and even collapse between the national debt and GDP have not been identified in terms of how much debt the economy can handle. As discussed in the Policy Dilemmas feature, several European nations reached that tipping point with severe economic consequences. Liberals/progressives and Democrats argue that the monetary policy of the Fed has, and will, continue to minimize any adverse impact of a national debt. A large national debt has the potential to limit future policy choices and significantly reduce the ability of Congress and the president to respond to unexpected challenges. Conservative economists argue that this level of debt results in slower economic growth with recessionary impacts. They also argue that now is the time to avoid ever encountering the tipping point for a future economic crisis by reducing deficits and reducing the growth of the national debt.

Monetary Policy

One view is that changes in monetary policy do not have long-term impacts on prices and interest rates. If the Fed restricts the supply of money, this will only defer demand, not eliminate it. When it lifts restrictions, demand will surge forward. Interest rates and economic activity tend to respond in only a short-term manner to changes in monetary policy. There is less agreement about the impact of long-term monetary policy changes on the GDP. The CBO has found that a gradual increase in the supply of money is necessary to support economic growth in order to avoid deficits without adversely affecting the economy by reducing growth of the GDP. Accordingly, actions by the Fed that tighten the supply of money may be counterproductive.

Balanced Budget Amendment

Past experience indicates that genuine deficit reduction comes only when the president and Congress together have the political will to make difficult choices about specific spending and tax programs.

A balanced budget amendment presents a number of problems. First, there is an absence of consensus concerning the composition of the federal budget. Defense spending, entitlement spending, spending for health care, and other programs compete for limited fiscal resources. Congress and the president can achieve balanced budget compliance on paper by using budgetary gimmicks as overly optimistic economic forecasts, moving some agencies and programs to an off-budget status, and transferring financial responsibility for programs to state and local governments. Such an amendment could restrict the ability of the government to deal with emergencies like military actions, economic recessions, and natural disasters that require an immediate federal response.

Line Item Veto

Most recent presidents have argued that they should have the power to veto specific budget items. Proponents of the line item veto claim that presidents would use it to eliminate unnecessary federal spending, known as pork barrel projects, due to their national perspective. Supporters note that forty-three of fifty governors possess the line item veto and that state governments operate with balanced budgets. Critics of granting this power to the president argue that it concentrates too much power in the hands of the president. Others observe that presidents would be tempted to use the line item veto to replace Congressional spending priorities and to support their own spending priorities rather than to reduce overall spending and reduce the deficit. Congress granted this power to the president in 1996 but the U.S. Supreme Court ruled that the law was unconstitutional and there have not been recent attempts to revive it.

Entitlement Programs

Outlays for mandatory spending, often called entitlements (for example, Social Security, Medicare, Medicaid), consume over half of the federal budget. Congress cannot easily impose caps on these programs. Social Security checks and medical benefits cannot legally be stopped when a budgetary spending ceiling limit is reached. In order to limit entitlement spending, Congress must adopt policy options that would modify the programs, restrict benefits, or transfer them to discretionary status. An inability to address the continuing growth of entitlement spending may produce a number of undesirable alternatives such as significant tax increases, a reduced rate of national economic growth, increased competition between entitlement (elderly and health) programs and other programs (defense, transportation, education) for funding, and a potential increase in generational conflict between the taxpaying young and the beneficiary recipient elderly population. Chapters 7 and 8 consider the difficulty of limiting spending in such programs.

Energy Costs

The price of oil has fluctuated since 1973 (see Chapter 5) with significant economic consequences. A drop in oil prices exerts a downward pressure on inflation. Increases in the market price for oil exert inflationary pressures on the American economy and affect economic growth.

Homeland Security

Following the terrorist attacks of September 11, 2001, the United States began an extensive program to strengthen homeland security. Spending for homeland security continues to increase. Given the open nature of American society, efforts to protect government institutions and the population from terrorist activities are expensive undertakings. There will be a continued emphasis on this type of spending. Its total impact on the nation's economy is uncertain.

SUMMARY

The role of the government in the American economy in the twenty-first century has expanded significantly from its role from that at the beginning of the twentieth century. Although the legitimacy of this role is now accepted by most Americans, the nature and extent of the role of government is a source of intense ideological debate. Major policy questions remain the subject of conflict over policy options. Issues relating to tax policy, spending policy, debt policy, and their link to social policy continue to produce profound disagreements within the American public which is reflected in conflict between their elected representatives over economic goals and the role of government. Policy conflict in this area will remain at a high level in the coming decade.

RESOURCES

American Enterprise Institute: **www.aei.org**

Brookings Institution: **www.brookings.edu**

Cato Institute: **www.cato.org**

Congressional Budget Office: **www.cbo.gov**

The Heritage Foundation: **www.heritage.org**

Homeland Security: **www.dhs.gov**

The Kauffman Foundation: **www.kauffman.org**

National Commission on Fiscal Responsibility and Reform:
www.fiscalcommission.gov

Office of Management and Budget: **www.whitehouse.gov/omb/**

Office of Tax Policy, United States Treasury: **www.treasury.gov/
about/organizational-structure/offices/Pages/Tax-Policy.aspx**

U.S. Department of Defense: **www.defense.gov**

U.S. Federal Reserve System: **www.federalreserve.gov**

Chapter 5

Energy and Environmental Policies: Policy Instability

U ntil the 1970s, energy policy was not a major public concern in America. Access to cheap energy and abundant natural resources contributed to the policy value that energy policies were unnecessary. The same was true for regulatory and protective environmental policies. These attitudes changed in the early 1970s due to uncertainty in access to imported oil from the Persian Gulf. Increased concern with the environment was evidenced by the first Earth Day in 1970, a product of the social activism of the 1960s.

ENERGY POLICY ISSUE BACKGROUND: COMPLACENCY AND CRISIS

In 1973, conflict between Israel and surrounding Arab states resulted in an embargo on oil exports to the United States by Arab nations. This oil embargo triggered a new era in U.S. energy policy before 1973 as the "traditional" period and the years following the Arab oil embargo marked by periodic shifts between crisis, uncertainty, and complacency.

Traditional Energy Policy

Before 1973, the private sector provided the nation with an unlimited supply of inexpensive energy. America had an abundance of domestic **fossil fuels**: coal, oil, and natural gas; and access to inexpensive imported oil and gas, all developed and provided by the private sector. Limited government regulations were primarily designed to protect energy producers by maintaining stable prices. Energy policy was a mix of state and federal actions designed to support consumption with little emphasis on conservation, efficiency, or national energy independence. Consequently, the United

States was not prepared for the events of 1973 in the Middle East that threatened the nation's energy supply and moved energy policy onto the public agenda.

Policy Values.   The private sector was allowed to engage in energy exploration and production on public lands by The Mineral Leasing Act of 1920. Energy producers paid royalties to both states and the federal government under this system. As oil and gas exploration moved offshore, the states obtained leasing responsibility for lands within their traditional boundaries (three to ten miles offshore) with the federal government exercising primary control over all other offshore lands such as the Gulf of Mexico.

Taxation.   Until 1973, energy tax policy emphasized tax breaks to energy producers in order to encourage exploration and production. The success of this tax policy resulted in both increased supply and overproduction, which led to states adopting prorationing. **Prorationing** involved governmental regulations that imposed production quotas on private companies in order to reduce supply, maintain market stability, and protect producers from unlimited competition.

Antitrust Policy.   The federal energy policy of limiting competition through prorationing conflicted with antitrust policies designed to promote competition. During World War II, the need to increase energy production caused the government to drop its antitrust efforts targeting the oil and gas industry and by the 1950s, antitrust actions targeting oil companies were viewed as counterproductive to meeting the increasing demand for oil.

Decentralization.   Traditional energy policy reflected a commitment to private-sector and free-market operations. No single level of government or regulatory body had responsibility for developing energy policy. Decentralization and fragmentation of policy responsibility was consistent with an emphasis on private-sector market operations and allowed the private sector to meet the energy needs of the nation.

Coal.   The abundant supply and cheap prices resulted in the nation relying on coal for almost 75 percent of the nation's energy consumption until the late 1920s. The oversupply of coal became so extensive that by 1932, only 300 of the 1,864 companies in operation reported a profit.[1] The Bituminous Coal Acts of 1935 and 1937 were attempts, similar to prorationing with oil, to impose production quotas in order to stabilize profits and protect wages of coal miners. The shift to oil as the preferred energy source after World War II reduced the role of coal as an energy source.

Oil.   Because most American oil initially came from Texas, the policy decisions of the Texas Railroad Commission (which regulated oil production in Texas) tended to define national oil policy between the 1930s and 1950s. Prorationing production limits set by Texas influenced other oil-rich states to adopt similar policies regulating production and distribution of this energy resource.

The **oil depletion allowance**, adopted in 1926 by the federal government, exemplified the protective nature of energy policies. At the end of World War I, the U.S. Geological Survey (USGS) predicted that the nation's oil reserves would be depleted within ten years. The oil industry argued that just as machinery wore out and buildings deteriorated, oil wells also lost their value over time as the underground reservoir emptied. Congress responded with legislation that allowed oil companies to deduct 27.5 percent of their gross income (not to exceed 50 percent of net income) from taxable income. The USGS prediction was inaccurate, as oil exploration efforts led to additional vast reserves in Oklahoma and East Texas by the 1930s. The oil depletion allowance was retained because it encouraged continued exploration across the United States and around the world as the tax savings and profits were used to fund new oil drilling expeditions.

Natural Gas.   Natural gas production requires very little refining before use and involves three major activities: production in the field, distribution through pipelines, and a specialized distribution network to consumers at the end of pipelines. The 1938 Natural Gas Act assigned federal regulatory authority to the Federal Power Commission (FPC). The FPC regulated pipeline construction and the price of natural gas in the interstate market.

The impact of these regulatory powers maintained a supply of low-cost natural gas. Interstate rates for natural gas were significantly less than the unregulated intrastate rates. Gas selling for $2.50 per thousand cubic feet in the intrastate market could be sold for only $1.00 in the interstate market. The low-price structure did not encourage efficiency or conservation. Interstate price control regulations encouraged increased demand for natural gas but also reduced profits for suppliers. This discouraged exploration for new gas supplies which then lowered production and supply of natural gas.

Nuclear Power.   During the 1950s and 1960s, nuclear power was viewed as a potential major source of energy for both the United States and Western Europe. Congress established the Atomic Energy Commission (AEC) to promote and regulate the development of nuclear power. Construction of nuclear reactors for commercial generation of electricity was assigned to the private sector.

Western Vulnerability: OPEC and the Arab Oil Embargo

Americans benefited from access to and control over foreign energy resources. The most important of these were the oil fields of the Middle East and North Africa. Before the 1973 Arab oil embargo, those oil-producing countries had minimal control over the oil industry within their borders. Major American and European international oil companies exercised extensive control over the production of oil, its market price, and the profit levels they chose to share with producing countries.

The Power of Western Oil Companies.   As the oil industry developed in the 1930s, seven major companies dominated oil production and distribution: Standard Oil of California (Chevron), the Texas Company (Texaco), Socony-Vacuum

(Mobil), Gulf Oil, Standard Oil of New Jersey (Exxon), Royal Dutch Shell, and British Petroleum (BP). These companies established cooperative arrangements for international oil exploration. One result was a reduction in competition in the international oil market. Competition decreased when the Arabian American Oil Company (Aramco) was organized by four companies (Standard Oil of New Jersey, Standard Oil of California, Socony-Vacuum, and Texaco) in 1947 to develop the enormous oil reserves of Saudi Arabia. These cooperative efforts were so successful that by 1952, the seven oil companies controlled over 90 percent of the total crude oil production outside North America and the communist nations.[2]

The Organization of Petroleum Exporting Countries (OPEC). The oil-producing states sought to create an organization that would provide control over price and production levels. OPEC was created in 1960 with the membership of seven Arab nations—Algeria, Iraq, Kuwait, Libya, Qatar, Saudi Arabia, and the United Arab Emirates—and six non-Arab nations—Ecuador, Gabon, Indonesia, Iran, Nigeria, and Venezuela. Several factors limited the strength of the new organization. First, the United States was nearly self-sufficient in the production of oil, with relatively little need for imports. Second, cooperative agreements among the major oil companies created an international oil cartel with near-monopolistic powers. Third, the production of crude oil exceeded international demand, which produced a buyer's market and limited the power of suppliers.

The 1973 Arab Oil Embargo. October 6, 1973, marked the opening date of the Yom Kippur War between Israel and the Arab states. This event provided a catalyst for Arab unity and demonstrated the power of collective action to OPEC members.[3] The Arab oil ministers resolved to use oil as a weapon in the struggle against Israel by imposing a 5 percent monthly reduction in exports to nations supporting Israel. Nations supporting the Arab cause were exempted from the embargo. The embargo had limited impact on oil imports by the United States, as non-Arab sources—primarily Venezuela and Iran—were available. The Arab nations lifted the embargo against the United States in March 1974, following the Egyptian–Israeli cease-fire. The embargo did achieve some of its original political objectives, as support for Israel in Western Europe and Japan softened. The real value of the 1973 Arab oil embargo was the dramatic example of power through unified policy that it gave to OPEC nations. OPEC realized that if action were taken in concert by all thirteen member states, their demands would be difficult to resist. This period marked the beginning of a rapid increase in the price for OPEC oil and regulation of production levels by producing nations. Figure 5.1 shows the price paid for oil between 1973 and 2013 for domestic and imported oil. The rapid increase in oil prices depicted in Figure 5.1 coincides with the 1973 embargo.

The increasing cost of oil exerted inflationary pressure on the economies of the oil-consuming West. During the late 1970s, OPEC could not agree on a fixed price for oil, so a price increase by one nation stimulated similar increases by other producers as well.[4] By 1982–1984, a combination of forces, including a

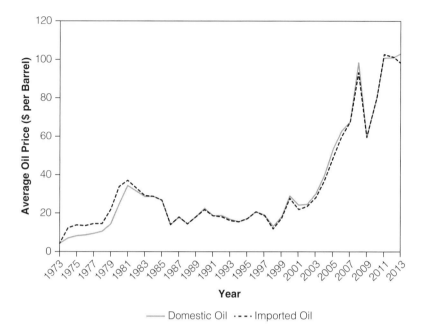

FIGURE 5.1   Average Price of Domestic and Imported Oil, 1973–2013

SOURCE: U.S. Energy Information Administration, *Monthly Energy Review*, February 2014, Table 9-1 Crude Oil Summary Prices, http://www.eia.doe.gov/emeu/mer/pdf/mer.pdf, accessed February 2014.

reduction in demand, discovery of reserves outside OPEC, overproduction, and OPEC disunity, brought about a drop in global crude oil prices, which stabilized in the $19-per-barrel range until late 1999 and early 2000. Oil prices again began to increase significantly to the $100-per-barrel range in 2008 and hovered near $105 per barrel in 2014.

CONTEMPORARY POLICY: A CYCLE OF COMPLACENCY, CRISIS, AND CONCERN

Energy Problems Emerge

The Arab oil embargo coincided with the end of American energy self-sufficiency. The United States began importing oil for domestic use in 1947. The minimal amount of less than one-half of 1 percent of total oil consumption increased to about 10 percent by the mid-1950s, because of the lower cost of imported oil, typically about half that of domestic.[5]

In order to protect the domestic oil industry, an import quota equivalent to 12 percent of domestic production was imposed in 1959. By 1973, American oil consumption reached nearly seventeen million barrels per day, with domestic production levels slightly less than eleven million barrels per day. This gap between domestic supply and demand prompted removal of all import quotas on oil in the spring of 1973, which allowed imported oil to reach the current 2013 figure of about 57 percent of total American oil consumption (see Figure 5.2).

Domestic natural gas production reached a peak of 24.1 trillion cubic feet in 1972–1973 and then began a gradual decline to some 19.1 trillion cubic feet in 1986. Increased demand for natural gas and the development of **fracking** technology to access natural gas from shale rock formations resulted in increased natural gas production to the 30.2 trillion cubic feet level in 2013. Current annual consumption levels are in the 24 to 25 trillion cubic foot level.[6] Nuclear power did not develop into a source of unlimited energy because of problems with the safety of the technology. A major accident in 1979 at the Three Mile Island nuclear plant in Pennsylvania and less serious incidents at other nuclear power facilities acted to shift American policy priorities away from this energy option in the 1980s. Coal furnishes a large percentage of energy consumption, but environmental problems and expanded federal regulations exist with coal as an energy source. Gases produced by the burning of coal contribute to acid rain, and strip-mining activities degrade the environment. Other sources of renewable energy such as solar power, wind power, and geothermal technologies have yet to develop sufficiently to offset any reduced dependence on oil and natural gas. The United States continues to depend on fossil fuels as the primary source of energy. This reality means continued reliance on oil imports.

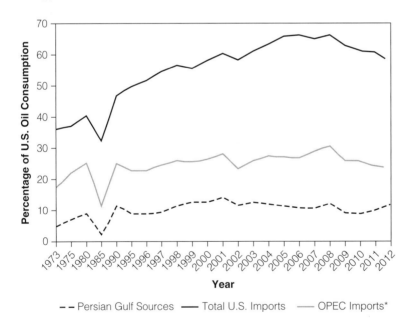

- - Persian Gulf Sources   —— Total U.S. Imports   —— OPEC Imports*

F I G U R E 5.2   U.S. Dependence on Oil Imports, 1973–2012 Persian Gulf, OPEC, and Total U.S. Imports (as percent of total U.S. oil consumption)

*Some Persian Gulf suppliers are members of OPEC.

SOURCE: *Monthly Energy Review*, U.S. Department of Energy, February 2014, Table 3.3a, "Petroleum Trade Overview," http://www.eia.doe.gov/emeu/mer/pdf/pages/sec3_7.pdf, accessed February 2014.

Global Dependence on Fossil Fuels

Dependence on oil as a primary energy source is a worldwide pattern. Figure 5.3 reflects the importance of oil and natural gas as primary energy sources. The proportion of energy provided by these two sources is now approximately 56 percent of total global energy consumption, an increase from some 36 percent in 1950. Coal has declined as a primary source of fuel in Western Europe from slightly over 85 percent to less than 19 percent of total energy consumption in 2012. The same pattern holds true for Japan, as its reliance on coal has dropped from over 86 percent to about 25 percent of total energy consumption in 2012. Oil and natural gas are now the world's primary energy sources, except in communist China where coal provides almost 70 percent of energy consumed, even though oil and natural gas are becoming increasingly important as fuels.

Dependence on imported oil is especially significant for the industrialized democracies of the free world.[7] The United States now imports about 40 percent of its oil. The figure is substantially higher for Europe and Japan, with oil imports accounting for 55 percent of European oil consumption and over 95 percent of Japanese oil consumption. Important sources of oil for Western Europe are the Middle East, North Africa, and Russia. Approximately 59 percent of the oil that Japan imports originates in the Islamic world. The United States has established a pattern since the mid-1970s of obtaining between 10 and 12 percent of its imports from Islamic nations. This means that the West's economic stability depends upon the uninterrupted flow of oil from the Islamic world and, therefore, upon political stability in the Middle East.

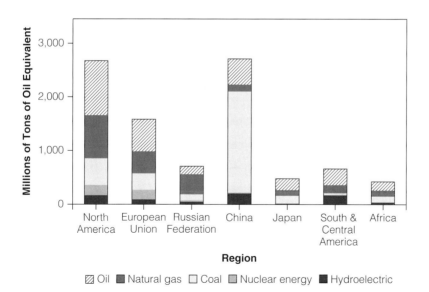

FIGURE 5.3   Regional Energy Sources, 2009 (millions of tons of oil equivalent)

SOURCE: British Petroleum, *Statistical Review of World Energy, 2013*. Primary Energy, Consumption by Fuel, http://www
.bp.com/content/dam/bp/pdf/statistical-review/statistical_review_of_world_energy_2013.pdf, accessed February 2014.

Energy Policy after 1973

The disruption of oil supply and the rapid increase in the cost of oil created by the 1973 oil embargo resulted in a dramatic expansion of the role of the federal government in energy policy.[8] Project Independence was announced in 1973 as a strategy to achieve energy self-sufficiency by 1980. With the lifting of the Arab oil embargo in the summer of 1974, the crisis atmosphere surrounding energy evaporated. Energy policy drifted as a unified energy policy could not be achieved.

During this period, the trans-Alaska pipeline was authorized over objections of environmental groups and a national 55-miles-per-hour speed limit was adopted in 1974. Two new governmental agencies were created to develop and coordinate federal energy policy: the Federal Energy Administration (FEA) and the Energy Research and Development Administration (ERDA). The emphasis on federal leadership led to the creation of the Department of Energy in 1977.

Legislation.   In an effort to move toward greater energy self-reliance, natural gas was deregulated and utility companies were encouraged to convert to coal from oil and natural gas to generate electricity by The National Energy Act of 1978. An important provision of the Act included a tax, paid by the manufacturer, on gas-guzzling cars. The tax initially ranged from $200 to $500 for the 1980 model year and has increased to a range of $1,000 to $7,700 for the 2013 model year for cars not achieving the 22.5-miles-per-gallon (mpg) fuel efficiency level. The **Corporate Average Fuel Economy** (CAFE) standard was implemented that required that the automobile industry produce a mix of cars with an average fuel efficiency of 27.5 mpg by 1985. The tax and CAFE standard contributed to a change in the size and fuel efficiency of automobiles, which reduced American oil consumption. In 2010, the Obama administration raised CAFE standards to 35.5 mpg for the 2016 model year. The popular sport utility vehicles, or SUVs, were classified as trucks and originally exempted from CAFE standards. Under the new CAFE rules, modified mileage and emissions standards apply to light trucks and SUVs. In 2014, CAFE standards were modified to require cars and light trucks to meet a 54.5 mpg standard by 2025. These new standards were developed with discussions and support of the major auto manufacturers in the United States and the United Auto Workers Union (UAW). The 1978 Act did not contain provisions to develop major alternative energy sources. Therefore, American dependence on oil continues.

Decontrol and the Windfall Profits Tax.   Federal energy policy moved in conflicting directions as illustrated by decontrol of oil prices and the imposition of a tax on oil profits at the same time. Domestic oil price controls began in 1971 as a mechanism to control inflation by keeping prices low. Proponents of decontrol argued that the removal of price controls would reduce oil consumption by up to one hundred million barrels of oil per year, because increased cost would reduce consumer demand. A second impact would be increased domestic production as higher profits encouraged oil exploration efforts. Critics of decontrol argued that significant social and economic problems would emerge because the poor and elderly would face increased financial burdens due to the higher cost of energy.

Federal policy then moved in two conficiting directions under the provisions of the Energy Policy and Conservation Act of 1975. All price controls on domestic oil were targeted for elimination by 1981, but Congress adopted the Crude Oil Windfall Profit Tax Act of 1980, which imposed a tax rate on profits in the 30 percent range (with a host of exemptions) with the tax being phased out by 1993. These revenues were intended to help the poor and elderly cope with energy costs.

Energy policy thus moved in two conflicting directions. Decontrol intended to provide economic incentives to spur domestic production and exploration. At the same time, taxes reduced the magnitude of the economic incentives provided by decontrol. Following decontrol there was a huge increase, followed by a decline, in the level of oil and gas exploration in the United States (see Figure 5.4). By 1995, exploration levels had dropped lower than in 1973. It was not until 2000, with rising worldwide oil prices, that exploration efforts for natural gas and oil began to steadily increase through 2010.

Energy Policy after 1980

Energy policy changed dramatically with the election of President Reagan in 1980. Federal energy policy shifted to the belief that the United States had an abundance of energy supplies.[9] Energy conservation and regulation strategies were rejected. The energy policies of the 1970s were viewed as counterproductive to domestic energy exploration and production. Policy efforts shifted to a focus on

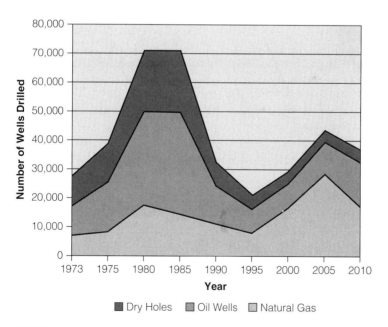

F I G U R E 5.4   U.S. Domestic Oil and Gas Exploration, 1973–2010 (thousands of wells)

SOURCE: U.S. Energy Information Administration, *Monthly Energy Review*, February 2014, Petroleum Overview, "Crude Oil and Natural Gas Exploratory and Development Wells," http://www.eia.gov/dnav/ng/hist/e_ertwo_xwc0_nus_cm.htm, accessed February 2014.

increasing production. The emphasis on "clean" energy was reduced as a guiding policy value. The environment was secondary to energy policy with environmental standards for clean air and water subject to relaxation. The operation of the market economy would create optimal environmental standards with a balance between energy for growth and a clean environment. Third, market operation, not government action, could best secure an abundant energy supply for the United States.

These policies encouraged offshore exploration for oil and gas, and favored opening more federal lands to oil and gas exploration. Conservation programs were reduced on the assumption that market forces are the most appropriate means of regulating energy consumption. One link to the past was a continued interest in nuclear energy in the form of federal research and development funding. Federal support for research and development of synthetic fuels and solar energy development was curtailed.

Energy Policy after 2000

Bush Energy Policy Values.   The Energy Policy Act of 2005 included four primary goals: promotion of energy conservation and efficiency, increasing domestic energy production, diversification of energy supply, and modernization of the energy infrastructure. Policy options to achieve these goals included: (1) tax credits of between $1,700 and $4,000 for purchasers of electric or hybrid vehicles; (2) increased funding support for the development of hydrogen-fueled vehicles; (3) tax credits for individuals of between $200 and $500 to offset the cost of installing high-efficiency home furnaces, air conditioners, and solar water-heating systems; (4) additional tax credits to support the use of alternative and renewal energy sources, such as wind, solar, and biomass gases; and (5) funding support for an expanded role of nuclear power as an energy source. No changes were made in the CAFE standards for automobile fuel efficiency, and there was an absence of any provision dealing with global climate change. The Act maintained a traditional emphasis on oil, gas, coal, and nuclear energy. Renewable energy sources such as wind, solar, geothermal, and ocean power received only marginal support in this legislation.[10]

Obama Energy Policy Values.

> We can't have an energy strategy for the last century that traps us in the past. We need an energy strategy for the future—an all-of-the-above strategy for the twenty-first century that develops every source of American-made energy.
>
> *(President Barack Obama, March 15, 2012)*

President Obama's "all of the above" policy values have resulted in several initiatives that may involve conflicting strategies. Higher CAFE standards for the automobile industry reflect acceptance of past energy policy values. President Obama focused on these higher standards as a strategy to reduce American consumption of oil. A policy allowing expansion of drilling for oil and natural gas was combined with an emphasis on safety and environmental concern. The devastating oil leak by *Deepwater Horizon*, a British Petroleum drilling platform, in the Gulf of Mexico in the spring of 2010 resulted in an announced policy of extensive regulatory reviews of offshore and public land oil and gas drilling activities. In another component of the "all of the above" energy strategy, President Obama is seeking to develop an oil and gas exploration policy on public lands that will expand development activities, reward rapid development of resources, and at the same time subject the new resource development to increased regulations that may reduce exploration and production. A third policy option involves a willingness to rely on nuclear power as a source of electricity. This involves increased federal funding for research and development of nuclear technologies for the future and a stated willingness to support expanded nuclear power for developing nations. A fourth initiative involves a number of actions to promote energy efficiency and conservation, including increased household appliance efficiency, weatherization programs for homes and public buildings, and improvements in the power transmission grid for the nation. The Obama administration is seeking to create a link between environmental issues (emissions, development of "green" industries, and "green" buildings) and energy policy. A defining policy value involves significantly expanded federal regulatory activity as opposed to reliance on the private sector to deliver energy to the nation.

The "all of the above" energy policy of President Obama has been challenged by both environmental groups and the fossil fuel industry alike as being contradictory and inconsistent. Environmental groups tend to oppose expanded oil and gas exploration offshore and on public lands, the construction of the Keystone XL pipeline, and nuclear energy. The fossil fuel industry is concerned that extensive regulations will effectively restrict oil and gas exploration efforts and that any restriction on the Keystone pipeline construction will deny the nation access to an important source of energy in North America. The president has emphasized the need for increased production of natural gas and has signaled that new technologies allow development of gas reserves in shale rock formations. Fracking is a process in which high pressure water is injected deep into shale rock formations to release natural gas. The potential supply of natural gas from this technology is extensive. Environmental issues are associated with this process. In some locations fracking has been accompanied by a number of small earthquakes. Critics of fracking are concerned about any negative impacts of injected water contaminating aquifers that cities and agriculture utilize. The role of fracking in early 2014 is an unresolved issue in President Obama's energy program.

POLICY EVALUATION: CONTINUED
FOSSIL FUEL DEPENDENCE

Energy consumption patterns reflect a continued reliance on fossil fuels. Imposition of reduced speed limits, the automotive fuel economy standards, energy tax credits, and other programs impacted energy usage. Some analysts argue that

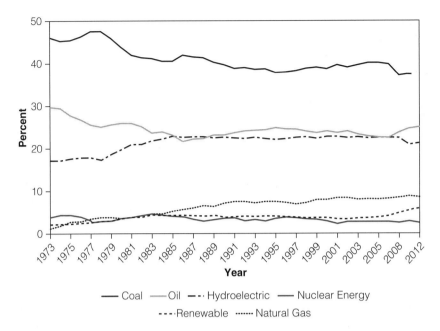

FIGURE 5.5   U.S. Energy Consumption by Source, 1973–2012 (percentage)

Note: Oil and natural gas includes domestic and imported products; renewable includes solar, wind, biomas, coke, and imported electricity.

SOURCE: *Annual Energy Review*, Energy Information Administration, U.S. Department of Energy, February 2014, Table 1.3, "Primary Energy Consumption by Source," http://www.eia.gov/totalenergy/data/monthly/pdf/sec1_7.pdf, accessed February 2014.

changes in consumption patterns have been the result of economic conditions, not energy policy or technological changes in energy. Figure 5.5 indicates U.S. energy consumption patterns since 1973.

Alternatives to Fossil Fuels

Research and Development.   The energy crisis of the 1970s and the accompanying increased cost of oil heightened interest in alternative sources of energy, such as solar, wind, and geothermal power. Prior to the rapid rise in the cost of fossil fuels, these alternatives were too expensive to utilize as major energy sources. When the price of oil decreased to the $17 per barrel range by 1992, the economic incentives for continued research and development of alternative energy sources were reduced because the costs were too great. Federal funding for energy research and development activities remains reduced as a national priority even as oil reaches the $105 per barrel range in 2014.

Solar Energy.   An energy program initiative in the 1970s was that by the year 2000, the United States should meet 20 percent of its energy need by solar power. This goal was not adopted by Congress and solar power experienced relatively little development in the United States. The Solar Heating and Cooling Demonstration Act of 1975 created a limited solar demonstration program and clearinghouse. To date, the president, Congress, and private-sector energy companies have not established specific goals for solar power as a major source of energy for the near future.

Coal Liquefaction.   The liquefaction of coal into a crude-oil substitute provides the ability to convert coal into a relatively clean-burning fuel. The 1980 Energy Security Act created the Synthetic Fuels Corporation and provided authority for federal funding for research and development of this technology. The costs associated with development and potential environmental impacts limited the economic viability of coal liquefaction. This energy source remains undeveloped.

Geothermal Energy.   Tapping the heat deep within the earth to convert water to steam for electricity generation is the objective of geothermal energy. Geothermal energy development is most promising in geologically active areas, such as Yellowstone National Park and Hawaii Volcanoes National Park. Concern over potential environmental damage led to congressional restrictions in 1994 on geothermal developments in the Yellowstone area. The Geysers, a complex of fifteen powerplants located in California, produces enough electricity to supply over 725,000 homes. Issues with geothermal energy include access to sufficient water to recharge the geysers and potential air and water contamination resulting from the deep wells. The Geysers injects treated wastewater from the region to maintain steam production. Expanding geothermal energy in the United States is not a current major policy priority.

Wind Energy.   Harnessing wind to generate electricity is a green energy strategy. As of 2013, wind turbine facilities in the United States have the capacity to generate over 60 gigawatts (GW) of electricity, an amount sufficient to supply over fifteen million American homes. Wind technology has evolved in that the wind turbines' efficiency continues to be increased from those used in 2000. Some estimates indicate that one turbine today can supply the electricity required for between four and five hundred homes. The industry continues to install facilities across the nation. As of 2013, the states with the greatest operating wind generators are Texas (12.3 GW), California (5.8 GW), Iowa (5.1 GW), Illinois (3.5 GW), Oklahoma (3.1 GW), and Kansas (2.9 GW). In the spring of 2014, wind power generated a temporary peak of 29 percent of the electricity within the state. Sustaining this capacity within all states is a function of wind constancy and wind speed. Wind energy has the advantage of being clean, renewable, and relatively inflation resistant. After initial construction, costs for wind energy farms remain stable and typically involve maintenance costs. As the cost of oil and natural gas increases, wind becomes an attractive energy source. Issues involving expanding wind power include mechanisms to integrate electricity from wind farms into the current electrical grid, a grid that was not designed to incorporate long-distance transmission of wind-generated electricity. A second issue involves implementation of funding for continued research and development to produce ever more efficient wind turbines and tax credits to encourage private-sector investment in wind as a source of electricity. Wind power remains a potentially significant source of environmentally friendly energy.

Peak Oil.   This concept holds that at some point in time, global production of oil must begin to decline as reserves of this finite resource are consumed at an ever-increasing rate. Proponents of peak oil observe that fossil fuels are not renewable and that much of the easily accessible petroleum reserves have already been accessed. Proponents also observe that new production technologies such as fracking for natural gas are increasingly expensive and serve to illustrate that more and more effort is required to maintain fossil fuel production levels. The date when peak oil production will be reached is subject to debate because estimates of petroleum reserves are difficult to accurately make. The erroneous USGS prediction in 1926 of American oil reserves is an example of the difficulty in predicting peak oil production.

Oil reserves are finite and the concept of peak oil is an impetus for energy conservation and the development of alternative renewable energy sources. The industrialized world depends heavily on petroleum products for economic stability and growth.

Nuclear Power

Nuclear power is a nonfossil energy source receiving increased policy attention. The development of the nuclear energy industry and the emphasis on nuclear technology as a source of energy were products of the government's desire to use nuclear energy for peacetime purposes. There are two different nuclear processes, fission and fusion. Fission is splitting atoms; fusion produces energy by fusing atoms. To date, fusion technology is still in the research and development stage. Nuclear-fission technologies grew out of the nuclear submarine program of the U.S. Navy, in which light-water reactors (LWR) use Uranium 235, a relatively scarce substance, to produce heat for steam generation of electricity. Current fission technologies use the more abundant Uranium 238, converting it into Plutonium 239.

Although nuclear power plants do account for nearly 10 percent of America's energy consumption, expanding nuclear energy remains questionable because it has yet to overcome three problems: safety, waste disposal, and decommissioning strategies.[11] Initial research indicated that nuclear safety would not be a problem. The 1975 Rasmussen Report issued by the Nuclear Regulatory Commission (NRC) concluded that nuclear accidents would probably never occur and provided a foundation for expanding nuclear power. The March 1979 accident at Three Mile Island in Pennsylvania dramatically demonstrated the inaccuracy of the Rasmussen Report.

Safety.   The issue of nuclear safety continues to have a significant impact on energy policy in the United States. Construction issues and adequate training and supervision of plant personnel remain a challenge to the nuclear industry. Adequate planning in the event of a major accident has also been difficult to achieve. Nuclear plants may also be at risk from attacks by international terrorists.

Waste.   Nuclear waste disposal has also proved to be a problem without a solution. Initially, experts assumed that spent nuclear fuel could be reprocessed into new fuel. This technology did not develop. Given the failure of the reprocessing option, the problem of long-term disposal of nuclear wastes remains unsolved. The amount of nuclear waste, however, will not reach the high levels projected during the 1970s, primarily because utility companies have not constructed any new reactors since 1990. While the volume of waste generated has not reached projected levels, the costs associated with nuclear waste management have skyrocketed dramatically. In 1983, DOE estimates for nuclear waste management were $23 billion. By 2012, cost estimates exceeded $100 billion. These cost estimates continue to escalate given the technological difficulties of managing nuclear waste.

Nuclear Plant Age and Decommissioning.   The nation's nuclear generating plants operate under forty-year licenses issued by the NRC. These licenses began to expire in 2000 for the oldest plants; by 2020, the licenses of over half of the current nuclear power plants will expire. The potential loss of these plants represents a serious energy problem since they generate almost 20 percent of the nation's electricity. One current strategy, adopted in 1991 by the NRC, is to extend their operating license on a case-by-case basis by an additional ten to twenty years.

License extensions are a source of intense controversy. Opponents argue that it is unwise to extend to fifty or sixty years the operating life of nuclear plants designed and manufactured for a forty-year life cycle. Neither the NRC nor the nuclear industry has data on the structural integrity of materials continuously exposed to radiation in a nuclear reactor. Supporters argue that proper maintenance and repairs can easily extend the life cycle. One controversial component of the policy involves the decision to use the plant's current license requirements as a basis for extension. Critics argue that the more rigorous safety standards based on today's increased knowledge should guide license extension, not the standards that were in place when a plant was first licensed some twenty to thirty years ago.

Decommissioning a nuclear power plant means shutting down and deactivating the plant to the extent that the site poses no environmental threat. To date, the NRC has not specified the guidelines and standards that will apply to future decommissioning activity. There are three options: dismantlement, mothballing, and entombment. Dismantlement presents problems of storage, because the fuel rods, containment buildings, and the reactor vessel will be radioactive for several thousand years. Some estimates indicate that up to 800 tons of radioactive material will require permanent storage from each nuclear unit dismantled. Mothballing simply means locking the facility behind a security perimeter and waiting several thousand years until the radioactive material decays on its own. This approach has been entitled SAFSTOR, or safe storage, by the NRC. Entombment takes mothballing a step further by constructing a large concrete structure around the facility. Both options present problems of protecting people and the environment from dangerous material for up to 80,000 years.

The actual costs for decommissioning a nuclear power plant are subject to debate. In 1978, the NRC estimated that costs would range between $43 million and $58 million, but the Rand Corporation published information that these costs might be in the $500 million range. The costs to achieve a partial decommission at Three Mile Island exceeded $1 billion. Actual costs vary significantly by the type of decommissioning selected: dismantlement is the most expensive, followed by SAFSTOR and the entombment strategy.

Costs associated with decommissioning may be transferred to utility customers over a protracted number of years. Customers of the utilities continue to pay for the decommissioning process of a nuclear power plant through rate increases for electricity. The costs of decommissioning a nuclear facility fall on future customers over ten to twenty years after the plant has closed. A national policy to apportion the costs of decommissioning a nuclear power plant has yet to be developed.

An unresolved policy issue is how to keep future generations informed (for 10,000 to 80,000 years) concerning the location and lethal nature of radioactive wastes. If such a mechanism had been in place since 1940, policymakers would know the location, nature, and the threat posed by nuclear wastes to the public and the environment today. No mechanism exists either for short-term (fifty to one hundred years) or long-term (thousands of years) transmittal of knowledge. Policy adopted by the Department of Energy in 1980 states, "Although this generation bears the responsibility for protecting future societies from the waste it creates, future societies must assume the responsibility for any risks, which arise from deliberate and informed acts, which they choose to perform."

The Future.   The United States has an uncertain policy related to nuclear technology as an energy option. In 2012 approval was granted to construct a new nuclear power plant in Georgia by the NRC. Applications have been filed with the NRC to construct an additional twenty-eight power plants but uncertainty exists about how many will actually be approved and constructed. Nuclear power plant construction was virtually complete by 1990 (see Table 5.1). President Obama supported the proposal to construct the new facility in Georgia and appears to advocate a significant policy change that would foster the construction of new nuclear power plants to replace aging nuclear facilities and increase utilization of this source of energy.

The March 2011 accident at the Fukushima nuclear power plant in Japan, in which an offshore earthquake and accompanying 45-foot tsunami wave resulted in damage to four reactors, raised concerns about nuclear power. The event required the relocation of over 100,000 residents due to the release of radioactive materials. Radioactive materials washed into the ocean and began to reach the western United States in late 2013, raising concern about contaminated fish and potential contamination of beaches and coastline. The impact of this event on the U.S. nuclear industry remains uncertain.

This pattern does not hold true for other nations. In 2014 there were 436 operating nuclear power plants in 30 countries with 72 more facilities under

TABLE 5.1 **Operating Nuclear Power Plants in the United States, 1960–2013**

Year	Number of Operating Plants	Percent of U.S. Electricity
1960	3	0.1
1965	13	0.3
1970	20	1.4
1975	57	9.0
1980	71	11.0
1985	96	15.5
1990	112	19.0
1995	109	20.1
2000	104	19.8
2013	100	19.6

SOURCE: U.S. Department of Energy. *Annual Energy Review, 2013*, Nuclear Energy, Table 8-1, Nuclear Power Plant Operations, 1957–2013, January 2014, http://www.eia.gov/totalenergy/data/monthly/pdf/sec8_3.pdf, accessed February 2014.

construction in 15 countries and still more in the planning phase. Table 5.2 depicts the status of global nuclear power plants. On a global scale, nuclear power generates over 12 percent of the world's electricity. Nuclear power provides over 25 percent of the electricity generated in 13 countries and continues to be a major source of global energy.

Global reliance on nuclear power traces to two factors. First, construction of nuclear power plants represents an investment of billions of dollars. The size of this investment exerts economic pressure to maintain the nuclear power plants in order to obtain a return on the massive construction expenditures. Second, many countries simply have no other currently available viable source of electricity. Even major nuclear accidents such as that at Chernobyl in the former Soviet Union and Fukushima, Japan, have not deterred emphasis on nuclear power plants on the international scene. Figure 5.6 reflects the relative importance of nuclear power in the generation of electricity for countries with nuclear power plants.

Political Impact of Continued Oil Dependence

There are political consequences of the free world's dependence on oil imports. The first is the uncertainty of supply. Interruptions or threats to the supply of oil can severely weaken the West's economic, political, and military power. The West's Achilles' heel is its dependence on imported oil. Interrupt the oil flow, and the West faces economic collapse. The oil reserves that the West must have to survive are located mainly in the highly volatile Middle East. Another consequence is that the Western world has been drawn into increased military and political involvement in the Persian Gulf region, with a primary goal of

TABLE 5.2   **Operating Nuclear Power Plants by Country, 2014**

Country	Reactors	Long-Term Shutdown	Under Construction	Country	Reactors	Long-Term Shutdown	Under Construction
Argentina	2		2	Lithuania		1	
Armenia	1			Mexico	2		
Belgium	7			Netherlands	1		
Brazil	2		1	Pakistan	3		2
Bulgaria	2		2	Romania	2		
Canada	19			Russian Federation	32		10
China	21		28	Slovak Republic	4		2
Czech Republic	6			Slovenia	1		
Finland	4		1	South Africa	2		
France	58		1	Spain	7	1	
Germany	9			Sweden	10		
Hungary	4			Switzerland	5		
India	21		6	Ukraine	15		2
Iran			1	United Kingdom	16		
Japan	48	4	2	United States	100		
South Korea	23		5	United Arab Emirates			2
				Taiwan	6		2

Total reactors: 435
Long-term shutdown: 6
Total under construction: 69

SOURCE: http://www.iaea.org/PRIS/WorldStatistics/OperationalReactorsByCountry.aspx, accessed February 2014.

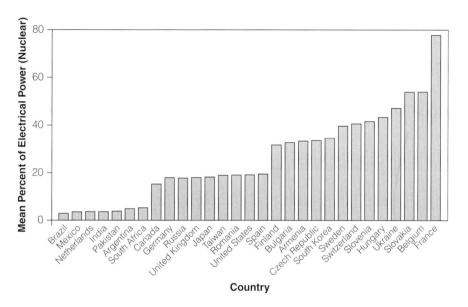

FIGURE 5.6   Percent Nuclear Electricity by Country, 2013

SOURCE: World Nuclear Association, Nuclear Basics, 2014, http://www.world-nuclear.org/Nuclear-Basics/Electricity-supplied-by-nuclear-energy/, accessed February 2014.

promoting internal stability in order to maintain an adequate oil supply.[12] Western involvement ranges from military sales and assistance to air and naval bases in the Middle East. Currently, the United States has either an established military presence or arrangements for military bases in Iraq, Oman, Egypt, and Saudi Arabia. The expanding role of Russia as an exporter of energy to the European Union (EU) is a policy issue. The EU imports over 30 percent of its oil and almost 40 percent of its natural gas from Russia. Gazprom, the Russian oil and gas company, is the largest company in Russia and one of the largest energy companies in the world. Energy exports provide Russia with financial resources for its economic growth and development. As the EU increases its dependence on Gazprom, the potential influence of Russia on EU domestic and international policy increases. This strengthening energy relationship for the EU may result in a reduced ability to resist Russian policy preferences in both neighboring nations of the former Soviet Bloc and in the Middle East.

Hidden Costs.   A consequence of dependence on imported oil is the impact on military and defense spending. In order to maintain economic stability within the United States, it is necessary to protect America's sources of oil from disruption. This involves a continuing military commitment in the Persian Gulf region. The cost of this military presence is not included in the price of imported oil. Imported oil adds significantly to military spending of the United States.

American reliance on imported oil contributed to a structural element to the trade deficit. Oil imports are a major element in the trade deficit of the United States. As domestic oil and gas production begins to increase, the impact of imported energy on the trade deficit decreases. In the absence of domestic oil and gas production that may result from extensive federal regulations, the cost of imported oil saddles the American economy with an international trade burden.

Organization of Petroleum Exporting Countries (OPEC).   An additional element of Western dependence on imported oil has been an inability to control the price of oil. When OPEC acted from a position of unity, the oil-consuming West demonstrated a marked inability to limit price increases. OPEC disunity is a function of disagreement over oil prices, production levels, and political conflicts. As the West began to become more energy efficient, demand for oil also began to decrease slightly. The most appropriate strategy to maintain price when demand drops is to reduce supply. OPEC has not been able to implement an allocation formula for reducing production levels. Member states—in need of revenues—have produced at levels higher than global demand, which acted to keep oil prices under control until 2004. The cost for oil has remained in the $100 per barrel range for the period 2011–2013.

Political disunity also is a factor. Military and political conflict in the Persian Gulf and in Syria contributes to uncertainty over oil production levels as the security of oil fields and transportation networks across the region remains a question. Conflict between Israel and the Arab nations has the potential to strengthen unity within OPEC. In 1973, the Arab members of OPEC found that oil was a common weapon to weaken support for Israel around the world. The possibility exists that any future Arab–Israeli conflict may provide a force to significantly strengthen OPEC unity again in the future.

Although the strength of OPEC has varied, it would be a mistake to minimize the potential impact that the organization can have on oil supply and costs. Internal events in the member nations can disrupt production, and external events can promote OPEC unity, as demonstrated during the mid- to late 1970s.

CONTINUING DEBATES: ENERGY
POLICY CONCERN

The energy crisis of the early 1970s evaporated, and the public concern that stimulated energy policy activity diminished. Lower energy prices and an adequate supply of oil mark the period until 2004–2006. The result was a return to an attitude of complacency toward energy policy.

One factor that contributed to the energy shortfall of the early 1970s was a product of faulty demand projections by the energy companies and governments. During the 1950s and 1960s, experts continually underestimated demand for oil. Ten-year projections were off by as much as 25 or 30 percent.[13] A gap of five to ten years exists between the decision to seek additional oil and gas reserves and actual production from new sources. Before the 1970s, the routine underestimation of demand failed to stimulate sufficient exploratory efforts to maintain a balance between supply and demand. By the early 1970s, energy consumption patterns, which were the cornerstone of forecasting, produced projections of dramatic increases in energy demand for the decade of the 1980s and beyond. The OPEC unity achieved in 1973, which provided a framework for price increases and limited production quotas, added credibility to the projections of a continuing future gap between supply and demand. Between 1973 and 1978, the growth in the demand for oil exceeded the growth in the oil supply, with several consequences. First, decisions were made to increase the oil supply by exploring the North Slope in Alaska, to increase exploration in the North Sea, and to intensify exploration efforts in other regions of the world as well as across the United States.

Second, the increase in the cost of energy produced slow but continuous changes in consumption patterns. Homeowners insulated their homes better. The efficiency of residential and commercial heating units increased. Fuel efficiency became an important value in the transportation industry as new trucks and aircraft were designed and manufactured. Changes in manufacturing techniques also provided increased energy efficiency. These changes acted to decrease the rate at which energy demand grew. A gradual change to more energy-efficient automobiles took place. During the late 1990s, however, consumer preference for less fuel-efficient vehicles began to increase with the popularity of trucks and SUVs. This shift in consumer purchasing preferences is another indication of complacency toward energy supply.

Third, OPEC economies were becoming more dependent on the oil consumption patterns of the West. Modernization and development programs created an ever-increasing demand for oil revenues within OPEC nations. The need to market oil and maintain production became a driving force within OPEC nations. Between 1974 and 1988, non-OPEC oil production increased by over 80 percent, from seventeen million to over thirty-one million barrels per day. This increase in production, combined with the improvement in energy efficiency and other conservation measures, acted to create an imbalance in which supply exceeded demand by 1988. The availability of an adequate energy supply and lower prices had a major impact on the United States. Complacency replaced public concern, as oil remained a primary energy source.

Renewed Concern

This complacency is not justified. Contrary to public perceptions, the energy system is considerably more volatile and dynamic now than in the past. Before 1973, the actions of the international oil companies largely controlled the supply and price of energy. During the 1970s, the OPEC oil cartel acted to control oil supply and prices. The power of these two systems of control has evaporated as oil supply, production, and cost respond to international market forces and competing international interests.

Global demand for oil continues to increase. One source of this significantly increased demand for oil is China. As China continues significant industrial and economic growth, its appetite for oil increases. One result of this new source of demand for oil is an increase in the price for oil on the global market.

Another area of concern is the potential for political unrest in the Middle East to disrupt the flow of oil to the West. Military and sectarian conflict in Iraq and other areas has the potential to reduce oil exports from that region. Potential actions by international terrorists also reduce the certainty of oil from the Middle East and force oil prices to ever-higher levels. Market uncertainty over the impact of political unrest also contributed significantly to increases in oil prices to the $100 range.

This has at least two policy implications for the United States. First, continued dependence on oil ties American economic strength to access to foreign energy sources. Any disruption in oil supply will have potentially profound economic consequences. One consequence of this dependence on imported oil is the requirement for what may be a prolonged military presence in the Persian Gulf to maintain the flow of oil to Europe, Japan, and the United States. Second, low international prices act to reduce domestic oil production in the United States and reduce investment in alternative energy sources. The dramatic increase in the price of oil provides the United States with an opportunity to invest in the development of wind, solar, geothermal, and ocean wave technologies that can potentially increase energy self-sufficiency and improve environmental quality through a reduced reliance on fossil fuels.

OPEC also faces challenges: In order to maintain high prices for its oil, it must (1) maintain a balance between production levels and prices to discourage the development of alternative energy sources, (2) encourage dependence on OPEC as a primary source of energy, and (3) develop strategies that will minimize the impact of political and military unrest on their ability to provide oil to the global marketplace.

Moreover, the American appetite for energy places energy companies in strong political positions. Concern about foreign imports, and about sufficiency of energy supply, impacts the environment. Natural disasters, such as Hurricane Katrina in 2005, also impact the supply of energy to the nation. As Katrina moved through the Gulf of Mexico, oil well platforms were forced to cease operation as crews were evacuated. Following the storm, it took time to repair the platforms in order to resume production. Hurricanes also present a significant danger to oil refineries located in Texas and Louisiana.

Drilling accidents impact offshore oil and gas exploration. Due to pressure from environmental groups, offshore drilling has moved into ever-deeper waters. British Petroleum's *Deepwater Horizon* drilling platform was producing oil from a well five thousand feet below the surface when a major accident destroyed the platform and created an unprecedented oil spill in the Gulf of Mexico in 2010. Because of the Gulf oil spill, Obama reversed himself and ordered a six-month moratorium on deep-water drilling.

The debate over construction of the Keystone XL pipeline between Canada and Texas remains an issue. The pipeline will provide the United States with a significant source of oil that is independent from the Persian Gulf and Venezuela. Construction of the pipeline has been opposed by environmental groups. Proponents argue that the pipeline will create both construction jobs and promote economic growth for the nation.

Important policy issues involve whether President Obama's "all of the above" energy policy will allow offshore drilling closer to shore where repairs are easier, allow drilling on federal lands such as the Alaska National Wildlife Reserve (ANWR), restrict drilling offshore and on federal lands, continue the current policy of encouraging deep-water drilling, encourage development of natural gas reserves through fracking, and aggressively pursue expansion of nuclear energy.

Environmental Policy

Public concern over the environment was minimal until the beginning of the twentieth century. Westward expansion of the United States reflected little concern for soil depletion, deforestation, or the impact of mining activities. Through the 1930s, conservation was the primary theme of environmental policy. Examples include the establishment of Yellowstone Park as the first national park in 1872 and creation of the national forest system in 1872. Although conservation provided a general policy framework, there was significant disagreement over specific strategies. Conservation can mean resource management for effective utilization, such as scientific forestry or viewed primarily as wilderness preservation. This conflict over strategy remains present today as a major policy issue.

Conservation policies did not reflect major concern with environmental protection through the 1950s. Publication of *Silent Spring* in 1962 was a major catalyst for environmental concern and drew attention to the dangers of pesticides, such as DDT, in the food chain.[14] The sense of social responsibility that emerged in the 1960s also moved environmental policy from the background to the forefront of the policy agenda.

ISSUE BACKGROUND: A LEGACY OF ENVIRONMENTAL ABUSE

The environmental problems of the nation are the product of indifference, neglect, and a historic lack of public concern with the unintended consequences of economic growth and development of an industrialized society. Air pollution, water pollution, solid-waste pollution, toxic- and hazardous-waste pollution, acid rain, and changing land-use patterns, as well as global climate change, all pose important problems.

Air Pollution

Air pollutants can be categorized in two groups: particles and gases. Particulate matter includes such material as ashes, soot, and lead (a noncombustible gasoline additive). Though particulate pollution is a problem, the dangers presented by the release of gases into the air are just as real but probably less well understood by the public. The major air pollutants sort into the following five categories.

1. **Carbon monoxide (CO).** Carbon monoxide is a colorless by-product of the incomplete combustion of carbon fuels. Gasoline engines are its primary source.

2. **Sulfur dioxide (SO_2).** The combustion of fuels containing sulfur produces sulfur dioxide. When combined with water vapor, it can form sulfuric acid and fall as acid rain.

3. **Hydrocarbons (HC).** Hydrocarbons, consisting of various combinations of hydrogen and carbon, are the unburned fuel resulting from incomplete combustion. The compounds have a major impact in the production of photochemical smog in urban areas.

4. **Nitrogen oxide (NO).** Nitrogen oxide is a by-product of fossil fuel combustion at high temperature levels. It combines with hydrocarbons to produce smog.

5. **Particulate matter.** Particulates include liquids or solids released into the atmosphere.

In 1980, the Environmental Protection Agency (EPA) estimated substantial increases in air pollution by the year 2000, with total emissions of particulate matter projected to double by that year.[15] As indicated in Figure 5.7, the emission level of these greenhouse gases has decreased in the United States since 2005.

A focus on measuring the raw amount of individual pollutants produced can be a deceptive approach to the problem, because serious health problems can result from either short-term exposure to high levels of these compounds or long-term exposure to relatively low levels. There is also evidence that these pollutants act synergistically on animal and plant life. This means that exposure

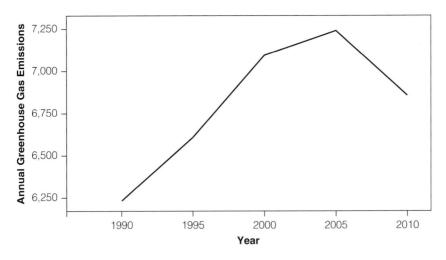

F I G U R E   5.7   Trends in U.S. Greenhouse Gas Emissions, 1990–2012

SOURCE: Environmental Protection Agency, *2014 U.S. Greenhouse Gas Inventory Report,* February 2014, Chapter 2, "Recent Trends in Greenhouse Gas Emissions and Sinks," http://www.epa.gov/climatechange/Downloads/ghgemissions/US-GHG-Inventory-2014-Chapter-2-Trends.pdf, accessed February 2014.

to the compounds together produces more harmful impacts than would result from exposure to them separately.

Not all emissions are easily categorized as either harmless or polluting. Such is the case with carbon dioxide (CO_2). (See Figure 5.8.) Scientists are concerned that high levels of CO_2 in the atmosphere may warm the earth and result in major climatic changes, known as the "greenhouse effect." Increased atmospheric levels of CO_2 trap the earth's heat by reducing the escape of infrared radiation from the surface into space. There is debate within the scientific community over the seriousness of the greenhouse effect. Debate also focuses on the origins of the rising levels of atmospheric CO_2. Some experts attribute high CO_2 levels to the use of fossil fuels; others believe that the rapid deforestation in Africa, South America, and Asia is the primary cause.[16]

Ozone Layer.   A thin layer of *ozone* some thirty miles above the surface protects the earth from excessive ultraviolet rays. The production and use of *chlorofluorocarbons* (CFCs) threaten the integrity of that protective layer. Scientists have documented a thinning of the ozone layer above North America and Europe. Depletion of the protective ozone layer could result in a higher incidence of skin cancer, cataracts, and other health problems. This is primarily due to the harmful nature of ultraviolet-B radiation from the sun.

Chlorofluorocarbons are viewed as a primary cause of ozone depletion. Air-conditioning and refrigeration units employed CFCs extensively. In 1987, the European Economic Community (EEC), the United States, and twenty-nine other nations initially approved the Montreal Protocol on Substances that Deplete the Ozone Layer, a group that represented 82 percent of the world's consumption of CFCs. A number of other nations have since signed the protocol with the result that CFC emissions significantly declined during the 1990s.

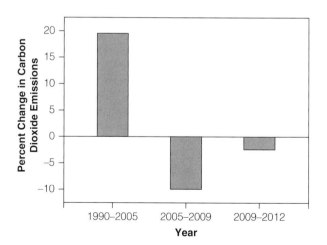

FIGURE 5.8   Trends in U.S. Carbon Dioxide Emissions, 1990–2012 (change in percents)

SOURCE: U.S. Environmental Protection Agency, *2014 U.S. Greenhouse Gas Inventory Report,* February 2014, Table 2-1: Recent Trends in U.S. Greenhouse Gas Emissions and Sinks (Tg CO_2 Eq.), http://www.epa.gov/climatechange/Downloads/ghgemissions/US-GHG-Inventory-2014-Chapter-2-Trends.pdf, accessed February 2014.

Water and Solid-Waste Pollution

Water Pollution.   Neglect of the nation's waterways has been a major environmental problem. Even though water pollution is a well-documented nationwide problem, its severity varies considerably among the different regions of the country. Waterways of the industrialized Northeast and Midwest have been especially abused. Even though sources of water pollution vary greatly, it is possible to classify most pollutants into four categories.[17]

Industrial wastes contain a wide range of organic and inorganic compounds, including heavy metals, such as mercury and zinc. A relatively new water-pollution phenomenon is thermal pollution; the cause is the discharge of heated water into rivers and lakes after cooling equipment used primarily in electric power plants. Thermal pollution heightens the toxicity of some other pollutants and, by accelerating the decomposition of organic matter, also lowers the oxygen level in surface waters.

Domestic and municipal wastes include human wastes and other compounds disposed of by people in their day-to-day lives.

Agricultural wastes include animal waste and other compounds that may pose health risks, such as fertilizers and pesticides that run off into waterways and enter the food chain. One of the greatest threats posed by agricultural wastes is the excess nutrients that enter lakes, rivers, and streams. These nutrients foster rapid growth of algae and other microorganisms that deplete the oxygen supply for fish and other organisms. The Centers for Disease Control and Prevention (CDC) notes that organisms harmful to fish and wildlife such as Pfiesteria typically occur in watersheds that drain large concentrations of chicken, hog, and other livestock operations.

Miscellaneous pollutants may be natural and include silt and sedimentation entering surface waters following rains. Also included are more serious pollutants, such as those from accidental oil spills. While offshore oil spills from supertankers and drilling accidents receive publicity due to their magnitude, the hundreds of other smaller spills that occur each year receive relatively little attention. Mining activity also adds to water pollution. Strip mining exposes sulfur compounds in the soil, which react with rain to form sulfuric acid, which then runs off into surface waters. One approach to reducing water pollution involves aggressive wastewater treatment by cities and industry to eliminate most of the contaminants before they enter surface waters. There are three levels of waste treatment. Primary treatment uses settling chambers to remove solid contaminants before the water returns to streams and rivers. Secondary treatment filters the remaining wastes through beds of rock and sand to remove organic contaminants, with the addition of chlorinates to kill bacteria. Tertiary systems use additional filtration (such as activated charcoal) to remove inorganic compounds and heavy metals.

There are numerous waste-treatment technologies available to municipalities and industry to minimize the discharge of contaminants. The major obstacle to their use is cost. Construction and operation of a tri-level treatment can cost three to four times as much as a bi-level treatment system. Economic costs act to shift policy options away from a completely aggressive waste-treatment strategy.

Solid-Waste Pollution.   Solid-waste pollution correlates directly to the level of economic activity. The United States produces a variety of solid wastes each year, including agricultural solid wastes, residential and commercial solid wastes, industrial solid wastes, and mineral solid wastes (slag and mill tailings). The traditional approach has been simply to bury the waste in landfills, an option that is less than satisfactory given the projections of continued growth in annual solid-waste production. Recycling is still an emerging priority in the United States with the majority of municipal solid waste sent to landfills.

As indicated in Figure 5.9, recycling is now at approximately 25 percent of municipal waste generated. The slow growth in recycling can be attributed to the fact that it is economically expedient, in the short run, to discard processed materials and utilize new raw materials in the production process. Government action mandating recycling has been adopted in some localities, but remains unlikely at the national level within the next decade. The proportion of waste transported to landfills has decreased since 1990 due to increased recycling and some components of municipal waste have been burned in the generation of electricity.

Toxic and Hazardous Waste

Hazardous wastes are those wastes that pose a significant threat to either health or the environment due to their "quantity, concentration, physical, chemical, or

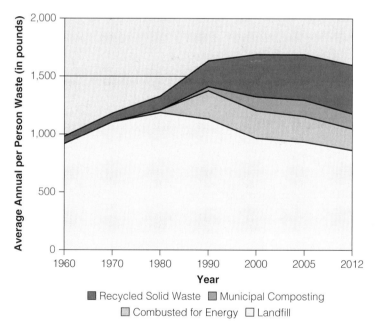

FIGURE 5.9   Municipal Solid Waste, 1960–2012

SOURCE: U.S. Environmental Protection Agency, *Municipal Solid Waste in the United States, 2014.* Adapted from Table 4, Generation, Materials, Recover, Composting, Combustion with Energy Recovery, and Discards of MSW, http://www.epa .gov/epawaste/nonhaz/municipal/msw99.htm, accessed February 2014.

infectious characteristics."[18] Estimates indicate that only a relatively small amount of toxic wastes are disposed of safely.

The impact of improper toxic-waste disposal may emerge only decades later. The event that moved the issue of toxic waste to the public agenda occurred at Love Canal in Niagara Falls, New York. The Hooker Chemical Company buried more than 20,000 tons of chemical wastes containing over 300 different chemicals at Love Canal in the 1950s. Two decades later, in the 1970s, residents in the Love Canal area experienced major health problems directly attributed to the buried toxic wastes. It took over $30 million to clean up the site and relocate all of the residents.

One type of increasingly important hazardous waste is radioactive waste. The two main sources of radioactive waste are the nuclear weapons program and nuclear power plants used to generate electricity. Some of these high-level wastes are so toxic that they must be stored for 500,000 years. Low-level wastes also pose a major problem. The United States produces over three million cubic feet of this waste, which requires safe storage for hundreds of years. Nuclear waste-management policy involves controversy and uncertainty.

Safe disposal of radioactive wastes remains an elusive goal. As the United States developed nuclear technology during World War II, there was minimal concern for safe disposal techniques. Radioactive wastes were typically burned, buried in shallow pits, or simply dumped into the existing solid waste systems. One guiding principle was that safe disposal involved the dilution of radioactive wastes, which facilitated dispersal of the wastes in the environment. During the late 1940s and the 1950s, the high volume of waste resulted in a new disposal system: ocean dumping. This technology involved using containers (primarily 55-gallon containers) to hold radioactive wastes. These containers were then filled with concrete and dumped off the coast of the United States.

Between 1945 and 1967, the United States dumped almost 100,000 of these containers into the waters off the Atlantic and Pacific coasts. This practice was terminated by 1970 because of the long-term environmental threats. The wastes can become exposed to ocean currents and potentially enter the food chain if the containers corroded. Currently, ocean dumping of radioactive waste is not a formal policy of any nation.

Land disposal has replaced ocean dumping of radioactive wastes. A policy problem is that a viable technology for long-term disposal does not yet exist. Current surface facilities are rapidly reaching or exceeding capacity. A safe, technologically feasible storage system is not in existence, and the level of radioactive waste continues to accumulate.

Another policy obstacle to solving the problem of toxic-waste dumps, nuclear and otherwise, is that many contaminated sites are not yet identified. The EPA has located over 17,000 potentially dangerous sites, but possibly thousands more still await discovery. Virtually every state in the union contains at least one hazardous toxic waste dump. Congress has not provided the EPA with the budget and the personnel to complete this critical first step of identifying them.

Acid Rain

A persistent environmental problem is the phenomenon of acid rain. This is produced when sunlight chemically converts air pollutants, primarily sulfur dioxide, nitrogen oxides, and hydrocarbons, into sulfates, nitrates, and other acidic compounds, which are returned to earth by rain and snow, and gradually change the acidic balance in both water and soil.

Acidity is measured in pH units on a scale ranging from 0 to 14, with the pH value of 7 representing neutrality. Values greater than 7 represent alkalinity, and values less than 7 represent acidity. The logarithmic nature of the scale means that a pH level of 5 is ten times more acidic than pH 6 and that pH 4 is one hundred times more acidic than pH 6. For example, a lake that increases in acidity from pH 4.5 to pH 4.2 has doubled its level of acidity. A lack of understanding of pH levels has minimized public concern with the potential threat posed by acid rain.

When acidity in a body of water exceeds the level of pH 5, the water loses the ability to support fish and plant life. Given that over twenty million tons of sulfur dioxides and twenty million tons of nitrogen oxides enter the atmosphere each year, the United States faces a potential problem of enormous magnitude. Data from the EPA indicate that the acidic level for rain and snow is below the level of pH 5 for the entire eastern half of the nation. This means that increased levels of acidity threaten the rivers and lakes in the affected region. There are geologic differences, however, that can reduce the impact on bodies of water in this region. For example, the limestone floors of some lakes in New England neutralize some of the acidity.

POLICY DILEMMAS   Balance, Compromise, and Policy Options

The linkage between energy and environment serves as a constraint on policy options that might be viable if each were independent of the other. Energy development impacts the environment. Economic growth gained from energy usage impacts the environment. Regulatory policies intended to protect the environment impact energy development and the economy. Another constraint on policy options relates to the international arena. Energy is a commodity that links the economies of diverse regions of the world and depends on political stability for distribution. Given the global nature of the environment, policy options in one country impact the environment of not just neighboring nations, but that of nations around the world.

1. If political compromise is required to develop energy and environmental policies, what are the values that policymakers should follow when developing effective energy and environmental policies?

2. Energy and environmental policy debates tend to be forward looking with a focus on future impacts. Yet the actions of the past have resulted in significant long-term environmental problems that require vast sums of dollars to correct. What are the available strategies or policy options that will support remediation of past problems, provide future protection, and be financially sound during a period of a weakened national economy?

The Environmental Legacy

The absence of an aggressive environmental-protection strategy produced potentially severe air, water, and toxic-waste problems. Land-use practices also pose problems for the nation. Both conventional and strip-mining activities had significant impacts. Without extensive reclamation efforts after strip mining, the land is permanently unusable for productive or recreational purposes. The tailings from conventional mining activity also present problems as wind and rain transport contaminants into the ecosystem. Uranium mining, for example, leaves radioactive debris in the open in mammoth piles of tailings. Land-use patterns can impact topsoil erosion, the loss of wetlands, and forestry management practices. Another area of concern is indoor air pollution. The traditional view presumed that pollution was an outdoor problem: People could escape the problem by remaining inside. Indoor health hazards, such as formaldehyde foam (used in building insulation), asbestos, and other toxic substances, are a source of indoor health hazards.

As with energy, the environmental policy legacy has been one of historical neglect of environmental protection, which allowed environmental abuse to develop into a significant public policy problem.

CONTEMPORARY ENVIRONMENTAL POLICY

Water-Pollution Policy

The federal government gradually assumed partial leadership in this policy area. The federal role began with the Refuse Act of 1899, which sought to limit the blockage of navigable rivers by municipal and industrial debris. Although largely ignored, the Act demonstrated the necessity for action by the federal government to respond to a problem that extends beyond state borders.

Congress gradually expanded the federal role with the Water Pollution Act of 1948 by providing federal funds for sewage-plant construction. In 1956, Congress amended the Act to assign the Public Health Service (PHS) a permanent role in monitoring water quality standards in municipalities across the nation. The 1961 Water Pollution Control Act and the 1965 Water Quality Act continued to provide federal funds for sewage-plant construction and to retain primary responsibility for water standards and enforcement to the states.

The underlying assumption of the emphasis on state responsibility held that states would be vigilant in protecting their own water resources, but this was not typically the case. State governments proved unwilling or unable to enact strict standards for fear of driving industry into other states with less stringent standards. Most states adopted very weak water-quality standards.

The Clean Waters Restoration Act of 1966 marked the beginning of the transfer of water-quality enforcement responsibility to the federal government. The Water Pollution Control Act Amendments of 1972 increased federal responsibility for water quality standards. The unrealized goal of this Act was to end the discharge of pollutants into waterways by 1985 by mandating that industry and municipalities adopt the "best available" sewage-treatment technology. The 1974 Safe Drinking Water Act continued the emphasis on federal action by assigning to the EPA responsibility for establishing minimum standards for drinking water.

Air-Pollution Policy

Attempts to control and improve air quality in the United States followed a similar pattern of a gradually expanding federal role. The first action taken by Congress, the Air Pollution Control Act of 1955, funded research on air quality. The federal role was increased as the Clean Air Act of 1963 provided funds for state air-quality programs, and the Motor Vehicle Air Pollution Control Act of 1965 empowered the former Department of Health, Education, and Welfare (HEW) to set automobile-emission standards. This was the first federal program to regulate emissions directly. The National Emissions Standards Act of 1967 expanded the program.

The 1970 Clean Air Act amendments signaled a major change in air pollution policy in the United States. This major piece of legislation sought to reduce all pollutants that constituted a health threat. Congress delegated primary responsibility for establishing and enforcing standards to the EPA. Initially, these standards reflected a primary emphasis on protection of public health and welfare, with a secondary emphasis on economic issues. The 1977 Clean Air Act Amendments responded to the energy crisis by relaxing emission standards. Emission standards for the automobile industry were delayed for four years. An important addition to the 1977 Act was adoption of a clean growth component designed to protect air quality in regions with air cleaner than that required by federal standards.

Congress enacted another series of amendments to the Clean Air Act in November 1990. These amendments aimed to move air quality toward the standards originally targeted for 1975. One specific provision included reducing SO_2 emissions in order to reduce the threat of acid rain. The amendments also allowed tailoring air-quality standards to the degree of pollution in individual communities, as opposed to setting uniform nationwide standards for all emissions. Critics of these amendments argued that they did not contain sufficiently stringent nationwide air-quality standards. Supporters held that these amendments did embody a move in the direction of the standards in the original Clean Air Act.

The National Environmental Policy Act (NEPA)

The National Environmental Policy Act (January 1, 1970) reflected a major change in environmental policy by the federal government.[19] The Act placed greater emphasis on federal leadership in formulating national environmental policy through the creation of the Council on Environmental Quality (CEQ), to provide advice to the president on environmental policy issues. Although the CEQ was largely an advisory body, its existence within the Executive Office of the President provided the framework for a strengthened federal role under the leadership of the president. The legislation also mandated that the president submit an annual environmental quality report to Congress and that federal agencies submit environmental impact statements to the CEQ on any action that would affect the environment. The Act required federal agencies to undertake a deliberate and thorough analysis of the potential environmental consequences of any projects under their control.

The EPA combined some fifteen offices and agencies into a single agency. The new EPA was assigned responsibility for (1) water pollution, (2) air pollution, (3) solid-waste management, (4) radiation control, and (5) pesticide and toxic-substance control. The legislation was designed to centralize federal power in environmental policy by eliminating the previous pattern of fragmentation and decentralization.

Unlike the advisory CEQ, the EPA is a regulatory agency with power to establish and enforce policy. The actual impact of the EPA on environmental issues is a function of the political values and assumptions of the president and of the administrator who guides the agency in interpreting and enforcing environmental rules and statutes. The EPA has been accused of making sweetheart deals with major industries and with scheduling EPA cleanup projects based on political considerations instead of environmental concerns. Critics have also charged that the White House has the ability to significantly edit EPA reports prior to their release. Other critics have argued that the EPA has been overly aggressive in developing environmental policy rules.

The Hazardous-Waste Superfund.   The Superfund was created by the 1980 Comprehensive Environmental Response Compensation and Liability Act (CERCLA). The Superfund provided the EPA with the authority and the funds to assist in cleanup operations at toxic- and hazardous-waste sites across the country. The creation of the fund allowed an active role for the EPA in dealing with emergencies and with abandoned toxic-waste sites. By 1984, the EPA had identified over 17,000 disposal sites, with estimates that an additional 5,000 sites exist. EPA estimates indicated in 1984 that the cleanup operations at the 2,000 most dangerous sites would cost between $8 billion and $16 billion, roughly five to ten times the size of the original level of the Superfund.

The provisions of the Superfund Act generated a limited number of site cleanups. In fact, a number of the sites have been cleaned by simply transferring the wastes to another toxic-waste site. This transfer of wastes from one location to another does not indicate progress in a cleanup program. The Superfund program has been hindered by a lack of federal financial support.

POLICY EVALUATION: SEARCHING FOR DIRECTION

Current Policy Direction and Values

The 1960s and 1970s were decades in which extensive environmental legislation was enacted and regulatory policies and agencies created. During the 1980s, the trend toward increased regulation and federal leadership changed, as new values became the source of environmental policy. The policy value during this period was to relax standards and to reduce federal regulatory activity.[20]

The bubble concept was developed during this time period. It applied clean-air standards to an industrial plant as a whole, rather than to the specific emission points. This meant that increased levels of pollution at one source within a plant were acceptable if the overall levels of contaminants for the particular plant remained within EPA guidelines. This concept made emissions enforcement easier but it acted to reduce pollution more slowly than shutting down specific pollution points. Proponents valued economic growth and advocated cost–benefit analysis and market forces as the most appropriate mechanisms for guiding environmental policy. Advocates saw market values as an appropriate mechanism for determining environmental policy. Environmental protection policies were to be minimized if the associated costs were higher than the monetary benefits. This approach favored a stronger role for state governments, as opposed to federal government regulation, in environmental legislation.

Environmental activists greeted the election of Bill Clinton and Al Gore with enthusiasm in 1992. Al Gore's book *Earth in the Balance*[21] reflected an emphasis on governmental action to remedy environmental problems. The new administration did not meet the expectations of environmental groups. President Clinton advocated a "peaceful coexistence" between environmentalists and the business community. His policy actions indicated an environmental policy that varied in style but not in substance from those of the 1980s. In 1995, he signed a logging exemption bill that expanded timber industry access to national forests. When signing the legislation President Clinton stated, "I've done more for logging than anyone else in the country."[22]

A significant shift in the federal role did not occur for two reasons. First, there was a growing concern that environmental policy had been based on popular opinion, not on scientific evidence. According to former EPA Administrator William Reilly, environmental policies have been "based on responding to the nightly news. What we have had in the United States is environmental agenda-setting by episodic panic."[23] Second, concern for reducing the federal deficit and achieving a balanced budget provided a basis for questioning the validity of environmental spending programs. Given the competition for increasingly scarce federal monies and strong reaction to unfunded mandates imposed by the federal government on state and local governments, environmental spending programs were challenged because they did not provide more benefits than they cost.

The administration of George W. Bush continued to pursue this course. He reduced a number of environmental standards, and his administration strongly favored energy exploration in environmentally sensitive areas, such as the Arctic National Wildlife Refuge. President Bush was unsuccessful in his support for amendments to the Clean Air Act in 2003, entitled the Clear Skies Act, that would have reduced a number of original Clean Air Act standards.

President Obama sought to advance an expansive environmental policy agenda. This included an emphasis on addressing global warming, dealing with toxic and hazardous wastes, increasing the emphasis on clean air and water and strengthening the role of the EPA in environmental policy. This involves the expanded use of federal regulations as an environmental policy tool. The emphasis on raising CAFE standards is linked to reducing oil consumption and reducing emissions.

This ambitious agenda was linked to his "all of the above" approach to energy policy which involves an element of conflict between two areas. Support for the development of clean energy involves increased reliance on natural gas that can be produced by the technology of fracking. Critics argue that expanding natural gas resources through fracking will adversely impact the environment. President Obama has stated support for the use of clean coal, while advocating regulations governing emissions from coal-fired plants and seeking to reduce the use of coal as a fuel for generating electricity. In order to provide oil resources, approval for offshore drilling was expanded.

An examination of the Obama administration's environmental policy seems to indicate it is moving in conflicting directions at the same time. The president supports a move toward energy independence but does not believe that the nation should seek to drill its way to energy independence. In terms of nuclear energy, the administration has voiced support for building new power plants that are opposed by environmental groups. Addressing climate change is an item on the president's agenda that is to be addressed primarily through regulation of emissions. As is true with most administrations, there exists a tension between developing energy policies that will promote economic growth and policies that will protect the environment. The announced "all of the above" strategy of the president seems to have disappointed environmental groups, the fossil fuel industry, and proponents of energy resource development as a mechanism for environmental growth.

Public Environmental Concern

The beginning of the twenty-first century witnessed marked changes in the intensity of public opinion supporting aggressive environmental policies. Conflicting scientific reports concerning causal relationships in environmental policy created differing levels of public confidence in environmental research findings. Costs associated with environmental protection escalated. Lifestyle values were in conflict with proenvironmental policies as the popularity of large, gas-guzzling SUVs in urban areas indicated a willingness to sacrifice environmental concerns with energy conservation and emissions reductions for personal lifestyle preferences. The public continues to verbalize a concern for the environment, but some public consumer behaviors became inconsistent with strict environmental policies and programs.

The Politics of Regulation

The regulatory process itself is subject to competing political pressures which can influence the formulation of a consistent environmental policy. One political factor that affects regulation is the pressure on administrators and elected officials to emphasize short-term economic benefits as opposed to long-term consequences of environmental damage. A second factor involves emphasis on the importance of economic growth as a basic value in the political system. Economic growth tends to carry some environmental cost. The American system has historically concentrated on the desirability of economic growth. A third factor that directly affects the regulatory process is the value placed on compromise in our political system. The Constitution itself is a product of compromise, and the American system places a great deal of importance on seeking the middle ground. Although compromise is a politically expedient technique for making policy, it is not necessarily the best approach in establishing a consistent environmental policy.

Given the nature of the political system, regulatory policy tends to be a product of political pressures and compromise, a fact that hinders development of consistent policy choices. Even if lawmakers could formulate policy without these factors, problems with enforcement would remain.

Enforcement Problems

Effective enforcement of environmental policy is difficult to achieve for a variety of reasons. A major obstacle is the climate in which the EPA must operate. The EPA has the mandate to provide scientific evidence to support the environmental standards established by Congress. The procedure of establishing a solid scientific base for its regulations required financial and personnel resources beyond what the EPA had available. The burden of proof rests on the EPA to defend the standards it proposes to enforce. Gathering and documenting this evidence is a time- and resource-consuming activity.

CONTINUING DEBATES: UNRESOLVED
POLICY ISSUES

International Treaties

The role of international agreements and treaties remains unresolved concerning environmental policy in the United States. There has been increasing interest in the international arena concerning the need for a coordinated international approach concerning threats to the global climate. The United Nations has been active in this area through the activities of the Framework Convention on Climate Change (FCCC). One product of U.N. activity was the Kyoto Protocol of 1997. The basic provision of the Protocol involved a global reduction in the emission of greenhouse gases to a level 5 percent below 1990 levels. This reduction was to happen between 2008 and 2012. Under the protocol, the European Union would reduce emissions by 8 percent, the United States by 7 percent, and Japan by 6 percent.

The protocol was rejected by the United States Senate vote of 95–0 in 1997 during the Clinton administration. The protocol would have had the force of law if ratified, and it could have had a significant impact on both environmental policy and economic activity within the United States. Critics of the Kyoto Protocol observed that China was exempt from the emissions standards even though it produces a significant amount of CO_2 emissions (2,893 million metric tons per year as compared to 5,410 million tons from the United States). Requiring the United States to reduce emissions while exempting China, a major source of pollution, would have placed the nation at a significant economic disadvantage compared to China.

An unanswered question involves the appropriate role of international agreements in defining American environmental policy. Opponents to these types of international agreements argue that such agreements restrict national sovereignty, will have a detrimental impact on the American economy, and rest on unverified scientific research.[24] They argue that the United States should be free to forge its own environmental policy path.

Self-Regulation of the Market

Should the federal government take an active role in planning and regulating activities that affect the environment? Should primary responsibility be shifted to the operation of the free-market system?[25]

Conservatives, advocating reduced environmental regulation and increased reliance on the market, point to the negative consequences of environmental regulations. Regulations mean higher costs and contribute to inflationary pressures on the economy.[26] These critics also contend that regulations interfere with business planning, are difficult to comply with, are often arbitrary, and lack a scientific consensus. They point to the once-stringent clean-air standards, which they contend are a good example of arbitrary and unrealistic standards forced to bend to more practical needs.[27]

Market-oriented individuals argue that the market economy would not produce rampant environmental spoilage. Rather, the free market would produce conditions that make it profitable for the private sector to recycle waste products and to develop technologies to reduce pollution at the source. Any level of pollution that did exist would be a product of the relationship between the costs and benefits to society.

Liberals and progressives strenuously disagree. They argue that consumers tend to purchase the least expensive item when quality is similar. Industry would never voluntarily install pollution-control equipment that would drive up the prices of its goods and put them at a competitive disadvantage. Thus, the market could not provide a basis for making intelligent environmental policy choices. Therefore, liberals/progressives argue that without governmental regulation the environment will continue to deteriorate. Pollution is an externality, an indirect impact of market activity, which will continue to have costly social and economic effects without the policy hand of government to minimize them.

Taxes and Legal Action

There are several alternative enforcement mechanisms for achieving environmental goals and compliance with environmental regulation.[28] First, taxes or fees for the discharge of pollutants might replace the system of rules, regulations, guidelines, and air and water-quality standards. Such a system represents a modified market approach popular with many neoconservatives. It would, they argue, reduce the administrative costs associated with regulation and allow industries to calculate the costs and benefits of environmental damage themselves. Critics of this alternative point out that some level of government would have to monitor discharges precisely in order to compute the tax; taxes would have to be set and adjusted continuously for particular pollutants; and companies in noncompetitive sectors of the economy could simply continue to pollute and pass the cost of the tax to consumers.

A second alternative, employed in some situations today, is the use of injunctions to halt pollution. This means obtaining a court order requiring that pollution be eliminated or reduced by a specified time or the polluter will be forced to cease operation. This strategy has the advantages of clarity and finality, but it is available only on a case-by-case basis.

A third alternative rewards enterprises that reduce pollution by awarding them tax subsidies or underwriting the cost of pollution-control equipment. This approach provides economic incentives to cease pollution activities and has a parallel in the tax credits already given to industries that install energy-conservation equipment. Yet, tax subsidies ultimately transfer the cost of environmental protection from the polluter to the public.

Stiff fines and jail sentences are a fourth approach to the problem. They would impose a strong negative incentive to cease pollution. Nevertheless, enforcement problems remain. Even when prosecutors obtain a conviction, perpetrators almost never receive jail terms in these types of crimes, and fines may be absorbed as business expenses.

Alternatives to enforcing environmental compliance have been debated and sometimes used, but, like those discussed here, they have met with limited success, and consensus has not been reached. An effective strategy to achieve compliance with pollution standards remains elusive.

The Role of State Governments

The issue of state responsibility for environmental enforcement remains unresolved. Early regulatory efforts concentrated authority in the hands of state government, with limited success. There is evidence that a reduction of the role of the federal government and transfer of responsibility for environmental policy to the states may result in a general weakening of standards.

One reason is that the governing coalitions within state governments have a relatively narrow political base. In other words, compared with the national level, the proportion of the population concerned with political events at the state level is relatively small. Public-opinion polls indicate that less than 30 percent of the electorate regularly follows state government actively. Consequently, it is relatively easy for a special-interest group to gain considerable power in state government.

State governments also face staffing problems in the regulatory agencies due to limited fiscal resources.

A third problem emerges when federal agencies, primarily the EPA, fail to issue regulations in a timely manner. The result is a negative impact on state enforcement procedures. Inconsistency, confusion, and delay follow as states operate individually without federal leadership.

A fourth problem grows from a perception that federal regulations fail to appreciate the unique needs of individual states, producing inflexible program requirements. The states view federal inflexibility as a barrier to state initiative, as states must implement rigid programs that may not meet their needs.

A fifth problem stems from the perception that federal EPA officials may not be interested in establishing meaningful communication with the states. A lack of responsiveness by the EPA builds perceptions at the state level that the feds do not understand and do not care about the problems and issues faced by state officials.

A sixth problem is conflicting interests among the states themselves. The same environmental pollutants do not threaten all states to the same degree. Acid rain is unevenly distributed across the nation and is not an issue in certain areas of the country. States vary with respect to their economic base. Strict environmental policies have differing levels of economic impact across the nation. Given the differences among the states, dissatisfaction with environmental policies adopted at the federal level will occur at the state level, and interstate conflict may lead to policy deadlocks in Congress and the EPA.

These six problems relate to the issue of dividing leadership responsibility between the federal government and the fifty states. Leadership requires the expenditure of financial resources. The states have not been overly eager to assume the leadership role in enforcement policy.

Public Attitudes

Attitudes within the American public have changed somewhat since 2000.[29] There has been a drop in the proportion of individuals who believe that the environmental movement has done more good than harm, from some 75 percent in 2000 to about 60 percent in 2014. This may reflect a slightly less sympathetic attitude toward aggressive environmental policies, as the nation's economy has weakened. Public opinion data do seem to suggest that politicians can lose votes by appearing uncaring about the environment, even though they cannot gain many votes by taking dramatic steps.

Energy and the Environment

Global Climate Change.   Global climate change, commonly referred to as **global warming**, is an issue on the policy agenda. Economic growth seems to produce energy consumption patterns that threaten the environment. Reliance on fossil fuels results in massive emissions of carbon dioxide that may generate a greenhouse effect, in which the earth's atmosphere warms excessively. Global warming is reflected in warmer winters, not necessarily hotter summers. Critics argue that there is an absence of direct, undisputed scientific evidence linking human activity to global climate changes and that the changes may be natural and cyclical in nature. Proponents argue that an undisputable linkage exists between human activity, the continued production of greenhouse gas emissions, and the phenomenon of a global warming.

The debate over the issue of global warming intensified in 2010 with reports that publications and reports from the Intergovernmental Panel on Climate Change (IPCC) of the United Nations were factually inaccurate and that IPCC reports contained a number of flaws and inaccuracies. One IPCC report stated that glaciers in the Himalayas would melt by the middle of this century and result in severe water problems for India. Critics discovered that the report was not based on scientific evidence but a statement in a graduate student's dissertation and nonscientific articles in mountaineering magazines.

The Copenhagen Climate Conference in December 2009 did not produce an agreement on climate change policy, nor an agreement to pursue a global strategy in 2010. Opposition to such an agreement was broad-based, with significant opposition from the European Union stemming from the negative economic impacts resulting from a strong environmental policy. Public opinion polls in the United States and Europe now seem to indicate that concern over the economy has significantly reduced public support for strict environmental policies.

The Thwaites Glacier, a large ice formation in Antarctic, has been melting over the past several years with a potential impact of rising sea levels. Melting of glaciers has been viewed as an indication of global warming. In 2014, researchers documented the presence of subterranean geothermal heat as one source of Thwaites glacial melting in the Antarctic. This is one indication of the need for continued research into the nature of generally accepted indicators of climate change.

The debate over the nature, extent, and causes associated with changes in the global climate will continue as an item on the policy agenda.

Other Issues.   Environmental regulatory policies often conflict with efforts to increase the supply of energy available to the nation. The onset of the energy crisis and the need for economic growth created pressures to postpone compliance deadlines and to relax environmental standards and rules. This linkage between energy policy, economic expansion, and environmental policy is a source of conflict. In April 2010, the *Deepwater Horizon* oil spill was the largest in American history. The extensive contamination of the gulf, coastline, and damage to wildlife illustrated a basic public policy conflict: the desire for a pristine environment and a commitment to produce energy to maintain economic stability. This event followed an announcement in April 2010 by President Obama that the federal government was expanding offshore drilling for oil and natural gas. Currently, there are over 3,500 offshore drilling platforms of various types in the Gulf of Mexico. Offshore drilling is an essential element in providing oil to the nation and remains a source of environmental risk. It will remain on the policy agenda for the foreseeable future.

The use of coal as a major fuel source intensifies several environmental problems. Increased utilization of coal generates higher levels of CO_2 because coal contains higher levels of carbon than either oil or natural gas. This strategy would also result in higher emissions of sulfur dioxides, a major factor in the acid-rain phenomenon.

The process of energy resource development also poses significant environmental threats. Strip mining for coal denigrates the environment, because it removes the ground surface to reach the underlying coal beds. Shaft-mining techniques for coal and uranium present problems because an effective policy for handling the tailings from the mines has yet to be developed and implemented. Offshore oil drilling efforts present significant environmental threats as well. Oil spills, leaks, and seepage threaten both water quality and wildlife.

Nuclear energy expansion also presents significant environmental threats. Miners are exposed to carcinogenic radon gas, and the mine tailings contain low-level radioactive materials that are scattered beyond the immediate mining area by the process of wind and water erosion. The wastes from nuclear plants present an environmental risk apart from the potential damage from a nuclear accident, such as the disaster at the Chernobyl facility in the former Soviet Union.

SUMMARY

Given the close relationship between energy-use patterns and the environment, basic values within society come into conflict. The American public values the environment and the record of environmental legislation reflects this. One example is the creation and expansion of the national park system. At the same time, the American public has come to expect continued access to relatively inexpensive energy, economic growth, and personal prosperity. The result is a willingness to accept potential risks to the environment to guarantee a ready supply of energy. Given its traditional confidence in science and technology, the American public finds it plausible to believe in an optimal scientific mix for energy and environmental issues.

The integral bonds between energy and environmental policies are the political, social, and economic issues and the conflicts they produce. The task for political institutions and actors is to resolve or minimize the conflicts and develop policies that promote growth in the energy supply and the economy while protecting the environment.

 **RESOURCES**

Energy Policy–Related Websites

American Petroleum Institute: **www.api.org**

International Atomic Energy Agency: **www.iaea.org**

Organization of Petroleum Exporting Countries (OPEC):
   www.opec.org/opec_web/en/

Solar Energy Association Listing:
http://www.energybible.com/solar_energy/Organizations.html

U.S. Department of Energy: **www.energy.gov**

U.S. Nuclear Regulatory Commission: **www.nrc.gov**

White House Energy Policy:
www.whitehouse.gov/issues/energy-and-environment/

Environmental Policy–Related Websites

CATO Institute: **www.cato.org**

Institute for European Environmental Policy: **www.ieep.eu**

U.S. Department of Energy, Environmental Policy:
www.energy.gov/environment/index.htm

U.S. Environmental Protection Agency: **www.epa.gov**

U.S. EPA Climate Change Website: **www.epa.gov/climatechange/**

Chapter 6

Crime and Criminal Justice: Dilemmas of Social Control

The public, throughout the late twentieth century, perceived crime as having reached intolerable levels, especially in America's major cities, not only with respect to the incidence of criminal acts but also with respect to the exponentially rising monetary costs to society. The earliest editions of this book reported the gloomy consensus that crime appeared to be out of control. That perception created a widespread demand that government do something to attack the problem. In the 1992 presidential campaign, the eventual winner, Bill Clinton, promised major legislation to attack the crime problem in America. The result of this pledge was the 1994 Crime Bill, and a dramatic reversal of the crime trend. Violent crime, the kinds of crime that Americans fear the most and that most affect Americans' lifestyle, has steadily declined since the 1990s to levels not seen since before the 1970s, as indicated by the *Uniform Crime Report*, issued yearly by the Federal Bureau of Investigation (FBI). As the crime rate has gone down, however, the number of people in prison in the United States has skyrocketed, and public confidence in our courts and criminal justice system is in decline. Furthermore, the technological environment of law enforcement has changed dramatically over the last couple of decades. Forensic science has advanced tremendously and technological advances in law enforcement have occurred as well. Since 2001, the federal government has also increased the presence of law enforcement and counterterrorism agencies such as Homeland Security and the National Security Agency (NSA). Some of these advances have been made under the auspices of fighting terrorism, but such technologies are increasingly being used in everyday law enforcement.

In a democracy, however, crime policies cannot simply be effective—they must also be perceived by the public as just and in accordance with our constitutional rights. This creates a dilemma for policymakers who are trying to control crime without violating peoples' rights or weakening public confidence in our justice system. In the current political climate, with crime at its lowest levels in decades, the public and politicians alike are beginning to question the widespread severity of punishments meted out in our criminal justice system. America has a larger percentage of people in prison than some of the world's most brutal total-itarian regimes, such as Iran or Belarus. The Obama administration's policy on crime has been to temper the harshness of previous presidential administrations. A centerpiece of President Obama's criminal justice policies is to reduce the number of overall people in prison and to steer nonviolent offenders toward alternative treatment programs. But, to understand how we became the country with the world's largest prison population, it is important to recall recent history regarding the crime wave that began in the 1970s and peaked in the 1990s.

In 1970, there were an estimated 16,000 murders within the United States. That figure climbed to 23,040 murders in 1980, declined slightly in the mid-1980s, and then shot up to 24,540 in 1993. By 2012, however, the number of murders declined precipitously to only 14,827. The rate of violent crime is down sharply from the 1980s as well. In 1986, the violent **crime rate** was 620.1 per 100,000 population; this decreased to 386.94 by 2012. The homicide rate, at 4.7 murders per 100,000 population in 2012, is down more than 50 per-cent from the 1991 figure of 9.8 per 100,000.

In general, the trends displayed in Figures 6.1 and 6.2 show violent crime and property crime rates continuing to decrease over the first decade of the twenty-first century.

Property crimes, far more pervasive than the more feared violent crime (an estimated 9.7 million offenses in 2008), have been cut almost in half since the early 1990s. In 2012, there were 2,859.2 reported property crimes per

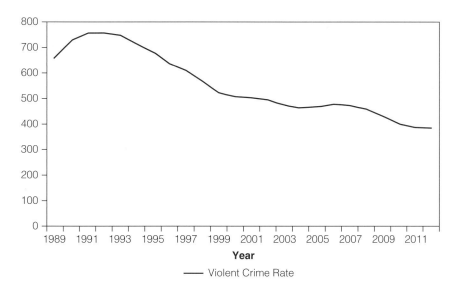

FIGURE 6.1 Violent Crime Rates per 100,000 People since 1989

SOURCE: www.fbi.gov, Federal Bureau of Investigation, *Uniform Crime Reports, 2008,* http://www.fbi.gov/ucr/cius2008/data/table_01.html.

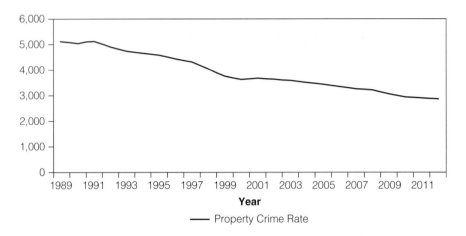

FIGURE 6.2   Property Crime Rates per 100,000 People since 1989

SOURCE: www.fbi.gov, Federal Bureau of Investigation, *Uniform Crime Reports, 2008*, http://www.fbi.gov/ucr/cius2008/data/table_01.html

100,000 people. This figure is 44 percent lower than the 5,140.2 property crimes per 100,000 people as reported in 1991.[1] Thus, while this chapter in earlier editions primarily focused on explaining the burgeoning crime rates of postwar America, the last several editions have tried to explain the clear and significant reversal of that trend. Is this reversal in crime due mostly to government policies, or are there also other social forces that are beyond the control of government? And while the reductions in crime are good news, when one considers the fact that our Constitution was founded upon principles of democracy and limited government, to what extent should we be troubled by government policies that lock up large numbers of our citizens for long periods of time?

In analyzing the impact of crime policy, this chapter focuses not only on how effective policies are in stopping crime, but also on the constitutional considerations that must be taken into account by government. As the title of the chapter suggests, when fighting crime, there are dilemmas faced by democratic governments regarding social control. Communist Russia, for example, was one of the safest societies in terms of private crime. The likelihood of being mugged while walking down the street in Moscow in the early 1970s was miniscule. The murder rate among private citizens was equally low. But the crimes perpetrated by the state on its citizens were a heavy price to pay for a law-and-order crime-free society. In this respect, democratic governments have to be circumspect in how they develop crime policies. Democracies must not only respect people's constitutional rights, but also must take into account public attitudes toward dealing with crime. This chapter focuses on one widely assumed strategy for the prevention of crime: **deterrence**. Deterrence refers to the discouragement of criminal acts by imposing prohibitive costs on criminals. In general, this means severe punishment. Research shows, however, that a high probability of punishment and the swift execution of the punishment are more conducive to deterrence than is increasing the severity of the punishment. If deterrence does not work (the fear of being locked up), then simply locking away the perpetrators of crime for long periods of time is another way to tackle the problem of crime. Yet, as this chapter will also note, policies of mass incarceration can exact a heavy toll on our democracy. Finally, the chapter also considers other explanations for the reduction in crime that are beyond the control of law enforcement.

Before evaluating the impact of public policy on crime, it is important to know the nature and extent of crime. It is therefore necessary to assess the extent to which the incidence of crime has actually changed one way or the other in recent years. Crime is not an undifferentiated phenomenon. There are different types of crime with different rates of occurrence and different causes, and they require different policies to reduce their incidence. Policies designed to reduce one kind of crime may have no effect on, or may even increase, other types of crime. The unintended consequences, or spillover effects, of public policy are crucial to the evaluation of crime policies.

Too often, politicians generalize about one type of crime, for example, "crime in the streets," as if that type of crime encompasses the universe of the crime problem. Actually, crime is any behavior that some duly constituted legislative body has chosen to make illegal. These behaviors include crimes against property (robbery and auto theft), crimes against persons (assault, murder, and rape), **white-collar crimes** (stock fraud and price-fixing), **"victimless" crimes** against a dominant moral code (public intoxication, vagrancy, and the sale of pornography), and political crimes (illegal campaign contributions and bribery). These are distinct types of activities, the causes and prevention of which differ. Even within these categories, many distinctions may be discerned. Carefully planned murders, spontaneous killing in anger or in a fight, and violent rape born out of a general hatred for women—all crimes against persons—will not respond to the same remedies. Because the concept of crime covers too diverse a category of actions to be analytically useful, this chapter distinguishes various types of illegal activities with respect to their causes and means of prevention.

ISSUE BACKGROUND: THE GROWTH AND DECLINE OF CRIME

The Extent of Crime

It is not difficult to find factual support for the perception that crime increased at an alarming rate in the first four decades after World War II. The crime rate, as defined by the FBI's *Uniform Crime Report,* rose dramatically for the two decades after the current method of tabulating the FBI index went into effect, until 1981. This **crime index** refers to the number of crimes per 100,000 population for seven categories of crime: (1) murder and manslaughter, (2) forcible rape, (3) robbery, (4) aggravated assault, (5) burglary, (6) larceny, and (7) auto theft.

Violent Crime.   Violent crime is defined by the FBI Uniform Crime Reporting Program as murder, nonnegligent manslaughter, forcible rape, robbery, and aggravated assault. They are offenses that "involve force or threat of force." James Q. Wilson argues that this type of crime—often referred to as **street crime**—has a more negative impact on America's sense of community compared to other types of crime.[2] Even for those who are not victims of crime, the *fear* of violent crime alters one's lifestyle and patterns of interaction. People may no longer feel free to walk the streets and in effect become prisoners in their own homes. In many cities, downtown businesses have failed to prosper because people no longer feel safe in those areas. Such failures can be considered to be an indirect cost or spillover effect of violent crime, which is a cost that does not enter into the crime statistics themselves.

The rise in index crimes of violence from 1967 to 1978 was 192 percent, and the rise in index crimes against property was 168 percent.[3] Clearly, these statistics represent significant increases, whatever the definitional problems. Significant increases were also recorded from 1988 to 1992 in those categories that generate the most fear among the population: violent crime, murder, aggravated assault, and forcible rape, with increases of 19 percent, 11 percent, 19 percent, and 14 percent, respectively. These are the kind of figures that caused a public perception of a public safety crisis.

Beginning in 1992, however, the crime rate reversed in a downward trend in all categories. Moreover, this downward trend was especially strong in those categories that generate the greatest fear among the population. Thus, the drop in homicide rates from 1994 to 2003 was 33.4 percent compared to a 23 percent drop in property crimes for the same period. Those numbers continued to drop through the first decade of the 2000s. By 2012, the homicide rate had dropped to 4.7, which is less than half of the rate of 9.8 homicides per 100,000 occurring in 1991. The total number of murders in the United States over the years is listed in Table 6.1. What is remarkable about these data is that the total number of homicides in 2012 is substantially *less* than the number of homicides in 1975 or

TABLE 6.1   Homicides by Year in the United States

1970	16,000	2005	16,740
1975	20,510	2006	17,309
1980	23,040	2007	17,128
1985	18,980	2008	16,465
1990	23,440	2009	15,399
1993	24,540	2010	14,722
1995	21,606	2011	14,661
2000	15,586	2012	14,827

SOURCE: U.S. Department of Justice, Bureau of Justice Statistics, www .ojp.usdoj.gov/bjs/, and Federal Bureau of Investigation, *Uniform Crime Report, 2012,* http://www.fbi.gov/stats-services/crimestats.

even 1970, despite the fact that America had a lot fewer people living in the country in the 1970s compared to today.

Property Crime.   Property crime consists of offenses such as burglary, larceny-theft, motor vehicle theft, and arson. Burglary is defined by the FBI as "the unlawful entry of a structure to commit a felony or theft." Larceny is defined as "the unlawful taking, carrying, leading, or riding away of property from the possession or constructive possession of another," and examples of larceny include theft of bicycles, shoplifting, pocket-picking, etc. The key distinction between property crime theft or burglary and violent robbery is that with property crimes, "there is no force or threat of force against the victims."

Table 6.2 shows that property crime, like violent crime, has been down significantly since the 1990s. Motor vehicle theft has declined by over 65 percent between 1991 and 2012. Burglary is down almost 50 percent and larceny is down by almost 40 percent. The FBI estimated that the cost of property crime

T A B L E 6.2   Crime Rates, 1991 and 2006–2012 (per 100,000 population)

	Violent Crime	Murder	Forcible Rape	Robbery	Aggravated Assault
1991	758.2	9.8	42.3	272.7	433.4
2006	479.3	5.8	31.6	150.0	292.0
2007	471.8	5.7	30.6	148.3	287.2
2008	458.6	5.4	29.8	145.9	277.5
2009	431.9	5.0	29.1	133.1	264.7
2010	404.5	4.8	27.7	119.3	252.8
2011	387.1	4.7	27.0	113.9	241.5
2012	386.9	4.7	26.9	112.9	242.3

	Property Crime	Burglary	Larceny-Theft	Motor Vehicle Theft
1991	5,140.2	1,252.1	3,229.1	659.0
2006	3,346.6	733.1	2,213.2	400.2
2007	3,276.4	726.1	2,185.4	364.9
2008	3,214.6	733.0	2,166.1	315.4
2009	3,041.3	717.7	2,064.5	259.2
2010	2,945.9	701.0	2,005.8	239.1
2011	2,905.4	701.3	1,974.1	230.0
2012	2,859.2	670.2	1,959.3	229.7

SOURCE: Federal Bureau of Investigation, *Uniform Crime Report, 2005 and 2008,* http://www.fbi.gov/stats-services/crimestats.

(excluding arson) to victims was around $15.5 billion. This figure is lower than the $17.6 billion in property losses that occurred in 2006.

Public Perceptions of Crime.   From 1960 to 1990, with respect to violent crimes per capita (the kind of crimes that generate the most fear and have a consequently severe impact on urban life), the crime rate grew a spectacular 355 percent. This included a rise in violent crime against random victims (unrelated to the identity or behavior of the victim), thus exacerbating a widespread fear of crime. This fear and the perception of victimization are illustrated by the fact that, according to the February 9, 1992, edition of the *New York Times*, sales of home alarm systems increased by 80 percent from 1986 to 1992.

As shown, crime then took a sharp downward direction; this was especially pronounced in those categories that generate fear of crime. The violent crime rate decreased 7.4 percent in the one year from 1995 to 1996, while the clearance rate for such crime increased from 45 to 47 percent in that same year.[4] Public perceptions of crime as an important issue for the United States continue to rank high in surveys when the issue is asked in isolation from other public policy issues. For example, a 2013 Gallup survey found that 55 percent of Americans described the "problem" of crime as an extremely serious or very serious issue.[5] But, when asked about the issue of crime in their own neighborhood in that same survey, a majority of Americans did not think that the issue was serious. Furthermore, when Americans are asked to describe the most important issues facing the country, the issue of crime barely registers in surveys today, as illustrated by Table 6.3. Thus, after a brief lag in the late 1990s and early 2000s, public perceptions of the threat of crime began to catch up to the data. Crime rarely gets mentioned as a high priority compared to other issues, and the reasons are probably due to the dramatic drops in violent crime and homicides across the country.

There is varied speculation but no consensus among social scientists trying to explain the drop in crime in the 1990s. Many refer to the demographic factor of the aging of the baby boom generation. Crime is most prevalent among males from the early teens to the mid-twenties. Accordingly, when large numbers of baby boomers were in that age category, crime rates went up. As they have aged beyond that category, the rates went down. Certainly, the "graying of America," the gradual increase in the average age of Americans continues; yet, crime is essentially a young person's activity. Other scholars refer to aggressive police

TABLE 6.3   Public Attitudes toward Crime: Percentage of Sample Naming Crime and Violence as "Most Important Problem"

1984	1994	1998	2000	2007	2012
4	37	20	13	3	2

SOURCE: *Sourcebook of Criminal Justice Statistics, 2012,* http://www.albany.edu/sourcebook/tost_2.html#2_o.

tactics and longer prison sentences instituted in the 1980s. These scholars point to the increase in incarceration rates as contributing to the decline in crime. These are discussed later in the chapter.

White-Collar Crime. When defining "crime," the crime index does not exhaust the universe of illegal activities. For example, the index does not include most white-collar crimes, which cost the American public more in lost dollar value than does the total of all the index crimes.[6] The scandals associated with the collapse of energy giant Enron Corporation in early 2001 cost employees and investors billions of dollars including, in many cases with employees, their entire life savings and retirement plans. The alleged fraud involved the upper management and their accountants covering up the financial state of the company, partly by hiding company losses in numerous covert "partnerships," and encouraging employees and investors to tie up their money in company stock, thereby inflating the price of that stock, just prior to management unloading their own stock at billions of dollars in profits. The accounting scandal of Worldcom, one of the largest telephone companies in the United States at the time, ended in one of the largest bankruptcy filings in U.S. history in 2002, eviscerating the investments of stockholders. The harm to American society from such "insider trading" and stock fraud cases is indirect. It may contribute to a loss of confidence in the integrity of the market, which would make it more difficult to accumulate capital from the growing source of millions of small investors thereby slowing economic growth. Hence, such white-collar criminals do not appear threatening to the average American, enabling them to retain a level of popularity and public acceptance unavailable to a convicted mugger, pedophile, murderer, or rapist.

Yet, white-collar crime can be far more damaging economically, and damaging across a wider area, than violent crime. Antitrust violations can cost consumers billions of dollars a year. The financial meltdown and mortgage crisis of the banking system in late 2007, which some financial experts blamed on the creation of credit-default swaps, cost American taxpayers hundreds of billions of dollars in the government-funded bailouts of banks and Wall Street brokerage firms. Congress, the state of New York, and the Justice Department of the Obama administration each launched their own investigations into the dealings of a number of Wall Street firms and large U.S. banks to determine whether wrongdoing had occurred. In 2010, for example, the Obama Justice Department opened an investigation into Goldman Sachs to figure out whether the firm had engaged in fraud or other federal crimes in the time leading up to and during the financial crisis.[7] Former Bush administration Treasury Secretary Hank Paulson, who orchestrated the 2007 bailout of banks and pressed Congress to pass the legislation, had also previously served as CEO of Goldman Sachs, which, as it turns out, was an indirect beneficiary of the taxpayer-funded bailouts (government bailout money paid to the insurance company AIG was then promptly used by AIG to pay off financial obligations to Goldman Sachs). While Paulson was not accused of breaking any laws, such cozy connections between those running the private-sector market and those in government erode the perception that market competition is "fair" and thus erode the legitimacy of unequal market-based outcomes.

In the end, despite demands from the public and the media for prosecutions of the people on Wall Street who either caused the financial crisis or unfairly gained from its excesses, the New York state government and the Justice Department of the Obama administration have engaged in very few prosecutions. Ponzi schemers such as Bernie Madoff have been brought to justice, but these peoples' illegal activities were exposed because of the financial meltdown. They were not necessarily the cause of it. In understanding why there have been so few criminal prosecutions, former federal prosecutors who are experts in white-collar crime wrote in the September 2013 *New York Law Journal* that government prosecutors (as well as potential jurors) would undoubtedly be confounded by the "financial instruments and transactions underlying the recent crisis" because they are "immensely complex and involve many individuals performing highly technical tasks with large volumes of data."[8] Moreover, they argue, nearly everyone was making poor business decisions at the time, making "it difficult to separate criminal behavior from business misjudgment." Clearly, white-collar crime can definitely impact the larger society, but its complexity and the difficulty that lies in distinguishing bad intent from bad judgment sometimes allows perpetrators to get away with their white-collar criminal activities.

"Victimless" Crimes.   Acts among willing adults that violate some moral principle supported by the dominant forces in society constitute a substantial fraction of crimes. Although some such acts may in fact inflict genuine harm—for example, drug use that leads to crimes to pay for the habit, or prostitution that spreads disease—they are called *"victimless crimes,"* because participation in such activity in and of itself is presumed to be voluntary. Estimates vary with the definition of the term and the range of activities proscribed, but in many estimates, arrests for victimless crimes account for over half the total number of arrests. Such laws often attempt to ban conduct that is widely practiced. Consequently, they are often ineffective in altering the actual behavior of people strongly disposed to engage in the proscribed conduct. Thus, the impact of these laws is not to prevent the conduct in question, but rather to criminalize large segments of the American population. A perfect example of this impact is represented by the large number of people in prison serving time for consuming illegal drugs.

The Rising Costs of Crime.   The dollar value lost to society because of crime has risen so sharply in the past three decades that it cannot be ignored. According to estimates by the Justice Department, insurance companies, and academic researchers, the overall costs to society of street crime by the mid-1990s were in the neighborhood of $163 billion, up from $43 billion (adjusted for inflation) in 1965—an almost fourfold increase. The value of stolen property alone for all reported index crimes in 2000 was $16.4 billion. Other factors contributed to the remaining costs of crime. The following example serves to illustrate the expense incurred by each crime. When on June 7, 1994, eighteen-year-old James Hunter was murdered in Washington, DC, police officers, detectives, and forensic experts came to the scene, costing the city $4,626. An emergency vehicle rushed Hunter to the hospital, costing another $1,310. The autopsy cost $1,046. Thus, even while police pursued his killer, the murder of one person cost that city about $7,000. The costs of the prosecutorial resources must be added if a suspect is apprehended, plus over $22,000 per year to keep someone in the district prison in the event of a conviction. This not-atypical crime was just one of more than 200 that occurred in the first three-quarters of 1994 in the DC area alone. When considering murder, rape, assault, burglary, etc., the Rand Corporation calculated that the cost of crime in 2010 in the United States was around $300 billion dollars.[9]

Reported Crime.   The FBI index includes only reported crimes. Sample surveys, on the other hand, report that two to three times more crimes are committed than are reported. This rate of underreporting, such "victimization surveys" indicate, varies according to geographical area. The crime rate as indicated by the official index, therefore, depends on what proportion of actual crimes is reported and becomes a statistic. A greater proportion of crimes being reported would lead to an increase in the crime rate even if the actual crime rate did not increase. Such a reporting increase occurred in the 1970s and 1980s.

There are two reasons for this. First, the development of computers and other data-processing equipment has facilitated the accuracy and completeness of collecting and tabulating crime data. Second, more stolen property is now insured, and in order for the benefits of a policy to be claimed, a police report must normally be filed. In past years, the likelihood that the perpetrator of a crime would be apprehended or that stolen property would be recovered was always low; therefore, there was little incentive outside insurance considerations to report crimes. This generates a rise in the crime index even if the number of actual crimes committed remains constant. Some types of crime (murder) are more likely to be reported than others (robbery). Rape was once seriously underreported, in part because of the kind of treatment rape victims received in court. With court reforms easing the potential embarrassment of victims who press charges, the rate of reporting rape may be going up significantly, in turn affecting the statistics for that crime.

Reasons for Crime

It is important to keep in mind that a "crime" is an activity that some legislative body has chosen to make illegal. This activity may be one that harms persons or property; it may be an activity that offends some ethical principle adhered to by the segment of society that dominates the lawmaking process; or it may be some silly or innocent activity, the illegal status of which is inexplicable. Old laws are seldom repealed, whereas new ones are continually being passed as each generation seeks to ban something that it finds odious. The number of proscribed activities has expanded over time. Clearly, the more things that are declared illegal, the greater the crime rate will be, even if behavior patterns remain constant. A statistical increase in crime does not necessarily reflect changes in behavior patterns.

There are a number of factors that can help explain crime, from socioeconomic status to changing demographics. We begin with one of the biggest areas of crime that continues to consume a lot of the resources of the criminal justice system: drugs.

Drugs.   Drug abuse may constitute a special category among victimless crimes. When a nonaddicted youth is seduced into drug use by a "pusher," the concept of voluntary, or victimless, behavior is stretched quite thin. Because many mind-altering drugs are physically or psychologically addicting—or both—the demand for them by the addicted is largely unaffected by costs, including potential punishments for their use. Consequently, the disposition to use such drugs is unlikely to be deterred by the threat of punishment. The legislative control of drug use in the United States is far from a recent phenomenon; however, this legislation has failed to stem a rise in the use of mind-altering drugs in recent decades. As the national surveys in Tables 6.4 and 6.5 indicate, a significant minority of students in high school and college have used drugs.

TABLE 6.4   Use of Drugs by High School Seniors in 2010 and 2012

	2010		2012	
Drug	Within 12 Months	Within 30 Days	Within 12 Months	Within 30 Days
Illegal drugs	38.3%	23.8%	39.7%	25.2%
Marijuana	34.8%	21.4%	36.4%	22.9%
Cocaine	2.9%	1.3%	2.7%	1.1%
Heroin	0.9%	0.4%	0.6%	0.3%
Alcohol	65.2%	41.5%	63.5%	41.2%

SOURCE: University of Michigan Institute for Social Research, sponsored by the National Institutes of Health, http://monitoringthefuture.org/pubs/monographs/mtf-vol1_2012.pdf.

TABLE 6.5   Drug Usage by College Students

	1995	2000	2005	2012
Marijuana				
Within last month	18.6%	20.0%	17.1%	20.5%
Within last year	31.2%	34.0%	33.3%	34.9%
Cocaine				
Within last month	0.7%	1.4%	1.8%	1.1%
Within last year	3.6%	4.8%	5.7%	3.1%

SOURCE: Institute for Social Research, University of Michigan, sponsored by the National Institutes of Health, *Monitoring the Future National Survey Results on Drug Use, 1975–2012, Volume II: College Students and Adults Ages 19–50*, http://www.monitoringthefuture.org/pubs/monographs/mtf-vol2_2012.pdf.

Drug users in search of money to finance their expensive habits have brought higher rates of property crime along with the drug epidemic. In the mid-1970s, the Drug Enforcement Administration estimated that an average heroin habit cost $57.50 per day, or $21,000 annually to support.[10] This cost is beyond the financial capability of typical upper-middle-class people, not to mention addicts who have a diminished capacity to pursue middle-class careers. Consequently, addicts have little choice but to turn to crime to support their habit. Given the rigid demand, the successful interception of the drug supply would only make the drugs scarcer and more expensive. This would produce the spillover effect of increasing the crime rate even further.

The high rate of drug addiction in the post-Vietnam period would therefore account for the high rate of street crime in that era. Heroin was relatively inexpensive and easy to obtain in the so-called "Golden Triangle" of Southeast Asia in an era characterized by widespread rebellion against "the establishment" and its taboos. The war involved a mixing of the conscripted middle class and the drug-using underclass in a situation of great stress. Hence, many middle-class veterans brought a drug addiction home from Vietnam. Since the 1990s, reported marijuana use within the last 30 days among high school seniors has increased from 12 percent in 1992 to 22.9 percent in 2012, but that is still much lower than the high point of 37 percent of high school seniors in 1978 who reported using marijuana within the last 30 days.[11] A number of states in recent years have either legalized medicinal marijuana, or decriminalized possession of small amounts of marijuana, or (in the case of Washington and Colorado) have legalized marijuana completely. Thus, it would seem unlikely that marijuana usage will decline in the future. On the other hand, cocaine use within the last 30 days among high school seniors is also sharply down in 2012 when compared to the high of 6.7 percent in 1985 and 5.7 percent in 1979.

According to the National Survey on Drug Use and Health taken in 2012, while only 19 percent of the population aged sixty-five or older has ever tried illegal drugs, over 50 percent of Americans aged twenty to sixty-four have tried illegal drugs at least once in their lifetime.[12] Regular cocaine use among Americans is down from 0.9 percent in 2002 to 0.6 percent in 2012. However, the overall percentage of regular drug users (i.e., used within the past 30 days) among persons aged twelve or older in the United States in 2012 was about 9.2 percent, and that rate has risen slightly since 2002, when it was 8.3 percent.[13] Current users of drugs other than marijuana aged twelve or older in the United States total about 3.4 percent of the population (or 8.9 million people).

More people are arrested by U.S. law enforcement for drug abuse than for any other type of crime, according to the FBI's 2012 *Uniform Crime Report* (1,552,432 persons arrested in 2012, accounting for 12.7 percent of all arrests). Total arrests for drug abuse are down slightly from the 1990s in terms of actual numbers of arrests, but when compared to other types of arrests, drug abuse arrests constitute a slightly larger percentage of the total arrests for crimes. In 1997, drug abuse arrests (1,583,600 persons) accounted for 10.3 percent of all arrests.[14]

While law enforcement may be arresting more people for drug abuse, the percentage of those arrests involving heroin or cocaine, or their derivatives,

T A B L E 6.6   Percentage of All Drug Arrests Involving Heroin or Cocaine or Their Derivatives

Arrest Offense	1995	1997	2001	2005	2008	2012
Sale or manufacture	14.7%	10.3%	9.7%	8%	7.7%	6.1%
Possession	27.8%	25%	23.1%	22.2%	20.1%	16.5%

SOURCE: FBI *Uniform Crime Reports*, http://www.fbi.gov/ucr/ucr.htm.

has fallen since the 1990s (see Table 6.6). For example, in 1995, possession of heroin or cocaine accounted for 27.8 percent of all drug arrests; but in 2012, arrests for possession of heroin or cocaine represented only 16.5 percent of all drug arrests. Heroin and cocaine (particularly crack cocaine) are most frequently associated with violent crime and property crime, and thus such a drop can account for much of the decline in street crime in cities such as New York. This decline contributed significantly to the reputation of urban leaders, such as former New York City Mayor Rudy Giuliani, as the increase in drug usage during the 1970s and 1980s accounted for the apparent wave of street crime in that period. One can only speculate about the reasons for the decline in drug usage, especially in the area of heavy drugs, in the early twenty-first century. Certainly, aging and rising economic status of the baby boom generation may be one factor. While the percentage of drug arrests compared to total arrests for other types of crimes has increased slightly over the last decade, Table 6.6 indicates that arrests for the most addictive drugs (heroin or cocaine or their derivatives) have gone down as a percentage of total drug arrests.

Demographic Change.   The influence of demographic trends, such as the urbanization of America, provides another explanation for trends in crime statistics. Cities offer a greater crime potential than do smaller towns and rural areas. The high concentrations of people in America's urban population centers mean more interaction among people, more opportunities for crime, and less chance of being apprehended. There is normally a greater selection of valuable, concealable, and transportable goods in cities than in rural areas. Furthermore, the anonymity of a city makes it easier for the perpetrator of a crime to escape detection or capture. As Table 6.7 illustrates, violent crime in urban areas is much higher than in rural or suburban America. Nevertheless, levels of violent crime have been decreasing recently among all population areas, bolstering other evidence in this chapter showing a decrease in rates of crime. Similar trends can be seen among urban, suburban, and rural areas for property crimes as well.

Another demographic trend that contributed to the increased incidence of crime in the past several decades is that those categories of people statistically more likely to commit crimes grew as a proportion of the total population. Youth is an important crime indicator, with 52.8 percent of persons arrested in 2012 registering between fifteen and twenty-five years of age. In contrast, arrestees in that year who were between forty and fifty years old only constituted 14.1 percent of all arrestees, while those above age sixty represented only 2 percent

T A B L E   6.7   **Urban-Rural Violent Crime, 2005, 2010, and 2012: Offenses Known to Police**

Population Crime Area	2005 Offenses (per 100,000)	2010 Offenses (per 100,000)	2012 Offenses (per 100,000)
Cities (250,000 and over)	941.2	751.4	769.4
Cities, (100,000 to 249,999)	616.2	519.6	494.1
Suburban areas	316.3	271.0	252.6
Nonmetropolitan counties	218.8	199.3	179.2

SOURCE: FBI *Uniform Crime Reports*, http://www.fbi.gov/ucr/ucr.htm.

of all arrestees. Some argue that crime is particularly concentrated within a small subset of youth. Marvin Wolfgang and his associates find that a small number of delinquents—juveniles who have had five or more recorded contacts with police—are responsible for a majority of all crimes and two-thirds of all violent crimes.[15] Until recently, there was a growing proportion of the population under twenty-five, due in part to the postwar baby boom. This trend has ended with the aging of the baby boom generation. With increasing longevity, the proportion of the older population is beginning to rise. This fact could also partially account for the recent downturn in crime rates.

Yet the criminal justice system does not fully accept the responsibility of minors for their actions, a fact exacerbated by the *Roper* case (discussed on page 169) in which the Supreme Court ruled the execution of anyone for a crime committed when younger than eighteen violates the Eighth Amendment's ban on cruel and unusual punishment. The perpetrator in the case bragged how he could escape serious punishment because of his status as a minor. Sentences usually are lighter; alternatives to actual incarceration are preferred; the police records of minors are erased; and in many cases they are released from the custody of the juvenile detention system when they become twenty-one years old. Long-term imprisonment is generally not a likely possibility until an adult record is well established, and, as we have seen, this is usually after the most active part of the criminal career is over. Hence, despite sharp increases in the prison population, an increasing number of inmates are older persons who do not present the greatest current and future danger to society. However, in recent years more juveniles are being tried as adults.

Another explanation (albeit a novel and controversial one) for the recent downturns in crime could be the changes in demographics resulting from the legalization of abortion in the Supreme Court case of *Roe v. Wade* (1973). University of Chicago Economics Professor Steven Levitt has suggested in his best-selling, coauthored book *Freakonomics* (2005) that the legalization of abortion in the 1970s cut down on crime in the 1990s. As Professor Levitt described on his blog at the *New York Times,* "The logic is simple: unwanted children have an increased risk of growing up to be criminals, and legalized abortion reduces the number of unwanted children. Consequently, legalized abortion lowers crime in the future."[16] Recently, however, rates of abortion have been declining, raising the question of whether crime will once again rise in the future due to the lack of abortions. But as Levitt has pointed out, it is unclear whether the most recent decline in abortion will cause a future rise in crime because researchers are still unclear as to why abortion rates are falling. There are a number of possible explanations for the decline, "and none of these have dire crime implications."[17]

Family Structure.   The divorce rate has climbed dramatically in the latter part of the twentieth century, to the point where half of the marriages in this country end up in the divorce court. Divorce rates declined in the wake of the recent financial crisis of 2008, but they are now on the rise again as the economy has recovered. Hence, a majority of America's children are not raised in a two-parent household. While many single parents successfully raise children with good results, the data show that in general, children raised in two-parent households tend to be more successful in their academic, professional, and personal lives. Therefore, the products of America's increasingly unstable family structure may be more likely to experience problems in their lives, problems that may involve perpetrating crime.

Socioeconomic Causes.   Certain types of crime are clearly related to poverty and unemployment, a fact that accounts for much of the apparent correlation between crime and race or ethnicity. The philosophical question is to what extent persons, regardless of their individual circumstances, remain free to choose between criminal and law-abiding behavior and hence are responsible for their actions. Conservatives tend to emphasize free will and individual responsibility for criminal behavior, whereas liberals are more likely to attribute such behavior to sociological circumstances, such as poverty and racism, which they argue cause the individual to act in aberrant ways. Of course, sociological conditions are more amenable to public policy solutions than are defects in individual character, and liberals tend to be more optimistic than conservatives are about the prospect of reducing crime by improving the environment in which people live.

Whatever conclusions one draws about this question, the fact remains that people in certain socioeconomic circumstances are statistically more likely to engage in criminal behavior. Accordingly, whether such circumstances are a cause of crime or a rationalization for it, a reduction in such circumstances may subsequently reduce the rate of certain types of crime.

ISSUES IN EQUAL PROTECTION AND GOVERNMENT RESPONSE TO CRIME

After outlining the extent of crime and the root causes of crime, it is tempting to jump immediately to the subject of public policy alternatives to deal with crime. As was noted at the beginning of the chapter, however, a democratic government must respect the civil liberties and civil rights of individuals when engaging in efforts to fight crime. Furthermore, sometimes the excesses that accompany an aggressive crime policy fall on those groups in society with the least political power. In this section, we look at some of the issues affecting African Americans within the context of crime policy and the criminal justice system.

The Supreme Court has interpreted the Equal Protection Clause of the Constitution's Fourteenth Amendment as prohibiting selective enforcement of the law based on race (see *United States v. Armstrong*, 1996).[18] Notwithstanding the Supreme Court's constitutional pronouncements, measures enacted by government to respond to crime do not always impact all racial, religious, and cultural groups equally. In fact, there is a strong sense among the African American population that they experience a particular injustice at the hands of the government's criminal justice system. The lower level of trust in the police and the criminal justice system on the part of African Americans as compared to whites is summarized in Table 6.8, and this is a fact that threatens the overall legitimacy of the system. These differences in perceptions have narrowed recently, perhaps due in part to the election of our first African American president. But, even in 2012, there were more African Americans who have very little or no confidence in the justice system (36 percent), as compared to 30 percent of whites with little or no confidence.

This gap in perceptions is not surprising given the huge differences in arrests in America between African Americans and other races. In 2012, African Americans were projected to make up approximately 13.1 percent of the national population; however, 28.1 percent of the persons arrested for a crime were African Americans, a figure down from 33.8 percent in 1978, but virtually unchanged from 28.9 percent in 1996.[19] The data for homicide in 2012 show a

T A B L E 6.8   Confidence in the Criminal Justice System and the Police, 2005 and 2012

		A Great Deal	Some	Very Little	None
2005	White				
	Justice system	36%	41%	21%	1%
	Police	66%	28%	5%	1%
	African American				
	Justice system	25%	40%	32%	3%
	Police	49%	37%	14%	0%
2012	White				
	Justice system	26%	44%	27%	3%
	Police	57%	27%	14%	2%
	African American				
	Justice system	24%	36%	28%	8%
	Police	32%	44%	23%	>.05%

SOURCE: *Sourcebook of Criminal Justice Statistics, 2005*, p. 113; and *Sourcebook of Criminal Justice Statistics, 2012*, http://www.albany.edu/sourcebook/csv/t2122012.csv.

TABLE 6.9   Arrests by Race, 2012 in Percentages (Hispanics Were Classified with Whites)

Crime Category	White	Black	Native American	Asian-Pacific Islander
Murder-manslaughter	48.2	49.4	1.2	1.2
Forcible rape	65.0	32.5	1.3	1.2
Robbery	43.4	54.9	0.7	1.0
Aggravated assault	62.8	34.1	1.4	1.6
Burglary	67.1	30.8	0.9	1.2
Larceny-theft	68.2	29.0	1.5	1.3
Motor vehicle theft	66.6	30.8	1.2	1.4
Arson	73.6	23.6	1.6	1.2
All violent crime*	58.7	38.5	1.3	1.4
Total all crimes	69.3	28.1	1.4	1.2

*Includes murder and manslaughter, forcible rape, robbery, and aggravated assault.

SOURCE: U.S. Department of Justice, Federal Bureau of Investigation, *Uniform Crime Report, 2012*, http://www.fbi.gov/about-us/cjis/ucr/crime-in-the-u.s/2012/crime-in-the-u.s.-2012/tables/43tabledatadecoverviewpdf.

disproportionate percentage of African Americans arrested. In that year, 49.4 percent of those arrested for homicide were black, up from 39 percent in 2000. Of course, a disproportionate number of murder victims in 2012 (over 50 percent of all murder victims) were also African Americans (separate data for Hispanics were not provided). The rates of arrest are summarized in Table 6.9. Some civil rights groups argue that these numbers are simply a reflection of a higher propensity on the part of the police to arrest African Americans for crimes that might otherwise go overlooked among whites. They argue that the evidence of arrests support suspicions that there is some racial bias in the dispensing of justice. Prominent scholars, such as Professor Charles Ogletree of Harvard Law School, charge that many of the young African American males in prison are in fact innocents caught up in a racist system.[20] Whether the disparity is entirely due to racial bias, however, is a much more complicated issue to statistically examine and understand. Certainly, differences in socioeconomics among African Americans and whites may also contribute to higher rates of criminal arrest among African Americans. Undoubtedly, the explanations could be a combination of both socioeconomic factors and racial bias by individuals in government.

Not only are African Americans disproportionately arrested, but they also disproportionately populate America's jails. In 2010, African Americans constituted about 37.8 percent of the prison population, despite representing only 13 percent of the population.[21] The fact is that African Americans who are arrested are much more likely than whites to end up incarcerated in prison.[22] Imprisonment rates for both whites and African Americans have risen since 1975, but the rate of African American imprisonment has risen much more rapidly.[23] But, of course, rates of imprisonment (as opposed to rates of arrests) are more likely to represent political decisions of the community rather than a reflection of rates of crime. Sociologist Pamela Oliver of the University of Wisconsin—Madison notes in one study that "[i]t appears that blacks are more likely to be imprisoned [in states and communities] where they are a smaller, politically weaker, and economically marginalized population."[24]

A related issue with regard to race and crime and the disproportionate percentage of incarcerated African Americans is racial profiling. This refers to the disposition on the part of numerous law enforcement personnel to regard the fact of being African American, in and of itself, as grounds for suspicion of past or prospective criminal activity. African Americans, without showing any other indications of criminality, are more likely than comparable whites to be stopped by police, interrogated, searched, and arrested for minor infractions. This issue undercuts perceptions by African Americans that the system is fair. Furthermore, the Civil Rights Division of the U.S. Justice Department argues that racial profiling is not only morally wrong, but also ineffective in terms of the public policy goal of reducing crime.[25]

The issue of racial profiling has also affected other minority groups. The issue has become a cause of concern for Muslims of Middle Eastern descent in America. The Justice Department's Civil Rights Division has issued guidelines that prohibit law enforcement in the federal government from outwardly profiling Muslims (in airports, for example) simply because of their ethnicity or religion. A notable exception to this guideline, however, is made for the realm of national security. Those same Justice Department guidelines state that "Federal law enforcement officers who are protecting national security or preventing catastrophic events (as well as airport security screeners) may consider race, ethnicity, and other relevant factors to the extent permitted by our laws and the Constitution."[26]

The issue of racial profiling of Hispanics became a political concern in Arizona in 2010 after the state passed a law to combat illegal immigration. Arizona has become a popular point of crossing for illegal immigrants, and a rise in crime in human trafficking and drug trafficking has resulted from this influx. In an effort to stem the tide of illegal immigrants and the resulting crime, the state passed a law, which allows law enforcement, when detaining an individual during the investigation of a crime or during a traffic stop, to inquire into the detained individual's immigrant status. Even though the law specifically prohibits authorities from engaging in racial profiling, some civil liberties groups and advocates for Hispanic rights are concerned that the law could nevertheless be used to unconstitutionally racially profile Hispanics. The passage of the Arizona law spurred a hail of protests and boycotts and even precipitated criticism of the law from President Obama. The U.S. Justice Department filed a lawsuit to block the state of Arizona from implementing the law. The case went all the way to the U.S. Supreme Court, which struck down several provisions of the Arizona law in 2012, including a provision that made it a crime for illegal immigrants to look for work. The U.S. Supreme Court reasoned that the state government had interfered with the exclusive power given to the federal government under the Constitution to regulate immigration. The Court left some provisions of the Arizona law intact, however, including a controversial provision that allowed state police to investigate the immigration status of anyone lawfully detained or arrested by the state police. Meanwhile, racial profiling continues to be an issue in law enforcement in Arizona. In a May 2013 ruling, a U.S. District Court found the Maricopa County Sheriff's Department had a practice of engaging in racial profiling and appointed a monitor to make sure it does not happen again.

The perception of justice denied is periodically renewed and exacerbated when the violent treatment of African Americans is apparently not prosecuted and punished with the same vigor as would be the comparable treatment of whites. Events that generate a perception of injustice include the 1991 videotaped beating by Los Angeles policemen of an African American, Rodney King, and the acquittal of George Zimmerman after he claimed self-defense for the 2012 shooting and killing of teenager Trayvon Martin in Florida.

Perceptions of an unfair and unjust system give rise to the phenomenon of "jury nullification," where a jury renders a verdict of "not guilty" even in the face of an overwhelming body of evidence to the contrary. The racial divide over the verdict in the case of former football star O. J. Simpson illustrates the level of African American distrust of our criminal justice system. When policymakers develop crime policy, healing this distrust (among *all* Americans) is essential to maintaining a fair and effective criminal justice system.

CONTEMPORARY POLICY: CONSTITUTIONAL RIGHTS AND DETERRENCE OF CRIME

Contemporary policies toward crime must comply with certain constitutional limitations, and these limitations came into full force by the 1960s. Conservatives attributed the problem of rising crime between the 1970s and 1990s in large part to a significant expansion in the rights of persons accused of crime, an expansion that was associated with the Supreme Court under the chief justiceship of Earl Warren (1953–1969). This expansion, however, was largely halted with the appointment of several Supreme Court justices under the Reagan and first Bush administrations, justices thought to be politically conservative and less sympathetic to an expansive view of individual rights implicitly protected by the Constitution. This Court, now headed by Chief Justice Roberts and buttressed by the addition of Justices Alito, Scalia, Kennedy, and Thomas, now has a more conservative profile. (See Chapter 13 for a list of current members of the Court and their judicial orientations.) President Obama placed two new justices on the court (Sotomayor and Kagan) who are liberal in orientation, but they simply replaced existing liberal justices on the court (Souter and Stevens). Thus, the George W. Bush appointments of Roberts and Alito give the Court a narrow conservative majority, despite some surprising liberal votes from Kennedy. (His opinion in the *Roper* case is discussed later in the chapter.) This apparent balance makes it unlikely that procedural rights will be significantly expanded in the near future. The respect that legal scholars in the Anglo-American common law system have for the force of precedent, however, probably limits the extent to which the Court can undo the revolution in procedural rights.

Because in our system the accused is presumed innocent until proven otherwise, the rights of the accused are the rights of the innocent. These rights require the judicial system to proceed according to the rules of evidence, rules that prevent people from being punished on the basis of hearsay, rumor, emotional prejudice, or other factors that do not objectively establish guilt. Given the choice of punishing all of the guilty, even if some innocent are also caught in the net, or taking care not to punish the innocent, even if some guilty people thereby escape punishment, Western society has opted for the latter alternative. It must be remembered that each of these procedural rights came into being in response to a particular abuse of government power. As Justice Felix Frankfurter once said, "The history of liberty has largely been the history of procedural safeguards."

This expansion of rights has come about in two ways. First, the Supreme Court has slowly expanded the meaning of the U.S. Constitution's Fourteenth Amendment to incorporate most of the federal **Bill of Rights**, making them applicable to state governments. The Bill of Rights (the first ten amendments to the Constitution) was originally written by the Founding Fathers only for the purpose of limiting the national government's criminal law and trial procedures in federal courts. In other words, until the Fourteenth Amendment was passed after the Civil War, state governments did not have to follow the Bill of Rights because it initially only applied to the federal government. Most crimes, however, are violations of state law. Consequently, most criminal trials happen in state court, not federal court. Since the Fourteenth Amendment provides that "no State shall deny any person life, liberty or property without due process of law..." the Supreme Court has ruled that due process requires that trials in state court must also follow most of the Bill of Rights. Consequently, now most state courts have to guarantee the same procedural rights as trials in the federal courts.

The second mode of expansion of the rights of the accused has been through a broadened interpretation of existing rights. With each of these rights, the question was not whether it existed, but rather what it meant or implied. The question of the implications and meaning of the rights of persons accused of a crime has come into sharper focus since the beginning of the "war on terror" and the USA PATRIOT Act, passed in the wake of the September 11, 2001 attacks, and the subsequent indefinite incarceration of citizens and noncitizens believed to be associated with terrorism. The Act significantly expanded the ability of law enforcement agencies to search telephone and e-mail communications along with medical and financial records, and enhanced the discretion of law enforcement agencies to detain and deport illegal aliens. The ability to indefinitely detain illegal immigrants has been criticized by civil libertarians and in September 2007, the American Civil Liberties Union filed a lawsuit challenging the ability of government agencies to monitor phone conversations. The Act was due to sunset at the end of 2005, but it was reauthorized and signed into law by President Bush on March 9, 2006.

The expansion of the rights of the accused has generated the most controversy in three areas:

1. The right to counsel and the admissibility of confessions
2. The exclusionary rule and the admissibility of illegally obtained evidence
3. Constraints on the use of capital punishment

Although these three rights greatly benefit the accused, some voices in society suggest that the pendulum has once again swung too far in favor of government in the area of criminal justice because of changes in technological innovations, the expansion of the federal government's power under the war on terror, and the dramatic increase in our prison population. Thus, we also take a look at:

4. Recent criminal policies designed to increase the technological advancement of police resources
5. The practice of locking away large segments of the population in prison for longer periods of time

Confessions and the Right to Counsel

It was decided quite early that the right to counsel applied to state criminal proceedings. What this right entails, however, has changed over the years. To the founders, it was understood by its common-law meaning: the right to hire an attorney. The concept that the state had any obligation to pay for one's attorney is a modern extrapolation from this earlier concept. The practice of providing defense counsel in federal criminal trials had long been standard procedure but not a constitutional requirement. The first expansion of the right to counsel occurred in 1932, when the Supreme Court held in the infamous Scottsboro case that the accused had in capital cases (cases in which the death penalty is a legal possibility) the right to be provided with effective counsel in state court.[27] The Scottsboro opinion noted that even intelligent laypersons lack "skill in the science of the law." Clearly, the prosecution is legally trained and, in an adversary proceeding, has a distinct advantage in knowing how to manipulate the rules of evidence and procedure. The logic of this argument prevailed as the Court extended the right to counsel at state expense to all indigent defendants facing felony trials in state courts in the 1963 case of *Gideon v. Wainwright*.[28] Finally, the courts have extended the right further to include "effective assistance of counsel." Thus, a federal appeals court in 2001 threw out a death sentence issued in a Texas state court after the defendant's court-appointed attorney slept through most of the capital murder trial. The federal appeals court stated that a sleeping attorney is like having no attorney at all.

Even this expansion of the meaning of the due process clause did not satisfy all the needs of defendants for counsel in state criminal processes. Most convictions in fact have been obtained from confessions, often through plea bargaining, before the cases ever come to trial. **Plea bargaining** is a frequently used process involving an agreement between the prosecution and the defendant by which the latter is allowed to plead guilty to a lesser crime than he or she is charged with. In return, the prosecution drops the more serious charge. The prosecution in this way avoids the necessity of satisfying the burden of proof for the more serious charge; the crowded court docket is relieved of another time-consuming case; the state thus saves money; and the defendant is freed from the threat of the more serious punishment.[29] This "bargain" is generally offered to a defendant with either the implicit or explicit threat that if the deal is rejected, successful prosecution under a more serious charge will be the outcome. Even innocent people may in such circumstances be persuaded to "cop a plea" in order to escape the threat of dire punishment. Furthermore, prosecutors sometimes overcharge in order to allow themselves room to bargain. At the same time, plea bargainers who have committed serious crimes may get by with more lenient punishment and early release from detention. The pressure from overcrowded court dockets on harried, overworked prosecutors to dispose of cases in this shortcut fashion can thus frustrate the goal of physically removing dangerous criminals from society for long periods of time and can detract from whatever deterrent effect serious punishment may exercise.[30] Potential criminals thus have good reason to assume that they can obtain leniency by plea bargaining.

Thus, for a period of time, many cases were being settled in the pretrial stage, when defendants did not have a guaranteed recourse to counsel. The *Escobedo*[31] and *Miranda*[32] cases extended the right of counsel provided by the state effectively to the point of arrest. Culminating in the famous "***Miranda* rule**," this right now includes: (1) the right to remain silent, (2) the right to know that anything said could and would be used against the accused in court, and (3) the right to be represented at that time by counsel, at state expense if necessary. Before any confession or damaging statement can be entered as evidence, all of the above rights must be consciously waived by the accused. Of course, the first thing that an attorney is likely to do is advise his or her client to say nothing, thereby placing the burden of proof on the police or prosecution to prove their case. This would seem on the surface likely to reduce the rate of convictions, because so many are obtained by confession. Furthermore, the decision seemed to mean freeing, on a legal technicality, a person who had voluntarily confessed to a heinous crime before being read her rights. For many, it epitomized a dangerous precedent for freeing other criminals on similar technicalities. Yet, despite the criticism of the case by conservatives, the concept of the *Miranda* warning offered by the Supreme Court in 1966 was not unique to America. Scotland already barred the use of confessions obtained through police interrogation, and in India, confessions to police without a magistrate present were excluded from evidence at trial since 1872, while England also had some provision (pre-*Miranda*) for police to caution suspects, before questioning, that they were not obligated to talk.[33]

The Exclusionary Rule and Search and Seizure

The **exclusionary rule** is the principle that evidence obtained in an illegal search and/or seizure may not be admitted in a court of law. The Fourth Amendment proscribes "unreasonable searches and seizures." A legal search and seizure requires one of two conditions. In the case of someone's home, police need to obtain a search warrant, issued by a judge, which authorizes the police to search private property without the consent of the property owner and specifies what is being sought. A judge can only issue the warrant on the showing by the police of probable cause that illegal activity may be occurring. In all other instances that occur outside the home or off private property, the police usually only need to prove to a court they had probable cause to make a search.

What happens when police conduct a search without a search warrant or without a showing of probable cause that a crime is being committed, and they then find evidence of a crime? The Constitution is altogether silent about what happens to evidence that is found during an unconstitutional search, and whether that illegal evidence can be used at trial. The Supreme Court held in the famous *Mapp* decision that the Constitution requires the exclusion from court of illegally obtained evidence.[34] In *Mapp v. Ohio* (1961), the Court rejected the argument that the exclusionary rule protects only the guilty. The Court found that other remedies were ineffective; hence, the exclusionary rule was a necessary means to enforce the admittedly fundamental right to be free from such illegal searches. The rule protects more than the guilty, because if illegally obtained evidence is inadmissible, there is no motive for police to make illegal searches of the guilty or the innocent.

Some law-and-order conservatives who oppose the *Miranda* rule argue that the Fourth Amendment ought not to be construed as excluding illegally obtained evidence, because such a principle would protect only the guilty, whereas constitutional rights are designed to protect the innocent. Furthermore, they say that if one is not guilty of a crime, an unreasonable search and seizure will not yield any incriminating evidence. The secondary argument against the exclusionary rule is that other remedies are available to deter police from illegal searches; namely, police can be sued or arrested for such behavior. But there are also valid arguments for having a rule to exclude illegally obtained evidence. First, the rule deters misbehavior by the police, for police cannot use evidence that they seize if they violate the Constitution. Police are less likely to undertake illegal searches if they know that they cannot use any incriminating evidence that they find through such searches. Second, the rule protects law-abiding citizens from arbitrary searches and harassment from the police. Third, law enforcement is forced to be more deliberate and circumspect in the deployment of resources. Of course, police could do wide sweeps of every home every day and undoubtedly find illegal contraband or criminal activity somewhere. Such behavior, however, wastes government resources and places a heavy burden on law-abiding citizens.

There are a number of exceptions to the exclusionary rule that allow police to search places without probable cause or a search warrant. For example, police do not need to have a search warrant or show probable cause that a crime is being committed in cases of exigent circumstances (such as when police believe a person may be dying in a home or suspect a bomb in a house). Nor are these rules necessary to search people at border checkpoints. The exceptions are too varied and complex to name all of them here, but many of these exceptions also revolve around the concept of protecting the safety of officers. Thus, in a lawful arrest in which a warrant has not first been obtained, the following forms of search may be made: (1) the person and pockets of the arrestee and (2) the arrestee's car or the room in which he or she was arrested ("the area under his possession"), but not the entire house.[35] A person merely stopped for questioning may be subjected to a pat down or frisk for weapons in the name of officer safety, even if that person is not suspected of engaging in any crime.[36]

Other exceptions have been made or debated within the context of counterterrorism policies begun under the Bush administration and continued by the Obama administration. For example, wiretapping someone's phone (even a public payphone enclosed in a booth) typically requires a warrant issued by a judge.[37] The Bush and Obama administrations argued for an exception to this rule in cases of national security, where a suspected terrorist is calling someone overseas. But, unbeknownst to the public and many members of Congress, the Bush and Obama administrations went much further than that, directing the National Security Agency (NSA) to vacuum up the telephone records of all Americans in the name of fighting terror. The NSA says that it needs data on innocent Americans in order to help it find terrorists. This "metadata" includes information on who you have called, who has called you, when you made a phone call, and the location of your phone call (which can yield a lot of data if one is using a cellphone). As of the writing of this chapter, dueling federal courts have come to opposing conclusions regarding the constitutionality of this NSA program. Although the Obama administration has claimed that such private information is only used in terrorism investigations, there has been some reporting that some information collected on Americans is being employed by general law enforcement, such as the Drug Enforcement Administration (DEA).[38] While the threat of terrorism continues to be real (as noted in Chapter 12), the biggest fear of civil liberties advocates is that this information being collected for counterterrorism will later be used against the American public for general crime-fighting purposes.

The complexity of these rules illustrates the difficulty that the courts have in trying to balance two conflicting values: the right of individuals to be free from governmental oppression or harassment and the control of crime and punishment of criminals.

The two biggest exceptions to the exclusionary rule occurred in the 1980s. The Supreme Court in 1984, driven by then Chief Justice Burger's avowed hostility to the exclusionary rule, chipped away at the rule without specifically overturning it. The Court announced a decision in the case of *Nix v. Williams* (1984) that held that illegally obtained evidence would now be admissible if the Court found that the police would have discovered the evidence sooner or later by legal means. This "inevitable discovery" rule pleased conservatives, who argued that it would render clearly guilty people less likely to be released on a mere "technicality." But liberals fear that this dampening effect on the disposition of the police to engage in illegal searches may be seriously weakened by this case. Subsequently, the Court made another inroad on the exclusionary rule in the case of *U.S. v. Leon* (1984), in which it held that if the police acted in "good faith" that the search was legal (for example, if a magistrate issued a search warrant, but it turns out the magistrate made an error because there was not sufficient probable cause), the fact that the search turned out to be technically illegal would not be grounds for suppressing any evidence found.[39]

Capital Punishment

The third area in which the expansion of the rights of the accused has provoked the most controversy is capital punishment. The relevant constitutional provision is the Eighth Amendment protection against "cruel and unusual punishment," which opponents of the death penalty have variously held either prohibits the imposition of capital punishment itself or, failing that, at least limits the mode and circumstances of its imposition. Given the ambiguity of the words "cruel and unusual punishment," their implications for the practice of capital punishment are something on which reasonable and informed legal scholars can and do disagree. The controversy is exacerbated by serious disagreement over the importance of capital punishment as a deterrent to capital crime.

The Supreme Court has affirmed that there are two legitimate social purposes that may be served by the death penalty: deterrence and **retribution**. Most of the published arguments supporting retention and use of capital punishment have focused on its putative value as a deterrent to future crime; the essentially normative, retributive argument is apparently distasteful to many scholars. Yet for the person in the street, retribution is also a real consideration. There are some crimes for which mere imprisonment seems an inadequate punishment. Many people's intuitive sense of justice is deeply offended when a brutal mass murderer, such as Jeffrey Dahmer, convicted in 1992 not only of killing but also of cannibalizing his victims, is allowed to live on in prison. (Dahmer was murdered in prison in 1994.) The issue of retributive justice was raised in 1997 in the case of the perpetrators of the bombing of the federal building in Oklahoma City that killed 168 people. For this act of terrorism, the worst in U.S. history prior to September 11, 2001, perpetrator Timothy McVeigh was sentenced to death, but coconspirator Terry Nichols was spared the death penalty by a jury. As an ethical argument, the issue of retributive justice cannot be resolved; yet, it may more easily withstand scrutiny than the more frequently relied-upon deterrence argument.[40] The retributive argument regards capital punishment as an end in itself, while the deterrent argument regards capital punishment as a means to the end of preventing serious crimes. Accordingly, the question of whether capital punishment serves as a deterrent is in principle an empirical question, a question potentially resolvable by observable data.

Deterrence?   If, on the basis of common sense, it seems clear that punishment deters proscribed acts, it follows that death should deter such acts more effectively than less severe punishment will. As the British Royal Commission on capital punishment stated in 1953, "*Prima facie,* the penalty of death is likely to have a stronger effect as a deterrent to normal human beings than any other form of punishment...." There is in fact evidence that punishment in general does deter crime. Another body of research, however, indicates that it is the swiftness and certainty of punishment, rather than its severity, that most effectively operates as a crime deterrent. Yet, the death penalty, in the American context, can neither be swift nor certain. It is hedged by automatic appeals and the right of almost any judge personally to stay an execution based on any question about the manner of arrest or conviction. These automatic appeals are in place to try and prevent error, though sometimes errors occur anyway. In some states over the last decade, there have been concerns that innocent people were inadvertently executed. In Illinois, concerns about error in the justice system prompted then-governor George Ryan to commute all 167 death row inmates to life in prison in 2003. In addition to the automatic appeals, the death penalty is limited also by the reluctance of judges and juries to impose the death sentence and the even greater reluctance of states to carry it out. Sociologist Thorsten Sellin has reported that, historically, the risk of suffering the death penalty in the United States if caught and convicted of capital murder during a period of widespread executions (1933–1950) was only 3.67 percent.[41] In 2008, there were 14,827 homicides; yet, in that same year there were only 3,170 inmates on death row and forty-three executions. There is a less than 1 percent probability that a convicted murderer will be executed; however, more important in terms of the deterrent effect of "swift and certain" punishment, there is virtually no chance that a murderer will be executed within two years of conviction. The relative frequency of people sentenced to death and the frequency of people actually being executed in recent years are indicated in Table 6.10. At the rate of the current high-water mark of ninety-eight executions per year, it would take more than thirty-three years to dispatch everyone currently under sentence of death, assuming no one else is so sentenced in that period.

There is very little doubt that if every person convicted of murder were to be immediately dispatched, other murders would be deterred. The foregoing data, however, suggest that there is very little likelihood of such a policy being

T A B L E   6.10   Death Sentences and Executions

Year	Under Sentence of Death	Executed
1996	3,219	45
1997	3,335	74
1998	3,465	68
1999	3,540	98
2008	3,207	37
2009	3,263	52
2010	3,261	46
2011	3,220	43
2012	3,170	43

SOURCE: *Sourcebook of Criminal Justice Statistics, 2000*, p. 549; http://www.albany.edu/sourcebook/tost_6.html#6_o and http://www.deathpenaltyinfo.org/executions-year.

implemented. First, the system seeks through appeals and rehearings to resolve all uncertainty before carrying out an execution. Second, America's more secularized society is uncertain about judging who deserves to live and die. Finally, there appears to be a cultural strengthening of the sanctity of life itself under way in the nation. Consequently, to execute promptly all or even most people convicted of murder is politically unthinkable. Failing that extreme approach of quick execution, it is hard to see how capital punishment can have a greater deterrent effect than do other forms of punishment. Despite these reservations about the deterrent effect of capital punishment, belief in that deterrent effect continues to be a widespread, although by October 2011, a minority opinion. Specifically, 3 percent of a national sample believed that the death penalty deters crime, and 64 percent said it does not, with 4 percent unsure.[42] Thus, supporters of the death penalty may be playing to public opinion rather than social scientific knowledge.

There are some data on the actual deterrent effect of the death penalty, but they are inconclusive.[43] For example, studies have compared the homicide rates of states that administer the death penalty with states that have abolished it. If the administration of executions were in fact a deterrent to capital crime, the murder rates in death penalty states should be significantly lower than those in the abolitionist states. It is worth noting that Texas, which far and away has the highest number of executions of all states (thirteen executions in 2011 and fifteen in 2012), had a homicide rate in 2012 (at 4.4 per 100,000 inhabitants) that is not much different from the national average (of 4.7). Louisiana, which also has the death penalty (although it does not execute as many people per capita as Texas), had an incredibly high murder rate in 2012 at 10.8 per 100,000. Meanwhile, Massachusetts and Minnesota, both of which have outlawed the death penalty, had murder rates in 2012 of 1.8. If the death penalty were working as an effective deterrent, one should think that Texas and Louisiana would at least rank closer in murder rates to Minnesota and Massachusetts. In 2012, about 35 percent of the executions in the United States occurred in Texas. Since capital punishment was reinstated in the United States in 1976, Texas has put over 500 people to death. In 2000, there were 85 executions in the United States, and Texas racked up 40 of them, its highest total of executions in recent years. Most executions in the United States occur in the South, yet it has a disproportionate share of the murders, given its population size, when compared to other regions of the country (see Table 6.11). According to Amnesty International, there are 58 countries that still actively retain the death penalty as a form of punishment, and of those, the countries with the most number of executions in 2012 included China (in the thousands, though it is difficult to estimate), followed by Iran (at least 314 or more), Iraq (at least 129 or more), Saudi Arabia (at least 79 or more), and the United States (43), then Sudan (at least 19 or more), Afghanistan (14), Gambia (9), Japan (7), and North Korea (at least 6 or more).[44] Out of the entire list of all countries worldwide that executed anyone in 2012, the only democratic industrialized country other than the United States to carry out executions was Japan. Most countries that executed people in 2012 were either dictatorial regimes or countries with poor records of human rights to begin with.

TABLE 6.11   **Percentage of Homicide Rates by Region, 2012**

	Percentage of U.S. Population	Percentage of Murders in the U.S.
Northeast	17.8%	14.2%
Midwest	21.4%	21.1%
West	23.4%	21.0%
South	37.4%	43.6%

SOURCE: U.S. Department of Justice, Federal Bureau of Investigation, *Crime in the United States, 2012.*

In 2014, 32 states, plus the U.S. government and the U.S. military, continue to provide for the death penalty by law. The death penalty has been abolished in the remaining eighteen states, most recently in New Mexico (2009), Illinois (2011), Connecticut (2012), and Maryland (2013). Table 6.12 compares murder rates in death penalty states to those in non–death penalty states. Contrary to expectations, the death penalty states in fact had slightly higher mean homicide rates than did the abolitionist states. These data clearly do not support the claim that the availability or exercise of capital punishment acts as a deterrent to the perpetration of murder.

This failure to find a significant impact of the death penalty on capital crime may be attributable in part to the fact that murder, the major capital offense is,

TABLE 6.12   **Murder Rates in Death Penalty and Non-Death Penalty States Compared**

Year	Death Penalty States Rates	Non-Death Penalty States Rates	(%) Difference
1991	9.94	9.27	7
1992	9.51	8.63	10
1993	9.69	8.81	10
1994	9.23	7.88	17
—	—	—	—
2005	5.87	4.03	46
2006	5.9	4.22	40
2007	5.83	4.10	42
2008	5.72	4.05	41
2009	5.26	3.90	35
2010	5.00	4.01	25
2011	4.89	4.13	18

SOURCE: http://www.deathpenaltyinfo.org/deterrence-states-without-death-penalty-have-had-consistently-lower-murder-rates.

relative to property crimes, one of intense passion. Whether much rational calculation goes on in the mind of a murderer about the probable costs (punishment) of the act is doubtful. It seems fair to conclude, then, that the death penalty as it may conceivably be practiced in the United States would not have a significant deterrent effect on the crime of murder. Therefore, the justification of capital punishment would have to rely on the retributive argument (an issue discussed shortly).

Capital Punishment and the Law.   The legal status of capital punishment itself has always been accepted by a majority of the Supreme Court. The Eighth Amendment prohibition of cruel and unusual punishment, however, does constrain the manner of execution. Reasonable people differ on what forms constitute cruelty. It is safe to presume that practices of medieval torture, such as the use of the rack or the screw, burning victims alive at the stake, drawing and quartering people, or crucifixion, would violate the amendment; however, beyond such obvious cases, states have been given wide latitude. Recent years have witnessed a trend in favor of adopting the method of lethal injection as the presumptively least painful execution method over other forms. All states have lethal injection as their primary method, but back-up methods or alternatives exist in some states either to allow the prisoner to choose, or to ensure that a method of execution exists in case lethal injection were ever declared unconstitutional. In the 2008 case of *Baze v. Rees,* the Supreme Court decided in a 7–2 vote that lethal injections (or at least, the three-drug cocktail employed in Kentucky) did not violate the Eighth Amendment's Cruel and Unusual Punishment. But, lethal injection has become more difficult for states to carry out because the European Union has banned the exportation of drugs to the United States for use in executions. With supplies of the drugs needed for executions dwindling, some states such as Texas have turned to private compounding pharmacies in order to concoct a deadly mix of drugs. This practice, however, is engendering a whole new series of litigation by defendants who face such new lethal drugs. Given the difficulties, some states are considering returning to older execution practices. As of the writing of this chapter, Missouri and Wyoming, for example, are considering readopting death by firing squad. Other states still have alternative methods on the books just in case lethal injections are ruled unconstitutional. Some of these states allow the prisoner to choose the method of his or her death. For example, among the eight states that have the electric chair as an alternative to lethal injection, four of them (Alabama, Florida, South Carolina, and Virginia) currently allow prisoners the choice of opting for the electric chair. In Utah, prisoners had the option (until 2004) to choose execution by a five-man firing squad. Ronnie Lee Gardner, who chose that method before the deadline, was executed by firing squad in June 2010. Although a few inmates have been grandfathered into the option in Utah and will be shot by firing squad, that state no longer allows the practice for any future death row inmates. Currently, only Oklahoma has execution by firing squad, and this is only available as a back-up method if lethal injection and electrocution were both declared unconstitutional. Given the controversy over a January 2014 lethal injection in

Oklahoma, in which the prisoner complained of his entire bodying "burning" after being injected with drugs, it is conceivable that the firing squad could return as the primary method of execution in Oklahoma as well.

Although practice and precedent in our common-law system support the legality of the death penalty itself, such common-law principles should also reflect "evolving community standards," a favorite phrase for those justices who argue for banning all or some portion of executions in the face of a long established legality of that punishment. Legal principles responsive to community standards have become more restrictive on the manner and circumstances of imposing the death penalty and categories of people to whom it should not be assigned, and it is in these areas that constitutional challenges to the death penalty have been based.

Capital murder is homicide for which the death penalty may be assessed. It is limited to premeditated murder and, since *Gregg v. Georgia* (1976), limited to certain types of premeditated murder, such as multiple killings, homicide committed in the course of another felony, or killing a police officer in the line of duty. Moreover, even conviction for capital murder in a death penalty jurisdiction far from guarantees that the death penalty will actually be assigned. In California, from 1950 to 1975, only 104 of the 2,111 persons convicted of capital murder were sentenced to die.[45] This raises the question of whether there are consistent criteria for determining why one murderer is sentenced to die and another is not, criteria based on the nature of the act itself.

Research shows that rather than the nature of the act, factors such as the defendant's race, socioeconomic status, or gender have proved to be better predictors of whether the death penalty will be assigned. African Americans have been executed in disproportionate numbers in American history, especially in Southern states. For instance, a study of executions in North Carolina from 1933 to 1937 showed eighty-one African Americans being executed, but only forty-five whites. A study of capital cases in Texas from 1924 to 1968 produced a higher percentage of convicted African Americans being executed than convicted whites, and the difference was statistically significant.[46] From 1930 to 1997, while African Americans made up only 12.5 percent of the population, they comprised 52 percent of those executed. In 2013, 13 African Americans were executed out of a total of 39 executions or 33 percent. These figures should be viewed in the context of the fact that African Americans are even more disproportionately likely to be convicted of murder. Furthermore, socioeconomic status has been an important determinant of suffering or avoiding the death penalty, because such status is related to the ability of one's lawyer. The disproportionate tendency for African Americans to suffer executions is shown in Table 6.13.

Such data on the impact of race constituted the bases of several challenges to the constitutionality of the death penalty. The Supreme Court under Chief Justice Rehnquist, however, did not appear to be receptive to such challenges, and the current Roberts court appears to be even less receptive. Most notably, in 1987, in *McCleskey v. Kemp*, the Court rejected the argument that the Georgia death penalty statute should be invalidated because the death penalty was more likely to be assigned when the victims of capital murder were white than when the victims were African American, as well as more likely when the perpetrators

T A B L E 6.13   **Executions by Race in the United States**

Year	Total	White	African American
1930–1997	4,291	2,016	2,228
1995	56	33	22
2005	60	38	19
2013	39	23	13

SOURCE: U.S. Department of Justice, Bureau of Justice Statistics, *Sourcebook of Criminal Justice Statistics, 2001* (Albany, NY: SUNY, Hindelang Criminal Justice Research Center), p. 560, updated via http://www.deathpenaltyinfo.org/executions-united-states.

were African American than when they were white. Julian Epstein, an aide to Michigan Representative John Conyers, reported a study of thirty-two states that revealed that killers of whites have an 11.1 percent chance of reaching death row, whereas the killers of African Americans have only a 4.5 percent chance. In some states, the discrepancy is even greater. For example, in Maryland, the killer of a white person is eight times more likely to receive the death penalty than the killer of an African American.[47] In another study, Professor Jack Boger and Dr. Isaac Unah of the University of North Carolina found that defendants whose victims are white are 3.5 times more likely to be sentenced to death than if the victims were black.[48]

Gender, though not widely discussed in this context, is perhaps an even better predictor than race. Women are far less likely to be assigned the death penalty than are men. From 1930 to 1967, of the 3,334 persons executed for murder in the United States, only 30 (or 0.8 percent) were women. Of course, such data should be seen in relation to a comparison of capital crime convictions of men with those of women. Unfortunately, such convictions are not broken down by gender in the available data. Statistics, however, do provide clues: in 1978, there were 12,736 arrests of men for murder and nonnegligent manslaughter (the index category that includes capital murder) and 2,234 such arrests of women. Because women, who accounted for about 17.5 percent of capital murder arrests, also accounted for less than 1 percent of the executions in earlier years, the conclusion that women are significantly less likely than men to be assigned the death penalty appears to be reasonable. Of the 3,122 prisoners under sentence of death in 1966, only 1.6 percent were women. In 1998, Texas—which has accounted for a third of the nation's executions since 1977—executed a woman, Karla Faye Tucker, for the first time in 135 years. Karla Faye Tucker had once claimed that she derived sexual pleasure with each blow of an ax to her two victims. She later claimed that she found God, and some religious groups sought to intervene on her behalf to stop the execution, but Governor George W. Bush declined that request.

Furman v. Georgia.   It was the importance of such determinants on who receives the death penalty—rather than the nature of the criminal act—that the Court found objectionable in the landmark case of *Furman v. Georgia* (1972), in which the Court laid down the first major explicit constitutional restraint on the practice of capital punishment in the United States.[49] A majority clearly rejected the notion that capital punishment is inherently cruel and unusual, but five justices agreed that it was cruel and unusual as it was then practiced in this country. There is no single pattern of reasoning to be discerned in these five diverse opinions, but one concept is that the imposition of capital punishment shall not be arbitrary. That is, its imposition must be on consistent criteria grounded in the nature of the criminal act.

Technology, Deterrence, and Crime

Whatever gains the criminally accused have made against the police in the rights revolution must necessarily be discounted by the enormous gains in technology made by police over the last two decades, both in forensic science and computerized technology. In forensic science, DNA analysis in crimes has improved remarkably since the 1990s. States have created DNA databases to house the DNA and fingerprints of prisoners and suspects indefinitely. Police employ experts in footwear impressions, tire tracks, fingerprints, ballistics, handwriting analysis, etc. Many of these tools allow police to catch criminals in crimes that otherwise would go unsolved. Furthermore, these advances have helped clear innocent people who were wrongfully convicted based on faulty evidence or unreliable eyewitness testimony.[50]

Other recent technological advancements in computers, cellphones, GPS tracking, and cameras provide further tools for police. In fact, cars, iPods, and cellphones come with GPS tracking options which do not allow a potential thief to get very far with your device. The near ubiquity of cellphone cameras and the relatively cheap cost of employing security cameras in businesses mean that oftentimes police can obtain pictures of the perpetrator of a crime. In the United Kingdom, the government has installed large numbers of "CCTV" (closed-circuit) cameras around public places all over the country in order to both deter and solve crime. In general, the U.S. government has declined to place a large number of cameras in public, though some people have called for such plans as a way to reduce crime.

Incarceration Rates

Incarceration has perhaps been the main policy promoted by conservatives in the Republican and Democratic parties as a way of stemming the crime wave that began in the 1970s and peaked in the 1990s. If criminals could not be deterred from committing crimes, another policy alternative would be to simply lock them up for a long period of time. In fact, that is what has happened in the United States over the last several decades. As crime rates have dropped, the prison population has increased, as illustrated by Table 6.14. In 1973, there were about 200,000 people sitting in federal or state prisons or local jails. In 1995, the number had risen to 1.58 million people. This amounted to an incarceration rate in the United States of around 592 people incarcerated for every 100,000 people. By 2012, that number had climbed to over 2.2 million Americans in jail, with an

TABLE 6.14   Trends in the U.S. Prison Population, 1995–2012

Year	Population*	Rate of Incarceration per 100,000 People
1995	1,585,600	592
2000	1,938,500	689
2005	2,195,000	743
2010	2,270,100	735
2011	2,240,600	719
2012	2,228,400	710

*These figures are estimated and rounded by the Bureau to the nearest 100. Data from 1995 come from the International Centre for Prison Studies, a partner of the University of Essex, http://www.prisonstudies.org/country/united-states-america.

SOURCE: Bureau of Justice Statistics, *Correctional Populations in the United States, 2012*, http://www.bjs.gov/content/pub/pdf/cpus12.pdf.

incarceration rate of 710. Not surprisingly, the expanding prison population has created overcrowding issues in state and federal prisons. In 2011, the U.S. Supreme Court ordered the state of California to reduce its prison population to 137.5 percent above the intended capacity of the prisons.

The full scale of this incarceration can be seen when one includes persons on probation or parole. In 2012, 6.93 million people in the United States, or about 2 percent of the entire population, were in some form of the correctional system, either in jail, on probation, or on parole. The number of people incarcerated in the United States far exceeds almost any other country, with the possible exception of China, whose actual prison population is difficult to know, because some people in China are put (euphemistically) into administrative detention or work camps instead of prison (see Table 6.15). Most Western democracies have prison rates that are typically seven times smaller than the United States. Germany's rate is only 77, Denmark 73, and England and Wales 149. The closest Western democracy to the United States in terms of prison rates was Lithuania. Many of the major countries that rank high in terms of rates of prison populations are serial violators of human rights, such as Cuba, Russia, and Iran. Most Europeans, observes one scholar, react "with horror" at America's system of punishment and prisons.[51]

There are several possible reasons as to why a democracy such as the United States locks up so many people. Americans are very different socially from other democratic societies in many respects. America is the only industrialized society that holds strongly religious beliefs, as most other Western democracies have become very secular societies. And Americans have an attitude of "rugged individualism" which puts a premium morally and financially on individual responsibility. Finally, Americans had been experiencing an unprecedented crime wave up through the 1990s. In such a society, the advocating of harsh punishments for criminals wins votes for politicians. Furthermore, unlike other countries, America largely elects its judges. State judges who appear soft on crime will routinely be

TABLE 6.15   Countries with the Most Prisoners, 2012

Country	Rate of Incarceration per 100,000 People	Prison Population
United States	710	2,228,400
Cuba	510	57,337
Russia	472	677,200
Lithuania	329	9,729
Iran	284	217,000
Mexico	210	246,226
United Kingdom: England and Wales	149	84,977
China*	124	1,701,344
Canada	118	40,544
France	100	67,050
Germany	77	63,317
Denmark	73	4,091
India	30	385,135

*Given the secret nature of the Communist Chinese government, it is difficult to know the actual number, as these official estimates are likely lower than the real count.

SOURCE: The International Centre for Prison Studies, a partner of the University of Essex, http://www.prisonstudies.org/highest-to-lowest. For U.S. data, see Bureau of Justice Statistics, Correctional Populations in the United States, 2012, http://www.bjs.gov/content/pub/pdf/cpus12.pdf.

voted out of office. Not surprisingly, studies show that in states that elect their judges, those same judges are more likely to vote for the death penalty, because to do otherwise could imperil their reelection.[52] In their reelection campaigns, American judges often focus on issues that show their ability to be tough on criminals.[53] These facts are not a criticism of electing judges, as such a system has both its advantages and disadvantages. Rather, the behavior of elected judges is really a reflection of the social norms largely present in American society regarding the punishment of criminals.

POLICY EVALUATION: FLAWS IN THE CRIMINAL JUSTICE SYSTEM?

In the preceding section, we examined the evolution of contemporary policy in the area of constitutional rights and the deterrence of crime, as well as the new realities of criminal justice in terms of the advancement of technology and the change in the prison population. In the next section, we analyze both the flaws and benefits of these policies.

Confessions and the Right to Counsel

As already seen, *Miranda v. Arizona* pointed up the legal ramifications of not informing a suspect of his or her rights before entering any confession or damaging statement as evidence. Many feared that the rights of the accused would be excessively protected at the expense of obtaining an otherwise valid confession and swift punishment.

Some argue that the fears by conservatives (or hopes by liberals, for that matter) of *Miranda* having a significant impact on law enforcement appear unfounded.[54] According to judicial scholar and political scientist Gerald Rosenberg, the empirical evidence suggests that "While warnings appear to be given routinely, and counsel is provided, *Miranda*'s effect on law enforcement has been negligible."[55] According to Rosenberg, some suspects continue to talk to police even after being informed of their rights, and to some extent, some of the worst practices of police brutality to force confessions were already disappearing from police forces even before *Miranda* had been decided. Yet even after *Miranda*, Rosenberg notes that police brutality still occurs and argues that the "evidence strongly suggests that the confession rate did not change because the *Miranda* warnings were unable to alter [the] imbalance" of power between police and suspect.[56] To illustrate Rosenberg's point, one study found that a third of eighty-five defendants processed did not choose even to avail themselves of the services of a lawyer on hand in the police station for that purpose; 75 percent of the defendants did not exercise their option for counsel other than the station house counsel; and 40 percent chose to make incriminating statements after having waived their *Miranda* rights.[57] These somewhat startling data become explicable in the light of the findings in the same study that 15 percent of the eighty-five defendants failed to understand their right to remain silent, 18 percent did not understand their right to the presence of counsel at that time, and 24 percent failed to understand that the state would appoint counsel at its expense.

Not everyone agrees with all of Rosenberg's conclusions. Others have found that *Miranda* may have lowered the rate at which confessions are obtained in the first place. One study found that in Pittsburgh in 1964, the police obtained confessions in 54.5 percent of the cases before *Miranda* procedures were implemented and in only 37.5 percent of the cases after the procedure was implemented.[58] Moreover, studies of the frequency of suppressing confessions on *Miranda* grounds do not take into account cases dismissed in preliminary stages or arrests not made because of the requirements of the *Miranda* rule.[59]

A related question is the extent to which confessions are necessary to dispose of cases. The *Miranda* case illustrates this point. The victim's bloodstained effects were found in Miranda's car; Miranda could not account for his whereabouts at the time the crime occurred; and he was identified by the victim. Hence, Miranda confessed when confronted with an overwhelming case against him. When the Supreme Court quashed the conviction on the admissibility of the confession, it did not acquit Miranda. Rather, when the Court nullifies a conviction on constitutional grounds, it is saying that there is a problem with the manner in which the conviction was obtained, but the Court is not determining guilt or innocence. The case is remanded back to the prosecution, which may then choose to retry the accused in a manner consistent with the Supreme Court ruling. Miranda was in fact convicted on other evidence.

The point is that if the only ground for conviction is a confession obtained from an uninformed suspect under the psychological stress of an intense interrogation, the possibility exists that the suspect may in fact be innocent. If the accused is guilty, there should be a good chance that physical evidence or witnesses can be found to implicate him or her in the crime without a pressured confession. Moreover, when it is easy to pressure a confession from any plausible suspect, police may be tempted to use that technique to avoid the difficulty of seeking evidence to find out who really committed the crime. In this respect, the *Miranda* rule helps protect against government overreach.

The Exclusionary Rule and Search and Seizure

We have already discussed the immediate importance of *Mapp v. Ohio*; that is, that the due process clause of the Fourteenth Amendment requires the exclusion from court of *illegally* obtained evidence. In effect, the Court rejected the argument that the exclusionary rule only protects the guilty; instead, it felt that if illegally obtained evidence is inadmissible, there is no motive for police to make illegal searches of the guilty or the innocent. Chief Justice Burger, who came onto the Court after the *Mapp* decision, disagreed, however, with such conclusions about *Mapp*'s effects. In his attack on the exclusionary rule, he made two claims: that it has a negative effect on successful prosecutions and that there is no evidence that it has a countervailing effect of deterring illegal police behavior.

But the empirical story is much more complicated. The reality is that it is difficult to prove statistically how and in what way *Mapp* has affected police practices: studies offer conflicting accounts of its effects. According to data cited by judicial politics scholar Stephen Wasby, Burger was wrong on both counts. With regard to Burger's fears that *Mapp* will allow guilty people to "get away with it," Wasby did note a substantial decrease of some 41 percent in the number of suspects actually reaching trial in New York in 1961, immediately following *Mapp*. He found, however, that the rate of successful prosecutions rose again the following year, suggesting that police were becoming adjusted to the new constraints on their behavior. Political scientist Stuart Nagel also found increased police adherence to the rules on legal searches and seizures.[60]

Political scientist and judicial scholar Bradley Canon looked at the rate of arrests for search and seizure offenses that occurred for several years before and after the *Mapp* case in nineteen cities. He found that about one-third of cities showed a decline in arrests for these types of offenses, leading him to conclude that the exclusionary rule "works sometimes."[61] But, as public law scholar Donald Horowitz has pointed out, Canon's findings do not say what proportion of those arrests after *Mapp* were illegal, and so cannot tell us whether illegal arrests declined. Horowitz also notes that, "Canon's findings could also be consistent with a continuing pattern of unlawful searches accompanied by greater discrimination in the making of arrests."[62] As Horowitz sees it, *Mapp* does not control police harassment of suspects, when police engage in illegal searches that do not result in an arrest. Furthermore, the case has encouraged some police to engage in false testimony or perjury in order to justify their search under the Fourth Amendment. Thus, *Mapp* has had consequences rather unintended by the Supreme Court majority, which authored the case. Still, Horowitz believes that the Canon study does indicate that police behavior did change to some extent after *Mapp*, but the effects are difficult to measure because states and locales have varied in the strictness with which they have applied the *Mapp* ruling. Police training also varies widely, and some police may not be aware of the rules of *Mapp*. Moreover, in many departments, there are no sanctions for engaging in illegal searches and seizures. In terms of Burger's assertions that many guilty would go free, Horowitz and others do not see much evidence that this happened. The dictates of the Supreme Court are not self-enforcing; the mere handing down of a ruling does not automatically alter behavior. That is why there is a growing body of research on the compliance with and the impact of such rulings.

Capital Punishment

After *Furman* outlawed capital punishment as practiced, but invited new statutes to conform to the standard of not being arbitrary, many states passed new laws that listed specific mitigating and aggravating circumstances as guides to be considered in deciding whether to assign the death penalty in a particular case, rather than making the imposition of the penalty mandatory for an entire category of crimes.[63] The legality of capital punishment applied in this way was explicitly reaffirmed by the Court. Liberals expressed the fear that this would bring about a flood of executions. The rate did increase, especially in the southern states (Texas and Louisiana alone accounted for 224 of the 598 executions carried out between 1977 and 1999), but the increase has slowed in recent years because of fears of the execution of innocent persons, intellectually disabled persons, and minors.

Debating Capital Punishment.   The capital punishment issue epitomizes widespread confusion with regard to the purposes of punishment. Although capital punishment is usually defended in terms of its deterrent effect, it is clear from the discussion earlier that capital punishment, as it can conceivably be practiced in the United States, is unlikely to have any significant deterrent effect on crime. It is possible, however, that many of those who defend capital punishment on deterrence grounds are really concerned about maintaining its role in retribution. The Court has explicitly said that retribution is a constitutionally valid purpose of punishment, stating in *Gregg v. Georgia* (1976) that

> … capital punishment is an expression of the society's moral outrage at
> particularly offensive conduct. This function may be unappealing to
> many, but it is essential in an ordered society that asks its citizens to rely
> on legal processes rather than self-help to vindicate their wrongs.…
> Retribution is no longer the dominant objective of the criminal law but
> neither is it a forbidden objective.

Many claim that the Eighth Amendment ought to be interpreted as banning capital punishment *per se*, but much of this argument is framed in ethical terms. Justices Brennan and Marshall, in making this argument, repeatedly evoked "the evolving standards of decency that mark the progress of a maturing society" to argue that a penalty that was permissible at one point in our history is no longer permissible today.[64] The precise content, however, of such "evolving standards of decency" is a subjective judgment on which reasonable people may disagree. The issue of whether the Eighth Amendment does or should prohibit capital punishment becomes instead the defining issue of how morally abhorrent capital punishment has become.

Execution of Minors.   The constitutionality of applying the death penalty to capital crimes committed while the perpetrator was a minor has been a hotly debated issue since the 1980s. Opponents characterized the practice as "killing our children" and pointed out that the United States was virtually the only remaining Western nation that executes teenagers. By 2005, thirty states prohibited the execution of minors. The presumption of these opponents was that minors are not fully aware of the nature and consequences of their actions; therefore, they should not be held as fully responsible for their actions as are adults. Justice Kennedy's opinion in the *Roper* case stresses that a worldwide consensus against the execution of minors had evolved; hence, Kennedy argued that we ought to interpret our constitution in the light of that consensus. In that case, *Roper v. Simmons* (2005), Kennedy, speaking for the Court, found that evolving standards of decency and world opinion entail the conclusion that the execution of a person for a crime committed before the age of eighteen violates the Eighth Amendment ban on "cruel and unusual punishment." Kennedy's opinion reversed *Stanford v. Connecticut* (1989), which held that the execution of sixteen- and seventeen-year-olds was not constitutionally barred.[65]

Those who support the application of the death penalty in such cases argue that violent and even vicious crimes increasingly are committed by teenagers. As noted earlier in this chapter, crime is to a large extent a young person's phenomenon; therefore, the policy of protecting the very sector of the population most likely to commit serious crimes from serious punishment weakens whatever deterrent effect that punishment might have.

Limits on the Death Penalty.   Although there remains significant public support for the retention of the death penalty, that support has declined over the years from a high of 80 percent in 1994 (during the peak of the violent crime wave) to 60 percent in 2012.[66] And the Court has established a general trend of circumscribing its application of death without invalidating the penalty itself. For example, in *Maynard v. Cartwright* (1988), the Court struck down an Oklahoma death-penalty statute on the grounds that the state's phrasing of aggravating circumstances as crimes that are "especially heinous, atrocious or cruel" was unconstitutionally vague.[67]

This trend of circumscribing the death penalty has been balanced by the tendency of the more conservative Court beginning with the 1990s to pull back from its previous defendant's rights emphasis, perhaps informed by the public's demand for a greater stress on victim's rights. This pullback began with *McCleskey v. Zant* (1991), which overruled the 1987 case of *Booth v. Maryland* and allowed victims' impact statements to be read with regard to sentencing decisions.[68] The *McCleskey* decision permitted statements read by the families of a murder victim testifying as to the devastating impact of their loss on their lives, statements that were followed by a death sentence to McCleskey. The liberal defense position continued to be that such statements constitute an emotional appeal that is extraneous to the hard facts of the case and therefore ought not to be salient in the assignment of appropriate punishment. Information about difficulties and deprivations in the background of the convicted perpetrator, however, have long been admissible in sentencing decisions.

As noted earlier, reservations about the death penalty have been reinforced in recent years with the introduction of DNA evidence into the criminal trial process. This genetic material often enables one to resolve questions of guilt or innocence definitively. DNA evidence has overturned several long-standing and seemingly solid death penalty convictions by proving that the condemned persons were innocent of the crime for which they were convicted. Renewed awareness of the reality of mistakes in the criminal process causes a reluctance to impose so final a punishment as death.

Is Technology Always Infallible?

DNA evidence and other advances in forensic science have changed the system of criminal justice. Sometimes DNA can offer definitive proof of a crime whereas eyewitness testimony is often unreliable. Such advancements in technology, however, are not without problems. If not dealt with carefully and diligently, the science of forensics can also create grave injustices. First, crime scenes can become contaminated. Concerns about DNA contamination in the case of American Amanda Knox, who was accused of killing her roommate in Italy in 2007, initially led to her conviction being overturned on appeal in the Italian courts (though at her retrial, these concerns were more or less ignored). Second, some forensic science is still not as clear-cut as one would think. The Innocence Project estimates that in 50 percent of cases where DNA exonerated a defendant, the underlying conviction had been obtained using "unvalidated or improper forensic science."[69] A number of cases convicting defendants based on bite-mark evidence have turned out to be in error, and in some, crime labs workers lack proper training.[70] Crime labs can also potentially mishandle DNA and other evidence. *Slate* magazine ran a story about how Massachusetts had to go back and review 34,000 cases and throw out over 1,000 convictions after a Boston chemist was accused of mishandling evidence during her nine years of employment in the state lab.[71] TV shows such as *Forensic Files* and *Body of Evidence: From the Case Files of Dayle Hinman* popularize the almost infallibility of forensic evidence, and thus it may be difficult to convince jurors that the persons behind this science can sometimes make mistakes. It is similar to a police officer who has captured you speeding on his radar. Even if you have reason to believe that the officer incorrectly deployed the electronic device or was not properly trained, it is extremely difficult to convince a jury that the computer (or person in position of authority) was somehow wrong about your speed.

Other types of technology deployed in police work to track our movements, record our activities, or collect information on our private life raise a different set of issues about not only the costs of policing but also the nature of our democracy and rights. Private security cameras and cellphone cameras have in many ways offered a good deal of help in criminal investigations where in earlier times there might be little other evidence. The presence of cameras is also thought to help deter crime as well. But Americans are a bit more wary of government deploying large-scale use of cameras around society. One concern about this practice is the shear cost to society. Britain's CCTV cameras have led some to complain that the cost of these systems is too much for the benefit. An internal report for the London Metropolitan Police found that "for every 1,000 cameras in London, less than one crime is solved per year" and that when CCTV cameras *do* help in a case, it costs an extra $33,000.[72] When considering the hundreds of millions of dollars that the U.K. government spends on this system, some wonder whether the money could have been better spent on improving street lighting or better neighborhood crime prevention initiatives.[73]

Deploying massive numbers of cameras in public in the United States, which is a much larger country geographically compared to Britain, not only seems a bit implausible from a financial standpoint, but also may not be consistent with our constitutional values. These constitutional limitations on police work also apply to some extent to GPS tracking by police. In the 2012 case of *U.S. v. Jones*, police attached a GPS tracker to the defendant's car and recorded his every move 24 hours a day for four weeks.[74] The Supreme Court found this a violation of the defendant's Fourth Amendment rights because it included a physical trespass, but left unclear how much privacy protection people have regarding the privacy of electronic data. As discussed earlier, the amount of legal protection Americans have to their privacy from government searches in the realm of cellphone use and Internet activities is still somewhat unclear. Currently, the NSA is building a multi-million dollar facility in Utah in order to house all of the information they are collecting on Americans' metadata activities on cellphones and the Internet. In the privacy rights debate over the collection of large amounts of electronic data on Americans by the NSA, most people have little to fear that they will somehow be labeled an "enemy combatant" and shipped off to a military detention center. Rather, the greater concern by privacy advocates is that this information might eventually make its way to general law enforcement or even worse, to a party or group of people in control of government who might use the information to go after political opponents. Thus, while law enforcement would always love more information, and undoubtedly more information would combat crime, it is not clear in a free and democratic society that more information is desirable, no matter how helpful it is in combating crime.

POLICY DILEMMAS   The Debate over Drugs and Incarceration Policies

Incarceration rates are up and crime is down in America. The Obama administration has slowly started to change the track of the incarceration policies of previous Republican and Democratic administrations alike. Here, we consider the effectiveness of the policy of mass incarceration and the dilemmas associated with the practice.

A large segment of the prison population in America is serving time for drug-related crimes. According to the Bureau of Justice Statistics, nearly half (48 percent) of all people serving in federal prison in 2011 were there due to drug offenses compared to 17 percent of prisoners in state prison.[75] Thus, large segments of the prison population consist of people who have committed drug crimes, and many of those are nonviolent offenders. As incarceration has increased, crime has gone down, but correlation does not always equal causation. Scholars dispute whether the correlation is meaningful or not, and even if it is, whether such policies are appropriate in a free society.

Conservatives and liberals in both parties have begun to rethink the "lock'em up" policies of the past decades. In 2010, President Obama signed the Fair Sentencing Act, which reduced the huge sentencing disparities between powdered and crack cocaine, disparities that fell disproportionately on minorities. In policy statements released by the President's Office of National Drug Control Policy, the Obama administration made aware its support for drug courts, to steer drug offenders away from prison and into treatment programs.[76] The White House and many state Republican leaders have also voiced their support for veterans' courts, as many in society believe that soldiers who return home from the battlefields in Iraq and Afghanistan and have trouble adjusting to society need mental health treatment, not prison time. In 2014, the Obama administration and libertarian-minded Republicans, such as U.S. Senators Rand Paul (Kentucky) and Mike Lee (Utah), began to work together to pass legislation aimed at softening the harshness of drug sentences by cutting them dramatically for nonviolent offenders.[77] The Obama administration also began moves in late 2013 and early 2014 to use the president's pardoning power more frequently to correct injustices in sentencing of nonviolent drug offenders.[78] But will easing the prison population produce more crime?

From a public policy standpoint of reducing crime, increased incarceration rates appear on the surface to be effective. If criminals are locked up, then it is hard for them to engage in crime—the "incapacitation thesis" as it is called. As recounted earlier in the chapter, some hardcore drug addicts engage in crime to feed their addiction. On the other hand, locking away nonviolent drug offenders costs money and leaves less space in prisons for more violent offenders. Finally, even if mass incarceration is effective at cutting crime, a governmental system in a democracy needs legitimacy to survive politically. Consider the earlier figures in the chapter about peoples' confidence in the criminal justice system. Among criminologists, there is no clear answer whether incarceration works or not.[79]

1.   Consider the "tough on crime" incarceration policies of past presidential administrations compared to the criminal justice policies of most other democracies in the world. Why has America responded differently to the problems of crime in the past compared to other democracies?

2.   In thinking about crime in the future, would you change any policies toward sentencing and incarceration or is the present system operating effectively?

Conclusion: Crime and Criminal Procedure

Although America's prisons are overflowing (and people who end up in American prison stay there longer than in other countries), it is still not easy to get into prison. It is important to keep in mind that in our criminal justice system, the theoretical route from criminal act to punishment is marked by numerous exit points, only one of which is an overturned conviction due to the expansion of defendants' rights (see Figure 6.3).

A justice system that lacks the swiftness or certainty of punishment might hobble deterrence. First, the rights of the accused can only come into play *after* a suspect is arrested. In fact, however, it is unlikely that any given criminal act will ever lead to an arrest. Even before the rise in crime rates in the 1960s and 1970s, one scholar estimated about twelve arrests for every one hundred crimes in the United States.[80] James Q. Wilson claims that the odds are fourteen to one that the perpetrator of any given felony will not be caught.[81] In any event, the chances that a given criminal act will never lead to an encounter with the criminal justice process are extremely high, probably over 90 percent; therefore, the nature and content of that process remain largely irrelevant to crime deterrence. Recall that there are *at least* twice as many crimes as are reported. In 2012, as reported in Table 6.16, about 22 percent of crimes for larceny-theft were cleared. Clearance rates tabulated by the FBI's report refer to instances where law enforcement solves the crime and the case is closed out. A cleared case does not mean the accused was put in jail, it basically only means that the case was solved by police and presumably the file was turned over to the prosecutor's office for further action. Let us assume that in the mythical city of X in State Y, there were 200 larcenies that year, and as previously noted, studies indicate that only about half of crimes are actually reported to the police (thus only 100 larcenies are reported to police in mythical City X). If only 20 percent of reported larcenies are cleared by law enforcement, that would mean that only 10 percent of all larcenies (i.e., 20 cases out of 200 in City X) get resolved by the police. That suggests that few crimes are ever really resolved. Even after law

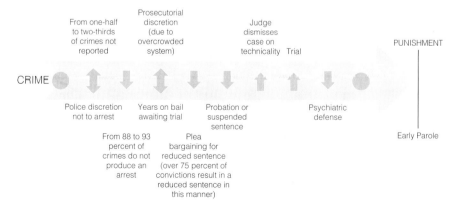

FIGURE 6.3 Exit Points in the Criminal Justice System

TABLE 6.16   Percent of Offenses Cleared, 2012

Type of Crime	Percentage Cleared
Murder	62.5
Aggravated assault	55.8
Forcible rape	40.1
Robbery	28.1
Total violent crimes	46.8
Larceny-theft	22
Motor vehicle theft	11.9
Burglary	12.7
Total property crimes	19

enforcement "clears" the crime, the accused criminal may still avoid punishment through any number of escape hatches listed in Figure 6.3, either through a prosecutor's or grand jury's decision not to bring a case, a plea deal, dismissal by the judge, acquittal at trial, early parole, etc.

A second factor detracting from the deterrent effect of punishment is the bail system together with the delay of trial. In those cases coming to trial, everyone except those accused of the most heinous capital crimes is accorded the option of posting bail and remaining free until the trial. For a large percentage of the accused who can afford the cost of bail, punishment is postponed until after the trial—and sometimes until after a series of appeals. Given the slowness with which our overburdened judicial system operates, punishment could and often does take years. Yet it is the swiftness and certainty of punishment that most deter crime. Studies show that from 30 percent to 70 percent of robbery suspects out on bail are rearrested for the commission of other crimes.[82]

As the clearance rates shown in Table 6.16 indicate, the overwhelming preponderance of crimes is not cleared. Violent crimes showed a significantly higher clearance rate for 2012 (46.8 percent, including 62.5 percent for murder), however, compared to the clearance rate for property crimes (19 percent). The possible explanation for this discrepancy is violent crimes are investigated more vigorously and such crimes often leave a victim who can identify the perpetrator; however, less than half of even violent crimes are cleared.

Finally, because of the overcrowded nature of the judicial system, 95 percent of convictions within one year of arrest are obtained through plea bargaining; about 80 percent of these convictions involve a felony. This fact also gives potential criminals reason to believe that they can escape serious punishment even if they are caught.

Given all of these exit points in the system, it is clear that the expansion of defendants' rights during the Warren Court played only a very small role in impeding or postponing the punishment of those who commit serious crimes.

In other words, even if we returned to a pre-expansion of rights period before the rulings of *Miranda* or *Mapp*, there is no reason to believe justice would be swift and operate as a useful deterrence against crime. On the other hand, these rights do help protect the innocent and enhance the perception of the system as a just one, thereby contributing to the legitimacy of the system. It can be concluded that the restriction of defendants' rights does not offer a cost-efficient method for controlling crime. However, alternative policy options do exist, and these will be explored in the following section.

CONTINUING DEBATES: POLICY OPTIONS FOR REDUCING CRIME

One obvious goal of public policy aimed at reducing crime is to increase the cost of illegal activity to the criminal, a result that a classic economic model predicts should reduce the quantity of crime.[83] These costs include material costs, time costs, and psychic costs as well as the familiar costs of expected punishment.

For example, encouraging, or even requiring, increased security devices in homes and businesses can add both to the time and the materials needed to commit a crime. Logically, it may be surmised that if the perceived opportunities for earning a better return by noncriminal means exceeds the opportunities for the return from crime (breaking into the now electronically secure business has become too much trouble), assuming an equal expenditure of time and effort, the potential criminal would find it rational to opt for noncriminal pursuits and crime would be reduced. (This kind of analysis points to an oft-cited conclusion: Programs to reduce unemployment and to provide jobs for the most crime-prone segments of the population would cut crime.)

The logic of this argument presumes that criminals are rational, economically motivated beings. This assumption is only imperfectly valid. It would most likely apply to property crimes, but crimes against persons are frequently acts of passion or anger or are conducted by sociopaths who are not interested in pursuing rational economic rewards. Even in the case of some property crimes the economic assumption remains imperfectly valid, most notably in crimes to support drug addiction.

Drug-Related Crimes

Estimates vary on what proportion of street crime (for example, mugging, robbery, and auto theft) is committed to support an addiction to illegal drugs; however, such estimates uniformly place the figure at over half and sometimes as high as three-quarters. As explained earlier, the high cost of addictive drugs on the illegal market combined with an inflexible and economically inelastic demand for such drugs almost requires the addict to commit crimes to support the addiction. Clearly, a reduction in the extent of drug addiction should lead to a reduction in crimes against property.

Attacking Supply.   The first strategy to reduce drug addiction—and perhaps the most popular to the public—is to try to intercept the supply, usually referred to as a "war on drugs." Though the heroic efforts of federal agents to catch drug smugglers, punish them, and confiscate their wares make sensational newspaper headlines, such efforts do not have a positive impact on the extent of drug addiction. The supply may be temporarily diminished, an unintended consequence of which raises the price of the remaining available drugs. The demand for drugs, however, is not sensitive to price, at least among chronic users. Therefore, the higher price probably has the effect of driving addicts to commit more crime in order to afford the higher prices, as recounted earlier.

Efforts to intercept the drug supply can never be completely successful. The nation's borders are too extensive, and the many ways of concealing smuggled illegal drugs make thorough searches impractical. Furthermore, the stakes are so high and the potential profits so great that there will always be someone willing to take virtually any risk or go to any lengths to supply the drugs.

Indeed, with the amount of money at stake, law enforcement officials can frequently be bought off. This is the case just across the border in Mexico, over which a large portion of illegal drugs enter. The high stakes have given rise to an escalating degree of violence among rival drug gangs. According to one 2010 *El Paso Times* article, the violence across the border has been so high that there were more homicides in Juarez (4,992) between 2008 and April 2010 than there were U.S. military deaths in Iraq since 2003.[84] There is, indeed, increasing skepticism about relying heavily on "drug war" tactics. In fact, Washington and Colorado legalized the sale of marijuana in referendums in 2012, a clear democratic disapproval of some aspects of the drug war. As seen by the Obama administration's approach to drug policy, there is a growing sentiment to approach drugs as a physical and mental health matter and to find different strategies to stem the demand for illegal substances.

Attacking Demand.   A second strategy in dealing with the drug problem is to attempt to prevent addiction in the first place and to rehabilitate addicts when prevention fails. This means assigning criminal addicts to a hospital-type facility rather than a prison. Here, addicts receive psychological counseling in conjunction with medically supervised withdrawal. Yet early studies placed the failure rate of such programs at well over 90 percent.[85] Drug courts, which specialize in alternative treatment programs, have become quite popular and have been promoted by the Obama administration. Some studies show that these courts do reduce the rearrest rate when compared to the regular prison and parole system, but it is not clear how effective they are. Moreover, addicts frequently return to heroin use even years after withdrawal.

Violence against Women

The crime of rape and other forms of violence against women have come into increasing focus in recent years, due in part to the rising prominence of the feminist movement.

Technically, rape consists of using force or the threat of force to obtain sexual interaction with another person against his or her will. Rape has come to be widely perceived not merely as a means of obtaining sexual gratification but rather as an extreme manner of expressing hostility toward women (misogyny). Far more often than not sexual aggression occurs within the context of courtship or friendship relationships (called "acquaintance rape" or "date rape") or even that of marriage. Susan Brownmiller, in *Against Our Will*, calls rape "nothing more than a conscious process of intimidation by which all men keep all women in a state of fear."[86]

Rape is an ongoing problem in American society, but along with other types of crime, it has seen a marked decrease in the last two decades (see Figure 6.4). Rape is 18 percent lower when compared to 1999 levels and is down over 37 percent since 1992. There were noticeable regional variations in rape, with the Midwest in 2012 showing the highest levels of rape at 31.7 per 100,000 people (followed by the West at 27.5, the South at 27.1, and the Northeast, which had a rate of only 19.7 per 100,000 people, far fewer than any other region). The number of rapes was down from 2011 to 2012 in the South and West but had increased in the Northeast and Midwest (see Table 6.17).

There can be no disagreement that men, who are typically stronger than women, all too frequently beat their wives and girlfriends, though estimates of this behavior are hard to determine. At the high end of the estimates, some have publicly alleged that as many as 4 million women are regularly beaten by their male partners. Others, including some feminists, dispute that estimate. Two sociologists who specialize in domestic violence, Murray Strauss and Richard Gelles, conducted a survey in which they found that fewer than

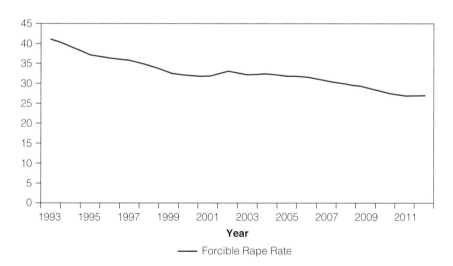

FIGURE 6.4 Rates of Forcible Rape in the United States per 100,000 Population, 1993–2012

SOURCE: http://www.fbi.gov/ucr/cius2008/index.html

T A B L E 6.17   Percent Change in Rates of Forcible Rape, 2011–2012

Total	−0.5%
Northeast	+0.8%
Midwest	+1.2%
South	−1.3%
West	−1.8%

SOURCE: U.S. Department of Justice, Bureau of Federal Investigation, *Preliminary Uniform Crime Reports*, December 2012, http://www.fbi.gov/ucr/ucr.htm.

5 percent of the families surveyed experience what they call "extreme violence," which would include punching and kicking.[87] These figures appear low, however, when compared to other studies. The Centers for Disease Control and Prevention (CDC) reports that 24 percent of women and 13 percent of men aged eighteen and older have experienced "severe physical violence by an intimate partner."[88] As for murder, the same CDC report states that in 2010, there were 241 men and 1,091 women murdered by an intimate partner. The public today is more aware that domestic violence is a serious public issue and not the private family matter that police, in the past, all too frequently regarded as none of their business.

Despite its vicious and exploitive nature, the crime of rape presents unique problems for the criminal justice system, which is, after all, dedicated to providing due process for those accused of even the most heinous acts. With an expanded definition of rape, it confounds a *sine qua non* of criminal law: that the behavior being proscribed is precisely defined. For sexual activity to be rape, it must occur against the will of the victim. Prosecutions for rape have always been weakened by problems of evidence and especially by the ages-old myth of implied consent, that is, the assumption or the assertion that although the woman said no, she must really have meant yes. Moreover, even expressed consent is frequently held by some to be implicitly coerced by the asymmetrical power relationship between men and women, a position reported by law professor Susan Estrich, who indicates, "Many feminists would argue that so long as women are powerless relative to men, viewing yes as a sign of true consent is misguided."[89]

Crimes of Violence and Gun Control

Drug-related crimes are primarily crimes against property, that is, theft in order to support expensive addictions. Of course, violence is frequently involved in such crimes as a means of obtaining the economic benefit. When the violence becomes the end in itself, the causes and the means of combating such crime are quite different from those in the case of crimes against property.

When the goal of the crime is material gain, a certain amount of rational calculation—cost-benefit analysis—may indeed go into the decision to commit the crime. Even drug-related crimes, with the addict's inelastic demand, can be curbed by removing the pusher's economic incentive and the addict's economic need. When the goal of the criminal act is violence to another person, however, the element of rational calculation diminishes. Although there may be certain psychic benefits that accrue to the perpetrator of a crime of violence, it is doubtful whether much rational calculation is involved.

A 2007 Small Arms Survey showed that the United States, with less than 5 percent of the world's population, accounted for 35 to 50 percent of the world's civilian-owned guns. U.S. civilians are estimated to own 270 million firearms as of 2007, about eighty-nine guns per 100 people. And these figures are probably only increasing. A 2011 Gallup survey found self-reported gun ownership was at its highest levels since 1993.[90] Contrast this to England and Wales, which has about six guns per 100 people or Spain, which has about ten guns per 100 people.[91] Such data have been used to infer a relationship between the pervasiveness of gun ownership in the United States and the much higher than average homicide rate in this country (see Table 6.18 for a sampling of homicide rates around the world). Perhaps it is not surprising that Spain, with one of the lowest gun ownership rates, also has one of the lowest homicide rates in the world at less than 1 person killed per 100,000 people. Note that the homicide rate in the United States is more than four times higher than Germany or Japan. Even less-developed Chile, for example, has a lower homicide rate than the United States. Albania, with about eight guns per person and representing one of the poorest countries in Europe, is on par with the United States in terms of the murder rate. For the most part, the U.S. homicide rate is exceeded only by third-world countries.

T A B L E 6.18   International Murder Rates per 100,000 Population in 2011

Liechtenstein	0.0	Chile	3.7
Japan	0.3	Albania	4.4
Switzerland	0.6	United States	4.71
Germany	0.8	Russia	9.7
Spain	0.8	Mexico	23.7
Denmark	0.8	South Africa	30.9
United Kingdom*	1.0	Jamaica	41.2
France	1.2	Venezuela	45.1**
Canada	1.5	Honduras	91.6

*Only England and Wales.
**2010 figures

SOURCE: United Nations Office on Drugs and Crime, http://www.unodc.org/unodc/en/data-and-analysis/homicide.html.

But it would be misleading and overly simplistic to claim that the large volume of guns in the United States is primarily responsible for America's higher murder rates. Germany, for example, is the fifteenth highest country in gun ownership in the world (at 30.3 guns per 100 people), yet its homicide rate in 2011 was only 0.8 per 100,000 people (see Table 6.18). Switzerland, which has the third highest rate of gun ownership in the world, at 45.7 guns per 100 people, also has one of the lowest murder rates in the world at 0.6 murders per 100,000 people. France ranks twelfth in gun ownership (31.2 guns per 100 people), but its murder rate is also very low. Honduras, on the other hand, was ranked eighty-eighth among countries in rates of gun ownership, with only 6.2 guns per 100 people, yet it had one of the highest homicide rates in the world in 2011 at over 91 persons murdered per 100,000 people. Venezuela and Jamaica also have very low rates of gun ownership (rates of 10.7 and 8.1 per 100 people, respectively), but these two countries also have staggeringly high murder rates. Thus, the number of guns in a society cannot be much of an explanation for high murder rates. If you live in Honduras, one of the murder capitals of the world in 2011, the cliché "Guns don't kill people, people kill people" must appear rather true, given the fact that most people in that society do not own guns. On the other hand, one cannot ignore the role of guns in crime in the United States, because firearms represent the most frequently used weapon to kill.

Guns and Violence.   Firearms are used to shoot over 200,000 people per year, some 29,573 of whom died in 2001. In that year, the U.S. homicide rate per 100,000 population was 5.5. In 2012, there were 14,827 murders known to police, of which 69.4 percent were committed by firearms (see Table 6.19). Firearm violence extends beyond criminal activity to suicide and accidents.

T A B L E 6.19   Murders in the United States by Weapon (percent)

	1995	2000	2008	2012
Guns (all)	68.2	65.6	66.9	69.4
Handguns (only)	55.8	53.4	47.6	49.9
Knives, etc.	12.8	13.5	13.4	12.4
Blunt objects (clubs, etc.)	4.5	4.7	4.3	4.1
Hands, feet, etc.	5.9	7.0	6.1	5.3
Strangulation	1.9	1.3	0.6	0.7
Fire	0.8	1.0	0.6	0.7
Poison	0.9	0.1	0.1	0.1
Explosives	0.1	0.1	0.1	0.1
Asphyxiation	0.6	0.7	0.6	0.8
Other	6.1	5.9	7.1	6.2

SOURCE: *Statistical Abstract of the United States, 1997*, p. 204; U.S. Department of Justice, Federal Bureau of Investigation, *Uniform Crime Report, 2000, 2003, and 2008.*

As for types of firearms, estimates indicate that some 20,000 to 22,000 people are killed by handguns each year. Clearly, while there are numerous ways to kill, guns constitute the easiest and surest way, which is why guns are used in such a high proportion of homicides and suicides.

Moreover, the proliferation of guns in society has meant that career criminals have easy access to them, particularly guns of the more high-powered variety. We have already alluded to the growth of gang warfare associated with drugs. Gangs frequently possess sophisticated weapons, especially semiautomatic assault rifles, such as the Israeli-made Uzi and the Chinese-made AK-47. Eruptions of gang violence often involve drive-by shootings in which innocent bystanders are killed. This caused geometric increases in the murder rates in some areas. A public outcry to control the widespread ownership of these weapons, stimulated by the random shootings of schoolchildren, motivated the previously anti–gun control president George H. W. Bush to impose a ban on the importation of assault rifles. This did not address the sale or manufacture of these weapons domestically. President Clinton's crime bill, passed with modifications in August 1994, included a ban on stipulated models of assault weapons. Despite vigorous lobbying efforts by the National Rifle Association (NRA), this provision was left in the final bill. The ban expired in 2004, however, and Congress declined to renew it.

Guns also often fall into the hands of children, who are less likely to use them responsibly. In 1987, an average of one child under the age of fifteen died in the United States each day from a handgun accident, and ten others were injured, according to the Center to Prevent Handgun Violence. Many of these tragedies occur because gun owners leave their weapons where children can find them. Accordingly, a number of state and local governments have either adopted or considered legislation holding gun owners responsible under both civil and criminal laws for any harm caused by leaving weapons accessible to children. Not surprisingly, the NRA opposes such legislation insofar as it covers young people fourteen years of age or older, claiming that fourteen-year-olds are capable of making their own decisions about guns. The NRA legislative counsel further opposes legislation that mandates criteria for storing weapons. As we shall see again below, this lobbying group for gun owners has consistently opposed any effort to regulate firearms possession and use, and its power and influence as an interest group is drawn largely from the fact that most Americans support the right to own guns.

Regulation of Guns.   Given the amount of gun violence in America, government has tried to respond by placing further regulations on the ownership and prevalence of guns. Because the vast majority of murders result from the use of handguns (more than any other type of firearm), state governments and the national government have focused regulations directed at this type of firearm. Thus, the Brady Bill, passed by Congress in 1994, required that prospective purchasers of handguns undergo background checks. The bill was named after presidential aide James Brady, who was critically wounded in John Hinckley's attempt to kill President Reagan in 1981, and after Sarah Brady, his wife, who has become one of the leading activists for handgun control. The bill mandates background checks for prospective purchasers of handguns to determine if they are part of a high-risk group (a convicted felon, a former mental patient, and such). These checks take a day or two, and purchasers have to wait five days before taking possession of guns, a period of time that also serves as a "cooling-off period." Opponents of this bill, led by the NRA, argue that criminals will get their guns by illegal means anyhow. Meanwhile, they argue, this bill creates unnecessary regulations adding to the costs of doing business for purveyors of guns and making for unnecessary inconvenience for prospective purchasers of guns. Supporters of the Brady Bill note that in the four years after its passage, over 100,000 applications to buy guns were denied under the Brady Bill because the applicants were in the proscribed high-risk categories: having a record of felony convictions or mental illness. If just 1 percent of these people were prevented from killing someone (assuming they did not buy a gun on the black market), that would be 1,000 lives saved. Supporters of the bill argued that the denial of so many applications constitutes evidence that some people who might misuse firearms do try to purchase them legally and may lack the resources to obtain them by other means.

A major loophole in Brady is that it only applies to licensed gun dealers; hence, one could purchase firearms at a gun show without either the waiting period or the background check. Gun control advocates have concentrated efforts in recent years to close that loophole. These efforts have thus far been unsuccessful as the next section illustrates.

Semiautomatic Weapons, Mass Shootings, and Obama Administration Gun Control Proposals.   The debate on the control of semiautomatic weapons, which hold many rounds of ammunition and allow many more rounds to be fired in less time, was activated by several mass killings, one having been the murder of five children and the wounding of some thirty others in a Stockton, California, elementary school in 1989 by a deranged man with a semiautomatic assault rifle. This debate continued when a Glock 17 was used by another deranged gunman, George Hennard, to kill twenty-two people and wound many others in a Killeen, Texas, cafeteria in October 1991. Not too long after this incident, the 1994 Crime Bill placed a ban on assault rifles, but this ban expired in 2004.

Another round of mass shootings occurred during the Obama administration. In the wake of the July 2012 Aurora shooting that took place in a Colorado movie theater, and the December 2012 Sandy Hook Elementary School shooting in Connecticut, the Obama administration responded with a number of proposals to regulate guns. The president's plan, unveiled in 2013, included closing background check loopholes, banning military-style assault rifles and high-capacity magazines, and increasing access to mental health services.[92] In a number of mass shootings, it was discovered that the gunman had mental health problems and should not have had access to a gun. At the time of this book's publication, there was not enough support in Congress to pass such legislation. Given public sentiment on the issue, few members of Congress will be punished for inaction. The Republican Party, which won control of the U.S. House of Representatives, is adamantly opposed to more gun regulations. Moreover, a Gallup survey in October 2013 found that only 49 percent of American adults favor stricter laws covering the sale of firearms, 37 percent were satisfied with current laws, and 13 percent wanted fewer restrictions.[93]

Debate over Gun Control. The question remains, however, whether these gun control laws had any significant effect on crime. The debate over gun control and whether it affects crime continues to be argued both among liberal and conservative ideologues and social scientists. As Table 6.19 illustrates, most murders are committed using a gun. Furthermore, supporters of gun control point out, quite logically, that it is both physically and psychologically easier to kill someone with a gun than with a blunt instrument or with a knife. It takes a greater degree of strength, passion, commitment, and insensitivity to bash in a head with an and-iron or to plunge a knife between someone's ribs than it does to stand across a room and pull a trigger. The possibilities of resistance are much greater in a knife or club attack, and requires physical proximity, rather than when one is shot from a distance. The proliferation of firearms makes the act of murder easier to carry out. It should be noted that despite the availability of numerous other means to commit suicide, firearms were used in over half the cases in the 1970s and since then, through the 1990s, account for almost two-thirds of all suicides. Taking one's own life is frequently an essentially irrational or impulsive act, and one that might not have taken place had the victim been forced to cool off in the light of day or to use some other, possibly unsuccessful, means.

Supporters of gun rights first point to two individual concerns that warrant allowing people to own guns. First, a number of people in America hunt game for recreation. Severe restrictions on guns or the banning of guns could adversely affect an activity that is seen by many, particularly in rural America, as an American tradition. A second, even more important individual concern arises from people who genuinely need a gun for protection. This would include those who work in high-crime neighborhoods, those who must travel late at night, and those whose safety has been threatened. The needs of these people constitute another important argument against gun control legislation. The argument is that law enforcement institutions and the justice process are unable to protect citizens from being victims of serious crime; therefore, such people have the right and the obligation to seek protection for themselves and their families. The argument states that if potential criminals believed that most people kept guns in their homes and knew how to use them, the number of break-ins would decrease dramatically. The death toll in cases of random violence would be lessened, it is argued, if armed citizens are able to defend themselves and others against the assailant.

Consistent with the logic of this argument, most states have now passed laws giving most persons the right, subject to a permit, to carry concealed weapons. To qualify for such a permit, the applicant has to have a record free from any felony conviction or mental illness and must take a course on firearm use and safety. In Texas, between January 1, 1996, when the law went into effect, and

January 1, 1998, the state had issued 163,096 licenses to carry weapons. Supporters of this law argue that it will lead to a decrease in street crime because potential perpetrators will be aware that their potential victim may be hiding the means to blow them away. Opponents of the law, especially groups and individuals actively working for firearms control in general, argue that many of the holders of these permits use their guns to commit crimes.

Supporters of greater gun control also point out that the majority of homicides are not premeditated, but are crimes of passion committed on the spur of the moment. The argument that would end with a punch when a gun is not available may end with someone dead if a gun is available. Many shootings occur in domestic quarrels or in drunken arguments in bars. If the combatants had to go out the following day and seek a firearm from illegal sources, surely some of their passion would have decreased in the sober light of day.

Advocates of gun control also may make comparisons to different states with varying gun control laws. For example, in 2012, Rhode Island, with strict gun control laws, had 3.2 total murders per 100,000 population, whereas Texas, with a high incidence of gun ownership and very loose gun laws, had 4.4 murders per 100,000 population. But such comparisons are not particularly meaningful, since there are a number of explanations for the difference in crime in these two states. For one, Rhode Island has a much different culture and is essentially devoid of large metropolitan areas that breed crime (such as Houston, Dallas, or San Antonio in Texas). Furthermore, this argument falls flat when one also sees that the District of Columbia, which had some of the strictest gun control laws in the country, also had murder rates (at 13.9 per 100,000 residents in 2008) that are higher than many third-world countries.

Given these data, many gun rights advocates argue that gun control regulations would not correct the crime problem. Opponents of gun control point out that guns are not the only available deadly weapon. Knives and blunt instruments can and do serve as instruments of violence, yet no one seriously advocates restricting the private ownership of such items. Opponents of gun control hold that persons determined to commit crimes will find illegal ways of acquiring firearms even if laws are made stricter. The only difference, say gun rights supporters, is that stricter laws make it more difficult for law-abiding citizens to obtain guns.

In fact, it is hard to draw definitive conclusions from the empirical research as to how guns relate to violence and murder. There is a battle over data and statistics among social scientists using a lot of sophisticated statistical analyses, but no definitive answers in the debate have evolved. No one, except for the most liberal of Democrats, is suggesting that guns should be completely banned. But current proponents of gun control do believe that it should be more difficult to buy a gun and that fewer guns existent in society would contribute to a safer society. They are also generally opposed to laws that license the carrying of concealed weapons. Gun control advocates were appalled when the Texas Legislature recently installed metal detectors at the state capitol for the general public, but then proceeded to create a fast lane that allows citizens to bypass the metal detector if they have a permit to carry a concealed handgun—even if they also have the handgun with them at the capitol. Many Texas legislators also wear their own guns in their state offices.[94]

In his book *More Guns, Less Crime* (1998), economist John Lott finds that rates of violent crime and murder fell a lot faster in states that adopted laws allowing for the carrying of concealed weapons when compared to states that did not adopt such laws. Lott analyzed crime data from more than 3,000 counties in the United States over twenty-five years.[95] A number of other social scientists have confirmed Lott's more general findings that more guns contribute to fewer murders and less violent crime.[96]

But not all social scientists agree with the findings or the analysis of the data in Lott's work and other studies. A 2001 study by a University of Chicago economist found that in the United States, "increases in gun ownership lead to substantial increases in the overall homicide rate," although there appears to be little relationship between gun ownership and other types of crime.[97] Coming at the issue from a public-health approach, Harvard professor David Hemenway finds that more guns cause more gun violence, that the deterrent effect of guns does not exist, and that all the available data show that arming people where they live, work, or go to school will only increase violence.[98] But even some skeptics of the notion that more guns reduce crime have had a difficult time explaining away Lott's findings. Hashem Dezhbakhsh and Paul H. Rubin reanalyzed Lott's data and questioned the statistical methods he employed to reach his findings. In the end, they grudgingly concluded that the effects of concealed weapons laws in reducing crime were real, but that the effects were much smaller than Lott claimed.[99] As two supporters of gun control conceded in the *Stanford Law Review*, "We conclude that Lott and Mustard have made an important scholarly contribution in establishing that these laws have not led to the massive bloodbath of death and injury that some of their opponents feared."[100] Still, these scholars think that the evidence that these laws reduced crime is weak. As noted earlier, an alternative explanation for drops in crime in the United States in the 1990s comes from economist Steven Levitt, who argues that the legalization of abortion in the 1970s contributed to that decline.[101]

In a 2007 article in the *Harvard Journal of Law and Public Policy*, criminologists Don B. Kates and Gary Mauser take a more cautious perspective on the current debate over the effects of gun policy. By drawing on evidence across a multitude of countries, they examine whether a total ban on guns would reduce homicide or suicide rates. They do not find a pattern of more guns equaling more homicide or suicide. For example, they point out that Greece has nearly three times as much gun ownership as the Czech Republic, and a somewhat higher rate of gun suicide, yet overall suicide rates among Czechs are 175 percent higher than among Greeks. And in Luxembourg, where handguns are banned and ownership of guns is severely restricted, the murder rate in 2002 was nine times higher than neighboring Germany, which has a fairly high rate of gun ownership. According to these criminologists, "whether causative or not, the consistent international pattern is that more guns equal *less* murder and other violent crime."[102] In other words, they point out that for the most part, there tends to be a relationship between having more guns and less violence in a society, but caution that this correlation does not necessarily imply that guns are the reason for less vio-lence (i.e., the old social scientist adage, correlation does not imply causation). Thus, these two researchers do not necessarily subscribe to the view that having more guns actually causes crime levels to go down. They suggest that there may be no causal link at all between either guns and lower violence/murder or guns and higher violence/murder. Instead, these two criminologists reiterate a very traditional view that "the determinants of murder and suicide are basic social, economic, and cultural factors, not the prevalence of some form of deadly mechanism."[103] In fact, an alternative explanation for the relationship of more guns and less violence could simply be because countries that are safer and have lower rates of crime are less troubled by the concept of allowing people to own guns and thus these countries choose to allow for more gun ownership.

It is unlikely that extremely strict gun control laws or bans on all guns could ever be adopted in the United States, based both on public support for gun rights in America and the Supreme Court's interpretation of people's Second Amend-ment rights to own guns. As noted earlier, public support for more gun regula-tion is just below 50 percent. This is down from a high in the 1990s of near 60 percent in favor of stricter gun laws. The trend in recent years has been toward a public that is more divided over the issue and less supportive of additional gun regulation laws. Americans are even less supportive of efforts to ban guns. In essence, Americans like their right to own a gun, so the idea that legislatures or Congress would attempt to ban, outlaw, confiscate all handguns (as was the case in the United Kingdom in 1997), or even offer mildly stricter gun regulations seems very unlikely in the near future.

Furthermore, even if Congress attempted to enact a ban, such legislation would be declared unconstitutional under the Second Amendment right to bear arms. In the 2008 Supreme Court case *D.C. v. Heller*, the High Court struck down the District of Columbia's onerous regulations on firearms as a vio-lation of the Second Amendment.[104] The 1976 District of Columbia law under scrutiny in the case banned private ownership of handguns, and stated that shot-guns and rifles could only be owned if they were registered, kept unloaded, and either disassembled or disabled by trigger locks. Some legal scholars have read the Second Amendment as only conferring a collective right to own guns because of its phrase, "A well-regulated militia, being necessary to the security of a free state...." The second part of the Second Amendment, however, seemingly con-fers an individual right because it reads, "the right of the people to keep and bear arms, shall not be infringed." To be sure, most constitutional law scholars agree that the Second Amendment is poorly worded. But the Court had never really directly answered whether an individual had a right to a gun until the *Heller* case. The Court rejected the notion that the amendment only conferred a collective right to bear arms, asserting that while the federal government could place some regulations on guns (that a person's right is not "unlimited"), the Second Amendment protects an individual's right to bear arms. Incidentally, an over-whelming majority of Americans agreed with the *Heller* decision that the Second Amendment protects an individual's right to bear arms (73 percent agreed with the Court decision in one 2008 Gallup Poll).[105]

Decriminalization and Deterrence

Recall that the swiftness and certainty of punishment are thought to be the major ingredients in deterring crime. There are two factors at work in the criminal justice system that greatly slow down the meting out of that punishment. One is the long period of time that criminals spend free between arraignment and trial, and the other is the enormous case load of "victimless crime" defendants.

A substantial portion of the total justice system case load is processing so-called victimless crimes. Arrests for such things as prostitution, public intoxication, or drug abuse take up a large portion of the court time in any large city, time that might otherwise be used to prosecute more swiftly the perpetrators of crimes against persons or property. Prosecutorial forces, court-appointed defense attorneys, and police efforts take up more time. Police are pressured to apprehend people who engage in victimless crime (i.e., prostitutes, addicts, and gamblers), not because of any threat they pose to public safety, but solely because they offend the dominant morality. These laws are also selectively enforced against social undesirables. Police arrest streetwalkers but rarely arrest expensive call girls. Lower-class people are arrested for public intoxication on the street, but middle-class people are rarely bothered for intoxication except when driving. These laws against prostitution, gambling, or drugs also encourage organized crime, which provides criminalized services. Finally, these laws fail to prevent the conduct they proscribe; they may not even substantially reduce such conduct. **Decriminalization**, the legalization of such conduct or the substantial reduction of penalties associated with it, is a policy option that would permit a reallocation of criminal justice resources to crimes against persons and property. As mentioned previously, Washington and Colorado have already moved to legalize marijuana, and many other states have sought to decriminalize possession of small amounts of the drug.

It is protested, however, that the legalization of such "immoral" conduct would in effect constitute a legitimization of it, an official stamp of approval that would result in its expansion. Laws against murder do not prevent the crime from occurring, but they reduce its incidence and place society squarely in the position of saying that murder is not tolerable. It is argued that there are principles of ethical conduct that define the essence of society as a community. Others argue that there is a basic difference between laws proscribing crimes against persons and property and laws proscribing conduct that a dominant group finds immoral. With the former case, there is a widespread consensus on the wrongful nature of acts, such as murder, robbery, and rape. With the latter, there is no such consensus on the immorality of such conduct as getting intoxicated, gambling, or smoking marijuana.

Strengthening the Police

Providing for more police or enhancing their technical law enforcement capabilities would seem to be an effective means of deterring crime. It is not clear, however, what effective actions specifically can be taken to secure this end.

Some studies have found that while a greater police presence can reduce property crime, violent crime is unaffected by police numbers. There are also significant costs involved for government in increasing the numbers of police. A British study published in 2012, however, found that a "one percent increase in police per capita results in a 1–2 percent decrease in the rate of victim-reported property crime and violent crime."[106] But these same researchers do not necessarily advocate for more police. Rather, using police more effectively (to patrol them in crime hotspots) is a more cost-effective way to reduce crime.

Increased physical equipment, such as riot control vehicles, or higher police salaries and sophisticated recruitment practices have not been shown to have a significant impact on police effectiveness. Although increasing the resources allocated to police may give the psychological satisfaction of supporting the forces of law and order, it does not hold out much promise of contributing to the goal of deterring crime.

Instituting cameras in public places, such as has happened in the United Kingdom, could deter crime and help police solve more crimes. However, the notions of privacy rights in this country (held by both conservatives and liberals), and the huge costs associated with such a project, mean that such an idea is likely not politically feasible. Other technological advances in forensic sciences such as DNA do help police solve murders, but problems in quality control can occasionally thwart the benefits of these technologies.

Penal Reform, Sentencing, and Recidivism

Criticisms of the disposition of our criminal justice system to impose insufficiently harsh penalties are frequently directed at the discretion available to judges to impose sentences. It is widely assumed that discretionary sentencing has resulted in excessive leniency for serious criminals, as well as resulting in unjustly harsh sentences that depended on which judge was presiding in a given case. These assumptions have led to a demand for standardization in sentencing. Mandatory sentencing at the state level may mean limiting the alternatives to jail time served, or it may mean imposing a minimum of time served before parole eligibility. Many argue that the mandatory sentencing laws have created an unduly harsh criminal justice system. Recently, some conservatives and liberals have looked at reforming sentencing laws so that valuable prison space is not wasted on nonviolent offenders but is instead reserved for more violent offenders.

The fact that most career criminals will serve prison time at some point in their lives renders the recidivism rate one of the more important facts about criminality. **Recidivism** is the rate at which crime is committed by people who have been convicted of previous crimes. A high recidivism rate indicates that people who have been punished for committing at least one crime have a higher probability of committing subsequent crimes than do people who have never been so punished. Widely accepted estimates suggest that recidivists account for around 60 percent of all felonies. A 2008 study reported that, in California, around 66 percent of inmates released from prison return to prison within three years.[107] The serious implication of the high recidivism rate is that rather than deterring individuals from committing additional crimes, punishment and incarceration appear to make it more likely that they will engage in criminal behavior again. The recidivism rate attests to the failure of our prison system. Its importance becomes even more obvious in light of the more than 2 million people incarcerated in American prisons, and the desire to curb this relentless relapse into criminality has inspired concern for the reform of the prison system.

Many charge that the prison system increases inmates' tendency toward criminality. First, the system is seriously overcrowded. This fact in turn results in the bitterness and dehumanization that occur when people must spend years in substandard conditions. Second, prisons are understaffed with respect to trained personnel who could help rehabilitate inmates. Third, improper supervision by staff and a lack of standards for choosing them result in such brutalizing experiences as beatings by guards, rape, and interracial violence.

Another characteristic of the prison system alluded to by its critics is a failure to prepare inmates to lead productive lives upon their release. Little is done to impart the skills needed to make the inmates more employable than when they turned to crime. Drugs are easily available within many prisons, and some prisoners become addicts under the pressures of prison life. This addiction, of course, almost guarantees the subsequent criminal activity of such inmates. It is within this perspective that many politicians have begun promoting the creation of veterans' courts and drug courts. These institutions are designed to move less violent offenders to treatment programs that can reduce their recidivism rate and avoid the damaging influences of prison life. There are other programs as well. **Work release** programs offer the added benefit of additional vocational training. But some reform proposals are controversial, and that is due in large part to confusion and ambivalence over the goals of the prison system. Liberals and many social scientists assume that the main purpose of the prison system is rehabilitative and correctional.

Still others see prisons as places to house and isolate crime-prone individuals from society, sociopaths who have no hope of rehabilitation, thus physically preventing them from inflicting any further harm. Among some law and order conservatives, the preferred strategy toward the crime problem is to lock up those individuals who are a threat to society and to keep them locked up. Specifically, the strategy would authorize judges to deny bail to accused persons whom they consider likely to commit additional crimes, as well as to target chronic offenders for long-term incarceration. These policies, however, have come under increasing criticism. Instead, reducing the prison population is discussed more frequently today by politicians because not only is crime down, but the enormous costs involved in running the current system and housing and feeding this large population behind bars seem less of a priority when state governments are pressed for cash in the wake of the Great Recession of 2008.

Zero Tolerance for Petty Street Crime

A number of policies instituted by former New York Mayor Rudy Giuliani have been given partial credit for the sharply reduced crime rate in that city during his administration that ended in 2001. One of these was a policy on cracking down on vandals and graffiti artists who deface a neighborhood. Once a neighborhood becomes so defaced, its demographic character may change and people may take less pride in the neighborhood. Moreover, the perpetrators of such petty crimes perceive that they can get away with flouting the laws and standards of society. New York believes this zero-tolerance policy has been a success.

Limiting the Alternatives to Punishment

The deterrent effect of prospective punishment is further reduced by the various mechanisms for circumventing the full weight of the law even when a person is convicted. The widespread availability of such mechanisms gives criminals reason to believe that the chances are remote that they will ever suffer the maximum punishment provided by law. These mechanisms include the defense of insanity, **indeterminate sentencing** with the widespread use of parole, probated or suspended sentences, and the separation of juvenile offenders from the regular criminal justice system. All of these mechanisms (except the insanity defense) reflect the problem of our overcrowded criminal justice system. They promote the release of inmates short of the maximum penalty provided by law, thereby freeing prison facilities for the continued influx of new inmates. Indeterminate sentencing means that the judge specifies a range of time for incarceration, say, two to ten years. The inmate then becomes eligible for parole any time after the minimum period is served. **Parole** is a process by which a convicted inmate is released from prison before serving the full extent of the sentence; a parole board decides whether an inmate can and probably will lead a socially constructive existence. Such a parolee must report for the duration of his or her sentence to a supervisory official known as a parole or probation officer. There is a movement to specify mandatory sentences of determinate length for certain types of crimes but it has not been widely adopted. Indeterminate sentencing is still the norm, however, because penologists feel that it offers the needed flexibility to fit the punishment to the unique circumstances of each case.

When a defendant is convicted of a crime, a judge or jury may, at their discretion, suspend the sentence, in effect waiving all incarceration for the convicted criminal. The only thing the convicted criminal suffers is the onus of having the conviction on his or her record. A probated sentence means that incarceration is not imposed, but the judge imposes a requirement that the convicted criminal must report to a probation officer at specified intervals. Judges and juries have the discretion to hand down suspended or probated sentences for a wide range of crimes. Although this discretion clearly lowers the deterrent impact of legally possible punishment, the mandatory incarceration of all convicted felons, especially for the length of their maximum sentences, would necessitate a substantial increase in available jail space.

Earlier we alluded to the fact that juveniles commit much of the violent crime in this country. Yet because we do not hold juveniles fully responsible for their actions, they are immune from the regular punishments of the criminal justice system. Whatever deterrent effect the punishments of the criminal justice system may provide, it does not apply to teenagers, the age group most likely to commit crimes against persons and property. The idea that children cannot be held responsible for their actions in the same ways as adults can appeals to our sense of fairness. After all, little children cannot be expected to possess the powers of judgment to discern right from wrong. But few would have problems with incarcerating a seventeen-year-old murderer, rapist, or mugger. It is this gray area in between where the lack of consensus exists. At what age do we draw the line?

SUMMARY

In looking at crime policy and the dilemmas of social justice, we first assessed the policy problem, examining the extent of crime in America today and providing a historical perspective. Unlike some of the early editions of this book, we can now report that both violent and property crime have greatly decreased in our society to levels not seen since before 1970. Murder, rape, robbery, theft, burglary, etc. are all down. We also examined the underlying reasons behind crime, including addictions to drugs, socioeconomic and family problems, as well as demographic changes and the graying of America. When it comes to race, African Americans have not received equal treatment in the criminal justice system, and policies in the courts and criminal justice system continue to evolve to address these concerns. We examined five changes in the criminal justice system and their effects on crime and police work, including the expansion of rights (confessions and the right to counsel, the exclusionary rule, and constraints on capital punishment), the advancement in technologies in forensic science and other criminological techniques, and the massive expansion of the prison population beginning in the 1970s and 1980s. In evaluating these changes in criminal justice policies, we found that the expansion of rights has not hampered police abilities to tackle crime, but advancements in forensic technology have the opportunity to help both the criminally accused and the police. It is unclear whether or not an increase in the prison population has caused a decrease in crime, but the financial costs and political toll have caused politicians on the Left and the Right to rethink the current system of incarceration. In terms of future alternative policies for combating crime, the least likely in the current political climate is stricter gun regulation. Instead, the Obama administration and others have advocated more politically realistic opportunities for policy change such as emphasizing drug courts and veterans' courts and reforming our sentencing laws with an eye toward reducing the number of nonviolent offenders in the prison system.

 **RESOURCES**

American Civil Liberties Union: **www.aclu.org**

Brady Campaign to Prevent Gun Violence: **www.bradycampaign.org**

Bureau of Justice Statistics: **www.bjs.gov**

Federal Bureau of Investigation Uniform Crime Report:
  www.fbi.gov/ucr/ucr.htm#cius

The Innocence Project: **www.innocenceproject.org**

Moratorium Campaign (Death Penalty): **www.moratoriumcampaign.org**

National Rifle Association: **www.nra.org**

Pro-Death Penalty: **www.prodeathpenalty.com**

Restorative Justice Online: **www.restorativejustice.org**

United Nations Office on Drugs and Crime:
  www.unodc.org/unodc/index.html

Chapter 7

Poverty and Social Welfare Policy

In response to problems associated with poverty and income insecurity, social welfare programs in the United States cover Social Security, public assistance, job training, public health, unemployment compensation, and education. This chapter discusses the following: **social insurance programs**, which are generally linked to individuals' past contributions and provide for those separated from the labor market due to age, injury, disability, or unemployment; and **social assistance programs**, which are means-tested and aim to minimize economic hardship and alleviate poverty for those not covered by social insurance. Chapters 8 and 9 cover social programs in health care and education. The policies discussed here comprise what most people consider to be the U.S. welfare state, charged with ameliorating the causes and consequences of poverty.

ISSUE BACKGROUND: POVERTY

The answer to the question "What is poverty?" is to some degree technical, but it also tends to be mired in political and policymaking controversy. Is poverty defined by income? By inequality? Or by hardship? It is important to know *what* the problem is before trying to solve it. After discussing issues that surround the definition of poverty, this section reviews historical responses to poverty and then describes the general characteristics of the U.S. welfare state.

Defining Poverty

Most societies have a view of poverty that is based on a combination of two views: economic need and behavioral malfunction. In terms of economic need, some people are simply unusually needy (orphans, the disabled, widows, widowers), and a minimum level of income is needed to support them.

Their situation is not self-created; rather, they are victims of unfortunate circumstance. In contrast, considering the behavioral dimension of poverty's definition, vagrants, for example, cannot function within society, so they are outcast, but considered victims by their own choice and actions. This is where the politically charged question of deservingness arises. Controversy surrounds our understanding of poverty because of attempts to suppress one or the other of these elements of its definition. Whether one considers the economic or behavioral dimension to be primary, the general concept of poverty is that one's resources are insufficient to meet basic needs. In the United States, poverty is defined by an absolute measure; in much of the rest of the developed world, poverty is measured relatively. In addition to these absolute and relative measures, some scholarship also considers hardship-based, psychological, and social exclusion dimensions of poverty.

Absolute Definitions.   The federal definition of poverty in the United States is economic only. In 1964, Mollie Orshansky in the Social Security Administration developed a guideline, an income threshold below which one is considered to be poor. Orshansky studied the consumption patterns evident in a 1955 data set and found that one-third of spending among lower-income families was on food. As a result, three times what the USDA called the "thrifty food plan budget" was identified as the **poverty line**. The amount varies by family size and is adjusted year to year for inflation by using the consumer price index. Each March, the **Current Population Survey (CPS)** documents people's previous year's earnings and derives the national poverty rate for that year by comparing their incomes to the absolute poverty line. In 2013, within the forty-eight contiguous U.S. states, the official poverty line for a family of four was $23,550; it ranged from $11,490 for a one-person family to $39,630 for a family of eight, with an additional $4,020 for each additional person thereafter.

Orshansky never intended this absolute measure to persist, but it has; and in recent decades, researchers have been examining the implications of changing the definition of poverty. Some problems with the U.S. poverty definition that have compelled this research *underestimate* income and therefore *overestimate* the proportion of people living in poverty. For instance, the official poverty rate is calculated by 1955 consumption patterns; however, the share of a family's budget now spent on food is less (some say a fifth or sixth rather than a third), primarily because of changes in technology and consumption patterns. Next, the official poverty threshold counts only cash income and not in-kind benefits. Since the 1960s, the value of in-kind benefits has increased substantially. In addition, people tend to underreport their income on surveys such as the CPS. Another problem is that assets are not considered, meaning that a family may have no income from work in a given year but may have a house and substantial savings—minimizing any hardship they may face—and these are not considered by the official U.S. definition of poverty. These criticisms suggest that the measure may be too high.

Conversely, some problems with the official definition serve to *overstate* income and therefore *understate* the proportion of the population in poverty.

Taxes (income, withholding) are excluded from the computation. A family near the poverty line before paying taxes may fall below the poverty line after paying taxes. The regressive nature of payroll taxes in particular disproportionately affects low-income workers. Moreover, expenses associated with work are ignored. This means that working people might not be considered poor by the official definition, but after considering their work expenses, their incomes may fall below the poverty line. Another criticism is that in the definition there is no regional variation. It is more expensive to live in New York City, for example, than in Mississippi, but the poverty line is the same in both places (the poverty line is computed separately for Alaska and Hawaii).

In the early 1990s, the National Research Council (NRC) proposed changing the poverty measurement by doing the following: (1) Define poverty using current consumption patterns. It would look at the budget for basic necessities and then use a percentage of that to identify the poverty line (that percent would be a political decision). The result would be to raise the amount of measured poverty. (2) Include in-kind benefits that are close to cash, such as housing and energy assistance and food assistance. This would raise measured incomes and therefore reduce the rate of poverty. (3) Consider only **disposable income** (after taxes and work expenses). The net effect of these changes, according to NRC, would be to raise the measured poverty rate by about four percentage points. It would change the shape of the income distribution, toward more working poor and less welfare-receiving poor.

Since then, debate and research on restructuring the poverty measure has been active, and for many years now the U.S. Census Bureau has produced a set of what it calls "experimental poverty measures," which incorporate and refine many of the NRC suggestions and allow us to understand the implications of varying poverty measures on the composition of the poor population. Most recently, the Obama administration has committed to creating an alternate poverty measure, which it now does annually under the label of "supplemental poverty measure" (SPM). Having both of these measures of poverty for comparison helps us to understand, by varying definitions, the extent to which the official rate is an inadequate representation of the proportion of poor people in the United States and also the extent to which government efforts are succeeding in helping the poor.

The World Bank is the other main institution that uses an absolute poverty line globally, which previously calculated it at $1 per person per day in developing countries. Beginning in 2005, it raised this threshold to $1.25–$2 per day, depending on the country. Clearly, this absolute measure is even less nuanced than the U.S. official poverty line. An important implication of using an absolute poverty line is that one can imagine raising the incomes of all of those below the line so that they might no longer be considered poor. In the United States, researchers sometimes use a "**poverty gap**" measure to identify the amount of money that would be needed in order to raise all those below poverty up to the poverty line. From some perspectives, using an absolute poverty measure represents an optimistic view since it suggests a possible cure.

Relative Definitions. The kind of poverty measure in use in most of the rest of the developed world is a relative one, which compels a focus on inequality. Most commonly, a relative poverty measure is defined as being below one-half of a nation's median income. That is, a family is poor if its income is insufficient to bring it to the current median standard of living in society. By this measure, in the last forty years, a constant one-fifth of the population has been in poverty; that is, about 20 percent of families earn less than half the median income.

The gap between those at the bottom and the richest Americans is widening. In 1970, the poorest quintile's share of income was 5.4 percent and the top quintile's share was 40.9 percent (see Table 7.1). By 2000, inequality had increased so that the poorest quintile's share of income had decreased to 4.3 percent and the top quintile's share had increased to 47.7 percent; and, remarkably, inequality has continued to increase since then: in 2012 the poorest quintile's share of income was just 3.2 percent, and the top quintile's share rose to over half (51.1 percent) of all income. As Figure 7.1 shows, the bottom 40 percent of the income distribution held about the same or slightly more income than the top 5 percent until 1985, which still represents marked inequality. Since then, the extent of this inequality has widened further, with the richest 5 percent of the population holding 22.3 percent of the nation's income in 2012; and the bottom 40 percent holding about half that (11.6 percent). The United States has the largest gap between rich and poor of any modern democracy.[1]

In addition to the absolute and relative definitions of poverty, some lines of debate center on defining material hardship, the psychological dimensions of poverty or social inclusion and exclusion. For the sake of simplicity, we will focus our next two questions—how many people are poor, and who are they?—by using only the official, absolute measure of poverty, because it is the most common perspective used in the United States.

T A B L E 7.1   Share of Aggregate Family Income Received, by Population Quintile, 1960–2012

Year	Poorest Quintile	Second Quintile	Third Quintile	Fourth Quintile	Richest Quintile	Richest 5 Percent
1960	4.8	12.2	17.8	24.0	41.3	15.9
1970	5.4	12.2	17.6	23.8	40.9	15.6
1980	5.3	11.6	17.6	24.4	41.1	14.6
1990	4.6	10.8	16.6	23.8	44.3	17.4
2000	4.3	9.8	15.4	22.7	47.7	21.1
2012	3.2	8.3	14.4	23.0	51.1	22.3

SOURCE: Table F-2, Share of Aggregate Income Received by Each Fifth and Top 5 Percent of Families, All Races: 1947 to 2008, http://www.census.gov/hhes/www/income/histinc/incfamdet.html, accessed June 3, 2010; and Table 2, Income Distribution Measures Using Money Income and Equivalence-Adjusted Income: 2011 and 2012, http://www.census.gov/prod/2013pubs/p60-245.pdf, accessed February 27, 2014.

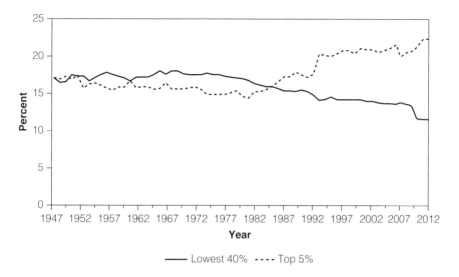

F I G U R E 7.1   Share of Aggregate Family Income Received by Bottom 40 Percent and Top 5 Percent, 1947–2012

SOURCE: Computed from Table F-2, Share of Aggregate Income Received by Each Fifth and Top 5 Percent of Families, All Races: 1947 to 2008, http://www.census.gov/hhes/www/income/histinc/incfamdet.html, accessed June 3, 2010; and Table H-2, Share of Aggregate Income Received by Each Fifth and Top 5 Percent of Households, All Races: 1967 to 2012, http://www.census.gov/hhes/www/income/data/historical/household/2012/H02_AR.xls, accessed February 27, 2014.

How Many Poor?

Debates over the definition of "poverty" link with disagreements about the cause of poverty and the number of poor persons in America. As can be seen in Figure 7.2, the proportion of the population that is poor, as measured by the official poverty measure, declined between 1959 and 1970, from 40 million poor (22 percent of the population) to 46.5 million poor (15 percent); since that time, however, the poverty rate remained relatively constant at roughly 12 to 15 percent. In 2012, 46.5 million persons, or 15.0 percent of the population, fell below the poverty threshold, with poverty increasing during periods of recession and declining during times of economic growth.

The Census Bureau data used in Figure 7.2 disguise a basic reality generally accepted by both conservative and liberal economists and elaborated in the section on the official federal poverty measure. These data reflect pretax cash income, including government transfer payments. That is, social insurance and public assistance cash benefits are counted as family income. Thus, if by "poverty" one refers to income earned without government help, removing even just cash public assistance payments (TANF and state general assistance) from the measure reveals that 16.2 percent (rather than 15.0 percent) of the population would be poor, as shown in Table 7.2. Without accounting for Unemployment Insurance, 17.6 percent of the population would be poor. Without considering Social Security income, the poverty rate would be 24.5 percent—nearly a quarter of the U.S. population—which highlights the substantial poverty-reducing effect that Social Security has. Further, the official poverty figures do not take

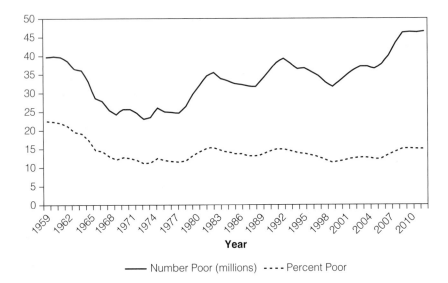

FIGURE 7.2 Poverty Trends, 1959–2012

SOURCE: http://www.census.gov/hhes/www/poverty/histpov/perindex.html for 1959–2006, accessed June 3, 2010; http://www.census.gov/hhes/www/poverty/detailedpovtabs.html for 2006–2008, accessed June 7, 2010.

account of the income value of **in-kind benefits**, such as medical care and food assistance, or employer-provided health care or other benefits, nor are they adjusted for the tendency of people to underreport income. Adjusting for these factors leaves about 10 percent poor, a figure cited in support of the enormous success of income maintenance and job programs. Although official statistics disguise the number of persons highly dependent on government aid, they also hide the success of federal programs in reducing poverty.

TABLE 7.2 **Effects of Selected Government Transfers and Taxes on Poverty, 2012**

Elements of the "Supplemental Poverty Measure"	Persons in Poverty (millions)	% of Persons in Poverty
Official poverty definition	46.97	15.1
Supplemental poverty measure	49.73	16.0
Without cash public assistance (TANF and state GA):	50.39	16.2
without SNAP	54.75	17.6
without unemployment insurance	52.26	16.8
without refundable tax credits	59.10	19.0
without Social Security	76.21	24.5

SOURCE: Table 5a, Effect of Excluding Individual Elements on SPM Rates: 2012, http://www.census.gov/prod/2013pubs/p60-247.pdf, accessed February 27, 2014.

Who Are the Poor?

The incidence of poverty does not fall evenly across the nation. Particular areas, groups, and classes bear a far higher incidence of poverty than others. Specifically, having or being a single mother, being young, being nonwhite, not working, and having a limited education are correlates of poverty, as is the location where one lives. Although a majority of the poor is white (they make up about 66 percent of those in poverty; see Table 7.4), the incidence of poverty is higher among racial minorities, reflecting racial prejudice, low job skills, and poor education. As Table 7.3 shows, although only 12.7 percent of whites are poor, 25.6 percent of Hispanics and 27.2 percent of blacks are poor. Poverty among Native Americans is even higher. Over time, however, the story of African Americans reflects success: in 1960 over half (55.1 percent) of blacks were poor, and that has been cut in half, at least in part to the successes of the civil rights movement.

Among children, almost one-quarter live in a single female–headed household, and more than half of these households are poor. Over time, change in the composition of who is poor has been referred to the "feminization of poverty," reflecting demographic trends discussed in Chapter 2.[2] In 1960, less than one in ten children lived with a lone mother. While that rate has more than doubled (to 25.3 percent in 2012), so too has the rate of poverty among these household types (from 23.7 percent in 1960 to 56.1 percent in 2012). High rates of divorce and unwed childbearing place a disproportionate share of women with small children in poverty. Lacking adequate child care and thus unable to work full-time and care for their children, they are much more likely to fall below the poverty line than are two-parent households. Sometimes these women do work full-time, but at jobs that do not pay enough to support their families.[3]

Employment in general is, not surprisingly, correlated with poverty. Among those who work full-time and full-year, poverty rates are extremely low (2.9 percent in 2012). Working only part-time or not at all clearly increases one's risk of poverty, and factors that complicate one's ability to work have implications for well-being. Nevertheless, as Table 7.4 reveals, among those who are poor, 9.1 percent still worked full-time in 2012, and 34.4 percent worked part-time, suggesting that work alone is not sufficient to prevent poverty or solve income insecurity.

Age is also associated both with poverty and with the government efforts to minimize poverty. Although the overall poverty rate was 15.0 percent in 2012, for those greater than age sixty-five, it was 9.1 percent. Poverty among the elderly has dropped sharply due to government assistance. As Table 7.3 shows, more than one-third (35.2 percent) of the elderly were poor in 1960 before substantial expansion of pension and health assistance, which has been touted as an enormous success for bringing elderly poverty as low as it is. In contrast, poverty among children is substantially higher, with more than one in five children being poor. Benefits to the elderly, principally Social Security, are generally indexed to keep pace with inflation. Benefits for others are not indexed and therefore decline over time in terms of real purchasing power. Subsequently, they have less potential to reduce poverty.

T A B L E 7.3   Percent of the U.S. Population That Is Poor (by characteristic), 1960–2012

Characteristic	1960	1970	1980	1990	2000	2010	2012
All people	22.2	12.6	13.0	13.5	11.3	15.1	15.0
All families	20.7	10.9	11.5	12.0	9.6	13.2	13.1
Families with lone female head	48.9	38.1	36.7	37.2	28.5	31.6	30.9
Age							
Children (<18 years)	26.5	14.9	17.9	19.9	15.6	22.0	21.8
children in lone-mother households	23.7	45.8	52.8	57.9	57.2	55.0	56.1
children in nonpoor lone-mother households	9.2	11.6	18.6	21.6	22.3	25.5	25.3
Elderly (65+ years)	35.2[1]	24.6	15.7	12.2	9.9	9.0	9.1
Sex							
Male		11.1	11.2	11.7	9.9	14.0	13.6
Female		14.0	14.7	15.2	12.6	16.3	16.3
Race and Ethnicity							
White	17.8	9.9	10.2	10.7	9.5	13.0	12.7
Black	55.1[1]	33.5	32.5	31.9	22.5	27.4[2]	27.2
Hispanic		22.8[3]	25.7	28.1	21.5	26.6	25.6
Geographic Location[1,4]							
Metropolitan area	15.3	10.2	11.9	12.7	10.8	14.9	14.5
Central city	18.3	14.2	17.2	19.0	16.3	19.7	19.7
Suburban	12.2	7.1	8.2	8.7	7.8	11.8	11.2
Rural	33.2	16.9	15.4	16.3	13.4	16.5	17.7
Region[5]							
Northeast		8.6	11.1	11.4	10.3	12.8	13.6
Midwest		9.6	11.4	12.4	9.3	13.9	13.3
South		17.9	16.5	15.8	12.8	16.9	16.5
West		10.4	11.4	13.0	11.8	15.3	15.1
Employment Status							
Worked full-time, full-year					2.6	2.4	2.6	2.9
Worked less than full-time, full-year					12.6	12.1	15.0	16.6
Did not work at all					22.1	19.8	23.9	33.1

SOURCE: Tables 2, 3, 6, 7, 9, 10, 25, http://www.census.gov/hhes/www/poverty/histpov/perindex.html, accessed June 7, 2010; Table 4, https://www.census.gov/prod/2011pubs/p60-239.pdf, accessed February 27, 2014; and Table 3, http://www.census.gov/prod/2013pubs/p60-245.pdf, accessed February 27, 2014; and Table 10, http://www.census.gov/hhes/www/poverty/data/historical/people.html, accessed March 1, 2014.

Notes:
[1] Year reported is 1959 rather than 1960.
[2] In 2008, black is measured as black-alone (not multiracial), whereas prior years include those of multiple races.
[3] Year reported is 1972 rather than 1970.
[4] 1960–2000 categories are metropolitan, central city, noncentral city (suburban), nonmetropolitan (rural); 2008 categories are inside MSA (urban), inside principal cities (central city), outside principal cities (suburban), outside MSA (rural).
[5] Year reported is 1969 rather than 1970.

TABLE 7.4   Selected Characteristics of the Poor, 1966–2012

Characteristic	1966	1970	1980	1990	2000	2010	2012
Age							
Children (<18 years)	43.5	41.1	39.4	40.0	36.7	35.1	34.6
People 18–64 years	38.6	40.1	47.3	49.1	52.8	57.2	57.0
Elderly (65+ years)	17.9	18.9	13.2	10.9	10.5	7.7	8.4
Race and Ethnicity							
White	67.7	68.8	67.3	66.5	68.5	67.1[1]	66.3
Black	31.1	29.7	29.3	29.3	25.3	25.0[1]	25.4
Hispanic (of any race)			11.9	17.9	24.5	29.2	29.3
Employment Status							
Worked at all			40.6	41.0	40.4	33.9	34.4
Worked full-time, full-year			8.7	9.8	11.6	8.3	9.1

SOURCE: Tables 14, 15, 18, http://www.census.gov/hhes/www/poverty/data/historical/people.html, accessed February 28, 2014.

Notes: Some figures do not add to 100 percent due to rounding, or, in the case of ethnicity, of excluded or nonmutually exclusive categories.
[1] Beginning in 2010, white and black are measured as white-alone and black-alone (not multiracial), whereas prior years reported in table may include those of multiple races.

Poverty also correlates with education and residence. People lacking a high school diploma are disproportionately poor: among workers with less than a high school diploma, 20.1 percent are poor, whereas poverty among workers with a college degree is just 2.4 percent.[4] In 1960, the distinctions in poverty by geographic location were much greater than they are today. Then, rural residents were poor at the rate of 33.2 percent: This has been cut in about half to 17.7 percent by 2012. The rural poor tend to be more chronically poor than the urban poor, more dispersed, and less likely to use public assistance. While poverty rates in metropolitan areas in general are about the same as the national average, this masks that urban cores tend to have higher poverty rates, with suburban areas having lower rates. Over time, these geographic trends have converged, making geographic variation less distinct. Further, those who live in the southern United States experience poverty at higher rates than in other regions of the country, a trend that has persisted but also become less distinct over time.

Although some characteristics are associated with greater or lesser poverty, as these tables and the corresponding discussion show, correlation does not infer causation. Substantial debate surrounds what actually causes poverty, and it is this topic we consider next.

What Causes Poverty?

What one considers the primary cause of poverty mirrors the general concept of poverty having economic and behavioral dimensions. Is poverty caused by external, economic forces or is it the result of one's own behavior and choices? Before 1973, poverty was much more directly responsive to changes in the macro economy than it has been since then. Generally, the liberal view is that the various characteristics of the economy are to blame for poverty; the conservative view is that the poor themselves are to blame for their own condition; and the radical view is that the fundamental nature of our capitalism system keeps poverty thriving. Historical moment determines the extent to which more evidence exists for one view or the other. Over time, collectively we have changed our view of who is deserving of assistance or not, related at least in part to the state of the economy. Each of these positions is summarized briefly next.

Liberal Views—External Locus.   Liberals and progressives dispute the notion that individual behavior compels poverty but claim instead that external forces in our economy are the main cause of poverty. The poor are no different from the nonpoor; they simply lack the opportunities for education, employment, and job training. Specifically, jobs are not available in the right place, at the right time, or with the right skill set. If employment opportunities were available, then the poor would take advantage of them. There is no firm evidence, the liberal perspective asserts, that government programs decrease work effort, increase illegitimacy, or promote family breakup.

Liberals emphasize that the opportunities offered to the poor must be real. Job-training programs must provide salable skills, not temporary, menial work with no future. Entry-level jobs must connect to higher rungs in the labor market, providing supportive career advancement. With lack of genuine opportunity as the root cause of poverty, the poor lack chances for success in a society and economy structured against them. Poverty is a result of the harmful side effects, the indirect costs, of a capitalist, free-enterprise economy where the pay for less-skilled jobs falls so low that even some full-time workers do not make a wage high enough to keep their families out of poverty. Changing that structure of the economy could break the cycle of poverty.

According to liberal theory, racial discrimination against blacks, Hispanics, and other minority groups and sex discrimination against women are important causes of poverty among these groups. Discrimination affects progress in school, employment choices, job advancement, wages, and housing conditions. Racial minorities and women have high poverty rates because of the pervasive discrimination they still suffer.

Conservative Views—Internal Locus.   Conservatives argue that the economy provides plenty of opportunities, is not at all as inhospitable as liberals would have us believe, and so consequently little involuntary poverty exists in the United States. Those who wish to work and to achieve a decent standard of living can do so by taking advantage of the free enterprise system's opportunities. For those unable to work because of age, physical handicap, or other disability, sufficient resources exist from social insurance programs and private philanthropy. Healthy adults who are poor, in this view, are poor because they lack the self-discipline to work hard, save, and to delay immediate pleasures for a better future—that is, the poor must choose not to pursue the educational and employment opportunities available to everyone. Conservatives also attribute these supposed qualities of the poor to a culture of poverty. Poor people learn attitudes and behaviors from the culture around them, which teaches immediate gratification, irresponsibility, and satisfaction with a life of casual social relationships. The religious right points to the decline of moral standards leading to family breakup, drug use, unwed pregnancy, and other social disorders as key causes of poverty.

Conservatives and neoconservatives argue that traditional government welfare programs cannot prevent or cure poverty because they do nothing to change the basic attitudinal causes of poverty. In fact, they contend, government programs have the unintended consequence of encouraging people to remain poor by guaranteeing support for this way of life. These programs encourage families to break up or not to form, by increasing benefits for additional, often illegitimate, children, and make only very weak work demands on recipients. Cheating and fraud are rampant in public assistance programs in the view of many conservatives. Policy, in turn, must be paternalistic in its delivery, forcing individuals to abide by a social contract to behave by a certain code.[5]

Radical Views—Capitalism. Radicals on the Left agree with much of the liberal analysis of the causes of poverty, but they see the roots of its family strife, unemployment, and discrimination lying deep within the American socioeconomic system itself. From a classically Marxist perspective, such radicals argue that capitalism necessitates poverty because it exists to create wealth for a small group of property owners. Poverty is necessary in a capitalist society because it provides a large pool of surplus labor to do menial and dirty tasks and to keep general wages low. Fear of the hardship and shame of poverty keeps the middle class hardworking and subservient to the attitudes and desires of the upper class. The culture of poverty is also useful to the middle and upper classes, as it offers them such outlets as gambling, prostitution, and charity work. Moreover, the violence, crime, and immorality of the poor provide a convenient focus for moral indignation, neatly deflecting attention from the corruption, injustice, and crass materialism of capitalist culture.

Welfare is publicly distributed in ways that keep it demeaning and despised, whereas handouts for the rich are dignified in hidden tax loopholes, investment credits, loans and loan guarantees, and government grants and contracts. Further, government support for the poor must remain low, but not too low as to incite revolution. Radicals scoff at the potential of government programs to create jobs and economic expansion. Such tactics will not work because poverty is built into the structure of the economy itself; only radical economic change that transforms the capitalist system can attack poverty.

Each of the liberal, conservative, and radical perspectives has been dominant at some point in the history of poverty and responses to it, as discussed next.

History. Discussion of social welfare has ancient roots.[6] The Greeks and Romans viewed love and charity as the highest of virtues. Ancient Judaic law called for caring for the needy: the Old Testament taught that giving was a duty, and the Talmud states, "Each and everyone should be supplied with what he needs." Central to Christianity are many of the same ideas, with emphasis on good deeds and loving the less fortunate; similarly, the central Islamic text, the Koran, exhorts believers to show charity to the unfortunate. Starting in the sixth century, monasteries were the basis of social provision. By the eleventh century, the system of governance known as feudalism prevailed; although it sharply curtailed individual rights, it had a built-in system of providing for workers and their families. Medieval hospitals served as social service agencies and were often governed by monasteries and then by municipalities as they appeared in cities. From this tradition came the civic-religious link in providing for the poor. The breakdown of feudalism saw the growth of urbanization and incipient industrialization, and with them new needs.

In England, the 1601 **Poor Law** codified several prior statutes into one coherent law. By our standards, it allowed for harsh treatment of the able-bodied poor if they refused to work, but it provided care for the dependent poor, and situated responsibility with local authorities. The Poor Law combined both "indoor" and "outdoor" relief. It was judged to be successful at helping many needy by putting the able-bodied to work and setting children up with apprenticeships. Underlying the law were two ideas. First, some poor people were deserving and others were not; the able-bodied poor were treated punitively if they did not work, and those less able were taken care of. Second, poverty is rooted in economic problems, not individual failings. The English Poor Law firmly established *civic* responsibility in dealing with poverty because it was in the state's economic best interest to do so.

The Poor Law also provided the basis for treating poverty in the American colonies, where they provided care as a civic responsibility, inspired by moral and spiritual duty. The American colonies imported the Poor Law, locating care for the poor locally. The early colonies set up systems of local social welfare provision for the poor, the aged, the disabled, the blind, and so on, by adopting laws quite similar to the 1601 Poor Law. During this period, the most common procedure was to place those who could not support themselves into private homes; others were given tax relief and some grants. As in England, beggars were treated harshly in the New World. As Cotton Mather proclaimed, "For those who indulge themselves in idleness, the express command of God unto us is, that we should let them starve."[7] Those deemed lazy faced compulsory labor, and children were sent to families to care for them and teach them a trade.

In the latter part of the eighteenth century, during the period of the American Revolution, there was an increase in spending on poverty to deal with the rise in poverty that came from a variety of sources, including immigration; military skirmishes or men lost at sea, both of which created widows and orphans as well as disabled soldiers and refugees of war; the seasonal nature of jobs; the rise in illegitimacy, through which children became the responsibility of the state; economic hardship and depression; illness and plagues; and growing overcrowding in cities.

The Enlightenment revered reason, and the ideas embodied in the Declaration of Independence emphasized individual equality, and these pointed to the need to improve the common person's lot. Living in the New World, with its abundant resources, instilled an *obligation* to eliminate poverty—as a condition, and not just to help the poor be relatively less destitute—so that all citizens could engage in democracy. As a result, the *state* became an "instrument for advancing the welfare of the entire population."[7] Before the revolution, local civic and religious authorities dealt with poverty. After the revolution, public poor relief became entirely a secular matter at the county level.

The federal system emphasized states' rights and did not explicitly provide for centralized poor relief. As a result, states had control, and there was therefore great variability in their codes as well as flexibility to meet local needs. Without any specific state action, counties and families continued to assume much of the responsibility in caring for the poor.

The nineteenth century saw the rise of individualism and a retreat from caring for the poor. At first, independence brought little change in the social welfare system, but the rise of market-based economics and of laissez-faire philosophy in England reached America, and Americans took it even further. Also growing was the Darwinian idea that the fittest will survive, and the idea that poverty was caused by individual weakness became increasingly widespread.

There was the desire to abolish support for the poor, and to make public aid harder to receive. Emphasis shifted to caring for the poor in institutions, alms houses, and workhouses, and those not institutionalized might receive moral assistance, but not material aid. When the Civil War broke out, care was nearly all local, mostly institutional, and there was a strong sense that poverty had individual roots and that widespread public care for the poor was not good or necessary.

The first federal effort to provide relief from poverty came in 1865, when Congress established the Bureau of Refugees, Freedmen, and Abandoned Lands, also called simply the Freedmen's Bureau. At first it was authorized to administer temporary relief during the war. Later, it aided blacks in making the transition from slavery to freedom through its wide range of functions: providing relief or employment; assisting settlement; offering educational, welfare, and health services; and providing legal aid. Although the Bureau closed in 1872, it provided a crucial demonstration that the federal government could provide welfare when local care broke down; reformers pointed to it when they called for further federal involvement.

After this, some states began coordinating otherwise incoherent efforts to serve the needy, but this was still less common than private charity efforts, which also followed a similar trend toward coordination across a variety of organizations. The federal withdrawal of involvement in social welfare in the 1870s came with the initiation and growth of the "Charity Movement," which created a new set of civic organizations, the Charity Organization Society (COS). These charity groups were highly organized, they had state-level associations aimed to consolidate diverse efforts to reduce duplication of services, and they kept detailed records, marking important beginnings of public administration research. The COS workers embraced the philosophy that material aid was harmful and should not be provided. Deprivation, they believed, was a crucial incentive.

Nevertheless, they thought that poverty could be alleviated via changing individual morals and behaviors. That is, the poor needed individual guidance and exposure to middle and upper class values and behavior.

The depression of the 1890s gave fresh rise to the view that the economy and not personal deficiencies was to blame for poverty. In this context and as part of the progressive movement arose the **settlement house** movement, which criticized the COSs for not providing enough and stressed that government must intervene. Four settlement houses existed by 1890, 100 by 1900, and 400 by 1910. Settlements were residences of highly educated social reformers, many of them women, who combined social service work with social reform. Their goal was to improve city life with less of a focus on the individual and more on social institutions and neighborhoods. Out of this movement came the founding of the NAACP (1909), the National Urban League, and an array of services, including day care, health care, education, public parks, and legislation that would influence housing and work conditions. Settlement Houses declined after World War I but ongoing professionalization of social work continued.

A significant event in the growth of a federal role in addressing poverty was the White House Conference (1909), which raised social work into prominence and reopened the question of a federal role in poverty alleviation. It emphasized the need for family preservation, challenging the prohibition of outdoor aid. The conference led to legislation in 1912 that established the U.S. Children's Bureau, primarily a research agency, which focused on the study of children's conditions and the protection of children. Based on her research on infant and maternal mortality, Julia Lathrop, the head of the Children's Bureau, introduced what became the **Sheppard-Towner Act** of 1921. This act established grants in aid from the federal government to the states in support of a range of child health–related programs. This was really the first modern federal effort to deal with poverty-related issues. Although the program ceased in 1929 because of physicians' opposition to government's takeover of medicine, the Act set the stage for the future relationship between the federal government and states in the provision of social welfare policy.

Between 1911 and 1919, thirty-nine states passed **mother's pension laws**. By 1935, all but two states provided legislatively based pensions to widows with children. The establishment of mother's pensions is recognized as a crucial turning point in social policy development. With the economic crisis of the Great Depression, one-fourth of the population was unemployed, and possibly as much as half to two-thirds were considered needy. This context and the policy activity earlier in the century poised the federal government to take an increasing role in combating poverty, which it did in several robust ways. From 1933 to 1935, the Federal Emergency Relief Administration (FERA) gave financial relief to people in need: in 1934, 20 percent of people received relief, and over the entire decade of the 1930s, 35 percent of the public received relief assistance. Even then assistance was unpopular. President Roosevelt recognized that cash assistance could be considered "a narcotic, a subtle destroyer of the human spirit," and so **work relief** substituted for simple cash assistance.

From 1935 through World War II, the Works Progress Administration, the Civilian Conservation Corps, and the Civil Works Administration created jobs at public expense.

Most notably in our social welfare policy history is the passage in 1935 of the **Social Security Act**, which combined welfare and pension programs to provide assistance to those disconnected from the labor market due to age, unemployment, or disability. In the decades that followed, the welfare state evolved and expanded in new directions. In particular the **Great Society** (1961–1978) included the "**War on Poverty**," which focused on antipoverty programs and was most active between 1964 and 1972. New civil legislation and court rulings provided important new protections for minority Americans. Confidence in macroeconomic policy saw executives using tax cuts to stimulate the economy to higher levels of production, growth, and employment.

While the Great Society initiated no major new social insurance programs, the old ones were massively expanded through both higher benefits and larger caseloads. For example, the Social Security rolls grew sharply due to aging population. Repeated benefits increases were followed in 1972 by the indexing of benefits to keep pace with inflation. This resulted in huge wealth transfer to the elderly, substantially reducing their poverty. Similarly, unemployment insurance rolls grew sharply in the 1970s due to recessions, extended benefits voted by Congress, and more lenient administration.

On the social assistance side, cash public assistance—then referred to as **Aid to Families with Dependent Children (AFDC)**—liberalized and grew sharply, and important in-kind (health, food) benefits were added. The **Food Stamp Program** was established in 1964. The program afforded poor families the opportunity to buy food and subsequently was reformed and liberalized in 1971 and 1977. The **Supplemental Security Income (SSI)** was established in 1972, providing income security to the aged, blind, and disabled. Welfare reforms in 1962 and 1967 allowed welfare recipients to keep more of their earnings if they work. And some important court cases liberalized public assistance receipt. During this welfare boom from 1965 to 1975, the AFDC rolls grew from about 4.4 to 11.4 million people due to higher benefits and liberalized procedures at the local level and driven by Community Action and the welfare rights movement.

Following the Great Society's expansion of a wide variety of educational and social supports, criticism that the welfare state compelled dependency and illegitimacy resulted in a new wave of welfare reforms that restricted assistance and tightened oversight. Conservatives had three arguments for cutting programs. First, the Federalist argument suggests that the national government should not tempt states and localities to run programs if they do not want to. This view asserts that states should initiate and design policy rather than respond to the availability of federal funds. Second, conservatives argued that social programs were failing, seizing on the modest impacts and lack of effects of employment and training and workfare programs, as documented by evaluations. To take this argument further, some noted authors—particularly George Gilder (*Wealth and Poverty*) and Charles Murray (*Losing Ground*)—argued that programs are not merely unsuccessful, but they make problems worse. In the 1980s, people began to listen to this line of reasoning. The third type of justification for cutting social programs was general opposition to *entitlement*; conservatives used moral arguments against the permissiveness encouraged by entitling individuals to receive social supports.

Conservative opposition to big government and concern for the permissiveness of welfare compelled a trend of enforcing work, and states began to experiment with reforms. By 1987, as many as forty states had developed workfare programs; research, however, presented a fairly negative picture of the results. In turn, a major piece of legislation was passed in 1988, the Family Support Act (FSA), which was one of the first expressions of "**civic conservatism**," that is, the idea that social rights should be secured by meeting some social obligation, such as working.[8] The FSA established the Job Opportunities and Basic Skills (JOBS) program, which required the states to set up workfare programs; required states to meet enrollment quotas and enroll welfare recipients in education or training programs; stiffened child support enforcement; and added transitional child care and health assistance for people moving off of welfare into work.

By 1994, welfare rolls covered 14.1 million people, representing 5 million families, an all-time high that represented about 5 percent of the U.S. population (see Figure 7.3). Public disdain for welfare resulted in a renewed effort to reform. Although presented as a radical shift in policy, President Clinton's vow to "end welfare as we know it" can be viewed simply as a continuation of prior policy evolution. The Clinton policy, which became known as the

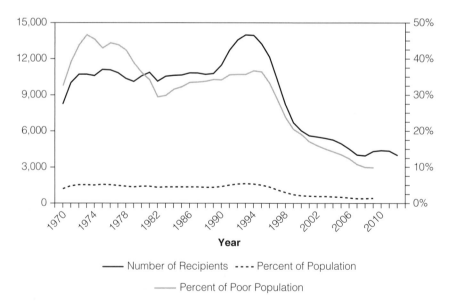

FIGURE 7.3 AFDC (1970–1996) and TANF (1997–2012) Recipients, Percent of Population, and Percent of Poor Population (1970–2012)

SOURCE: Appendix A, Table TANF 2, U.S. Department of Health and Human Services (2010). Indicators of Welfare Dependence: Twelfth Annual Report to Congress. Available at http://www.aspe.hhs.gov/hsp/13/indicators/rpt.cfm.

Personal Responsibility and Work Opportunity Reconciliation Act (PRWORA), contained four conservative themes: it cut the budget by $54 billion, further devolved cash public assistance to the state level, limited the assistance teen mothers could receive, and imposed tougher work requirements. Most notably, it placed a time limit on how long one can receive assistance (at least supported by federal dollars), ending what had been an entitlement since 1935. The act, with minor changes, was reauthorized in the Deficit Reduction Act of 2005. It was scheduled for subsequent reauthorization in 2010 but debates over the Affordable Care Act delayed it, ultimately remaining policy through a series of extensions. In recent years, without active policy action, the value of TANF benefits has eroded, with 2013 benefits being 20 percent lower than they were in 1996 in thirty-seven states, affecting 99 percent of TANF recipients.[9]

TANF caseloads remain low across the states, relative to their high in 1994, and most programs are characterized by their requirements: individuals generally must engage in job search and comply with a wide variety of program rules—from ensuring children's immunization and attendance in school to submitting documentation of their participation in work-related activities. While fundamentally today's TANF programs aim to assist individuals in returning to work quickly, they must do so with a caseload whose needs are varied and sometimes extreme, and some focus on job quality and persistence in order to reduce the likelihood and frequency of individuals' return to welfare.

The Welfare State

As this brief history of social policy history reveals, dozens of federal programs provide social insurance and social assistance to Americans. They range from huge programs such as Old Age, Survivors, and Disability Insurance (OASDI) and Social Security, to relatively small programs such as the Women, Infants, and Children (WIC) nutrition program. Federal expenditures were roughly $4.8 billion in 2012 with additional state contribution covering 8.9 million individuals.[10] Administration varies by program. Many programs are joint federal–state ventures, requiring fifty different sets of rules; this state variation has implications for policy delivery and the experience of claimants contingent on state of residence. At the federal level alone, jurisdiction is divided among numerous committees in the House of Representatives and the Senate and among various executive departments and agencies. The majority of federal aid recipients benefit from two or more programs, with most receiving aid from three. The package of supports that families receive at the state level has them interacting with many different agencies and receiving assistance through varied means.

The U.S. welfare state is commonly described as "bifurcated," with social insurance policies and programs being contributory and valued, and with social assistance programs being means-tested and generally stigmatized. The way in which programs within each of these two tracks of social welfare policy are administered mirrors the extent to which they have political and public support. The top tier of programs tends to be federally administered, universal and respected, while the lower tier tends to involve much state discretion, and is categorical and devalued. Whether separations from the labor market are compelled by internal or external forces, policy responses to dealing with poverty and income insecurity have four main purposes: to replace lost earnings, provide minimum income security, offset unavoidable expenses, and motivate work. The programs discussed in the next section do one or more of these things in responding to poverty.

CONTEMPORARY POLICY: SOCIAL INSURANCE AND SOCIAL ASSISTANCE PROGRAMS

This section describes the main social insurance and social assistance programs and policies that make up the U.S. welfare state. Generally, the social insurance programs are contributory in their funding, universal in their coverage, effective in reducing poverty, and popular among the public and politicians. In comparison, the programs that provide social assistance are categorical and means-tested in their eligibility, limited in their coverage, stigmatized in their receipt, and subsequently not well regarded publicly or politically. Nevertheless, these are the programs that exist to provide a minimum level of well-being among those dislocated from work for a variety of reasons, and together they form a package of assistance from government.

Social Insurance

Social Security.   Originally a retirement program only, Social Security added survivors' benefits in 1939 and disability insurance in 1956. Health insurance (Medicare, covered in Chapter 8) was added in 1965. Today, Social Security and National Defense roughly tie as the two largest items of federal spending. In 2010, of the $3,456 billion in federal outlays (Table 7.5), $707 billion was Social Security and $694 billion was Defense (2011 estimates have Social Security at $748 billion and Defense at $768 billion). Together, these programs account for half of federal spending.[11] Social Security covers over 95 percent of the working population, including the self-employed. Over 16 percent of the population (about 50 million persons) currently receive benefits; Social Security accounts for almost one-quarter of federal expenditures and revenues. In addition to the Social Security program covering most workers, the federal government also administers special retirement programs for federal workers, railroad employees, and veterans. These programs constitute the vast bulk of government entitlement spending; that is, benefits to which persons have a legal right because they meet program criteria.

The program is administered by the Social Security Administration, an independent federal agency, headed by a commissioner and deputy commissioner, advised by a seven-member, bipartisan advisory board. This status and independence signify political support for Social Security and the political power of its growing number of aged recipients.

TABLE 7.5   Federal Outlays Overall and on Social Insurance and Assistance, 2010–2011, Estimated (in billions of dollars)

	2010	2011 (estimated)
All federal outlays	3,456.2	3,818.8
Income security	622.2	622.7
General retirement and disability insurance (excluding Social Security)	6.6	7.6
Federal employee retirement and disability	119.9	127.1
Unemployment compensation	160.1	134.8
Housing assistance	58.7	69.4
Food and nutrition assistance	95.1	107.2
Social Security	706.7	748.4
Education, training, employment, social services	127.7	115.1

SOURCE: Computed from Table 473, U.S. Census Bureau, *2012 Statistical Abstract*, http://www.census.gov/prod/2011pubs/12statab/fedgov.pdf, accessed February 27, 2014. The education, training, employment, social services category includes the value of charitable contributions and education tax credits, among other items.

Social Security is financed by a payroll tax, in theory paid in equal shares by employer and employee. Most economists, however, believe that the burden of the employer's share is nearly always passed on to the employee in the form of lower wages. The bulk of the tax goes to two trust funds, Old Age and Survivors' Insurance, and Disability Insurance, which finance the benefits paid out of these programs. Originally set quite low, both the payroll tax rate and the wage base on which it is applied have steadily risen, from the original 1 percent each for employer and employee on the first $3,000 of wages to 6.20 percent each (for a total tax of 12.4 percent) on a wage base of $117,000 in 2014. In addition, Medicare imposes a payroll tax of 1.45 percent on *all* wages, without an upper limit. (This portion goes to a Hospital Insurance Trust Fund, discussed in Chapter 8.) The most rapid increases have come in the last three decades.

Benefits under OASDI follow a complicated formula using the worker's previous average monthly earnings and a schedule that pays higher percentages of average earnings for lower income brackets. Thus, the highest-paid workers receive higher benefit amounts up to the maximum amount, but lower-paid workers receive higher percentages of their average wages in monthly benefits. In 2012, the average benefit for a retired worker was $1,230 per month. The maximum depends on the age of retirement; for a worker retiring at age seventy in 2013, the maximum would be $3,350 per month. Disability benefits are calculated in a similar way. A divorced spouse (male or female) can receive benefits on a former husband's or wife's Social Security record if the marriage lasted at least ten years. The divorced spouse must be at least sixty-two and unmarried and must wait until two years after the divorce to receive benefits for the first time. Benefits and expenditures have risen rapidly with growth in the number of aged recipients, their longer life span, and liberalized definitions of disability.

Inflation is also an important factor, because benefit levels have been indexed since 1972 to increases in the cost of living through **Cost-of-Living Adjustments (COLAs)**. The 2013 COLA, for example, was 1.5 percent, and has been a topic of contention. Total OASDI expenditures were about $707 billion in 2010. It is important to note that Social Security benefits are not the only source of income for retired workers and their dependents, particularly those who have earned high wages. Private retirement plans have proliferated in recent decades, and Congress acted in 1974 to ensure retirees' rights to benefits and the financial integrity of such plans.

Unemployment Compensation. Unemployment Insurance and **Workers' Compensation** are the other two main programs that provide social insurance. Unemployment insurance benefits and wage replacement rates vary across the states, but are generally sufficient to support the temporary unemployment they were designed for, particularly when combined with the benefits available from some unions and from other forms of public assistance. Long-term unemployment is a more serious problem, but the unemployment insurance system was never intended to handle it. During the 2007–2009 recession, about half of the unemployed received unemployment insurance. This rate is as low as it is because of eligibility restrictions and limited benefit periods. Unemployment insurance is of most help to those with stable work histories and good prospects for finding a new position rapidly. Those with weak job skills and erratic work experience frequently find themselves ineligible for benefits. Low benefit levels and complex eligibility requirements also discourage many low-income workers from applying when they become unemployed. Although federally mandated, unemployment insurance is funded through state systems that collect funds from employers, usually via complex state-specific formulas that often preference employers with little experience laying off employees that would then collect from the system. Since the 2007–2009 recession, the federal government has required that states extend the period of eligibility, from twenty-six to ninety-nine weeks; and federal funds have been made available to the states to cover the increase in unemployment insurance payments both due to this eligibility extension and to overall greater demand.

Unemployment insurance and workers' compensation provide the supports that workers need in situations where labor market disconnections occur, be they from employment terminations or injury. Together with Social Security, these programs benefit from public and political popularity. Their contributory funding structures and generally streamlined administrative processes minimize stigma associated with claiming these benefits; nevertheless, the universal programs have meaningful redistributive properties that make them effective antipoverty policies, despite not being viewed by the public explicitly as such. Between 2008 and 2009, federal outlays in unemployment insurance—despite it being a predominantly state-funded program—doubled in direct response to extreme need caused by recession and high and persistent unemployment. Although public response to this expansion was favorable, the persistence of these benefit

---

POLICY DILEMMAS   Unemployment during Recession

Fifteen million U.S. workers lost their jobs during the 2007–2009 Great Recession—
the most severe recession since the 1930s. Although state Unemployment Insurance
(UI) usually lasts for twenty-six weeks, the federal government historically extends
the duration during hard times. For example, during the Great Recession, benefits
were extended to ninety-nine weeks (later reduced to seventy-three weeks). On
December 28, 2013, however, the extended benefits that were supporting more than
1.7 million long-term unemployed (defined as those searching for work for more
than twenty-six weeks) expired when Congress recessed. At the time, the rate of
unemployment in the United States was 6.7 percent, with state figures ranging from
2.7 percent (North Dakota) to 9.3 percent (Rhode Island).

Democrats were committed to restoring the extended UI benefits promptly when
Congress resumed in January 2014, but benefits remained unextended while Congress
as a whole debated the issue. As of this writing, seven bills had been introduced into the
House and Senate, including provisions to provide federally supported UI benefits
beyond the twenty-six-week state policy for up to an additional two years.

Democrats, led by Senate Majority Leader Harry Reid (Nevada), argued that—
despite no longer being in a formal recession—the economy was still not welcoming
to those searching for work, especially those with long-term absence from the workforce. They argued that it was the government's responsibility to help out-of-work
Americans who were struggling to pay their bills and get back on their feet. President Obama called for private businesses to prioritize the long-term unemployed
in their hiring.

Republicans argued that UI extensions provide a serious disincentive to work.
Because UI gives people the option to hold out for a "better" job offer, they may let
other job offers pass them by. Moreover, the price tag for reinstating the extension
was too high (depending on the bill's specifics, as much as $6.4 billion) and, Republi-
cans argued, should warrant cuts elsewhere.

Democrats rebutted that UI payments are not a disincentive to work because
they are much lower than jobs pay. Democrats also argued that the cost of the
extension should be considered "emergency" and not permanent spending, so
cutting the budget elsewhere was unnecessary.

This policy debate represents a classic partisan political road block, with each
party standing firm on its position with little interest in compromise. In the meantime, many people whose UI benefits expired remained unable to find work and
began to face even greater hardships. While the UI extension debate raged, a Gallup
Poll reported that 25 percent of Americans viewed unemployment as the nation's top
problem, with an additional 20 percent citing the economy.

1.   In addition to the benefits themselves, what other costs should be considered
      when debating the extension of UI?

2.   Which argument do you find most convincing: that having longer access UI ben-
      efits reduces the imperative to accept a job, or that government has the
      responsibility to help those whose long job searches have not been successful?

3.   What alternatives to extending UI benefits might support workers who cannot
      find jobs?

expenditures into the post-recessionary period became politically wearing, ultimately resulting in heated debates about the appropriate role for government in
assisting the long-term unemployed.

Social Assistance. Among social assistance (sometimes called public assistance) programs, cash public assistance is generally thought of as "welfare." This assistance intends to help certain categories of persons whose circumstances place them in poverty. Its goal is to assist families who are temporarily unable to support themselves and to help persons who are ineligible for social insurance but need help because of age or disability. Historically, we have assumed that cash public assistance should go only to people who deserve it, that is, those not responsible for their own poverty; therefore, cash public assistance has traditionally been available to children and to adults who are aged, blind, disabled, or guardians of small children. Adults who are none of these are assumed to be undeserving and are seldom eligible for assistance.

As identified in the history section, these federal programs to assist the poor have their origins in the Social Security Act of 1935. General tax revenues pay for public assistance programs, and any person within an eligibility category may qualify to receive benefits, making these programs categorical in their eligibility. In addition, benefits are related not to previous earnings, but to present need. They are means-tested. Examples of these social assistance programs are Temporary Assistance to Needy Families (TANF), Supplemental Security Income (SSI), and the Supplemental Nutrition Assistance Program (SNAP).

Public assistance programs come in two forms: cash assistance and in-kind assistance. Cash assistance is simply a transfer of money from a government agency to an individual. In-kind assistance refers to programs in which a tangible benefit, but not cash, is given to the recipient. SNAP benefits, for example, are convertible into food but not into money, and subsidized child care pays providers part of the fee associated with day care, thereby reducing parents' out of pocket costs. Assistance to the poor also comes in the form of services. Examples are literacy training, job training, job search assistance, family planning, and foster care.

Cash Transfer Programs

Temporary Assistance to Needy Families. Most people are familiar with the phrase "welfare reform," but welfare programs have been in a state of reform almost since their inception. The most recent incarnation of these reforms was the 1996 welfare reform legislation—the Personal Responsibility and Work Opportunity Reconciliation Act (PRWORA)—which accelerated devolution of cash assistance provision for families and children to the states. Under a new system of block grants to states, PRWORA ended the federal entitlement to assistance and imposed new work requirements and time limits on recipients.[12] The goals of PRWORA were (1) to assist needy families so that children can be cared for in their own, or a relative's, home; (2) to end welfare dependency by promoting work and marriage; (3) to reduce unwed pregnancy; and (4) to promote two-parent families.

TANF replaced the former Aid to Families with Dependent Children (AFDC) program. Instead of reimbursing the states for expenditures linked to eligible individuals (as in AFDC), TANF is a block grant to the states of approximately $16 billion per year since 1996, meaning that its value has eroded due to inflation. States have wide discretion in determining who is eligible for assistance under TANF and in setting various requirements for recipients. In the earlier years of PRWORA, incentive grants helped states encourage marriage, deal with fast-growing populations or high unemployment, and move welfare recipients to work.

States have a constellation of federal rules to choose from and modify to meet their own needs and interests. For example, states may deny federal TANF funds to adults who have received welfare for more than a cumulative total of five years in their lifetime or for adults who do not work after two years of assistance. States may impose shorter time limits and may exempt some of their caseload from the five-year time limit, reflecting the reality that many adults are so limited in their abilities as to be nearly unemployable. States also may deny assistance to unwed mothers under eighteen and to children born to TANF recipients. States vary substantially in their eligibility criteria, administrative practices, and choice of other rules that recipients must abide by. States are free under TANF to divert some funds from income support to pregnancy prevention, job training, or other services. There is also no guarantee that devolution of responsibility must stop at the state level. States can transfer financial responsibility to county or city governments. Some states have contracted with private businesses to perform eligibility and other functions formerly done by state employees. Recognizing that child care assistance is vital for public assistance recipients seeking to find and keep employment, PRWORA folds all major federal child care programs into the existing Child Care and Development Block Grant (CCDBG). In fiscal year 2012, federal funding was $5.2 billion. Like TANF, the CCDBG has been set to expire since 2010 but temporarily reauthorized through a series of short-term extensions.

Supplemental Security Income.   Some states have created explicit "diversion" programs as part of TANF, where they may offer families a lump sum of, say, three months' worth of cash assistance, in lieu of not enrolling in the program for the longer term. Related to this, some states have taken their much-harder-to-serve population, those with severe problems who are unlikely to be employable in the short term, and diverted them to the Supplemental Security Income (SSI) program, which provides a cash transfer to those with disabilities. Established in 1974, the SSI program replaced the jumble of state and federal programs for the aged, blind, and disabled with a single, centrally administered program. It is the only guaranteed minimum-income program in the United States funded from general revenues. The Social Security Administration sets benefit levels, adjusting them annually for cost-of-living increases. In December 2012, the federal plus state benefit averaged $519 per month, with those under age eighteen receiving slightly more ($621) and those over age sixty-five receiving slightly less ($417).[13]

Although initial SSI recipients were predominantly aged, higher Social Security benefits and rising rates of Social Security disability reduced the aged proportion of SSI recipients to about one-third. Slightly over half of all benefi-ciaries are disabled adults between eighteen and sixty-four years of age. Despite the expectation of one simplified, consolidated program, SSI has turned out to be quite complicated. First, the benefits have been insufficient, with benefit levels low enough that most states supplement SSI with their own funds. Sec-ond, the federal government is not the only administrator; some states administer their supplemental programs directly. Third, SSI supplements OASDI when its payments are below SSI standards. In fact, about 60 percent of all aged recipients and nearly 30 percent of all blind and disabled recipients use SSI to supplement Social Security. Federal and state SSI expenditures totaled $52 billion in 2012 for 8.3 million recipients.

Earned Income Tax Credit.   First established in 1975, the **earned income tax credit (EITC)** for low-income working families has been an increasingly important form of social assistance. It was substantially expanded in 1986, and again in 1990, 1993, 2001, and 2012. As of this writing in 2014, President Obama had proposed another EITC expansion. The EITC is now the largest federal, means-tested cash benefit program, and, as of 2014, twenty-five states and the District of Columbia had adopted state earned income credits as well. The federal EITC gives taxpayers a credit from the government for each dollar earned up to a certain point; the credits gradually phase out as income rises. This credit is refunded to eligible taxpayers who claim it on income tax forms. The EITC provides a benefit of anywhere from a few hundred dollars to a maximum of $6,044 in tax year 2013 for a family with three qualifying children. This pro-gram is a very important part of antipoverty efforts, because it rewards workers, a strong emphasis for both Democrats and Republicans. In 2013, for families with two children, a couple's earnings up to $51,567 generated a very small credit, with the largest credits going to those earning between about $10,000 and about $25,000. In 2012, over 27 million tax filers received credits amounting to $55.4 billion dollars.

In-Kind Benefits

Public assistance in the form of in-kind benefits now constitutes a higher propor-tion of public assistance than cash benefits. Medicaid (described in Chapter 8) is the largest in-kind public assistance program, and in most states its eligibility is administered jointly with cash and food assistance. The in-kind programs dis-cussed here include food and housing assistance.

Food Assistance.   The Supplemental Nutrition Assistance Program (SNAP) was established as the Food Stamp Program in 1974. Families below certain income levels receive a near-cash benefit (now in the form of a loaded debit card) that can be used in grocery stores specifically for food items. The fact that cash does not go directly to recipients reveals basic assumptions about welfare and poverty in America, rooted in the desire to see the poor adequately fed but also in a distrust of their spending habits.

The program is administered by the Department of Agriculture, which pays the entire cost of the food and almost two-thirds of each state's administrative costs. Benefits follow the price of food, the cost of a decent diet, family size, and income. Most recipients between the ages of sixteen and sixty now must be either seeking work, working an average of twenty hours per week, or in work training in order to receive SNAP benefits. PRWORA requires states to terminate food stamp benefits after three months in any thirty-six-month period for recipients not working or participating in employment programs, although states may exempt 15 percent of such recipients. States also have the discretion to align SNAP with TANF and other parts of public assistance, creating a uniform set of eligibility and work requirements.

Because eligibility guidelines differ from the income levels in cash assistance programs, many persons ineligible for the latter are eligible for SNAP. Because TANF and SSI income are counted in determining eligibility, those in states with high TANF and SSI benefits receive less in food stamps, and vice versa. This feature of the program tends to narrow the interstate disparities of cash assistance. SNAP is very sensitive to changes in the economy; in times of recession and unemployment the program expands.

Federal expenditures for SNAP totaled approximately $74.6 billion in 2012 for 46.6 million recipients. The federal government operates other nutrition programs, such as the Women, Infants, and Children (WIC) program and the school breakfast and lunch programs. WIC expenditures of $4.8 billion in 2012 covered 8.9 million recipients; the school breakfast program expended $3.3 billion for 12.9 million recipients; and the school lunch program expended $10.4 billion for 29 million recipients. Combined, these programs make major efforts to ensure the food security of our population, with SNAP being considered an essential part of our social safety net and the other programs serving children and other vulnerable, nutritionally needy populations.

Housing Assistance.   On a single night in 2012, there were 633,782 homeless people in the United States, including 394,379 who were homeless as individuals and 239,403 people who were homeless in families. Almost two-thirds (62 percent) of homeless people were living in an emergency shelter or transitional housing, and about one-third were living on the street.[14] The U.S. Department of Housing and Urban Development (HUD) aims not only to tackle this problem of homelessness, but also aims to help the millions of Americans who live in substandard, dilapidated, and overcrowded dwellings or who are paying too much for shelter. In 2011, one in four working households had a "severe" housing cost burden, meaning that they spent more than half of their incomes on housing; and among households with the lowest incomes (those below 30 percent of their area median income), the rate of high housing cost burden was 81 percent.[15] Programs to meet housing needs include public housing, rural farm labor housing, housing for the homeless, service-supported housing, homeownership assistance, rent and mortgage subsidies, the Community Development Program, and neighborhood rehabilitation. All attempt, in one way or another, to restore urban and rural housing and to provide decent shelter for low-income persons. Yet federal housing aid makes only a small contribution toward this goal.

Among the many HUD programs is public housing, which involves the federal government funding local housing authorities to build and maintain subsidized public housing units for qualified low-income individuals and families. Public housing accounts for about 1.1 million housing units and is much smaller than the housing choice and Section 8 tenant-based rental assistance programs and vouchers. Together, HUD spent about $33 billion in 2012 to assist about 5.4 million low-income individuals with its housing choice vouchers, project-based rental assistance, and public housing.[16] This level of assistance means that only one in four eligible households can receive any form of housing assistance.

In addition, federal policy, through the deductibility of mortgage interest payments and home loan guarantee programs, provides more housing assistance to middle- and upper-income than to poor families. Indeed, federal tax expenditures provide a wide array of benefits for the nonpoor and are much larger in magnitude.[17]

In addition to assistance with affording housing itself, the federal government also administers the Low-Income Home Energy Assistance Program (LIHEAP) to help people afford the energy costs associated with heating and cooling their residence or to weatherize for improved efficiency and lowered costs. Federal LIHEAP dollars are allocated to states in the form of a block grant, which was $5 billion in 2011.

Work Supports—Subsidized Child Care, Health Assistance, Employment Programs, and Other Services.   Through cash transfers, made either directly or through the tax system, and through in-kind assistance, intended to offset important costs, usually associated with work, the federal government, in partnership with the state, provides substantial work support to otherwise vulnerable households. The most important of these are health assistance (Medicaid; see Chapter 8) and child care subsidies. As noted in the section on PRWORA, the Child Care and Development Fund (CCDF) provided $2.9 billion to states in 2012 to assist low-income families in obtaining child care in support of work, training, and education. Some of these funds must go toward improving the quality of child care and coordinating resources to serve families through an integrated child care subsidy program.

In addition to the in-kind work supports that low-income households can access, the federal government and states also provide assistance in the form of services, including, importantly, remedial and vocational job training. The primary purpose of job-training programs is to help nonworkers attain marketable skills or to retrain dislocated workers for better jobs. These programs provide funds for training welfare recipients and others in job skills. They offer grants to state and local governments for skills training, counseling, remedial education, subsidized employment, and job creation in areas with high unemployment. They also fund the Job Corps, summer youth employment, and the Young Adult Conservation Corps. Since the mid-1980s, job training has been redirected toward the private sector. The Job Training Partnership Act (JTPA) placed most job-training programs in the hands of local Private Industry Councils, constituted by business persons, educators, labor officials, and other community representatives. This has since been replaced by the Workforce Investment Act (WIA) programs, which provide training services. PRWORA directed major attention to job readiness and job training for public assistance recipients.

What Is Missing?

Although here we describe the welfare state as being bifurcated into the social insurance and social assistance sets of policy responses to poverty, some have made the argument that the state is actually trifurcated. What we have ignored is the substantial assistance that goes to middle- and upper-income households through either employers or the government. For example, many jobs carry with them employer-provided health insurance and benefits; and major tax benefits come to homeowners in the form of the home mortgage interest tax deduction. These are very costly benefits that raise the well-being of those who are already in a relatively favorable position in society. The amount expended in this third tier of assistance is even more substantial than what we spend to minimize poverty and provide a safety net for those more vulnerable members of society. For example, the tax revenue forgone by having the home mortgage interest tax deduction amounted to more than $70 billion in 2012, which is more than four times the size of the federal TANF block grant to states.

POLICY EVALUATION: DO SOCIAL WELFARE POLICIES REDUCE POVERTY?

Growth in public assistance caseloads and associated spending during the 1970s and 1980s, as well as the media's "welfare queen" images, contributed to the unpopularity of these assistance programs among the American public.[18] One reason for that growth was demographic: as divorce and unwed childbearing rates climbed, so did public assistance expenditures. These programs grew also because of high unemployment generally characteristic until the mid-1990s. Programs designed for the working poor and the unemployed grow rapidly in such periods. This led ultimately to PRWORA's passage in 1996. Since then, public views have softened, first in response to rapidly declining caseloads and later in response to greater sympathy among the public compelled by real hardships caused by the most recent recession. In terms of their impact on the total budget, social insurance programs, which account for 70 percent of income support expenditures, dwarf public assistance. Moreover, all federal expenditures for public assistance, other than medical care and education, amounted to $322 billion in 2008, which represents 10.8 percent of the federal budget and about 2 percent of GDP. Even within public assistance itself, the relatively popular EITC and food stamps are the two largest programs. Widespread dislike of, and dissatisfaction with, public assistance in the 1990s had shifted by the turn of the twenty-first century, when caseloads appeared to have eliminated anyone perceived to be undeserving, retaining only the hardest to serve. Since the 2008 shift in the economy, the view that the economy, not personal failings, cause poverty is once again more dominant; this has resulted in broader public support for a strong safety net, since a greater number and diversity of people are now forced to access it. This section summarizes the accomplishments and criticisms of these two tiers, the social insurance and social assistance programs.

Accomplishments and Criticisms of Social Insurance

Although social insurance spending greatly exceeds spending for public assistance programs, until the late 1970s it generated comparatively little controversy. First, these programs, particularly OASDI, have a good record of accomplishing their goals. Their direct impact on the target populations of retirees, survivors, and disabled workers has been favorable. In terms of intended consequences, Social Security has achieved its goals. Moreover, because benefits are related to the self-contribution mechanism under the insurance aspect of OASDI and unemployment compensation, they are compatible with American values. Most see benefits as a return on an investment, albeit a mandatory one, rather than as a handout.[19]

OASDI and unemployment insurance have done a good job of keeping recipients out of poverty, particularly when combined with tax breaks, private pensions, and other benefits, such as SSI, Medicare, Medicaid, and food assistance, for which beneficiaries may also be eligible. Social Security helps keep the elderly poverty rate lower than the national average, making it America's most successful antipoverty program. Social Security gives retirees, survivors, and the disabled a fair return on their investment, as most can expect to receive more in benefits than their taxes. Current retirees, especially those with lower incomes, will likely recoup their payroll tax contributions, but middle- and higher-income workers will find their contributions and benefits closer to equivalence.[20]

Despite the fears of many younger workers that the Social Security system will be bankrupt by the time they retire, Congress regularly acts to ensure its financial stability. In 1983, for example, Congress raised the tax rate and the wage base for Social Security contributions and mandated a gradual increase in the retirement age from sixty-five to sixty-six by 2009 and to sixty-seven by 2027. At the same time, it subjected to federal taxation half of the Social Security benefits of approximately one-third of retirees with the highest incomes. These provisions will keep the program solvent until the late 2030s. In the next decade, Social Security will require further adjustments to maintain solvency.

Accomplishments and Criticisms of Social Assistance

The strong economy of the late 1990s made it possible for many former welfare recipients to find work. The economy plus restrictive TANF provisions produced a dramatic decline in public assistance enrollment, and, along with it, the public's disdain for welfare and those who rely on it softened. The recession of 2001 made it more difficult for persons to find work, but strict TANF restrictions still kept enrollment falling. With the renewal of TANF in 2005, Congress kept TANF's basic structure, but strengthened work requirements and state account ability for job placement, made it more difficult for recipients to attend college while on TANF, and reduced treatment length for substance addictions and mental illness. The renewal also appropriated $150 million for healthy marriage and responsible fatherhood initiatives. The most recent recession has carried with it many budget crises across the states, and public assistance has been less able to minimize hardship among those affected by the poor economy than in the prior recession. But, TANF is just one of the many programs that form the social safety net in the United States. Because there are so many social assistance programs and policies and because all aim at the general problem of poverty and its manifestations in poor health, nutrition, and housing, each program cannot be evaluated separately. Rather, this section considers both particular programs and the successes and failures of public assistance as a whole.

Because of the radical differences in their perspectives on poverty and its causes, critics of various ideological stripes have different evaluations of income support, with little agreement on their impacts or outcomes, direct or indirect. Conservatives, given their belief that poverty is the fault of the poor and of misguided welfare spending, generally evaluate public programs negatively, though they tend to believe that PRWORA has been a success. Liberals, believing that poverty is involuntary and related to lack of opportunity, have a generally favorable attitude toward welfare and income support programs, but find PRWORA restrictions counterproductive. Radicals see poverty programs only as bandages on a wound, neither intended to nor able to accomplish prevention or cure. It is the economic system itself, not government programs, that causes persistent poverty.

Americans are highly ambivalent about public assistance programs. Most believe that government programs are ineffective in relieving poverty and that most recipients do not deserve help. Yet a majority also are highly compassionate, believing that government should spend more money, not less, on helping poor persons with food, housing, medical care, and income.[21]

Despite these highly critical public attitudes, the welfare system has accomplished many intended goals. First, social assistance, through its combination of cash and in-kind aid, moves many Americans out of poverty. For many unfortunate enough to suffer from poverty, it will be a transitory experience ending in economic health. The public assistance programs, examined in isolation, have important shortcomings and inequities, but taken together, they provide a basic minimum living standard for many of the poor. This combination effect is the reason that many liberals oppose cutting what, to some, may appear to be excessive spending in particular programs.

The EITC has been the most effective mover of persons out of poverty. In 2012, 10.1 million people, including 5.3 million children, were lifted out of poverty.[22] One estimate suggests that the poverty rate for children would be a full one-third higher than it is if it were not for the EITC.[23] It is highly effective also in reaching its target: people who work hard but on earned income alone cannot support a family. The EITC encourages single parents to enter the workforce and to work more hours. At the same time, it enables some married couples to have one parent spend more time at home with the children or rewards two-parent households who work but still have low earnings. Moreover, the EITC is efficient and affordable to administer, as it uses the existing tax structure. On the other hand, the EITC has very high error rates, as it is difficult for many persons to determine whether their family situation qualifies them for EITC. On the whole, however, the EITC retains strong liberal, conservative, and popular support.

Food assistance programs contribute to improved nutrition among the poor. More than half of all recipients are children, who would have severe nutrition problems in the program's absence. Moreover, the near-poor can maintain decent living standards when economic hard times place severe restrictions on income. SNAP in particular is more than an antihunger program; it is now an essential part of the network of supports that provide a safety net. Housing assistance, subsidized child care, and other in-kind programs also supply many basic needs while supporting work. America's great wealth makes its residual poverty shocking; even more shocking would be the extent of poverty if no public assistance programs were available. Without government programs almost double the proportion of individuals would be poor than the official poverty rate reveals.[24] Public assistance is more successful than usually acknowledged in alleviating poverty, hunger, ill health, and inadequate housing. But the fact remains that, even with these programs in place, 46.5 million of our population are poor; and living under such resource-constrained conditions has long-term and important consequences, especially for children.

The use of public assistance by most American families conforms to the policy's intention, to provide temporary help until jobs are found, health is regained, or the divorced or widowed are remarried. Accessing welfare is primarily an economic decision influenced by the unavailability of jobs and by prevailing wage rates. Despite widely held opinion, fraud and corruption are no more or less of a problem than in most other government programs or in private business, for that matter. Moreover, social science research consistently shows that public assistance does not produce an increase in illegitimacy or additional children as a means of receiving more money.[25]

Liberal critics obscured these successes by shifting the issue from poverty to income inequality. During the 1960s, liberal action focused on remedying absolute poverty. During the 1970s, the focus implicitly changed to an attack on inequality. Although public assistance made strides in minimizing the former, it did little about the latter.[26] Loyalty to government's responsibility to support low-income persons remains strong among progressives. Liberals, however, tend to confuse their strong sense of justice and compassion for the poor with the ability of public assistance to solve the poverty problem. Conservatives, on the other hand, are ideologically predisposed to oppose public assistance programs. Yet public assistance has protected American private enterprise from its own shortcomings. The very success of social assistance (and social insurance) programs in reducing poverty smothers demands for a more radical reform of the American political and economic system, as radicals lament.

Did the policy change that created TANF, in particular, improve the performance of the system of social assistance? The liberal, conservative, and radical differences in perspective on public assistance and on poverty and its causes suggest highly divergent responses to this question.

Cost and Administration.   Conservatives are generally pleased that TANF has kept low the cost of cash public assistance to mothers and children. The program's block grant feature ensures this result. SSI, EITC, and SNAP expenditures, however, continue to grow, which displeases conservatives. Yet, the total cost of all federal nonhealth social assistance is only about 10 percent of the federal budget and is dwarfed by other public expenditures in areas that are much less publicly and politically contentious. The total amount spent, however, is not inconsequential, administrative expenses are high, and the multitude of overlapping programs creates inefficiency in getting funds to the target populations and numerous unintended consequences. Moreover, social assistance, especially in times of economic slowdown, just when people most need this assistance, puts a severe financial strain on some state and local governments.

The problem of administrative complexity is a serious dilemma for public assistance programs of all modern nations and an important cause of high administrative costs. Confusion and complexity are inherent in categorical and means-tested programs because hundreds of questions, forms, and regulations are needed to define categories and levels of need and to establish whether particular persons are needy and fit the defined categories. Multiply this by the determination process for other programs, add periodic rechecking of eligibility to reduce fraud and waste, and the administrative burden of these programs becomes staggering. On top of all this is the complexity of having separate rules and regulations at each level of administration: federal, state, and local.

Paradoxically, antifraud regulations unintentionally contribute to high error rates. As regulations to close loopholes pile up, program complexity increases. As this happens, program employees are more prone to mistakes; caseworker turnover increases, and new workers—having had less time on the job—are even more prone to mistakes. A double bind operates. Public assistance can be either lower in administrative costs and higher in fraud and mistakes, or higher in administrative costs and lower in fraud and mistakes. Low overhead and low error rates cannot be achieved simultaneously. PRWORA did not change this equation.

Adequacy of Benefits and Reduction of Poverty.   Traditionally, liberals and progressives have evaluated public assistance programs by their ability to support individuals and families in dignity (adequacy) and in their ability to reduce the number of poor persons. Poverty rates in the United States remain much higher than in comparable nations. TANF, SNAP, SSI, and other benefits barely provide any kind of decent living standard. Moreover, there are substantial gaps in public assistance coverage, particularly for single individuals and childless couples under sixty-five. Pegged as they are to the "deserving" poor, social assistance programs contribute little to relieving the poverty of these people. Few programs provide assistance solely on the basis of need; most exclude certain categories of people. The prosperous economy of TANF's first five years reduced poverty rates and masked the seriousness of the adequacy problem. The economic slowdown beginning in 2001 threw many out of work, pushed poverty rates higher, and highlighted the inadequacy of benefit levels from the liberal perspective. The more recent recession, beginning in 2008, is both deeper and lengthier, and these assistance programs have been more intensely accessed, though at a time when state governments' budgets have been in crisis, thereby limiting assistance just when it is needed most. With evident hardships extending further up the income distribution, the programs that make up the social safety net have gained somewhat wider popularity. Because of the lack of entitlement and time-limit placed on cash assistance receipt, the change to TANF likely makes the adequacy problem worse for many families, particularly during recessionary economic times. Although no longer currently in recession by 2014, the U.S. economy's recovery has been sluggish, with those with the lowest skills being chronically unemployed and little opportunity for them to find jobs.

Work.   Whatever their disagreements on cost, administration, and adequacy of benefits, conservatives and liberals, Republicans and Democrats, agree in preferring an economy and a system of public assistance that encourage work, equip persons to work, and reward work. Commentators often frame this issue in terms of dependency: the extent to which citizens depend on government programs for their basic needs, rather than being able and willing to find work to provide for these needs. In this regard, PRWORA presents a decidedly mixed picture, one that conservatives tend to interpret favorably and liberals unfavorably.

The most universally recognized problem of public assistance prior to 1996 was that, despite work requirements, there were discouragements to work (and thus encouragements to dependency) built into program structures, particularly given the effect of multiple programs and the lack of time limits. Little empirical evidence shows large effects, but some were real. Work disincentives keep recipients dependent even when work is available to them, obviously an unintended and undesirable effect. These disincentives come into play because in many programs benefits are phased out as earned income increases. Yet, in too many cases, for every dollar earned, the recipient lost a dollar or more in benefits. In addition, there were points in the benefit scale (notches) at which an additional dollar of earnings did not simply reduce benefits, but made a family totally ineligible for benefits. The loss of Medicaid for families with health problems was a particularly strong work disincentive. The work requirements, transitional health assistance, and child care support built into TANF were designed to create work incentives.

Now almost two decades since PRWORA's passage, it is possible to evaluate its strengths and weaknesses in terms of work and poverty rates among former recipients.[27] TANF caseloads dropped precipitously so that fewer people rely upon government cash assistance. Evidence shows that 60 to 70 percent of adults leaving TANF worked at least some time, and the percentage of income derived from work among low-income, female-headed families rose from

30 percent of all income to nearly 60 percent. At the same time, liberal predictions of rising poverty among adults and children were not fulfilled. Poverty rates either remained the same or declined, until the economy turned again in 2008.

These good results are not all attributable to TANF. The economy of the 1990s was exceptionally strong, helping provide jobs and reduce poverty. The EITC expanded in these years as well, as did health care benefits and the child tax credit, helping to make low-income families better off. Moreover, poverty remains persistently high, and nearly 40 percent of those leaving public assistance because of exhausting their limits do not work consistently. Most have the kinds of handicapping conditions of low education, poor mental or physical health, and lack of job skills that make it unlikely that they and their children will ever escape poverty. PRWORA has made their living conditions worse.

Finally, job training and job advancement are critical if former public assistance recipients are to remain off the rolls and out of poverty. Progressives contend that too much of PRWORA's efforts have been on having recipients land in a job. After that, they are on their own. Moreover, the simple truth is that work plus the EITC often is not enough to support a family in dignity, if its wage earners have little education or job skills, and particularly if their jobs do not include health insurance and other benefits, as many low wage jobs do not. The poverty rate among working single-mother families (after government benefits and taxes) remains stubbornly high. Local food pantries continue to report an increase in long-term need for food assistance, especially among working families. As many as 12 million American families currently report not having enough food or fear of going hungry. Many more must weekly decide whether to pay medical bills or buy gas for the car to get to work, whether to buy food or clothes for the children.[28]

Equity.   Inequity, in two senses, is a problem in social assistance. Horizontal inequity refers to the fact that poor persons with the same degree of need frequently do not receive the same degree of aid. Vertical inequity refers to a twofold imbalance: the neediest often do not receive aid, and the system sometimes offers high benefits to some of the poor, while providing none for the near poor. These inequities have two main sources: benefit level variation from state to state and the categorical nature of the programs. Because each state sets eligibility and benefit levels for TANF, a poor family receives different income depending on where it lives. A family with an income of $10,000 in California receives higher benefits (even adjusting for differences in cost of living) than a family in similar circumstances with the same income in Alabama.

Additionally, families with an earned income slightly above guidelines receive no support, where others without such income are eligible for a variety of programs, the combined benefit of which makes them better off than the working family. SNAP, the EITC, and other programs available to the working poor reduce some of these inequities, but substantial ones remain. Because many in-kind programs are funded at a low level, their benefits are not available to all those technically eligible. Only a fraction of those who could qualify receive housing assistance, for example.

Family and Marriage.   The family and marriage goals of PRWORA have been the least enthusiastically pursued by state governments, as most bureaucrats and most Americans remain ambivalent about government responsibility to intervene in private choices about marriage and family. Liberals support this reluctance and wish to minimize attention to these aspects of welfare reform; conservatives advocate strongly for attention to these.

The goals of child care and child support are central to welfare reform. When work is required of adult guardians of children, where will good quality child care be found? Conservatives argue that existing child care funding is adequate and that strong efforts at requiring absent fathers to pay child support are needed. Liberals argue for increased child care funding, contending that good quality, affordable child care remains difficult to find. The fact of the matter is that it is cheaper to pay welfare recipients to stay at home and take care of their children than it is to pay for job training and placement and to pay for the child care of persons in low-skill jobs with minimum wages. Unless the child care available to now-working, former TANF mothers is relatively high quality, then PRWORA may produce higher rates of crime, poor education, and addiction as unintended consequences of child neglect and lack of quality supervision.

Summary of Accomplishments and Criticisms.   It is now abundantly clear that the poor are not an undifferentiated group. First, there are the elderly and disabled, for whom direct income assistance is considered to be the most appropriate form of aid. Indeed, it is this group that has been most assisted out of poverty, particularly by Social Security. A second group of the poor is single mothers with young children. To move out of poverty, they need flexible, quality child care, child support from absent fathers, health insurance, and assistance in finding jobs along with secure jobs that pay enough to support a family and offer advancement opportunities. Another group is the working poor, who are underemployed or employed only part-time or at minimum wage. Their primary need is a solid EITC, remedial education and job training for higher-wage skills, a labor market that includes good jobs with advancement opportunities, and health insurance; and they need unemployment insurance for protection when jobs run out. This complexity is the deepest challenge for the future of social insurance and social assistance programs.

CONTINUING DEBATES: SOCIAL WELFARE POLICY CHANGE

While social insurance programs enjoy broad popularity and are relatively efficient and effective in meeting their goals, social assistance policies remain charged with addressing two primary intractable dilemmas: (1) the large number of children spending all or part of their childhood in poverty, and (2) the availability of jobs that lift people out of poverty. (The discussions of family demographics in Chapter 2 and family policy in Chapter 13 are particularly pertinent in this regard.)

Children and Poverty

The number of children spending years in poverty, living in squalid conditions, dependent on public assistance, and learning few job skills became one of the most striking indictments of public assistance before 1996. Public assistance had been designed many years ago as a temporary support for children and their mothers. For many, it served that purpose. For others, poverty became a way of life linked to many social problems—drug abuse, crime, poor housing, chronic unemployment—and their consequences.

One important goal of welfare reform has been to reduce nonmarital child-bearing and to strengthen family life, by extension reducing the high proportion of children growing up in poverty. By any standard, to have one-fifth of children in poverty is too much. In part for the favorable increase in mothers' labor force participation, more children are in child care and after-school programs. Child support enforcement on absent fathers has raised the percentage of support judgments and collections, though these rates remain stubbornly low. PRWORA was one marker for a reorientation of public assistance away from entitlements toward an idea of reciprocity in American social policy.[29] In return for cash assistance, child care support, increased EITC, and other supports, adults should exercise responsible parenthood—take care of their children, work to support their families, seek out job training when needed, and so forth. Families that fail in their responsibilities can expect to be sanctioned. At this writing in 2014, President Obama has proposed expansion of the EITC and child tax credits; and generally, Republicans appear supportive. Because the EITC is a credit to *working* families, and the most generous amounts go to families with *children*, the EITC is in sync with the notion that individuals need to meet some obligation (such as work) in exchange for help.

It is difficult, however, to say that this new reciprocity—or paternalism, as some call it—has been fully developed in welfare policy to the extent as is represented in the EITC, for example.[30] In fact, many states have devoted very little attention to implementing the child and family provisions of TANF, instead focusing on increasing employment and reducing welfare rolls. The states vary widely in their efforts and success in reducing child poverty.[31] Some evidence shows that low-income young children are doing better in school, but adolescents may be faring worse in terms of their criminal activity.[32] Finally, welfare rolls declined far more rapidly than the child poverty rate.

As reported in the first section of this chapter, children are disproportionately poor. More than one of every five lives below the official poverty line at any given time, and many more live in poverty for at least part of their childhood. Moreover, children are increasingly living in single-parent families, most of which are headed by lone mothers. Twenty-five percent of all children under eighteen live in such households, and about half of all children will do so at some time. Many go for years without seeing their fathers, even for short visits. A growing proportion of TANF benefits are directed to "child only" cases, meaning that the children receive aid while parents do not, either because the parents have exceeded their time on TANF, or because the child lives with grandparents or other relatives, or because the parents are ineligible for benefits because of their immigration status.

The consequences of child poverty and family breakup are severe, including poor education, teenage pregnancy, child abuse, suicide, drug addiction, and high crime rates. Moreover, poorly educated, addicted, abused, or imprisoned children have a difficult time growing up to be productive citizens. Government spending on children is not very effective, especially when compared with spending on the elderly. In 1965, government spending on the elderly was 21 percent of all income maintenance and other social welfare spending, while 37 percent went to children. By the late 1980s, spending on children was 24 percent, and spending for the elderly reached 33 percent. These expenditures lifted out of poverty 82 percent of the elderly who would have been poor without government programs. Only 32 percent of children were lifted out of poverty.[33] Today, the poverty-reducing effect of Social Security is clear, whereas other forms of assistance remain less efficient and less effective.

Other wealthy, democratic nations have far more generous programs for children, without slighting the elderly. Most, for example, have a universal children's allowance, amounting to from 5 to 10 percent of the median wage. They also provide cash benefits to parents at the time of childbirth, as well as allowances that support a parent for taking time away from work in the first months (and in some cases years) of the child's life. Other nations generously support preschool and child care programs. In the United States, recent debate has centered on the potential for the Head Start program to prepare disadvantaged children to enter kindergarten and thereby achieve at the same levels as their nonpoor counterparts. Early childhood education has been a hallmark of President Obama's State of the Union addresses.

Children's advocates advance many proposals to attack the problem of child poverty and associated social problems. Reducing the tax burden on families with children finds support among both liberals and conservatives; recent tax legislation went some distance in this direction by creating a per child tax credit, providing tax credits and deductions for college expenses, and reducing the tax burden on married families. But these will do little for *poor* children unless their parents find and keep jobs with reasonable income and benefits. Cash public assistance, TANF, itself cannot have a large effect on child well-being since it is merely one part of a whole constellation of policies and programs that share poverty alleviation as a goal. As Table 7.2 notes, adjusting the poverty measure for TANF assistance changed the supplemental poverty measure from 16.0 to just 16.2 percent in 2012; and while 0.2 percentage points still represents 622,000 individuals, the poverty alleviating effect is negligible, compared to other government efforts. Given the lessons from the success of social insurance programs—their nearly universal coverage and wide popularity—policies to address the causes and consequences of poverty for children would be most effective if universal, maximizing coverage and minimizing stigma.

Employment Issues

In responding to PRWORA, many state public assistance programs focused first on those recipients most job-ready because of their education, former employment history, and motivation. These were easiest to place and to take credit for under the new PRWORA rules and expectations. Recipients who are more difficult to place because of long-term dependency, low education, drug or alcohol abuse, criminal record, or histories of being sexually abused are far more difficult (and far more costly) to work with.[34] This is doubly so because, under current federal law, all persons required to work must receive a minimum wage and be covered by employment rights, such as health and safety regulations. Moreover, the children of public assistance recipients are more likely than average to have health or behavioral problems that make it difficult for their mothers to obtain and hold full-time work, especially considering related day care needs and supply. Expenditures for training, educating, and placing such people, when it is done well, are more costly than traditional welfare.

Job training alone is insufficient to ensure work for all, as is made particularly evident in the current economic climate, where even skilled workers are being laid off or seeing their wages cut. In poor neighborhoods, there are multiple applicants for the few jobs that open up. All the training in the world will not produce a job when no jobs are available. Job creation strategies must accompany work requirements for welfare reform to be effective. Yet, there is little consensus and less experience in making more employment available in areas suffering high rates of poverty and economic decline, as well as high rates of addiction and other challenges.

Progressive and conservative welfare reformers agree that work is the best and most permanent path out of poverty. It is not clear, however, how to make that path available. Proposals run from the most extreme, cold-turkey approach on the libertarian side (abolition of all public assistance with each individual responsible for finding work in the private sector) to proposals to imitate the German system of apprenticeship, in which schools and businesses combine for three-year education and job training programs. In the middle of these extremes is reform of the current system to expand on work expectations and opportunities while also considering the role of education in reducing poverty. At this writing, the broader state of the economy is taking policy priority over additional tinkering with a policy, as reauthorized under PRWORA, that elected officials find generally acceptable.

In addition to considering employment for welfare recipients in particular, it is important to consider more broadly the hard-core unemployed and the challenges they face. Often with long-standing substance abuse problems, criminal histories, or mental instability, this small part of our population finds employment difficult. Work requirements or job training requirements that are part of TANF do not tackle these problems and therefore are unlikely to be successful. Addressing these problems is very difficult and costly.

Next, the jobs available to those with low skills, whether they receive public assistance or not, are likely to be low paying, without such benefits as health care, and without decent possibilities of advancement. Even successful workfare programs have only marginally improved the lives of participants, in large part due to the inhospitability of the lower rung of the labor market. Even if those leaving welfare for work secure jobs paying near the minimum wage, these jobs are very likely to carry with them little or no benefits, meaning that these workers must still access housing assistance, health assistance, and possibly food assistance in order to support a family. In times of economic stress, both government and charitable services are burdened not only with the long-term chronically poor but also with an influx of those with short-term needs. Neither those who escape welfare for work nor those who are working but remain poor can fully escape some dependence on government help. What happens when they lose their jobs, become sick or injured, or grow old? If perceptions of public assistance lead Americans to think that work and dependence are mutually exclusive alternatives, they will be sadly surprised.

SUMMARY

Current social insurance and social assistance programs in the United States combine features in tension with each other. Sympathy for the plight of the elderly, widows, widowers, and children drives policy in a progressive direction; that is, toward the notion that all members of society deserve an income and sufficient economic dignity to support a decent life in a prosperous, democratic society. On the other hand, commitment to the free market and suspicion that government programs encourage dependency drive policy in a conservative direction. It may well be that recent changes, particularly in public assistance, signal not so much liberal–conservative tension as movement toward a more communitarian political ideology. Here, the focus is on opportunity and responsibility, where government programs should provide opportunities and support to persons so that they can succeed if possible on their own; at the same time, every person has a responsibility to use his or her talents to make the most of the opportunities furnished by government and the market.[35] The primary challenge is to discover what combination of public policies best enacts opportunity and responsibility with respect to income support and with respect to health care, the topic of the following chapter.

 **RESOURCES**

AARP: **www.aarp.org/issues**

Brookings Institution: **www.brookings.edu**

Center on Budget and Policy Priorities: **www.cbpp.org**

Heritage Foundation: **www.heritage.org**

Institute for Research on Poverty: **www.ssc.wisc.edu/irp**

Joint Center for Poverty Research: **www.jcpr.org**

Spotlight on Poverty and Opportunity: **www.spotlightonpoverty.org**

Urban Institute: **www.urban.org**

U.S. Department of Health and Human Services: **www.hhs.gov**

Chapter 8

Health Care: Transformation or Continued Crisis?

Spring 2010 witnessed historic change in Washington. After nearly a century of struggle, debate, false starts, and incremental change, major health care reform legislation passed both houses of Congress and was signed by President Obama, achieving what presidents Franklin Roosevelt, Harry Truman, Richard Nixon, and Bill Clinton (and their respective congresses) had failed to accomplish: significant movement toward universal health insurance coverage and the promise of substantial change in the way health care is delivered and financed.

Yet, that victory occurred by the narrowest of margins in an extraordinarily rancorous political climate, following an ideological and political battle of epic scale and complexity. That the passage of the **Patient Protection and Affordable Care Act (PPACA)** was historic cannot be doubted. What is very much in doubt is whether the legislation will be successfully implemented and produce its intended effects. If it *does* achieve its goals, then the transformation of the American health care system will have begun. If it *does not* achieve its goal, the system will remain in continued crisis.

Judging the outcome will take many years, because the U.S. health system features deeply embedded disruptive tensions. "Health care is caught in an 'iron triangle' of conflicting expectations among patients, clinicians, and public health and government policy makers. Not all the forces can be satisfied and some are mutually exclusive."[1] The general public (patients and voters) prefers unfettered choice of medical providers and comprehensive, low cost insurance. Medical professionals want practice autonomy and access to the latest science and technology. Government and public health professionals desire low cost care, access to care for all, and effective treatments. The ACA is caught in this high level struggle to reconcile this iron triangle of conflicting expectations that create intense political and policy conflict. Health care reform either will exacerbate these contradictions, or it will begin to alleviate the fundamental distress at the heart of one of our largest social systems.

The same perplexing logic and inherent goal conflicts that characterize the income support policies described in Chapter 7 plague health care policy. High medical bills plunge many Americans into poverty. The poor and the aged are more likely than the rest of the population to suffer illness and to struggle with gaining access to health care.

ISSUE BACKGROUND: THE CHANGING HEALTH CARE SYSTEM

The Structure of American Health Care

The traditional American health care system combines public and private institutions without central planning or coordination. "Independence" and "autonomy" are the watchwords. At the highest level of the health care profession—among physicians, dentists, and psychologists—solo, **fee-for-service (FFS)** practice was the rule until recent decades. That is, the professional provider of health services established his or her own office, with perhaps one or two others sharing the same specialty, saw only his or her own patients, and charged a separate fee for each individual service performed. Institutions such as hospitals, clinics, and laboratories operated primarily on the same FFS basis. Hospitals were primarily public (city or county owned) or else were nonprofit community hospitals owned and operated by religious groups or nonprofit foundations. Laboratories, nursing homes, and other providers were largely for-profit, independent operations. There were many independent health insurance companies offering products to businesses or individuals with some state regulation. Patients also were independent, free to choose among any providers willing to accept them as patients.

Medical care in this kind of environment is fragmented, difficult to coordinate for persons with multiple or serious medical conditions, and very expensive. In FFS, the economic incentives are clearly to provide more services to patients, even if they are of questionable or limited value. Such a structure is particularly problematic as the population ages and chronic conditions (instead of sudden acute illness or accident) become predominant. This traditional system shifted during recent decades, moving away from FFS toward coordinated care systems, driven by two different often contending forces: (1) government programs attempting to control spending and to improve quality and (2) organizational consolidation and integration by insurance companies, hospitals, and physicians. These changes began to restrict patient choice of hospitals, physicians, and other providers.[2] Limited networks of providers emerged as a force in American health care in the 1980s as a method to hold down the increasing cost of health care. At the same time, consolidation in the insurance industry gave these companies leverage in negotiations with hospitals, physicians, and other medical providers. In response, independent hospitals consolidated into systems, many smaller hospitals closed, and physicians joined into larger single- or multispecialty groups, in order to achieve efficiencies of scale and to have bargaining power with insurance companies. In the first decade of the 2000s, for example, the share of physicians in solo or small practices declined from 53 percent to 23 percent. Physicians also sought employment by hospitals and other organizations better to control their quality of life, working conditions, and income.

Thus, a corporate model of economic organization began to characterize health care. Now many health care systems combine physician practices, hospitals, specialty care companies, and insurance products into one hierarchically organized structure. The growth of information technology in the form of electronic medical records, Smartphone health applications, and web-based search engines facilitates such consolidation. Currently, patients are becoming (or asked to become) smarter health care "consumers," investigating and testing medical treatments and providers in much the same way they purchase automobiles, groceries, or other products.

Medical bills are paid through complicated arrangements among government agencies, individuals, and private insurers. Federal, state, and local governments provide a number of health-related services directly, for example, inoculations, health inspections, vector control, veterans' care, and epidemic control. They also operate some hospitals and other facilities and reimburse private medical providers through direct payments for services. Individuals pay for a variety of services directly, but they also pay indirectly by purchasing health insurance from private insurance companies. These companies reimburse providers for covered services, which vary widely according to the terms of particular policies. Most private insurance is purchased through employers, with the employers passing their share of premiums to employees in the form of lower wages.

Despite radical changes under way in health care delivery, fragmented and expensive care continues as a legacy of the system's origins. Consolidation should improve the ability of providers to seamlessly meet the needs of persons with chronic conditions; yet, that promise is seldom recognized in practice, because patients, physicians, insurance companies, and medical organizations have competing incentives. As advances in medicine reduce admissions and length of stay, hospitals are closing or are redirecting their missions. Outpatient surgeries and freestanding surgical units, or specialty hospitals, as well as minor care clinics (which are often located within pharmacies or grocery stores) direct care away from physician offices and hospitals. These changes have occurred without overall strategy or design, resulting in disjointed and wasteful delivery of medical care. Proponents of health care reform hope that the ACA will help to rationalize care delivery.

The Institute of Medicine has described what a properly functioning health care system should look like.[3] Health care should be STEEEP—safe, timely, effective, efficient, equitable, and patient-centered. Achieving these goals of a properly functioning health care system has proven elusive. The main shortcomings are deficient quality, gaps in access to care, and unsustainable costs.

Quality: How Healthy Is America?

Genetic endowment, the physical environment, social class, and behavioral choices have a larger effect on health status and longevity than medical treatment.

Medical technology, however, certainly keeps many persons alive and in good physical condition. Intensive care units, coronary bypass surgery, and hemodialysis, as well as immunizations, fillings of dental cavities, and antibiotics, lessen pain and prolong life for millions.

The most widely used statistics on health are encouraging. By 2013, life expectancy at birth in the United States averaged just over 78.5 years, and the death rate for infants during the first year of life had fallen to 5.9 per 1,000 live births, the lowest rate ever. These figures represent considerable improvement over previous decades, but they are more than matched by other nations (see Table 8.1). Even though American medical technology is the most advanced in the world, the United States ranks behind countries such as Sweden, Japan, the Netherlands, Canada, France, England, and many others in life expectancy and infant mortality. Life expectancy for the very aged in the United States, however, is slightly above the median, reflecting an emphasis on the elderly in American health care policy. Although the United States and Canada started from the same point in the late 1960s, universal coverage in Canada seems to have produced better outcomes on most measures and at lower cost. The perception is widespread among professionals and the public alike that, despite improvements in health statistics and advances in medical knowledge and technology, Americans are only marginally healthier now than in previous decades. Despite massive increases in health care expenditures, most Americans, although satisfied with their individual care, believe that there is a crisis in the system as a whole.[4]

If the basic ills of the American health care system are looked at generally, a pattern is clear: the system emphasizes some kinds of care at the expense of others. In particular, cure of acute medical conditions (lasting less than three months and requiring immediate medical attention or restricted activity) takes priority over care for chronic conditions (debilitating illnesses lasting over three months). Yet, chronic conditions are far more prevalent and (in the aggregate and over time) more expensive to treat. Expensive, curative care receives more attention than disease prevention, health education, rehabilitation services, chronic care, primary care, or public health measures.

Health statistics are improving, and most Americans are satisfied with their personal health care. American medical technology and health care innovation are the best in the world. Yet, fear of high health costs, possible loss of insurance, and increased complexity of health care leave Americans feeling uneasy. Formerly convinced that the *quality* of health care was uniformly high, Americans are discovering a different reality; medical care often is not safe, effective, or patient-centered (three of the STEEEP goals).[5]

The focus of American medicine on new technologies in drugs, diagnostic tests, and surgical procedures produces a **service intensity** that not only increases cost, but also produces a greater likelihood of medical errors that harm patients. Even though the *percentage* of errors is low, the large number of procedures per patient produces a high *number* of errors. In 1999, the Institute of Medicine shocked the nation with an estimate of up to 100,000 hospital deaths per year resulting from medical errors. There is no single government or private agency responsible for measuring the quality of American health care.

T A B L E 8.1   Salient Features of Health Care Systems (selected nations)

	Type of System (all with universal coverage except USA)	Spending as % GDP (2012 or latest year)	Spending per Capita (2012 or latest year)	Rank: Life Expectancy at Birth (all OECD nations)	Rank: Infant Mortality (all OECD nations)	Rank: Avoidable Hospital Admissions: Diabetes (all OECD nations)	Government Percentage of Health Spending
Australia	Public insurance, limited private supplements	8.9	$3,800	7	23	11	68
Canada	Single-payer, public insurance	11.2	$4,666	17	27	6	70
France	Public insurance, limited private supplements	11.6	$4,118	6	18	n/a	77
Germany	Regulated competing private insurance	11.3	$4,495	18	20	18	77
Netherlands	Regulated competing private insurance	11.9	$5,099	11	22	n/a	85
New Zealand	National health system (public), limited private supplements	10.3	$3,182	12	30	15	83
Norway	National health system (public), limited private supplements	9.4	$5,901	10	4	5	85
Sweden	National health system (public), limited private supplements	9.5	$3,925	8	2	10	82
Switzerland	Regulated competing private insurance	11.3	$5,914	1	24	3	65
U.K.	National health system (public), limited private supplements	9.4	$3,405	15	25	4	83
USA	Public-private mix	17.7	$8,508	27	31	17	49

Note: OECD = Organisation for Economic Co-operation and Development (see http://www.oecd.org/about, accessed February 24, 2014).

SOURCES: Cathy Schoen et al., "Access, Affordability, and Insurance Complexity Are Often Worse in the United States Compared to Ten Other Countries," *Health Affairs, 32* (December 2013): 2205–2215, appendix 1; and www.oecd.org/els/health-systems/oecdhealthdata2013-frequentlyrequesteddata.htm, accessed March 14, 2014.

The severe problems of uninsured Americans and unequal access to care also contribute to poor quality. America cannot claim to possess the highest quality of care in the world when a high proportion of the population lacks access to it and suffers unnecessary disability, pain, and death.

Another quality problem is overspecialization among physicians. Primary care physicians (internists and family medicine) now constitute a small proportion of American physicians. Other nations have significantly higher percentages. Serious consequences flow from the predominance of specialists. Poor performance on measures of infant mortality and life expectancy is more sensitive to high-quality routine care than to sophisticated, exceptional procedures. Overspecialization contributes to the high cost of medical care, because specialists charge more and use hospitals more than do general practitioners. It also leads to poor coordination of care and confusion about prescriptions.

Inequities in Access to Health Care

The Uninsured.   The percentage of the population lacking health insurance coverage is unacceptably high. Although the vast majority of Americans are insured via connection with employment, that form of insurance has been in steady decline, only partly offset by increases in Medicare and Medicaid insurance (see Figure 8.1). For 2012 (the most recent data available), the U.S. Census Bureau counts 48 million persons (nearly 18 percent of the population under age sixty-five) lacking public or private health insurance coverage and thus with serious difficulty obtaining health care services. Uninsurance is a dynamic condition, with people moving into and out of insured status constantly. For some, uninsured spells are brief; however, for about 26 million persons, being uninsured lasts more than a year.[6] Low-income working adults, young adults, and persons living in the South and West are particularly likely to be uninsured. Sixty percent of those without insurance live in families with at least one full-time worker, but whose employer does not provide insurance or who cannot afford the premiums.

Of course, health insurance is not health care, and health care is not health itself. Health *practices,* such as fitness, adequate rest, and the avoidance of smoking, contribute more to life and well-being than health *care*. Yet, if illness or injury strikes, medical care becomes vital to a person's health. Health *insurance* is the ticket to medical care in the United States.

Many Americans believe that persons without insurance do not go without health care, because they can receive treatment in a hospital emergency department if they are truly sick. Such care, however, is often too little and too late.[7] Moreover, persons treated in this fashion remain ill longer, have more disability, and experience more obstacles to productive work. In addition, uninsured persons, even when admitted to hospitals, receive less care, fewer tests and other procedures, and are dismissed earlier than insured persons with the same conditions; their death rates are substantially higher. Finally, the "safety net" of public hospitals, clinics, and charity care has become decidedly frayed. Competition,

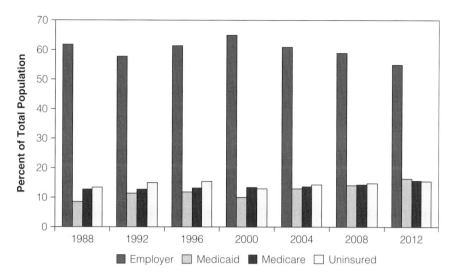

F I G U R E 8.1   Sources of Insurance (selected years)

SOURCE: DeNavas-Walt, Carmen, Bernadette D. Proctor, and Jessica C. Smith, U.S. Census Bureau, Current Population Reports, P60-245, *Income, Poverty, and Health Insurance Coverage in the United States: 2012*, U.S. Government Printing Office, Washington, DC, 2013; Table C-1.

mergers, and financial belt-tightening have reduced the number of beds for the poor and have made it more difficult for clinics providing free or reduced cost care to remain open. Physicians and other health professionals have reduced their levels of charity care.

Lack of access has other dimensions. Because health insurance is so closely tied to employment, many persons experience "job lock"; that is, they are tied to jobs that they may wish to change but fear changing because a new employer may not provide insurance. Similarly, unemployed persons with health problems find difficulty securing employment, because prospective employers cannot afford to carry them on their health insurance policies. These problems are now beginning to affect the middle class, and they are growing worse. Employment is falling in the traditionally well-insured manufacturing sector, and growing in the service and part-time sectors, which have high rates of uninsurance. The direct costs of being without insurance are felt by individuals and families. The indirect costs are experienced by businesses in the form of greater absenteeism and lower productivity. They are experienced by government and taxpayers in the form of higher taxes needed to cover charity care and bad debt in public hospitals, and by health insurance policyholders in the form of higher premiums. It is precisely these trends that the ACA intends to alleviate.

Medical care is maldistributed; that is, the areas and persons with the greatest needs for health care are not the areas and persons with the greatest access to care. Hospitals, clinics, doctors, and dentists are disproportionately located in well-to-do urban and suburban areas. This phenomenon is particularly true for access to specialized institutions and personnel, but it is also true, to a lesser extent, for general practitioners and basic care institutions. Ability to pay rather than need determines who receives medical care.

Disparities refer to unjustified inequalities in the receipt of health care and differences in health outcomes according to race and ethnicity, income, education, and occupation. Limited access contributes to poor health and shorter life expectancy for those who are poor or live in rural communities. African American infant and maternal mortality rates are nearly twice those of whites and comparable to many countries in the Third World. The average life expectancy for African Americans is seven years lower than for whites. Nearly 30 percent of Hispanics and 20 percent of African Americans are uninsured, compared to about 11 percent of whites. Poor children tend to be inadequately immunized and to suffer more from chronic and acute conditions, such as vision problems, low hemoglobin, upper respiratory ailments, and elevated blood lead levels. A quarter has severe dental problems. Substantial racial gaps exist in incidences of heart attack and stroke, kidney disease, meningitis, and pneumonia. African Americans are less likely than whites (even at the same income levels) to receive coronary bypass and kidney transplant surgery. The poor suffer as well from significantly higher rates of mental illness, and they have many more days of restricted activity, bed disability, and lost work than those who are not poor.

High Cost

The U.S. health care system absorbs a massive share of national resources. Total spending from all sources was $2.8 trillion in 2012, a sum that amounted to 17.2 percent of the GDP for that year, an average of $8,915 for every man, woman, and child in the nation. Health care's share of GDP has been growing; fifty years ago, medical expenditures were less than 6 percent of GDP. By the mid-2000s, nearly one-third of uninsured Americans had major financial burdens from health care costs. Public sources now pay about half of the total bill, households pay 28 percent (through premiums, co-pays, and deductibles), and businesses pay 21 percent (mainly by funding employment-based insurance).[8] These percentages, however, vary greatly with the type of service. For example, direct out-of-pocket payment by individuals for hospitalization is generally a small portion of the bill, but direct payment for dental care represents a high percentage.

Cost escalation in the medical field has been constant. Table 8.2 and Figure 8.2 illustrate this trend. Although the rate of health care inflation slowed in the mid-1990s, it resumed at a high rate by 2000 and remained well above the general rate of inflation in the economy, slowing only when the recession struck all economic sectors in the late 2000s. Since then, health care inflation has remained at historic low levels.

The cost of health care (far beyond levels in other developed nations) has significant consequences that subsequent parts of this chapter explore. Costs that increase so rapidly are unsustainable for individuals, families, businesses, and government. For the average working American, any wage increases in the last decade and a half have been more than consumed by the cost of health insurance or health care itself, crowding out other life necessities. Moreover, the expense

TABLE 8.2   Aggregate and per Capita National Health Expenditures (selected years)

	Aggregate ($ billions)	$ per Capita	Percentage of GDP
1960	27.4	147	5.0
1970	74.9	356	7.0
1980	255.8	1,100	8.9
1990	724.3	2,855	12.1
2000	1,377.2	4,879	13.4
2005	2,035.4	6,889	15.5
2010	2,599.0	8,411	17.4
2012	2,793.4	8,915	17.2

SOURCES: http://www.cms.gov/Research-Statistics-Data-and-Systems/Statistics-Trends-and-Reports/NationalHealthExpend
Data/downloads/tables.pdf, accessed January 21, 2014.

of insurance has risen so fast as to become unaffordable for many workers, thus contributing to the growth of the uninsured population. Businesses, in response to these trends, have either increased the premiums and co-pays for employer-based insurance or have reduced the level of benefits. Because federal and state governments fund nearly half of all health care spending (primarily through Medicare, Medicaid, Veterans Health, and military health), the rising cost of health care has placed tremendous pressure on federal and state government budgets. The ACA was designed to respond to these financial pressures.

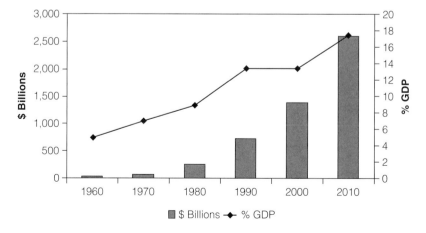

FIGURE 8.2   Health Expenditures, 1960–2010

Note: Data is presented in ten-year increments.

SOURCE: Data from Table 8-2.

Other Nations

The United States is unique among industrial nations in its mix of private insurance, public financing, and direct patient spending.[9] There are two main types of health care systems. The central government can operate a national health service, such as in Great Britain. Or, the central government mandates universal insurance coverage through employer or other private policies, plus government insurance for the population unable to obtain private insurance, such as in Canada, Germany, Sweden, France, and Italy. England's National Health Service is the only health care system in the developed world that may properly be called **socialized medicine**, for in it health care institutions are government owned and operated. Specialist physicians and many other providers work for the government; only general practitioners have private practices. **National health insurance** systems, on the other hand, vary widely in the amount of government control and are not socialized medicine.

The health care systems of developed democracies (excluding the United States) have other important features in common (notwithstanding wide differences in organization). In these nations, virtually the entire population is covered by mandatory insurance for all, or the major part, of health needs (see Table 8.1). The only exceptions in some nations are higher-income persons, who may opt out of the mandatory system and seek private health care. In the United States, however, prior to the ACA, government-guaranteed insurance covered only the military, veterans, the elderly, and some of the poor, although tax subsidies encourage it for others. Thus, gaps in U.S. health care coverage are far more substantial than elsewhere, with millions of persons lacking appropriate access to needed health care.

Insurance in other nations is generally broader than coverage by public or private insurance in the United States. Coverage for nursing home care, medicines, eyeglasses, and dental services is common, as is home health care. In Sweden and the Netherlands, social service agencies visit the elderly regularly to care for their health and other needs. In the case of children, these visits provide low-cost preventive services; in the case of the aged, they limit the need for expensive nursing home care.

Although some systems, such as those in France, New Zealand, and Sweden, employ relatively high deductible and coinsurance requirements, generally third-party payments cover a higher percentage of medical bills than in the United States, with deductibles and out-of-pocket expenses capped. Financial burdens from medical care are largely absent. None of these nations allows medical bills to place a catastrophic financial burden on families. The ACA does cap out-of-pocket expenditures for the first time, but it still allows relatively high deductibles and co-pays compared to other nations.

Despite more extensive coverage than the United States, costs in other nations are lower. Virtually all, however, face cost escalation. Even in systems that serve all, regardless of financial status, there are inequities in access to care and in the health of different social classes. Rural areas have less access to good medical care than urban locations. Most nations have introduced some elements of cost control and limitation on services. All nations seek ways to hold down health care spending; most succeed better than the United States. There seems to be no correlation between the type of health care system and the amount of money, public and private, spent on health care. Nor is there any correlation with general levels of citizen health; indeed the population of most of these nations enjoys health quality higher than American citizens.

Americans have higher rates of hospitalization for preventable illnesses than citizens of other nations, as well as far higher rates of deaths from homicide and motor vehicle accidents, higher rates of teen pregnancy and sexually transmitted diseases, and more obesity and diabetes. The United States does perform better on rates of suicide and smoking, as well as on survival after diagnoses of cancer, stroke, and heart disease. Americans are more likely to put off care due to the expense of health care and to experience long waits to see primary care physicians, especially if they are uninsured or suffer from chronic conditions. Finally, Americans are more dissatisfied with their health system than citizens of other nations and more likely to want to see fundamental change or rebuilding.[10]

CONTEMPORARY POLICY: MEDICARE, MEDICAID, AND THE AFFORDABLE CARE ACT

In the mid-1960s, the volume and complexity of federal health legislation increased dramatically, and government expenditures exploded. Medicare and Medicaid were enacted in 1965 and expanded until the present day. In 2010, another major step was taken with the passage of the Patient Protection and Affordable Care Act (popularly known as "Obamacare"). The degree of government involvement with the nation's health care system deepened. The federal **Department of Health and Human Services**, principally through its **Centers for Medicare and Medicaid Services (CMS)** has primary responsibility for administering ACA, Medicare, and Medicaid. The Internal Revenue Service (IRS) and other federal agencies also have responsibility for some parts of the ACA. Particular programs for military personnel, veterans, Native Americans, and others are housed in the Defense Department, Veterans Affairs, and other federal agencies. The states, as we shall see, share administrative oversight of parts of the ACA and Medicaid.

The assumption behind federal involvement, frequently challenged by conservative health policy advocates, is that the free market cannot efficiently or fairly allocate medical resources. The conditions for an effectively operating market (see Chapter 3) are not sufficiently present, a concept known as "**market failure**." In the case of health care, market failure derives from barriers to entry of competing providers (principally through medical licensure requirements), inequality of information between buyers (patients) and sellers (health care providers), the large presence of not-for-profit hospitals, nursing homes, and other institutions, the high degree of uncertainty and fear that surround medical decisions, and other factors related to the presence of insurance.[11]

Medicare

Congress designed **Medicare** as a supplement to Social Security for elderly persons, who have more extensive medical needs and expenses than the general population.[12] Medicare protects this population against the risks of medical disaster. At its establishment fifty years ago, Medicare transformed health care for the elderly from charity care to a public right. With Medicare, primary responsibility for the health needs of elderly and disabled persons shifted from them, their families, and philanthropic organizations to the federal government. Low-income seniors needed no longer to beg health care providers or relatives for a handout, but became entitled to medical care as a right. The primary justification of this shift was that the health care system had evolved in complexity and expense beyond the capability of private responsibility and charity.

Medicare covers 41 million elderly for hospitalization, physician services, post-acute care, and pharmaceuticals. In addition, 9 million younger persons with disabilities also receive support from Medicare. Eighty percent of recipients report satisfaction with the program and with their ability to obtain and afford medical care when needed.

Medicare consists of four parts: Hospital Insurance (**Part A**), Medical Insurance (**Part B**), **Medicare Advantage** (**Part C**), and Prescription Drug Coverage (**Part D**). Part A Hospital Insurance covers a broad range of hospital and posthospital services, subject to some **deductibles, coinsurance**, and **co-payments**. A deductible is a set dollar amount that a patient must pay directly before insurance benefits begin. Coinsurance is a percentage of the bill that a patient must pay out of pocket after meeting the deductible. Co-payments are fixed amounts due at the point of service. Beneficiaries pay a yearly deductible for hospital care set at the approximate cost of one day of care ($1,216 in 2014), after which Medicare pays the first sixty days in the hospital. Patients pay coinsurance for stays beyond sixty days, though Medicare covers the bulk of the cost. To encourage early discharge from expensive hospital care, Medicare covers certain types of posthospital care, such as skilled nursing facilities and home health service. Beneficiaries have a daily co-pay of $152 from twenty-one to one hundred days in a skilled nursing facility. Thereafter benefits cease. Medicare does not pay for ordinary nursing home or routine home care, but it does cover hospice care for terminally ill patients.

A special payroll tax finances Part A of Medicare. Both employer and employee pay a tax of 1.45 percent of the employee's total wage (2.35 percent on earned income above $200,000). In addition to the aged, since 1974 Hospital Insurance covers persons with end-stage renal (kidney) disease and disabled persons, if they have been entitled to Social Security disability payments for at least two consecutive years.

Medical Insurance (Part B) is a voluntary insurance program for persons sixty-five and older. Monthly premiums were $104.90 in 2014. (Recipients with taxable incomes over $85,000 single or $170,000 joint return pay higher premiums, up to $335 per month for the highest income groups.) These premiums cover 25 percent of the total cost of Part B; general tax revenues pay for the remaining 75 percent. Ninety-three percent of the elderly elect to buy coverage. Part B covers physicians' services, outpatient hospital services, some home health, and various other medical services. After a yearly deductible, Medicare pays 80 percent of allowed charges (the maximum fees set by the government) for most covered services. (Under ACA, Medicare will pay 100 percent for preventive services.) Parts A and B constitute "Traditional" or "Original" Medicare.

Part D, the voluntary prescription drug plan created by the Medicare Modernization Act of 2003, funds outpatient prescriptions. It has a base monthly premium and a complex set of co-payments, as well as a coverage gap (beginning at approximately $2,900 combined drug spending by patient and insurance) often referred to as the "**doughnut hole**." At this point coverage decreases substantially until another limit is reached (approximately $4,500), when full coverage begins again.

Private insurance companies contract with CMS to offer Medicare Advantage (Part C), which combines Parts A and B (and often Part D) into one contract for all Medicare services, plus other services that the company may offer. Part C is funded by recipient premiums and by per capita government payments to the insurance companies for Part A and B services.

Recipients may choose to enroll in a Medicare Advantage Plan or to remain in traditional Medicare. Many of the elderly in traditional Medicare retain private insurance coverage from their previous employers or choose to purchase private health insurance to cover those parts of their care not covered by Medicare Part A or B. This insurance is referred to as **medigap**. Federal law regulates coverage and rules for these policies. Medicare Advantage takes the place of medigap policies for those with Part C. Elderly persons whose low income makes them eligible for Medicaid are automatically covered by Medicare in most states, which have elected to "buy in" by paying the recipient's premiums, deductibles, and coinsurance. Persons with both Medicare and Medicaid are "**dual eligibles**."

Half of Medicare beneficiaries live on less than $23,000 annually (2012), one-quarter on less than $14,000. Recipients bear the burden of rising costs. These low-income recipients often pay out-of-pocket substantial deductibles and co-payments. In recent years, half of Medicare recipients spent more than 15 percent of their income on premiums, deductibles, and co-pays. One-third spent 20 percent or more.

Medicare costs have been prime contributors to health cost inflation, rising from $215 billion in 2000 to nearly $550 billion in 2012. Figure 8.3 shows the increases of the last thirty years. The reasons for this growth are clear: inflation in hospital prices, physician's fees, drug prices, and technology. Moreover, because the proportion of the elderly is growing and they are living longer, increases in beneficiaries contribute substantially to cost escalation. In the most recent period, care of recipients with chronic conditions such as diabetes, hypertension, and arthritis has accounted for more of Medicare's growth than hospital-based treatment of acute illnesses such as heart attacks.[13]

Congress has worked over many decades to slow the growth of Medicare spending, and its current growth per beneficiary is lower than private insurance.

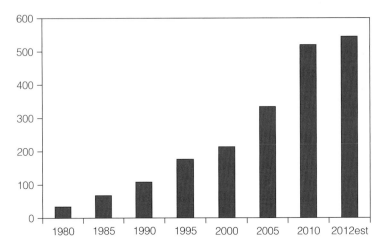

F I G U R E 8.3   Medicare Benefits (in billions of dollars)

SOURCE: http://www.cms.gov/Research-Statistics-Data-and-Systems/Statistics-Trends-and-Reports/DataCompendium/
2011_Data_Compendium.html, Table 1.2, accessed January 24, 2014.

The **prospective payment system (PPS)** for inpatient care utilizes a fixed scale for treating over 500 different conditions (Diagnosis-Related Groups, or DRGs). Hospitals have incentives for cutting costs and making sure that only necessary services are given to patients, for if their costs are higher than the set fee for their treatments, they must still accept the DRG-established fee as payment in full and may not charge the patient for the difference. On the other hand, if their costs are below the PPS payment, they keep the difference as profit. The Centers for Medicare and Medicaid Services have developed similar prospective payment systems for outpatient, skilled nursing, rehabilitative, and home health treatments.

In order to restrain spending for physician services, Congress periodically changes the way Medicare reimburses doctors. There is now an annual cap on Medicare physician payment increases, the so-called **sustainable growth rate (SGR)**. Over time, the primary care specialties, such as family practice and internal medicine, saw reimbursement rates increase, while surgeons, anesthesiologists, ophthalmologists, and other specialists saw their rates rise more slowly or, in some cases, even decrease. The intended effect is to encourage more lower-cost primary care and less use of high-cost specialists, as well as to provide incentives for physicians to enter primary care fields.

Universally acknowledged flaws in the sustainable growth rate formula have produced chaos in physician payment schedules and widespread physician dissatisfaction with Medicare. Over the last decade the formula, if it had been applied fully, would have *reduced* Medicare payments to doctors (a 21 percent reduction in FY2010, for example). Physician resistance to reductions and fears that doctors would cease accepting Medicare patients prompted Congress to suspend the formula each year. At the time of this writing, proposals circulated in Congress to devise a new physician payment system that would reward primary care and quality improvement.

Medicare has grown to 16 percent of the federal budget, and is headed higher with the retirement of the baby boom generation and rising health care costs. It is expected to grow from 3.6 percent of gross domestic product in 2010 to 7.1 percent in 2040. Medicare's actuaries project that the Trust Fund (funded by the Medicare payroll tax) that supports Part A will be exhausted by 2030. After that and without changes, payroll taxes will be sufficient to pay for only about four-fifths of expenditures. Proposals to address this problem will be discussed in the Continuing Debates section.

Medicaid

Medicaid is a public assistance program funded out of general revenues. Like Temporary Assistance for Needy Families (TANF) (reviewed in Chapter 7), it is a federal–state program with benefits varying among the states. Prior to ACA changes taking effect in 2014, states had to cover certain categories: Supplemental Security Income beneficiaries, persons who would have qualified for Aid to Families with Dependent Children under pre-TANF rules, and certain other poor persons, particularly young children and pregnant women. Medicaid had to cover all children in families with incomes below the poverty line. In addition, states could choose to cover children in families with incomes up to 185 percent of poverty and other "medically needy" persons as defined by state law. Because of state variations in eligibility and difficulties in enrolling eligible persons, the proportion of the poor actually enrolled varies by state. Nationally, only about half the poor and near-poor received Medicaid coverage prior to 2014. ACA included a significant expansion of Medicaid to include all adults and children living in families with incomes below 138 percent of poverty. This change (in those states that choose to implement it) created two classes of Medicaid recipients and two different federal reimbursements to state governments (pre- and post-ACA eligible persons).

To receive federal Medicaid matching funds, states must offer basic medical services without cost to the patient. These include inpatient and outpatient hospital services, physician's services, prenatal care, laboratory and X-ray services, home health services, skilled nursing, nursing home care, treatment of physical and mental defects in those under twenty-one, and family-planning services and supplies. Additionally, states may include other services for which the federal government will reimburse a portion of costs. Optional services include dental care, physical therapy, drugs, dentures, and eyeglasses. All states offer some optional services. Depending on the state's per capita income, the federal government reimburses 50 to 80 percent of the costs of these services for pre-ACA eligibles and 100 percent of costs for post-ACA eligibles (from 2014 to 2016, dropping gradually to 90 percent of costs for 2020 and after).

The states can "buy in" to Medicare for elderly Medicaid recipients by paying Part B premiums. The reverse is also true, as many poor Medicare recipients also are eligible for Medicaid, particularly for nursing home care and other services not covered by Medicare. About 20 percent of Medicare recipients are dually eligible, and Medicaid costs reflect this, with two-thirds of expenditures covering health care for elderly and disabled recipients. Medicaid supports

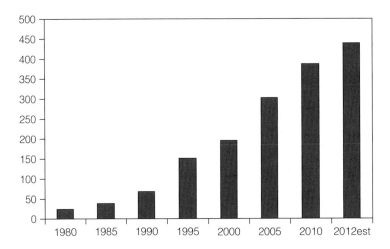

FIGURE 8.4 Medicaid Benefits (in billions of dollars)

Note: Combined federal and state expenditures for years indicated.

SOURCE: http://www.cms.gov/Research-Statistics-Data-and-Systems/Statistics-Trends-and-Reports/DataCompendium/2011_Data_Compendium.html, Table 1.2, accessed January 24, 2014.

60 percent of all nursing home residents. Although the aged, blind, and disabled are only 25 percent of Medicaid recipients, their care accounts for 70 percent of the program's cost. The remaining 30 percent of funds care for children, their mothers, and other non-aged, nondisabled recipients.

Just as with Medicare, the costs of Medicaid exploded far beyond original estimates, accounting for two-thirds of all public assistance spending by the mid-1990s. This explosive growth severely strained federal and state budgets. Combined federal and state expenditures were about $400 billion in 2010 for over 55 million recipients. Figure 8.4 shows the program's growth. Medical inflation and the high cost of care for the impoverished elderly and disabled account for most increases. The recession of the late 2000s made increasing numbers of persons eligible for Medicaid.

Patient Protection and Affordable Care Act

In late March 2010, President Obama signed historic legislation that generated major health system changes in response to the access, cost, and quality problems. The politics surrounding the writing and final passage of the Patient Protection and Affordable Care Act and the accompanying budget reconciliation bill, the **Health Care and Education Reconciliation Act**, were the most intense in recent memory. (The pages to follow will refer to these laws either as "ACA" or as "Reform.") The political polarization was profound, and the Reform debate contributed in no small measure to the rise of the Tea Party movement. Reform evoked intense political, philosophical, religious, and moral beliefs, and there were passionate lobbying efforts by supporters or opponents in Congress, interest groups, and the public.

The ACA reformed large parts of Medicare, widened access to insurance, including Medicaid, promoted quality improvement, acted to restrain spiraling cost increases, and aimed to change long-term care for an increasingly aging population. See Box 8.1 for a summary of major Reform features.[14]

In June 2012, the Supreme Court upheld the constitutionality of the ACA with the exception of its Medicaid expansion, turning back numerous challenges from states and private organizations.[15] The decision pleased friends of the ACA and disappointed its opponents. Supporters had argued that the Constitution's Commerce Clause furnished legal grounds of the ACA's requirements for insurance coverage and its regulation of health insurance. Opponents argued that the Constitution did not authorize what they see as a "government takeover" of the health care system. The Court upheld the insurance purchase requirement and Reform's various industry regulations, but on the basis of Congress's *taxing* power, not the Commerce Clause. This gave strong, but qualified support to the law, mightily disappointing opponents. On the other hand, the Court gave opponents a major victory by ruling that the ACA's Medicaid expansion was not simply a change in dimensions of the Medicaid law, but rather a fundamental alteration of the law. Therefore, the ACA could not *require* the states to adopt Medicaid expansion. Indeed, about half of the states have decided not to implement Reform's Medicaid expansion.

ACA and Access to Insurance.   Deep ethical and political disagreements surround the question of universal access to health care. Those who argue that there is a right to health care and that it is an equal right (primarily persons on the Left of the political spectrum) support expansion of health insurance to all Americans. This view drove ACA design, although certain groups remain outside of its coverage provisions, chiefly undocumented immigrants.

Advocates base the right to health care on the principle that health is a requirement for a decent life, as important as food, clothing, shelter, and political and civil freedom. Government has the responsibility to see that all persons, insofar as humanly possible, have access to the care needed to preserve health. Those who oppose this position contend that the Anglo-American constitutional tradition recognizes political and civil rights (such as freedom of speech and the right to a trial by jury), but it has never recognized rights to the public distribution of economic goods, such as food, health care, and shelter. Health care for those unable to afford it should be given by churches and other private organizations and, in emergency cases, by government public assistance, as charity. They also argue that this form of charity is already available to uninsured persons, because a federal law from the 1980s guarantees that all persons must receive treatment in a hospital emergency department for injuries or illnesses.[16]

During the 2008 primaries and general election, Democratic and Republican presidential candidates advanced significant reform proposals. With the election of Barack Obama and a Congress with a strong Democratic majority, the stage was set for the Reform ultimately produced in 2010. In general, Congress had only three options to reach universal or near-universal insurance coverage: a "single-payer" system, mandated universal employment-based

Box 8.1   Major Features of the Affordable Care Act

Features	Description
Medicare Changes	Leaves the structure of Medicare intact, but makes significant changes in benefits and taxes.
Doughnut hole	Shrinks and then eliminates entirely by 2020 the Medicare Part D coverage gap.
Preventive care	Beneficiaries entitled to annual wellness visit and to preventive care with no co-pays. Reimbursements for primary care physicians and general surgeons increased.
Medicare Advantage	CMS overpayments to Medicare Advantage plans reduced with savings helping pay for added benefits and ACA insurance access expansion.
Taxes	Medicare payroll taxes and Part B premiums increased for upper income earners.
Quality/cost initiatives	Numerous quality improvement and cost reduction programs and experiments: CMMI, PCORI, payment for value, bundled payments, ACOs, Patient-Centered Medical Homes, and penalties for excessive hospital readmissions and failures to follow evidence-based care guidelines.
Medicaid Changes	Medicaid expanded, but Supreme Court ruling leaves decision to states.
Eligibility	Expanded to all individuals under age 65 in families with income lower than 138 percent of the federal poverty level, subject to state acceptance of expansion.
State reimbursement	State governments reimbursed 100 percent of cost of expansion from 2014 to 2016; then gradually reduced to 90 percent for 2020 and beyond; state flexibility in design of Medicaid delivery.
Physician payment	Reimbursements for primary care physicians increased to Medicare levels.
Insurance Reform/Access to Care	Major goal of ACA is to expand insurance coverage among low-income working adults, in order to reduce the number of uninsured from approximately 50 million to 20 million persons (see also Medicaid Changes above).
Individual mandate and subsidies	With certain exceptions, all citizens must purchase health insurance or pay a penalty on income taxes. Federal subsidies available to persons with incomes up to 400 percent of Federal Poverty Level to help make insurance affordable.
Exchanges/marketplaces	Federal or state web-based insurance marketplaces designed to make purchase of individual and small-group insurance transparent and efficient.
Minimum essential benefits	Federal standards to guarantee all employer-based and individual insurance policies include a minimum package of benefits.

(continued)

Box 8.1 *(continued)*

Features	Description
Preventive care	ACA-qualified insurance plans must cover certain preventive care services with no co-pays.
Mandatory issue	Health insurance plans barred from denying coverage to persons with preexisting conditions and from dropping persons from coverage after expensive illnesses or injuries.
Maximum deductibles	Yearly deductibles in qualified health plans cannot exceed a maximum amount.
Modified community rating	Insurance plans may change older persons no more than 3 times what they charge younger persons.
Elimination of caps	Requires that insurance plans eliminate all annual and lifetime maximum payments

insurance, or mandated individual purchase of health insurance. Absent mandated coverage, lower-income workers, relatively healthy young workers, and some higher-income workers will opt out of coverage, keeping rates of uninsurance high.

Congress rejected the single-payer option quickly and, after many political twists and turns, adopted a combination of the employer mandate and individual mandate. Ironically, the individual mandate or voucher approach, usually associated with conservatives and Republicans, evolved during the 2009–2010 debates into the "Obamacare" reform that congressional Republicans in both houses unanimously opposed. One analogy is automobile insurance. All states have laws requiring drivers to purchase a minimum insurance policy in order to protect themselves and the general population, but the states allow wide latitude for citizens individually to purchase policies above the minimum. In the same way, health insurance could be divorced from employment and left to individuals to determine their own needs, as long as everyone purchased a basic minimum policy for themselves and their families. This approach formed the heart of the 2006 Massachusetts health care reform signed into law by then-governor Mitt Romney, the Republican nominee for president in 2012, who disavowed the idea during his presidential campaign. Instead, Republicans criticized the ACA as a "government takeover" of health care that would evolve into the single-payer system rejected in 2010.

Access Expansion. Congress designed Reform with multiple strategies unfolding over nearly ten years. American health care itself is complex, touching every person, thousands of different interests, and 18 percent of the economy. Such complexity requires long lead time to design new programs, create the regulations and hire the personnel to implement them, and to roll them out in such a way as not suddenly to disrupt insurance that people rely on. Box 8.2 illustrates how ACA coverage expansion works.

Box 8.2   Health Coverage Under the Affordable Care Act (ACA)

How to Get Coverage Beginning in 2014

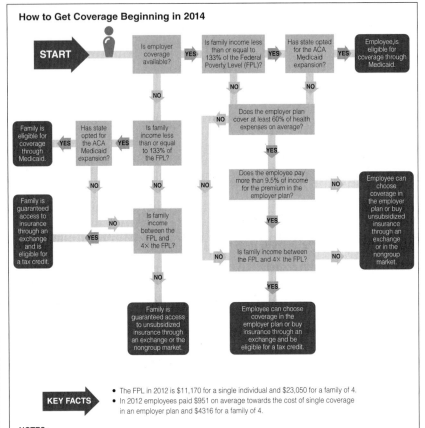

KEY FACTS
- The FPL in 2012 is $11,170 for a single individual and $23,050 for a family of 4.
- In 2012 employees paid $951 on average towards the cost of single coverage in an employer plan and $4316 for a family of 4.

NOTES:

- Some states may have higher income eligibility levels for Medicaid.
- In general, individuals who are currently eligible for Medicaid in their state of residence (who are mostly parents and children today) will continue to be eligible for Medicaid after ACA implementation. Those below 133% of the FPL who will be newly eligible for Medicaid after implementation are mostly adults without dependent children.
- For a discussion of the tax credit that may be available for insurance purchased through an exchange, please see Levitt L. "The Middle Class Tax Break Hardly Anyone Is Talking About." The *JAMA* Forum. http://tinyurl.com/chogalp. August 2, 2012.
- In some cases, children may be eligible for public coverage through Medicaid or the Children's Health Insurance Program (CHIP) while their parents are covered through an employer or an exchange.

- Undocumented immigrants are ineligible for Medicaid and may not purchase coverage in an exchange or receive a tax credit.
- In general, people are required to obtain coverage or pay a penalty, but those whose health insurance premiums exceed 8% of family income (after tax credits or employer contributions are taken into account) will not be penalized if they choose not to purchase coverage.
- Final regulations specifying how dependents of workers with employer coverage available are treated have not yet been issued. Draft rules indicate that the affordability of employer coverage (ie, whether it costs more than 9.5% of income) will be based on the required premium for a single worker rather than family coverage.
- Small businesses may choose to buy insurance through newly created small Business Health Options Program (SHOP) exchanges or directly from insurers.

SOURCE: Kaiser Family Foundation (http://www.kff.org) analysis.

Produced by: Larry Levitt, MPP, Anne Jankiewicz, and David Rousseau, MPH.

Intended to expand access to 32 million persons, the ACA created three fundamental requirements. First, the **individual mandate** (effective 2014) requires most citizens and legal residents to purchase an insurance policy with "minimum essential benefits." Federal subsidies are available for persons with incomes up to 400 percent of the federal poverty level (approximately $95,000 for a family of four). Some persons are not subject to the mandate and not required to purchase insurance (though they are permitted to purchase it if they wish). These are individuals for whom the insurance premium (even with a subsidy) is still too expensive (more than 8 percent of their income), or whose income is below the federal income tax filing threshold of about $10,000 for an individual. Original estimates were that nearly half of the 32 million newly insured would come from this mandate. (The other half would come from expanding Medicaid eligibility.) Those subject to the purchase mandate are penalized beginning in 2015 (based on 2014 coverage) if they fail to buy insurance. The penalty begins at $95 per person or 1 percent of income (whichever is larger) and rises in 2016 to $695 or 2.5 percent of income. (There are no *criminal* penalties for refusal to purchase insurance.) Whether the size of these penalties will be enough to encourage persons to buy insurance is a major item of speculation. The vast majority of persons lacking insurance, however, does want to buy coverage, but cannot afford it without the kinds of subsidies available under the ACA.

Persons in the United States illegally are not allowed to purchase insurance on the exchanges or to receive subsidies; therefore, the vast majority will not be covered. They will constitute most of the estimated 15 to 20 million persons still without insurance when the Reform is fully implemented.

The second prong of the three-prong approach is insurance market reform. This includes two kinds of **Health Insurance Marketplace (HIM)**, originally called "Exchanges" to be established by states: one for individuals and the other (**Small Business Health Options Program**, or **SHOP**) for small businesses, which are defined as employers that average fewer than 101 employees. States may combine the two exchanges, collaborate with other states to form exchanges that serve residents and employers in multiple states, or may establish more than one exchange within the state to serve different geographical areas.[17] If a state fails to establish its own marketplace, the law directs the federal government to establish a federally run marketplace for that state. At the end of 2013, there were only seventeen state-operated HIMs (including one for the District of Columbia), leaving twenty-seven federally facilitated exchanges and seven federal-state partnerships. Buyers will use information available in the HIMs to compare insurance options, including quality of care and price.

One size of insurance coverage does not fit all; therefore, the ACA provides for four coverage levels (bronze, silver, gold, platinum) based on varying percentages (60 percent, 70 percent, 80 percent, and 90 percent, respectively) of the actuarial risk that the insurer will assume. (The complement, 40 percent, 30 percent, 20 percent, and 10 percent, constitutes the purchaser's premium plus the average patient cost-sharing for her rating class.) The HIMs also make available "catastrophic" plans to individuals under thirty and those exempt from the mandate. Such plans would be less expensive and cover only major medical costs.

Thus, (1) consumers of health insurance in an HIM must consider which metallic level to buy and then compare (2) various insurance policies at that level, and (3) each policy's price for coverage within the desired plan tier. Finally (4), purchasers must determine which physicians and hospitals are part of a plan's network of preferred health providers. Thus, even with strict regulation restricting unnecessary variation and forcing insurers to offer comparable products, purchasers are faced with complex evaluations that may make choice difficult.

Other insurance market reforms began in 2010 and were fully implemented by 2014. These include required dependent coverage for children up to age twenty-six on parents' policies; prohibition of annual or life-time coverage limits; prohibitions on denials of coverage (or cancellation of coverage) for preexisting conditions, and limits on the ability of insurance companies to charge different rates for different persons (modified community rating). These early provisions of the ACA are among the most popular with the general public.

The third prong of the three-prong approach is a mandate on some employers to provide insurance under certain circumstances, or to pay a fine if they do not. Small businesses will be eligible for subsidies to assist them in providing insurance for their employees, and employers with fewer than one hundred employees will be eligible to access marketplace insurance (SHOP) as a source of affordable employment-based insurance. Beginning in 2017, states have the option of opening the exchanges to firms with more than one hundred employees.

The employer mandate works this way. The vast majority of large employers currently offer insurance to their employees with policies that meet ACA requirements. They and their employees will see few changes. Firms with fifty or more full-time employees will have to pay a penalty of $2,000 per employee if they do not offer insurance and if some of their employees enter the exchanges to receive government subsidies. Firms that do offer insurance will have to pay a fine of $3,000 for any employee who refuses to take the firm's insurance, but instead uses a federal subsidy to purchase individual insurance on the exchange. Firms with fewer than fifty employees do not have a mandate, but they are eligible for a complex set of federal subsidies if they do offer insurance. Because of the rocky rollout of the HIMs in late 2013 and because of the complexity of compliance for small and medium employers, the Obama administration decided on a series of delays to these requirements, postponing penalties until 2016 to allow a smoother, less disruptive implementation.

Medicaid.   In addition to these measures, the ACA requires state Medicaid programs (beginning in 2014) to cover all individuals living under 138 percent of the federal poverty line.[18] The federal government picks up most of the cost to cover the newly eligible: 100 percent from 2014 to 2016, declining to 90 percent by 2020 and subsequent years. Medicaid payments to primary care physicians are to rise to the level of Medicare rates by 2013. The federal government will also more heavily subsidize the **State Children's Health Insurance Program (SCHIP)**, and states must maintain SCHIP eligibility levels until 2019. The 2012 Supreme Court decision upholding the ACA modified the law to make state participation in Medicaid expansion voluntary. About half the states (as of early 2014) decided not to participate. These are the states controlled by conservative opponents of the ACA who objected to and wanted to undermine the ACA as a whole. They believe that its Medicaid expansion would inflate what they consider a failed social program. They also do not trust the federal government will keep its funding promises. Notable is that these states also have some of the largest populations of uninsured persons, and their failure to participate severely blunts the ability of the ACA to reduce the uninsured population.

New Revenues. For the most part, Reform is paid for by taxes and fees on upper income earners. Individuals with taxable income of $200,000 per year (and couples with $250,000) now pay a Medicare tax of 2.35 percent (instead of 1.45 percent) on income over those amounts. They also pay a 3.8 percent "contribution" to Medicare on unearned income (such as dividends, interest, and capital gains). In addition, beginning in 2018 there will be a tax on expensive "Cadillac" health plans provided by employers (plans costing more than $10,200 per year for individuals and more than $27,500 per year for family coverage). The penalties on individuals and employers for not obtaining or not providing insurance also generate revenue. Finally, the health insurance industry, in return for getting so many millions of additional subscribers, must pay new fees, as must pharmaceutical companies and medical device makers.

Spending Reductions. Medicare Advantage payments to insurance companies will be reduced by nearly $140 billion by 2020. In addition, hospitals and other providers of patient care agreed to Medicare fee schedule reductions of nearly $200 billion during the same period, as a trade-off for a major decrease in their charity care and bad debt costs, since so many more patients will have insurance. The ACA projects as well that medical cost increases will be reduced by the quality and delivery system changes described next. Finally, the ACA provided for an **Independent Payment Advisory Board** to begin 2014. It would submit recommendations for fee schedule reductions and other cost-saving changes if Medicare spending targets are not hit. This board, however, proved so controversial that Congress reduced its available funding and members were not appointed; thus, this ACA provision likely will never be implemented.

Delivery System Reform and the Quality of Health Care. Improving health care quality is difficult because there is no definitive location of responsibility, no national system for error-tracking or for tracking unqualified providers, and only rudimentary information technology. Payment mechanisms are not aligned. The traditional FFS system contains built-in incentives to overtreat patients, because it rewards the *quantity* of visits and procedures. Every time a physician or hospital or other provider *does something*, a fee is generated for that service. Moreover, the system rewards *sickness* care rather than *wellness or health* promotion. Illnesses generate visits and procedures that generate income. Promoting wellness receives no reimbursement.

During the 2000s, private and public insurers tried to devise methods to improve quality and to promote wellness without abandoning the FFS foundation of health care.[19] With the ACA those efforts accelerated, and private and public payers began to promote movement away from FFS toward **capitation** and employment models. In such systems, providers have financial incentives to keep patients well and out of expensive hospital care. In these models, services create expenses to the provider instead of income. This change is especially important as chronic conditions dominate in the patient population. These conditions require prevention, wellness initiatives, and continuity of care in the right setting.

On the governmental side, CMS years ago instituted a major pay for performance program, which has become **payment for value** under the ACA. The idea is to give financial incentives or bonuses to hospitals and physicians that employ (or payment reductions if they fail to employ) proven, evidence-based medicine to improve the quality of patient care. Initially, incentives were created for publicly documenting use of such measures, but gradually the incentives (and disincentives) moved toward use of best practices and toward improvement of health outcomes.

The ACA includes numerous measures, mainly experiments and pilot programs, to address quality and to build upon these early efforts. The law created a new agency, the **Center for Medicare and Medicaid Innovation (CMMI)** to fund and evaluate such quality improvement experiments. Most measures aim to persuade hospitals and specialist physicians to reduce the use of high-cost care focused on episodes of illness. The goal is to reduce the number of such episodes by better coordinating care for chronic illnesses before, during, and after a hospital stay. One goal is to decrease admissions and readmissions; another is to shift as much care to primary physicians as possible.

The new law creates pilot programs based on "bundled payments" to hospitals and physicians who cooperate on measures to coordinate care and to reduce the number of unneeded physician consults and testing. Reform also creates a demonstration project to encourage providers to care for high-need patients at home, instead of in the hospital. The most talked about pilot project involves cooperation between doctors and hospitals and other providers to establish **accountable care organizations (ACO)** and **patient-centered medical homes**. Such pilots aim to remove current legal barriers to physician-hospital sharing of savings resulting from higher quality, lower cost care. Medicare will save dollars if such experiments are successful, and the ACOs would be allowed to distribute bonus payments to members if the savings are realized.[20]

Quality and cost savings are also the aim of various *penalties* created by Reform. Starting in 2012, Medicare payments were reduced for hospitals with high rates of preventable readmissions and hospital-acquired infections. In the same year, CMS established a value-based purchasing program in which hospitals will be paid more based on whether they achieve higher quality care, as evidenced by their hitting certain performance measures.[21]

Improving the ability of health care professionals, hospitals, and clinics to deliver quality medicine is only part of what is needed to improve the overall quality of American medicine. Primary care physicians, nurses, radiology technicians, surgical technicians, and other auxiliary health care providers are in short supply—leading to understaffing, long hours, low morale, and difficult working conditions that endanger quality. Both ACOs and medical homes, along with millions of newly insured patients, will depend upon the availability of primary care physicians to take the lead in their evaluation and care. Therefore, the model of one patient seeing one physician at a time on each visit cannot be the future of medicine. Rather, a team-based, medical home approach must evolve in which patients see the right person (sometimes the primary care physician, but sometimes a nurse, physician assistant, social worker, or care coordinator). Reform appropriates additional funding to train nurses, nurse practitioners, and physician assistants to staff the new care models contemplated by the legislation.[22]

A major contributor to quality improvement (and cost reduction) is enhanced focus on electronic health records. The 2009 American Recovery and Reinvestment Act provided incentives for doctors to install such records in their practices. CMS established similar incentives for hospitals to implement electronic records. The United States lags behind European nations in systems that automatically check for adverse drug interactions, right dosage, and previous medical history, thus helping to reduce both errors and unneeded and duplicative tests and procedures. Hospitals and physicians are allowed to cooperate to create such records, and (as incentive) they will receive additional Medicare payments if they meet "meaningful use" targets. By 2015, reimbursements from CMS will be reduced if they do not use electronic medical records.

Quality would be improved by effective methods of disease prevention and modification of unhealthy behaviors that lead to high risk for cancer, diabetes, and other diseases. The ACA contains numerous provisions to research the best means of enhancing prevention, to make such preventive measures more affordable in public and private insurance plans, to create incentives for individual behavior modification toward better health, and to help employers to adopt qualified wellness plans for employees.[23]

Other Federal Programs

The Balanced Budget Act of 1997 (BBA) established a federal block grant to the states, which could use funds to expand Medicaid to children not presently eligible, or they could use it to establish a separate child health insurance program (State Children's Health Insurance Program, SCHIP). States' plans must meet minimum federal standards and receive approval from the Department of Health and Human Services. The ACA leaves SCHIP in doubt. The law specifies that the program must continue until at least 2019, but it does not appropriate funding past 2015. The most likely scenario is that those states which expand Medicaid under the ACA will simply fold SCHIP into expanded Medicaid and the HIMs. Those states that do not expand Medicaid will have to continue SCHIP indefinitely as a separate program.

Though Medicare, Medicaid, and SCHIP account for most public health expenditures and for nearly one-fifth of the entire federal budget, there are other important federal health programs designed to attack the problem of access. Thousands of Federally Qualified Health Centers, rural health centers, and similar organizations receive special federal funding to serve the uninsured (an estimated 20 million persons after full ACA implementation) as well as Medicaid and low-income persons with HIM insurance. They receive special appropriations from Congress, and that funding was greatly increased by the ACA. Approximately 1,150 Community Health Centers are a major part of this effort, operating at over 8,000 sites, and serving nearly 20 million persons.[24] In addition to the system of local public hospitals, they are the key "safety net" health care institutions. Through its spending on medical research and education, the federal government helps to support the medical and allied health schools that train physicians, nurses, and other medical care providers. Medicare and Medicaid pay teaching hospitals to train resident physicians and other health personnel.

POLICY EVALUATION: HEALTH CARE AT THE CROSSROADS

U.S. health care, for acute life-threatening conditions and injuries, is superb. Medicare and Medicaid have reduced the financial burden of health care for the elderly and poor and have lowered financial barriers. The ACA's goal is to build on these successes and extend them to a larger portion of the population. Yet, even if the ACA is successful, burdens will remain for many, and serious problems of access will persist. Health statistics have improved continually, and government support of medical research, federal training programs for health workers, and public financing of medical care for the aged and poor have assisted this advance. The United States, however, lags behind the rest of the developed world on many health status measures.

Patient Protection and Affordable Care Act

Will the ACA succeed in its goals of increasing access, controlling cost, and improving the quality of care? Although it has been law since 2010, Reform's provisions are so complex and extensive that it is too early to make a definitive assessment. This section furnishes a preliminary evaluation of the law's first years along six dimensions: politics and public opinion, legal challenges, 2010–2013 implementation, promoting prevention, implementation of exchanges/marketplaces and Medicaid, and employment-based insurance.

Politics and Public Opinion.   Evaluation of the ACA falls along ideological and partisan lines, highly exaggerated for political advantage. Republicans continue to make Obamacare the focus of attacks on President Obama and on Democrats in general. Tea Party activists especially tout the "failures" of the

ACA and its (alleged) potential to "socialize" American medicine. For them, the ACA was created on false promises. The law's implementation has been, they allege, an unmitigated disaster. They even allege that the ACA was *designed* to fail to pave the way for a complete government, "single-payer" takeover of the system. Such attacks helped the Republicans gain control of the House of Representatives following the 2010 elections, although the strategy did not work in the presidential election of 2012. They hope that continued problems in the rollout will propel the Republican Party to further victories in 2014 and 2016.

The ACA's supporters have been less vociferous and confident than its opponents. Indeed, the relentless attacks on the ACA have undermined implementation and diminished its short- and long-term potential.[25] Supporters of the ACA believe that its greatest potential is to eliminate insurance company unfairness in the form of denials and cancelations of coverage for health-related reasons; to expand insurance to as many as 30 million Americans; to improve the quality of care; and to make inroads on the increasing cost of care. They have had an uphill battle in making this case, and the botched marketplace rollout in late 2013 undermined their position.

Indeed, public opinion has consistently revealed a plurality (not a majority) opposed to the ACA with a slightly lower percentage consistently supporting it. Paradoxically, the same opinion surveys have shown strong support for all the specific provisions of the law, with the exception of the individual mandate to purchase insurance. The public has little awareness of what is actually contained in the law.[26] As more persons acquire ACA-based insurance during 2014, supporters hope that favorable opinion will grow and will help Democrats at the 2014 polls. Supporters of the law also count on the lobbying efforts of health care industry stakeholders that will benefit from the provisions of Reform, especially health insurance companies, hospitals and health systems, pharmaceutical companies, large physician practices, and primary care physicians.

Legal Challenges.   The Supreme Court upheld the ACA against its most serious legal challenges in June 2012. The insurance market reforms, the mandate to purchase insurance (and the fines levied for failure), and other key provisions passed constitutional muster, much to the dismay of its opponents. The Supreme Court severely complicated the Medicaid provisions of the law, however, when it ruled that Reform changed the very nature of the Medicaid program. Therefore, the federal government could not *require* the states to expand Medicaid. About half of the states subsequently refused the expansion. Because most of these were Republican-dominated states in the South and West, with very large numbers of uninsured persons, this meant that the law's potential for reducing uninsurance was severely hampered.[27]

Two main legal challenges remained to be decided in 2014. The first involved language in the legislation that raised a question about whether federal subsidies and other financial support were authorized for individuals purchasing insurance on the federally operated marketplaces. (There is no question about the state-operated marketplaces.) Lower federal courts have ruled that they are.

A Supreme Court ruling otherwise would be a major setback for the ACA. The second challenge was to a relatively obscure, but politically sensitive, topic—whether employers that have religious objections could be required to furnish contraceptive drug coverage as part of the ACA's minimum essential benefits. The Court decided in June 2014 that the contraceptive mandate violated the religious freedom of "closely held" private companies. It has not yet decided the question of the mandate as it applies to faith-based, nonprofit employers. The question is not central for the operation of the ACA; so the Supreme Court decision against the Obama administration did not damage the law significantly, but it is a political setback.

Early Implementation.   During the time that virulent political debate and legal challenges dominated the news from 2010 through 2013, most ACA early provisions took effect relatively smoothly. Some early provisions included that children would be allowed to remain as dependents on their parents' insurance until age twenty-six, the prohibition of canceling or refusing to sell policies covering children with preexisting conditions, and the removal of life-time and annual limits on coverage. (See Box 8.3.)

Other early Reform provisions affecting a broad swath of the health care industry rolled out uneventfully. These included beginning the phaseout of the Medicare doughnut hole in prescription coverage; increased Medicare and Medicaid payments to primary care physicians; funding increases for community health centers; payment reforms and quality improvement experiments in Medicare; and increased Medicare taxes on high-income earners and new taxes on tanning salons, pharmaceutical companies, and makers of medical devices.

Promoting Prevention.   There is widespread agreement that the U.S. health care system does not do enough to encourage wellness, illness prevention, and personal responsibility for health. Chronic conditions related to health behaviors are difficult to manage and costly to treat. Diseases such as diabetes, various cancers, and heart and lung disease are directly related to behavior (obesity, smoking, alcohol consumption, and so forth) and to access to good primary, preventive care.

The ACA contains numerous provisions designed to affect wellness and health behaviors. Medicare and private health insurance plans must cover the entire cost of preventive services rated by the U.S. Preventives Services Task Force as highly effective based on scientific evidence. These include vaccinations, and certain age- and behavior-related screenings (for example, colorectal cancer, cervical cancer, Type 2 diabetes, and high blood pressure). Primary care physicians will receive higher reimbursements from Medicare and Medicaid to encourage them to do such screenings and to encourage more medical students to choose primary care specialties. The ACA authorizes employers to develop employee health and wellness programs and to reduce premiums for employees who participate.

Many of the bundled payment and medical home experiments described above include provisions to encourage and remove barriers to patient compliance

---

Box 8.3   Timeline of Affordable Care Act Implementation: 2014–2020

Between 2010 and 2013 a series of changes prepared for the major changes in health care policy that take effect between 2014 and 2020. The early changes principally affected children's coverage, high-risk individuals, Medicare, and health industry taxation. See text for summary.

2013

- October—State and federal health insurance marketplaces (HIMs) open. Major problems with federal and some state HIMs emerge.

2014

- Individual health insurance coverage under the ACA's Health Insurance Marketplaces begins January 1.

- Premium credits and cost-sharing subsidies become available to help persons afford insurance.

- Health plans cannot exclude adults with preexisting conditions or charge such persons higher premiums.

- Individual mandate begins, with most citizens and legal residents required to buy insurance or pay a fine in 2015 for failure to have insurance by March 31, 2014. *(Note: Some persons are exempt from the fine until 2016, if their existing policies were canceled in late 2013 because they were not compliant with the ACA.)*

- Employers with fifty or more employees who do not offer coverage and who have employees buying insurance on the exchange with government subsidies pay a fine. *(Note: Penalties to be paid in 2015 on 2014 reporting of employee enrollment postponed until 2016.)*

- Insurance companies begin paying a fee based on market share.

- Medicaid expands to all individuals under age sixty-five with incomes below 138% of federal poverty level. *(Note: 2012 Supreme Court decision made this expansion optional for the states. As of early 2014, only half the states have adopted ACA's expanded Medicaid.)*

- Medicare and Medicaid Disproportionate Share (DSH) payments to hospitals decreased.

2015

- Medicare creates a physician payment plan rewarding quality of care rather than volume of services.

- Small employers allowed to use HIMs to shop for ACA-compliant employee insurance plans.

2016

- Employer penalties take effect that were originally scheduled for 2015, but were postponed because of HIM rollout problems.

- Individuals who had insurance policies canceled in 2013 because plans were not compliant with ACA must obtain ACA-compliant policies or pay fine.

(continued)

Box 8.3   *(continued)*

2017

- States have option of opening Small Business Health Options Program (SHOP) to firms with more than one hundred employees.

2018

- Excise tax imposed on employer-provided insurance plans that cost more than $10,200 per individual or $27,500 for a family.

2020

- Medicare prescription coverage "doughnut hole" is completely eliminated.

with medical directives and patient responsibility for healthier behaviors, especially patients with major chronic illnesses.

Implementation of Health Insurance Marketplaces and Medicaid.   Despite the success and the popularity of most of the early provisions and the prevention components of the ACA, controversy focused on major elements that took effect on January 1, 2014: the mandate for individuals to purchase insurance, the state and federal health insurance marketplaces (HIMs) designed to facilitate enrollment in individual policies (and to generate the federal tax subsidies to make the policies affordable), and the expansion of Medicaid eligibility to adults in families with incomes below 138 percent of the federal poverty level. The implementation of these provisions was difficult and error-plagued at best. Significant opposition, monkey wrenches thrown into the works, and refusal of most states to implement state-based marketplaces and of half of the states to implement the Medicaid expansion also hindered implementation.[28]

On October 1, 2013, as customers first began to access the website for purchasing insurance on the federal HIM, the site crashed continually and was plagued with delays and errors when it was up and running. Millions of persons who tried to visit in the early weeks of October were unable to log in or locate information. It was an unmitigated administrative and political disaster for the most crucial component of the ACA. In those states that established their own HIMs, the picture was mixed. Some state HIMs worked as smoothly as intended (California and Kentucky, for example); others were no better and in some cases worse than the federal HIM (Minnesota and Maryland, for example).

On top of this failure, millions of individuals who previously had individual insurance through commercial insurance markets received notices that their policies were being canceled, the result of two factors coming together at the most inconvenient political and administrative time. First, the individual market is highly volatile in normal times with frequent policy cancelations and premium swings. Second, many pre-2014 policies did not meet the minimum essential benefit levels specified under the ACA for *all* health insurance (preventive care, limits on cost sharing, no exclusion of preexisting conditions, and so forth). After 2013, these policies could no longer be sold. Some persons with canceled policies obtained a new policy through their old insurer, though mostly at higher rates. Many others, perhaps most, had to go to the HIMs (that were not working) in order to obtain insurance or, crucially, to apply for the new subsidies that would help them afford the new policy. In light of these problems, the Obama administration decided to allow insurance companies to continue to offer non-compliant policies to prior policyholders and to postpone the fine for such individuals until 2016.

Finally, in early 2014, the magnitude of the cost sharing expected of patients with new ACA policies began to become apparent. The most popular bronze and silver level HIM policies require significant deductibles and co-payments (the trade-off for keeping premiums low). Moreover, many insurance companies created only "narrow networks" of hospitals and physicians who agreed to accept lower insurance payments in the bronze and silver policies. Many patients were faced with changing from familiar to unfamiliar physicians. Although insurance companies were moving already before the ACA toward high deductibles and narrow provider networks, the ACA took the brunt of the anger. On the positive side, millions of persons who were uninsured or who had to change insurance discovered that their ACA policies had better coverage and that they were income-eligible for substantial federal subsidies that lowered their premiums (sometimes to $25 per month) and their deductibles (sometimes as little as $500 per year).

The Obama administration created multiple exceptions to ACA regulations and deadlines in response to implementation failures. Particularly important were a one-year delay in the requirement for employers to report the insurance status of their employees and a similar delay in the ability of small employers to use the federal HIM to shop for ACA-compliant coverage for their employees (though they could still shop for such policies directly with insurance companies or through insurance agents). The administration funneled millions of dollars into repair of the federal website, and these efforts were largely successful by December 2013. The administration had accepted a target of 7 million enrollees on the HIMs by the end of March 2014 (the deadline for persons to enroll and avoid tax penalties). By May 2014, it appeared that approximately 8 million persons had received marketplace insurance with another 4 million receiving expanded Medicaid, exceeding administration expectations. Reports in summer 2014 showed that rates of uninsurance had declined substantially (from 20 percent to 15 percent of working age adults), although there was far less improvement in states that did not expand Medicaid.

Employment-Based Insurance.   Most Americans obtain their health insurance through their employers, and their insurance has not had a major impact from the ACA implementation, except for some improvements—requirements for preventive care without cost sharing, limits on annual and lifetime caps, and so forth. With recent slowing of health care cost increases, employee premiums have increased gradually for the most part, though such restraint is unlikely to last. Moreover, employers are designing the same kinds of unpopular high deductible and narrow network plans for employees as in the individual market.

The principal controversy regarding employer insurance related to the status of part-time employees and to employees of small to medium-sized businesses. Because of complex coverage requirements for such employees, numerous employers announced that they will no longer offer insurance to part-time employees or will keep other employee hours under the insurance requirement target (30 hours per week). These employees likely will move to the HIM market, where most will be able to find more affordable policies than with their employers. Some employers are considering keeping their employee numbers under the fifty employee point at which they will be required to offer insurance.[29]

Medicare and Medicaid

Successes.   Approximately 56 million persons each month benefit from Medicaid and about 50 million from Medicare. These two programs pay for about 18 million hospital stays per year, and about 42 million persons receive physician services annually. Over four million receive home health services.[30] Measures of health show improvement, with the last three decades witnessing declines in death rates from diseases particularly afflicting the elderly. Moreover, Medicare and Medicaid achieve these results with extremely low administrative costs, less than 2 percent for Medicare and less than 5 percent of expenditures for Medicaid, a result far better than private health insurance carriers.

The ACA builds on these successes by adding free preventive care services to Medicare and by closing the Medicare Part D doughnut hole by 2020. It expands access to the benefits of Medicaid to all below 138 percent of the federal poverty level (in those states accepting Medicaid expansion), and it raises fees paid to primary care physicians to encourage them to accept Medicaid patients.

Problems.   Medicare and Medicaid, however, have increasingly high costs, and they have structural flaws that inhibit their ability to deal most effectively with the major problems in health care. Access to health care remains a problem, along geographical, racial, and income lines, especially in Medicaid because of its very low physician reimbursement rates. Large differences between upper and lower income groups in death rates, life expectancy, and infant mortality persist. Burdensome qualification procedures keep millions of persons from receiving benefits for which they are otherwise qualified. The ACA would have changed this for Medicaid by transforming Medicaid into a universal, means-tested (noncategorical) program, if all states had accepted its expansion.[31]

Medicare has no dedicated long-term care component; therefore, it is highly restrictive on nursing home and home care. Elderly persons who need this care indefinitely, unless they are well-to-do, must "spend down" their financial resources until they are poor enough to qualify for Medicaid.

Structural problems also inhibit the effectiveness of Medicare and Medicaid, preventing them from accomplishing all their goals. They contribute to cost escalation in health care by underwriting the most expensive forms of care. Medicare regulations allow its most generous payments for acute hospitalization.

Medicaid pays nearly half of all nursing home costs and has largely financed the expansion of that industry. State governments have been reeling under the burden of rapidly increasing Medicaid costs. These costs and problems in state health care for the indigent led many states to work toward structural reform of their Medicaid programs. Medicare spending places severe pressure on both the Hospital Insurance Trust Fund and the federal budget. Its financial problems parallel those of Social Security (described in the previous chapter), but are more imminent and more severe. The retirement of the baby boom generation that began in 2011 puts extreme pressure on the Hospital Insurance Trust Fund, which is projected to be solvent only for the next ten years. Finally, Medicare's structure largely reflects the practice of medicine and methods of insurance coverage prevalent in the 1960s when the program was created. Acute care is more richly rewarded than preventive or chronic care. Delivery and payment reforms begun in the early 2000s and accelerated by the ACA respond to these shortcomings, and recent data show significant slowing in Medicare expenditures per enrollee.

Ideology and the Health Care System

It is difficult to assess the ACA, Medicare, Medicaid, and other government health programs, because there is sharp ideological disagreement over the U.S. health care system and government's role in it (see Box 8.4).

From the *political Left* come charges that the health care system discriminates against rural residents, low-income persons, and racial minorities. According to this view, persons in these groups are less healthy than others because they are powerless, unable to control access to quality health care. The growth of for-profit health care, the decline of public hospitals, and the new emphasis on cost cutting in Medicare and Medicaid may lead to *reversing* the gains made in health care for low-income persons. The medically indigent patient, even when covered by Medicaid, is not a source of profit, and such patients may be turned away to overcrowded, declining public clinics or hospitals, or to nowhere at all, if public facilities are not locally available. These trends produce severe financial pressure on the "safety net" of public and nonprofit hospitals and clinics, placing their survival in doubt. Liberals, therefore, strongly defend Medicare's current structure, fight to protect and expand Medicaid, and defend the ACA. They seek greater federal regulation of the health care industry and removal of financial barriers to access. Most favor making the benefits of private insurance and Medicaid available to more persons (as in the ACA). A smaller group favors radical conversion of American health care to a single-payer system.

Conservatives and those on the Right, such as the Tea Party, find no hope in government regulation. Making the medical market more competitive would produce efficiencies that will lower the rate of cost growth and serve patients better. Excessive government intervention leads to lower quality and higher costs. Conservatives believe that, if government were to cease regulating the medical market and subsidizing third-party payments, consumers' freedom of choice, coupled with the availability of alternative types of health insurance, would make the market more competitive and less costly. Associated with this perspective is an emphasis

Box 8.4	Ideological Division over U.S. Health Care System			
	Right to Health Care	Favored Payment Mechanism	Favored Delivery Mechanism	Other Emphases
Liberals and the Left (most Democrats)	Yes. An entitlement to comprehensive health and sickness care, independent of one's income or health status; guaranteed through federal regulations and subsidies. Younger and healthier persons mandated to purchase insurance.	Most: ACA-type expansion of private and public insurance; social responsibility to furnish medical care for all. Some: Single-payer at federal or state level; social responsibility to furnish medical care for all.	Capitation and bundled payments; medical homes; and other new forms of delivery; government regulation of quality of care.	Wellness programs by employers are acceptable, but should operate through incentives, not penalties. Providers should receive payment incentives to remove social and financial barriers to patient compliance with medical advice.
Conservatives and the Right (most Republicans)	No. Entitlements produce dependency. Individuals are responsible for their own health; health status and age should influence premiums. Minimal government regulation and assistance only to the truly needy for acute medical conditions. No mandate to purchase insurance.	Insurance should be an individual responsibility, not employer-based. Medicare should be furnished on a defined contribution basis. Medicaid should be transitioned to greater state control.	Fee-for-service. Malpractice insurance reform. Experimentation with new delivery models, so long as they are driven by market mechanisms and give financial incentives to patients to spend more wisely.	Employer-based wellness programs that encourage healthy behavior or penalize unhealthy behavior such as smoking. Individuals and voluntary agencies, not governments or health providers, are responsible for addressing barriers to compliance.

(continued)

Box 8.4 *(continued)*

	Right to Health Care	Favored Payment Mechanism	Favored Delivery Mechanism	Other Emphases
Skeptics (Left and Right)	Left: Yes. Right: No. Both skeptical about the ability of the current health care system to create gains in health.	Depends on whether the skeptic is primarily liberal or conservative in outlook. Generally believe that the health care system is corrupt and too influenced by money.	Tend to favor paraprofessionals, such as nurse practitioners, physician assistants, nurses, social workers, and public health personnel working closely with patients with chronic conditions. Also more favorable to alternative medicine, such as acupuncture.	Left: Main emphasis is on robust funding of federal and state public health measures and on environmental factors, such as clean air and water and on safe housing and neighborhoods. Right: Limited public health measures; individuals should be primarily responsible for healthy eating and other behavior choices. Environmental protection is primarily a market function.

on informing and empowering health care consumers. One mechanism is greater transparency of provider quality outcomes; another is making patients responsible for a larger share of treatment cost, an incentive for more prudent spending decisions, and more responsibility for healthy behavior. They favor the growth of **health savings accounts (HSAs)** and "**consumer-driven health plans**" and strongly oppose government-mandated health insurance coverage. Personal responsibility should be the path toward health improvement.

Skeptics of the Left and the Right challenge overemphasis on medical care, which they see driven by large corporations for financial gain. More funding, Left skeptics argue, should go toward the environmental causes of ill health. They emphasize the public health system and educating individuals to take responsibility for their own health by making healthy behavioral choices. The great advances in health and life expectancy made early in the last century came through immunizations, inoculations, and public health measures, creating a more sanitary environment. Comparable gains likely will not come through cancer and heart research and treatment, or increased spending on doctor, hospital, and nursing home care. Rather, progress will come from attending to cancer- and other disease-causing agents in the workplace, air, and water. Environmentally induced cancers, lung diseases, kidney diseases, and other ailments are already costing billions of dollars for health care and lost work time.

The Right especially argues that the greatest potential for improving health and extending life lies within the personal control of the individual. You can add years to life through basic health habits, such as regular exercise, moderate alcohol consumption, not smoking, and regular sleeping and eating patterns. The greatest determinants of premature death, apart from individual genetic makeup, are behavioral, followed by socioeconomic status, and environmental conditions. Inadequate medical care is responsible for only 10 percent of premature deaths.[32] The medical system generally treats only the *results* of adult and childhood obesity—diabetes, hypertension, heart disease, and so forth. At this point, Left and Right diverge.

The Left believes that greater public investment in social prevention strategies is more likely to have a benefit than investment in medicine's treatment of preventable diseases. A recent example is wellness programs offered by employers as a method of keeping employees more healthy (and thus more productive), but also as a way of holding down insurance premiums. Advocates differ over whether employers should be allowed to *penalize* employees who refuse wellness programs or who engage in unhealthy behaviors, such as smoking. There is limited and conflicting evidence about the effectiveness of workplace wellness programs in enhancing health or reducing health care costs.

Individual control also appeals to those on the Left and Right who distrust the medical establishment and turn to "alternative medicine" practices, such as herbal remedies, acupuncture, and massage therapy. Patients often find in these practices the individual, holistic concern that often seems missing in conventional medicine.

Progressives who emphasize these ideas also strongly support government programs of occupational safety and health, strict controls on disease-causing chemicals, efforts to clean up the environment, and antiobesity campaigns. Government's responsibility for public health cannot be avoided. Without strong public health measures and good individual health practices, the cost of health care based on acute, curative medicine will be unaffordable in the future. Moreover, worries about bird flu mutating into the next worldwide influenza pandemic, and the potential of terrorists to use biological weapons, strongly support a far greater investment in public health infrastructure.[33]

CONTINUING DEBATES: RESHAPING
A COMPLEX SYSTEM

Medicare

Republicans and their ideological allies portray Medicare (as well as Social Security, Medicaid, and public assistance) as "entitlements" with a pejorative connotation. "Entitlements" are harmful, they argue, because they encourage

POLICY DILEMMAS   Ideology, ACA, and Health Care

Conflicting ideological commitments help to explain the intense political controversy and partisan conflict the Affordable Care Act generated.

Democrats see the ACA as a moderate attempt to fulfill Americans' right to health care and to move the delivery system away from a high cost, quantity-driven system to a focus on quality, prevention, and integration of care across the lifespan. The law even includes a large measure of conservative focus on individual responsibility to provide for one's own health care through buying insurance and incentives for prevention and healthy behavior.

Republicans view the law as a big government "takeover" of health care, moving the country further away from individual responsibility. You cannot, they argue, mandate responsible behavior. Moreover, the idea that health care is a right to be enforced by government borders on socialism. Although conservatives support some aspects of the law, the ACA as a whole takes the nation in the wrong direction and must be repealed.

Although they might accept specific components of the ACA, skeptics of the Left and Right find the law as a whole misguided in its overreliance on the medical care system. The best way to improve the health of the nation, they argue, would be to encourage individuals to take better care of their health (Right) and to improve social and environmental conditions (Left).

1. Is health care a right? If so, is it an equal right? If not, then what responsibility, if any, does public policy have for improving individual access to care and for promoting a healthy society?

2. How might government fulfill its health care role and still foster individual responsibility for health and wellness?

3. Given your own values and ideological commitments, what part or parts of the ACA should be retained and what repealed or replaced?

"dependency" on government and produce an "entitlement culture" that will bankrupt the nation. Their ideological orientation is toward personal and family responsibility, supported by free market economic structures and by personal charity when individuals are genuinely unable to fund their vital medical needs. Although most conservatives would not abolish Medicare, they would alter it to maximize personal responsibility and to enhance the role of medical markets.

Democrats and their ideological allies, on the other hand, describe entitlements favorably; they are "social insurance" earned by hard-working Americans. Entitlements allow Americans to live in dignity during aging or declining health. Moreover, the size, cost, and complexity of the medical system for elder care are beyond the capability of all but the healthiest and wealthiest of Americans. These protagonists also argue that the free market does not (and cannot) function effectively in most parts of the health care system. Thus, they favor a dominant role for government to ensure the health of elderly and disabled persons.

These two general positions have solidified and now resist compromise. Medicare politics has evolved into a battle to the death between irreconcilable ideologies and two irreconcilable approaches to reforming Medicare: (1) modest changes within Medicare's current structure and (2) fundamental structural changes to the program.[34]

Modest Changes in Medicare's Current Structure.   In general, Democrats and progressives wish to preserve Medicare's current structure, while making modest changes to improve its quality and efficiency and to ensure its financial sustainability. Medicare, they argue, has served patients and providers well. Fundamental changes would place those gains in jeopardy, especially for low-income seniors and disabled persons. Moreover, the ACA already is reforming Medicare and has pushed the estimated exhaustion of the Part A Trust Fund from 2017 to 2030. In addition, the ACA accelerated payment and health care delivery system reforms described in earlier sections. If successful, these would reduce Medicare's rate of cost growth as a side-effect of quality improvements, thereby making the program even more sustainable into the future.

The modest changes that Democrats and progressive advocates believe will improve Medicare and sustain it financially are a mix of revenue increases and spending controls, plus quality improvement initiatives. Modest revenue enhancements would come from income-related premiums under Medicare Parts B and D, as well as small changes to the Part B deductible for new beneficiaries and a surcharge on new beneficiaries who buy Medigap policies with very low cost sharing. Expense reduction proposals are to continue ACA experiments and quality improvements with a goal of reducing the target growth rate for Medicare spending from GDP + 1 percent to GDP + 0.5 percent for 2020 and future years. Progressives would also require drug manufacturers to provide rebates for Part D plans equivalent to the current discount they provide to the states under Medicaid. Finally, they would move more rapidly away from FFS payment to acute care providers toward "bundled payments" for episodes of illness. Another measure, favored by fewer progressives (and some conservatives), would increase the age for recipients of Medicare from sixty-five to sixty-seven or even seventy (paralleling Social Security proposals).

The principal argument in favor of some combination of minor changes to Medicare is that these changes would maintain Medicare's familiar structure, which has worked well for fifty years. Depending on the combination of changes adopted and their starting date, minor alteration would extend the financial solvency of the program from the current 2030 date to sometime in the mid-2030s or beyond.

The arguments against modest changes boil down to their being too modest. Medicare's chassis and engine were designed fifty years ago when the practice of medicine was far different from what medicine is like today or will be like twenty to forty years from now. Critics of minor changes argue that, even were they somewhat successful (and they challenge that assumption), they do not create a modern Medicare program.

Fundamental Structural Changes.   These critiques lead naturally toward fundamental structural changes to ensure Medicare's future. In general, Republicans and conservatives wish totally to reform Medicare's organization and financing. Democrats and progressives fear such changes would impair Medicare's benefits for low-income seniors and disabled persons. The most well known of such proposals has been advanced in various formulations by Congressman Paul Ryan, the 2012 Republican vice-presidential candidate. These proposals in general call for Medicare to transition from "**defined benefit**" to "**defined contribution**" (often called "premium support"). Current recipients and those currently over (say) age fifty-five would have the right to continue in the current form of Medicare; they also would have the choice of moving to the new design. Those turning sixty-five in (say) 2024 would be automatically enrolled in the new premium support Medicare. (The ages and dates vary from proposal to proposal. Moreover, some variations would retain traditional Medicare as an option even for new recipients.)[35]

Currently Medicare guarantees a menu of benefits to each disabled person and to each person who turns sixty-five. This menu includes preventive services, acute care services, and rehabilitation services within a wide array of settings, such as physician offices, hospitals, postacute facilities, and hospice services. Medicare guarantees that it will pay for whatever services are consumed by recipients (apart from co-pays and deductibles). Under this defined benefit structure, expenditure control is difficult because decisions by providers and recipients about services delivered determine spending levels. Government simply pays the bill, attempting to hold down spending by reducing provider fees from time to time.

Under defined contribution, government would control Medicare spending by, in effect, eliminating the guaranteed menu of benefits, replacing it with a prespecified payment (in effect, a voucher) to each recipient, who would take this payment and shop on the private insurance market (a Medicare HIM) for whatever package of benefits best meets her or his needs. If the package costs more than the Medicare payment, the difference would be paid by recipients themselves. By controlling the voucher amount, government controls its annual Medicare spending.

Proponents of defined contribution proposals identify two chief advantages. First, it would preserve Medicare indefinitely, since government could peg how much it spends to annual growth in the economy and thus to available revenues, taking health spending pressure off the entire federal budget. Congress does not have the political discipline directly to modify Medicare's benefits in order to maintain fiscal stability. Premium support introduces this discipline through annual financial targets. Second, this new structure would remove government from being a dominant buyer of health care; instead, individual recipients would hold the power as informed consumers in a market-driven health care system.

Opponents make three criticisms. First, unless the government contribution rose as fast as health care inflation, the voucher over time would buy less insurance coverage, forcing more people to use their own funds to purchase adequate coverage. This would particularly burden low-income seniors.

Second, the market has never worked effectively in health care, for reasons discussed earlier in the chapter. Most medical spending is not the result of voluntary, informed decisions, but rather follows doctor-recommended treatments needed to address injury or illness. Informed patient consumers would have only minimal impact on these kinds of expenditures.

Third, since premium support, even if adopted, would not begin for over a decade, traditional Medicare would still require complex and politically difficult reform in the short run. Moreover, the ACA is already implementing reforms in Medicare delivery and payment structures. It is prudent to wait for the results of these changes before committing to even more radical reforms.

Health policy scholar Paul Ellwood and others have proposed a reform in which, first, Medicare payments (and ultimately, all government health spending) would be indexed to GDP growth and then, building on current Medicare Advantage plans, all Medicare would transition from fee-for-service to capitation.[36] Under capitation the financial incentive is to reduce expenses by keeping the patient as well as possible, an improvement in quality of care delivered. The idea is to develop a new model of health care, moving from illness to wellness by aligning payment incentives to quality medical care delivered. To keep patients from requiring expensive hospital care, particularly for chronic illness, develop care teams of primary care physicians, nurses, and allied health professionals focused on removing barriers for patients to stay as healthy as possible for as long as possible.

The principal criticism of such proposals is that incentives for quality under capitation can slide into incentives to *undertreat*, to skimp on services to patients in order to meet the bottom line. In addition, it will be very difficult to change a medical system that from its beginning has been oriented to aggressive, fee-based treatment to a system based on capitation and wellness.

A recent proposal from the liberal side of the spectrum would change Medicare's structure by relying on current ACA reforms and building in financial incentives (reduced cost sharing) to recipients who seek care from providers in high-quality networks (those that engage in comprehensive primary care, care coordination for complex, chronic conditions, and other innovative approaches). They call this proposal "Medicare Essential."[37]

Its proponents argue that this structure of incentives and modern features reduces administrative costs, motivates high-quality, lower-cost care, and produces substantial savings. It could be implemented very rapidly and produce salutary effects quickly, unlike premium support proposals. Critics point out that Medicare Advantage already contains many of the elements of Medicare Essential and that the innovation experiments on which it depends are so far unproven for improving quality and reducing costs.

Because virtually all political capital on the Left and Right currently flows to fights over Obamacare, there seems little prospect for significant Medicare change in the next five years.

Medicaid and the States

Major Medicaid debate is occurring in the states. As of early 2014, about half the states had adopted the ACA's expansion of Medicaid into a universal entitlement for persons with incomes under 138 percent of federal poverty level. The ACA contains strong financial incentives for states to adopt the expansion, reimbursing 100 percent of their cost to cover newly eligible persons between 2014 and 2016 and at least 90 percent of cost in subsequent years. In sum, the states could cover millions of their citizens with health insurance at very little cost to their own taxpayers. Why have so many states turned down that bargain? First, one way for opponents to undermine the ACA and ultimately to overturn it is to limit its effectiveness by limiting Medicaid expansion. Second, Medicaid is unpopular with Republicans because it is a "welfare" or "entitlement" program run by government. The only way many Republican resisters would accept Medicaid is if the program were changed from a federal–state program to a block grant, in which the federal government sent its portion of Medicaid dollars without strings to the states to run their own programs according to their own rules. Third, conservatives do not trust the federal government to keep its promise to fund expanded Medicaid at 90 percent of cost. They believe that the states will ultimately be left holding the bag.

The harsh reality is that states lack the financial flexibility to lead the drive to cover the uninsured. The recessions of 2001 and 2008 underscored this truth, as one state after another imposed either enrollment limits or sliced provider reimbursements in Medicaid and SCHIP in order to restrain accelerating health care spending.

During the next few years, health care stakeholders will continue to pressure resistant states to accept ACA Medicaid expansion. Hospitals, which are vital economic engines in electoral districts, possess particularly strong incentives to lobby their representatives. Millions of dollars are at stake, because the ACA reduces hospitals' special Medicaid payments for taking care of the uninsured. Reform assumed that *all* states would expand Medicaid and the number of uninsured would shrink dramatically, so hospitals would no longer need these payments. Relatedly, even though hospitals *lose* money on each Medicaid patient, they lose less than when they treat uninsured patients. Local "safety net" public and nonprofit hospitals, clinics, and community health centers especially benefit from Medicaid expansion. This same incentive exists, though to a lesser degree, for physicians and other providers. In addition, because the extra Medicaid dollars would flow to providers in local communities, local Chambers of Commerce and other business leaders sometimes see it in their community's interest to accept the expansion.

The amounts at stake can be very persuasive. About 6 million persons (half of them in Texas, Florida, and Georgia) will not receive the new Medicaid if the current situation holds. These states would lose approximately $50 billion federal dollars in 2016 alone and nearly $500 billion over ten years. That's a great deal of money *not* coming to the states for health care needs.[38] Given the toxic and divisive political climate, it is not clear how persuasive even these amounts of money will be on resistant governors and state legislators.

Debating the Future of the ACA

By 2014, despite ferocious political opposition to Reform and despite the disastrous rollout of HIMs, the ACA was well established. Attempts to repeal the law that dominated the legislative agenda from 2010 to 2013 gave way (except in election commercials) to discussion about modifying the ACA.

Modifying the ACA.   The most obvious need is error correction. All major legislation contains drafting errors and unforeseen consequences. The unique parliamentary maneuvering that created the ACA in 2010 generated errors that normally would have been reconciled in the legislative process, but which were not corrected because of the political stalemate in Washington, DC. For example, a drafting error seems to indicate that ACA subsidies are available only to persons who obtain insurance on *state* HIMs, but not *federal* HIMs. There also are problems with the affordability standards for employer-based insurance that determine whether an employee may obtain family insurance on the HIMs instead of through the employer. Other adjustments need to be made following the Supreme Court ruling about Medicaid expansion. Beyond such technical adjustments, there are sound arguments to revise the design of the employer mandate, especially as it applies to medium-sized businesses and part-time employees. The Obama administration delay of these mandates in early 2014 suggests needed revision. Some liberal and progressive groups have even gone so far as to accept the idea of eliminating the *employer* mandate from the ACA. They estimate that doing so would reduce complexity, eliminate significant employer opposition to the ACA as a whole, and affect relatively few persons, who would then be able to obtain insurance through the marketplaces.

Most Democrats are open to making typical legislative adjustments to the ACA as problems are discovered, as well as to some small modifications of the law. Republicans, however, are reluctant to engage in this exercise. The technical errors and problems give them political leverage against the law. Their price for making minor adjustments is to open the law to major changes, something that the Democrats will not countenance. The short run thus offers little prospect for the normal legislative process for modifying the ACA. Therefore, President Obama has taken controversial steps to modify or postpone some parts of the ACA using executive authority. This seems to set the pattern at least until 2017.

There are parts of the ACA that are so popular, especially after some years in place, that it would be very difficult to leave them out of any modified ACA. (See Box 8.1 for the list of ACA features.) Unlikely to be changed under any modification are the guaranteed issue, preventive care, maximum deductible, and elimination of lifetime caps. Ideologically, Republicans do not favor these, but politically they cannot *take away* such popular benefits. Yet, there are ACA features that conservatives would eliminate and replace with different reforms. The results of the 2014 congressional and 2016 presidential elections will determine whether they have the opportunity to do so.

Conservative Alternatives to ACA.   Most Republicans favor an alternative to the ACA that would entirely repeal it, and start over, but mainstream Republicans, recognizing the political popularity of parts of the ACA, would keep them in any politically feasible alternative, what some critics have described as

"Obamacare Lite." These proposals, such as the Patient Choice, Affordability, Responsibility, and Empowerment Act, proposed in early 2014 by a group of influential Republican senators, expand coverage and reduce the number of uninsured by using principles of freedom of choice without requiring health insurance purchase (eliminating the ACA's individual mandate to purchase).[39] These Republican plans would also eliminate the ACA's Medicaid expansion and make Medicaid a block grant program. A prominent proposal on their agenda is expansion of HSAs and consumer-directed health plans (CDHPs). HSAs are individual tax-free savings plans used to cover medical expenses. They can be set up by employers or purchased on the individual insurance market. Customers purchase a high-deductible insurance policy at relatively low cost for coverage of very expensive illnesses or accidents. Ordinary medical care is paid for out of tax-favored saving accounts. Republicans argue that this encourages people to conserve on medical care, using it only when necessary, thus slowing the rising cost of health care and making it more affordable.

Republican proposals also include a feature similar to the ACA, using the income tax system to provide health insurance vouchers in the form of refundable tax credits to assist low-income persons to purchase individual health insurance policies (basically the ACA's HIMs, but without the mandate). Employers would not be required to provide or purchase insurance for workers, but small businesses would be encouraged to band together into voluntary "association health plans" to obtain better rates from insurance companies. Republicans advocate making such plans available across state lines, bypassing state insurance regulations that mandate benefits and regulate insurance company operations (which the ACA does at the federal level to a great extent). Republicans also favor malpractice reform to hold down cost increases.

More extreme conservative and Republican reform proposals eliminate or reduce the decades-old tax benefits available to encourage employers to offer health insurance to employees. They believe that employer-based insurance distorts markets. They would as well eliminate even the popular provisions of the ACA, allowing insurance companies once again to deny coverage for preexisting conditions and to charge higher premiums for older and sicker persons. Instead, these plans would set up state-based high-risk insurance pools for persons unable to obtain or afford regular commercial insurance.

Progressive Alternative: Single-Payer Plan.   In light of the complexities of the current system of public and private insurance, some progressive policy advocates support a complete restructuring of American health insurance. This restructuring, known as the **single-payer plan**, would provide public health insurance to every person as a right of citizenship. Health providers would still be private; government would not take over private hospitals or physicians' practices. But such a program would eliminate all private insurance, as well as Medicaid, in favor of a national or state-administered single health insurance program. It would be financed by payroll taxes, supplemented by other government revenues. It would vastly simplify administration. Patients would have complete freedom of choice among physicians and other providers, and the public system would reimburse such providers for all covered care at the same rate. The single-payer plan has no chance of passage unless two things happen: (1) continued major ACA implementation failures, coupled with failure of the ACA to control costs and/or to reduce substantially the number of uninsured, and (2) election of a Democratic president and an overwhelmingly Democratic Congress following (1). Both conditions seem highly unlikely in the foreseeable future.

Controlling the Cost of Health Care

As discussed earlier, the cost of health care is rising too rapidly to be sustained, negatively affecting state, federal, and family budgets. (See Table 8.2 and Figure 8.2.) Although cost increases have abated recently, there is no universal agreement why. Moreover, despite its intentions and some successes, the ACA so far has not shown sufficient evidence of cost control. The most widely cited reasons for the high and rising cost of medical care in the United States compared to other nations are administrative costs, higher prices, and more medical care consumed, largely due to technology.[40]

Administrative Costs. The complicated system of multiple private insurance companies selling multiple products, combined with complex Medicare and Medicaid systems, means that the United States spends high and growing dollars on administration compared to other nations with simpler systems. Thousands of persons and their associated equipment, offices, and support consume nearly one-quarter of health expenditures selling insurance, processing claims, billing for care, devising forms, and collecting money. None of this expenditure provides actual care to patients.

Prices and Labor Costs. U.S. health care costs far more than other nations because health care professionals in the United States are paid considerably more than their international counterparts. The prices of drugs and medical equipment are higher as well.[41] Medical care remains highly labor intensive, despite its high technology. The fact that medicine is the only major industry that is both labor and technology intensive is a primary contributor to its high cost. American hospitals employ a higher ratio of staff to patients than any other nation. Because it has become more difficult to find registered nurses and some other medical professionals, salaries and bonuses are rising, an additional cost pressure. Other nations also more closely regulate the prices that can be charged for drugs and for medical devices, and they limit the number of expensive devices that can be purchased, all without noticeable reduction in patient outcomes.

Technology. Continuing advances in medical technology, including new prescription drugs, are the most important cause of rapidly growing spending. Diagnostic and treatment procedures—such as magnetic resonance imaging (MRI) (for exact images of internal tissues and organs), neonatal intensive care units, chemotherapy, coronary bypass surgery, and fiber-optic surgery—are tremendously expensive, because of the equipment and materials themselves and the specialized personnel needed to operate them. Yet there is little scientific assessment of the effectiveness of most new treatments in extending life or improving well-being.[42]

Some new technologies do reduce costs. New drugs can treat conditions formerly requiring surgery. MRI scanners can look inside the body to make diagnoses that formerly required exploratory surgery. Such cost reductions apply, however, to the cost of individual procedures. Because they are noninvasive, doctors now perform such procedures more often than the old ones they replaced, adding to the total cost of the health care system. This is an example of technological change producing increased service intensity. Patients tend to receive more procedures today than they did before. Of course, the system of payment for procedures is also an incentive to service intensity. FFS rewards volume, not quality.

Serious cost problems associated with medical technology flow from status competition among hospitals and doctors. Helicopter ambulances, open-heart surgery units, and chemotherapy units have become items of high prestige, and often hospitals in the same area duplicate technology, irrespective of actual need. Each patient entering the hospital helps subsidize the equipment.

Chronic conditions, especially those related to obesity, sedentary living, smoking, and other behavior and cultural changes generate higher spending. The aging of the population also drives health cost increases. Life expectancies at ages sixty and eighty-five began to increase significantly in 1950. By 2010, male life expectancy at age sixty-five had increased to an additional 17.7 years; for females, an additional 20.3 years. This means that the average sixty-five-year-old male will live to age eighty-three (female to age eighty-five). Presently, there are about 19 million Americans over age seventy-five; in thirty years, there will be close to 30 million. The aged have more severe health care problems than working adults or children. They also have more instances of disability and of inability to perform the ordinary activities of daily living. The elderly require substantially more acute care, more chronic care, and more assisted living care than persons of other ages.

The public's exaggerated expectations of medical science, coupled with its unprecedented fear of illness, old age, and death, also contribute to the cost increases. Americans treat these as abnormal conditions, instead of part of human life. The sick and aged increasingly use medical specialists, hospitals, and long-term care. Medical science discovers more "risk factors" for disease and at earlier ages, thus placing more and more people under medical care.

A small proportion of health cost increases is owed to medical malpractice suits filed by injured or disgruntled patients. Malpractice insurance companies raise their premiums to providers, who in turn raise their fees to consumers to cover the additional costs. Moreover, doctors practice "defensive medicine" by ordering more extensive tests and procedures than strictly necessary, in order to guard themselves against possible lawsuits. Malpractice, however, has been exaggerated as a reason for the high cost of health care. Physicians and the public often attribute to defensive medicine tests and procedures that would have been performed anyway because of the desire for absolute certainty in diagnosis and because of service intensity.

Cost Control Measures

Earlier sections described the ACA's multiple provisions to reduce health spending's rate of growth. Quality improvement provisions assume that higher quality care will in the long run save money by reducing duplicative tests and procedures, using primary care rather than specialists, and avoiding preventable hospitalizations. In addition, two new organizations were created within CMS to kick-start better quality care and explore expenditure reduction proposals. The first is the *Center for Medicare and Medicaid Innovation*, which tests innovative payment and service delivery models to reduce program expenditures. The second is the *Independent Payment Advisory Board*, which was to recommend changes in Medicare to hold down projected costs, especially after 2018. These entities use **comparative-effectiveness research** to establish the highest quality, low-cost care paths for the treatment of certain illnesses. The board, however, is not likely to be created, at least in the short run. Its members have not been appointed as of early 2014. Slowed health spending growth, combined with strong opposition to comparative-effectiveness research from many physicians and from Republicans, has made its future highly uncertain.

Comparative-effectiveness research studies are widely used in other nations to assess the relative success of medical treatments, tests, and pharmaceuticals in curing or alleviating medical conditions.[43] Sometimes this research includes comparison of the cost of different treatments in conjunction with their effectiveness. Those treatments found to be most effective and least costly are promoted and are covered by public and private insurance. Comparative-effectiveness research uses experiments and the experiences of numerous physicians to establish "best practices." Such practices have the potential to improve the quality of medical care and to reduce cost growth.

Comparative-effectiveness research must have some "bite," if it is to be effective. That is, it must employ substantial financial incentives for providers that follow evidence-based protocols for treatments where they exist, or financial penalties when providers fail to follow such protocols. Critics worry that comparative-effectiveness research will produce "cookie cutter" medicine or even will be used to "ration" care.

Many deny that *rationing* exists in the United States and worry that Reform's comparative-effectiveness research will lead to rationing. Yet Reform will only alter the *type,* not the *fact* of rationing, which exists in *every* health care system. At present, American medicine rations by insurance status, place of employment, income, insurance policy coverage limitations, willingness to wait in line, and other factors. These will continue, though perhaps in less severe form, under Reform. Extending coverage changes the dimensions of some factors, but it neither creates nor eliminates rationing. Similarly, cost control measures raise issues of whether it is ethical to ration care according to the age of patients, according to the imminence of their death, according to the quality of their life, or other considerations. These questions are forbidden in American policy debate. Indeed, one of the most emotionally powerful arguments in Congress and the public during the 2009 and 2010 debate over Reform was that it would lead to "European-style rationing." So powerful was this fear that the ACA explicitly forbids CMS from using results of comparative-effectiveness research to "ration" care.

Because the principal driver of medical cost inflation is the development of new technologies, there is no way to rein in the cost of health care without either slowing technological innovation (an idea rejected by most Americans and by both political parties) or by limiting insurance coverage of expensive new technology (also a politically unpopular idea).

Public policy has limited tools at its disposal for grappling with technology's contribution to the rising cost of health care. It could, for example, place limits on technology growth, for example, by the Food and Drug Administration refusing to certify new drugs or devices or by the Medicare program refusing to pay for them until they are well established. The popularity of new technologies has made Congress reluctant even to consider such methods. Or, public policy could employ strong comparative-effectiveness guidelines. The ACA, especially in its Medicare payment and delivery experiments, moves hesitantly in this direction. Or, public policy could place ceilings on the prices it pays to doctors, hospitals, and other providers. These measures have been used frequently, but with mixed success (especially in the physician payment realm) and with much political pain.

Cost control's ultimate goal is to index health care cost to the growth of the economy as a whole; that is, keep health care at 18 percent of GDP. Although with difficulty government could do so for Medicare and Medicaid, it does not have the tools to require private insurance companies to do the same. Moreover, for government programs unilaterally to reduce reimbursements has the danger of providers withdrawing from Medicare and Medicaid, leaving their patients without caregivers. One promising idea mentioned above and currently evolving with payment and delivery system reform is to do away entirely with FFS and move all payments to providers to a capitation basis.[44] Under capitation, more treatments *cost* the provider income; therefore, the incentive is to keep patients well and out of expensive hospital or nursing home care. Delivery reforms under the ACA begin to move in this direction, but very slowly.

Beginning and End of Life

The abortion debate nearly killed Reform at different times in the House and Senate. Ultimately, a complex compromise was achieved; one that supporters of the ACA argue preserves current prohibitions against federal funding of abortion. Insurance plans on the exchanges are forbidden to use federal subsidy funds for abortion coverage. Instead, persons who wish to purchase insurance with abortion coverage must use their own funds to pay the difference between a plan with coverage and a plan without it. Insurance companies must keep federal funding and monies to cover abortions strictly segregated. Opponents, however, argue that these provisions are not strong enough, allowing federal dollars to fund abortions for the first time.[45]

At the other end of life, debate includes whether society should fund or encourage the use of sophisticated medical technology to keep alive those suffering terminal illnesses. Should some expensive procedures be available to all persons, or should they be denied to persons beyond a certain age, if they are unlikely to prolong the quality or length of life significantly? Examples are kidney dialysis, heart transplants, and chemotherapy for the very old. Should government discontinue funding such treatments in order to use the resources elsewhere? The myth of "death panels" in the legislation crystallized this concern during the 2009 phase of the ACA debate.[46]

Reform and Long-Term Care

A major issue for the future is financing long-term care for the elderly and disabled. Expenditures on long-term care have risen dramatically in recent decades, along with the increase in the number of aged persons (see Figure 8.5). As the baby boom generation began to retire in 2011, the problem intensified. Medicare does not pay for ordinary nursing home care, although Medicaid does. Therefore, Medicare recipients who need such care must pay out of their own resources. Once resources are exhausted, they may be poor enough to be eligible for Medicaid. Those living past sixty-five now average three years of disability at the end of life. Half of those living past eighty-five will have serious cognitive decline. Increasingly, those living to these ages have only limited family support and limited personal savings upon which to draw.[47] The number of Americans needing long-term care will double by 2050.

Policymakers must find ways to fund less-expensive care and to develop continuity of care for the many different health-related needs of the aged. Current programs are highly fragmented, with responsibility for establishing a continuum of care falling largely to the elderly themselves or their children, who often lack the ability to navigate complex regulations and agencies to build a

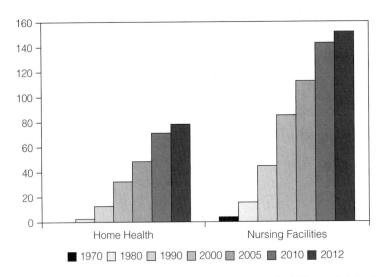

FIGURE 8.5 Long-Term Care Spending Growth (in billions of dollars)

SOURCE: http://www.cms.gov/Research-Statistics-Data-and-Systems/Statistics-Trends-and-Reports/NationalHealthExpend Data/Downloads/tables.pdf, Table 2, accessed February 7, 2014.

coherent system of care. The coordination of care experiments in Reform nudge medicine in this direction. Nevertheless, any solution will be costly.

To address this dilemma, the ACA included the Community Living Assistance Services and Supports (CLASS) Act. This part of the ACA promised availability by 2012 of affordable long-term care insurance. Premiums were to be tiered to the age of the enrollee, and employers would be encouraged to offer CLASS insurance as an employee benefit. Unfortunately, it became clear that funding CLASS would be impossibly expensive if its benefits were to be adequate. The Obama administration formally notified Congress in October 2011 that it would not move forward with the legislation because it could not meet the Act's certification of financial sustainability requirement. At present there is no policy close to enactment that addresses long-term care. Into the future, Medicare and, especially, Medicaid will remain the primary public policies supporting aged and disabled Americans.

SUMMARY

The ACA introduced disruptive tensions into the U.S. health care system, making fundamental changes to private insurance (both individual and employer-based), as well as to Medicare and Medicaid. A medical system on the verge of collapse clearly required *some* disruptive tension. The preceding pages address whether the ACA was the *right* measure.

Of course, there is no agreement on how to assess the *rightness* of the ACA or of associated changes in Medicare and Medicaid. Nor how to continue to revise these three major government programs in the future. Ideological divisions and partisan arguments, prominent throughout American public policy, became particularly strong in health care policy during the last ten years.

The next ten years will witness how the policy and health systems absorb and modify the provisions of the ACA, Medicare, and Medicaid. The true yardstick for success will not be political gains or losses, but health outcomes.[48]

RESOURCES

Centers for Medicare & Medicaid Services: **www.cms.gov**

Hastings Center: **www.thehastingscenter.org**

Health Affairs: **www.healthaffairs.org**

Health Insurance Marketplace: **www.healthcare.gov**

Henry J. Kaiser Family Foundation: **healthreform.kff.org**

Modern Healthcare: **www.modernhealthcare.com**

U.S. Department of Health & Human Services:
  www.hhs.gov/healthcare/rights

Chapter 9

Education: Conflict in Policy Direction

The pluralistic nature of American society produces disagreement over the basic values that guide education policy. Consequently, controversy and conflict accompany the education policy debate. Much of this conflict can be traced to two opposing traditions within education theory: conservative and liberal/progressive thought.

Conservative thought links personal development and educational achievement to individual initiative and responsibility. Most resulting economic and social inequalities should be attributed to differences in personal initiative and ability. This emphasis on the individual places traditional conservative thought in general opposition to an expansion of federal involvement in education policy. Conservatives emphasize the responsibility of the family, local school boards, private institutions, such as the church, and state government as the appropriate structures for determining education policy. Societal rewards are accumulated through individual initiative not intrusion by the federal government.

Liberal/progressive thought reflects a conviction that government has an obligation to compensate for social inequities resulting from individual differences. Liberals emphasize programs designed to eliminate the effects of privilege, discrimination, and individual differences in ability. Liberalism favors the creation of an educational system that promotes equality of opportunity. This concern with equality leads progressives to advocate an expanded role for the federal government in education policy as a means to remedy past state and local policies that produced unequal educational opportunity. One example of these state and local policies was the enforcement of school segregation, which was eliminated by federal court actions.

These two traditions generate cross-pressures and conflicting goals in American education policy. Schools are responsible for multiple and sometimes conflicting tasks of teaching students basic skills (reading, writing, arithmetic, science), promoting high self-esteem, defining a lifelong value system, laying the groundwork for an integrated society through contacts with individuals from different racial and ethnic backgrounds, providing the nation with an adequate supply of highly trained citizens for scientific and technical enterprise, and creating a sense of loyalty to American values.

ISSUE BACKGROUND: HISTORICAL PERSPECTIVES AND THE ONSET OF FEDERAL INVOLVEMENT IN EDUCATION

Two principles directed education policy in the United States: first, education should be free and universal, and second, control over education should be centered on the local level.

The Tradition of Free Public Education

Thomas Jefferson advocated a system of free public education as a basic requirement for democracy. He wrote in 1816, "If a nation expects to be ignorant and free, in a state of civilization, it expects what never was and never will be."[1] Jeffersonian thought embodied three educational goals: first, literacy training; second, expanding access to education; and third, providing an educational system in which leaders could be trained in the United States rather than in Europe. The American free public education system reflects these values. Free education was viewed as the means to enable the public to make choices consistent with democratic values, maintain stability of the republic, and promote social order.[2]

Education served as a tool for political socialization in the melting pot approach to nation building. Immigrants brought a variety of religions, languages, customs, and political values to the new nation. Individuals arriving from countries without democratic institutions needed to develop an understanding of democracy and establish a new identity as Americans. A free public education system promoted integration into the American social and political system. Education served as an instrument for promoting national unity, and the tradition of free public education became entrenched in American thought.

The Tradition of Local Control

The U.S. Constitution does not specifically provide for federal involvement in or control over education policy. The American educational system reflects its English heritage in which the church and home were responsible for education. This heritage produced the district school in America. Residents of each independent district decided policy issues relating to education such as taxes, hiring teachers, school calendar, and curriculum selection. Community control remains a basic tenet of American education as demonstrated in the local school district of today. Federal control over education was viewed as an inappropriate exercise of national power in the early years of the nation.

An Emerging Role for State and Federal Governments

State governments gradually expanded their role in education policy. State government creates local school districts, which can exercise only those powers specifically granted to them by the state. As state funding for local schools increased, states exercised greater control over education policy. State education departments now determine education policy guidelines for local districts, specify curriculum models and teacher certification standards, and establish guidelines for education programs.

State governments also control the framework for financing education. Local districts are free to tax and spend only within guidelines established by the state. State governments have primary responsibility for establishing minimum expenditure levels for local districts.

In the last half of the twentieth century, the role of the federal government in education policy emerged as a major issue. Yet the federal government played some role in education from the earliest years of the republic. A partial history of significant federal education programs appears in Box 9.1.

Box 9.1   Federal Education Programs

1787 Northwest Ordinance: Required one section of land in each township of the Northwest Territory to be reserved for the support of education.

1862 Morrill Land Grant Act: Provided public land for colleges that would specialize in agricultural and mechanical arts.

1867 Office of Education Act: Created the U.S. Office of Education.

1917 Smith-Hughes Act: Provided limited federal funds for vocational education.

1920 Smith-Bankhead Act: Provided for vocational rehabilitation grants to the states.

1935 Social Security Act: Provided for vocational rehabilitation of the handicapped.

1941 Amendment of the 1940 Lanham Act: Provided federal funding for construction of schools in areas with extensive federal tax-exempt property.

1944 Servicemen's Readjustment Act (GI Bill): Provided financial assistance to veterans in education programs; these benefits were extended to Korean conflict–era veterans in 1952 and to Vietnam-era veterans in 1966.

1946 National School Lunch Act: Provided students nutrition subsidies through school lunch programs.

1950 Federal Impacted Areas Aid Program: Authorized federal funds for aid to school districts in which large numbers of federal employees and tax-exempt federal property contributed to high school enrollment and a reduced local tax base, such as school districts serving military institutions.

1950 National Science Foundation (NSF): Created with the goal of promoting scientific research and improving the quality of teaching in the areas of science, mathematics, and engineering.

1958 National Defense Education Act: Provided federal financial support to strengthen the areas of science, mathematics, and foreign language instruction, and to establish a system of direct loans to college students.

1964 Economic Opportunity Act: Provided federal work study grants to students from low-income families.

1965 Elementary and Secondary Education Act (ESEA): Provided limited financial assistance to local schools for textbooks, libraries, and other instructional materials.

1968 Elementary and Secondary Education Act Amendments: Provided financial assistance for educating handicapped children.

1974 Educational Amendments: Consolidated some federal programs and established the National Center for Educational Statistics.

1978 Career Educational Incentive Act: Provided for the creation of career education programs in elementary and secondary schools.

1979 Department of Education Organization Act: Created the cabinet-level Department of Education by consolidating education programs from other federal departments.

1985 Montgomery GI Bill: Provided education benefits to veterans entering active duty after 1985 (extended in 1991).

1994 Goals 2000: Educate America Act: Created the National Education Standards and Improvement Council to develop voluntary national skills standards for local districts.

1997 Taxpayer Relief Act of 1997: Created the Hope Scholarship Program for college students.

1998 Charter School Expansion Act: Provided for expansion of charter schools.

2002 No Child Left Behind Act (NCLB): Reauthorized the Elementary and Secondary Education Act and contains the policy initiatives of President George W. Bush, which include testing and accountability measures and school choice provisions for parents of children attending low-performing schools. NCLB is subject to reauthorization as of early 2014.

The various programs do not represent a major federal financial role in education. Federal aid to education today remains limited in scope. Federal programs generally represent limited solutions to specific problems. Given this orientation, most Americans accepted a limited federal role in education.

The Elementary and Secondary Education Act of 1965: Expanding the Federal Policy Role

The baby boom at the end of World War II produced a dramatic increase in school enrollment beginning in the 1950s. During the Great Depression and World War II, capital expenditures for education had been either reduced or suspended. After the war, the nation's schools faced a challenge to accommodate dramatically increased enrollment resulting from the baby boom.

Even though public opinion generally supported expanded federal financial aid to education, federal aid legislation failed to pass because it was entangled in two broad areas of social conflict: public education versus private sectarian education (the problem of separation of church and state) and integrated versus segregated schools (the problem of racial discrimination).

Interest groups also divided along national versus local control lines. Liberals/ progressives tended to support increased federal aid and viewed federal funding as a means of improving education quality and as a solution to inequality in educational spending. An increase in federal dollars could help eliminate inequality by equalizing per-pupil spending across geographical regions. Given a commitment to the tradition of local control, many conservatives felt that federal funding would create expanded federal control over education policy. Federal control over education policy was in basic conflict with their commitment to limited government.

Even more controversial than the issue of federal control were the issues of race and religion. Minority groups, such as the National Association for the Advancement of Colored People (NAACP), and many liberal groups opposed federal aid to segregated schools. For this reason many liberals worked to prevent the enactment of such legislation until segregation had been abolished, as mandated by the Supreme Court in its landmark decision *Brown v. Board of Education* **(1954)**, which outlawed "separate but equal" educational facilities.

In 1964, President Johnson adopted an approach that emphasized a range of categorical assistance programs designed to remedy specific problems, especially the educational needs of disadvantaged children. The *Elementary and Secondary Education Act (ESEA) of 1965* provided federal funding to local public schools. Under the concept that ESEA gave aid to children but not to schools, the law authorized funds to parochial schools for the purchase of nonreligious textbooks and library materials, but excluded teachers' salaries.

Intergovernmental Conflict on ESEA.   Despite the passage of ESEA, the role of the federal government in providing financial aid remains relatively minor, although federal regulations increased in number and scope. Figure 9.1 indicates that the federal government today still accounts for only 12 percent of funding for public schools, with about 88 percent of education revenue provided by state and local sources. ESEA had the long-term effect of significantly expanding the federal regulations in education policy without a corresponding increase in federal dollars. Unfunded policy mandates became a mechanism for expanding federal control. Congressional reauthorizations of ESEA in 1994 and again in 2002 (as the **No Child Left Behind Act**) contain provisions that require states to comply with additional federal regulations without providing a significant increase in federal funding dollars.

State governments are an important source of revenue and now supply nearly 45 percent of the revenues of local districts. State funding has translated into increased power over education policy. For example, curriculum content and structure as well as competency standards for students and teachers are now the domain of state governments. The tradition of local control was weakened as the role of state government in financing schools expanded.

Problems also have surfaced with the federal government's expanding role. Federal officials continue to impose policies and mandates on state and local

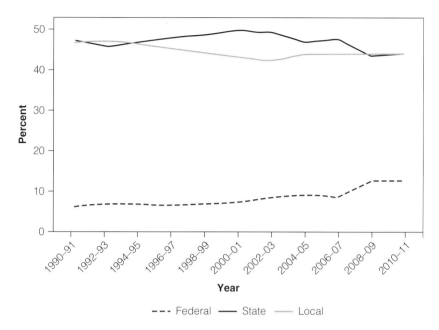

FIGURE 9.1 U.S. Elementary and Secondary Education Expenditures by Source, 1990–2011 (percentages)

SOURCE: U.S. Department of Education, National Center for Education Statistics, *Digest of Education Statistics,* Table 235-10, Revenues for Public Elementary and Secondary Schools by Source of Funds: Selected Years 1919–20 through 2010–11, http://nces.ed.gov/programs/digest/d13/tables/dt13_235.10.asp, accessed March 2014.

authorities, often without the funding necessary for implementation. State and local officials resent the financial burden that typically accompanies this federal policy intrusion. Many state and local officials fear that the federal government will increasingly control policy through a strategy of withholding financial aid without adequately considering the values of local residents.

The Federal Role in Higher Education

Tax-supported public institutions dominate higher education in the United States today. The enactment of the Morrill Act in 1862 resulted in the rapid and extensive development of public higher education. The agricultural and mechanical colleges resulting from the Morrill Act had a practical orientation that increased public support for universities. Today, almost 80 percent of the nation's college students attend public institutions of higher education. In the words of a former Department of Education official, "In a democratic society there is really no choice but to accommodate the educational demands of the people."[3] This demand for access to higher education presents the issue of maintaining a quality education while allowing almost unrestrained public access to higher education.

State institutions of higher learning rely primarily on state funds and tuition payments for operation, but a variety of federal funding programs do exist.

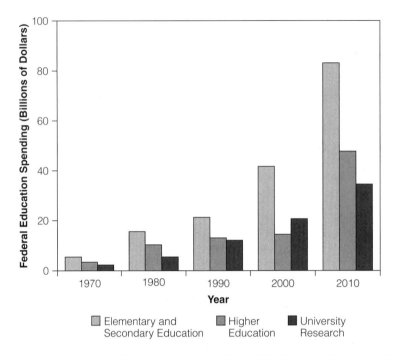

FIGURE 9.2   Federal Education Spending, 1970–2010 (in billions of dollars)

SOURCE: U.S. Department of Education, National Center for Education Statistics, *Digest of Education Statistics*, Table 419, Federal Support and Estimated Federal Tax Expenditures for Education, by Category: Selected Fiscal Years 1965 through 2012, http://nces.ed.gov/programs/digest/d12/tables/dt12_419.asp, accessed March 2014.

Work-study programs, loan programs, and veterans' benefits provide financial assistance to university students. Federal aid in the form of grants for research also subsidizes higher education (see Figure 9.2). Universities have utilized this additional money to offset some instructional costs through support of research activities and the funding of faculty positions. Federal research dollars have increased the ability of the federal government to exercise influence over the educational policies of recipient institutions. Universities find it necessary to comply with federally mandated policies in order to receive research grants and contracts.

CONTEMPORARY POLICY: REMEDYING SOCIAL INEQUALITY THROUGH EDUCATION

Disagreement on the objectives of education is a source of policy conflict. Education can serve as an equalizing and leveling institution, or it can be a mechanism that relies on individual responsibility. The concept that education is to function as an equalizer was not widely accepted at the time of Washington and Jefferson. Attempts to use education for such purposes only served, in the opinion of many, to "pull down what is above, never raise what is below." This conservative orientation conflicts with the liberal concern for the creation of an egalitarian education system.

Leveling is central to the socioeconomic goals of education directly related to educational equality. Equalization of educational opportunity provides students with the potential for social and economic advancement. Yet, *Plessy v. Ferguson* (1896) legitimized inequality for much of American education. In this ruling, the U.S. Supreme Court established the doctrine of "separate but equal" resulting in the establishment of a dual education system in the South based on race. This segregated system was unequal in physical facilities and in the quality of education provided. The Supreme Court recognized the effects of separate educational systems and rejected the "separate but equal" doctrine in 1954. Equalizing educational opportunities gradually became a national education policy priority.

The Issue of Unequal Financial Resources

Because of the uniquely American tradition of local control, local tax sources, primarily the property tax, generate about 44 percent of elementary and secondary school revenues. The result is a system in which local school district tax revenues are limited by the value of taxable property, which varies widely from district to district within a state. This unequal distribution of resources works to the disadvantage of residents of poor districts. Revenue is a product of the tax rate multiplied by the value of taxable property (the tax base).

Districts with extensive property wealth can generate a large amount of revenue with a relatively low tax rate. A less wealthy district must tax at a higher rate to generate the same amount of revenue. The result is a disparity in per-pupil expenditures. In many cases the districts with low levels of spending are taxing at a relatively high rate, yet they lack the financial base to support spending at higher levels. This situation exists at the state and regional levels as well.

The national per-pupil spending average for 2010 was $11,184, ranging from $6,775 in Utah to $19,075 in New York.[4] Education spending per pupil is a function of wealth (tax base), the willingness to tax (tax rate), and the number of students to be educated. Another significant, yet difficult, factor involves the relative cost of living. In states with a lower cost of living, per-pupil spending tends to be less than in those states with higher costs of living.

One policy option to equalize per-pupil spending across the nation would involve a massive infusion of federal dollars. This approach is not feasible for two reasons. First the state governments and local districts desire to retain primary responsibility for education policy which would be threatened by significantly increased federal funding. Second, and probably most important, competing demands on the federal budget and the significant federal deficit prevent such action. The federal government has not played a leadership role in encouraging education financial reform, nor has it attempted to provide assistance to states that are wrestling with the problem. The result is an emphasis on state assistance to local districts, with the result of uneven spending across the nation and within individual states.

There are often high levels of financial inequality among districts within a given state. Per-pupil financial disparities within a state can be profound. As illustrated in per pupil spending between districts in the fifth and ninety-fifth percentiles in such states as Texas ($9,190 to $25,554), Illinois ($8,590 to $20,018), and New York ($15,094 to $37,937). Similar patterns hold true for most other states.[5] State court challenges to finance formulas have cited such significant gaps.[6] Financial inequality remains a policy issue in many states, with a ratio of unequal spending of two or even three or four to one being common. Urban school districts in large cities tend to face the problem of low fiscal resources to a greater extent than suburban and rural districts. Federal aid has not been a factor as a remedy for fiscal inequities between districts within a state.

Efforts to Reform Financial Disparities.   Attempts were made at the state level to force school finance reform to foster greater equality. The California Supreme Court ruled in *Serrano v. Priest* (1971) that under the provisions of the California constitution, education is a fundamental right that cannot be a condition of the wealth of a child's parents or neighbors.[7] This doctrine of fiscal neutrality found that reliance on the property tax resulted in excessive financial disparities among school districts. Following the *Serrano* decision, lawsuits were filed in about thirty states in an attempt to spread the California reform to other states.

The U.S. Supreme Court, in 1973, declared the issue of school finance reform off-limits to lower federal courts. In the case of *San Antonio Independent School District v. Rodriguez*, the Court refused to equate inequities in property values and the resultant differences in educational expenditures with violation of the equal protection clause of the Fourteenth Amendment.[8] The Court reasoned that the United States Constitution did not explicitly or implicitly guarantee the "right" to an education. Furthermore, differences in spending levels could not be equated with "interference with fundamental rights." The Court supported the continued use of the property tax in Texas by stating that there was no evidence that the arrangement deprived Texans of "an adequate minimum educational offering." Because many state constitutions do guarantee the right to an education, litigation concerning school finance reform was restricted to state court systems.

Since the 1990s, lawsuits in state courts attempting to change the existing approach to funding education have met with some limited success, as supreme courts in states, such as Montana, Kentucky, and Tennessee, ruled that school funding practices violated provisions of their state constitutions. The record is mixed regarding developing and implementing funding formulas that achieve a degree of equality in per-pupil spending. Although some state court systems acted as a lever to stimulate change, state legislators remain hesitant to redistribute money from wealthy districts to poor districts.

Conflict over School Finance Reform.   The reform movement embodies significant policy conflict.[9] Conservatives often see finance reform as an attempt to solve a problem by simply spending more money. Accordingly, they argue that reform efforts should focus on education philosophy, not spending. Education finance has been traditionally distributive in nature, with little emphasis on a redistribution of financial resources within a state. The redistributive nature of school finance reform is in conflict with conservative thought. Redistributive policies are often liberal in orientation and involve far more conflict than distributive policy. Increased power and control over education exercised by state governments also concerns proponents of local control. This type of financial reform is therefore viewed as a threat to a basic tradition in the American educational system.

The controversy over financial equalization reflects the conviction that expenditures affect quality of education.[10] The relationship between expenditures and educational achievement remains less than clear. Conventional wisdom holds that the future opportunities of students attending poor districts are restricted when compared with the future opportunities of others. Consequently, it is assumed that deprived students will achieve less in life, have lower incomes, find it more difficult to advance economically and socially, and contribute less to making America economically competitive than will students from wealthier schools. Studies in this area have not resolved the question because of conflicting results and differing interpretations.[11]

There is little doubt, however, that expenditures do affect the educational environment provided to students. Wealthy districts do spend differently than poor districts.[12] Poor districts tend to (1) have a higher student–teacher ratio, (2) spend more on core instructional programming and less on college preparatory electives, (3) spend less on capital projects (building construction and maintenance), and (4) have lower teacher salaries than wealthier districts.

It is clear that the educational options available to students in poor districts are less extensive than to those attending wealthier schools. What we do not know relative to school district spending for specific education purposes complicates the issue of financial equity. First, it is possible to assess total per-pupil spending between districts, yet information relative to the costs of elementary education as compared to secondary education within a district are less easily understood. Understanding the relationship between cost of providing instruction across subjects (for example, high school chemistry as compared to high school social studies or English) and student achievement is also less than clear. Related issues involve the issue of per-pupil spending within a district. "Should per-pupil spending be the same for all schools, for all grade levels, and for all subject areas within a district?" remains an unanswered question in the debate surrounding financial equity.

A second factor involves differences surrounding cost-of-living issues for various regions within a state. Schools in higher cost-of-living areas face higher costs (teacher salaries, land acquisition costs, student transportation costs, labor costs for support staff) in the delivery of equivalent education programs than do other schools within the same state. A mechanism for adjusting these differences remains elusive.

A third factor involves establishing measures of adequate funding levels necessary to promote student achievement. Adequacy implies a sufficient minimum level of funding that will support student achievement, the desired outcome of the education system. Historically, adequacy was simply assumed and defined in terms of available tax revenues raised by a local district. This approach was modified over time as states adopted foundation formulas that provided a mechanism for distribution of additional state dollars to local districts designed to guarantee a minimum spending level across the state. These spending levels were never equal. Increasingly, adequacy is now defined in terms of goals related to student achievement. This means that the school finance policy debate may increasingly emphasize student performance gaps as the foundation for changing funding patterns, rather than claims based solely on differences in per-pupil spending.

Equality in Education

All, regardless of race or class or economic status, are entitled to a fair chance and to the tools for developing their individual powers of mind and spirit to the utmost. This promise means that all children by virtue of their own efforts, competently guided, can hope to attain the mature and informed judgment needed to secure gainful employment, and to manage their own lives, thereby serving not only their own interests, but also the progress of society itself.[13]

The concept of equality remains a central tenet of American ideology. Yet, most Americans find it difficult to provide an explanation of equality that is free of contradictions. Initially, conflict centered on the appropriate role of government in guaranteeing equal opportunity. The notion of equality of opportunity implies that the rules for success and failure are fair. The concept of educational equality varies along a liberal–conservative continuum. The conservative orientation holds that individuals possess differing levels of ability. Intelligence and motivation rather than equal opportunity determines the individual's life chances. This conflicts with the liberal/progressive orientation, which emphasizes equality of opportunity. All external barriers should be removed to allow complete development of individual potential. Government should use its power to assure each child an equal education independent of social and background characteristics. The emphasis lies on the inputs of education through the expansion of special programs for disadvantaged students.

This concern for equality of opportunity gradually gave way to a concern for proportional equality as reflected in affirmative action policies. The focus shifted from the inputs to the outputs of education policy, that is, to the occupational outcomes of education. Increasingly, education policy is assessed by the degree to which employment patterns reflect population demographics. (In the perfect model, for example, the same percentage of blacks as in the total U.S. population would be found employed in, say, engineering careers.) Effectiveness then would depend on the advancement experienced by previously disadvantaged groups. This shift of concern from the inputs to the outputs of education policy has widened the gaps between conservatism and liberalism.

Educational Inequality Outside the United States

Equality as an issue in education is not limited to the United States. There has been concern in Western Europe with the relationship between educational opportunity and life chances available to citizens. Various surveys and studies indicate the existence of a general lack of equality of educational opportunity. Although the GI Bill greatly expanded education opportunities in America after World War II, only 2 to 5 percent of the same age group in Western Europe enrolled in higher education.

In Europe, education tends to select individuals based on test scores and early tracking of students, devices that tend to reflect society's class structure. In postwar Sweden, over 60 percent of university students came from the upper and upper-middle classes. Only 6 to 7 percent had origins in the lower socioeconomic strata (which made up about 55 percent of the population). The same was true for all of Western Europe. Studies in Germany, England, and France revealed similar patterns: only a small percentage of university students were drawn from the lower and lower-middle classes. European reform efforts in recent decades have moved to change these patterns.

Equality of educational opportunity is also restricted in the former communist countries. Although the data are not so readily available, some pertinent observations exist. The vast majority of students attending universities come from the upper socioeconomic levels. Even though the United States is not alone in the struggle to increase educational equality, it has made greater efforts than has Western Europe to achieve equality of opportunity.

POLICY EVALUATION: EDUCATIONAL QUALITY IN THE UNITED STATES

Concern with the educational system in the United States has led to a variety of efforts to evaluate the quality of education provided to students. A range of measures of quality have been employed, and there remains considerable debate about how best to measure educational quality. In the following section, attention will be given to some of the common measures of the various dimensions of quality: SAT scores, minimum competency tests (MCTs), teacher competency, master teachers, bilingual education, and multiculturalism.

Concern over Poor Student Achievement

During the 1960s and 1970s, many school districts adopted innovative programs that reduced the emphasis on the traditional three Rs and instead focused on students' emotional growth, self-direction, and individualism. Because these changes coincided with a decline in student achievement, the public came to believe that these curriculum reforms were not academically adequate. Performance levels of students on such standardized tests as the SAT declined since 1967, as indicated in Table 9.1.

In 1996, this pattern of declining SAT scores artificially appeared to be reversed because the test was recentered to provide an average score of 500 for both the verbal and math scales. In the words of the College Board, "Setting

TABLE 9.1   SAT Scores (Average), 1967–2013

	1967	1975	1980	1984	1988	1992	1996*	1996**	2000***	2004	2013
Verbal	466	434	424	426	428	423	427	505	505	508	496
Math	492	472	466	471	476	476	484	508	514	518	514

*1996 scores on original scale.

**1996 recentered scale scores.

***2000 and later scores based on recentered scale.

SOURCE: College Board, http://professionals.collegeboard.com/data-reports-research/sat/equivalence-tables (discusses recentering), accessed April 16, 2010; http://media.collegeboard.com/digitalServices/pdf/research/2013/TotalGroup-2013 .pdf (for SAT scores), accessed March 2014.

the average verbal and math scores at 500 means that most students' scores will be higher."[14] On the new recentered scale, a verbal score of 500 would have been a score of 422 on the original scale, and a math score of 500 would have been a score of 474 on the original SAT scale. Recentering means that interpreting SAT scores should now be based on a contemporary rather than a historical reference group. Critics of education policy and curriculum argue that recentering SAT scores to a higher level is indicative of a loss of overall rigor and quality in the nation's schools.

Although there is little debate on the fact that the average performance on standardized tests declined over an extended number of years, there remains disagreement concerning the causes of the decline. Many analysts cite parental attitudes and societal changes as the major factors contributing to low levels of performance. On the other hand, many parents and taxpayer groups believe that the departure from education basics—reading, writing, and arithmetic—fostered the decline in student achievement.

Investigators of the decline in the SAT mean scores have attributed it to several factors.[15] More students are taking the test now than in any previous period. Specifically, there has been a marked increase in the number of students from families that have not traditionally attended college. Low scores by this group tend to lower the mean score on the test as a whole (see Figure 9.3). Accordingly, the SAT average scores may not be an accurate barometer of student achievement in the society as a whole. Television viewing and family instability have lowered the motivation of students to excel. The findings of these studies have not been conclusive, and research into factors that might explain the decline has remained problematic. Figure 9.4 indicates the variation in average scores between demographic groups on the SAT. White students had higher average verbal and mathematical scores than did all other demographic groups, with the exception of Asian American math and writing scores. This pattern has persisted over time.

If high school curricula decline in rigor, a pattern of declining SAT scores could result. The College Board, which administers the SAT, has indicated that the decline in SAT scores indicates a "disturbing pattern of educational disparity" in the nation's schools. There is concern that the nation's schools may be

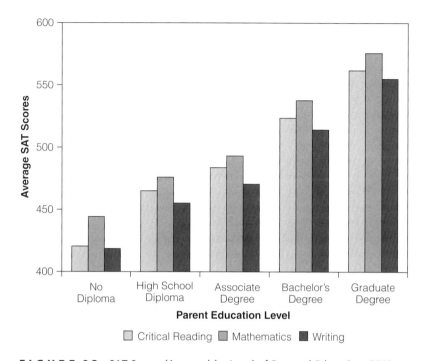

FIGURE 9.3   SAT Scores (Average) by Level of Parental Education, 2013

SOURCE: Table 11, Student Background Information and Characteristics, http://media.collegeboard.com/digitalServices/pdf/research/2013/TotalGroup-2013.pdf, accessed March 2014.

producing two categories of students: a group of well-educated students and another group of ill-educated students.

Family background characteristics clearly affect student SAT performance, as indicated in Figure 9.3. The higher the level of parental education, the higher the average SAT score earned by the child. Children of parents with a graduate degree had average reading and math scores of 560 and 576, respectively. Children of parents without a high school diploma had average reading and math scores of 464 and 477, a difference of 96 points on the reading scale and 99 points on the math scale. Because level of education is one indicator of socioeconomic status, a positive relationship between socioeconomic status and student performance appears to exist. Analysis of SAT score patterns is complicated by the recentering of the test and will be further complicated due to the revision of the SAT examination that will be used beginning in spring 2016. The revised SAT will replace the required essay with an optional essay, reflect an effort to focus on evidence-based reading and writing, and move away from what was traditionally described as critical reading. Scoring the test will change with elimination of penalities for wrong answers on multiple choice questions and a change in the total points possible on the test. The revised SAT will also report subtest scores for each individual. The utility of using SAT scores as an indicator of educational achievement can only be established after a period of extensive analysis of test score patterns and student performance.

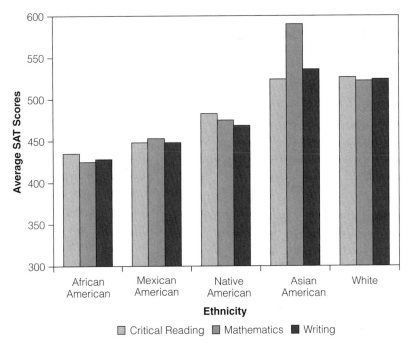

FIGURE 9.4   SAT Scores (Average) by Selected Ethnicity, 2013*

*Ethnicity as reported by College Board.

SOURCE: College Board, *Total Group Profile Report 2013,* Total Mean Scores by Ethnicity, Table 10, http://media
.collegeboard.com/digitalServices/pdf/research/2013/TotalGroup-2013.pdf, accessed March 2014.

Student performance on the ACT has remained stable over time. The ACT
is a different type of test than the SAT. ACT scores range from 1 to 36, and
questions on the test are designed to reflect high school curriculum, with scores
reported in English, mathematics, reading, and science. ACT scores would not
necessarily reflect a decline in the rigor of high school curriculum. Since 1970,
the national average on the ACT, about 20, has remained very stable, varying
less than a half-point.

Minimum Competency Tests.   Concern over low student achievement levels
led to the adoption of minimum competency tests (MCTs) in over forty states by
1990. The tests were developed to serve a variety of purposes: criteria for student
promotion, diagnostic tools to determine the need for remedial training, or
assessments of the quality of local instruction. A passing grade on the MCT
became a requirement for receiving a high school diploma in over twenty states.
Most of the MCT exams required performance on an eighth- or ninth-grade
level.[16] Minimum competency testing was advocated as a way to force schools
to stress the basics of education, to add value to the high school diploma by
confirming the graduate had mastered specified levels of knowledge, and as a
method to combat what the public perceived as a trend toward lower academic
standards.

Critics of MCTs charged that the examinations were biased, statistically unreliable, and a simplistic solution to a complex problem. Given their disproportionate impact on minority students, it was argued that MCTs measured the impact of racial discrimination in education, not student achievement.[17] The vast majority of high school students (some 99 percent) eventually passed the test by the end of their senior year.[18] Critics argued that MCTs emphasized a narrow range of academic abilities as a means of determining the quality of the education system and emphasized teaching of test content, which narrowed the curriculum. The proliferation of MCT examinations reflected a belief that testing was the appropriate mechanism to measure student academic performance. Adoption of the No Child Left Behind Act (NCLB) in 2001 resulted in testing analogous to that of MCTs becoming national education policy. Under NCLB, terminology was changed to place an emphasis on proficiency rather than minimum. In reality, the proficiency levels of NCLB testing have become the new minimum levels for both students and schools.[19] Due to the emphasis on assessing student achievement through testing, conflict concerning their use continues as high stakes-testing under the requirements of NCLB has become a fixture on the educational landscape.

Questioning Teacher Competency

Accompanying the concern for student performance is a concern for the level of teacher competency. Today, every state uses some form of competency testing for initial certification of classroom teachers. The National Teacher Examination (NTE) developed by the Educational Testing Service (ETS) was replaced by a series of exams known as Praxis I (measuring basic academic skills), Praxis II (measuring general and subject-specific knowledge), and Praxis III (Teacher Performance Assessment). Most states require either passing selected Praxis examinations or a test developed and approved by that specific state.

The validity of the competency tests remains in question. There is an absence of data to support the assertion that the tests actually measure competency. There are two components to effective teaching: mastery of knowledge and mastery of teaching strategies. Even if competency tests do validly measure mastery of academic material, their power to assess mastery of teaching skills remains unconfirmed. Despite the problems with determining teacher competency, the use of such testing will continue in this decade.

A related problem centers on the starting salaries of teachers. Average starting salaries for teachers range from $5,000 to $15,000 less per year than for other career fields, such as business administration, engineering, sales and marketing, and liberal arts. This salary gap does not disappear as teachers gain experience and earn master's degrees. Many experts argue that, given the lack of financial rewards after graduation, teacher education programs have a disadvantage in recruiting students. A counterargument to the need to dramatically increase teacher salaries involves job security and retirement. This view holds that teachers benefit from greater job security and from defined retirement pay plans more than do other career fields.

Second, projections indicate that the demand for teachers exceed the supply in some disciplines, primarily in the areas of math and science. The challenge is to produce an adequate supply of high-quality teachers in an environment that has made it difficult to recruit and retain teachers. The issue of teacher competency is bound up in the policy of teacher compensation as reflected in the issues of merit pay and master teachers.[20]

Merit Pay and Master Teachers

Merit Pay. The emphasis on quality education led to an advocacy of merit pay as one appropriate way to attract, reward, and retain quality teachers. State governments and individual districts have experimented with various types of merit pay provisions for teachers. Although merit pay does appeal to the public, there are problems in implementing the concept. First, because the merit pay concept intends to attract and retain exceptional teachers, it is best implemented after teachers' salaries are elevated to levels competitive with those of the private sector. Merit pay is not a substitute for an adequate salary scale.

A second problem with the concept is the issue of the validity of merit pay as a motivating force in teacher behavior. Because many of the nation's quality teachers remain in the profession despite salary scale issues, salary may not be the main factor in recruiting and retaining the highest-caliber teaching force.

A third problem involves establishing an unbiased operational definition of merit as applied to teachers. No group, whether teacher organizations, school boards, state education commissions, or federal agencies, has been able to determine exactly what constitutes merit or effective teaching. For example, student test performance is not an acceptable measure, because such performance is primarily related to parental education and economic status; therefore, teachers are very much captives of the students assigned to their classrooms. Because the students taught by individual teachers change every year, the ability to measure teacher performance over time becomes complex. Does student performance in a fifth grade class change over several years because of teacher performance or is the change the result of a different group of students taught by that teacher? Answering this question is a problem for advocates of merit pay.

A fourth problem with merit pay is associated with impact on teacher behavior arising from development of unambiguous terms and standards defining merit. In order to qualify for merit pay, teachers may abandon their own creativity in order to comply with a rigid set of standards. Merit pay may become a threat to teachers' experimentation and creativity if teachers follow established guidelines to meet merit standards.

A fifth problem with merit pay is cost. A genuine merit plan would increase costs to local districts. Given the climate of opposition to local property taxes, school boards find it difficult to pass tax increases necessary to fund a merit pay system. This means that state governments are the only viable source of revenues to pay for a merit plan. At the same time, because of fiscal limitations, state legislatures resist demands to assume greater responsibilities in financing programs.

During the 1920s, the concept of merit pay was widely supported in the United States and the rhetoric of that period closely resembled that of today. Nevertheless, merit pay plans failed to overcome the problems of defining merit and evaluating teachers. The impact of merit pay plans for teachers on teacher performance, student learning, and educational outcomes is unresolved and is a topic for continued investigation.

Master Teachers. The concept of classifying master teachers closely relates to the concept of merit pay. This system may include merit pay components as well as career ladders for teachers as they progress. Master teachers are to provide a variety of services and fill a range of roles, depending on the educational climate and needs of each school district. Typically, a master teacher plan includes the identification of exceptional teachers, a system of merit-based financial rewards, and the use of master teachers as resource personnel in a supervisory capacity over other teachers to encourage higher levels of teaching effectiveness.

The master teacher movement remains a factor in education across the nation as teacher organizations, universities and colleges, states, and local school districts develop this designation for teachers. Selection criteria, the role of teacher organizations in the process, and financial compensation procedures vary from state to state.

Bilingual Education

Bilingual education programs grew out of Title VI of the Civil Rights Act of 1964 and the Equal Educational Opportunities Act (EEOA) of 1974. The U.S. Supreme Court interpreted these Acts to mandate that states and local school districts create programs to remedy language deficiencies of students from non–English speaking families. Program development and implementation remained in the hands of state and local education officials. The **Bilingual Education Act of 1974** provided federal funds to meet the language needs of non–English speaking students. Throughout the 1970s, bilingual education was favored as the appropriate method to remediate language difficulties. Over 70 percent of these programs were created in the Southwest and Pacific coast areas where districts had high concentrations of non–English speaking families.

There are two primary types of bilingual programs. In two-way bilingual programs (TWBE), students receive instruction in both English and their native languages throughout their elementary education. In transitional bilingual programs (TBE), instruction is in English only after students achieve a specified level of proficiency in English. Evaluation of the effectiveness of bilingual education programs remains inconclusive.[21] In the absence of federal mandates to provide bilingual programs, any reduction in federal funds for these programs would place their future entirely in the hands of the state governments. Given the costs of the programs and the financial pressures on state governments, bilingual education programs remain a topic of debate.

Multiculturalism

In order to establish a greater appreciation for the contributions of the various ethnic groups in the United States, the multicultural movement emerged with a direct impact on education policy. One objective is to change public perceptions by reexamining traditional views of the Western European impact on the Americas. The resulting emphasis on redefining the diverse and disparate ethnic elements in American society and revising history books accordingly has significant consequences for curricula. In fact, multicultural education has been defined, in social reconstructionist terms,[22] as a program designed to create social changes beyond increasing tolerance and understanding. In 1973, the American Association of Colleges for Teacher Education (AACTE) defined multiculturalism as a rejection of "the view that schools should seek to melt away cultural differences or the view that schools should merely tolerate cultural pluralism."[23] The AACTE defined multiculturalism in terms of embracing such concepts as multilingualism, multidialectism, empowerment, equity, and cultural and individual uniqueness. The political dimensions of multicultural education are extensive, and any attempt to depoliticize was recognized as inconsistent with its very nature.[24]

Redefinition of the African American contribution, for instance, requires that African culture and values be identified and taught. Such curriculum revisions have the effect of expanding students' knowledge of cultures often ignored in traditional curricula. The emphasis on Afrocentrism arises from a conviction that African American students' educational performance improves with a heightened sense of cultural pride.

The curriculum changes that accompany the multicultural movement generated considerable conflict. The emphasis on self-definition by various ethnic groups requires revision of both their contributions and the Western heritage. The result can be a significant alteration of traditional views. Some critics argue that basic American values brought from Europe—democratic principles, the Anglo-Saxon legal system, the importance accorded the individual, and science and technology—will not receive sufficient attention in a revised curriculum. The 2010 Arizona legislature went so far as to ban public schools from offering ethnic studies classes because of these fears and in direct reaction to a Tucson school's Mexican American Studies curriculum.

Multiculturalism is also at odds with the view of America as a melting pot, wherein an undeniable measure of political and social integration was synthesized from innumerable ethnic elements. The multicultural curriculum may be better characterized as a salad bowl view of America, stressing and encouraging diversity rather than homogeneity. Advocates of multicultural curricula reject the concept of mainstream America as being nothing more than an attempt to foster an emphasis on Eurocentrism in education.

Opponents of the multiculturalist current express concern that an emphasis on cultural diversity could lead to societal fragmentation and weakness.

Minority Teachers.   Currently, minority teachers make up slightly more than 14 percent of the teaching profession. Some analysts argue that the salary structure for teachers causes many minority college students to reject teaching as a profession.

Projections continue to indicate that minority Americans continue to be underrepresented in the teaching profession. This occurs at a time when minority children attending public schools comprise about 36 percent of the school-age population.

Changing Priorities in Federal Education Policy

The changing priorities of education policy are reflected in the changes of policy preferences at the federal level. The Great Society domestic policies of President Johnson (1963–1968) encouraged new and innovative programs aimed at the educational needs of disadvantaged groups. Although the level of federal education spending did not increase dramatically, there was a general expectation that the proportion of federal aid would increase. This expectation was not met. President Nixon (1969–1974) sought to shift the direction of federal education policy by placing greater emphasis on the role of state and local governments. The Carter administration (1977–1980) shifted slightly toward federal leadership in education policy with the creation of the Department of Education and renewed emphasis on governmental involvement in fostering equal educational opportunity.

President Reagan (1981–1988) led another shift in education policy, with attempts to transfer responsibility for education policy back to the state level. The 1980s also saw debate over curriculum content and reform. The Department of Education developed two model curricula: *James Madison High School* (1987) and *James Madison Elementary School* (1988), which embodied an emphasis on classical education with a college-preparatory focus. For example, the English requirement consisted of a four-year literature sequence: introduction to literature, American literature, British literature, and world literature. Three full years of mathematics included an emphasis on algebra, geometry, trigonometry, statistics, and calculus.

Although the approach pleased conservatives, because of its emphasis on traditonal values, others were critical. Liberals, although commending the model's rigor, felt that it was overly narrow. While students were to read Homer, Shakespeare, the Bible, and other great literature, they would not be exposed to the works of contemporary women, minority, or ethnic authors.

In mid-1991, President George H. W. Bush released *America 2000: An Education Strategy*. Although *America 2000* presented very broad goals for the United States, some very specific policy preferences were included: adoption of a nationwide achievement test, publication of annual national and state report cards by the U.S. Department of Education to document student achievement levels, expansion of **school choice** options through the use of vouchers, and maintaining a limited federal financial role in funding education initiatives. Implementation of *America 2000* was not achieved, primarily because the absence of federal funding made the plan unattractive.

President Clinton proposed *Goals 2000* as the centerpiece of his education policy agenda. This program contained the same basic goals as those announced by President George H. W. Bush in his *America 2000* initiative. Clinton's education policy provided states participating in the program the option of either adopting the national standards developed by the National Education Standards and Improvement Council (NESIC) or developing their own standards, which were to be of "equal or higher quality" than NESIC standards.

Goals 2000 involved a strategy of federal policy leadership in the areas of curriculum and education outcomes, but with minimal federal funding. This policy initiative involved a greater role for the federal government using mandated policy guidelines. These goals generated considerable debate between conservatives and liberals. Conservatives supported many of the individual goals, such as school choice and technological literacy, but opposed the creation of national standards developed by a federal education bureaucracy. Conservatives were concerned about the impact of mandatory national testing programs and of the cultural values that might be mandated for inclusion in the school curriculum. Progressives tended to support these initiatives, but had reservations about some components, such as school choice and the creation of charter schools. Liberals tended to be less concerned about national standards and the values that education professionals would include in curriculum.

CONTINUING DEBATES: COMMUNITY CONTROL, PRIVATE SCHOOLS, A CHANGING FEDERAL ROLE, AND CONFLICTING PRIORITIES

Questions regarding equality and education, the ability of schools to educate minority students, and the competence of both students and teachers produced calls for alternatives to the traditional public school system. Two frameworks dominate current discussion of educational reform. Liberals or progressives tend to emphasize federal leadership in establishing education policies and programs. Such leadership is necessary if schools are to achieve their social purposes. An acceptance of a strong role for education professionals as policy experts also marks this perspective. Liberals tend to combine an emphasis on public schools with a somewhat skeptical view of private and church schools. Conservative thought generally emphasizes local governance through community control of schools. This orientation is skeptical of using schools to advance the social agenda of education professionals, which may conflict with local values. Yet a conservative president, George W. Bush, made national education standards the signature of his education policy with the No Child Left Behind Act.

Community Control and Decentralization

Cutting across ideological lines, members of minority groups advocate effective local participation in school decision making in order to exercise power over the institutions that directly affect their lives. Other groups resisting federal and state intervention in local schools have made this same demand. Examples include controversies over textbooks, school prayer, and student drug abuse. Today, citizens expect education to be both technically advanced and responsive to the public.

The Role of Professional Educators.   Professional education associations resist the movement toward decentralization and community control. One reason they cite is the public's alleged lack of expertise, which prevents the effective evaluation of educational alternatives. However, the public often has strong opinions about education and usually agrees on general criteria for judging a school: qualified teachers, classroom discipline, and physical equipment.

Historically, professional educators tended to dominate state and local education bureaucracies and to mold education policy. Professional educators are inclined to resist giving power to groups they perceive as less well informed and unqualified. Yet, community participation in education also serves to move minority Americans into wider-ranging positions of power and responsibility. Conservative Americans have become more interested in local control as a way of challenging the educational bureaucrats who control the public education system.

The Issue of Private Schools

Most parents justify the shift to private schools as a concern for quality education. Parents also objected to mainstreaming, whereby students with severe disabilities (mental or physical) are integrated into regular public school classrooms. This practice has led to charges that teachers have to spend excessive time with the special needs students and neglect other students. Parents then claim that their children are simply warehoused through the twelve grades.

Parental concern over religious beliefs and values has added to the enrollment support of private schools. Approximately 78 percent of all private school students attend a school with religious ties. Today about six million children attend private schools of various types. A major factor now appears to be a desire for an educational system that follows traditional curriculum and is committed to teaching moral values.

As reflected in Figure 9.5, the percentage of students attending private schools of all types has remained somewhat stable, varying by less than 1 percent since 1970. This indicates that public schools have not lost ground; nevertheless, they will continue to face competition from private schools throughout this decade, especially under any voucher system. Competition to public schools from **charter schools** may also increase in the near future. Parents may choose to send their children to specialized charter schools instead of public schools. Under the current provisions of No Child Left Behind, parents may send their children to another school if their public school fails to meet prescribed standards. Charter schools may benefit from this provision. This competition will involve not only enrollment numbers but also curriculum content, student achievement levels, social values, and financial support.

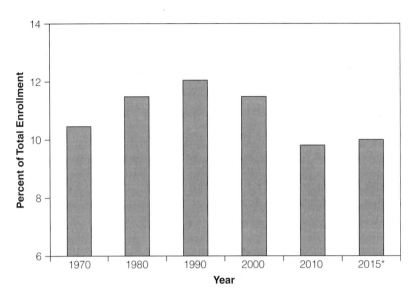

FIGURE 9.5 Private School Enrollment, 1970–2015 (as a percentage of total enrollment)

*2015 reflects estimated data.

SOURCE: U.S. Department of Education, National Center for Education Statistics, *Digest of Education Statistics* (2012), Chapter 1, Table 3, Enrollment in Educational Institutions, by Level and Control of Institution: Selected Years, 1869–70 through Fall 2021, http://nces.ed.gov/programs/digest/d12/tables/dt12_003.asp?referrer=report, accessed March 2014.

Education Vouchers and Tax Credits.   One proposed reform of education financing is a system of **education vouchers** or **tax credits** that would allow parents to select the school best suited to the needs of their children. This reform has strong conservative support as well as support from private schools. Vouchers allow public tax dollars to be redeemed at private schools for education services. A voucher system allows parents to use them as tuition payment at either public or private schools. The origin of the voucher concept can be traced to economist Milton Friedman's contention that the education system would be strengthened by free-market competition between public and private schools;[25] public and private schools would either develop quality programs or cease to exist as their enrollments evaporated. Others have long supported vouchers or tax credits as a way of facilitating parental control over their children's education.

Proponents of the voucher plan argue that it is necessary to overcome the inflexibility of the existing local public school districts. This view holds that public schools, dominated by rigid professional education bureaucracies, are incapable of developing the programs and incentives necessary for an effective teaching and learning environment. The concept of school vouchers enjoyed significant public support. By 1999, some 60 percent of public school parents indicated support for the voucher system with elected officials (both Republican and Democrat) evenly split on the issue. By 2012, only some 30 percent of the public supported a voucher system. Support for charter schools, however, was in the 70 percent range.[26]

School choice plans vary significantly. Some concern public schools only, and allow parents to send their children to any public school regardless of district of residence. Other plans encourage the option of attending private schools (including religious schools) through vouchers, tax credits, or tax deductions. Tax credits would allow parents to deduct educational expenses from their actual federal or state income tax bill. In effect, parents would use money for private education expenses instead of paying it as income tax and would therefore be free from the burden of paying both tuition costs for a private education and contributing to the upkeep of public schools that their children do not attend.

The adoption of a system of vouchers or tax credits might spur an enrollment shift toward private schools, which progressives and public educators oppose on egalitarian grounds. Professional educators also have an interest in maintaining their control over local schools. Before desegregation, a duality existed in the education system based on race. If middle-class students are removed from the public system, a new duality could arise based on socioeconomic status, and a two-tiered educational system would be the final result. Private schools, funded with public tax monies, could constitute the upper tier, with public schools relegated to the bottom. Supporters of vouchers and credits counter that students from all economic classes would use the financial aids and that suburban/urban schools are already two-tiered, as well as socially and economically segregated.

The use of a voucher system might create nationwide social problems, according to opponents. The educational system acts as a major vehicle for political socialization through which the young achieve a common set of values and level of knowledge concerning the political and social system. A common curriculum and the opportunity to interact with students from diverse backgrounds achieve this result. A voucher system could segregate students in accordance with parental preferences, and the diversity of experiences available to public school students could disappear.

Private religious schools provide students with an educational environment in which religion is an integral part of the curriculum. Financial aid from government for religious education instantly evokes the doctrine of separation of church and state. Here, it is sufficient to say that the Court has struck down as unconstitutional state programs of general aid to religious schools but has allowed aid directly to students attending religious schools. However, at the same time, the Court has allowed public funding to support a variety of services to private religious schools, as well as limited voucher programs. Proposals for assisting private and religious schools continue to face a serious constitutional challenge; this issue will remain on the education policy agenda.[27]

Educational Concern

If an unfriendly foreign power had attempted to impose on America the mediocre educational performance that exists today, we might have viewed it as an act of war. As it stands we have allowed this to happen to ourselves.[28]

Thus stated the 1983 report of the National Commission on Excellence in Education. The report was critical of the state of the nation's education system and concerned about the implications for the future. The ability of the United States to maintain a preeminent position in commerce, industry, science, and technology was, in the words of the commission, "at risk." Competition from Japan, South Korea, and Western Europe places a burden on our education system to produce skilled, creative individuals in order to ensure economic strength.

The commission's report was significant because it reflects a continuing concern of elected officials, education professionals, and the general public about the perceived decline in the quality of education. The commission's recommendations focused on curriculum reform, with a renewed emphasis on the basics of education (English, science, math, and social studies) and on a longer school day and year (seven-hour day, 220-day academic year). The commission also endorsed the concepts of merit pay, competency testing for students and teachers, and the implementation of a master teacher program. It gave the primary responsibility for financing education to the local school districts and the states, limiting the federal government's fiscal role.

The challenge for the United States to make significant progress toward overall educational excellence remains and can be linked to several factors. First, the average performance of American students has remained stable and has not increased relative to other industrialized nations. In a competitive global economy, stability may be equated with stagnation and translated into a competitive disadvantage. Second, wide disparities remain between high-achieving and low-achieving students in the areas of science and mathematics, with significant numbers of students lacking what may be defined as basic literacy in those two areas of learning. Data also suggests that the disparity between high- and low-achieving students in reading and language arts is now increasing in the United States. And third, in the area of science and mathematics, the average performance scores of American students are below those of Western Europe, the industrialized Pacific Rim nations, and Russia. Historically, the lack of rigor in the curriculum of American schools has been viewed as the source of much of these differences.[29]

The high school dropout rate remains a continuing problem, the magnitude of which appears in Figure 9.6. The national dropout rate is slightly under 7 percent with the Hispanic rate at 12 percent. The failure of a significant proportion of the population to earn a high school diploma encourages the development of an undereducated minority class.

Education Policy Priorities in the Twenty-first Century

President George W. Bush developed an education policy initiative when the No Child Left Behind Act of 2001 (NCLB) was signed into law in January 2002 as a reauthorization of the Elementary and Secondary Education Act. NCLB is best understood as a continuation and expansion of the education policy initiatives of President George H. W. Bush and President Clinton. Box 9.2 presents the significant provisions of this education initiative.

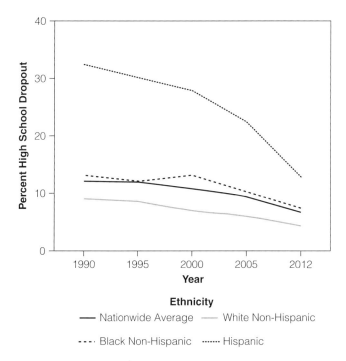

F I G U R E 9.6 Dropout Rates of 16–24-Year-Olds by Race/Ethnicity, 1990–2012

Race/ethnicity used in the *Condition of Education, 2009* "… are in accordance with the 1997 Office of Management and Budget (OMB) standard classification scheme…. The 1997 standards emphasize self-reporting and self-identification as the preferred method for collecting data on race and ethnicity." (Supplemental Note 1)

SOURCE: U.S. Department of Education, National Center for Education Statistics, *The Condition of Education, 2013,* http://nces.ed.gov/programs/digest/d13/tables/dt13_219.70.asp, accessed March 2014.

NCLB as a Source of Policy Conflict. The debate surrounding potential reauthorization of NCLB continues in 2014. Provisions of the act continue in force, but it was not reauthorized in 2007 and remains on the policy agenda. First, federal funding levels to public schools have not increased significantly as a result of the Act. The primary funding source for education programs continues to be from state governments and local school districts. Liberals' criticism of NCLB is linked to this lack of federal funding for implementation across the fifty states. They argue that this federal program initiative should be accompanied by sufficient federal dollars if the local districts are to successfully comply with the requirements. Conservatives are opposed to increased federal funding for NCLB, holding that implementation funding should rest with states and local districts in order to retain a degree of local autonomy in education policy. At the same time, conservatives tend to oppose NCLB because component parts of the Act control and direct curricular decisions that historically are the domain of local districts. Liberals find reason to support NCLB precisely because it seeks to establish national standards and is therefore a potential mechanism to promote equality of educational opportunity. NCLB is a source of conflict both within and between conservatives and liberals.

Box 9.2   President George W. Bush's Education Policy Initiative

The No Child Left Behind Act of 2001 (Reauthorization of ESEA in 2002)

Accountability and Assessment: Annual assessment of student achievement in reading and math in grades three to eight, accompanied by school and state report cards. Districts required to demonstrate "proficiency" for all groups of students enrolled.

State and Local Flexibility: Reduces the number of ESEA programs from fifty-five to forty-five and allows states to transfer up to 50 percent of non–Title I funds into other ESEA areas without advance federal approval. Local districts may participate in "flexibility demonstration projects" to consolidate all federal funds in exchange for agreements to produce higher student achievement.

Expansion of Parental Choice: Parents of children in "failing schools" are allowed to transfer their child to a higher performing public school or charter school and to obtain supplemental education services from either public- or private-sector providers.

Emphasis on Reading: Provides federal funding assistance to local districts in order to achieve the goal that every child can read by the end of third grade.

Improvement of Teacher Quality: Provides federal grant funding to states to improve teacher recruitment and retention in exchange for agreements to improve student achievement.

Promoting English Proficiency: Consolidate bilingual and immigrant education programs with emphasis on improved teaching methods and testing of student achievement after a student has been in the school system for three consecutive years.

Safe Schools: Districts must use federal funding to implement drug and violence prevention programs with provisions that students in "persistently dangerous schools" be allowed to transfer to another public or charter school.

SOURCE: U.S. Department of Education (2004). A Guide to Education and No *Child Left Behind*, www2.ed.gov/nclb/ overview/intro/guide/index.html, accessed March 2005.

Critics of NCLB hold that the Act is a mechanism that imposes an unfunded mandate on local school districts and the states. In order to continue to receive existing limited federal funding, the states will be required to absorb the costs associated with implementation of the Act. Critics hold that any federal policy mandate should be accompanied by sufficient federal funding associated with that policy. Proponents of NCLB hold that the requirements accommodate significant latitude for states to establish their own goals, and therefore the states should assume primary responsibility for program costs.

NCLB generates conflict relating to the issue of national versus local control of education policy. A central component of the Act is the concept of adequate yearly progress (AYP). The NCLB initially required that **adequate yearly progress (AYP)** be achieved such that 100 percent of students in each class and each school are rated as proficient by 2014. Education professionals found that these requirements applied to all students regardless of their individual level of intelligence, motivation, learning disability, and family background. Each state established standards that measure the AYP of students as a mechanism to hold local districts and schools accountable for their educational performance. Each state is also required to establish clearly defined goals for student and school performance. Students in school that fail to meet their AYP goals become eligible to transfer to other schools.

Proponents of the program argue that states have significant flexibility to define their own performance goals. Advocates of local control argue that NCLB will ultimately evolve into a mechanism for the imposition of national standards and national goals on local districts. Advocates of a more centralized education policy are concerned that the provisions allowing states to develop their own standards will not strengthen the curriculum and improve performance, but will foster continued decentralization. In the absence of renewal of NCLB some forty-four states by 2014 had applied for or were granted waivers from achieving the national AYP standards and allowed flexibility to establish their own AYP standards.

An integral component of NCLB involves reliance on a program of regular testing of student performance to assess AYP. These tests have been identified as high-stakes testing for schools. Student performance on the tests are used to assess school performance and are reported to the general public. Schools not meeting their AYP goals may qualify for corrective action and students attending those schools may be allowed to transfer to other, higher performing schools. One result of this provision is a linkage between NCLB and the school choice movement. Proponents of school choice argue that students should have the freedom to move to higher performing schools if their own school is performing at a low level. Some proponents also see this provision for school choice as a potential mechanism for students to transfer to higher performing private schools. Critics of this provision argue that such high-stakes testing acts to weaken the commitment of the public to the public school system as parents may be given the ability to shop for higher performing schools. One potential result could be a renewed emphasis on charter schools that target students from low-performing schools.

Classroom teachers and school principals find themselves under intense pressure to demonstrate that the students under their care achieve proficient test scores. In order to adapt to the requirement for ever-increasing student performance on tests, two strategies have developed. One involves a narrowing of the curriculum to teach primarily material on the standardized tests. The second involves beginning the school year in early August in order to provide more time to prepare students to take the tests that are typically administered in the fall. Professional educators and other critics have argued that NCLB guarantees that virtually all of the nation's schools will eventually receive a failing grade.

Finally, to return to the writings of Thomas Jefferson, education in a democracy was intended to focus on such values as judgment, critical thinking, justice, civic responsibility, and independent thinking. The emphasis of NCLB on achieving proficiency on standardized test scores seems to be in conflict with this view of education.

POLICY DILEMMAS   Accountability and Performance in Education

A recurring issue in education policy involves the role of the federal government in establishing educational standards and education programs. President Obama's Race to the Top initiative involves federal grants totaling $4.35 billion to encourage innovation in state and local education policy. This spending level represents less than 1 percent of education spending in the United States, and funding is provided only to education policy innovations that meet federal guidelines and standards. As of 2013 some fifteen states had received funding under Race to the Top. The U.S. Department of Education created an Implementation and Support Unit to work with states and local districts in developing reform initiatives that will ultimately meet federal standards. One such manifestation is the continued development and implementation of testing as a preferred mechanism to establish benchmarks of student achievement. Another element involves development of performance-based funding for schools. This emphasis on testing and school performance measures has been embraced by both conservative (President Bush) and liberal/progressive (President Obama) federal leaders.

1. What should be the role of the federal government in establishing educational standards and assessment procedures within the context of very limited federal funding for education?

2. What is the appropriate role for high-stakes testing (such as that mandated by NCLB) in determining student achievement and school performance?

Education Policy Initiatives of President Obama

> My Administration's blueprint for reauthorization of the Elementary and Secondary Education Act is not only a plan to renovate a flawed law, but also an outline for a re-envisioned federal role in education. (President Obama, *A Blueprint for Reform*, 2010)

The education policy preferences announced by President Obama reflect an expanding emphasis on federal education policy leadership with only a marginal increase in federal funding. President Obama's policy initiatives remain under discussion and are generally consistent with the philosophy of NCLB. One element involves reauthorization of modified NCLB legislation with an emphasis on requiring students to demonstrate progress in their test scores rather than achieving a specified level of proficiency as measured by testing. States receiving federal funding would also be required to strengthen teacher and administrator evaluation systems in order to improve school performance and enhance teaching effectiveness.

Under his plan, charter schools should be encouraged and receive support as a mechanism to give parents more choice in the education of their children. Federal education funding to states would require states and local school districts to encourage the growth and development of charter schools.

President Obama also seeks to increase the emphasis on science, technology, engineering, and mathematics (STEM) in local school districts. This initiative involves cooperation with the National Science Foundation (NSF) and other agencies in the development of education strategies in this area. Federal policy leadership would also be expanded through a range of initiatives targeting education such as Race to the Top, Promise Neighborhoods, Early Childhood Education programs, 21st Century Community Learning Centers, and a variety of other program initiatives.

Critics of the initiatives advocated by President Obama argue that the programs serve to expand federal control with an absence of federal funding. For example, Race to the Top provided minimal levels of new federal dollars ($100 to $700 million) to individual states if the developed programs were consistent with federal policy guidelines. Critics cite the fact that expansion of federal funding for elementary and secondary education was only in the $4 billion range for FY 2011. Under the Race to the Top program, federal influence continues to increase through a system of federal grant programs. Federal funding levels will not change from historic levels in the 8 to 10 percent range because annual funding of the Race to the Top program is minimal, less than 1 percent of all education spending (see Figure 9.1). Given the significant federal budget deficit, federal aid to education will not be expanded in the foreseeable future. Federal education initiatives have been designed to influence education policy, not expand federal funding.

The education policy initiatives of President Obama remain fluid in early 2014 without congressional action. Debate over the federal role in education will continue as federal policy initiatives continue to mandate policy direction without an increase in federal funding.

Unresolved Education Issues: Teachers and Curriculum

A number of unresolved issues remain on the education policy agenda. Drug abuse, violence, and crime present significant challenges to the education system. One response has been the development of zero tolerance codes for weapons, fighting, drugs, and other student behaviors in an effort to promote student safety.

National Teacher Certification.   The qualifications of teachers remain an important issue. Professional educators created the nongovernmental National Board for Professional Teaching Standards in 1987 in response to the publication of a report by the Carnegie Forum on Education and the Economy titled *A Nation Prepared* (1986). The primary focus of this report was the establishment of national standards to assess and certify teachers, as opposed to the decentralized process used by the fifty states today. Proponents argue that teacher certification has too much of an impact on education quality to continue reliance on the states with their decentralized uncoordinated standards.[30] Before 2000, there were only some 9,500 nationally certified teachers; by 2014, this number had increased to over 100,000.

Workforce Preparation.   Historically, the American public education system produced two types of graduates. One group was students on a college track, who would later become managers, decision makers, and scientific or technical experts. The second group consisted of students who would enter the workforce after graduation and assume nontechnical positions in the nation's factories. Today's economy requires workers who are capable of rapid and continuous learning to improve productivity and enhance the global competitiveness of the nation. Some federal programs provide limited financial assistance for partnerships among school districts, businesses, labor unions, and community groups that provide high school students with work experience and insights into the education requirements for specific careers.

Proponents of these programs argue that students should be exposed to the relationship between education and careers while in high school, rather than after graduation. Such exposure will translate into increased student motivation in the classroom and an appreciation of the need for lifelong learning. Critics argue that the program simply provides academic credit for low-level, part-time jobs that have little relevance to a genuine career.

Moral Education.   Conservatives argue that the schools have an obligation to provide a moral foundation for the nation's children through an emphasis on traditional values. The Northwest Ordinance in 1787 clearly linked "religion, morality, and knowledge" to good government. Federal legislation in the twentieth century did not emphasize moral foundations, but stressed values, such as national security, equality, and separation of church and state. Both liberals and conservatives are increasingly concerned that moral foundations be linked to the education process.[31] Differences over substance, however, are divisive. Conservatives emphasize values that stress the importance of the individual as shaped by institutions, such as the church, the family, and traditional political values. These values then shape collective societal values. Liberals, however, place greater emphasis on social values that shape institutions such as the church, the family, and the political culture. These collective values then shape the values of the individual.

A related movement, back to the basics, advocated an increased emphasis on basic skills, such as reading, writing, and arithmetic, but also traditional values of respect, obedience, and moral content.[32] The movement first emerged in the late 1950s after the Soviet Union launched Sputnik, the first space satellite. During this early period, the emphasis was on basic education as a foundation for national security. Basic skills of the 1950s did not focus on individual and personal goal attainment, but rather on the individual's responsibility to use basic skills to contribute to the national good. Current debates over curriculum can be traced directly to the back-to-the-basics movement.

Intelligent Design and Evolution.   A significant policy issue involves conflict over inclusion of intelligent design in the curriculum as either a balance or opposing position to evolution. The issue is complex and involves two elements. The first element involves discussion relevant to the presence or absence of conflict between religions and generally accepted scientific precepts. When conflict is present (such as between theistic creationism and evolution), does the education system have the obligation to present materials advocating both positions?

The conflict between evolution and intelligent design will continue in the next several years.

The second factor involves the issue of the establishment clause in the U.S. Constitution as related to separation of church and state. In 1968, the U.S. Supreme Court in *Epperson v. Arkansas* ruled that states could not ban the teaching of evolution due to a conflict with religious beliefs.[33] In 1987, the U.S. Supreme Court in *Edwards v. Aguillard* ruled that states could not mandate that teachers include a discussion of creation science when discussing evolution.[34] The federal courts tend to hold that teaching of either creation science or intelligent design involves establishment of religion and is therefore in violation of the Constitution. This topic remains a hot button issue on the policy agenda and will continue as a source of conflict.

Unresolved Education Issues: Structural Questions

Charter Schools.   The concept of the charter school was introduced in the mid-1980s and is designed to allow the creation of an independent legal entity with responsibility for delivery of education programs.[35] Under this concept, state boards of education grant a charter to either a public or private group to organize and operate a school. A charter school is a tuition-free entity that is publicly funded and provides educational choice to students and parents. Charter schools blur the distinction between public and private school systems since they can be considered as either quasi-public or quasi-private entities. The charter school movement began with two schools in 1991 in Minnesota and has experienced significant growth. The number of charter schools increased from about 1,500 in 2000 to about 5,270 in 2012. Charter schools are in operation in over forty-one states. Enrollment in charter schools has expanded from around 300,000 in 1990 to slightly under two million students in 2014.

Local school boards tend to have minimal responsibility for the operation of a charter school within their jurisdiction. Proponents of charter schools argue that they present a unique opportunity for education reform and serve as a mechanism for educational reform and innovation. Critics of charter schools see the movement as simply a modification of a voucher system for private schools.

Proponents state that charter schools may serve as a new approach to create autonomous schools that respond to specific educational needs and develop creative strategies to improve student performance that are unattainable by current school systems. Advocates of charter schools emphasize characteristics defined as unique strengths of charter schools. School choice is one of these strengths. Parents are able to select an alternative school that best meets the needs of their children, independently of the public school system. This provides students from poor and disadvantaged areas the opportunity to attend a higher quality school outside of the attendance zone of their traditional public school. Charter schools are able to specialize their curriculum to meet the needs of students through innovative and creative approaches. For example, some charter schools build their programs around the arts, others emphasize the sciences, and still others focus on college preparation.

The ability of charter schools to operate independently of a sometimes complex and inflexible educational bureaucracy is cited as a strength. One result is that charter schools are presented as having a higher level of responsiveness and accountability to parents than do traditional schools. Charter schools are typically created with a requirement for student performance and achievement. Proponents state that the standards for charter schools are higher than for traditional public schools and that this contributes to an improved learning environment for students.

President Obama continued to signal his support for charter schools through his proclamations, declaring a week in May as "National Charter Schools Week." This is consistent with the practice of his predecessor. The role and extent of charter schools in the American education system continue as a policy debate.

Privatization. Another educational reform movement involves the creation of privately managed public schools. Education Alternatives, Inc. (EAI), in what is now known as the Edison Project, promoted this idea as a mechanism to improve the performance and quality of local schools.[36] Under this concept, the operation of either a single school or an entire district may be contracted out to a private firm. Proponents argue that initiative provided by the private sector provides a mechanism to improve the performance of schools by reinventing the curriculum and teaching techniques. Proponents also believe that **privatization** is consistent with the charter school movement. Critics argue that there is no evidence that privately operated public schools actually perform at a higher level than their public-managed counterparts do and that concern for profitability of the enterprise will require that student needs become a secondary priority. Often, privatization emerges as a last-ditch effort to salvage failing urban schools.

The authority granted to the private contractor varies from district to district. Mixed evaluation results produce significant conflict. Benefits included an increase in student attendance rates, a drop in suspension rates, increased access to computers in classrooms, and improved building maintenance. Privatization varies in scope, from contracting for limited services, such as cafeteria, maintenance, and transportation, to managing an entire school. Because privatization experiments are so diverse, it remains an unsettled issue on the education policy agenda.

Home Schooling. Perhaps the ultimate form of privatization in education is the development of **home schooling**. Under this model, parents assume primary responsibility for the education of their children. Some parents undertake this effort because of dissatisfaction with their local public schools; others wish to provide a religious education specifically in keeping with their beliefs. Still other parents wish to allow their children to develop their learning more naturally, instead of through the perceived artificial organization of standardized public school curricula.

Estimates are that almost two million students participated in home schooling in 2014. Based on the limited evidence available, children participating in home schooling perform at a level higher than their public school contemporaries do. Parents involved in home schooling have organized at the state and national level to defend their right to educate their children at home with considerable success. Virtually all states now recognize the rights of parents to supervise their children's education in this setting; colleges increasingly accept home-schooled students, despite the lack of conventional transcripts and recommendations.

Single-Gender Schools.   Public education in the United States evolved from single-gender (boys only) to coeducational schools by the mid to late 1800s. During the colonial period, formal education tended to be limited to boys, with girls receiving informal education at home. By 1890, coeducation was the norm across the nation. In 1972, **Title IX of the Education Amendment Act** prohibited discrimination against students based on sex and imposed limits on single-gender institutions. The Citadel and the Virginia Military Institute are two public universities forced to abandon their single-gender status and to admit women students. Some educators now advocate single-gender elementary and secondary schools as a viable alternative to increase student achievement. Proponents argue that single-gender schools for girls reduce distractions, provide greater self-confidence, enhance the development of leadership skills, and reduce the risk of educational failure. In 2006, the U.S. Department of Education's Office of Civil Rights (OCR) issued new policy guidelines that allowed waivers to Title IX and other statutes. Flexibility was provided to schools to provide single-sex schools, classes, and extracurricular activities.

Common Core State Standards Curriculum Reform.   This 2009 initiative grew out of work done by the staff of the National Governors Association and the professionals of the Council of Chief State School Officers. While the federal government did not directly initiate the reform, the Race to the Top initiative of the Obama administration provided funding to support development and encourage adoption of the Common Core. The logic behind the Common Core is that uniform nationwide standards should be developed and applied to all students across the nation for each grade level in the areas of language arts and math. Advocates claim that the standards ensure that students in all fifty states will master the same skills at the same level of proficiency. They also argue that these skills reflect proficiencies that will allow American public school graduates to compete for jobs in an international arena.

Opposition to the Common Core is derived from two diverse groups. Conservatives are concerned about the uniform social and political values that may be incorporated into the initiative's lessons. Many of these values concerning family relationships, the role of government, and social standards are in conflict with traditional values of conservatives. Conservatives, liberals, and educational professionals have challenged the Common Core for other reasons as well. First, the emphasis on standards seems to require all teachers to use the same instructional approach with all students, regardless of learning level. Creativity, diversity, and flexibility of instructional technique (especially valued by educational professionals) seem to be discouraged with the emphasis on universal standards. The standards also assume that all students can and will master the same material within the same time period. This assumption ignores differences in student ability. A second reason for opposition is that the emphasis on standards requires an ever-expanding testing mechanism that will be used to measure both student learning and teacher effectiveness. Issues with this type of testing served to create dissatisfaction with NCLB.

Four states never adopted the Common Core (Texas, Virginia, Alaska, and Nebraska). In early 2014, Indiana formally withdrew from the initiative and several other states are considering withdrawing from the program based on costs, concerns over federal intrusion, and the issue of high-stakes testing associated with the Common Core.

Another national standards curriculum, Next Generation Science Standards, has been developed with the goal of providing consistent science education to all students across the nation. This curriculum follows the same philosophy of an emphasis on nationwide standards and testing as that of the Common Core, but has yet to achieve widespread adoption by the states.

Development of the Common Core and the Next Generation Science Standards indicate that standardized curriculum, high-stakes testing, and uniformity of instruction will remain on the education policy agenda throughout this decade.

Issues in Higher Education

Diversity and Affirmative Action.   Justice Powell introduced the concept of diversity as a rationale for group preferences in the *Bakke* decision dealing with the issue of reverse discrimination. Diversity became a value embraced by colleges and universities across the nation. Higher education flourishes when varieties of racial, economic, ethnic, and social groups interact on the same campus. Moreover, graduation from college increasingly is necessary for economic and social advancement in American society. Minority groups and women see pursuit of diversity in higher education as a way to remedy the effects of historical discrimination. Diversity thus served as the primary legal justification in the admissions process for over fifteen years. It continues to be a significant value in higher education.

Affirmative action in admissions has been one of the primary means to achieve diversity in higher education. The future role of affirmative action admissions programs for colleges and universities, however, is unclear. California's passage of Proposition 209 in November 1996 (an amendment to the state constitution that prohibits the use of race-based and gender-based preferences in hiring, contracting, and education) signaled a significant education policy shift. The amendment survived a challenge in the federal courts and affected 1997–1998 admissions policies. The U.S. Supreme Court has interpreted the Constitution to permit limited forms of preference in higher education, in which race and ethnicity are among a variety of factors that admissions officers may take into account.

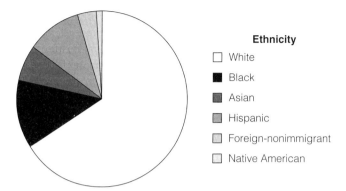

Ethnicity

☐ White

■ Black

■ Asian

■ Hispanic

▨ Foreign-nonimmigrant

☐ Native American

FIGURE 9.7   Higher Education Enrollment by Ethnicity, 2012 (as a percentage of total enrollment)

SOURCE: U.S. Department of Education, National Center for Education Statistics, Fast Facts, 2009, p. 344, Table 9.8, Percentage Distribution of Students Enrolled in Degree-Granting Institutions by Race/Ethnicity, http://nces.ed.gov/programs/digest/d12/tables/dt12_264.asp, accessed March 2014.

Affirmative action programs have had their greatest impact primarily in highly selective colleges and universities where there is considerable competition in the admissions process. At other colleges, the impact of granting an advantage based on race or gender is actually relatively minor. This means that the elimination of affirmative action preferenced-based programs in university admission standards will not have a uniform effect on all university campuses. It does mean that some of the most selective public institutions may no longer be as accessible to some groups in society. Figure 9.7 indicates enrollment in higher education by ethnicity. Hispanics and African Americans tend to be overrepresented in two-year institutions and underrepresented in four-year colleges and universities. Indications remain that race and gender-based standards in state university admission processes will remain an area of policy conflict.

Cost of Higher Education.   One issue on the policy agenda involves the ever-increasing cost of higher education. Tuition increased dramatically for both public and private four-year colleges between 1975 and 2008 (see Figure 9.8), a rate significantly greater than the median household income increase for the same period. After that, it declined somewhat.

Two factors contribute most to the increase in tuition: spending increases by colleges and a greater dependency on tuition and a reduction in state funding as a source of revenue. Public universities are increasingly state-assisted rather than state-funded institutions. Figure 9.9 shows that state funding has decreased as a source of revenue. The decrease in public funding must be offset by an accompanying increase in tuition. Universities have been able to use research funding, gifts, and endowments only as a small buffer for tuition charge increases. If the goal of higher education for most Americans is to be attained, state legislators will have to make difficult choices about raising taxes to fund higher education or cutting other programs to free up funds.

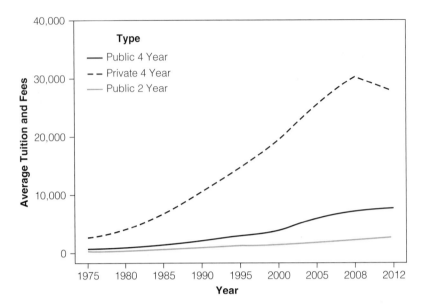

F I G U R E 9.8   Average Undergraduate Tuition, 1975–2012 (excluding room and board)

SOURCE: National Center for Education Statistics, *Digest of Education Statistics*, 2013, Table 381, http://nces.ed.gov/programs/digest/d12/tables/dt12_381.asp?referrer=report, accessed March 2014.

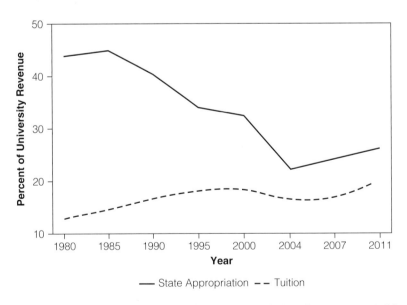

F I G U R E 9.9   Tuition Dollars and State Appropriations for Four-Year Public Colleges, 1980–2011

SOURCE: U.S. Department of Education, National Center for Education Statistics (2006), *Digest of Education Statistics*, 2007, Tables 337 and 338, and *Digest of Education Statistics*, 2013; http://nces.ed.gov/programs/digest/d06/tables_3asp#Ch3aSub7, accessed July 2007; and http://nces.ed.gov/programs/digest/d12/ch_3.asp, accessed March 2014.

SUMMARY

American education policy is characterized by a tension between local control and the expanding role for the federal government—without the infusion of federal dollars. The expansion of the federal role has been motivated by a concern about school performance, as well as a perceived issue with the educational achievement of students across the nation. Education policy reflects the concern for accountability and performance with adoption of what can be described as high-stakes testing of students. Policy conflict remains regarding the issue of the appropriate role for the federal government, the issues of student achievement, and accountability of the school system.

 **RESOURCES**

American Association of University Professors: **www.aaup.org**

American Federation of Teachers: **www.aft.org**

Annenberg Institute for School Reform: **www.annenberginstitute.org**

Charter Schools: **http://nationalcharterschools.org**

Education Resources Information Center (ERIC): **www.eric.ed.gov**

Homeschooling website: **www.home-school.com**

National Board for Professional Teaching Standards: **www.nbpts.org**

National Catholic Educational Association: **www.ncea.org**

National Center for Education Statistics: **www.nces.ed.gov**

National Center for the Study of Privatization in Education: **www.ncspe.org**

School Choices: **www.schoolchoices.org**

United States Department of Education: **www.ed.gov**

Chapter 10

Legal and Social Equality: The Struggle against Oppression and Bigotry

F ew concepts in the context of either domestic or international politics are capable of generating as much symbolic and emotional appeal as equality. Traceable in some form as far back as the concept of justice, its roots precede Plato. The term *equality* is certainly a familiar and recurring one in the history of Western thought. The enduring strength of the appeal of the concept was made apparent when, in early 2014, President Obama announced that income inequality would be the number one priority in the remainder of his presidency.

Yet, despite its strong symbolism and cultural familiarity, the substantive content of the term has remained imprecise, inconsistent, or both. A central theme of this chapter is that three distinguishable conceptualizations of equality have existed: **equality under law**, **equality of opportunity**, and **equality of material well-being**. Each conceptualization implies different goals for public policy, and the dominant reading of the term has changed over time. Indeed, definitional quarrels in the matter of race have become so pervasive that Stephen and Abigail Thernstrom contend that "today we argue without a common language" in this area.[1] A generation ago a widespread conception of racism involved judging the qualities of people by the racial group to which they belong and treating them accordingly. We will see later that a current conceptualization of symbolic racism includes a demand that race be used as a factor in selecting people for employment or admission to selective universities. Terms in this area are used as much for their emotional and symbolic content as for their precise meaning.

Not only has the meaning of the concept of racism evolved but the dominant attitudes about questions of race and equality have undergone tremendous changes in the past generation. In the early 2000s, when prominent African

Americans such as Jesse Jackson or Al Sharpton put themselves up as candidates for the presidency, these candidacies were widely regarded as symbolic gestures. The decisive electoral victory of Barack Obama in 2008, however, when he carried 52.9 percent of the national vote, suggested to many that the racism that would prevent a white person from voting for an African American simply because of his/her race has become the exception rather than the rule.[2] Even in the Republican primary in 2012, African American candidate Herman Cain ran credibly for the nomination but was not successful. While there is undoubtedly lingering racial bigotry in the United States, Obama's election, and subsequent reelection in 2012, suggests that race is no longer the absolute impediment for racial minorities to attain any high office to which they might aspire.

Other scholars, however, argue that substantial racism continues to exist in the United States. This chapter demonstrates that an expanding sense of equality of material well-being has come to dominate the policy process. Meanwhile, the roster of groups identified by the policy process and the media as official victims of discrimination have been expanding. To the evils of racism (referring to discrimination against African Americans, Hispanics, and Native Americans) and sexism (referring to discrimination against women) have been added ageism (discrimination against the elderly), ableism (discrimination against people with disabilities), homophobia (discrimination against homosexuals), and nativism (discrimination against foreign born or immigrants). The law has further developed the concept of the rights of children independent of their families. Children have acquired the right to sue their parents and even to "divorce" their parents. The status and rights of foreign-born citizens and legal immigrants to this country is the ongoing controversy over the question of whether illegal immigrants have rights and whether these persons should be granted citizenship (see Chapter 11). This issue came to national attention with the 1994 passage of a referendum in California of Proposition 187, a vote that amended the California Constitution to deny public benefits, including welfare, access to public health facilities, and even the right to attend public school, to illegal aliens and their children. Spokespersons for Hispanic immigrants challenged the constitutionality of that proposition in federal court. A permanent injunction was issued and the proposition was never enforced. Meanwhile, the issue of illegal entry into the United States, largely over our Southern border with Mexico, exploded in 2010 as one of the most divisive and passionately felt issues in the country. Many business and farming interests want to protect the flow of illegal immigrants, especially those coming across the Mexican border, as they provide a supply of cheap labor. Others, however, are concerned with security considerations and the costs to public facilities (e.g., schools, hospitals, and welfare programs), as well as the high crime rate among the illegal immigrants. They want to stem the flow and secure the border before addressing the question of the status of those already here. Some states have issued driver's licenses to undocumented persons, which have been used to obtain other documents, a policy which some argue could be used by potential terrorists.

In the spring of 2010, the state of Arizona, one such border state that has borne a disproportionate share of the costs of illegal immigration, passed a highly controversial state law to control the flood of illegal immigrants across its southern border. The law states that if someone is detained for other legitimate reasons, such as a traffic violation, the police may demand that the detainee produce documentation of immigration status if "reasonable suspicion exists" that the person is in the United States illegally. A strong wave of criticism of the Arizona law argued that the law encourages law enforcement officials to detain and harass individuals just because they look Hispanic, an example of the widely denounced policy of **racial profiling**.

Racial profiling refers to the practice of selecting people of a given race or ethnicity for examinations to which others are not subjected merely because the selected group is believed to be disproportionately responsible for crime, violence, or terrorism. In Florida, racial profiling became an issue in 2014 as Trayvon Martin, a black teenager, was killed by George Zimmerman. Martin was in a neighborhood where Zimmerman seemed to think he did not belong, and he claimed self-defense in the shooting trial. Zimmerman was not convicted of murder, which caused outrage regarding profiling.

Although the Arizona law seemingly does not authorize detaining and checking the identifications of people based on how they look, some people who were detained by the Maricopa County sheriff's deputies sued. In 2013, the federal district court ruled that the sheriff's office had actually engaged in profiling and it was upheld by the Ninth Circuit Court. A federal monitor was put in place to make sure that the profiling stopped. Nevertheless, criticism of the law remained strong.

ISSUE BACKGROUND: THE IDEA OF EQUALITY

Equality under Law

The first conceptualization, equality under law, may be thought of as the minimum position, in that if the term means anything, it means at least this much. The concept of equality under law implies that government should treat people as individuals rather than as members of social groups, and that when those categorizations are used, they impose a heavy burden of proof on government to show that there is a valid and widely accepted public purpose behind them. This concept clearly implies that government should not allocate rewards and punishments to people on the basis of the racial, ethnic, or religious groups to which they belong. Clearly, the law does make many categorizations of people. It distinguishes criminals from noncriminals, the psychotic from the sane, children from adults, and so forth. The reason why law permits these categories is that there is widespread consensus that these categories are based on behavioral distinctions. Thus, we assume that criminals behave differently from noncriminals, psychotics from those defined as sane, and children from adults. Insofar as the law has now completely rejected the belief that there are behavior patterns or dispositions that are intrinsic to members of a given race, at the very least, however, classification by race is inconsistent with the concept of equality under law.

POLICY DILEMMAS   Social Justice: Legal and Social Equality

The controversies generated by the struggle for social, racial, ethnic, and economic equality are exacerbated by disagreement over the question of what is a "fair" or "just" distribution of material well-being. To what are individuals or groups entitled by the mere fact that they exist as human beings? Conversely, are a person's or group's entitlements determined by that person's or group's achievement of competitive success that contributes to the social good? The top one and a half percent of the population owns one-third of the privately owned wealth in the country. While the top 20 percent of the population has just under half of the nation's income, the bottom 20 percent has only 4 percent of the nation's income.* While the President has raised income inequality as one of the most important issues of the time, he has had difficulty in getting Congress to act to address it–even on the issue of minimum wage, which is currently set at $7.25 an hour. Some congressional Republicans suggest that the earned income tax credit should be adjusted instead. None of these suggestions have been acted upon.

President Obama has said famously that we "spread the wealth around" and "there is a point at which a person has enough money."** There is the implicit suggestion in such statements that a disproportionate distribution of wealth is due to the reality that the "playing field is not level."

1. Should government address the issue of income inequality? Why or why not?
2. If government were to address the issue, what should it do? Explain.

---

*Kathleen Miles, "Next Time Someone Argues for 'Trickle-Down' Economics, Show Them This," *The Huffington Post*, February 6, 2014, http://www.huffingtonpost.com/2014/02/06/rich-richer_n_4731408.html.

**Natalie Gewargis, "Spread the Wealth?" *Political Punch*, October 14, 2008, http://abcnews.go.com/blogs/politics/2008/10/spread-the-weal/.

Categorization of people on the basis of the group into which they are born, such as race and ethnicity, is generally presumed unconstitutional unless government can satisfy the burden of proof to demonstrate that they satisfy a "compelling public interest." Therefore, such categorizations are not always unconstitutional. Government conceivably could satisfy the required burden of proof. In recent years, the compelling public interest used to justify race-based selection has been given as diversity in the racial makeup of the workforce or student body. We will see that the current Supreme Court has recently questioned whether such diversity is a sufficiently compelling interest.

Some categorizations, such as gender, may be constitutional for some purposes but not for others. The law has come to reject the assumption that men are intrinsically more intelligent than women; therefore, laws banning women from occupations in which intelligence is the main qualifying criterion violate equality under law. The law, however, may protect some residual assumptions that women are intrinsically less aggressive than men by excluding them from combat roles in the military. Even this assumption has been substantially eroded in the law by the recent acceptance of women for many combat roles in today's military, including that of combat pilot. In 2014, however, consistently applied standards of upper body strength (such as the ability to do two pull-ups) remained as obstacles to women joining such special forces as the Navy Seals. It will become apparent from our discussion of sex discrimination that society's assumptions about the intrinsic properties of women are undergoing a process of evolution and that this process is affecting law and policy. Legal principles distinguishing the sexes that went unchallenged a generation ago are now being found to be in violation of the right to equal protection of the law or are now banned by statute, and women are increasingly appearing in roles previously assumed to be beyond the competence of the typical woman. A similar flexibility of roles is beginning to emerge for men. Thus, one can now find women working as doctors, lawyers, or judges, and men working as nurses, flight attendants, or grade-school teachers. Despite the breakdown of the exclusive domination of certain roles by one gender or the other, many roles remain dominated by the gender conventionally associated with that role. Most lawyers, doctors, and professors are men despite the inroads of the feminist movement, and most housekeepers, raisers of children, secretaries, receptionists, and grade-school teachers are women (see Figure 10.1). The progress of women entering formerly male-dominated professions became apparent when prestigious business schools, such as The Wharton School at the University of Pennsylvania, announced that they would seek male student applicants to counter the fact that a strong majority of their students are female.

In the political maneuvering done up to the 2014 congressional elections, Democrats accused Republicans of conducting "a war on women" because the GOP supported the right of Catholic (and other conservative Christian)

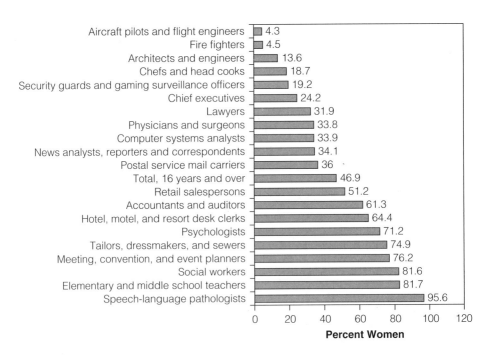

FIGURE 10.1 Women as a Percent of Total Employed in Selected Occupations, 2011

SOURCE: http://www.bls.gov/opub/ted/2012/ted_20120501.htm, accessed March 21, 2014.

institutions to be exempt from including coverage for birth control in their health care plans. These religious institutions have a long history of moral opposition to barrier and chemical birth control. The GOP also supported strong restrictions for Planned Parenthood clinics that have been the major provider of abortion services. In February 2012, Sandra Fluke, a Georgetown Law School student, gained fleeting fame in her complaint that Georgetown's refusal to provide her with free contraception was an infringement on her lifestyle. The GOP was not helped by the fact that many Republican officials and candidates expressed extreme positions on women's issues.

Equality under Law in U.S. History.   The concept of equality under law historically has had a liberal implication. For many years in Western history, it was directed against legally mandated privileges of the various aristocracies or other dominant groups. These privileges included weighted voting and laws stipulating who could or could not own land, enter prestigious occupations, and so forth. Even in the United States, dominant groups were legally able to restrict the accessibility of social values to subordinate groups. For example, before the historic Supreme Court decision in *Brown v. Board of Education of Topeka, Kansas,* which struck down legally required racial segregation in public schools, state-mandated racial segregation reserved the best public schools and facilities for whites. Furthermore, laws sanctioned discrimination in facilities licensed by the state to serve the public. Inns and restaurants across the country freely and openly, with the blessing of the Supreme Court, restricted their clientele to the dominant groups. Until a decade or so after World War II, many major law schools and graduate schools overtly or covertly maintained quotas restricting the admission of Jews—who, it was feared, constituted a disproportionate share of such professions—regardless of the credentials of the individual applicants. In the 1920s, Harvard University, under the direction of the president, A. Lawrence Lowell, attempted to reduce the number of Jewish students by various means: limiting the amount of scholarship aid available to them, devising disguised quotas, requiring photographs on admissions applications, and making "character" a qualification for admission and then defining the term in such a way as to exclude negative attributes that Jews were considered to possess.[3] Also tried was a system of geographical balance whereby applicants from New York City, with its large Jewish population, were passed over in favor of candidates from the South and West, regions with sparse Jewish populations. No method worked satisfactorily. In 1926, admissions officers began to reject candidates known or presumed to be Jewish without any stated reason. The number of Jewish students did in fact drop from 25 percent to 15 percent.

It was alleged in 1988 that the University of California was using such an unofficial quota to restrict the proportion of high-achieving Asians among the students accepted to its several campuses. Although the university denied the charge, it is a fact that the percentage of Asians admitted was substantially lower than that of successful applicants whose objective qualifications (grade point averages and SAT scores) were inferior to those of the Asian students.[4] In 1989, Berkeley rejected more than 2,500 Asian and white students with a straight-A average. Asians as a group suffer from this more than whites because a higher percentage of them attain such credentials.[5]

In mid-nineteenth-century California, Chinese victims of crime were unable to obtain justice because the courts would not allow the Chinese to testify against a white person. Special taxes were levied against their laundries. In the first half of this century, laws prohibited intermarriage with Asians and segregated Asian schoolchildren. Asians were virtually excluded from immigration to the United States in the 1920s, and those who were already here were denied citizenship and were prohibited from owning agricultural land. This anti-Asian discrimination in official policy culminated in one of the most blatant examples of inequality under American law in this century, the compulsory internment during World War II of Americans of Japanese ancestry in what critics called concentration camps.

For much of American history there was an explicit legal denial to Native Americans of equal access to the values of our society, a fact manifested in their being herded off their land and confined to residual pieces of unwanted territory called reservations.

Of course, the denial of equality under law to African Americans has been a well-known and widespread phenomenon. The Black Codes were one of the more blatant examples of this. These were a series of laws passed in many parts of the Old South after Reconstruction in an attempt to nullify the reality of the Thirteenth Amendment's prohibition of overt slavery. The effect of these laws was to restore the almost complete black dependence on, and subservience to, the former slaveholders. African Americans were forbidden to hold jobs, receive an education, or even to walk the streets of cities and towns without permission from whites. General Colin Powell, chairman of the Joint Chiefs of Staff during the first Gulf War and secretary of state under President George W. Bush, recalls that in 1962, as he was driving through Virginia and about to leave for Vietnam, he and his wife were unable to find a bathroom they were allowed to use.[6] Until the impact of the *Brown* school desegregation case was finally established in the late 1960s, blacks continued to be singled out by law for specified disadvantages. They were routinely excluded from public facilities in the Old South.

Women have also been denied equality under law. Until the passage of the Nineteenth Amendment, only a few states allowed them to vote in state or national elections. Political wisdom was apparently held to correlate with gender. Historically, many states also prohibited women from going into business or from owning property, though those provisions no longer exist. Historically, there has been a gender gap in pay with women earning less than men for the same work performed. The **glass ceiling** demonstrates that women have a much more difficult time moving into management positions, or increasing status positions, than men do. Women are still very underrepresented in corporate management, although they have made some progress. Even in the public sector, women tend to be pigeonholed into certain types of work. In the military, women have had a hard time rising through the ranks because they have been precluded from serving in some functions, especially those that are combat related. Issues such as these reflect gender inequality and are discussed in later sections of the chapter.

It is argued that although the United States has never had a formal aristocracy to unseat and despite the commitment in American ideology to the idea of equality under law, there has been a more or less identifiable dominant group in this country, a group definable by gender and race or ethnicity, which directly or indirectly has used the law in addition to social discrimination to maintain other groups in a subordinate status. This dominant group has been white, male, and largely Protestant, especially the older, nonevangelical denominations, such as Episcopal, Congregational, or Methodist—as opposed to Baptist, Church of Christ, and Pentecostal.

Inequality in the Western World.   Dominant groups throughout the Western world create institutional arrangements to perpetuate their status and to minimize social mobility. The educational system has often functioned as this kind of selective institution in Western nations. In Great Britain and France, for example, rigorous competitive examinations determined who goes on to a university. England had its "eleven plus" exams until the early 1970s, and France still uses the baccalaureate; what these exams really test are those skills and attributes passed from parent to child in middle- and upper-class families. In England, there are private and expensive secondary private boarding schools, paradoxically called public schools, the most prestigious of which have been the major avenue to Oxford and Cambridge, which educate most of Britain's elite. There is a similar system of preparatory schools in the United States that improves the chance of admission to prestigious higher education for the children of the affluent. The children who go to these selective prep schools are overwhelmingly children of parents who attended these schools, almost rendering the elites of these countries a semiclosed caste.

The culture defines dominant groups along ethnic, racial, or religious lines in situations where there is diversity of such attributes. In nations where there is more ethnic or racial homogeneity, stratification is mainly along the lines of social class. Nations with distinct subcultures, such as Belgium, the Netherlands, Canada, and Austria, usually contain one such subculture that is perceived as dominant and others as subordinate. Frequently, these divisions are along religious or linguistic lines. In general, whenever cultural, religious, racial, ethnic, or linguistic attributes are congruent with socioeconomic divisions, the political conflict between dominant and subordinate groups is intensified.

Equality of Opportunity

Laws that treat each individual equally do not necessarily have an equal impact on each individual. The impact of a law on an individual is a function not only of the substance of the law itself but also of the circumstances and attributes of the individual. Equality under law does not necessarily create genuine equality of opportunity. Equality of opportunity refers to the right of all individuals to realize their human potential to become whatever their wishes and personal abilities allow them to become, free from barriers imposed by society and its institutions. When government reserves certain roles or rewards in society for particular groups or classes of individuals, irrespective of performance or behavior, this in effect impedes the goal achievement of others. This would constitute a violation of equality of opportunity as well as of equality under law.

It is clear, however, that social and economic barriers exist, even though neither law nor public policy assigns privileges or disabilities to specified groups or individuals. The unequal distribution of such resources as wealth, abilities, and health will bestow advantages or disadvantages on individuals in competition for social or material values even when law and policies are neutral. People acquire things they value through the successful investment of resources they already possess. Those who lack such resources cannot use them for self-improvement even when permitted to do so by law. This is especially true in a capitalist system in which capital (resources deferred from consumption to investment) is used to generate more resources. One may need to be clever to succeed in the stock market, but one first needs capital to invest. Even such things as leisure time, transportation, and good health are resources that can be invested for self-improvement, but they are not evenly distributed throughout the population. Furthermore, people and institutions may make goal achievement more difficult for some than for others through mechanisms, such as prejudice.

Thus, it may be argued that governmental or legal neutrality perpetuates the existing inequalities of opportunity by permitting those who have superior resources to use them to maintain or increase their status relative to the have-nots. Without governmental regulation of the market, the gap between those who have more and those who have less tends to increase. This fact has been thought to epitomize the attitude of the Obama administration—as implied in Obama's comments during the 2008 presidential campaign—that substantial inequality in the distribution of material well-being constitutes a denial of "social justice." As Vice President Biden put it, it is good to "spread the wealth around." In the 2012 presidential campaign, inequality was a major theme again with Republican candidate, John McCain, talking about 47 percent of Americans being takers and President Obama again focusing on inequality.

The fact that many American families could not qualify for a mortgage loan was regarded as a denial of social justice. In the Bush administration, the elevation of home ownership to an "entitlement" (something a society owes everyone regardless of their competitive success) precipitated the 2007–2008 "subprime mortgage crisis" (in which major lending institutions succumbed to pressure to issue mortgages to people whose financial status would not ordinarily have qualified them to receive the mortgage). The fact that all Americans do not have access to the level of health care available to our most affluent families was regarded by the Obama administration as another denial of social justice resulting in the health care reform act of 2010 (see Chapter 8).

It is clearly unrealistic to assert that a child born to and raised by a poor, semiliterate, African American, single teenager in one of America's urban ghettos has the same chance of achieving high socioeconomic status as does the child of upper-middle-class, well-educated parents in an affluent suburb, even assuming that all legally imposed distinctions between these groups have been eliminated. The latter set of parents will impart skills, values, and resources to their offspring that the former parent is unlikely to be able to offer. The best single predictor of academic achievement is the educational level of one's parents. Although it is true that some individuals with superior talents and motivations may rise from rags to riches, when genetically acquired properties are about equal, the child of affluence has a much higher probability of reaching his or her potential.

The principle in operation here is that equal laws have unequal impacts on unequal persons. The French socialist Anatole France put it eloquently when he said, "The law, in its majestic impartiality, forbids the rich as well as the poor to beg in the streets, sleep under the bridges, and steal bread." Obviously, such laws do not prevent the rich from doing anything they are likely to do. Consequently, the discrimination that makes a group of people socially and economically unequal will tend to cause the offspring of that group to continue to be socially and economically unequal after the original discrimination is discontinued and the current rules of the game apply equally to all. Thus, unequal opportunity may be generated from previous, legally imposed inequalities. A somewhat different unequal opportunity stems from differences in the talents and values that one is either born with or acquires early in life that do not stem from any socially or legally imposed discrimination.

A major controversy emerged in this regard with the publication of a book, *The Bell Curve*, written by the late Harvard psychologist Richard Herrnstein and Charles Murray, which argues that there is a greater genetic component to IQ than society has been willing to admit.[7] Because they further argue that IQ is a major determinant of wealth and social status, they offer the pessimistic conclusion that poverty and inequality are largely beyond the power of social policy to remedy, a conclusion that deeply offends many Americans. It should be clear, however, that their conclusions and the implications of them are vehemently challenged by a broad spectrum of scholars, writers, and policy analysts.

The idea of meritocracy, essentially a conception of what is meant by social justice, holds that the allocation of social values and status should be on the basis of performance standards in part derived from perceived contributions to the public good. Meritocracy entails the following assumptions: (1) some social roles contribute more to the good of the community than others do, and so rewards should be proportionate to such contributions; (2) the fulfillment of such roles frequently requires long and difficult training or rare talents; (3) special inducements are required to persuade people to fill these important and difficult roles; and (4) both justice and public need require that the occupants of some roles be rewarded a disproportionate share of social values. It is important to note that the concept of meritocracy entails the principle that people are rewarded on the basis of what they do rather than who they are.

It is also important to keep in mind that the assumption that performance is a function of material reward is one that has not been conclusively or even, to some, convincingly demonstrated. People contribute to the social order for many reasons, and it is unclear the extent to which such behavior is caused by the prospect of material reward. Thus, when President Obama declared in his 2014 State of the Union address that greater income equality would be a central focus for the remainder of his presidency, he was assuming that great income inequality violates the concept of social justice, as opposed to the assumption that one's contribution to the social good has a market value.

It might be said that a consensus exists in America that people ought to be rewarded differently on the basis of performance standards, based in turn on talent, effort, and contribution to the social good; there is, however, a lack of consensus on how performance or social contribution should be measured. There is the question, for instance, as to whether the standards for admission to higher socioeconomic status in the United States, such as success in the educational system, reflect talent and potential social contribution or merely the cultural experiences of the dominant middle-class group. Does a higher grade point average, a standard on which certain groups consistently fall short, indicate a probability of being a superior physician, lawyer, or scientist? For example, Linda Wightman argues that race-based selection to America's law schools has been successful because the graduation rates of blacks admitted on race-based selection are not significantly different from those of whites. Stephen Thernstrom retorts, however, that because 89 percent of the whole sample graduates, this was a deceiving measure of black performance. A more accurate figure, he claims, is that whites were six times more likely to pass the bar examination on their first attempt.[8] To answer such a question of who is better in certain roles, one would have to be able to precisely measure performance in such roles. Because such measurement cannot now be made to the satisfaction of everyone regardless of their values, it remains impossible either to demonstrate or justify the social relevance of the performance standards on which a meritocracy is based.

Equality of Material Well-Being

Because of the aforementioned difficulties in using the principle of meritocracy to legitimate the material inequalities that exist in all societies, spokespersons for relatively disadvantaged groups and individuals have been arguing that government has a moral obligation to engineer a more equal distribution of material values, irrespective of traditional performance standards. Furthermore, because actual opportunities for upward social mobility depend on the resources with which one starts life, it is argued that equality of opportunity requires equality of material well-being. In short, equality of opportunity is held to be inseparable from equality of result. Thus, the list of entitlements continues to grow.

Proportional Equality.   The concept of equality of material well-being (sometimes called equality of result) would have to be precisely defined in order to be applied to actual social policy. This policy goal has been formulated in terms of the **proportional equality** of designated social groups. Proportional equality refers to the idea that a social group's percentage in the overall population should be equaled by its share of certain benefits, such as income and wealth, or the holding of desired social roles, such as membership in the professions, high socioeconomic status, and admission to professional schools. For example, if African Americans make up 12 percent of the population, they should make up approximately 12 percent of doctors, lawyers, and executives. It is inferred that if a group

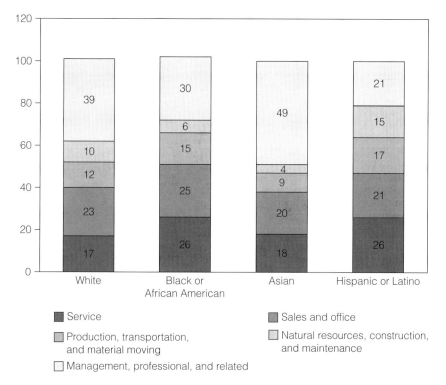

FIGURE 10.2   Employed People by Occupation, Race, and Hispanic or Latino Ethnicity, 2012 Annual Averages (percent of employed)

SOURCE: http://www.bls.gov/cps/epsrace2012.pdf, accessed March 22, 2014.

has less than its share of social values—for example, the 12 percent of African Americans comprises less than 6 percent of the nation's physicians—this is evidence that institutional factors, such as systematic discrimination or its pervasive effects, are operating to bring about underrepresentation. It is therefore implicitly assumed that if discrimination were not present, each group would acquire its proportionate share of society's goods. The distance between proportional equality and the actual inequality of the races is illustrated in Figures 10.2 and 10.3.

The concept of proportional equality is important because it ultimately became the key goal of the social reforms championed by the American civil rights movement. That movement, however, came to this consensus only after a lengthy period of trial and error with other political tactics.

The Civil Rights Movement and Equality

The civil rights movement appears to have gone through three distinct stages in its political evolution. The first stage, dating from the early years of the twentieth century and the establishment of the National Association for the Advancement of Colored People (NAACP) and other organizations, was to attack denials of equality under law. Early cases addressed particular denials in law

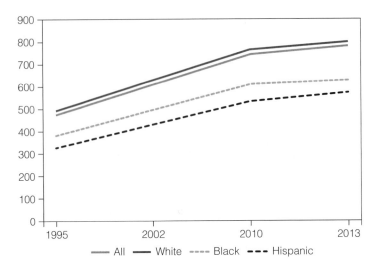

F I G U R E 10.3   Median Family Weekly Income by Race and Hispanic Origin

SOURCE: http://www.bls.gov/cps/earnings.htm, accessed March 22, 2014.

school admissions and public school facilities, culminating in the great school desegregation cases of the 1950s and 1960s. Goals were formulated for the elimination of Jim Crow laws that segregated African Americans and imposed legal disabilities on them.

Although this first stage was mostly successful, expectations for a more profound change in the lifestyle of the typical African American individual were not realized, leading to disappointment and dissatisfaction among civil rights leaders. With the goals of legal equality largely realized, the second stage of the movement, from the mid-1960s into the 1970s, concentrated on other goals, particularly equality of opportunity: (1) legislation to secure access to jobs and to public facilities, such as restaurants and places of accommodation (the 1964 Civil Rights Act); (2) legislation to secure the right to vote (the 1965 Civil Rights Act); and (3) legislation to end discrimination in the sale and rental of housing (the 1968 Civil Rights Act). In other words, the second stage largely had to do with access to values and facilities privately owned but ostensibly available to the general public. Finally, the movement began to press for proportional equality, the third stage of the movement.

CONTEMPORARY POLICY: STRENGTHENING CONSTITUTIONAL GUARANTEES OF EQUALITY

The Erosion of the Fourteenth Amendment

After the Thirteenth Amendment (1865) ended outright slavery in the United States, laws continued to exist that singled out African Americans and other racial and ethnic groups for discriminatory treatment. The Fourteenth Amendment (1868) was intended to end such discriminatory legislation by state governments, but two important decisions by the Supreme Court, *The Civil Rights Cases* (1883) and *Plessy v. Ferguson* (1896), greatly weakened the amendment's role and in fact legitimized existing forms of discrimination, specifically in education and access to public facilities. It is important to understand this weak interpretation of the intent of the Fourteenth Amendment because, in varying ways, each of the policy areas to be discussed in this section—school desegregation and integration, equal opportunity in employment and higher education, and equal rights for women—was an attempt to circumvent this eroded interpretation.

Restrictions on the Concept of State Action.   A key portion of the Fourteenth Amendment has been the subject of much litigation concerning the struggle for equality over the years. It reads "... nor shall any state deprive any person of life, liberty or property without **due process of law**; nor deny to any person within its jurisdiction the equal protection of the laws." Among the important points to note about this passage are (1) that the language does not prohibit purely individual discrimination; and (2) that the language is passive—it tells what the state cannot do, but it does not explicitly command the state to do something actively.

After the Civil War and the enactment of the Fourteenth Amendment, it was assumed by many that the scope of the amendment was intended to encourage state governments to take action per se and also to extend such actions to businesses licensed by the state to serve the public. Because it is assumed by established common law principles that such businesses perform a public function under state aegis, they have customarily been considered state agents. In other words, because they derive their income from the public, they have an obligation to the public. Such an interpretation would have brought this form of discrimination, the most pervasive in our society, within the purview of the Fourteenth Amendment.

The Supreme Court rejected this traditional interpretation of the amendment in the *Civil Rights Cases* (1883) when it ruled that businesses licensed by the state to serve the public did not come under the concept of state action, an interpretation that still is in effect.[9] This ruling emasculated the amendment's effectiveness in dealing with this form of discrimination.

Ending Segregation

The emasculation of the Fourteenth Amendment as an effective instrument against segregation soon went even further than it had under the *Civil Rights Cases*. The Court ruled in 1896 to legalize active state intervention to segregate public facilities, including public schools. In *Plessy v. Ferguson,* the Court held that the equal protection clause of the amendment did not forbid laws requiring separation of the races.[10] Separation, the Court held, did not necessarily mean inequality. The opinion of the Court argued that any implication of African American inferiority derived from such Jim Crow laws was solely a function of the perceptions of African Americans themselves. Hence, in enunciating the so-called separate-but-equal doctrine, the Court officially legitimated such segregation laws. Moreover, in asserting that separation was legal, neither the Court nor society paid much heed to the equality portion of that doctrine. The public facilities available to African Americans in localities where segregation was officially practiced, the states of the Old South, were not equal to facilities for whites.

The *Plessy* separate-but-equal principle remained in effect until 1954. After a series of cases that made inroads on its logic, *Plessy* was formally overruled in the 1954 landmark case of *Brown v. Board of Education of Topeka, Kansas,* which held that any state-mandated segregation in the field of education inherently violates the equal protection clause of the Fourteenth Amendment.[11] That 1954 decision is now known as *Brown I.* Chief Justice Warren, speaking for a unanimous court, held that the fact of segregation was widely understood as a badge of nonwhite inferiority and that this perception was likely to have a permanent destructive impact on the psychological development of African American children, irrespective of the physical equality of the facilities in question. In fact, Topeka, Kansas, was deliberately selected because the physical inequality of African American schools was not a serious issue there; therefore, the issue of the inherent inequality of segregated schools was brought to the fore. The unconstitutionality of Jim Crow laws was eventually applied to all other public facilities, such as parks, cemeteries, and hospitals.

It was one thing to hand down a principle of law; it is quite another to see that it is carried out. The response of the Southern state governments was by and large to resist the integration of their school systems as forcefully and as long as possible. Recognizing that the immediate dismantling of the dual school system would be disruptive and expensive, the Court had, in a separate opinion (known as *Brown II*), ordered the implementation of its *Brown I* decision "with all deliberate speed."[12] There was sufficient ambiguity in that standard to permit those Southern politicians who wished to do so to interpret the phrase as referring to the indefinite future. The South moved slowly toward the termination of its dual school systems. By 1964, only about 2 percent of the African American school children in eleven Old South states were attending integrated schools. As late as 1969, the Court was forced in *Alexander v. Holmes County* to inform a Mississippi school board that the time for "all deliberate speed" had run out and that further delays could not be granted.[13]

Meanwhile, under the **Civil Rights Act of 1964**, pressure was placed on local school districts to comply with the intent of *Brown I* by the threat of withholding federal funds from districts that did not satisfactorily respond. Under such pressures, desegregation in the Old South finally proceeded rapidly in the late 1960s. By 1970, a greater percentage of African Americans were attending schools with whites in that region than in the North. Thus, the first major goal of the civil rights movement, the elimination of Jim Crow laws, had succeeded. The movement had already turned its attention to the reality that the demise of such state-mandated segregation had failed to provide integration.

Enforcing Integration

Persisting discrimination against African Americans and Hispanics in the sale and rental of housing has exacerbated a widespread tendency in urban America toward racial and ethnic homogeneity in housing and residential patterns. Although each group of immigrants, Italian, Irish, Greek, Polish, and so forth, had displayed some tendency to seek out and live in neighborhoods peopled by those of its own derivation, housing discrimination against African Americans and Hispanics has added to the racial homogeneity of the neighborhoods of these latter two groups. Because assignment to public schools has traditionally been on the basis of sending children to their neighborhood schools, the traditional policy perpetuated racially homogeneous public schools. This racial separation of students due to the effects of discriminatory housing patterns is a form of **de facto segregation**. (De facto segregation is that not caused by law or public policy. **De jure segregation** is that so caused.)

Dissatisfaction with merely ending de jure (state-mandated) school segregation was given impetus by the Coleman Report of 1966, a study of the causes of educational achievement involving over a half-million students.[14] This report found that among educational attributes, the one factor that had a significant effect on scholastic achievement was an intermingling of higher achievers and lower achievers. Peer group influence tended to upgrade the performance of the lower achievers without harming that of higher achievers.

In any event, the goals of the civil rights movement with respect to education came to be redefined in terms of the racial balance of the student body and faculty of each school, a goal first stipulated by the Supreme Court in *Green et al. v. County School Board of New Kent County* (1968).[15] Once this standard is accepted as the imperative of the Fourteenth Amendment, an active governmental role in assigning students to schools on a racial basis is inescapable. The explicit judicial mandate for compulsory integration, achieved by busing, came in *Swann v. Charlotte-Mecklenburg Board of Education* (1971).[16]

The Struggle for Racial Balance in Employment and Higher Education

Civil Rights Act of 1964.   Busing dealt with the integration of the public schools. This left the underrepresentation of the designated disadvantaged groups—usually African Americans and Hispanics, but occasionally including all nonwhites and women—untouched in various sectors of the American economy and in higher education. The Civil Rights Act of 1964, in its Title VII provisions, set up the Equal Employment Opportunity Commission (EEOC) to implement policy toward ending discrimination by any employer or labor union with twenty-five or more persons engaging in interstate commerce. Title VI of the same act requires that it shall be the responsibility of each federal agency to require an end to discrimination in any program or institution to which it allocates federal funds. The Office of Federal Contract Compliance is responsible for implementing this policy. As discussed earlier, the goal of ending discrimination has been interpreted as the achievement of proportional representation for designated groups in various valued social roles. Although the EEOC cannot require either **quotas** or **preferential treatment** from the mere fact of racial imbalance, it can use such imbalance as evidence of discrimination. The assumption again is that if discrimination were not at work, these groups would be present in various sectors in rough proportion to their numbers in society as a whole.

Expanding the Constitution's Commerce Clause.   Because the *Civil Rights Cases* weakened the Fourteenth Amendment, review of the constitutionality of the Civil Rights Act of 1964's provisions guaranteeing all citizens access to restaurants, motels, and other places of public accommodation required drawing on an expanded meaning of the Constitution's commerce clause. Federal power to regulate interstate commerce was used to forbid discrimination by businesses directly or indirectly involved in such commerce. This was upheld in the *Heart of Atlanta Motel* case in 1964. Another case that year, *Katzenbach v. McClung*, permitted the extension of the law's application to businesses whose only connections to interstate commerce were purchases from a national market.[17]

Equality of Result in Education and Employment.   The adoption of proportionality as a criterion of discrimination came into being largely because much discrimination is covert rather than overt and is thus hard to prove. For example, a school wishing to keep African Americans out may deliberately adopt entrance requirements that it knows African Americans will disproportionately fail; similarly, it is frequently difficult to establish why a particular job applicant was not hired for a job.

The remedies to imbalance in employment, in the composition of professions, or in admissions to higher education consist of some form of preferential treatment for members of the underrepresented groups or of a challenge to the standards by which people are selected. Accordingly, the Office of Federal Contract Compliance and the EEOC laid down guidelines to the effect that any test for employment, promotion, or membership that is disproportionately failed by members of the designated groups constitutes evidence of illegal discrimination unless the job relevance of that test can be shown. In other words, it must be shown that those who score higher on the test or selection criteria actually perform better in the roles for which they are being selected.

Beginning with the case of *Washington v. Davis* (1976), the Court tended to shift the burden of proof to the plaintiff to demonstrate the test was instituted with the intent to discriminate.[18] Subsequent decisions in the appellate courts applied the latter standard of placing the burden of proof on the plaintiff alleging discrimination. It is this new rule of law that the controversial 1991 Civil Rights Act (described later) sought to overturn.

Another approach to proportionate equality is the idea of preferential treatment. Preferential treatment plans vary from using membership in one of the designated groups as one positive factor to be taken into account in employment or admission decisions to rigid quotas that require a set proportion of those selected to be members of such groups. But strict quotas generate considerable emotional hostility among some groups, for example, among Jews, because quotas were once used against them to exclude them from prestigious schools and professions. Often preferential treatment finds support in federal **affirmative action** policies. These require businesses and educational institutions guilty of past discrimination or in receipt of federal funding to demonstrate by positive action that they attempt to hire and admit minorities and women.

The Challenge to Race-Based Selection.   The opposition to selection on the basis of race, although frequently emanating from perceived self-interest, has been argued in terms of an interpretation of the equal protection clause of the Fourteenth Amendment. It is contended that preferential treatment for nonwhites unconstitutionally discriminates against whites, the idea of reverse discrimination.

In the *Alan Bakke* case in 1978, the constitutional issue was addressed with great expectation that the Court would resolve it. This case involved the admissions procedure for the University of California Medical School at Davis, which had rejected Bakke's application for admission. This school had set aside a fixed number, sixteen places out of one hundred, for nonwhites. Because scores were compiled for each applicant on grade point averages (GPA), the Medical College Aptitude Test (MCAT), and a personal interview, the procedure created two separate applicant pools.

Although the applicants for the sixteen minority seats had to meet minimum standards on the given criteria and in that sense were qualified, the records of those selected from the minority pool on the two objective scores (GPA and MCAT) were significantly inferior to those selected from the regular pool and, perhaps more significantly, well below the record of some of those, like Bakke, who were rejected under the regular admission process. In fact, the average percentile ranking on MCAT scores of those admitted under the special program were from 36 to 52 percentile points below those selected from the general applicant pool in the years studied.[19] The GPA of regular admittees averaged 3.5 and 3.4 for those years, where the special admittees averaged 2.6 and 2.4.

The Court found itself as divided on the legality of such a program as society is divided over the issue. Four justices (Burger, Rehnquist, Stevens, and Stewart) held that the use of racial criteria violated Title VII of the Civil Rights Act of 1964. Therefore, these judges held that Bakke should be ordered admitted without considering whether such admissions policies violated the equal protection clause. By deciding the case on statutory rather than constitutional grounds, these justices gave Congress the opportunity of overriding the decision by ordinary legislation rather than constitutional amendment.

Four other justices (Blackmun, Brennan, Marshall, and White) argued that neither the Constitution's equal protection clause nor Title VII prevented the use of racial categories to remedy the effects of past discrimination.

It was left to Justice Powell to cast the swing vote to dispose of the case. His opinion constituted the official Opinion of the Court. Agreeing that racial categorizations are suspect categories that place a severe burden of proof on the state to show a compelling public purpose, Powell held that this burden was satisfied by the need to secure "a diverse student body." Powell, however, saw fit to distinguish a fixed quota of student slots assigned on the basis of race—a policy he found incompatible with the equal protection clause—from the use of race as one among several factors in selecting from an open applicant pool—a policy known as **racial preference plans** that he approvingly endorsed. Powell found the Davis program invalid on equal protection grounds, whereas the Burger group invalidated it on Title VII grounds, making a motley majority of five to order Bakke admitted.

Today, government and educational institutions continue to strive to ameliorate the underrepresentation of targeted groups in the economy and in higher education. However, programs to do so inevitably displace nontargeted people who are increasingly challenging such programs. The Court dealt affirmative action a serious blow in 1995 when it ruled unconstitutional a University of Maryland scholarship, the Banneker Scholarship, that was set aside for African Americans only. This is consistent with *Bakke* and other cases in that the scholarship went beyond racial preference by restricting competition to African Americans only. The Court's 1997 decision in upholding the California Civil Rights Initiative, discussed later, struck another blow against affirmative action.

Equality and the Women's Movement

With the rise of the feminist movement in the United States, women pushed for social policies designed to bar and redress the repression of women and their consequent underrepresentation in valued social roles. In *Craig v. Boren* (1976), the Court set standards for when gender may be used to classify people: The government must convince the Court that its purpose is an important one and that the gender classification is "substantially related" to achieving that purpose. This case invalidated a law that set a higher legal drinking age for boys than for girls.[20]

Women's suffrage was the first big push for women's rights in the United States. With the Nineteenth Amendment in 1919, women were guaranteed the right to vote across the country. This was something that had only been available in a few states until this time. With the right to vote, women then began to press for equality in the workplace, equality in education, and reproductive rights, among other issues. Among acts supporting equality were the Equal Pay Act of 1963, Title IX of the Civil Rights Act of 1964, and the Equal Opportunity Act of 1972. The Supreme Court decision in *Roe v. Wade* marked a major milestone in women's rights to abortion.[21]

In the sense of proportional equality, women have been, and remain, underrepresented in higher-status positions such as doctors, lawyers, business executives, and aircraft pilots and flight engineers, and overrepresented in typically lower-status positions such as elementary school teachers, social workers, and hotel–motel resort administrative assistants. (See Figure 10.1.) Even the minimal goal of equal pay for equal work has been difficult to obtain. The median income for women was only 77 percent that of men in 1993. Gradually, the

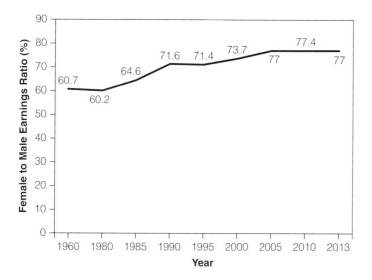

FIGURE 10.4   Gender Pay Gap: Percent of Female to Male Earnings

SOURCE: U.S. Bureau of the Census, Historical Income Tables, Table P37, http://www.census.gov/hhes/www/income/data/historical/people/index.html, accessed March 26, 2014; and Bureau of Labor Statistics, Household Data Annual Averages Table 39, http://www.bls.gov/cps/cpsaat39.pdf, accessed March 26, 2014.

gap has decreased, but even in 2014, the median income for women is still only about 88 percent of that of men (see Figure 10.4). In *Ledbetter v. Goodyear Tire and Rubber Co.* (2007), the Supreme Court rejected the claim of Lilly Ledbetter, who found out that her employer paid men substantially more for the same position of supervisor and had been doing so for years.[22] The Court ruled that she could not pursue the action because it was outside the 180-day statute of limitations required for filing a claim under the Equal Pay Act. The Court said that the 180 days started on the first day the difference in pay occurred, even though Ledbetter did not learn of it until years later. The decision became an issue in the 2008 elections, with Senator Obama arguing for a correction in policy. President Obama made remedying the situation a top priority for his administration. The first law that he signed in office was the Lilly Ledbetter Act of 2009. Although feminists hail the limited progress, they point out that the gap remains unjustifiably large. Part of this large differential reflects the tendency for women to still be channeled into lower-status and thus lower-paying roles. Nevertheless, part of so large a difference probably also reflects the tendency to pay women less for some of the same jobs that men have. Pink-collar jobs, those traditionally held by women, often pay less than do those jobs traditionally held by men when the levels of skill or training demanded by the respective sets of jobs are comparable.

Now, the movement for gender equality concentrates on requiring equal pay for jobs of comparable worth (equal pay for different jobs requiring equal levels of skill, training, or responsibility). There is no reason, it is argued, why administrative assistants should be paid less than plumbers, when comparable levels of specialized training and responsibility are involved. The concept of **comparable worth**, however, has not made progress at the federal legislative level. It was feared that the concept would unleash a flood of litigation without providing precise standards for measuring comparable worth and thereby resolving such lawsuits.

Women in the Western world still fare far better than women in parts of the Islamic world and other traditional societies where it is illegal to educate women, women must keep their entire body covered except for eye holes, and women may not choose their mate. Overcoming these gender-role stereotypes is one of the most difficult tasks for the women's movement because they appear to retain a greater persistence in the public mind even than racial stereotypes.

Part of the denial of marketplace equity to women may be traced to the fact that access to business opportunities was long restricted to male-dominated bastions. The effort of feminists to penetrate traditional male domains received a boost when the Supreme Court upheld a New York City ordinance that banned discrimination by private clubs on the basis of race, gender, creed, or national origin in *New York State Club Association v. City of New York* (1988).[23]

The issue of the right of clubs to selectively determine their own membership was addressed in June 2010, when the Court ruled by a 5–4 margin in *Christian Legal Society v. Martinez* that a public university is not required to subsidize student groups that it considers discriminatory. The Christian Legal Society, defined by a commitment to conservative Christian values, did not admit homosexuals and non-Christians.[24] This case follows the precedent of the *Dale* case discussed later in this chapter. Although private clubs have the right to choose their members, public pressure often causes them to become more inclusive. Thus, one of the most prestigious golf clubs in the world, Augusta National Golf Club, finally admitted blacks in 1990 and women in 2012.

Although gender-role stereotypes have had much to do with the formation of discriminatory laws against women, it is helpful to distinguish between their subtler effects and the blatant use of law to define the female role. The legal disabilities that women have faced should not be minimized. They did not obtain the right to vote, for example, until 1920, fifty years after African American men were accorded the right. Women also were once denied the right to serve on juries, work in bars, and pursue various other callings. Some laws with the ostensible purpose of protecting women—such as limiting the amount of weight they could be required to lift on the job or the maximum hours they could be required to work—had the negative effect of keeping women out of many jobs. Some critics have argued that this was deliberate. Such laws assume an inexorable connection between gender and physical strength, a relationship that is far from perfect. Nevertheless, most of the discrimination against women has been the product of social attitudes and gender-role stereotypes rather than the law per se.

It is not unusual, for instance, for men in hiring positions to avoid considering women for jobs in the belief that they will soon quit to get married or to have children. Prospective employers can continue to apply such sexist standards surreptitiously as long as they do not have to justify not hiring any particular applicant.

Furthermore, for years, colleges and universities spent many times as much on men's athletics as on women's, principally for two discriminatory reasons. First, society in general regards athletic prowess as a male prerogative; that is, male athletes are admired, whereas their female counterparts were chided for being unfeminine. Second, given such attitudes toward women athletes, their sports have not been good collegiate revenue producers because, until recently, they did not attract large paying audiences. However, Title VII of the Civil Rights Act of 1964 bans discrimination on the basis of sex as well as race, and Title IX of the Educational Amendment Acts of 1972 forbids any institution from receiving federal funds to engage in gender discrimination. Accordingly, the government now requires colleges and universities to equalize the amount spent on interscholastic athletics. This caused vociferous opposition from supporters of expensive but profitable football programs, and so the cost of these programs was exempted from the cost equation. The requirement has also resulted in the cancellation of a number of men's minor sports programs, such as swimming.

Nonetheless, gender equity still does not exist in college athletics. While women make up roughly 54 percent of college students, they are represented by only 43 percent of all college athletes. Men receive more than one-third more scholarship money than do women. In fact, men's sports receive more money in every aspect of athletics programs than do women's sports. Women are very underrepresented in athletic department administration, representing only about 17 percent of athletic directors and only 44 percent of women's team coaches.[25]

Issues central to the concerns of the leaders of the women's movement include the control of one's childbearing, which entails both access to information and support of effective contraception as well as freedom to receive legal abortions and the achievement of equity in job status and indices of material well-being. These are issues of symbolic and emotional as well as of substantive content. Control of one's fecundity is of crucial importance because becoming a parent is perhaps the most all-encompassing commitment that one can experience, one that will inevitably constrain one's life choices. The complex issue of access to abortion is discussed in detail in Chapter 13. Feminists are also concerned with the issues of rape and sexual harassment. The former offense is discussed in detail in Chapter 6, the latter in this section.

As was seen in the expanded conceptualization of rape in Chapter 6, the asymmetrical relationship between the sexes defined by the putative dominant power position of men over women in our society has given rise to an effort by feminists to utilize law and policy to protect women from sexual harassment. Here again we encounter a fundamental shift in the meaning of terms and the lack of a common language. While traditionally **sexual harassment** referred to a situation in which a man who holds a position of dominance over a woman repeatedly attempts to establish a form of sexual relationship (broadly defined) with her, a quid pro quo arrangement in which the dominant male offers professional or educational benefits in return for sexual cooperation, now sexual harassment also includes actions that offend the victim or render her uncomfortable, producing what is perceived as a hostile environment.

Sexual harassment continues to be a serious problem. In 2014, the mayor of San Diego, California, was forced to resign after being charged by numerous women of both quid pro quo and hostile environment harassment. In the corporate world, Julie Gallagher of C.H. Robinson Worldwide Inc. experienced a "locker room" style of harassment and sued the company. She endured unprofessional behavior and an environment that was hostile to women. Gallagher won her case and the decision was affirmed by the Sixth Circuit Court of Appeal.[26] The military has also been the subject of many sexual harassment charges of late. In 2013 and 2014, Congress considered new legislation to address sexual harassment in the military, but as of March 2014, Congress has not been able to settle its differences.

Clearly, some harassment cases are filed frivolously, such as a case in which a female writer claimed that she endured hostile environment harassment because of banter of her team members. The courts found no basis for a claim because the team's purpose was to come up with lewd, provocative material. While frivolous claims will be made, people who file them are subject to penalties for doing so, such as having to pay court fees for the defendants in such cases in court.

Female critics of the goals and policies of the feminist movement include not only traditionally oriented women who aspire to domestic and child rearing roles but also women who consider themselves feminists and are very active in professional roles. Women, such as Camille Paglia and Katie Roithe, argued that the feminist portrayal of women as a victimized group demeans them. Roithe argues that the concept of sexual harassment as an "actionable offense" (one over which one can file a lawsuit) implies that women, unlike men, are incapable of warding off unwanted sexual advances.[27] The legal protection of women against the broadened conceptualization of sexual harassment demeans the strength and independence of women. Thus, the feminist movement remains divided between equality feminists—those who wish to abolish gender-based classification in law and policy so that women can be treated equally with men—and difference feminists, who wish to emphasize the distinct status and needs of women as a victimized group in need of special protection and treatment.

The difference between these two positions was illustrated by the controversy surrounding January 2005 remarks by then-president Lawrence Summers of Harvard at a conference concerning the underrepresentation of women in the fields of engineering and science. Summers speculated that, rather than this underrepresentation solely being the product of gender bias, women might be genetically less attracted to those fields than men. Biology Professor Nancy Hopkins was so upset at this opinion that she exited the meeting complaining that his remarks put her on the verge of vomiting. Whatever the merits of Summers's opinion, Hopkins' reaction typified the image of women as victim rather than an image of strength. Meanwhile, Summers's suggestion was so politically incorrect that he was forced to resign over this and other politically incorrect positions. Insensitive remarks about women are a continuing problem. The 2012 election saw numerous candidates running for the House of Representatives and the Senate making comments that outraged many. Senate candidate Todd Akin of Missouri referred to "legitimate rape" when suggesting that pregnancy would not occur in such circumstances and Richard Mourdock, an Indiana Senate candidate, suggested that pregnancy resulting from rape was something God intended. These types of comments reflect a lack of respect for the equality of women with men.

The question remains, to what extent are there essential or natural differences between men and women, or are all differences socially conditioned? Though they would disagree with Summers's particular example, difference feminists would accept the assertion of some inherent differences between the sexes, while equality feminists would minimize such differences.

Bias against Homosexuals, the Handicapped, and Native Americans

Homosexuals are another group in American society increasingly asserting legal and constitutional rights to combat discrimination. Incidents such as the beating and brutal murder of gay student Matthew Shepard in Wyoming in 1998 underscored the scope and intensity of the problem of antigay feeling. The public was reminded of the incident when Jason Collins, the first openly gay NBA player, chose to wear "98" as his jersey number to honor Matthew (the year he was killed). Out of this increased awareness has come the increased visibility of the presence of lesbian, gay, bisexual, and transgender (LGBT) individuals. As of 2012, there were 639,440 known same-sex couples in the United States. While many Americans remain uneasy about the expansion of gay rights, by 2014, 55 percent supported same-sex marriage while 35 percent opposed same-sex marriage and the rest were indifferent.[28]

One of the primary concerns of opponents of homosexual rights is the fear that homosexuals will somehow influence or recruit heterosexual, but impressionable, children to join their "ranks." This fear conflicts with the prevailing psychological opinion that homosexuality is more an involuntary than a conscious choice, by either school-age children or adults. A study done in 1991, moreover, concluded that there are measurable genetic differences between the brains of homosexual men and those of heterosexual men. In 2014, Northwestern University scientists reported that they had found the "gay gene." The implication of these studies is that one is born with one's sexual orientation and that orientation will be unaffected by any system of rewards and punishments—the danger of heterosexual minors being "recruited" into homosexuality is virtually nonexistent. Therefore, it does not make sense to regard homosexuality as something that can be deterred through criminal law.

A 1978 Oklahoma law typified the widespread efforts to bar or remove homosexuals from teaching positions. The law criminalized "advocating, soliciting, or promoting public or private homosexual activity in such a manner that creates a substantial risk that such conduct will come to the attention of school children...." Note that the law criminalized the advocacy of homosexuality, not the attributes of being a homosexual. A U.S. Court of Appeals struck down the law, however, on free speech grounds and the Supreme Court upheld this ruling in 1985. Ironically, Russia adopted a similar law in 2014 using similar justification and some African nations adopted virulently antigay policies as well.

Efforts continued to bar homosexuals from leadership or role model positions relative to young people with respect to the Boy Scouts of America instituting a ban on avowed homosexuals from scout leadership positions. Gay rights advocates challenged this ban, but the Court upheld the ban in *Boy Scouts of America v. Dale.*[29] Dale was a gay activist who sought a position as assistant Scout master. He had an outstanding record as a former Scout, reaching the rank of Eagle Scout, and was therefore otherwise well qualified for the post. The Court treated the Boy Scouts as a private organization and the issue as one of freedom of association as in the New York Club and the Christian scholars cases discussed above. In 2013, the Boy Scouts voted to allow gay youth to participate, but maintained a ban on gay leaders. In response, a new organization, Trail Life USA, was created as an alternative with continuation of antigay policies.

President Bill Clinton sought to defuse the issue of gays in the military with a "don't ask, don't tell" plan. The plan was that the military would no longer inquire into the sexual orientation of their personnel or recruits; hence, gay recruits could serve in the military as long as they do not make that orientation public. Gays were still subject to dismissal, however, if they revealed their sexuality or were caught in homosexual acts. In the course of the debate, it was revealed that many gay people had served with valor and distinction in this nation's wars; however, many feared that the presence of gays in such close, and often intimate, quarters would detract from the central mission of the military. Reports on the implementation of the policy indicate that some military officers circumvented the intent of the policy by putting pressure on suspected homosexuals to reveal their orientation and then proceeded to discharge them on a less than honorable basis. The policy was repealed in 2010 and ended in September 2011 after the president, Secretary of Defense, and the Chairman of the Joint Chiefs of Staff certified that the repeal would not harm military readiness.

In the 1986 case of *Bowers v. Hardwick,* the Court upheld the Georgia sodomy statute with reference to its ban on homosexual behavior, a statute that criminalizes sex "against the laws of nature." The Court reversed this decision in 2003, however, in *Lawrence v. Texas,* a decision that banned the criminalization of consensual homosexual acts on privacy grounds.[30] The movement toward greater social acceptance of homosexuals and toward reducing the discrimination against them received a setback in the 1980s because of the spread of acquired immune deficiency syndrome (AIDS), a contagious and deadly disease. Homosexual men have constituted one of the high-risk groups in the United States for the disease and have widely been perceived as one of its major sources of contagion.

The leadership of the LGBT community has evolved from merely seeking tolerance from the rest of society to a goal of legitimating homosexuality as a morally equivalent alternative lifestyle. It was this goal that caused gays to demand a specifically gay contingent marching with their fellow Irish Americans in the Boston and New York annual St. Patrick's Day Parades. It was not an issue of whether gays could participate in one of the other units in the parade without declaring their sexual orientation; gays demanded recognition as gays. The ban and controversy continued in 2014.

The issue of same-sex marriage has come into prominence in recent years as another means of gaining the legitimation of moral equivalency that gays seek. Part of the issue involves the question of whether normal spousal rights— inheritance, visiting rights to an ill partner in hospital, custodial rights of adopted children—apply to the long-term partners of gays. Many of these concerns can be addressed in a formal legal arrangement called civil union, an arrangement that grants all the aforementioned legal rights without calling it marriage. Such an arrangement was first adopted under state court order in Vermont in 2000. By the end of 2006, Connecticut and New Jersey had also enacted such civil union laws, with New Hampshire following in 2007. The resistance of straight social conservatives to allowing the term *marriage* to define gay relationships stemmed from their unwillingness to grant moral equivalence to the gay lifestyle. This resistance, however, is breaking down. This evolution of attitude combined with several state court rulings has spread the equality of gay marriage to the point that as of February 2014, seventeen states had legalized same-sex marriage. The legality of gay marriage in these states alarms social conservatives in the rest of the nation because "the Full Faith and Credit clause" of the U.S. Constitution requires each state to recognize the rights and credentials of citizens, possibly including marriage, of all the other states. Hence, the availability of same-sex marriage in one state could lead to its prevalence throughout the country.

To counter this perceived threat, many states have adopted constitutional amendments to their respective state constitutions defining marriage as a heterosexual union. The federal government enacted the Defense of Marriage Act (DOMA) in 1996. It advanced the same goal. The Supreme Court struck down DOMA in *United States v. Windsor* (2013). Some federal judges have ruled such state policies as unconstitutional.[31] Comparatively, eight Western countries sanction same-sex marriage: Belgium, Canada, the Netherlands, Norway, Portugal, South Africa, Spain, and Sweden. Israel recognizes gay marriage, but will not perform it. This battle over the legitimacy of the gay lifestyle reflects the cleavage between religious conservatives and secularized Americans, a cleavage that will not disappear any time soon.

Defining New Victims: People with Disabilities.   People with disabilities have also recently become a visible minority recognized in law. The nature of their demands, however, differs considerably from those of the aforementioned groups. People with disabilities concentrate on access to public places and various public benefits—for example, demands for ramps where only stairs had been present, the availability of material in Braille for the blind, closed-captioned television for the hearing impaired, and the like—with much less concern for proportional equality, the placement of set or targeted proportions of people with disabilities in valued roles. The concern of their leaders appears to fit the idea of equalizing opportunity and competition rather than the idea of equality of results.

The goals are the amelioration of the present effects of their disabilities rather than any compensation for the effects of past discrimination, and so their claims have generated less controversy than have those of the other groups previously discussed.

The most important legislation protecting the rights of persons with disabilities is the **Americans with Disabilities Act (ADA)** of 1990 and various amendments. Its primary provisions extend to people with disabilities the kinds of protection granted to minorities and women in the 1964 Civil Rights Act. This legislation prohibits discrimination on the basis of disability in employment, public services, and public accommodations. In employment, a qualified disabled person is one who, with or without reasonable accommodations, can perform the essential functions of a particular job. The law also requires new buses and trains, as well as public buildings, to be accessible to the disabled, and it mandates communications companies to operate relay systems that will allow speech and hearing-impaired persons access to telephone services.[32]

Native Americans.   Native Americans constitute another group that has historically been subject to oppression by the dominant culture. From Plymouth, Massachusetts, to Wounded Knee, South Dakota, their numbers were systematically reduced, and they were forced onto desolate and often infertile reservations. They were caricatured as malevolent and ignorant savages in countless Western films. Their standard of living is substantially below the national norm, and they are beset today by structural unemployment, alcoholism, and other symptoms of alienation.

In 1991, Native Americans took up as a target of protest the names of certain athletic teams. They organized demonstrations when the Atlanta Braves played in the World Series and in early 1992, when the Washington Redskins went to the Super Bowl. The issue of the Washington Redskins was strongly debated again in 2013, but the issue of a possible name change has yet to reach a conclusion. Several universities abandoned their traditional mascots including the University of Illinois in 2007, with its Chief Illiniwek, who had been a central part of the university's athletic tradition since 1926. Defenders argued that the team names had never been meant to disparage, and that, in any case, the protests were a distraction from addressing the undeniably deep social and economic problems of the Native Americans. The 500th anniversary of Christopher Columbus's voyage also became an opportunity to debate the effect of American society on the original population.

POLICY EVALUATION: THE DRIVE
FOR PROPORTIONAL EQUALITY

The impact of public policy on the issues of inequality examined in the preceding section is complex, but focusing on racial preference programs will tell us much about present general trends.

Busing for Racial Balance

Busing children to achieve racially balanced schools historically generated intense social and political conflict. Busing for racial balance, however, has become increasingly rare on the American political landscape: it has been replaced by other programs such as magnet schools or the Seattle program discussed in Recent Assaults on Racial Preference. Busing was used to overcome de facto segregation in schools resulting from the fact that different ethnic and social groups tend to congregate in segregated neighborhoods. In *Milliken v. Bradley* (1974), the Court held that busing could not be required across school district lines.[33]

Retreat on Preference Programs: Weber and Title VII

The *Bakke* case, discussed earlier, appeared to cast doubt on the validity of direct quotas in educational admissions. In *Kaiser Aluminum v. Weber* and *United Steelworkers of America v. Weber* (1979), the Court confronted the legality of a voluntary quota to balance racially a training program leading to promotion at Kaiser Aluminum.[34]

The Kaiser program, which led to promotions, selected individuals on the basis of seniority. For every white selected, however, one African American had to be selected, regardless of seniority. Thus, though Weber was excluded, some African Americans with less seniority than Weber were selected. There was no evidence or allegation of previous discrimination by either Kaiser or the union.

The *Weber* case focused on whether the Civil Rights Act banned discrimination when whites were the victims. This question was revisited in the 2009 case of *Ricci v. DeStefano*, a case involving a test for promotion in the New Haven Connecticut fire department.[35] Frank Ricci, afflicted with dyslexia, had gone through considerable personal effort and expense to prepare himself for the test which he passed along with 116 other whites. When no African Americans scored high enough for promotion, however, the city, fearing a lawsuit on behalf of the African Americans, threw out the test denying promotion to the successful whites. The Court in June 2009 ruled that the action of New Haven discarding the test violated the Civil Rights Act of 1964.

Careful examination of the legislative debate over the adoption of the 1964 law may lead to the conclusion that Congress intended Title VII to prevent race from being used as a basis for hiring, firing, or employment status whether for or against target group interests, and at least one scholar, quoting the leaders of the House and Senate in this debate, made a powerful case for that interpretation.[36]

This trend of undermining judicial support for affirmative action policies was reinforced in two 1989 decisions (*Richmond v. Croson* and *Wards Cove Packing Co. v. Antonio*), in which the Rehnquist Court moved to limit the force and effectiveness of affirmative action. The *Croson* case concerned a Richmond, Virginia, statute requiring that 30 percent of all city contracts go to firms in which a targeted minority had at least 51 percent ownership. These targeted groups, according to the statute, include "citizens of the United States who are African American, Spanish-speaking, Oriental, Indians, Eskimos, or Aleuts," although groups other than blacks amounted to just 1.82 percent of Richmond's population. The statute was clearly aimed at African Americans, who account for about half of that city's population. The J. A. Croson Company challenged the law, and the Supreme Court overturned the law. In July 1995, the Court reinforced *Croson* with its ruling in *Adarand Constructors v. Peña*.[37] A 5–4 majority, speaking through Justice O'Connor, held that an affirmative action plan must be shown to satisfy a "compelling public interest." That interest must be directed at redressing specific discrimination by the parties involved. Merely creating "a more diverse society" will not pass the rigorous "strict judicial scrutiny" demanded by the **compelling public interest** test. This criterion placed much of the network of affirmative action programs in constitutional jeopardy because in recent cases diversity was the value that justified race-based selection.

The 1991 Civil Rights Act and the Judicial Assault on Racial and Gender Preference.   Although, the term *affirmative action* is rarely invoked anymore, the issue of affirmative action remains far from settled. The key issue that emerged from the *Croson* case is whether racial preference plans may be implemented in the absence of evidence of specific discrimination by the firm or institution instituting the plan and, if past discrimination must be shown, what kinds of evidence must be used as the basis of that conclusion. The *Croson* and *Wards Cove* cases showed that the Court was unprepared to accept simple statistical evidence to justify racial preference policies.

Congress sought legislative reversal of the *Croson* and *Wards Cove* decisions in the **Civil Rights Act of 1991**, *which* reverses the burden of proof in charges of employment discrimination, making it easier for minorities to succeed in such disputes. The law requires employers charged with discrimination based on statistical underrepresentation of targeted groups in their workforce to justify their hiring criteria on job relevance or "business necessity," effectively negating the *Wards Cove* decision.

Critics branded the legislation "a quota bill," a charge its supporters denied. The law specifically outlaws quotas but made statistical disparities in the workforce prima facie evidence of employment discrimination and placed the burden of proof on employers to show business necessity for hiring qualifications that lead to such disparities. The effect of the provision putting the burden of proof on the employers to justify statistical imbalance, opponents of the bill argued, is to invite a deluge of litigation against employers in whose workforce target group members are statistically underrepresented, lawsuits that are expensive, time-consuming, and stressful even if one wins. Therefore, it would be rational for employers to try to avoid statistical disparities in their workplaces, in other words, to institute voluntary quotas. In effect, the *Wards Cove* and *Croson* decisions have been overturned, and the burden of proof is upon employers to justify any statistical discrepancies in their workforce.

Recent Assaults on Racial and Gender Preference

The preference plans implicitly approved in the *Bakke* decision were challenged in a case emanating from the University of Texas Law School and resolved at the Fifth Circuit Courts of Appeals. In that case, Cheryl Hopwood and four others claimed the school's admission policy discriminates against whites.[38] The case grew out of the following facts: The Law School, with many more applicants than it can accept, is highly selective. The median Law School Admission Test (LSAT) score of white students admitted is in the ninety-third percentile and the mean GPA is 3.5. As of 1992, the median LSAT score for African Americans was in the seventy-eighth percentile. The white student criteria would have admitted only 1 out of 280 African American applicants, resulting in a virtually all-white student body. Nearly 700 higher scoring white applicants were passed over before the first blacks were denied admission; therefore, race was clearly the deciding factor in selecting African Americans over whites. The school set a different set of criteria for target group members in order to meet a goal of 10 percent Mexican Americans and 5 percent blacks and to ensure racial and ethnic diversity. Although race was one factor in the admissions process for the University of Texas Law School, the school insisted that it admitted blacks who were qualified to meet the academic demands of a legal education. Yet, while some 90 percent of the nontarget group passed the bar exam on the first try, the corresponding rate for the African Americans admitted under the race-sensitive selection criteria was a pass rate of less than 50 percent. Without race as a decisive factor, the University of Texas Law School soon became virtually an all-white institution, as even the most well-qualified African American students elected to apply elsewhere.

The Hopwood principle was challenged in two Supreme Court cases involving the University of Michigan decided in June 2003, *Grutter v. Bollinger* and *Gratz v. Bollinger*. The former case emanates from the law school while the latter case concerns undergraduate admissions. The law school took race into account for each individual in an imprecise way that the Supreme Court found did not isolate the target group applicants from competition with other applicants, but considered all in the same applicant pool. Moreover, the Court found that the policy was "narrowly tailored" to the public purpose of achieving a diverse student body. However, in practice race had a decisive weight. The university, however, admitted undergraduate students on a point system. An excellent essay on the admission form was worth three points and an SAT score over 1,360 out of a possible 1,600 was worth twelve points, but being a member of the right target group was worth twenty points, more than any other single factor except the twenty points given to scholarship athletes. The precise weighting given race in undergraduate admission was rejected by the Court in *Gratz*, but taking race into account in law school admissions was upheld in *Grutter*, a decision that effectively overruled Hopwood.[39]

Meanwhile, the use of racial preferences by the University of Texas for undergraduate admissions was challenged by Abigail Fisher in 2008. The Fifth Circuit Court upheld the ruling in favor of the University in 2009; however, this decision was vacated by the Supreme Court of the United States (SCOTUS) which remanded the case back to the lower court for reconsideration. At the time she applied to the University of Texas, Fisher had a GPA of 3.59 and an SAT of 1,180 from Stephen Austin High School, which placed well above some of the target group applicants who were admitted. As of February 2014, the case is pending.[40]

The "compelling public interest" used to justify race-based selection, the criterion discussed previously for overriding the principle of equality under law and using the suspect category of race, has been diversity defined in terms of race. Critics charge that other possible criteria of diversity, such as religion, socioeconomic background, or even ideas are ignored by race-based selection. Eminent social scientist James Q. Wilson recently reported a body of research that found that, contrary to current conventional wisdom, people were better off "by every measure of social well-being" in racially homogeneous neighborhoods rather than ethnically diverse ones.[41] The Court followed such critics of race-based selection in a landmark case in 2007, *Parents Involved in Community Schools v. Seattle School District Number 1*, in which the school district assigned students to public schools specifically to keep the racial mix within specified limits. This case was merged with a case posing the same question emanating from Louisville, Kentucky.[42] The Court struck down the Seattle plan for racially balancing its schools, stating that diversity as conceptualized above was not a compelling enough public purpose to justify the use of the suspect category of race. This decision casts doubt on the legality of most preference plans in the country to engineer a racially diverse student body.

Meanwhile, another far-reaching assault on preference-based selection, led by African American entrepreneur Ward Connerly, was in the form of a constitutional referendum that handily passed first in the state of California in 1996 and was upheld by the Supreme Court in 1997. While the referendum was focused on affirmative action, his particular concern (as an African American) is that such policies demean the many blacks who achieve on merit and ability and they exacerbate the opposition to other legitimate claims of the civil rights movement. Proposition 209, known as the California Civil Rights Initiative, reads as follows:

> Neither the State of California nor any of its political subdivisions or agents shall use race, sex, color, ethnicity or national origin as criterion for either discriminating against, or granting preferential treatment to, any individual or group in the operation of the state's system of public employment, public education or public contracting.

Nebraska adopted a similar civil rights initiative in 2008. States across the country have adopted similar laws and the courts have generally upheld them. The result is that affirmative action has become discredited as a tool for achieving diversity.

CONTINUING DEBATES: THE CHANGING CONCEPTION OF EQUALITY

The Debate over Affirmative Action

With the recent judicial and political assaults on affirmative action, it is no longer championed as a way of achieving equality in the United States. Nonetheless, some governments still attempt to use preference systems to achieve diversity and equality. Challenges to such approaches inevitably are successful as illustrated by the preceding discussion. Perhaps the main logical or philosophical objection to affirmative action is that it seems to deny the principle of equality under law. In the final analysis, affirmative action policies reward or penalize individuals on the basis of who they are—their racial, ethnic, or gender attributes—rather than on the basis of what they do. Furthermore, this aspect of affirmative action reintroduces the relevance of racial, ethnic, and gender categories as permissible in American legislation. Yet, as was noted in the discussion of equality under law, the struggle to label certain categories as suspect has been viewed as a liberal and progressive struggle, and the triumph of meritocracy over privilege based on the accidents of birth has been traditionally seen as one of the attributes of both a liberal and a more developed society. Some opponents of affirmative action warn that if specific traits can be used for benign purposes, it will henceforth be more difficult to prevent them from being used in other ways. After all, defining what constitutes a benign policy becomes a judgment by those in power. Thus, critics claim, affirmative action works against the principles of individualism and meritocracy.

Underlying the goal of proportional equality that is at the heart of preference programs is the presumption that in the absence of pervasive and continuing discrimination against target group members, they would attain a proportionate representation in valued social and economic roles. Yet, others suggest that different groups have cultural backgrounds and widely held values that dispose their members to seek certain roles more than others. Without denying that cultures are equally valid and of value, they are not identical and do not disseminate the same values, attitudes, and skills to their progeny.

It should be noted that some of the opposition to affirmative action programs is based in part on grounds of self-interest rather than principle. Those who are not members of the designated beneficiary groups, such as white men, find that with selected social rewards being set aside for members of designated minority groups, there are fewer rewards for white men to allocate among themselves.

Equality

The most clearly discernible trend in the struggle for equality is the evolution of the generally understood meaning of the term, which has changed its goals and issues. The meaning of the term once referred to the struggle for eradication of discrimination, based on racial, religious, sexual, or ethnic attributes, and of laws or social policy that burden or penalize people on the basis of such attributes. It has, in recent decades, come to imply that each identifiable racial or ethnic group and each sex has a right to a proportionate share of the benefits of society. The legitimacy of an uneven distribution of material well-being and of the dominance of certain groups over others has increasingly come under attack.

The changing conception of equality has been accompanied by a changing conceptualization of racism. More recently, supporters of target groups have been using the term symbolic racism to refer to opposition to programs and policies advocated by target group leaders or to statements not overtly racist as a racial or ethnic slur, but statements to which target group members nonetheless take offense as "insensitive." Thus, someone who criticizes busing for racial balance or some affirmative action policy may be accused of using such critiques as a cover for deeply held racist attitudes. Of course, the charge of symbolic racism is hard to avoid. One can with care avoid using direct racial slurs, but one may find it more difficult to anticipate those statements or opinions to which some target group member may take offense or regard as insensitive. For example, at the University of Pennsylvania in early 1993, a graduate student, an Israeli named Eden Jacobowitz, shouted to a group of African American women celebrating beneath his dorm window, "Shut up, you water buffalo!" Jacobowitz had translated an Israeli term that connotes coarseness or crudeness, but has no particular racial connotations. Still, Jacobowitz was pursued for an entire semester with charges of racist insults under Penn's rigorous speech code.

Clearly, there are arguments to be made for some form of compensatory justice in view of the history of discrimination against certain groups. However, because of the confusion between the bigotry or discrimination of groups and those of individuals within those groups, the justice of the matter becomes muddled. The white race may, in the aggregate, be guilty of discrimination; however, individuals—Brian Weber, Cheryl Hopwood, or Alan Bakke—pay the debt, even though they may not personally have so discriminated. To change the rules of the game and deny benefits to the Hopwoods, Webers, and Bakkes of society, benefits to which they were entitled under the old rules, is perceived by some as a denial of their rights.

Yet minorities do have a right to combat the persisting impact of the history of social discrimination. The point is that rights conflict. The intractable difficulty of the equality issue is that it is not a clear case of right and wrong, but one of conflicting rights. Plausible ethical arguments can and have been constructed to support conflicting claims based on powerful interests. In addition, in an economy in which hopes of perpetual economic growth confront the reality of scarcity and the finite supply of resources, society is increasingly in a zero-sum situation. Members of nontargeted groups increasingly perceive that they cannot help target groups without giving up something themselves. Thus, the strongest opposition to affirmative action frequently comes from those segments of white society most likely to be displaced by members of target groups, the middle or lower-middle classes. Members of the upper class are less likely to be so displaced, and therefore the support for affirmative action by so-called limousine liberals is without cost. Because of this conflict among plausible rights, issues concerning equality promise to continue to be among the most intractable and divisive of issues facing the country for the indefinite future. The issue of racial equality in higher education was given new life in a 1992 case in which the Supreme Court ruled that Mississippi's system of predominantly African American and white universities is discriminatory. Similar systems in nineteen other states were strongly affected by this ruling.

The struggle for equality by African Americans has resulted in an inevitable rise in tensions between African Americans and the rest of society, many of whom perceive the progress of the targeted groups toward greater material well-being as coming at their expense. In particular, racial, ethnic, or gender preference plans are deeply resented. A new phase of the struggle of the less well-off groups has been entered, in which it is perceived that the goal of such groups has shifted from seeking integration or assimilation in the liberal democratic system, as symbolized by the renowned "I Have a Dream" speech of the Reverend Dr. Martin Luther King, Jr., to challenging the legitimacy of the system itself. Thus, the sympathy of such current African American leaders as the Reverend Jesse Jackson, singer Harry Belafonte, or the Reverend Jeremiah Wright for third-world antidemocratic leaders such as Fidel Castro or Hugo Chavez was perceived as a threat to the dominant system in a way that King's goals of assimilation were not. Thus, despite all of the progress toward equality documented throughout this chapter, tensions between the targeted less well-off groups and the rest of society remain high. These racial tensions are exacerbated by highly publicized incidents, such as the conflict between African Americans and Jews discussed earlier. The question of whether African Americans can receive equal justice in the American judicial system is likely to remain salient for the foreseeable future.

Just how difficult it is for African Americans and other racial minorities to achieve just treatment is dramatically revealed by periodic housing studies. A study conducted for the Department of Housing and Urban Development by Syracuse University in the early 1990s employed 3,000 paired African American, white, and Hispanic prospective homebuyers and renters. It found that African Americans experienced some form of discrimination 56 percent of the time they sought to buy and 59 percent of the time they sought to rent a house. Comparable figures for Hispanics were 50 percent and 56 percent. Follow-up studies by the Fair Housing Alliance used a similar methodology and discovered the same patterns of discrimination as recently as 2006.

The levels of racial antagonism and African American alienation from American society were shown in the celebration of the acquittal of accused murderer O. J. Simpson in 1995. Simpson's attorney Johnny Cochran had urged the jury to send a message to the white community in the face of a mountain of incriminating evidence. The right of a jury to return a verdict in the face of contradictory evidence is known as jury nullification, an option that was frequently used by Southern white juries to free whites who committed crimes against blacks. Now it was being used in defiance of the white criminal justice system. It had also been used in acquitting Lemrick Nelson, despite his admitted role in the murder of Yankel Rosenbaum (discussed earlier). Not only was there generalized outrage at the criminal justice system and at the living conditions of many African Americans in urban America, there was specific hatred directed at whites, Hispanics, and Asians. Such outrage persisted as George Zimmerman was acquitted of murdering Trayvon Martin, a black teenager, who was walking from a convenience store to his father's home in 2013. Similarly, Jordan Davis, a black teenager, was shot by Michael Dunn, a white former policeman, because Jordan and his friends were playing loud music on the car radio outside a gas station in 2014. The jury could not reach a verdict on the murder charge.

SUMMARY

Equality is a seemingly simple concept, but in the American experience, it has evolved to mean different things over time. There are three conceptualizations of the term: equality under the law, equality of opportunity, and equality of material well-being. Historically, government has institutionalized inequality through its laws and practices. Various groups have had to make their case for equal rights. Thus, nonproperty owners pushed for the right to vote as did women, both of whom were denied such rights in early America. Then the push for ending slavery and eventually full equality for blacks spanned the late nineteenth and much of the twentieth centuries. During the middle of the twentieth century, legislation and court decisions expanded equal rights for women and minorities of all types. People with disabilities were guaranteed their rights in the late twentieth century and the gay, lesbian, and transgender community saw their turn come as well. While much progress has been made, there are still challenges to ensure that all are really equal in the United States.

 RESOURCES

American Civil Liberty Union's Lesbian Gay Bisexual Transgender Project:
www.aclu.org/lgbt-rights

Center for Equal Opportunity: **www.ceousa.org**

Center for Race and Ethnicity at the Manhattan Institute:
http://www.manhattan-institute.org/

Feminist Majority Foundation: **www.feminist.org**

National Association for the Advancement of Colored People (NAACP):
www.naacp.org

National Organization for Women (NOW): **www.now.org**

U.S. Supreme Court Multimedia Database: **www.oyez.org**

Chapter 11

Immigration Policy: The Barely Open Door

The romanticized notion of America is that anyone could come to the United States and succeed through hard work. Immigrants helped the nation's westward expansion and helped fuel the industrial revolution that defined the U.S. economy for over a century. Beneath the romanticization of immigration, however, there always lurked some fears of the impact of immigrants on the social, cultural, economic, and political fabric of the country.[1] Even in colonial days, the nation's founders feared that immigrants might foster challenges to the political system being developed in the new country.[2] Nonetheless, it was not until the late nineteenth century that significant debate developed over immigration, waxing and waning as a major concern ever since. Since the 1970s, immigration policy has commanded a great deal of attention in political debate, as it has been tied to issues of the rate of flow of immigrants, effects on racial/ethnic mix of the population, economic well-being of citizens, and demands for public services. Since the early 1990s, the issue has been prominent in public policy debates in many parts of the country and in national elections.

Michael LeMay notes that shifts in immigration policy follow major recessions or depressions and come during periods of social unrest and turmoil.[3] According to LeMay, each major shift also resulted from one or more of the major political parties including a change in immigration policy as part of its party platform and after the formation of interest groups focusing on the issue. In most instances, groups used immigrants as scapegoats for the problems they identified, although, on occasion, the groups advocated greater support for immigration. This chapter examines immigration policy in light of the forces advocating either opening the doors to or advocating limits on immigration.

ISSUE BACKGROUND: FROM AN OPEN DOOR
TO INCREASING LIMITS

The Open Door

Traditionally, people viewed the United States as a nation of immigrants, implying that it is open to immigrants from around the world. As part of that view, the expectation arises that immigrants are part of the social contract the nation has with its citizens. The social contract "implies that citizens (and, in certain instances, other residents) who work hard and obey the law are eligible for government assistance in the form of health and education benefits and other social services at certain points in their lives, including those times when they are especially economically vulnerable."[4] The poem by Emma Lazarus inscribed inside the pedestal of the Statue of Liberty symbolizes the values of liberty and opportunity that attract many immigrants and that reflect the openness of American society:

> Give me your tired, your poor,
> Your huddled masses yearning to breathe free,
> The wretched refuse of your teeming shore.
> Send these, the homeless, tempest-tost to me,
> I lift my lamp beside the golden door.

For most of its history, U.S. government policy officially reflected these ideals. Nonetheless, implementation of policy did not always live up to the ideal, and there always has been sentiment to restrict entry.

Although some founders of the nation expressed concern about the effects of immigration, such as the potential for undermining the political values of the new nation, little formal policy emerged during the developing years of the United States. Instead, immigrants were welcomed to populate the country and aid in its economic development. Early concerns focused mostly on moral character and loyalty to the country. Some of these concerns arose from colonial days, when authorities objected to acceptance of criminals, paupers, or others of undesirable character. For example, in 1717, the Pennsylvania Colony imposed a fine of five pounds on every criminal brought in and made shipmasters post a year's bond for the good behavior of some passengers. Religious compatibility also affected colonial acceptance of immigrants. Beginning in Massachusetts in 1637, all colonies but Rhode Island imposed limits on settlers based on religious belief. Massachusetts, for example, restricted settlement of non-Puritans. Still, economic development and the abundance of land overshadowed these concerns and little regulation took place.[5] Citizenship could be acquired in state courts after five years of residence. This laissez-faire approach to immigration held until the mid-nineteenth century.

Use of Quotas

From the 1780s until 1819, approximately 250,000 immigrants arrived in the United States. Beginning in 1820, the pace of immigration quickened, with over 140,000 arriving during the 1820s and an annual average of almost 164,000 from the 1830s until 1860. A total of 5.1 million arrived during the 1860s and 1870s.[6] The increasing pace of immigration created the conditions for opposition to arise. Because more than 80 percent of the immigrants came from Western and Northern Europe, however, opposition was not widespread before 1820. Because most immigrants who came after 1820 looked for work in the developing factories and textile mills, they tended to settle in the Northeast, especially in New York and Pennsylvania. As many of these immigrants were different from the existing population, coming from southeastern Europe, being non–English speaking, and being predominantly Catholic and Jewish, opposition began to arise and quotas were imposed.[7]

Immigrants became "ghettoized" and many urban pockets of poverty developed. To many of the "native" population, these ghettos were spawning grounds for social problems, such as poverty, housing deterioration, lack of social cohesion, and crime.[8] Violence erupted in some places, such as in Philadelphia, which experienced a riot in 1844. The Native American Party (also known as the Know Nothing Party) arose in the 1850s out of anti-immigrant sentiment and enjoyed success in electing governors and members of Congress in the northeastern states. The party built on the beliefs of many native-born citizens that immigrants were a threat to their job security and threatened their religious foundations and the political culture.[9]

After the 1850s, negative responses of native-born citizens continued to build, and states expanded their exclusionary policies. The Civil War created a temporary diversion from the immigration issue and split the Know Nothing Party, but after the war, sentiment against immigrants grew again. California, in particular, excluded people based on their nation of origin, focusing on the Chinese, who arrived in large numbers in the West. California also imposed fees on Chinese immigrants, but this policy and all other state laws restricting immigration were invalidated by various decisions of state and federal courts based on the fact that immigration was a national and not a state issue. In 1882, the U.S. Congress acceded to the pressure from California and the Asian Exclusion League by passing a law setting a *quota* on the number of Chinese who could immigrate to the United States, and in 1888 further targeted Chinese immigrants through the Chinese Labor Exclusion Act. Congress also established a national policy on immigration through the Immigration Act of 1882, excluding ex-convicts and the mentally ill. These policy initiatives foreshadowed future limitations to immigration. The notion of excluding undesirables led to a long list of those to be excluded, such as polygamists, those convicted of crime, and those with certain illnesses.[10] Congress also responded to the concerns of organized labor with the Alien Contract Labor Act of 1885, banning the importation of contract labor, which often commanded lower wages than domestic labor.

By the end of the nineteenth century, Japanese immigration to the United States emerged as an issue, again in California. Efforts to limit Japanese immigration resulted in cities, such as San Francisco, segregating Japanese from the white population in schools. California again turned to the national government to stem the tide of Japanese immigrants. With pressure from President Theodore Roosevelt, Japan agreed to limit issuance of passports for nonlabor individuals going to the United States.[11] California went so far as to prohibit Japanese residents from owning agricultural land, and eventually, even from owning leases or any other real estate interests. Other states, such as Arizona, Texas, and Washington, followed suit.

In 1881, Congress established the Office of Immigration in the Treasury Department to coordinate the evolving immigration policies. The 1906 Naturalization Act renamed the office to the Bureau of Immigration and moved it to the Commerce and Labor Department. The Act also established the requirement that immigrants be able to speak English to gain citizenship. Reflecting continuing growth of anti-immigrant sentiment, Congress passed the 1917 Immigration Act, which incorporated all the earlier exclusions, required a literacy test, and specifically banned immigration of most Asians and Pacific Islanders. During the first two decades of the twentieth century, immigration averaged over 700,000 per year. During World War I, immigration dropped off, but it resumed at a higher pace after the war, peaked at 1.8 million in 1991, and has hovered around 1 million since (see Figure 11.1).

Social problems, such as unemployment, economic sluggishness, and a shortage of housing, fueled anti-immigrant sentiment. Groups such as the Ku Klux Klan, the American Coalition, the Immigrant Restriction League, and the American Protective League of True Americans advocated greater restriction on immigration. At the same time, others, such as the Hebrew Sheltering and Immigration Aid Society and the Anti-National Origins Clause League, opposed the restrictions. Congress passed the 1921 Quota Act, restricting the number of

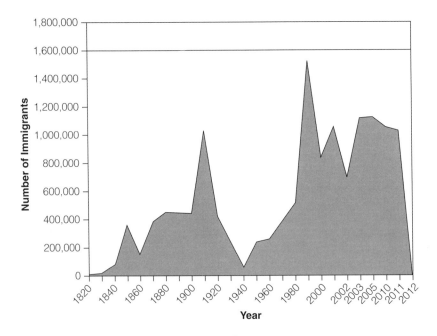

FIGURE 11.1 Legal Immigration Trends

SOURCE: http://www.dhs.gov/yearbook-immigration-statistics-2012-legal-permanent-residents, accessed March 24, 2014.

immigrants, and also established a quota limiting immigrants of any given nationality to 3 percent of those of the same nationality living in the country in 1890 as the base year for the quotas. The National Origins Quota Act of 1924 helped enforce the provisions by requiring immigrants to obtain visas from U.S. embassies in their native country. These acts attempted to maintain the ethnic balance of the United States and made it especially difficult for people from Italy, Spain, Russia, and Africa because their proportions in the population already living in the United States were small compared to Western or Northern Europeans. Thus, the intent of the Act was to shift the balance of immigration flow back to northwestern Europe by establishing low quotas for others. An unintended consequence of these new policies emerged as illegal immigration through Mexico and Canada by those from countries with very low quotas, because they had no other way of entering the country. Unlike the economies of the affected nations, the economy of the United States was very strong and opportunities abounded. The increase in illegal immigration prompted the Bureau to create the Border Patrol.

Because of the Depression, immigration declined dramatically in the 1930s. Most people seeking residency in the United States during this time were attempting to flee Germany and other Nazi-dominated countries, although the quota acts led to restrictions on the number admitted. By 1940, national security concerns prompted Congress to pass the Alien Registration Act, requiring fingerprinting and registration of new immigrants. It also required deportation of criminals and subversives. The bombing of Pearl Harbor by Japan led to relocation of many Japanese living in the United States. Whether they were new immigrants, long-time residents, or citizens, public officials considered Japanese potentially disloyal. The national government moved them from the West Coast to internment camps. Many lost their property because they defaulted on property taxes while in internment or were unable to secure it. Many were imprisoned. Also in 1940, the Bureau of Immigration was moved to the Department of Justice and renamed the Immigration and Naturalization Service (INS).

World War II and the draft created shortages of labor resulting in a policy allowing temporary workers (especially from Mexico) to enter the country. The lower wages paid to these workers led to industries pressuring for continuation of the program after the war. The United States and Mexico signed a Migrant Labor Agreement in 1951 making the program permanent. Called the Bracero Program, it survived until 1964. In 2001, some businesses and political leaders, especially in the Southwest, argued for a return to allowing temporary workers to enter the country. The recession of 2001–2002 temporarily eliminated the support for such programs; the recession of 2007–2009 again dissipated support.

In 2004, President Bush proposed a plan for a temporary worker program that included provisions for immigrant workers to be matched with employers willing to hire them. Permits could be renewed for up to three years. Bipartisan groups drafted legislation to address the issues in 2005, 2007, and 2013. Controversy arose each time over whether a guest worker program (a revived Bracero Program) should be included, over whether border security needed to be established first, and over a proposed pathway to citizenship for those already here. Rhetoric cast the debate in terms of amnesty versus deportation of immigrants.

Despite the bipartisan support and support of Presidents Bush and Obama, the efforts failed. After the failure of the proposed legislation, the administrations aggressively enforced sanctions against employers who knowingly hire illegal immigrants thus stirring up new controversy. The Obama administration promised to continue to push for comprehensive immigration reform.

The many applications of refugees just prior to and during World War II called attention to the problem of refugees and the fact that the United States did not differentiate among potential immigrants. Eventually, the 1948 Displaced Persons Act addressed the issue by setting up a separate refugee system. During the 1950s, the Act accommodated those fleeing communist countries. The refugee system permitted people to be accepted outside the quota system for their nations of origin. These refugees were granted permanent resident status and were permitted to apply for citizenship. The Cold War and anticommunist frenzy stimulated closer scrutiny of immigrants as well to ensure exclusion of suspected subversives. After the terrorist attacks of September 11, 2001, similar pressures led to measures imposing greater scrutiny of immigrants and visitors.

Transition to a Preference System

In 1952, Congress enacted the Immigration and Nationality Act, which consolidated much of the earlier policy into one general policy. The Act maintained the quota system and alien registration. It also gave preference to skilled labor and relatives of citizens and resident aliens. Later, the Immigration and Nationality Act of 1965 abolished the national origins quota system and established numerical limits in order of preference to:

1. unmarried children of U.S. citizens,
2. spouses and unmarried children of permanent resident aliens,
3. people in the professions and exceptional scientists and artists,
4. married children of U.S. citizens,
5. siblings of U.S. citizens,
6. workers with skills needed in the U.S. labor market, and
7. refugees.[12]

The Act set a limit of 170,000 annually from the Eastern Hemisphere. It also established a limit of 120,000 annually for the Western Hemisphere after July 1968. The new policies resulted in large increases in illegal immigration and mounting pressure within the country for policies dealing with it. Much of the illegal immigration increase resulted from the fact that many of the Braceros who worked legally in the United States until the unilateral termination of the program by the United States still were welcomed by employers, especially in the agricultural sector. The workers now just came across the border illegally to work in the same jobs. The deterioration of the Mexican economy also contributed to the increase.

After 1965, immigration again surged and backlogs developed in applications because of the ceilings imposed, especially on immigration from the Western Hemisphere. To some, the reforms of 1965 represented a method of maintaining the same effect of the national origins quota system without being overt about it, since Asians and Africans would still find it difficult to immigrate because relatively few of them had relatives here.[13] The concept of family reunification drove the development of the new system that still underpins much of today's policy. The huge backlogs led to long waits for applicants, especially from Mexico. In 1976, Congress responded by creating the appearance of equality of treatment by establishing a limit of 20,000 immigrants from each country in the Western Hemisphere. Another change in 1978 imposed a ceiling of 290,000 visas per year for the world as a whole, thus deleting the differentiation between the Eastern and Western Hemispheres. The preference categories established in 1965 provided the basis for immigration under the 1978 policy.

Congress addressed the refugee issue again in 1980, separating refugee policy from overall immigration policy. The Refugee Act of 1980 created a separate admissions process for refugees and established a ceiling of 50,000 per year. It also gave the president, in consultation with Congress, the power to act in emergency situations involving refugees.

In 1986, Congress confronted the illegal immigration issue through the Immigration Reform and Control Act of 1986. The Act granted **amnesty** and temporary resident status to illegal immigrants who had lived in the United States continuously after January 1, 1982. It also attempted to address the employment of illegal aliens by banning employment of undocumented workers and imposing sanctions on employers who knowingly hired illegal aliens. It created a program to help alleviate labor shortages, which might result from the sanctions on employers. Border patrol and inspection were strengthened by the Act as well.

The Immigration Act of 1990 built upon the 1965 reforms and serves as the foundation for current policy. The Act provided that, after 1995, immigration would be limited to 675,000 per year for all types of immigration. Family reunification remained the primary criterion for the policy, but some new categories also were created. For example, those who would invest $1,000,000 in urban areas or $500,000 in rural areas and create at least ten new jobs would be eligible above the overall ceiling. The Act created a classification of diversity immigrants to allow people from countries with very low representation in the U.S. population to immigrate through a lottery process.

Illegal Immigration

The Illegal Immigration Reform and Immigrant Responsibility Act of 1996 addressed numerous issues concerning illegal immigration. The Act responded to growing pressures among the public, especially in states along the Mexican border, to stem the flow of illegal immigration. To achieve that objective, the Act almost doubled the size of the Border Patrol and provided resources to acquire sophisticated technology and otherwise improve the tools for securing the border and for detection and apprehension of those entering the country illegally. Stiffer penalties were enacted for smuggling illegal persons into the country and for production and use of fraudulent documents. Illegal immigrants caught also face stiffer penalties under the law.

The 1996 reform also attempted to deal with the problem of employment of undocumented workers. Specifically, the Act provided sanctions for knowingly employing illegal immigrants and created some programs to assist employers in confirming the eligibility of the employee to be hired. The programs emphasize the need for the Immigration and Naturalization Service, Social Security Administration, and the attorney general to work together and to develop systems for speedy confirmation of information to employers. They developed the **E-Verify** system for employers to check the eligibility of applicants to work in the United States.

The 1996 law requires family members who sponsor immigrants to earn 125 percent of the federal poverty income guideline in order to sponsor a relative. The law also addresses some of the provisions of the 1996 welfare reform affecting immigrants. In particular, the provisions make clear distinctions between legal and illegal immigrants relative to benefits that states can or may provide. Generally, illegal immigrants may be denied benefits, but some benefits also will be denied to legal immigrants. Specifically, Social Security benefits may not be paid to immigrants who are not legally present in the country; higher education benefits to illegal aliens are restricted; food stamps and Supplemental Security Income (SSI) are phased out for most noncitizens; and states are permitted to deny benefits, such as nonemergency Medicaid to illegal aliens and sometimes to legal permanent residents. By 1997, Congress and the president faced pressure to change some of the provisions to assure benefits to immigrants in the country legally and who worked and paid taxes. SSI benefits were restored for legal immigrants in the country prior to enactment of the 1996 reforms. Congress also approved changes that allow immigrants with green card applications filed by January 4, 1998, to remain in the country while the application paperwork is processed. Congress also passed legislation making Nicaraguan and Cuban refugees automatically eligible for permanent status and allowing refugees from El Salvador, Guatemala, and Eastern Europe to apply for suspension of deportation under pre-1996 provisions less stringent than those in the 1996 Act.

CONTEMPORARY POLICY: RESPONDING TO CHANGING IMMIGRATION DYNAMICS

As with all public policies (see Chapter 1), contemporary immigration policy serves diverse purposes. Most pieces of immigration policy reflect attempts to deal with a particular concern rather than a comprehensive approach, thus resulting in a complex patchwork of items. Thus, efforts to limit immigration often are justified in terms of meeting security and prosperity needs of people. Specifically, many opponents of immigration argue that immigration is an internal threat to the extent that it is related to social problems, such as crime and poverty, and to the extent that it undermines the political and social covenants on which American society is built. At times immigration also is linked to external threats, such as terrorism or, as during the Cold War, to subversion. These threats to security provide one rationale for limiting immigration. The threats became very real with the September 11, 2001, terrorist attacks in New York, Pennsylvania, and Washington, DC. In response, Congress passed the USA Patriot Act of 2001. The Act enhanced immigration enforcement with particular attention to potential terrorist threats. Many calls for even more restrictive policies use the terrorist threat as a rationale.

The Homeland Security Act of 2002 created the Department of Homeland Security and integrated immigration services and programs into the department. Specifically, the Act created the U.S. Citizenship and Immigration Services (USCIS). In March 2003, USCIS fully absorbed INS and renamed it the U.S. Immigration and Customs Enforcement (ICE). The Homeland Security Department also includes U.S. Customs and Border Protection (CBP).

Regulation of immigration is often based upon prosperity needs. Many of the arguments against immigration are couched in terms of economic impact. Opponents argue that immigrants take away jobs of native-born citizens and put downward pressure on wages and the standard of living. Others contend that immigration should be encouraged because our economy needs people to take jobs that native-born citizens are unwilling to take. Also, many supporters of immigration point to the many highly skilled immigrants in technical fields as important to our ability to compete in the global economy. Thus, both proponents and opponents of immigration point to effects on the prosperity needs of the society to support their positions.

Policies on illegal immigration also rest on arguments about security and membership purposes. The same contentions as those regarding immigration generally are used, but others emerge as well. Membership is used as a basis for limiting access to various social programs. For example, denying noncitizens and illegal immigrants education and welfare benefits is based on membership as defined by citizenship.

The myth of immigration in U.S. history claims that the country opens its doors to the world and represents the best and most generous aspects of humankind. It has become a part of what is known as the American spirit. Some label it a myth because the specifics of immigration policy, as they developed, support anti-immigrant sentiment arising from people's anxieties and self-interest.[14] Despite restrictions, the United States ranks "as the principal immigrant-receiving nation in the world."[15] Others, however, argue that while absolute numbers of immigrants place the United States at the top, other nations, such as Australia, Canada, and Germany, admit more immigrants as a ratio of their total population.[16]

Part of the debate over immigration policy emanates from the national origin of immigrants and the large concentrations of some ethnic groups. Current policy gives preferences to those who have family already in the country, reflecting the family reunification philosophy of the policy. The family reunification policy supports maintaining the ethnic balance of the country and makes immigration from Africa particularly difficult. Furthermore, perceptions are that the number of Hispanics, and especially Mexican Americans, has increased dramatically in recent years. Data indicate that immigration from Mexico and other Latin American countries remained stable from the 1920s to 2000 at 35 to 45 percent, but then increased to 54.6 percent by 2007 with more than 31 percent coming from Mexico.[17] The concentration of immigrants from Central America and Mexico in the Southwest and of Cubans in Florida gives the appearance of huge waves of immigrants from these areas and results in their being targets for the frustrations of native-born citizens.

Current policy is based on the 1965 Immigration and Nationality Act with modifications made in the 1990 Immigration Act and the Illegal Immigration Reform and Immigrant Responsibility Act of 1996. The policy establishes family reunification as the primary criterion for immigration and sets limits on the flow of immigrants. The 1996 Act, in particular, attempts to control the influx of illegal persons and imposes penalties on employers of illegal immigrants. Immigration to the United States reached an all-time high of 1.8 million in 1991. Tougher policies reduced those numbers dramatically in succeeding years. The reforms of 1990 provided a ceiling of 675,000 beginning with fiscal year 1995. The ceilings have been exceeded because of various exceptions granted and because the family reunification philosophy allows immigrants to include their immediate families beyond the limit. In 2001 and 2002, for example, total immigration numbered just under 1.1 million; it dipped to 705,827 in 2003, and then gradually rose again to 1.27 million in 2006. It gradually declined to 1 million in 2012 (see Table 11.1). Immediate relatives of U.S. citizens account for roughly 65 percent. Included are spouses, parents, children, and siblings of U.S. citizens.

Approximately 12.7 percent of immigrants are admitted under employment-based preferences. These include people with advanced degrees or of exceptional ability, skilled professionals, unskilled workers filling special needs, and other special categories, including students covered under the Chinese Student Protection Act who might face persecution if they return to China. The category also includes investor immigrants, who receive admission to the United States based on their investing large sums of money into the economy. Employment-based immigration often is justified in terms of the increasingly global economy and the need for the United States to remain competitive. Often, highly technical skills are available in other nations and the ability to communicate and penetrate other economies through language and culture also are addressed in these approaches.

Refugees and **asylees** constitute another category. These are people who face persecution in their native countries. Refugees are usually people displaced from their countries because of political instability or persecution by a political regime against a particular group. Asylees claim political persecution for their ideas or political activities. They may be granted political asylum because of the harm they face by going back to their native countries. Refugees and asylees made up about 16 percent of immigrants in 2009 and diversity immigrants represented approximately 4.7 percent.

The top countries from which immigrants came in 2012 were Mexico, China, India, the Philippines, and Dominican Republic (see Table 11.2). Until the 1960s, Europe dominated in sending immigrants to the United States. With the new face of immigrants, especially the large numbers of Asians and Hispanics, public attitudes have changed. Assimilation is not as easy as it was for the Europeans of early immigration waves. Resentment grows and is exploited by many interest groups and political opportunists. Anti-immigrant sentiment peaked in

TABLE 11.1   Immigration since 1991

Year	Number of Immigrants Admitted
1991	1,826,595
1992	973,445
1993	903,916
1994	803,993
1995	720,177
1996	915,560
1997	797,847
1998	653,206
1999	644,787
2000	841,002
2001	1,058,902
2002	1,059,356
2003	703,542
2004	957,883
2005	1,122,257
2006	1,266,129
2007	1,052,415
2008	1,107,126
2009	1,130,818
2010	1,042,625
2011	1,062,040
2012	1,031,631

SOURCE: U.S. Department of Homeland Security, *2012 Yearbook of Immigration Statistics*, Table 1, http://www.dhs.gov/yearbook-immigration-statistics-2012-legal-permanent-residents, accessed March 26, 2014.

2001. Polls in 2001 found that 59 percent of Americans believed that legal immigration should be reduced; by 2014, only 36 percent responded that way.[18]

Immigration patterns have changed so that now more immigrants come from Asia and the Caribbean and Latin American countries. Their settlement patterns are different; they settle in the coastal states, with the Pacific states and Southwest attracting Asians and Mexican Americans. Florida and the Northeast coast are the destinations of most of those from Cuba and the Caribbean. Currently, California, New York, Florida, Texas, New Jersey, and Illinois attract the largest numbers of foreign-born people (see Table 11.3).

Racial and ethnic origins of immigrants also have changed over recent decades.[19] Prior to 1970, 86 percent of the foreign-born population was white, while in 2010, only 48 percent of those arriving were white. Hispanics increased from 32 percent pre-1970 to 47 percent in 2010. Asians increased from 9 to

TABLE 11.2   Legal Immigrants by Top Ten Countries of Origin, Fiscal Year 2012

All countries	1,031,631
Mexico	145,326
China	78,184
India	63,320
Philippines	55,541
Dominican Republic	41,535
Cuba	32,551
Vietnam	25,578
Haiti	22,446
South Korea	20,802
Jamaica	20,300

SOURCE: U.S. Department of Homeland Security, *2012 Yearbook of Immigration Statistics,* Table 2, http://www.dhs.gov/yearbook-immigration-statistics-2012-legal-permanent-residents, accessed March 26, 2014.

TABLE 11.3   Concentration of Legal Immigrant Populations by Top Ten States of Residence, Fiscal Year 2012

California	196,622
New York	149,505
Florida	103,047
Texas	95,557
New Jersey	50,790
Illinois	38,373
Massachusetts	31,392
Virginia	28,227
Georgia	26,134
Pennsylvania	25,032
All states	1,031,631

SOURCE: U.S. Department of Homeland Security, *2012 Yearbook of Immigration Statistics,* Table 4, http://www.dhs.gov/yearbook-immigration-statistics-2012-legal-permanent-residents, accessed March 26, 2014.

25 percent of the foreign-born population in the same time period. Blacks represent about 8 percent of the foreign born.[20]

The education level of immigrants varies somewhat from the native-born population as well. Interestingly, three times the percentage of foreign born (31.5 percent) than native born (10.6 percent) lack a high school degree, but approximately 11.5 percent of foreign born have graduate or professional degrees compared to about 10.5 percent of native born. Immigrants are a little less likely to have a bachelor's degree (16.0 percent) than are native born (18.3 percent). Native born are more likely to have graduated high school and have some college (50.6 percent) than foreign born (41.1 percent).[21]

The Illegal Immigration Reform and Immigrant Responsibility Act of 1996 addresses the problem of illegal immigration, which reached a peak in 2007 at 12.2 million, and fell during the Great Recession to 11.3 million in 2009. By 2012, it had increased again to 11.7 million and appears to be continuing to increase slowly (see Table 11.4).[22] Much of the pressure for reform of immigration arose out of the frustration that many people felt about illegal immigration and their beliefs that illegal immigrants are the cause of many of the country's social ills. The 1996 reforms addressed this problem directly. Figures on illegal immigration are difficult to ascertain with accuracy, as illegal immigrants shy away from census takers. The number of illegal immigrants apprehended (currently approximately 650,000 per year) by ICE serves as one measure of the magnitude of the problem. ICE apprehensions increased steadily from the 1960s to 2000, declined until 2011, and began to increase thereafter.[23] Increased enforcement and Mexico's improving economy and fewer economic opportunities in the United States are pointed to as reasons for recent declines, along with the 1996 Act and stricter border controls under the 2001 USA Patriot Act. The improving U.S. economy seems to be behind the latest increase. Illegal immigration is a very emotional issue as many Americans are convinced that illegal immigrants are a burden to society and create economic problems by taking jobs away from native workers.

Additionally, the distinction between legal and illegal immigration is not always clear. Past law has allowed illegal residents to become legal; many families in the United States contain some legal and some illegal members; and the status of many is unclear, awaiting adjudication. The next section explains the different views about the effects of current immigration policy.

TABLE 11.4   Estimated Unauthorized Immigrants in the United States

Year	Number
2000	8,500,000
2005	10,500,000
2007	11,800,000
2008	12,200,000
2009	10,800,000
2012	11,700,000

SOURCE: Office of Immigration Statistics, *Annual Report, Immigration Enforcement Actions*, 2012, http://www.dhs.gov/sites/default/files/publications/ois_enforcement_ar_2012_1.pdf, accessed March 27, 2014.

POLICY EVALUATION: CONTRASTING PERCEPTIONS

Current Policy Concerns

Immigration policy is a very emotional issue that does not lend itself easily to ideological splits. Instead, people's views are shaped by their family ties, their experiences with immigrants, their fears of the impact of immigration, and the areas of the country in which they live, to name a few. LeMay argues that economics, race, nationalism, and foreign policy play pivotal roles in all U.S. immigration policy.[24] The opposing perspectives presented in the following discussion bear out LeMay's contention. Negative or positive perspectives on immigration revolve around several issues, including the impact on the economy, with special emphasis on employment, dependence on public services (such as welfare and education), quality of life, and impact on the social and political culture.

Economic Concerns

Much of the debate over immigration policy focuses on its impact on the economy, with those favoring a more restrictive policy claiming that immigrants are a drain on the economy and take jobs away from the native population.[25] Those who support immigration and even argue for more immigration point to many positive effects on the economy and the need for the labor provided by immigrants.[26] Certainly, traditional immigration provided a supply of labor that helped develop the United States into a leading economic power. Even during the nineteenth and early twentieth centuries, however, the arrival of many immigrants led to resentment and policy changes attempting to limit or exclude some groups, as noted in the first part of this chapter. During economic boom times, the issue usually is not as visible as during periods of economic sluggishness.

Opponents of immigration argue that immigrants take jobs held by natives or are willing to work at very low wages, thus depressing the income of the native population.[27] This argument has considerable emotional appeal and seems very logical. Examples of the Vietnamese who fish on the Gulf Coast of Texas or the prevalence of Hispanics in hotel and food service industries in Florida and California support critics' contentions that immigrants take jobs from native-born citizens. While these examples illustrate real problems in specific locales, they do not reflect the overall impact on the labor market. Critics of immigration argue that the unemployment rate is evidence of the availability of native-born labor. Some cite the inability of people to live on the minimum wage and blame immigrants for depressing wages because of their availability in the workforce. Traditionally, labor unions have opposed immigration as a means of protecting their own interests. Cheap labor might undermine the efforts of labor unions to share in the profits of business. Additionally, they argue that the cheap labor does not reflect the type of skills that the United States should be encouraging to help it in global competitiveness.[28] Nonetheless, some unions now embrace immigration as they have seen their numbers grow with the addition of immigrant workers to union rolls.[29]

People on the other side of the issue argue that immigration has negligible impact on the labor market and that rather than taking jobs from others, immigrants actually help create jobs.[30] Immigrants are still attracted by employment opportunity. As they take jobs, they become productive participants in the economy and spend money, thus helping to create demand for more products and thus more employment. Proponents of immigration also note that immigrants tend to have a very strong work ethic because they were motivated to come to the United States to seek opportunity. They have not differed from nonimmigrants in their rates of unemployment until the recession of 2007–2009, which seems to have had a larger effect on immigrants.[31]

Proponents of immigration also cite the entrepreneurial activities of immigrants and how those activities contribute to the growth of the economy and employment. U.S. data indicate that 5.1 percent of immigrants start businesses compared to 3.7 percent of the native population.[32] Though the enterprises tend to be small, small enterprises are the source of nearly a quarter of new jobs since the early 1970s.

Although many immigrants work in low-wage jobs, many also are highly talented and skilled professionals. Clearly, many industries depend upon the unskilled laborers who harvest produce and work in the garment, restaurant, and hotel industries. Significant numbers of immigrants also are scientists and engineers and have been important parts of the success of high-tech industries.[33] Additionally, as noted earlier in the chapter, the children of immigrants tend to achieve college education and enter the professional ranks at very high rates. Asians appear to be the most successful and arrive with high levels of education and skills. Indians and Arabs also tend to be highly educated and skilled. Not surprisingly, Mexicans tend to be less educated and more unskilled as they generally are immigrating to escape poverty and the lack of opportunity in their society. Generally, facts suggest that immigration has positive impacts on the economy. At the same time, the negative impact in a given community with high concentrations of immigrants can be very significant and can put a strain on resources in that community.

Impact on Public Services

Opponents of immigration raise the specter of overloaded public services as another major issue. They argue that our schools are overrun with children of immigrants, and that immigrants burden the welfare system. The issue created much pressure in many states and in national politics to limit the access of immigrants, especially illegal immigrants, to these governmental benefits. Several states passed laws, often citizen initiatives, to prohibit illegal immigrants from receiving benefits such as publicly funded health and welfare benefits and in-state tuition at institutions of higher education. All but a few states now prohibit illegal immigrants from having driver's licenses; although so-called **Dreamers** are allowed to in most states. Dreamers are individuals who were brought to this country when

---

POLICY DILEMMAS   **Unanticipated Impact of Effort to Help Dreamers**

In 2012, President Obama announced a deferred action program to allow children who were brought to the United States as undocumented immigrants (Dreamers) to remain in the country for two years and to obtain work permits. At the time, Arizona had a very strict law targeting undocumented immigrants and the governor, Jan Brewer, issued her own executive order banning Dreamers from obtaining driver's licenses in the state. (In July 2014, her executive order was ruled unconstitutional by the 9th Circuit Court and she has promised to appeal.)

Rosalie Perez is a twenty-year-old social work student who needs to serve an internship to complete her degree. She was offered an internship fifteen miles from her home, but unfortunately, as a Dreamer, she is unable to accept the internship because there is no public transportation serving the area of the internship, and under the governor's executive order, she cannot obtain a driver's license.

Carl Shaller, born a U.S. citizen, retired from his job as a financial analyst in his native Ohio and looked forward to relocating to Arizona for retirement. When he arrived, he went to the Motor Vehicle Division to get a driver's license and turned in his Ohio license. The Motor Vehicle Division told him that the governor's executive order meant it could not accept his Ohio license to apply for an Arizona one. He had to return later with a valid identification showing that he was a U.S. citizen. Even though he was not a Dreamer, he was affected by the decisions regarding them.

1. What institutional factors affect the experience of the two people in these scenarios? Do you see any political forces at work?

2. Was the president right in creating the deferred action program? Was the governor right in issuing her executive order? Do you see any unintended consequences of either executive order?

---

they were under the age of sixteen, have lived here for five consecutive years, and have recently graduated from high school. They must be currently under the age of thirty and have no criminal record. Under an executive order by President Obama, they may apply for a waiver to stay in the country. Some municipalities have adopted ordinances prohibiting landlords from renting to illegal immigrants, but a court in Pennsylvania found such an ordinance in Hazelton, Pennsylvania, unconstitutional, saying that immigration is a federal government responsibility. Arizona Senate Bill 2010 was challenged on the basis that immigration is a federal responsibility and the courts ruled most of its provisions unconstitutional on those grounds. Nonetheless, several states continue to pass restrictive immigration laws and face the inevitable legal challenges.

Immigration poses many challenges to public school systems in the areas in which there are large concentrations of immigrants. Clearly, these challenges have existed for long periods of time in the major cities, such as New York and Chicago. Recent immigration patterns, however, have brought the challenges to new areas, especially in Florida, Texas, California, and generally the Southwest.[34] School districts in these areas experience difficulty in handling the numbers of students and in meeting their needs because of the language barriers and the lack of resources to serve many of their students, immigrant or nonimmigrant. Typically, the most affected school districts are the large urban districts that long have suffered the most from lack of adequate funding and from overcrowding in poorly maintained facilities. These problems mean that they cannot meet the educational needs of immigrant and native-born children alike. All the problems of large urban school districts make the assimilation of immigrant children more difficult than it otherwise would be. Because immigration law, specifically the 1996 Act, permits states only to limit higher education benefits, public schools are required to provide education for immigrant students. The Supreme Court in *Plyler v. Doe* (1982) ruled that illegal immigrants could not be denied public education. Restrictions do apply, however, to some students, particularly those who live on the Mexican border and enter the United States for their education. Under visa restrictions, they are denied access to public schools. Nonetheless, studies indicate that children of immigrants have better attendance, are less likely to drop out, and are more likely to do better in school than U.S.-born children.[35] While not much research exists on the subject, a few studies indicate differential performance by immigrant groups. A study of San Diego high school students indicated that, with the exception of Hispanics, performance of children of non–English speaking immigrants had higher test scores than all other students. Other studies indicate that students of immigrant families from China, Korea, Japan, Vietnam, the Philippines, Laos, and Cambodia outperform native-born students. Also, Mexican-born immigrant students tend to outperform U.S.-born students of Mexican descent.[36]

According to many opponents of immigration, the welfare state is a major attraction of immigration to the United States. Many of the concerns are raised by state government officials because state and local governments bear much of the cost of social services, especially as the national government has cut back in recent years (see Chapter 7). Studies indicate that recently arrived immigrants are slightly more likely to use public services than is the general population, but that over time, they are less likely to do so.[37] More recent research, however, suggests that immigrants are more likely than the rest of the population is to use social services.[38]

All immigrants are eligible for public school education, but eligibility and use of other benefits differ somewhat by category. Until 1996 reforms in welfare and in immigration, most legal immigrants were eligible for most benefits. With the 1996 reforms, higher education benefits and welfare benefits, such as food stamps and disability benefits, are denied to some legal immigrants. Children born in the United States of illegal parents, however, are citizens and thus eligible for benefits. Some states are considering legislation to ensure medical and financial assistance to legal immigrants by replacing the federal funds with state money. Refugees and asylees generally are treated like legal immigrants when it comes to benefits. Illegal immigrants, however, are unlikely to see much support for their access to services.

Proponents of immigration also present data on the taxes paid versus the costs of services. By these calculations, immigrants represent a positive investment for the country. Immigrants contribute more to the system in taxes than they use in benefits, thus pay their own way. Ironically, illegal immigrants contribute at an even higher rate than others because they work and pay taxes, but are less likely to be eligible for or to apply for public services because they fear deportation.[39] A disproportionate share of the taxes, however, is paid in income tax to the national government while the burden of providing services falls to state and local governments.

Much has been made of older relatives of immigrants coming to the United States to take advantage of Social Security or SSI benefits (see Chapter 7). After the 1965 reforms, it appears that there was an increase in such immigration, but some observers suggest that immigrants actually provide support for the survival of Social Security programs. Given the fact that the native population is aging and increasingly qualifying for Social Security benefits, workers are faced with increasing taxes to support the system. Many argue that the system will be bankrupt by the time the baby boomers retire. Some scholars argue that immigrants usually come to the country while they are in their prime working years and that they help ensure the survival of the Social Security system by their contributions to the trust fund.[40]

Clearly, many state and local governments feel the pressures of immigration, both legal and illegal. The pressures on social services, roads, and bus systems can be very heavy, leading to frustration on the part of the taxpayers who have to pay for the services and for those needing the services when they are unavailable. The burden is distributed unevenly. Because of large numbers of immigrants in states such as Florida, California, Arizona, and Texas, and especially in major cities, such as Miami, San Diego, and Los Angeles, the pressures on these states and cities are especially large. At the same time, the contributions of working immigrants to the tax base support the economy and society as a whole. Both supporters and opponents of immigration have pointed out the uneven distribution of the costs and make suggestions for federal government support for services that cannot be denied because of the Constitution or other federal policy. The restriction of many benefits to citizens or legal immigrants resulted in part from this pressure as well.

Quality of Life

Quality of life issues arise relative to immigration mostly among those who oppose more immigration. They argue that continued immigration will lead to overpopulation of the country, resulting in increasing poverty and harm to the environment. Opponents also argue that the culture of the society is being changed and that the social fabric is being destroyed. In particular, they hearken back to the idea that the United States has been a melting pot, but that with the new waves of immigration, the society is being fragmented. Assimilation occurs more slowly because larger concentrations of people of similar background sustain old customs and traditions. Some suggest that the United States no longer is a melting pot but a pluralism of ethnic groups that do not become assimilated.[41] In recent years, many new groups have tried to preserve their ethnic identities by celebrating their ethnic and cultural traditions. These developments lead to resentment by many people who believe they should make efforts to assimilate more fully. Immigrants often become scapegoats for many of the problems of society.[42]

Overpopulation. Overpopulation is often cited as a problem by those opposing more immigration. Some people fear the sheer growth in numbers of people as putting a strain on all aspects of American society.[43] Many social critics blame immigrants for the decline of some of the major cities, citing crime statistics, exodus of whites to the suburbs, housing deterioration, poverty, and loss of business and jobs in the central cores at the same time that immigrants are moving into those areas.[44] The rhetoric often is very inflammatory and leads to policy proposals that might not necessarily address the real problems. Blaming immigrants for threats to economic security, for example, diverts attention away from the causes of the slow wage growth, as the data indicate that immigrants have little overall impact on the issue. Closing the doors to immigrants seems like an easy solution, but the problems of America's major cities are much more complicated than immigration.

One of the issues raised concerning population growth is the impact on the environment. Some critics suggest that the pressures on production of food and the waste produced will lead to effects such as global warming, air pollution, water pollution, and the destruction of the physical environment (see Chapter 5).[45] There is no question that increasing population puts a strain on many environmental features. What those on the other side of the issue say, however, is that the United States is nowhere near its capacity to handle the population and that efforts should be made to improve environmental policy to protect the environment rather than using immigrants as the scapegoat. They also counter that the native birthrate is declining, and that immigration is barely replacing the decrease in population due to this decline.[46]

Crime. Crime is another issue opponents of immigration use. They blame immigrants for a high crime rate, especially in the major cities and along the border with Mexico. Although immigrants themselves appear to be less likely than the rest of the population to be involved in crime, critics still blame them for crime by their argument that they take the jobs of U.S.-born natives, thus increasing the unemployment rate. High unemployment in the urban centers then contributes to a life of crime by people who are disenfranchised from the system.[47] Given the evidence that immigration has a negligible impact on employment issues, proponents of immigration note that the argument does not follow. They also cite the vitality of many ethnic neighborhoods fostered by immigrant groups and that those neighborhoods foster a sense of community, which helps discourage crime.[48]

Social and Political Culture. Perhaps the most controversial issue raised about the impact of immigration on the quality of life is the impact on social and political culture.[49] Many opponents of immigration claim that it is threatening the values of our society and that ethnic groups have separatist notions, which lead to balkanization of American society. Some claim that these developments are leading to culture wars, and that our borders must be closed to stop the march to disappearance of America's distinctive social and political culture.[50] These arguments are not new. The founders of our nation raised the issue at the very beginning, as did many of the colonists. The Know Nothing Party of the 1850s and 1860s brought the ideas to the electorate. Depending on the time and circumstances, critics perceived threats to religious homogeneity, the family structure, and social cohesion of communities, to name a few. Thus, these critics of immigration continue a long tradition of appealing to the fears and anxieties of citizens. Clearly, the concentrations of Mexican Americans in the Southwest and Haitians and Cubans in Miami are examples for many people of the ability of new immigrants to hold on to their cultures. Because they have distinct cultures, they are easy targets for those who have an idealized view of Americans as a homogeneous culture. Sometimes it is easier to strike out at the identifiable group than to accept that society evolves constantly. There is much evidence of identifiable ethnic groups attempting to continue their homeland cultural traditions, but there is no evidence that it undermines the political democracy of the United States.

Because of the cohesion of some groups, critics also fear the political power they represent. These fears helped proponents in their efforts in Arizona in 2004 to pass Proposition 200, which required proof of citizenship to vote. Similar measures have passed in other places especially running up to the 2012 and 2014 elections. In March 2014, a federal court judge in Kansas ruled that such a requirement was constitutional. The decision is being appealed. Of course, immigrants in the past helped political machines of both political parties in many of the major cities. Their support was given in return for services provided by the machines, and the process helped assimilate many immigrant groups into the political culture. Modern-day immigrants are unlikely to have the same close relationship with political leadership, but political parties certainly can exploit the opportunity to address their interests in hopes of gaining their support. It is unlikely, however, that the type of patronage that the nineteenth and early twentieth centuries witnessed will arise. Politicians, however, will pay attention to issues that affect new citizens. President George W. Bush and others, for example, were criticized for their support of a path to citizenship for those here illegally. It also is an issue that continues to derail comprehensive reform efforts.

Some proponents of immigration charge that the culture issue is a code for racism.[51] They are concerned that opponents are worried primarily that the white majority is declining and that opponents fear competition with the many ethnic groups emerging as serious social and political forces. Opponents claim that the effects of immigrants on jobs and on public services create divisiveness and pit groups against one another.[52] These efforts create what the opponents of immigration claim is a culture war, but in many ways the opponents themselves provide the fuel for the culture wars through the rhetoric they use to support their positions.

CONTINUING DEBATES: OPENNESS
OR RESTRICTION?

Although there is much disagreement about whether immigration *per se* is a problem, there seems to be consensus that immigration policy needs improvement. Depending upon whether people believe that there is too much or not enough immigration or somewhere in between, views on future policy options range from closing down immigration to encouraging more immigration, with options between the two extremes as well.

Some people argue that immigration should be stopped completely. Pat Buchanan spoke for them when he suggested that the borders of the United States be closed down and that the military be used to enforce the policy. In some instances, he seemed to support a temporary suspension; at other times, he seemed to be suggesting a permanent closure to immigration. His arguments usually focused on preserving the national culture and on preserving jobs for the native born. Congress did pass legislation to secure the border with fences or walls and technology, and the National Guard has been sent to help the Border Patrol do its job. Many critics of militarizing the border claim that the military is not equipped for law enforcement. The terrorist attack of September 11, 2001, however, led to the military being involved in many activities to deal with terrorist activities as well as border security.

Most people recognize that a complete stop to immigration is impractical and maybe impossible even if they are troubled by the degree of immigration at present. Thus, they advocate a moratorium[53] or a reduction.[54] The reasons vary according to the way in which they define the problem. For the most part, advocates of a moratorium or a reduction in immigration believe that the nation needs to catch up with the absorption of those who have already arrived. They also see a moratorium or reduction as an opportunity to consider improvement in immigration policies to deal with the problems they believe immigration has created. Reforms have attempted to address concerns about the numbers of immigrants entering the United States, thus taking some cues from advocates of reductions.

Some of the specific recommendations for limiting immigration suggest that the policy should focus on what needs the country has, especially in job skills. They argue that the majority of immigrants are unskilled and do not help revitalize the economy or support U.S. competitiveness in the global economy.[55] To correct this perceived problem, it is suggested that immigrants be allowed in, based primarily on having skills that will contribute to advancing the economy. Others argue that economic policy, not immigration, is the issue and that the United States needs to align its immigration policy with its trade policies, which focus on opening borders to trade.[56]

Others argue that immigration should focus primarily on people who are committed to becoming U.S. citizens.[57] Applications for citizenship give some indication of the prevalence of commitment to citizenship. After enactment of the Immigration Reform and Control Act of 1986, granting amnesty to illegal aliens who had lived in the United States continuously since January 1, 1982, and providing for restrictions and renewal of green cards allowing employment, applications for citizenship increased. Similarly, when Proposition 187 was being proposed in California, many people applied for naturalization so that they could vote in the election. Naturalizations peaked at 1,046,539 in 2008 but dropped to under 750,000 in 2009. In 2012, 757,434 people were naturalized.[58] The concern of people arguing that citizenship should be the focus is that most debates over immigration take a short-term perspective on the problems and contributions of immigration. The long-term view considers the assimilation of immigrants and their becoming citizens as having positive outcomes because they imply commitment to the system and greater likelihood of learning the language and culture of the United States. Most studies indicate that the issue of language and culture is not nearly as important as many critics of immigration contend. In fact, children of immigrants prefer English and adapt very quickly to American culture.[59] It appears that those groups that come to the United States with little hope or intent of returning to their native lands (e.g., the Vietnamese and Laotians) achieve citizenship and adapt to the culture more quickly, while those who expect to return to their homelands someday are less likely to do so (Central Americans and those from the Caribbean, for example).[60]

Still others contend that the various criteria for determining who can immigrate are not realistic and that immigration should be based on a "first come, first served" basis.[61] People taking this position suggest that some spots should be reserved for family reunification and other criteria, but that the majority of slots should be based on review of applications as they are received. The position harkens back to the ideological basis for immigration, namely, that the country opened its doors to people from around the world primarily because Americans believed that everyone should be given a chance. Proponents of this position contend that other bases for including or excluding immigrants have not worked and should be scrapped for this more rational approach, which does not accept the premises of the proposals at either extreme of the debate.

The arguments over immigration often appear to be driven by anxieties that actually have nothing to do with immigrants.[62] Immigration is easy to exploit as the cause of many of the nation's problems because immigrants are an easily identifiable and usually relatively powerless element of society. The nativist arguments resonate with people who fear what they do not know or understand. Those who suffer economic dislocation or fear poverty and crime find an easy target in immigrants. Immigrant rights groups also often oversimplify the issues and see immigrants as victims in every effort to gain some control over the problems related to immigration. Most observers of immigration policy recognize that some regulation of the flow of immigration is desirable. How to achieve that regulation and how to ensure fairness and humane considerations are at the root of the controversies over immigration policies.

In the 2008 presidential election, Senator Obama called for comprehensive immigration reform, but he did not push it aggressively early in his presidency. In the meantime, a strong advocate of comprehensive reform, Senator Edward Kennedy, died; another strong advocate, Senator John McCain, changed his stance as he faced a very strong anti-immigration candidate in his Republican primary in Arizona. Because the national government failed to act, anti-immigration forces gained support, especially in places like Arizona, where Senate Bill 1070 (SB1070) was passed by the legislature. This law made it a crime to be in the state without legal documents, among other provisions. The author of the legislation, State Senator Russell Pearce, boasted that one purpose of the legislation was to make it so uncomfortable for illegal immigrants that they would leave the state. The courts declared virtually every provision of SB1070 unconstitutional, in part, saying that immigration is a national, not a state, issue. Russell Pearce was recalled in a special election because voters in his district grew weary of his constant anti-immigration efforts. He tried a comeback in 2012 but was soundly defeated.

In 2013, immigration again became a major item on the national policy agenda. A bipartisan group of eight senators crafted proposed comprehensive immigration reform legislation and the Senate passed it, but it was never acted on in the House of Representatives. Instead, the Republican majority in the House crafted a set of guidelines but never actually put them into proposed legislation. President Obama has also outlined his proposals for immigration reform in numerous speeches.

The major differences in reform proposals involve whether immigration reform should be comprehensive or should be done piecemeal. The Senate bill, the Democrats, and President Obama favor a comprehensive approach, while Republicans in the House insist on addressing reform issue by issue in separate pieces of legislation. President Obama's proposal has four major items: to continue efforts to strengthen border security, to enhance efforts to hold employers that hire undocumented workers accountable, to require undocumented immigrants to pay back taxes and a penalty and pass a criminal background check if they pursue citizenship, and to streamline the system for legal immigration. The Senate plan provides more money for border security while the House Republican guidelines insist on border security verification before any other action would be taken. All the proposals call for verifying eligibility for employment by employers using some version of the current E-Verify system. Because the House has not taken action on immigration reform, President Obama decided to act on his own executive authority which further inflamed Republican opposition. In the summer of 2014, a surge of young children crossing the Mexican border created more controversy with each side blaming the other for it. Because of federal law, the children (largely from Central America) must be accorded judicial hearings before being sent back prompting some legislators to propose changing the law to allow immediate removal.

All of the proposals also call for the tweaking of work visas, with special attention paid to a temporary work visa system for scientists, engineers, mathematicians, and people in technology. The proposals also call for temporary work visas for agricultural workers with the House guidelines requiring that something be in place to be sure that they do not displace native workers.

In the Senate bill, Dreamers would be accorded the protections provided under President Obama's executive action discussed earlier. Children under the age of sixteen would be granted a five-year path to citizenship. The House Republican guidelines would allow young people brought here illegally by their parents to gain legal residency if they graduated from college or served in the military but not a path to citizenship.

The president and the Senate bill provide for a path to citizenship for people here illegally. They would be required to learn English, pass a background check, and pay a fine and fees. The House Republican guidelines would not allow a path to citizenship for illegal immigrants, but they could live in the United States legally if they met certain conditions such as criminal background checks, paid back taxes and fines, demonstrated English proficiency, demonstrated understanding of American government, and were able to support themselves and their families.

With the 2014 elections looming at this writing, the prospects for resolving this difference seem remote. Nonetheless, the proposals provide a basis for discussion and future action.

SUMMARY

Immigration policy has been a contentious issue from the founding of the country. The immigration debate revolves around how easily immigrants are assimilated into the society, their impact on the economy and environment, and their effect on politics, culture, and public services. Crime and national security also divide people on immigration. These issues are as important today as they have been historically. Immigration policy will remain a controversial issue for the foreseeable future. It is an emotional issue that does not lend itself to consensus.

 **RESOURCES**

Center for Comparative Immigration Studies: **www.ccis-ucsd.org**

Center for Immigration Studies: **www.cis.org**

Center for Migration Studies: **http://cmsny.org/**

Ellis Island National Monument: **www.ellisisland.org**

Federation for American Immigration Reform: **www.fairus.org**

U.S. Department of Homeland Security: **www.dhs.gov**

Chapter 12

Foreign and Defense Policy: Security and Interests in a Dangerous World

The events of September 11, 2001, brought home to America the realization that retreat to a fortress America, the recurring isolationist approach to foreign policy in American history, is no longer (if it ever had been) a realistic option. The ongoing threat of massive terrorism cast this country into the maelstrom of world conflicts suddenly and to a degree for which the nation was quite unprepared and unwilling to support on a long-term basis. The catastrophic destruction of the World Trade Center was but the most destructive of a number of terrorist attacks on American lives and properties perpetrated in recent years by militant Islamist groups. Some commentators, comparing these attacks to the Japanese assault on Pearl Harbor in 1941, have declared that America has been propelled into World War IV, a conflict that these commentators claim is directed against Western Civilization as we know it.[1] Others disagree that America faces such a direct threat, especially from those opposing American efforts to reshape Iraq, and advocating a withdrawal of American troops from the Middle East. A growing libertarian movement within the Republican Party, led by former Congressman Ron Paul of Texas and his son, Senator Rand Paul of Kentucky, aggressively opposes the projection of U.S. military strength overseas unless the United States is directly threatened or attacked. The Obama administration withdrew American troops from Iraq, as well as announced its withdrawal of all American forces from Afghanistan in November 2013. The administration focused negotiations on a weakening of sanctions against Iran, apparently seeking a diminished assertion of American power in that part of the world and displaying faith in the nation's ability to achieve its goals by persuasion.

The natural borders on the east and west coasts of the United States, provided by two major oceans, together with nonthreatening neighbors on the northern and southern borders, seemed (for much of U.S. history) to insulate the country from the need for active involvement in the affairs and conflicts of the world outside of the Western Hemisphere. Two world wars in the twentieth century did much to puncture belief in such insulation. The **Cold War** with the Soviet Union left the United States feeling uniquely vulnerable to the Soviet's intercontinental thermonuclear capacity (what the aforementioned commentators call World War III).

America experienced a wave of violent assaults on its personnel and property by militant Islamist groups since the 1970s. The wave of assaults (successful and unsuccessful) on American lives and property continued in the aftermath of the September 11, 2001, terrorist attacks through spring 2010. In November 2009, U.S. Army Major Nidal Malik Hasan began randomly shooting personnel at Fort Hood, Texas, while shouting the Muslim cry of "Allah Akbar" (God is great), killing thirteen people and wounding another thirty. On December 25 of that year, Umar Farouk Abdulmutallab boarded a flight to Detroit with a bomb in his underwear. Fortunately, the bomb failed to detonate and merely singed Farouk. In May 2010, Faisal Shahzad parked a van with a homemade bomb inside in Times Square, New York. The bomb failed to detonate; Americans were fortunate again. In each of these incidents, the government initially claimed that the perpetrators were isolated and deranged individuals without ties to external forces. In each case, however, it was established that the perpetrators had direct contact with, and trained with, Al Qaeda forces. These events triggered a debate among America's political and journalist elites as to whether we should consider ourselves in a state of war with an extreme and militant segment of the Islamic world or whether we should regard these events as criminal acts. The Obama administration, concerned with provoking the rest of the vast Muslim world, decided to eschew the terms terrorism, **jihad**, or Islamic extremism and to refer to these acts as "overseas contingency operations." In this spirit, the Obama administration has hoped that its successful locating and killing of Islamist leader Osama bin Laden significantly ameliorated the threat from Al Qaeda, the international terrorist network. This would enable the Obama administration to pursue its primary goal of the transformation of America's domestic economy while reaping the credit for "winning" the "war on terror."

Accordingly, when confronted with a clearly organized Islamist attack on the American embassy in Benghazi, Libya, in 2012 killing the American ambassador and three American Navy Seals, the administration declined to send reinforcements and initially labeled the event as a spontaneous demonstration gotten out of hand caused by a reaction to an obscure video critical of the prophet. This attack, combined with the detonation of two bombs near the finish line at the 2013 Boston Marathon by two terrorists, which killed three and wounded hundreds, served as notice that Islamist militants still posed an existential threat to Americans.

Attorney General Eric Holder, testifying before Congress in May 2010, refused to suggest that the perpetrators of the attacks of 2009 through 2010 might have been motivated by a connection to Al Qaeda. President Obama pursued his belief that he could ameliorate the tensions between the Islamic world and the West by negotiation although he continued to say that all options were on the table, including use of American military power. Meanwhile, the threat of the exercise of American military power became less credible in the context of cuts in the defense budget. Doubts about President Obama's reputation as a strong leader were exacerbated by his lack of response to Russian President Putin's military seizure of the Crimea section of Ukraine in April 2014.

The bombing of Tripoli was the last serious response to the wave of assaults from militant Islamists until 2002 when President Bush mounted an armed offensive aimed at removing the Taliban regime from power in Afghanistan. The Taliban had provided a safe haven for the militant Islamist group, Al Qaeda, which mounted the devastating attack on the World Trade Center in 2001. The World Trade Center had already been the target of a terrorist bombing in 1993. Before a replacement regime could attain legitimacy in Afghanistan, in spring 2003 America launched a preemptive strike (attacking them before they could attack) at Saddam Hussein's Iraqi regime. The war in Iraq, and the entire concept of preemptive war on which it was based, has generated some of the most bitter political controversy in decades, a topic examined in this chapter. As noted already, however, the Obama administration, citing a failure to attain a status of forces agreement with indigenous Iraqi leaders, withdrew all American forces from that country. President Obama had been a strong critic of that war throughout his campaign for the presidency. Meanwhile, President Obama did order a surge of additional troops be sent to Afghanistan to concentrate on what he called "the good war" against the origins of the World Trade Center attack. Critics, however, claimed that he squandered the gains of this surge by announcing a set date for a complete American withdrawal from that country, in effect telling our enemies there that they only had to wait until we left before beginning activity again.

ISSUE BACKGROUND: COMPETING APPROACHES TO FOREIGN POLICY

Realism or Classical Diplomacy

There is a style in the conduct of international diplomacy that characterized relations among European and other Western powers for much of the modern era. This style, based upon a set of assumptions about the nature of the world order and about the nature of humanity, is widely known as **classical diplomacy**. This approach to foreign policy is also known as political realism or power politics. Scholars such as Hans Morgenthau, E. H. Carr, and Kenneth Thompson were leading proponents of this approach.[2] This chapter will show that a perspective different from realism has primarily influenced the foreign policy of the United States in the twentieth century.

The first premise of classical diplomacy is that there are no universally self-evident principles of justice, right and wrong, or truth that nations are morally obligated to pursue. Hence, the national interest is not only a legitimate goal of foreign policy, but, in the view of political realists, the only defensible goal. States function and are morally obligated, in this view, to protect the interests of their societies. Realists point to the widespread public support that has existed for policies that the mainstream West regards as obscene, such as genocide (the systematic slaughter of an entire racially, religiously, or ethnically defined people).[3] Regimes based on widespread public support carried out such genocide not only in World War II, but in the former Cambodia (now called Kampuchea), in the former Yugoslavia, and in Rwanda since World War II. The defiant lack of remorse by Slobodan Milosevic, the former president of Serbia, during his trial in an international tribunal for a policy of ethnic cleansing against Bosnian Muslims, the growing popularity among Islamist militants of using their children as suicide bombers to maximize slaughter and mayhem among civilians, the deliberate starvation and slaughter of tens of thousands of black Sudanese by their militant Arab government, as well as the aforementioned other acts of modern genocide, cast doubt on the assumption that universal principles of justice are self-evident to all reasonable persons. This was underscored by a continuing rebellion in 2013 and 2014 against the Syrian regime of Bashar Assad in which Assad slaughtered thousands of his own people with chemical agents, despite a warning from President Obama that there would be "consequences" for such action. The eventual consequences were economic sanctions and isolation of the Syrian regime.

Because of considerations of geography, demography, resources, and history, each nation develops a set of objective and perceived interests, some of them considered vital, that are unique to that nation. Moreover, the interests of nations naturally come into conflict. Hence, conflict among nations is normal. What is good for some nations logically conflicts with what is in the interests of other nations. The goals of foreign policy to the realist, therefore, ought to be framed in terms of such interests and the costs of protecting them, rather than in terms of abstract principles of justice or universal morality. Thus, some critics of President Obama argue that his stated aim of being universally liked as a "citizen of the world" conflicts with his first duty, to represent and defend his country's national interests. Of course, different members of the elite of any country may define the interests of their country differently. Thus, the Obama administration is less likely than other administrations to perceive an American interest in projecting its military power to other parts of the world.

For example, contrary to realist principles, the American Cold War policy of **containment**, the resistance to any expansion of communist control or influence between World War II and 1990, was based more on the presumption that communism was a bad thing, and the antithesis of many of the fundamental values of the West, than upon any consideration of how much a particular expansion of communist influence affected our national interests. Many realists criticized our involvement in the Vietnam War on the basis that we did not have enough at stake in who controlled the Indochinese Peninsula to justify the costs of keeping South Vietnam in the hands of an anticommunist regime. Similarly, the brutality with which Saddam Hussein treated his Iraqi subjects,

including torture and mass murder, would not for the realist constitute an adequate justification of our invasion of that country unless the invasion could be
justified in terms of American interests. Foreign policy goals, in the realist perspective, can be framed in terms of whether the national interests in question are
achievable and in terms of an analysis of the costs of achieving them in relation
to the benefits to be derived. Thus, the question is not whether we are better off
with Saddam Hussein not in power, defying the international community,
funneling money to terrorist groups, and threatening his neighbors. The question
is whether the benefit to our interests is worth the considerable cost in blood and
treasure to remove his regime (4,489 American lives and 32,021 wounded), a
little more than half the number of troops lost in the first day of the Normandy
invasion in World War II. Some estimates of the wounded ran as high as
100,000. In Afghanistan, the United States suffered 1,834 killed and 11,786
wounded. The aims of foreign policy, to the realist, should not be separated
from consideration of the relative power of the concerned nations and the costs
of achieving one's goals.

Power Politics.   Force, in this classical or realist perspective, is neither moral
nor immoral in itself, but rather an extension of diplomacy intended to pursue
the national interest. Power is a central concept in the realist perspective.[4]
Power is defined here as a relationship between two or more actors such that
the power wielder can get others to do what the power wielder wants them to
do and which they otherwise would not have done. The powerful accomplish
this by manipulating the threat or promise of potential rewards and punishments
to make the others perceive that they would be better off doing what the power
wielder wants. Such use of power is the essence of politics. Thus, leaders of
democratic countries must be prepared to give up some of what they want to
persuade leaders of competing interests to accommodate other goals.

Realists define broadly the resources involved in creating the threat of
rewards or punishments; they may include such things as economic power, the
appeal of one's principles, or the intensity or degree of one's commitment to the
goals in question, as well as military might. Power in the realist perspective is
therefore based in large part on a country's reputation for using its strength in
the pursuit of its interests; a nation that is perceived as relentless in the use of
power to pursue its interests is less likely to have those interests challenged.
Therefore, President Obama's apologies to numerous segments of the world
community for America's alleged sins were widely perceived as conveying an
image of weakness, making it more difficult for America to assert its national
interests. Critics also say that his weakness led to the unimpeded Russian annexation of Crimea from Ukraine in 2014.

Given the natural conflict of interests among nations, politics or the use of
power is inescapable in this perspective. **Diplomacy** or negotiation is not a substitute for the application of power or force, because diplomacy without an
understood ability and willingness to back up one's goals with force or power
becomes equivalent to supplication (begging). Nations, in this view, must be
perceived as willing to use force or power to pursue their interests to the extent

---

POLICY DILEMMAS   The Cost of Involvement in Foreign Affairs

The ubiquitous dilemma in the conduct of foreign affairs is the identification of national interests and the strength or intensity of those interests. This task is complicated by the costs of pursuing the goals of foreign policy, as costs that are normally borne by a reduction in the resources devoted to domestic goals and values. The pursuit of foreign policy goals entails a cost–benefit analysis. Thus, in spring 2014 the United States may have had an interest in the preservation of pro-western independent nation states in eastern Europe, such as in the case of Ukraine. But, not at the cost in blood and treasure of preventing a determined President Putin of Russia from dominating or absorbing that country into a greater Russia empire.

Foreign policy goals do not have the direct impact on people's lives as do domestic policies such as President Obama's Affordable Care Act that cost millions of Americans hundreds of dollars. Hence, while much of the population does not care very much that President Putin defies President Obama's expressed demands without concern for consequences, millions of Americans are angry about the immediate costs of Obamacare.

1.   What are some of the costs borne by the United States in the pursuit of its foreign policy goals in the twenty-first century? How do those costs affect our pursuit of domestic policy goals?

2.   What is the importance of using force on the one hand, versus persuasion on the other, in the pursuit of America's foreign policy goals in the twenty-first century?

---

that the likely benefits of achieving one's goal exceed the costs. This cost–benefit analysis does not include a moral judgment of the inherent goodness or evil of one's opponents. **Foreign policy realists** would therefore agree with British statesman Lord Palmerston (1784–1865) who famously said, "Nations have no permanent friends or allies, they only have permanent interests."

Realists, therefore, are willing to engage in limited war for limited objectives, something with which Americans have traditionally felt uncomfortable, preferring to define conflicts in moral terms. Thus, in the case of the Iraq crisis of 2003, the United States led a movement in the United Nations (U.N.) to pass a number of Security Council Resolutions regarding such concerns as cooperation with the U.N. weapons inspectors, adherence to the no-fly zone over Kurdistan and southern Iraq, and allocation of the revenues from the oil for food program, resolutions that were defiantly ignored or rejected by Saddam Hussein. There was concern that an unwillingness to back up these resolutions with force in the face of that defiance would have left the United States with an image of impotence, rendering it unable to defend its interest in that part of the world. Despite U.S. warnings to give up any pursuance of nuclear weapons or nuclear programs, Kim Jong-un, the aggressive leader of North Korea, has developed a nuclear arsenal and missiles to deliver just such weapons to countries including Pakistan. Similarly, Russian President Vladimir Putin sent his troops, without provocation, to annex the Crimean peninsula of Ukraine in the spring of 2014 with only weak economic sanctions against a half dozen Russians in response.

Spheres of Influence.   Because principles of justice are not universal, the legitimate interests of nations are greater in some parts of the world than in others. Normally, nations have a greater interest in territories contiguous to their borders than in other parts of the world. Hence, in the Monroe Doctrine, the United States proclaimed to the world that it had a vital interest in the politics of the Western Hemisphere. Similarly, near Yalta at the end of World War II, Roosevelt yielded to the claims of the Soviet Union that they had a greater interest in the affairs of Eastern Europe than did the United States. This was not, as critics of the Yalta agreements charge, a case of selling out the freedom of Eastern European people as much as a case of not having as great an interest or a willingness to expend as many resources in shaping the politics of that region as did the Soviets. Similarly, opponents of the second Iraq War argued that the United States did not have enough interests in shaping the character of that country to justify the cost in blood and treasure to achieve that goal. The same argument of **spheres of influence** may be used by Russia regarding the just mentioned annexation of Crimea.

In a reaction against American participation in the Vietnam War, many people identified the lessons of Vietnam as indicating that the United States ought not to attempt to shape the internal politics of other countries as they did in trying to prevent South Vietnam from becoming part of the communist orbit. These lessons were the basis of a scathing critique of U.S. opposition to the pro-Marxist Sandinista regime in Nicaragua during the 1980s. Yet the sphere of influence principle was also used to argue that America had a legitimate interest in the affairs of Central America that it did not have in the affairs of Indochina. After all, an anti-American regime in Central America, able to influence if not subvert other regimes in the region, including Mexico which shares a long, porous border with the United States, could pose a realistic threat to American interests that did not exist from a small, nonindustrialized country in Southeast Asia.

It seemed heartless, or at least ethnocentric, that the United States did not commit blood and treasure to intervene in the mass slaughter between the Hutu and Tutsi tribes in Rwanda in Central Africa in the early 1990s, or the mass slaughter of black Sudanese beginning in 2004 by the Muslim government in Khartoum, while it did commit such resources to halt ethnic cleansing in the former Yugoslavia. Critics of the failure of America to act more decisively to halt the slaughter in Africa have suggested it was because the victims were black. Yet realists make the argument that the United States had more interests at stake in the affairs of central Europe, a region that provided the spark to ignite the two world wars in the twentieth century, than it did in Rwanda or the Sudan. Such a conclusion would be an implementation of the concept of spheres of influence as opposed to the idealist conception that America should fight injustice with equal vigor wherever it occurs. The spheres of influence argument could also be used to add to the criticism of U.S. efforts to impose a multidenominational, pro-Western government in Iraq.

The concept of spheres of influence provides a criterion for rationing the expenditure of scarce resources. Political realists argue that if the United States appointed itself as a world police force or guardian of international justice, it would have to raise and support a considerably expanded defense and military establishment. By confining efforts to the protection of one's own vital interests, the expenditure of resources becomes more manageable. George W. Bush may have been articulating this position in the 2000 presidential campaign when he argued against our assuming the role of the world's policeman. He was reacting to the unsuccessful insertion of our military forces in Somalia during the Clinton administration. The apparent inconsistency between this position and his later action in Iraq may be explained for some by the enhanced awareness of the terrorist threat after the events of September 11, 2001.

This kind of realism in Bush's 2000 position is not equivalent to the isolationist sentiment of the interwar period (between the two world wars), which asserted that events outside of our borders were none of our concern. The spheres of influence concept acknowledges American vital interests at stake in the Western Hemisphere and Western Europe, among other places. Due to modern technology, however, U.S. interests are no longer defined only geographically. The affairs of an economic superpower such as Japan may have a serious economic impact on Americans.

The Balance of Power

Another major concept of this realist, or power politics, approach to foreign policy is that of the **balance of power**. The key principle of this concept is that no one power or coalition of powers should be allowed to gain such dominating power as to be able to dictate terms of the relationships among nations without having to compromise its interests with the demands of competing interests. **Hegemony** designates a situation in which one state so dominates other states that it may dictate the terms of the relationship between them without the need to compromise its interests. When one nation acquires hegemonic power over other nations, the other nations lose their ability to protect the vital interests of their citizens.

Nations that pursue the balance of power strategy do so by shifting alliances so that one power always allies with the weaker of competing states or alliances. If a nation joined the stronger alliance, once that alliance eliminated the competing weaker alliance, the strongest power in the victorious alliance would have hegemonic power. By joining the weaker alliance or power, and thereby increasing the strength of the weaker forces or diminishing the strength of the strongest power, the balancing nation could force the strongest power in the stronger alliance to bargain and come to terms with competing powers and interests.[5] The idea is to check the imposition of the goals and values of the strongest and potentially hegemonic powers by establishing equilibrium among the nations.[6] Consistency in the balance of power strategy does not mean you always either support or oppose a given regime. Thus, in the first Gulf War, the United States sided with Kuwait against Saddam Hussein to prevent Iraqi hegemony in the region, even though it had sided with Hussein's regime in its earlier war against Iran when it perceived the latter country was threatening to achieve hegemony in the region.

The roles of Britain and eventually the United States in World War I were an exercise in balance of power politics with the goal of checking Germany's Second Reich under Kaiser Wilhelm from obtaining a hegemonic domination of Western Europe. Thus, Professor Nicholas Spykman, a staunch political realist, wrote that "Twice in one generation we have come to the aid of Great Britain in order that the small offshore island might not have to face a single gigantic state in control of the opposite coast of the mainland."[7] Of course, U.S. idealists did not see it that way. Instead, they defined the American mission in apocalyptic and idealistic terms, such as "the war to end all wars" and "saving the world for democracy." The balancing strategy epitomizes classical diplomacy in that normative policy considerations are irrelevant and power considerations are everything.

Deterrence.   As opposed to the strategy of avoiding aggressive action by potential foes by reconciling differences and accommodating grievances by negotiation, realists avoid attacks on their vital interests with a strategy known as **deterrence**. Deterrence is a strategy based purely on power politics considerations without concern for the relative merits or justice of the respective policy goals. This strategy involves the possession of sufficient and varied power to survive the best first strike by a potential foe with enough power and willingness to inflict unacceptable damage on such an attacker.

There are psychological dimensions to the strategy of deterrence. The implied threat of the use of power or force against the potential foe must be credible. That is, the potential foe must believe in one's willingness to actually use the deterring force. The key here is to cultivate a reputation for a strong and certain response to attacks on or even threats to our vital interests. Thus, the U.S. Cold War strategy of relying on masssive nuclear power to deter Soviet encroachment on its vital interests did not deter the Soviets from numerous encroachments on lesser interests, because they did not believe in U.S. willingness to launch a thermonuclear strike and risk nuclear retaliation for any interest short of the very survival of our country. Moreover, the deterrent effect of the undeniably most powerful U.S. armed forces may have been diluted had we been unwilling to exercise force in Iraq without the approval of our reluctant allies. After Saddam's humiliating capture in a hole in the ground, Libyan strongman Kaddafi abandoned his earlier defiance of the United States and United Nations and voluntarily surrendered his nuclear arms program to Western weapons inspectors. When a political leader such as President Obama threatens "consequences" on Syrian President Assad if he used his chemical weapons and then does nothing when Assad does in fact slaughter thousands of civilians with gas as occurred in 2013, Obama's reputation for strength and his consequent ability to influence behavior and events is weakened.

The second psychological dimension is the question of what damage the leadership of a potential foe considers unacceptable. Authoritarian leaders in some countries have shown a willingness to accept a considerable amount of misery and even death among large segments of their citizenry in order to pursue their policy goals. Both Stalin and the rulers of communist China were willing to accept massive starvation in order to collectivize agriculture. Saddam Hussein of Iraq was willing to accept considerable deprivation among his people to ride out U.N. sanctions and protect his freedom to pursue weapons programs. Iran's Prime Minister Rafsanjani said in 2007 that the loss of two-thirds of ordinary Iranians would be an acceptable price to pay for the extermination of all of Israel in a nuclear exchange, while the Ayatollah Khomeini, the founder of the Iranian Islamic Republic, declared that "We do not worship Iran. We worship Allah … I say let this land go up in smoke …" More recently, Bashar Assad brutally slaughtered thousands of his people in Syria in order to put down a rebellion. These leaders have provisions meaning that they could survive even nuclear retaliation against their countries. There is therefore a serious question as to whether the prospect of massive losses among their populations would be enough to deter such leaders. Deterrence thus presumes a certain level of rationality among the leaders of potentially hostile states.

Nevertheless, deterrence has a record. Despite an announced desire to do so, the Soviet Union never attacked the West directly during the Cold War, the longest period in modern history without a general war in the West. Throughout the Cold War period, however, many American idealists criticized the American arms buildup to implement the deterrence strategy. On the other hand, the strategy used between 1919 and 1939 to avoid future wars was negotiation unsupported by the credible threat of power, combined with mutually negotiated disarmament.[8] World War II attests to the failure of this latter strategy.

The American Style in Foreign Policy: Wilsonian Idealism

The previous discussion of classical diplomacy or power politics implicitly contrasted that approach to foreign policy with a different American style. Scholars characterize that American style as **idealism**. Because President Woodrow Wilson's Fourteen Points speech to Congress in 1918, in which he proposed the League of Nations, epitomized this approach, it is often called **Wilsonian idealism**. Americans have been more prone to exercise the idealist style in foreign policy than other Western nations; however, the United States has not been consistent in that regard and at times has exercised hardheaded realism in making foreign policy. The Obama administration has epitomized the idealist approach in its repeated offers to negotiate with its implacable enemies without preconditions and without the implicit threat of force.

Universal Justice and the Nuremberg Principle

To the idealist perspective, the pursuit of the national interest is an inadequate justification for resorting to the horrors of armed conflict. There are, for idealists, knowable and universal principles of justice over and above the laws and policies of any particular state. Hence, the governments and people of nation-states can be held accountable for the protection and pursuit of those principles. Thus, the leadership and even the population of the sovereign nations of the world are morally obligated to disregard and disobey the laws and policies of their countries to the extent that these laws and policies violate these knowable principles of justice. This position is sometimes called the **Nuremberg principle**, because without the assumption of such knowable universal principles of morality and justice, the war crimes trials of top Nazi leadership in Nuremberg, Germany, would have made no sense. The Nazi elites, after all, were obeying the laws and orders of their lawful superiors in their nation-state.

The Universal Harmony of Interests. With this assumption of a knowable universal good, idealists view human nature as essentially good and cooperative. Most people, therefore, share basic values (health, prosperity, family). President George W. Bush, in defense of his policy to import democracy to Iraq, claimed that given the choice, any man would choose freedom. The world, therefore, possesses a **universal harmony of interests** marred only by the selfish motives of a small group of unaccountable rulers. Thus, in their concern for just treatment of Muslims, American leaders reassured the American public in the wake of the attacks on the World Trade Center and Pentagon of September 11, 2001, that these events were the work of a few extremists who distort Muslim principles and that the vast multitudes of ordinary people in the Muslim world would never condone such attacks. Thus, following the events of September 11, students at a number of major universities, for example at the University of North Carolina, were required to read accounts of Islam that treated it as an essentially peace-loving faith. In positing the clear distinction between the allegedly selfish and out-of-touch rulers and their ordinary masses, the idealist perspective rejects the claim of realist scholars, like Harvard's late Samuel Huntington, that Islamic civilization has been based upon and has pursued values and goals in direct conflict with the West for 1,400 years, and that the Muslim masses increasingly see the West as "materialistic, corrupt, decadent and immoral."[9]

Because of this universal harmony of interests, calm reasoning or negotiation can generally resolve conflicts, and war is usually wrong and unnecessary. When war becomes unavoidable, however, it becomes a crusade against these selfish and autocratic rulers. War is never justified in terms of a pursuit of the national interests alone, but only as a moral crusade. President Bush, in his 2002 State of the Union speech, defined conflict in such moral terms when he characterized Iran, Iraq, and North Korea—nations whose professed aims and whose potential weaponry render them a threat to the vital interests of the United States—as "the axis of evil." When one defines conflicts in such normative terms, the goals of the utilization of force frequently become unconditional surrender or the total destruction of one's opponents. After all, one does not bargain and compromise with pure evil. When it was obvious by the fall of 1918, following America's 1917 entry into World War I, that Germany would be unable to obtain the hegemony that it sought over Europe, Germany sought a negotiated peace. The American president, however, insisted upon an unconditional surrender involving the abdication of the "evil" Kaiser Wilhelm and the creation of a democratic republic completely incongruent with the German culture and experience. The war dragged on for another year before the capitulation of the Second Reich. The inevitable failure of the Weimar Republic that followed created a power vacuum in Central Europe that would be filled by Hitler's Third Reich some fourteen years later.

Because they see principles of justice as universal, idealists reject the premise of the spheres of influence principle of classical diplomacy. Thus, to the idealist, this assumption of universal justice is that the same moral imperatives that led to our intervention in the former Yugoslavia against the Serbian "ethnic cleansing" should have led to our intervention in the mass slaughter in Rwanda or the Sudan. Evil is evil, whether it occurs in Central Europe or in Africa.

Diplomacy, Force, and American Optimism

In the American idealist perspective, diplomacy is an alternative to the use of force. Because people are essentially cooperative by nature and motivated by the same basic values, mutual reasoning and persuasion can resolve differences among peoples. From the Kellogg-Briand Pact of 1928 that renounced war as an instrument of national policy and the mobilization of antiwar sentiment by Charles Lindbergh and others on the eve of World War II, to the mobilized opposition to the Vietnam War, our entry into the 1991 Gulf War, the U.S. intervention in the former Yugoslavia, and the war in Iraq in the first decades of the twenty-first century, Americans have been reluctant to commit military force for any purpose short of the survival of the country. The disappointing outcome of U.S. intervention in the Vietnam War reinforced this reluctance to the point where American hesitancy to use force has sometimes been called the Vietnam syndrome. President Obama's oft-pronounced willingness in his presidential campaign to sit down and talk without preconditions with the leaders of the most aggressively anti-American countries in the world, such as the Islamic Republic of Iran and the government of North Korea, epitomizes this belief that talks unsupported by power can productively resolve issues with such countries that do not share our most fundamental values. This faith in the ability to resolve conflict with reasoned negotiation downplays the significance of conflicts of interest. American leaders, epitomized by President Obama in dealing with Iran, posit a choice between force and diplomacy. Realists, however, would argue that effective diplomacy cannot be divorced from the threat of force.

This persisting faith in diplomacy rests upon the deep-seated American faith that all conflicts are ultimately resolvable by reasoned negotiation. Former Secretary of State Henry Kissinger has written of the American confidence in the bargaining process in which our diplomats view themselves as mediators between Washington and the country with which they are negotiating.[10] All of this presumes that there is a scenario to which all parties, given their values and goals, can plausibly agree. For example, it will be shown that advocates of the Middle East peace process, in which America has been so heavily engaged, assume that all of the major parties ultimately would be satisfied with a two-state solution. This perspective also assumes that the conflict is really about borders rather than mutual acceptance by Palestinians and Israelis of the right of the other to exist. Yet, it is doubtful that all relevant parties would agree to such an outcome regardless of the borders.

Besides divorcing diplomacy from power, idealists tend to divorce the formulation of foreign policy goals from the costs and possibilities of achieving them. Our Cold War goal of containment, the policy of resisting any further encroachment of governments labeled communist in whatever form or context, framed foreign policy in terms of the moral presumption that communism was a bad thing. Although, other things being equal, the United States may have been better off with a non-communist government in place in a given country than an avowedly communist one, it was not clear that all regimes labeled communist posed an equal threat to American interests. Therefore, the costs of preventing the expansion of a particular communist regime may or may not have been justified in terms of those interests.

Moreover, aside from considerations of cost, it is not clear that all foreign policy goals are ultimately achievable. Regardless of the desirability of having a stable and legitimate noncommunist and pro-Western government ruling South Vietnam, knowledge of the history of Vietnamese nationalism suggests that goal may never have been achievable.

This disposition to define foreign policy goals independently of the costs and possibility of achieving them is a result of defining international conflict in terms of the pursuit of some conception of universal justice, rather than in terms of the national interests. American idealists have tended to seek an alternative to power politics and to define military conflict as "a holy crusade against evil incarnate ... holy wars of 'unconditional surrender' against solitary infidels ..."[11]

Collective Security and Institutional Solutions to World Conflict

Idealists reject the balance of power strategy for deterring aggressive behavior and its underlying premise that war is a normal instrument of policy. Among the institutional means of preventing conflict offered by idealists is the principle of **collective security**. This system assumes that the preponderance of states in the world share values of peaceful coexistence and wish to prevent aggression by one state on another. It assumes that the states in the system will subordinate their particular national interests to the collective good. It further assumes that there is agreement among the states as to the status quo that is to be preserved. It also assumes there is agreement about what constitutes an act of aggression.[12] Given that the term is normative (the other fellow's military action is aggression; mine is self-defense), identifying acts of aggression could be a problem. Is an act of violence terrorism, aggression, self-defense, or an act of war? Such regional alliances as the North Atlantic Treaty Organization (NATO) and the Southeast Asia Treaty Organization (SEATO) are examples of the principle of collective security, where each participant declares that an attack on one is an attack on all. With the end of the Cold War, the purpose and future of such collective security arrangements has been rendered uncertain. The September 11 attacks on the United States did not bring a collective security response from the other NATO members. Surveys showed that a majority of the European populace believed the claim that attacks were carried out by Americans to justify the U.S. attack on Iraq and Afghanistan or by the Israeli Mossad. Indeed, a book making this claim was the best-selling book in France for part of 2007.

One of the critiques of the second Bush administration's attack on Iraq has been that it was virtually an act of **unilateralism**, policies undertaken without first obtaining political and material support from most major allies. The converse concept, **multilateralism**, means that serious foreign policies ought to be implemented in concert with and presumably with the blessing of one's major allies. If one cannot obtain the cooperation of major allies for a foreign policy operation, the policy may lack justification according to widely accepted standards of international justice and morality. Critics of multilateralism claim it gives other countries a veto over our foreign policy options. Unilateralism implies that a country is acting according to its own narrow (and, by implication, selfish) conception of its national interests, virtually the epitome of classic realism. Indeed, the very concept of **sovereignty** implies that a nation-state should be able to define its own national interests. President Bush was criticized for launching the attack on Iraq without getting U.N. approval and especially without the approval or cooperation of France and Germany. Defenders of the war in Iraq point out that France and Germany each imported a substantial share of their oil from Iraq and that these governments had special arrangements for obtaining Iraqi oil that substantially enriched the leadership of these three countries. Then-President Jacques Chirac reportedly received substantial sums of money from the Iraqi oil for food program, giving him and France a particular interest in preserving Saddam's regime.[13] The United States, by contrast, gets most of its imported petroleum from Mexico, Canada, and Venezuela. Hence, the lack of cooperation on Iraq between the United States and its allies stems largely from the fact that their interests diverged. Unilateralism is based on the principle that each nation is responsible for defining and acting to preserve its own national interests, the essence of the realist or classical style in foreign policy.

Policymakers in the American idealist tradition have thus often sought an alternative to what they regard as the corrupt power politics of classical diplomacy. We will now turn to how the formulation and implementation of major foreign policies in the post–World War II world reflected these assumptions and dispositions and how these policies differ from the classical style of diplomacy.

POLICY PAST AND PRESENT: COLD WAR, CONTAINMENT, AND AFTER

The alliance of the United States and the Soviet Union quickly fell apart at the close of World War II, when the Soviets engineered the installation of regimes in Eastern and Central Europe hostile to the West and its values. What Winston Churchill called the "**iron curtain**" descended across Europe, separating the democratic states of Western Europe from these Soviet puppet regimes united in a collective security arrangement called the Warsaw Pact. Meanwhile, the Western democracies formed their own collective security arrangement, the North Atlantic Treaty Organization (NATO).

This arrangement seemed necessary in light of the failure of the collective security provisions of the newly established United Nations. Collective security in the United Nations depended upon the unanimous agreement of the great powers (as noted earlier in the discussion of collective security). The effective veto power of the Soviet Union over decisions of the U.N. Security Council meant that organization could not mobilize a U.N. response to Soviet aggression.

The success of the communist revolution in China and other parts of Asia did not seem initially in the early postwar era to alter the apparent bipolar nature of the postwar world order. The essential nature of that order was perceived in the West as the freedom-loving, democratic states of the West threatened by a monolithic bloc of communist nations directed from the Kremlin in the Soviet Union.

The reality of the Chinese–Soviet split and the emergence of a wave of newly independent nations in Africa and Asia in the 1950s and 1960s following the breakup of European-dominated imperialistic empires challenged this perception of a bipolar world. These newly emergent states, however, appeared to many Americans as a similarly monolithic third world independent of the communist and noncommunist blocs of nations.

Nevertheless, the United States viewed the postwar world as dominated by the threat of the aggressive communist bloc of nations to the security of the democratic West. Although ideological tension between the putatively capitalist West and what the Soviets called communism goes back to the Bolshevik Revolution of 1917, these ideological stances were more of a justification for action in pursuit of national interests than a cause of conflict. The ideological conflict, however, took on a life of its own once the Cold War became a reality.[14] Fear of communist expansion and assaults on the vital interests of Western nations was not unrealistic in this early Cold War period. Aggressive action by communist bloc nations did occur (for example, the invasion of South Korea by its northern neighbor in 1950), as did instances of Soviet-directed espionage and undermining of noncommunist regimes. However, this bipolar view of the world dominated all other interests and became normatively defined as a struggle against what President Ronald Reagan called "the evil empire."

It was clear that the publics of the West were not ready to undertake military action to wrest control of the communist bloc nations from the Soviets, especially when it became clear that the Soviet Union had acquired the capability to manufacture and deliver nuclear weapons. The alternative adopted as the defining principle of American foreign policy during the Cold War was what George Kennan, a diplomat in the U.S. embassy in the Soviet Union, called containment.[15] Kennan and those who thought like him believed that the Soviet Union was going to be an aggressively expansive power, a conclusion reinforced by Soviet leader Joseph Stalin's speech in February 1946, in which he discussed "the inevitability of conflict with capitalist powers."[16] The essence of the concept of containment was that the United States would act to resist the expansion of the influence of communist powers over previously noncommunist powers. The policy glossed over the distinctions among the nation-states in each of these broad categories. Clearly, some structures bearing the label communist posed a very different level of threat to American interests than other such structures.

Moreover, noncommunist states varied greatly with respect to whether they supported or challenged American interests. The United States supported some very authoritarian and unsavory regimes during the Cold War because such regimes identified themselves as being anticommunist. For example, it supported a military junta in Greece headed by an autocratic Colonel Papadopoulos because he replaced the elected previous Greek head of government who was a leftist too closely associated with a Marxist point of view. This simplistic division of the world into the good-guy capitalists and the bad-guy communists reflects a characteristically American moralistic perspective that ignores the national interest in particular cases. Thus, although the Soviet Union collapsed in 1989, under President Vladimir Putin (president from 2000 to 2008 and again from 2012 to present), a former KGB agent, Russia regressed into a new authoritarianism that pursued policies frequently in conflict with the West. Especially troublesome was his announced intention in 2013 to reassemble the Russian empire as manifested in the Soviet Union.

The war in Korea that began when the North Korean regime invaded the South in 1950 was a classic implementation of the principle of containment. There was little or no discussion of how communist control of the Korean peninsula would affect American interests, other than to invoke the Munich analogy, referring to the infamous appeasement of Adolf Hitler on the eve of World War II. **Appeasement** means accommodating the announced grievances of aggressive leaders in the hope that they will then abandon their aggressive behavior. At Munich, British Prime Minister Neville Chamberlain gave Hitler the Sudetenland, the German-speaking part of Czechoslovakia, in return for empty promises of peace analogous to acquiescence to Russian President Putin's seizure of the Russian speaking segment of Ukraine in 2014. The analogy presumes that Europe under the control of the Nazi war machine posed no greater threat to American interests than the Korean peninsula under the control of the less-modernized North. The American effort was successful in saving the noncommunist status of South Korea, because its military had a legitimate political system to defend. That was not the case in the next major American military commitment in Vietnam.

The Failure of Containment in Vietnam

The success of Ho Chi Minh in gaining control of first the government of the North and the support of much of the population of the South was that he co-opted the strong nationalist and anti-imperialist passion among the Vietnamese people for his political and communist purposes.[17] Indeed, the success of the Communist movement in Southeast Asia was proportional to its ability to become identified with the struggle for national independence.[18] While we perceived the struggle there as between the yoke of communist oppression and the freedom of the noncommunist world, many Vietnamese saw the struggle as between Western imperialism and national liberation.

The Leninist modifications of Marxism in fact offered an ideal ideological vehicle for mobilizing movements of national liberation. Lenin explained the failure of capitalism to collapse as Marx predicted by **imperialism**. Imperialism, he argued, gave capitalism artificial life by providing cheap foreign raw materials and captive markets to siphon off the surplus value that Marx predicted would bring down capitalism. It was therefore not hard to combine a passion for Marxism–Leninism with a nationalist opposition to Western colonialism. In this way, Ho Chi Minh was able to co-opt the Vietnamese nationalist front, the Viet Minh, for the goal of a communist dictatorship. Because it identified Ho Chi Minh as a communist, the United States financed and supported a French invasion of Indochina to resume French colonial control after the war. When the French armies were defeated, the United States gradually assumed the role of fighting the Viet Minh. Many of the Vietnamese, however, saw our role as a defense of Western colonial control of their homeland.

At that point in history, Western imperialism was not a defensible system. Because much of the native population perceived South Vietnam as an instrument of Western colonialism, it lacked internal legitimacy. Our military can certainly defend a sovereign, legitimate government, but it cannot as readily create one. This may also speak to America's difficulty in creating a stable post–Saddam Hussein regime in Iraq, and the goal of a pro-Western South Vietnam was possibly never achievable.

The realists' position that some goals are unachievable seems to be supported by the frustrating outcome of American policy in Vietnam, the loss of South Vietnam to the North in the mid-1970s.

The Search for a Comprehensive Peace in Palestine

Foreign policy idealism appears also in the active engagement of the United States on several occasions, including the 2013 pressure by the Obama administration on the Israelis to sacrifice land to lure the Palestinians to the "peace table" to broker a comprehensive peace agreement between the state of Israel, the various Arab and Muslim countries in the area, and the various groups that support the nationalist aspirations of the people known as the Palestinians. From the active role played by President Carter to engineer a peace agreement between Israel and Egypt, and the intense effort by President Clinton in 2000 to broker a comprehensive settlement between Israel and the Palestinian Authority (PA) represented by the late Yasser Arafat, to the U.S.-sponsored conference in Annapolis in November 2007, the United States continues to expend considerable diplomatic capital on this effort. President Obama has further pursued this elusive goal with the appointment of Dennis Ross and former Senator George Mitchell as permanent negotiators followed by the direct involvement of Secretary of State Kerry in 2013 for an Israeli–Arab peace process, based upon the two-state resolution (separate states of Israel and Palestine peacefully coexisting side by side). This faith in a negotiated comprehensive settlement led to Secretary Kerry jetting back to the Middle East in January 2014 with a proposal to secure an Israeli withdrawal from the **West Bank** secured by a ten-year Israeli military presence on the West Bank. PA president Mahmoud Abbas has firmly declared that no Jews should be permitted in a new Palestinian state.

This continued American effort is justified by the recognition of having important American interests in the region, by the presumption that a settlement is desired by both parties and is possible, and by an American disposition to end violence and correct perceived injustices throughout the world. Furthermore, the ongoing conflict between the Palestinians and Israel is perceived by President Obama as a major obstacle to the goal of reaching out for friendlier relations with the Muslim world, a goal clearly stated in a speech from Cairo early in his presidency.

POLICY EVALUATION: REALISM VERSUS IDEALISM IN THE MIDDLE EAST

The contemporary foreign policy challenges that stem from American policy in the Middle East particularly involve the conflict between Israel and the Palestinians, the politics of oil, and the terrorism directed at the United States and its allies. Realism and idealism seem intertwined in the policies of the United States toward the region.

America perceives that it has several important interests at stake in the region, interests that could be threatened by an eruption of the tension into a general conflict. These interests include access for the United States and its Western allies to the world's largest proven reserves of crude petroleum; hence, it feels the need to maintain a working relationship with those Arab and Muslim states in the area that control those reserves. Actually, our European and Japanese allies are even more dependent on Middle East oil than the United States is, but the United States has an interest in the health of their economies. Secondly, the Middle East is geographically at a strategic crossroads in the world (see Map 12.1). It therefore is to America's benefit to have a reliable ally who can provide logistical support for American military forces, such as facilities to land and refuel planes, store supplies, dock ships, and give liberty to crews, as well as to share intelligence about movements and forces in the area that affect our interests. For example, the United States used bases in Saudi Arabia during the Gulf War of 1991. Middle East policy, then, tests the limits of classical diplomacy and of foreign policy idealism. The American pursuit of peace (the absence of open warfare) in the area may be in conflict with the American interest in preventing the vigorously anti-American regime in Iran from becoming a nuclear power, which would give Iran hegemonic control over other states in the region. As of fall 2013, the United States (through Secretary of State Kerry) had engineered an agreement with Iran to loosen sanctions on that country while allowing the continued enrichment of uranium, apparently in the belief that Iran could be persuaded to voluntarily abandon its decades old quest for a nuclear weapon. In return for America's relaxation of sanctions against them, the Iranians agreed to slow the enriching of uranium, an easily reversible action. The United States has apparently fallen back to the goal of containing a nuclear Iran. Containment, however, assumes a degree of rationality on the part of the leaders of the country being contained, an assumption that many feel is not present in the Iranian Mullahs.

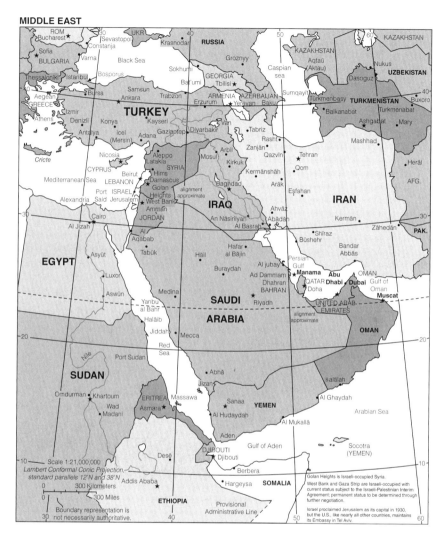

MIDDLE EAST

M A P 12.1 Nations of the Middle East

© 2009 Cengage Learning®

An Israeli attack on Iranian nuclear facilities may soon be the only way to prevent Iran from getting the bomb, which is an option strongly opposed by the United States but favored by other Gulf states, such as the Saudis fearful of a hegemonic Iran. Many people feel that such an attack would lead to the outbreak of general war in the region.

The Emerging Threat of Iran's Nuclear Ambitions

American interests have been threatened in recent years by the increased radicalization of the Islamic regime governing Iran, while that regime appears to be acquiring the ability to deliver nuclear armed missiles in the near future.

Former Iranian President Mahmoud Ahmadinejad asserted his intention to "wipe Israel off the map" and claimed to envision a possible world without the United States. Claiming to be driven by an eschatological vision of a world dominated by the Shiite version of Islam, the Iranian Mullahs threaten to establish Iranian hegemony over the entire Middle East region, while the Iranian regime remains militantly hostile to the West and the values it entails. The election of a new president in Iran in 2013 brought hope to the minds of some that the new president signaled a more moderate regime in Iran. Others were skeptical that the new president was actually different from his predecessor. If Iran is allowed to acquire a nuclear capability, Western interests and the very survival of America's formerly close ally Israel will be in grave jeopardy.

This situation has caused some speculation about a possible military strike to destroy or at least delay Iran's capability to acquire usable nuclear weapons.[19] The total elimination of all of Iran's nuclear operations is apparently unfeasible; however, some argue that key links in the chain needed to produce the weapon could be put out of commission for a period of time. It is rumored that Israel has been actively training for such an operation. Such a strike would fall under the concept of preemption discussed later with reference to the second Iraq War. In an effort to slow up Iran's drive to nuclear capability, a computer virus, reportedly developed by Israelis, invaded computers used in Iran's nuclear program in October 2010.

Oil, U.S. Foreign Policy, and the Middle East

The idealist position assumes that there is a just and legitimate Palestinian **nationalism** and a just and legitimate Israeli nationalism. Under this assumption, the goal of a peace process is a Palestinian state that would coexist with the Jewish state of Israel, and this goal can be achieved by trading for peace land that Israel seized in the 1967 war. Therefore, efforts to broker peace presume that the issue is where to draw the borders between a Jewish and a Palestinian state. These efforts further presume that there is some scenario or outcome to which all contending parties might conceivably agree. This presumption was dealt a serious blow at the Annapolis Conference of November 2007, when Israeli Prime Minister Olmert declared that Arab recognition of Israel as a Jewish state is a prerequisite for any further concessions. All of the Arab leaders immediately and unequivocally responded that they would never consider such recognition. Together with their insistence on a right of return for some six million descendents of the Palestinian refugees which would undermine the Jewish character of Israel which, after all, was the whole point of the Zionist enterprise. This "peace process" presumes that the preservation of a Jewish-free East Jerusalem could be the foundation of a Palestinian state, which could lead to the end of the Israeli–Palestinian conflict. Yet the Arab leaders have been repeatedly saying for the past sixty years that they are not interested in any Jewish state living peacefully with Israel. This illustrates the American refusal to conclude that there is no possible scenario for a settlement of the dispute. The peace talks aggressively pursued by Secretary of State Kerry in the spring of 2014 broke down again as PA

President Abbas reiterated his refusal to consider granting Israel the right to exist as a Jewish state. Other Arab leaders also have not backed off from their firm commitment to the extermination of Israel as a Zionist regime.

The Obama administration operates under the apparent assumption that if Israel makes enough concessions to the Arabs, such as giving them more land or in unilaterally disarming themselves (as in Obama's push in spring 2010 to pressure Israel to dismantle its nuclear capability under the terms of the Nuclear Non-Proliferation Treaty), that the Arabs would agree to live peacefully with Israel. This assumption by the Obama administration was illustrated by its publicly expressed anger in May 2010 at Israel's plans to build apartments in a Jewish neighborhood in East Jerusalem, because the Arabs insist that the entire eastern and holy parts of Jerusalem be reserved as the capital of a future Palestinian state. These strained relations were further manifested in a lengthy and angry phone call by former Secretary of State Clinton to Israeli Prime Minister Netanyahu that took on the nature of a scolding.

This strained relation was further manifested and magnified by America's public neutrality over an anti-Israeli group (HHI, operating out of Turkey with ties to Al Qaeda) that attempted to break a blockade of **Gaza** in June 2010. Blockades are an accepted tactic under the rules of war. Lincoln's blockade of the American South probably hastened the victory of the Union in the Civil War; America blockaded German and Japanese ports in World War II; and John F. Kennedy's blockade of Cuba in the 1960s resolved the "missile crisis." The Israeli blockade is intended to separate out materials (e.g., arms and weapons) that could be used in that war. After the separation of potential war materials, hundreds of thousands of pounds of humanitarian aid (mostly food and medicine) was delivered by Israel to Gaza in the first half of 2010.

The value at stake here is Western access to the oil reserves of the Middle East. How an American-brokered settlement would enhance that access or whether the continued tension between the parties would impair that access is a key unanswered question. The Arab world has sold oil to the West since the value of that resource became manifest. This has occurred despite the fact that the 1,400-year history of relations between the Muslim world and the West has been one of tension.[20]

Moreover, supporters of Israel argue that the United States has an interest in the preservation of the one nation in that part of the world that is democratic and has been consistently pro-Western. With the possible exception of Iraq, the Arab world has yet to produce a single transition to democracy, despite waves of such transitions in other parts of the world. America, partly out of a feeling of kinship to a Western-style democracy, partly out of sympathy for a nation born out of the Holocaust, and partly out of the domestic power of the American Jewish community, has felt obliged to offer considerable financial support to the beleaguered state of Israel, without which that nation could not survive. American financial support of Israel is entirely military aid which is mostly spent on U.S. arms providing thousands of American jobs in the defense industries. Moreover, America gets more intelligence from Israel than it gets from the CIA and NSA combined.

This support angers the Muslim world, which refers to the establishment of the Jewish state as the *nakba* (catastrophe), hardly an orientation implying either recognition of or a propensity to live peacefully with that state.

Meanwhile, Israel has come under almost universal condemnation from elites throughout the Western world. There is a growing and increasingly aggressive segment of American society that argues that it is not in America's interest to continue its level of support for Israel. Indeed when **Hamas** launched a missile attack on Jerusalem and Tel Aviv in July, 2014, Israel mobilized for a retaliatory strike against Gaza. One of the foreign policy advisors in the Obama foreign policy team blamed the escalated tensions on Israel for continuing to "occupy" the disputed West Bank. Another of President Obama's foreign policy team, Samantha Powers, advocated using the American military to drive the Israelis out of the territories and behind the 1947–1967 borders. This segment of our society, which is joined by most of the leadership of other Western societies, characterizes Israel as an oppressive society that is largely to blame for the tensions in the Middle East and is therefore a major threat to peace in the region. They argue that a disproportionately strong Israeli lobby (AIPAC, or the American–Israeli Political Action Committee) distorts American foreign policy to serve Israeli interests at the expense of American interests.[21]

Critics of the anti-Israel perspective argue that it exaggerates the influence of AIPAC, which cannot even get the United States to recognize Israel's capital of Jerusalem and move its embassy there accordingly. Mainly, they argue that the interests of America and Israel are largely compatible and aligned against antidemocratic, aggressive regimes, especially aggressive Islamist movements. Yet, the anti-Israeli chorus continues to be strong. Leaders of the EU have argued for ending European investment in Israel and for a boycott of Israeli products.

Palestinian Nationalism

The question for American interests in the area is what can the American government do to reduce the likelihood of renewed war? It is assumed by many that America also has a realist or pragmatic interest in the survival of the pro-American state of Israel within the bounds of acceptable costs. Yet American pressure on Israel to make unilateral concessions (such as the American pressure in 2013 to release over a hundred violent terrorists from Israeli prisons), rather than produce a settlement, may likely increase the odds of war or at least of continued violence by making Israel appear more vulnerable. The Arabs have used their acquisition of control of Gaza in 2006 to launch an unrelenting barrage of missiles and rockets into southern Israeli towns (see Map 12.2). Arab control of the entire West Bank would place Israel's major population centers within rocket and even mortar range. The barrage from Gaza was so intense that the Israel Defense Force (IDF), in Operation Cast Lead, invaded Gaza in 2009 to seek out and eliminate the sources of these rocket attacks. Israel was roundly condemned in the world community for this operation. Despite efforts of the IDF to minimize collateral damage to civilians, casualties did occur among civilians fueling this condemnation.

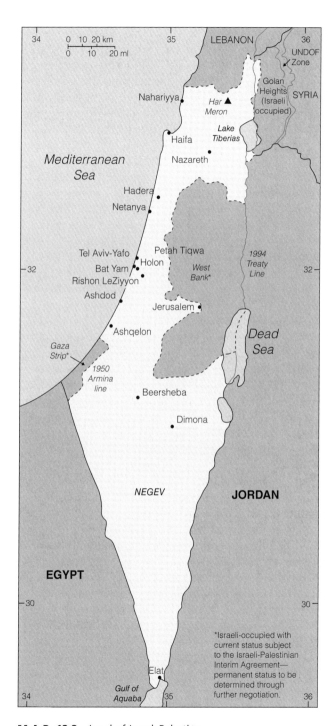

M A P 12.2 Land of Israel–Palestine

© Cengage Learning®

The idealist argument for the Palestinian cause reflects an assumption that the Israelis are settlers who have occupied land that has been Arab or Palestinian since "time immemorial." This widely held assumption about that area was most succinctly stated by author Joan Peters. She refers to "the myth that 'the Jews arrived only in 1948 where they displaced a teeming Arab population from its rooted homeland since time immemorial.'"[22] Peters came to a different conclusion than the one she set out to prove. She found that while some Arabs and some Jews had always lived in the area of the Palestine Mandate, it was sparsely settled and run down. Many of the people we call Palestinians descend from people who migrated to the area about the same time as the Zionists in the early twentieth century, taking advantage of an expanding Westernized economy.[23] (The late Palestinian Authority Chairman Yasser Arafat himself was born and raised in Egypt.) Critics of Israel reject Peter's research and conclusions as flawed, however.

Moreover, the argument for the justice of a borders-based settlement to the conflict reflects the widespread belief that this particular self-proclaimed nation deserves self-determination and a sovereign state that allows it to act in the world as an identifiable people. However, there are numerous national groups whose stateless conditions do not seem as pressing to the world as that of the Palestinians (e.g., the Kurds, the Chechens, the Basques, the Catalonians, the Armenians, and the Tibetans). The irreconcilable positions taken at Annapolis in 2007 suggest that a resolution in the short run may not be possible; America may have to live with continuing tension. Given the Palestinian determination to settle for nothing less than the elimination of Israel, America's pushing Israel to make territorial concessions may encourage the Arabs to aggressively pursue that goal. In other words, it may make war more likely, which is not in America's interest. The status quo may not make life pleasant in Israel but it may be the option that least threatens American interests. The Palestinian determination to exterminate Israel as a Jewish state may be inferred from their repeated eschewal of a two-state solution described in the following historical summary.

When the British abandoned its mandate after World War II, the United Nations Security Council voted to partition the mandate into three states: a small Jewish state on the shores of the Mediterranean, an Arab state east of the Jordan River called Trans Jordan to be governed by the Hashemite monarchy, and another Arab state between the West Bank of the Jordan River and Israel. Israel and Trans Jordan accepted the partition and declared their states. The rest of the Arab world rejected the partition and mobilized to destroy the Jewish state by armed force. The point here is that a Palestinian state was formally offered by the United Nations and Israel and rejected by Arab leaders. This is the second of four times that a formal offer of a Palestinian state was rejected, the first being the Arab rejection of the 1938 Peel Commission Report by the British as a proposal to dispose of its League mandate. Although the Arab attempt to destroy the Jewish state did not succeed, Jordan occupied the West Bank, leaving the Jewish state eight to twelve miles wide at its neck, not a defensible position.

The third rejection of such an offer came in the wake of the 1967 Six Day War. Declaring once again their intention to destroy the Jewish state, the Muslim states massed their troops on its borders. Israel's ports were block-aded, an act of belligerency under international law. Facing this situation and with their indefensible borders, Israel launched a **preemptive strike** (a concept discussed later in the context of the second U.S.–Iraq War), destroyed the Egyptian air force on the ground, and defeated the combined Arab powers in six days. The Israelis now controlled the West Bank, the Sinai Desert through which the Egyptians had launched three armed attacks against Israel in twenty years; the area known as Gaza; and the Golan Heights, through which Syria had launched its assaults on Israel. Although Israel now had defensible borders, its government offered to return the territories it had captured in return for peace treaties and formal recognition from its neighbors. The immediate Arab response was the so-called Khartoum Doctrine: "no negotiation, no recognition, no peace." However, after Egyptian president Gamal Abdel Nasser died, President Anwar Sadat negotiated a peace treaty with Israel. The entire Sinai, with its valu-able oil reserves and strategic passes, was returned to Egyptian control. Relations between the two states, however, remain cold and hostile.

The fourth refusal of an explicit offer of a state for the Palestinians came after weeks of intense negotiations under the mediation of President Bill Clinton in 2000. The offer included the return to Palestinian control of over 95 percent of the territory under dispute. This offer went further than anyone familiar with Israel thought its government would ever go. Nevertheless, Chairman Arafat of the Palestinian Liberation Organization refused the offer, believing that the offer did not include a right of return for all of the descendants and their relatives of the 700,000 or so Arabs who fled to escape the oncoming war. This would amount to some six million Arabs flooding into Israel, which would of course render the Jews a second-class minority in their own land; thus, Israel would no longer be a Jewish state.

The Clinton-led negotiations were the culmination of a lengthy process known as the Oslo Peace Process after an agreement negotiated in that city. The agreement committed the Israeli and Palestinian parties to a land-for-peace process. The Palestinians committed themselves in this pact to recognize Israeli's right to exist and to curb violence against Israeli citizens. The Israelis committed themselves to withdrawal from territories occupied in the 1967 war. The Israelis argue such a withdrawal should be tied to the aforementioned Palestinian Authority steps while the Arabs argue withdrawal should be total and precede any negotiation.

The PA charter, committing the organization to the destruction of Israel, has not been changed. Moreover, in mid-May 2004, the late chairman of the PA, Yasser Arafat, ordered an escalating wave of violence following the an-nouncement of Bush's "Road Map" to a peaceful settlement, involving numer-ous suicide bombers in public places. In the first eleven weeks following the announcement of the Road Map, there were 321 attempted suicide attacks resulting in 51 murdered civilians and 317 serious injuries. Following a bus bombing in September 2004 that killed 16 Israelis, the PA turned out 20,000 individuals to dance in celebration while Arafat told the crowd, "We will march to Jerusalem; we will sacrifice millions of martyrs."[24] The hoped-for negotiated reconciliation between Israel and the PA has been rendered more difficult by the election of Hamas to lead the PA. While **Fatah**, the faction headed by the late Arafat, occasionally hinted at a willingness to negotiate, Hamas has been unambiguous about its goal of the elimination of Israel. Meanwhile, the current (as of June 2007) speaker of the PA legislature has publicly called for "the extermination of all Jews and Americans."[25] Supporters of the peace process argue that such statements are mere rhetoric for local consumption. Israelis, however, take promises to exterminate them seriously.

Meanwhile, the Israelis have withdrawn from over 90 percent of the West Bank. The late Israeli Prime Minister Ariel Sharon, in a move drawing strong opposition from within his own country, ordered an Israeli retreat from and abandonment of its remaining settlements in Gaza as well as some of its remaining West Bank settlements in order to unilaterally establish defensible borders for the Jewish state. The forced evacuation of all Israelis from Gaza, some of whom had lived there for three generations and had built thriving cities and businesses, caused intense controversy among Israelis. Rather than govern their newly acquired Jew-free territory, the Arabs have chosen to turn it into a platform for the daily launching of Kassam rockets into southern Israel and a base for the collection of arms and explosives; meanwhile, armed gangs roam Gaza, killing and terrorizing local inhabitants in pursuit of the deadly conflict between the Fatah and Hamas factions of the Palestinians. The latter group, being more explicit in its genocidal aims regarding Israel, is regarded by the United States as more militant. Hence, the United States in mid-2007 pressured the Israelis to allow the importation of thousands of assault rifles, RPGs, antitank missiles, and hundreds of armored personnel carriers into Gaza to support Fatah. However, Fatah is so weak that many of these weapons would fall into the hands of Hamas. The alliance forged in 2014 between the so-called moderate Fatah wing of the PA and the more militant Hamas, who explicitly embraces the goal of exterminating Israel and its people, renders the achievement of a negotiated settlement between Israel and the PA even more unachievable.

Gaza fell into chaos as armed gangs roamed, killing children (in front of their parents), doctors working in hospitals, and other civilians, while Israel continued to provide essential water and electricity to Gaza for humanitarian purposes. At the same time, Fatah was killing Hamas people in the West Bank. The implication for U.S. policy is that continuing pressure on Israel to make further concessions is not likely to produce a peace agreement. Rather, such concessions would be perceived by Arab militants as a sign of weakness of Israel and its American supporters and an incentive to increase efforts to eliminate Israel.

Apparently, Israel's strategy is to unilaterally set what it determines is its defensible borders in the absence of a serious negotiating partner. In order to carry out this decision that six million Jews cannot indefinitely govern thirty million Arabs, the Sharon forces decided to voluntarily relinquish control of most of the disputed territories. Although Sharon was felled by a stroke in 2006 that left him comatose, his successor Ehud Olmert was determined to carry out the plan of Sharon and his Kadima (Forward) Party. Sharon remained comatose until his death in January 2014.

To curb the almost daily slaughter of its civilians, Israel has undertaken the construction of a wall or fence along these unilaterally declared borders. In the first four years after the current **Intifada** was launched, after the failure of the summit at Camp David and Taba, 1,017 Israelis have been killed, 70 percent of whom were civilians, and 5,600 injured, 83 percent of whom were civilians.[26] At this writing (in spring 2014), the wall has been completed on the northern border between Israel and Samaria (the Israeli name for the northern West Bank) and construction continues along the border with Judea (the Israeli name of the southern West Bank). Since the construction, successful suicide bombings in Israel have been reduced by over 90 percent. A suicide bombing occurred in September 2004, allegedly in retaliation for the targeted assassinations of the last two well-known leaders of the radical group Hamas, Ahmed Yassin and Abdel Rantisi, six months earlier. It took that long for Hamas to launch a successful attack, and these killings occurred south of the completed wall between Israel and Judea. Meanwhile, life in Israel has returned to near normal. The economy grew in 2004 at 4 percent a year and Jerusalem's King David Hotel has reached full occupancy.[27] That rate slowed to 3.1 percent in early 2014, still a healthy rate. Israel, however, remains a garrison state under siege with armed soldiers patrolling throughout Israel, with armed checkpoints along every major roadway, and guards questioning and searching patrons to virtually every restaurant, examinations based upon unabashed ethnic profiling.

In light of widespread condemnation of the wall, the International Court at The Hague issued a judgment that the wall is illegal based on the premise that the West Bank is legally Arab land, an assumption addressed earlier in this chapter. The wall apparently presents a major obstacle to the goal of Hamas, Islamic Jihad, and the PA to destroy the fabric of Israeli society, with an intolerable level of killing of innocent men, women, and especially children.

A number of Israeli settlements remain in the contested territory. Some of these are quite large with elaborate, modern edifices and are generally surrounded by a wall. But as discussed earlier and reinforced by their reaction to the pullout from Gaza and large parts of the West Bank, the decisive grievance of most Arab elites is not the settlements or the retaliation against terrorist leaders and the launchers of rockets, but the existence of the Jews themselves, especially in the Middle East.

Given the offer rejected in 2000, it is hard to see any plan on which the parties can agree. While classical diplomacy involved mutual concessions in which no party got all of what it wanted, the Arab position, in the wake of Arabs having launched and lost at least three wars in less than half a century, seems to demand that the victorious target of those attacks surrender to Arab demands unconditionally. Moreover, several strong and well-armed Palestinian groups have never wavered in their declared intention to completely destroy the Jewish state: Hamas, Islamic Jihad, Hezbollah, the Popular Front for the Liberation of Palestine, Black September, and even Arafat's Fatah movement, although the Fatah made some conciliatory statements in its discussion with Western leaders and media. Arabs call the founding of Israel *nakba* (catastrophe). The supposedly moderate president of the PA, Mahmoud Abbas, has made it clear that he has neither the power nor the will to compel the Hamas prime minister to eschew continued violence against Israeli civilians. On the other side, a vocal but tiny orthodox Jewish minority claims the right of Israel to the entire territory of Palestine as a biblical mandate.

American Options in the Area: A Ray of Hope Dashed

It therefore has been hard to imagine the basis for any conceivable settlement. Yet the American government continues to dispatch representatives to the region as with the 2013 negotiations personally led by Secretary of State John Kerry. Israel had seemed more amenable to American pressure than their Arab foes, so the temptation was to lean on that country to make additional concessions, most notably the coerced release in 2013 of over a hundred convicted terrorists with civilian blood on their hands. Since the ascension of harder line Binyamin Netanyahu of the hawkish Likud Party to the prime minister's office in Israel, Israel has been less amenable to American pressures. Indeed, Prime Minister Netanyahu defied the Obama administration's demand that he extend a moratorium on the construction of Jewish housing in East Jerusalem in September 2010.

A ray of hope emerged in late October 2004, when Chairman Arafat died rather suddenly of still undisclosed causes and was succeeded by Mahmoud Abbas as president of the PA. Abbas had been identified as a Palestinian moderate. Of course, moderate is a relative term. Abbas earned the designation by stating that the Intifada was a tactical mistake (not a moral one). Nevertheless, he also said that "a crackdown on Hamas (the main perpetrator of suicide bombings) … is not an option." Abbas said that he would never compromise on an unlimited right of return, and authored a book denying that the Holocaust occurred. Abbas won the weakly contested Palestinian election in January 2005. These hopes, however, have been dashed by the maximalist rhetoric by the Hamas leadership of the PA and the outbreak in 2006 of renewed fighting in southern Lebanon. This fighting came in response to Hezbollah (the Party of God) kidnapping two Israeli soldiers from Israeli soil and the raining of Katyusha rockets on Israel's northern cities, killing forty-four civilians. Meanwhile, tensions in the area have been further exacerbated by the aforementioned rain of Kassam rockets from Gaza. This fusillade of rockets left the Israeli town of S'derot virtually uninhabitable, although the Israeli antimissile operation (known as the "iron dome") can now intercept almost 90 percent of incoming missiles.

Meanwhile, continued American military aid to Israel is crucial in enabling that state to survive. The continuation of tension and stalemate between Israel and the Palestinian and opposing Arab forces do not in themselves harm American interests, which consist of access to Middle East petroleum reserves and maintaining the existence of the single consistently pro-Western democratic state in the area. Given the unyielding refusal of Arab leadership and of the majority of Palestinian people to accept a Jewish state in the area, America's acceptance of that stalemate while ensuring Israel's ability to defend itself may be America's only realistic option in the immediate future. The alternative policy pursued by the Obama administration is to pressure Israel to cease the construction of housing in Jewish neighborhoods in East Jerusalem and to release hundreds of convicted Arab terrorists as a "confidence building measure" to get Abbas to the negotiating table. Abba continues to refuse to recognize Israel's existence as a Jewish state; hence, the hoped for outcome of these negotiations remains doubtful.

America and the Arab Spring.   In 2013, several nations in the Gulf experienced popular uprisings and revolutionary protests and demonstrations against autocratic regimes, a movement referred to as the Arab Spring. American policy was to take no action to encourage these rebellions with the exception of the uprising against Libyan leader, Muammar Gaddafi. Western leaders and intellectuals held out hope that this movement would bring about a more democratic and pro-Western Middle East. Militant Islam, however, remained prominent and largely in control of that area. As of 2014, Egypt remains in the hands of the military that ousted Muslim Brotherhood president when he tried to assume unchecked power. The Mullahs remain firmly in control of Iran when thousands of additional secularized Iranians took to the streets to protest the theocratic regime.

CONTINUING DEBATES: RESPONDING TO TERRORISM AND NUCLEAR PROLIFERATION

The events of September 11, 2001, brought the specter of terrorism to the forefront of American consciousness to a greater extent than ever before. Although Americans have suffered acts of terrorism on several occasions in recent years, as noted at the outset of this chapter, foreign terrorism had never struck so violently so close to home. Moreover, the threat of large-scale terrorism against Americans appears to be an ongoing danger. In 2007, the United States and British agents uncovered plots to blow up ten U.S. airliners carrying hundreds of passengers over the Atlantic, to slaughter as many GIs as possible at Fort Dix, and to cause massive explosions at Kennedy Airport in New York. More recently, there were shootings at Fort Hood (2009 and 2014) and the failed underwear and Times Square bombings mentioned at the outset of this chapter. The Obama administration, seeking to assume credit for removing Al Qaeda as an imminent threat to America after the killing of Osama bin Laden, has downplayed the use of the term "**terrorism**." Thus, there were expressed doubts that the Fort Hood shootings were terrorist acts. The term *workplace violence* was used to describe the events at Fort Hood in 2009 even though the Palestinian perpetrator yelled "Alihu Akbar" as he shot, and the Benghazi attack was initially characterized as a spontaneous uprising in response to an offensive video about the prophet despite the sophisticated weaponry used in the attack. By contrast there was no evidence that the 2014 shooting at Fort Hood was terror related.

Terrorism appears to be an increasingly popular tool for militarily weak, but disaffected, forces against the democratic West, today a tool almost exclusively used by young and radically religious Muslims. In the wake of the events of September 11, our government under President Bush fully committed itself to a war on terror. Critics of the Obama administration charge that administration is more concerned with bringing that war (which is over ten years old) to an end. In order to assess the effectiveness of that war, we need to examine the nature of terrorism and the policy options for confronting it.

Defining Terrorism

Terrorism has acquired an ideological connotation: what your enemy does is terrorism, while your perpetrators of political violence are called freedom fighters, or some equally positive term. Terrorism, however, has a particular meaning. Terrorism is not merely violence to achieve political objectives. Wars, and even guerilla tactics by irregular troops, use violence for political goals, but these are not normally designated as terrorism. Rather, terrorism consists of random violence against civilian or noncombatant populations to compel another power to change its policies by generating widespread anxiety or fear among its people. The randomness of the violence is a function of the soft or indefensible nature of the targets. Even the victims of the Fort Hood shootings were impersonally and randomly selected. Thus, the events of September 11 were clearly terrorism, as was arguably the June 1996 attack on the Khobar Towers in Saudi Arabia, where military personnel in a noncombatant mode were sleeping. A major attempt to explode bombs in the London Underground in July 2005 was partially successful, and inflicted numerous casualties. Because it is virtually impossible to avoid being a potential target, terror can paralyze the ordinary daily life of the target population. For example, many Israelis routinely ride the bus to school or work; hence, after several attacks killed the occupants of buses, Israelis were afraid to put their children on the bus to school or to commute to work. Even those who were not killed or maimed were unable to carry on their ordinary life. Thus, terrorism, if successful, paralyzes the ordinary life of the target society. This tactic appeals to weaker forces with grievances against stronger powers, because such acts have been almost unpreventable. No nation can constantly guard every possible target of such attacks. Moreover, when terrorists are willing, as they frequently are, to risk or sacrifice their own lives, it is very difficult to prevent these tactics. Hence, as detailed at the outset of this chapter, America, as the world's strongest power, has been the target of terrorist tactics numerous times in recent decades.

Options for Confronting Terror

Some policy analysts and political activists from the idealist perspective urge that we try to address and remedy the grievances of those who commit or are likely to commit such acts, a strategy that realists give the now pejorative name of appeasement, as explained earlier. Idealists argue that although we cannot stop people from committing acts of terror if they are determined to do so, we can remove the incentive by remedying the alleged injustices and the poverty that breed suicidal rage at American interests. From this perspective, a just peace in the Middle East and economic development in the Islamic world would reduce the conditions of terrorism.

Realists, however, dispute this. They note that the head of the leading Islamist terrorist organization, Osama bin Laden, came from a wealthy family and that most of the perpetrators of the events of September 11 were not poor.[28] (**Islamism** refers to the radical and militant aspects of Islam, not to the entire Muslim world.) A typical suicide bomber, Zainab Al Issa Abu, who blew herself up in Jerusalem in mid-September 2004, came from a wealthy family whose parents owned a television station. Ms. Abu, one of an increasing number of women suicide bombers, was the hostess of a children's show on that station. While suicide bombings of this sort have become more rare since the construction of a fence separating pre-1967 Israel and the West Bank, other spectacular killings of Americans may still occur. The destruction of the American consulate and the killing of an American ambassador, as well as three other Americans, in Behghazi in 2013 have been widely identified as terrorism.

The realists argue that one should never grant the grievances of terrorists, even to the extent of not doing something one might have been disposed to do if such policy were a terrorist demand, and even to the extent of refusing to negotiate with the terrorists or discuss their grievances because America must not let the terrorists perceive that their tactics are achieving their objectives.

Despite the tactical reasons for Israel's withdrawal from Gaza discussed above, Islamist groups have claimed that they have driven the Jews out of Gaza; they have argued that terrorism is working and ought to be stepped up. They made this same argument after the unilateral Israeli withdrawal from Lebanon after both incursions into that country. For example, in the *Al Ahram Weekly* of September 30 to October 6, 2004, Yasser al-Zaatrah argued that Islamist groups had made good their pledge to drive Israel out of Lebanon, and they have driven them out of Gaza. The realists argue that the first principle in preventing acts of terror is to remove the incentive to commit them by making it clear that the potential terrorists cannot realize their agenda with these acts. They further argue that the strategy of granting their demands and remedying their grievances is impossible, because such grievances tend to be infinitely expansive and to conflict with the vital interests of the stronger power. Thus, Daniel Pipes argues that the agenda of the Islamist militants (not all Muslims) is to impose an Islamic theocracy on the United States with Islamic law (Shira) trumping American law, obviously not a viable policy option for most Americans.[29] The impression that weaker powers can advance their agenda by committing acts of terror invites such acts in the future, according to the realist position.

To take this position means that the potential target nation must consider victims and potential victims of terror as expendable. When terrorists seize hostages, the media always consults the families of the hostages, who urge meeting the terrorists' demands. Realists argue that these are the last people to have any perspective on balancing the concern for the victims with the interests of the whole nation and the prevention of future acts of terror. Thus, despite a stated Israeli policy of not accommodating the grievances of terrorists, they released over one thousand imprisoned Arab terrorists in 2011 in order to secure the return of a kidnapped Israeli soldier, Sergeant Gilad Shalit, who had been held captive by Hamas militants for five years. Critics of his release argue that it provides an incentive to other militants to seize other hostages whenever they want something from the Israelis. Yet, it would be difficult to confront a soldier's parents and inform them that their son or daughter is expendable.

The second realist principle in fighting terrorism is to impose costs on those who make the decision to commit such acts and who plan and support them. This means that one should hold accountable not merely the perpetrator, such as the suicide bomber, but the states or large organizations who increasingly plan and sponsor such acts. Until the 2001 war on terror, the United States was reluctant to take action against such states or organized terrorist networks.[30] The United States had known for some years about the Al Qaeda network that planned and sponsored not only the September 11 attacks but also a number of the other acts against the United States previously discussed. Increasingly, complex acts of terror involve either the sponsorship of nation-states or well-organized networks like Al Qaeda. This is a phenomenon known as state-sponsored terrorism. A related version of this has been terrorism sponsored by the governing authority in the Palestinian-controlled territories or the organizations affiliated with them, such as Hamas, Islamic Jihad, and Black September.

These organizations, including an arm of the late Chairman Arafat's own Fatah group, the al-Aqsa Martyrs' Brigades, unleashed a rash of nine suicide bombings in nine days in the heart of Israeli cities, killing dozens of men, women, and children in March 2002. A sense among the Arab world that such a strategy is effective was encouraged by a wave of anti-Israeli and anti-Semitic violence throughout Europe. Israel, following the realist formula, responded with a military push into the West Bank town of Ramallah against the headquarters and leaders of these groups. Further seeking to impose costs on the leaders of this new Intifada, Israel began a policy of targeted assassinations of the leaders of Hamas, the group behind most of the recent attacks and more recently the leaders of the Islamist Taliban in Afghanistan using pilotless drone aircraft. Using helicopter-launched missiles, the Israelis killed Ahmed Yassinin in spring 2004, and then two weeks later killed his successor, Abdel Aziz al-Rantisi. No visible Hamas leader willing to be publicly identified emerged for some months; after the almost-daily attacks, six months passed before the next Hamas attack. The Israelis, meanwhile, even attacked the sense of a safe haven for terrorist leaders by killing another Hamas leader, Izz al-Din al-Sheikh Khalil, in Damascus, Syria, in September 2004.

The sharp reduction in the incidence of successful suicide bombings in 2004 suggests to some scholars that the policy of targeted assassinations of Hamas leaders caused the group to become more cautious in their attempts to paralyze Israeli life. Meanwhile, the Obama administration has vigorously pursued the targeted killing of terrorist leaders using strikes conducted by pilotless "drone" aircraft. In 2013, a targeted attack carried out by Navy Seals succeeded in killing terrorist leader Osama bin Laden. Critics of attacks are concerned with collateral killing and with the killing of some American Jihadists without due process of law. With the reduced incidence of terrorist violence, tourism was up sharply in Israel; the economy grew in 2004 at around 4 percent, and life returned to a kind of well-guarded normalcy.[31] The result of imposing costs on terrorists and those who sponsor terrorism may be seen in the actions of the late Libyan leader

Muammar Gadaffi voluntarily surrendering his nuclear weapons program after seeing the spectacle of Iraqi leader Saddam Hussein reduced to rags when he was taken into custody. Yet, some argue that the Obama administration has weakened the deterrent effect of swift justice for terrorists by treating them as ordinary criminals entitled to all the procedural rights afforded such accused perpetrators of ordinary crime. In particular, such critics of our treatment of captured Jihadists object to the practice of affording them "Miranda rights," with a state-appointed lawyer advising his/her client of a right to silence and cutting off a potentially valuable source of intelligence about other terrorist plans. It was argued by supporters of the harsh interrogation of captured Jihadists that it yielded information that led to the killing of Osama bin Laden. Defenders of the administration's opposition to harsh interrogation argue that harsh treatment of Jihadist prisoners is a "recruiting tool" causing Muslim individuals to join terrorist organizations. The alternative to affording Jihadists "due process of law" is military tribunals, a process that was used against Nazi saboteurs in World War II.

Such interrogation of prisoners is part of another option in the struggle against terrorists, to try to uncover and foil terrorist plots before they occur. To this end, the USA Patriot Act authorized a variety of intelligence-gathering techniques, including the interception of phone calls from suspected militants and other Muslims to overseas recipients without prior judicial authorization. Critics of the USA Patriot Act raise privacy issues and paint the specter of a police state. The conflict between national security and the privacy inherent in the very concept of a free society came to the fore in the summer of 2013 when Edward Snowden, a former employee of the CIA and the NSA, turned over to the media thousands of classified documents and then fled to Russia. The documents revealed a pattern of widespread surveillance of American citizens among others. Defenders of the Patriot Act claim that exigencies often do not permit the luxury of hunting down a judge without losing the opportunity for crucial information. The USA Patriot Act was scheduled to sunset and had to be reauthorized in 2005 in the Senate and 2006 in the House with amendments. The amendments now require high-level (FBI director or deputy director or official in charge of intelligence) approval of requests for sensitive information, such as library or medical records, and require court notification within ten days of surveillance of new objects. Supporters of the administration policy point out that no successful terrorist plots were carried out in the United States since the events of September 11, while several major attempts have been foiled. Occurrences such as the underwear bomb attempt or the foiled Times Square truck bombing reminds us that plotting such mass murder is an ongoing enterprise. The ongoing threat of such terrorist violence was once again brought home with the detonation of two pressure cooker bombs at the finish area of the 2013 Boston Marathon by two Chechen brothers. The explosions killed three and injured over two hundred. The elder brother was killed by police and the younger one is still awaiting trial. Some defenders of civil liberties on the left argue that threat of terrorism is exaggerated and is used as an excuse to infringe on those liberties.

Idealist attempts to remedy the grievances of the Islamists may be frustrated by the depth of their hatred of Western civilization itself. It has now been reported that Islamist academies not only in the Middle East, but in the United States and other Western countries as well, are teaching children that it is their sacred duty to kill Jews and convert other Americans. These academies are run by the militant Wahabi wing of Islam, financed by our putative ally, Saudi Arabia. Muslim schools in the territories and even a Muslim Mickey Mouse preach hate and the glory of *shahada* (dying for Islam) to very young children.[32] Bernard Lewis, perhaps the leading Western authority on Islam, stated on July 28, 2004, that Europe would be Islamic by the end of this century at the latest, a recognition of the intensity of the commitment of the Islamists to convert or exterminate the infidels of the Western world.[33] This has led some Western leaders to try to accommodate demands of the Muslim leaders. Other Western leaders reject the assumption that terrorism is an essentially rational act to achieve certain goals. However, it may be that such acts are just as much an expression of raw hatred and shame at one's powerless situation. The danger here is magnified by recent efforts by the leaders of states and organizations sponsoring terrorism to acquire chemical, biological, and nuclear weapons of mass destruction, especially the Iranian progress in the development of a nuclear bomb. The efforts of the Obama administration to dissuade the Mullahs from pursuing their nuclear program by rational negotiation was described above.

The War in Iraq and the Struggle with Terror

America's first response to the events of September 11, 2001, was to invade Afghanistan and militarily bring down the Islamist Taliban regime that had been providing a territorial haven for the Al Qaeda group responsible for those events. There was little quarrel with this response. However, while a number of Al Qaeda leaders were captured, the top leadership, including Osama bin Laden, the head and main financial support of that group, escaped capture until 2012, when he was caught and killed by American Navy Seals while in hiding in Pakistan. While his death provided a sense of justice for the September 11 attack, there was disagreement over whether the killing of bin Laden made Americans safer from the threat of terrorism.

President Bush had ordered a U.S.-led invasion of Iraq in March 2003, a move that generated intense domestic criticism. This criticism had two targets. First, critics questioned the decision to go to war in the first place, a decision that was in part justified by the claim that Saddam Hussein had weapons of mass destruction (WMD) that included chemical, biological, and nuclear weapons. When no stockpiles of these weapons were found after the collapse of Hussein's regime, critics of the war alleged that Bush had deceived the nation to justify a war either for oil or to settle old scores for his father.

The major justification for this invasion was Iraqi leader Saddam Hussein's repeated noncooperation with a U.N.-sponsored weapons inspection regime and his defiance of several U.N. resolutions demanding his cooperation and an accounting of his weapons programs. President Bush argued that given the destructive power of such weapons, he could not rely on deterrence and retaliation, granting Hussein the first shot. This is the newly asserted doctrine of **preemptive war**;

it replaced the old doctrine of deterrence because we can no longer rely on a second strike in this era of WMDs. It turned out, however, that after we toppled Hussein's Baath Party regime, no stockpiles of WMDs were found. Critics argue that the threat that Hussein's regime posed to the United States was not clearly imminent. Moreover, they argue that we should have assembled more international support for our actions to clothe them with international legitimacy. The Obama administration has emphasized the importance of such a multilateral approach to foreign policy to secure the approval of other nations for its actions. Realists respond by saying that we cannot give other nations an effective veto on how we defend our national interests. Idealists also question the morality of the doctrine of preemptive war and the use of force based upon the unproven inference that the object of the attack is likely to threaten one's vital interests.

Prewar Intelligence on WMDs and on a Connection between Iraq and Terrorism

The United States knew that Saddam's regime had chemical weapons and had used them in the 1980s to kill millions of Iranians in the Iraq–Iran War and thousands of its own Kurdish citizens. Saddam's son-in-law briefly defected to the West and told of a chemical weapons plant at which he had been employed in the late 1990s. Clearly, Saddam had the know-how to replenish his supply of chemical weapons. Moreover, it is clear that Saddam had sought and acquired some technology and material used in the development of a nuclear weapons program, but it is not clear how far he had progressed on that quest. Saddam and his associates discussed restarting chemical weapons programs as soon as the inspections ended. Given the fact that he had the knowledge and technology to acquire such weapons, he could have had a small stockpile in a matter of months. However, in hindsight, it may simply be that the intelligence available to President Bush prior to the attack on Iraq, suggesting that Saddam Hussein had recently been involved in the acquisition of WMDs, was flawed.

Saddam had supported terrorism in a variety of ways. He sent large cash payment to the families of Palestinian suicide bombers to encourage that activity. He offered his country as sanctuary to a number of prominent terrorists. Moreover, despite the denials by many of the critics of the war, there were ongoing and repeated, although not formal and institutionalized, connections between Saddam's regime and Al Qaeda leadership. We know that these contacts were discussed in a memo from Undersecretary of Defense Douglas Feith to Jay Rockefeller and Pat Roberts of the Senate Intelligence Committee dated October 27, 2003. Between 1992 and 1995 meetings were held in Khartoum, Sudan, between Iraq Intelligence officials and Al Qaeda leader Faruq Hijazi. Iraqi Intelligence Officer Ahmed Hikmat Shakir facilitated the entry of several September 11 hijackers through customs in Kuala Lumpur, Malaysia, in January 2000 and attended a meeting with them.

While there is no evidence that Hussein was involved in planning the events of September 11, there is no doubt he supported radical Islamist terrorism in general. The question is whether this connection in and of itself justified a preemptive invasion of Iraq. Idealist critics of the war strongly argue against the morality of initiating the horrible human cost of war without a direct and imminent threat to a nation's vital interests.

It is, however, too late to argue whether we should have invaded Iraq. Now that we have overthrown Saddam's regime, our options are different and difficult. At this writing, U.S. forces in Iraq and Iraqi civilians were being killed and wounded although at a much reduced rate since a "surge" of twenty thousand additional troops were deployed in 2007. However, a persisting insurgency of former Baathist militants and itinerant Islamist fighters remained and by 2013, with the total withdrawal of American troops, Iranian sponsored fighters have reestablished their presence in Iraq. This violence was exacerbated by internal warfare between armed gangs of Sunnis, the minority sect that had ruled Iraq under the aegis of Saddam's regime, and armed Shiite militias bent on exacting revenge upon their former Sunni oppressors.

President Obama vigorously opposed the war in Iraq throughout his campaign. Accordingly, he publicly announced a timetable for the withdrawal of all American troops from both Iraq and Afghanistan claiming he was unable to engineer a status of forces agreement from Iraqi leaders, but he first increased activity in Afghanistan saying that it should have been the focus instead of Iraq. War critics demanded that we have an exit strategy for terminating our participation in these wars (which, war hawks point out, is not the same as the goal of victory).

Realists respond that if we withdraw from Iraq without realizing our objective, the Islamists would likely convince themselves that they had driven us out, thereby justifying a renewed commitment to terrorism. Moreover, they point out that an announced timetable for the withdrawal of allied troops will tell the insurgents and other Islamist opponents of the pro-American forces that they only need wait us out. Potential friends among Iraqis or in Afghanistan will believe that the Americans will not protect them after that date. It would in fact become an unconditional surrender to those who wish to end American influence in that country. These realists further argue that the hostility of the Arab street to the West exists independently of our policy. While the death of any American serviceperson is a tragedy and an unbearable loss to his or her loved ones, in perspective, we lost twice as many troops on D-Day alone in World War II as lost in four years of fighting in Iraq. Supporters of the war argue that the assertion of our national interests sometimes requires such tragic costs.

A surge of some 20,000 additional troops were deployed in Iraq in the summer of 2007. The idea of the surge is to allow the allies to clear a contested area of insurgents and then have enough personnel to hold that area, where previously, when the allies drove the insurgents out, they would soon have been redeployed and the insurgents would have moved back into the area. As of spring 2010, experts agreed that the surge helped to stabilize Iraq, gains that were relinquished when America withdrew all of its troops. The antipathy between the Shiite Muslims, the Sunni Muslims, and the Kurds overrode a widespread sense of an Iraqi nation. The distinguished scholar and expert on the concept of community, Amitai Etzioni, has argued for a communitarian solution to the question of how such a segmented society could provide essential security. He advocates that the three geographically defined subcultures—Sunni, Shia, and Kurd—each provide security for its own people and area.[34] Yet, realists argue that failure to achieve some plausible approximation of our goals would render it difficult for America to assert its interests in that region for many years.

Rogue Regimes and WMDs

The threat posed by countries who challenge American vital interests is infinitely exacerbated when **rogue states**, states that operate outside acceptable patterns of international behavior, acquire the capacity to build and deliver WMDs. North Korea and Iran constitute the major examples of such regimes. In the era of widespread availability of information, it is increasingly difficult to contain that capacity. A less-developed and otherwise weak country could deliver devastating carnage and destruction to the strongest of nations. Hence, many Americans advocate that we keep the option of a preemptive strike against hostile nations on the verge of acquiring that capacity. It will be recalled that Israel took such preemptive action in destroying Iraq's nuclear reactor in 1983. Obama, however, has discouraged Israel from such action against Iran claiming success in negotiation with Iran in December 2013. Iran, however, only agreed to slow the pace of enriching uranium to weapons grade, an easily reversible commitment. In return, America weakened a regime of sanctions that had created considerable hardship to the Iranian economy.

Such is the case today with Iran, a nation with a nuclear program close to having the ability to use that power to produce nuclear weapons, and with North Korea, a nation that already has such weapons and some capacity to deliver them. Iranian medium-range missiles could easily reach Israel as well as parts of Europe with a nuclear warhead. It is uncertain how effective the Arrow antimissile system fielded by the United States and Israel would be against such an Iranian strike.

Iran is controlled by radical Muslim clerics, while North Korea is a hard-line communist state. Obviously, it would be much more difficult and dangerous to confront North Korea with its existing nuclear capacity and its massive, well-armed military. Talks with North Koreans have resulted in it breaking promises not to push ahead with its nuclear program, which directly threatens South Korea. North Korea has, in the past, shared its nuclear and missile technology with anti-American forces such as Iran and could provide a nuclear capability to terrorists. While many strategists and scholars such as Zbigniew Brzezinski and Brent Scowcroft point out the possible calamitous consequences of alienating the Arab world with such a strike, Israel may also be considering another preemptive strike as it did in Iraq if Iran nears success in producing deliverable weapons, but its task would be much harder this time without the benefit of surprise and because Iran's program is spread to several sites. However, some experts, including some Arab leaders, encourage the possibility because of the equally dire consequences of a nuclear armed Iran and its ability to "Finlandize" the region (or politically dominate the region so that other countries could not act contrary to Iran's wishes).[35]

A pair of MIT scholars has presented research on the feasibility of such an operation given the status of Israeli military capability and Iranian defenses against such an attack. They conclude that "... the IAF now possesses the capacity to destroy even well-hardened targets in Iran with some degree of confidence. The operation appears no more risky than the earlier attack on Osirak."[36] Two scholars, one a nuclear engineer and the other a political scientist, concluded that the Israelis would have a reasonable chance of successfully accomplishing that task by concentrating on three key links: the heavy water plant at Arak, a uranium conversion facility at Ishfan, and a uranium enrichment facility at Natanz. A successful Israeli operation would clearly be in America's interest. Not only had former Iranian President Mahmoud Ahmadinejad promised to wipe Israel off the map but has stated the eventual goal of a world without the United States. Therefore, while it would be very difficult to completely destroy Iran's widely dispersed nuclear program, some think that Israel could prevent Iran from assembling a bomb by taking out key links in the nuclear chain. Other Arab states feel threatened by the prospect of a nuclear Iran. Saudi Arabia, for example, has granted Israel permission to use its air space en route to such a raid.

The United States tried to engineer an economic boycott of Iran to pressure it to abandon its nuclear program, but America's European allies have eschewed support for such a boycott. The Bush administration, however, assembled a large enough boycott to place serious strains on the Iranian economy until the Obama administration loosened the strictures in the 2013 negotiations with the Mullahs. American options regarding a nuclear Iran are limited. However, Seymour Hirsch, writing in *The New Yorker* in late January 2005, charged that the United States had special operations units infiltrating Iran to determine the location of that nation's nuclear facilities (possibly for an air strike on said facilities).

AMERICA FACES A CHANGING MIDDLE EAST

The second decade of the twenty-first century revealed a Middle East in the throes of popular turmoil as popular uprisings unfolded throughout the area. America hoped this would lead to the transformation of long-entrenched Arab autocracies to something approaching liberal democracy. Hosni Mubarak was ousted from the presidency of Egypt, and Libyan strongman Muammar Gadaffi was overthrown. In Iran, masses took to the streets to protest the apparently corrupt reelection of Mahmoud Ahmadinejad in 2009. They looked to the Americans to give them some kind of support; however, the Obama administration, apparently hoping for negotiations with the Mullahs, remained silent through what some saw as an opportunity for regime change. Hosni Mubarak as president of Egypt had supported American interests and kept the treaty with Israel. Nevertheless, the American administration offered Mubarak no support as he was ousted by Mohamed Morsi, leader of the Muslim Brotherhood, a group many considered supportive of Islamist extremism.

CONTINUING DEBATES: ISSUES ON THE FOREIGN POLICY HORIZON

Americans hoped that the demise of the Soviet Union would end the decades of tension between the democratic West and Russia, perhaps forgetting the foreign policy goals of the Soviet Union reflected the long-standing foreign policy interests of Russia. Although Russia flirted with democratic institutions for a while under President Boris Yeltsin, a colorful character who had been instrumental in bringing about the collapse of the Soviet Union, a former hard-line MKVD (an espionage and police agency) leader, Vladimir Putin, succeeded Yeltsin in the Russian presidency. On a range of issues, such as backing sanctions and embargoes on Iran and North Korea to keep them out of the nuclear club, Russia has been very noncooperative. Meanwhile, Putin has been suppressing opposition to his rule within Russia and aggressively suppressing a separatist movement in the province of Chechnya. Meanwhile, former communists have been emerging in key leadership posts. With Russia suffering deplorable economic and social conditions, it is apparent that the Russian people value a strong and effective government more than they do civil liberties, making the emergence of a Western-style democracy disappointingly unlikely. Meanwhile, Putin has declared an interest in reassembling the old Soviet empire. In that vein, he put down a movement in Georgia during the Bush administration, and in April 2014 he moved troops into Ukraine and annexed the Crimean Peninsula that contains a Russian-speaking population. The United States and its allies have used economic sanctions but have few options to counter the military force, thus projecting a widespread image of weakness.

The other great communist power, China, has been rapidly growing from a less-developed country to a military and economic superpower. With very cheap labor, China has become a major exporter of consumer goods, creating a massive trade imbalance with the United States. This means we buy far more from China than it buys from us, weakening the value of the dollar. As China becomes an industrial power, it adds significantly to the body of pollution that threatens the air and seas of the world. This is an age of what is called globalization, the fact that we live in world economic and industrial systems in which the impact of economic and other activities transcends international borders. The United States has little if any control over the activities of this China, whose activities pose a threat to our interests. This is especially true as China has become the creditor for much of the enormous debt the United States amassed in the first decade of the twentieth century.

Similarly, the West is virtually without leverage in protecting its security interests in the face of an expanding nuclear club. Countries such as Iran and North Korea that do not share basic Western values have or are about to acquire the means to wreak devastating destruction on their foes. While President Obama claims to envision a world without nuclear weapons, any action toward that goal seems to be unilateral with the United States relying on a reduced supply of overaged and untested weapons. Some feel that weakens the deterrent effect of our nuclear capability in the face of the threat of nuclear power in the hands of powers that do not like us. Clearly, America faces unprecedented challenges from the globalized world system. The solutions to these challenges are still being sought as the nation attempts to cope with a perilous future.

Conservatives and liberals differ from one another with respect to the issue of unilateralism and the defense of national sovereignty versus globalism and transnationalism. While conservatives are generally more concerned with the defense of sovereignty and the capacity of unilateral action without the approval of allies, liberals are inclined to favor a global or transnational approach. This issue emerged in August 2007 in the meeting of the heads of government from the United States, Canada, and Mexico in Montebello, Canada, to "harmonize" their respective economies, regulatory systems, and policies through what they call a Security and Prosperity Partnership (SPP), which is an umbrella for two dozen trilateral working groups. Professor Robert Pastor, a former Clinton administration insider now working with SPP, has already come out in favor of a common currency that he would call "the Americo," a proposal sure to offend conceptions of American national sovereignty.

SUMMARY

This chapter places the conduct of foreign affairs in the context of two major approaches, classic and idealist. It is assumed that nations will act to protect their national interests. Because this defined how foreign policy was conducted from the outset of the nation-state system, it became known as the classic approach. Others see nations acting to pursue social or political justice, or ideals, thus the idealist approach.

The chapter identifies the major foreign policy crises of the post–World War II era: the Cold War, Vietnam, globalism, the Middle East, the unsolvable conflict between Israel and Palestinians, terrorism, and national defense.

 **RESOURCES**

American Enterprise Institute: **www.aei.org**

Brookings Institution: **www.brookings.edu**

Century Foundation: **www.tcf.org**

Ethics and Public Policy Center: **www.eppc.org**

Independent Media Review and Analysis: **www.imra.org.il**

Middle East Media Research Institute: **www.memri.org**

Terrorism Research Center: **www.terrorism.com**

Chapter 13

Private Morality and Public Policy: Moral Values, the Constitution, and the Open Society

The concept of the **open society**, which provides for tolerance and diversity of all political, social, and religious points of view, is a philosophy that the U.S. Supreme Court has appeared increasingly more willing to side with when interpreting the constitutional rights of individuals. Yet, this idea of the open society sometimes runs counter to the moral values of groups on both the Left and the Right of the political spectrum. As these groups attempt to enact their moral values as public policy, their plans can sometimes conflict with individuals' constitutional rights. As this chapter lays out in further detail, the courts and the Constitution are often at the center of these debates over controversial social issues such as abortion, gay and lesbian rights, assisted suicide, the regulation of intolerant speech on university campuses, and prayer in school.

The 1960s brought tremendous social change in the United States, and in many respects, the U.S. Supreme Court was in the middle of this change. During this time, the Court became more involved in upholding the ideals of individual liberty that flow from our Constitution, particularly in the area of rights of crime suspects, rights to privacy, and freedom of speech. Even before the 1960s, the Court had been moving toward greater involvement in protecting individual liberties and away from the New Deal controversies of government regulation of the economy. The Court's move to protect such individual rights precipitated a backlash among conservatives (both conservative Republicans and Southern conservative Democrats). In a speech in 1969, President Richard Nixon appealed to the "silent majority" in the hope of uniting conservatives

417

against the permissiveness of the more liberal counterculture of the 1960s. In 1973, the Supreme Court ruled in *Roe v. Wade* that the constitutional right to privacy included a woman's right to an abortion, providing an even greater rationale for Southern Democratic conservatives to begin uniting politically with conservative Republicans. Christian evangelist Jerry Falwell created the Moral Majority in the late 1970s as a conservative political movement designed to promote Christian family values and fight the open society. The Moral Majority heavily supported Ronald Reagan in the 1980 presidential election.

Ronald Reagan's election in 1980 heralded a process of transformation of the American Right that had been occurring for decades (as Reagan captured a large portion of the Southern conservative Democratic vote). The traditional Republican Party of Calvin Coolidge, Herbert Hoover, and Robert Taft, a party whose principles included a hierarchical sense of human nature and a commitment to **neoclassical (free market and probusiness) economics**, was partially transformed into a **neopopulist** party of the Right. This blue-collar Republicanism reflects a well-established populist tradition in American history and transformed the issue focus of the American Right from a preeminent concern with the protection of the self-regulating market and the interests of the business and capitalist classes of society to a preeminent concern with social issues and the protection of their view of public morality. Some elements of this social conservatism can be seen in the rise of the Tea Party activists in the 2010 midterm elections, though other elements of the Tea Party also contain more libertarian-minded groups who are more supportive of the open society, making for a motley crew of populist elements.

Social conservatives are not the only group opposing the concept of an open society. In recent decades, some on the political Left have also begun to oppose this concept through their support of laws designed to promote morality in the area of racial and cultural tolerance.

THE IDEA OF THE OPEN SOCIETY

The Neopopulism Emergence on the Right and Its Challenge to the Open Society

Populism is one of those social science terms without precise meaning or content; however, there is widespread agreement on several attributes associated with the concept. Rather than accepting the hierarchical view of human nature associated with traditional conservatism, populism presumes a commonsense wisdom of the working class and average person. Thus, Pat Buchanan, a well-known figure of the populist Right, alluded to being backed by "the peasants with their pitchforks," while Bill O'Reilly of Fox News claims to be "looking out for the folks." Populism is not confined to the ideological Right. From the political center, billionaire presidential candidate Ross Perot ran a populist campaign for president and later turned his populist rhetoric to fight against the adoption of the North American Free Trade Agreement, claiming it would hurt the regular working American. On the political Left, John Edwards ran a populist campaign for president in 2008 with a theme about "Two Americas." Also on the political Left, Ralph Nader has made a career out of claiming to protect the interests of working Americans against what he perceives as big corporations trying to take advantage of them. In this respect, populism further perceives that the interests of these common people are opposed by conspiratorial elites such as bankers, big business, bureaucrats, and politicians. This antielitist faith in the commonsense wisdom of the masses frequently degenerates into anti-intellectualism.

The populist tradition in the United States mobilized in the 1890s with the first nominating convention of the People's Party in 1892. Then it was basically a movement of Midwestern and Southern farmers. It eventually became expressed through such charismatic mobilizers of the marginalized masses as Democrats Huey Long, William Jennings Bryan, and Tom Watson. The populist tradition appealed to marginalized individuals such as unskilled workers, small shop-keepers, smaller farmers, and others whose economic roles and well-being seemed threatened by the forces of modernization. These people evolved into a **New Right** which was distinct from the old Republican conservatism of people like Calvin Coolidge. The clientele of the Old Right was dominated by big business, professionals, and other examples of the social and economically successful in our society. These well-educated members of the classic Right tend to be more tolerant on social issues such as moral questions or civil rights. With the new clientele of the Right, evangelical and fundamentalist Protestants and traditionalist Catholics joined such main stream Protestants as Congregationalists, Episcopalians, and Presbyterians as the core support of the GOP. The relationship between the New and Old Right may be seen graphically in Figure 13.1.

The populist revolt on the American Right was to a large extent a revolt against the **secularization** and increasing social permissiveness of the American

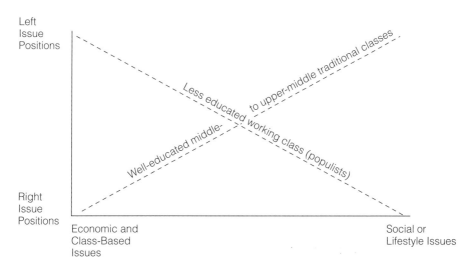

FIGURE 13.1 The Relationship between the Old and the New Right

SOURCE: American Public Policy: An Introduction 9e; Cengage Learning © 2009.

culture. In particular, the evangelical and fundamentalist clientele of the new populism were offended by the extent to which this secularization became a goal of official policy. Much of the New Right's outrage is directed at *Roe v. Wade*, which created a right to an abortion, but their angst extends to other areas as well. The religious Right has also voiced opposition against policies conferring rights to gays and lesbians, including the 2003 U.S. Supreme Court decision in *Lawrence v. Texas*, which provided protections based on privacy rights to consenting adults who engage in same-sex relationships, as well as the 2013 Supreme Court decisions allowing for gay marriage in California and the recognition of same-sex relationships for purposes of obtaining federal benefits. In short, these elements of the GOP emphasize social issues and government-mandated restoration of traditional Christian morality. Since 2008, libertarian populists have also been on the rise in the GOP, thus creating a struggle within the party, at times, between the goals of social conservatives and libertarians. Unlike social conservatives, libertarians are not concerned with private morality at all, but are instead more focused on enacting policies that create a smaller government with lower taxes and less regulation. Along with social issues, the emerging threat of militant Islamism brought foreign policy and national security issues to the forefront as discussed in the previous chapter, issues that differentiated what we have called the Old Right from the populist New Right. The Old Right tends to emphasize tolerance, cosmopolitanism, openness toward other cultures, and a belief that most international issues can be resolved through diplomacy. Libertarians have also been supportive of the Old Right positions. The New Right is more chauvinistic and hawkish toward potential foes, bringing these social issues to the forefront of the American political agenda.

The importance of these social issues to the Republicans, as well as the tensions they cause with the economic conservatives and libertarians of the party, played out in the 2011–2012 presidential primary campaign for the Republican nomination. Many social conservatives supported former Pennsylvania Senator Rick Santorum. Santorum made opposition to abortion and gay marriage the linchpins of his presidential campaign. Santorum also supported a hawkish military policy and a continuation of Bush's foreign policy. On the other side of the fence was libertarian Ron Paul, who—while nominally opposed to abortion—did not focus on the issue at all. Paul also had voted to change military policy by allowing gays to serve openly and advocated for legalizing marijuana. Rather, the focus of Paul's campaign was to drastically reduce the spending of government and to reject Bush era policies that advocated military intervention in furtherance of democracy. The GOP nominee Mitt Romney tried to thread this needle by choosing Paul Ryan as his vice-presidential nominee, as Ryan was strongly opposed to abortion but also supported some libertarian viewpoints.

Challenges to the Open Society on the Left

As noted earlier, though most challenges to the concept of an open society come from populists on the Right, there are some on the Left that are not completely comfortable with the concept. Some feminists, civil rights activists, and communitarians on the Left have sought to impose their own moral values by promoting the regulation or abolition of speech or conduct that they believe is offensive, insensitive, or intolerant toward women or people of other races or cultures. Somewhat ironically, these groups seek to enforce the value of respect for tolerance of all peoples and views by regulating or criminalizing expressions of views that they consider to be intolerant or offensive. In this respect, these groups have advocated hate crimes legislation, laws against hate speech, and laws against speech that might be considered sexual harassment in the workplace. Other examples include the rise in speech codes on university campuses. In some instances, those on the Left have resorted to protests and other political tactics to stop someone they believe is intolerant from speaking. When former Colorado Congressman Tom Tancredo, a strong conservative opponent of illegal immigration, attempted to give a speech at the University of North Carolina–Chapel Hill in the spring of 2009, hundreds of student protesters showed up, forcing university officials to shut down the speech before it even started. One student activist told the *Raleigh News and Observer,* "We don't think Tom Tancredo has the right to go around spewing his hate speech."[1] Many of these groups support laws making hate speech a crime. Thus, some liberal communitarians, like some social conservatives, seek to promote public policy that enforces their moral view of the world on others, in contradistinction to the idea of an open society, where all lifestyles and points of view are respected.

The Open Society and Tolerance of Diverse Ideas

The emerging importance of these social issues exists in a state of tension with another emerging force in American politics: the legitimation of a diverse and open society. The concept of the open society entails tolerance of diversity in *all* social, political, and religious points of view, that is, acknowledgment that different judgments on these subjects all have a right to be held and advocated. Democratic political institutions in the modern world are characterized, at a minimum, by genuine, regular competition among alternative political elites for the occupancy of decision-making roles.[2]

It is therefore presumed that the different conceptions of the public good, emanating from different interests, will be resolved by a process of bargaining and compromise in which no one group or interest will completely get its way. Each will be restrained by competing interests. The concept of an open society thus means that in matters of social, political, or ethical judgments, no one has a monopoly on truth or wisdom; therefore, it makes sense to leave the channels of communication open. As Justice Oliver Wendell Holmes said in perhaps one of the most eloquent of all expositions on the concept of freedom of thought:

> Persecution for the expression of opinions seems to me perfectly logical. If you have no doubt of your premises or your power, and want a certain result with all your heart, you naturally express your wishes in law, and sweep away all opposition. To allow opposition by speech seems to indicate that you think the speech impotent, as when a man says that he

has squared the circle, or that you do not care wholeheartedly for the result, or that you doubt either your power or your premises. But when men have realized that time has upset many fighting faiths, they may come to believe more than they believe in the very foundations of their own conduct that the ultimate good desired is better reached by free trade in ideas—that the best test of truth is the power of thought to get itself accepted in the competition of the market, and that truth is the only ground upon which their wishes safely can be carried out. That, at any rate, is the theory of our Constitution.[3]

The notion here is that if opinions or philosophies are untrue or pernicious, they will be rejected in an open society aware of competing ideas. It should not be necessary to use the enforcement machinery of the state to repress any set of ideas, even if such ideas are considered immoral by conservatives or intolerant by liberals. Rather, differences in opinion should be dealt with by discussion—the interchange of ideas. The open society further entails the principle that each perspective on these essentially subjective matters on which reasonable people will always disagree is equally legitimate—that there is no official position on matters of morality and religion. The open society refers to a libertarian view of how government treats morality. The new politics of social issues, however, centers on such concepts as family values, community, and political correctness that entail the assumption that some positions on such issues are preferable to competing positions and thus ought to be protected or encouraged with public policy. More importantly, competing positions are penalized and therefore not tolerated by public policy. The principle that all perspectives on religious, philosophical, and political positions are equally legitimate was tested in the 2012 campaign of Republican Mitt Romney, a Mormon, for president. Some religious Christians said they could never vote for a person of the Mormon faith, which they perceive as not being a Christian religion. Survey evidence from the 2012 American National Elections Studies indicate that Romney lost a small percentage of Republican votes due to his Mormon faith (as these voters stayed home); though, it is important to keep in mind that Romney's loss was undoubtedly due in large part to other factors (i.e., an economy and a foreign policy record that marginally favored the incumbent President Obama).[4]

The open society position—that all political and social points of view should not only be tolerated but may be advocated—has been put to the test in the first decade of the twenty-first century by the widely perceived threat of militant Islam to perpetrate acts of terror in the United States. There have been calls to silence radical mullahs who allegedly preach to their young followers in their madrassas (Muslim day schools) the duty to carry out violent attacks on Americans. Here, the value of the open society comes into tension with the need to provide the security that would prevent random killings of civilians. This tension was epitomized in the controversy surrounding the USA Patriot Act. The Patriot Act was enacted in 2001 in the wake of the events of September 11 of that year: it authorized the gathering of data about potential terrorists, including the interception of phone calls from known Islamist radicals to other Islamists overseas; Section 215 authorized access to such sensitive data as library and medical records. This bill was widely attacked by liberals and libertarians as an invasion of the right of privacy but defended by conservatives as a necessary tool to allow the government to protect the lives and property of its citizens against a severe and ongoing threat. Questions about who should be monitored arose again in 2013 when NSA worker Edward Snowden facilitated the unauthorized release of scores of classified secret documents. These documents outlined programs where the NSA routinely violated American citizens' privacy in an effort to find Islamic terrorists or people who may be sympathetic or verbally supportive of the goals of Islamic terrorists.

The various parts of the First Amendment all may be seen as protecting the concept of the open society, that some perspectives and values may not be suppressed by dominant majorities. The whole point of the concept of civil liberties is that there are some things that majorities may not do, no matter how politically dominant they are. This position that majorities may need to be suppressed is in a state of tension with the populist perspective, which places great faith in the wisdom of the masses and generally seeks procedures to guarantee that majorities of the moment can determine the course of public policy.

Community and Family Values versus the Open Society

The central precepts of the open society and of multiculturalism, that all perspectives are equally legitimate, exist in a state of tension with the recently rediscovered concept of community. The principle of community, as advocated by such communitarian spokespersons as Amitai Etzioni, entails the idea that the essential nature of a society is defined by a set of shared values and assumptions.[5] Thus, it may be argued by conservative communitarians that the United States is a Western society defined by the traditions of Western political thought and the Judeo-Christian religious tradition. Competing religious and philosophical perspectives, while tolerated, are not equally legitimate in defining this social system. There has been a widespread perception among conservative communitarians that the radical Islamist movement poses a direct threat to Western civilization and its values. This perception created a challenge for the multiculturalist view that all religious perspectives are equally valid and should be given equal tolerance. Thus, some scholars since at least the mid-1990s have been arguing that radical Islam is an enemy of the West—that a clash of civilizations is inevitable—while other scholars have cautioned that we should avoid stigmatizing Muslims.[6]

Conservative communitarians in general argue that these shared Judeo–Christian Western values are the cement that binds the social system together as a coherent entity and gives it meaning. America, in this perspective, stands for something; it is not merely the collection of individuals who happen to reside there. Moreover, it is argued that multiculturalism carried to its logical conclusion can lead to a segmented society—a society in which the different cultural segments are mutually isolated from one another. Such societies in the world with mutually isolated and alienated segments have not generally fared well as coherent entities able to effectively resolve issues. Our neighbor Canada has been beset with secessionist sentiment among its French-speaking subculture for some time. Belgium, where the Flemish (similar to Dutch) have often been at odds with French-speaking Walloons, has gone from a unitary state to a confederation. Nigeria has experienced a civil war between its Muslim elite and one of its Christian tribes and is proving ungovernable. The list could go on, but the message is that some level of community may be necessary in order for a political system to retain stability and effectiveness. The Christian Right in the United States, although in disagreement with the communitarians on a number of issues, has advocated widespread acceptance of traditional, bourgeois moral values— what are referred to as family values—as precisely the kind of social cement of which we have been speaking. Moreover, political scientist Robert Putnam of Harvard finds in a study published in 2007 that a culturally diverse and segmented society weakens the institutions that sustain communities and increases interpersonal distrust.[7]

"Family values" is a somewhat imprecise term that has acquired a great deal of symbolic content as a code word for many of the values that are held to delineate America as a community defined by its Western heritage. It appears to refer to many of the principles of the Judeo–Christian tradition that underlies the sense of America as a community. Family values has therefore been used to advocate against equal moral and social status for gays and lesbians; against redefinition of appropriate gender roles, and therefore for the traditional two-parent family with a male breadwinner and a female bearer and nurturer of children; and even against the promotion of effective contraception. In other words, family values has come almost to symbolize a defense of middle-class morality against the forces of secularization and change that seem to accompany modernization. To its opponents, the concept of family values suggests the idea that only a particular set of values are legitimate and that there are distinct limits to the extent to which contradictory values will be tolerated. The issues generated by the defense of family values are particularly divisive in the United States, where religious conviction and regular church attendance are quite high compared to other industrialized nations. Thus, while about 39 percent of Americans attend church weekly according to one 2013 Gallup survey (about the same level as reported by Gallup in 1950), regular attendance in the United Kingdom and other Western European countries is less than half that number. A 2012 Gallup Poll indicated that 46 percent of all Americans believed in creationism and rejected evolution. Thus, Americans are more likely to be committed to support policies designed to reinforce Christian doctrine symbolized by the concept of family values.

The movement for equal rights and equal treatment for gays and lesbians is a natural extension of the open society, but this movement offends the goals of some groups that promote family values. For example, gays and lesbians have asked (successfully) that they be allowed to serve in the armed forces without regard to their sexual orientation, and they have also pursued the right to be treated equally in marriage—working for the legal recognition of same-sex marriage.

The concept of the open society is therefore in logical conflict with the support of family values. A theme of this chapter is how this tension generates political issues that often play out in the courts. Among these issues, the following are dealt with: reproductive freedom, including access to effective contraception and medically supervised abortion; freedom in sexual relations; the suppression of pornography and the pursuit of sexual pleasure; the right to die and end-of-life care; and the protection of the practice of traditional institutional religion. This chapter also addresses the conflict between the open society and efforts to suppress hate speech, offensive conduct, and other points of view that some on the Left believe are morally intolerant and unworthy of expression.

Meanwhile, it is important to recognize that the concept of the open society is not merely of philosophical value, but is an important bulwark for the structure for democracy itself. Without acceptance of the legitimacy of positions with which one disagrees, those in power will tend to use the powerful administrative tools at their disposal (e.g., command of law enforcement and the tax structure) to suppress those who advocate those positions and thereby to suppress political opposition itself. But democracy by definition entails regular and meaningful competition for political office. Therefore, governmental imposition of a given perspective on social and moral issues is held by libertarians to threaten the political competition that is one of the cornerstones of a democratic system. Yet granting equal status to all perspectives on such issues is held by conservatives and some liberals to threaten the sense of community that is the glue that binds society and enables it to function as a coherent entity.

The Courts and Social Policy

Over the last several decades, the battleground for political fights over moral values often end up in the courts, where contentious public policy issues such as abortion, prayer in school, and hate speech, among others, often implicate constitutional rights to privacy and the First Amendment's clauses on free speech and the establishment of religion. This chapter illustrates how the U.S. Supreme Court and Constitutional law often govern the parameters of public policy options available to government when it seeks to implement social policy on hotly debated moral values questions. In these moral values fights, the U.S. Supreme Court has increasingly interpreted the Constitution in favor of the open society concept.

Political scientists and court watchers have long noted how political American courts can be. Alexis de Tocqueville famously believed that there was hardly a political question in the United States which does not sooner or later turn into a judicial one. Numerous statistical studies by political scientists confirm that while there are a number of factors that affect a Supreme Court justice's decision, his or her political ideology is not infrequently the key to understanding the justice's decision.

Before World War II, the political and ideological fights in the Supreme Court mostly dealt with how much authority the federal government (and state governments) had in regulating the economy. These fights culminated in the showdowns between the Court and President Franklin Roosevelt during the Great Depression in the 1930s. When the conservative justices on the

Court kept striking down President Roosevelt's New Deal economic plans, Roosevelt threatened to pack the Court with as many of his supporters as needed in order to get his plans approved by the Court. The Constitution does not set a limit to the number of justices who can serve on the Supreme Court. The Court eventually backed down from the president's challenge and retreated from challenging the power of the federal government and states to regulate the economy. After World War II, the politics of the Supreme Court focused a great deal on civil liberties issues before eventually wading into the culture wars of abortion and contraception in the 1960s and 1970s.

In recent decades, the process of nominating judges to the U.S. Supreme Court and the lower federal courts has become quite politicized. Hot-button cultural issues such as abortion dominate the confirmation politics of Supreme Court justices in the U.S. Senate. Lawmakers realize that judicial nominees, once confirmed to the federal bench, will be heavily influenced by their political ideology (e.g., conservative, liberal, moderate, libertarian) when making fundamental decisions on the constitutionality of laws and government regulations that deal with moral values.

Presidents therefore appoint justices to the Court who, they predict, will reflect the values that the president purports to represent. The importance of who controls the presidency is magnified by the power to shape the direction of the Court even long after that president leaves office. President George W. Bush, for example, altered the ideological makeup of the Court by appointing the conservative Samuel Alito to replace the more moderate Sandra Day O'Connor. President Barack Obama has not had a chance yet to change the ideological direction of the court, as the only justices who have retired are liberal justices, and Obama has replaced them presumably with more liberals. In 2009, liberal Justice David Souter retired, and President Obama replaced him with another liberal, Sonia Sotomayor. When liberal justice John Paul Stevens retired in 2010, he was replaced by Elena Kagan, another liberal. As of summer 2014, the makeup of the Court is shown in Table 13.1.

Rights are legally or constitutionally imposed limits on what government may choose to do. Government actions to encourage and protect family values have come into conflict with variously interpreted rights from the First Amendment, as well as with the right of *privacy,* a right not expressly stated as such in the Constitution but inferred by judicial interpretation. The fact that the exercise

TABLE 13.1   The Supreme Court in 2014

Conservative	Liberal
John Roberts, Chief Justice	Ruth Bader Ginsburg
Antonin Scalia	Elena Kagan
Samuel Alito	Sonia Sotomayor
Clarence Thomas	Stephen Breyer
Swing Vote: Anthony Kennedy	

of the right of privacy is based upon judicial inference has been used by some conservatives as a point of argument to claim that the Constitution does not explicitly guarantee such a right. The inferential basis of the right of privacy is in three amendments: the Fourth Amendment protection against "unreasonable searches and seizures," in the Fifth Amendment Due Process Clause, and in the much-overlooked Ninth Amendment that tells us "the enumeration in the Constitution of certain rights shall not be construed to deny or disparage others retained by the people." The origins of the Ninth Amendment arise out of the founders' natural law view of rights—that rights are derived from God, not from government, and thus are unalienable. The Constitution conferred limited powers upon the federal government, as designed by its original drafters. There was a fear at the time of its drafting that if explicit rights were listed in a bill of rights, there would be the assumption by implication that those rights not listed could be regulated by the government. The Ninth Amendment was placed in the bill of rights as a catch-all phrase for our rights, designed to check the federal government from regulating rights which may have been inadvertently omitted from the Constitution. Thus, the Ninth Amendment essentially reiterates the premise that the Constitution confers limited powers on the federal government and that the people retain all of their rights. The conceptual problem with the amendment is about who decides what these other rights are that are not listed. This is nothing less than an invitation for future generations and courts to find unlisted rights by inference, an elastic clause for the Bill of Rights. Yet the concept of a right of privacy—that some areas of behavior or life are none of the government's business—is one of the core attributes by which a relatively liberal society is differentiated from one with totalitarian tendencies and aspirations.

Among the purposes for which the right of privacy has been used are to protect access to information and technology for effective contraception and to professionally performed abortions, goals that conflict with the principle entailed by the family values belief that human sexuality should primarily be confined to the instrumental goal of reproduction within the bonds of marriage. The privacy right was first explicated by the Court in *Griswold v. Connecticut,* a case that struck down Connecticut's ban on the practice of artificial contraception (contraception using chemical or barrier methods). When the Court later used this inferred right to resolve the sensitive and controversial issue of the legal status of abortions by judicial fiat, this resolution proved unacceptable or illegitimate to the antiabortion or pro-life forces on the losing side. The legal status of abortion is perhaps the issue that generates the most passion and intensity of conflict of all the issues that involve the clash of inviolable moral principles of conservatives on the one hand, and the secularized, more libertarian concept of the open society on the other.

ABORTION, BIRTH CONTROL, AND THE LAW

Prior to 1973, most states criminalized abortions. The common exception was an abortion permitted when necessary to save the life of the mother. As noted earlier, *Roe v. Wade* (1973) overturned these laws as a violation of the right of privacy, a right not specifically mentioned in the Constitution, but inferred from the Fourth, Fifth, and Ninth Amendments and applied to the states through the Fourteenth Amendment.[8] Specifically, the opinion said that states are forbidden to ban abortions in the first trimester (three months) of pregnancy; states may regulate abortions in the interest of the health of the mother in the second trimester; and the state may choose to ban abortions in the final trimester unless the health (broadly considered) of the mother is in danger. The Court found that states had no "compelling interest" to intervene during the first trimester in the private decision of a pregnant woman to abort. Abortions are statistically safer than child birth for the mother during the first trimester, when performed by competent medical personnel in sanitary surroundings. Abortions become progressively more dangerous, however, during the second trimester; this gives states a compelling interest in protecting the health of the mother. At around the beginning of the third trimester, the fetus becomes viable outside the womb, and the now potentially independent new life becomes another compelling interest. These three legal distinctions in time are, of course, approximations. Fetuses born in the second trimester have survived, and fetuses born after the second trimester sometimes do not live. Moreover, the trimester division comes increasingly under question as medical advances place the viability of fetuses earlier in pregnancy. A Missouri law upheld in 1989 requires fetal viability tests on any fetus over twenty weeks old.[9] Critics argue that no fetus could survive at that early age and that the tests are dangerous and inconclusive. Antiabortion (or pro-life) forces view the fetus, no matter how small, as no different from a baby. Pro-life forces often use graphic images of aborted fetuses in protests to make their point. The recorded rate of abortion has almost doubled since *Roe v. Wade* from about 15 per 100,000 live births to about 26. It should be noted, however, that the pre-*Roe* figure may be low because illegal abortions were not accurately recorded. Despite charges that *Roe* grants the right to abortion on demand, that case affords no absolute constitutional right to a third-stage abortion. And despite the imagery employed by pro-life forces, as in Bernard Nathanson's film, *The Silent Scream,* well over 95 percent of all abortions are performed in the first trimester. Second-trimester abortions occur principally because of the availability of amniocentesis, a procedure that shows whether a fetus (or unborn child) is seriously flawed, as with spinabifida. Amniocentesis is possible only in the fourth month of the gestation period. Although hundreds of third-trimester abortions do take place, it is difficult to find physicians willing to perform them, as a recent *Los Angeles Times* notes, and those that do are subject to violent threats from extremists on the pro-life side. In 2009, Dr. George Tiller, a provider of late term abortions in Kansas, was gunned down inside his own church by a pro-life extremist.

Despite the rarity of late term abortions, attention in the late 1990s began to be focused on a particularly brutal form of late-stage abortion known as partial birth abortion, a procedure in which the unborn baby is extracted from the womb except for the head. The base of the baby's skull is pierced and the brain is sucked out, collapsing the size of the head, at which point the head is removed from the woman. This procedure is defended as being less threatening to the health and well-being of the mother, although these details do not serve to enhance public support of the pro-choice positions. Proponents of the availability of this procedure argue that there may be circumstances in which the health problems of the pregnant woman could not have been known until too late in the pregnancy and that alternative methods are effectively unavailable or unnecessarily risky to the pregnant woman. Even many of those who support a woman's right to choose to have a legal abortion, however, were repulsed by the details of this procedure, as well as by the claim that many of these procedures are performed on healthy women bearing healthy fetuses. Disagreements exist as to the frequency with which this procedure occurs; estimates range from a few hundred to a few thousand. The widespread public revulsion to partial birth abortion has led to repeated attempts to ban the procedure.

An attempted federal ban on this procedure was vetoed by President Clinton; however, the state of Nebraska passed such a ban in 2002. This ban was struck down in the case of *Stenberg v. Carhart*. With the recent changes in the makeup of the Court, a federal ban on the procedure, the Partial Birth Abortion Act signed by President George W. Bush, was upheld in *Gonzales v. Carhart* in April 2007.[10] The Supreme Court was bitterly divided in a 5–4 vote with the two new Bush appointees effectively reversing the majority in the *Stenberg* case and upholding the ban. It is not clear that this more conservative court would overturn *Roe,* however, as Chief Justice Roberts has stated his respect for precedent and "settled law."

The ease by which a pregnancy may be terminated was enhanced by the development of a pill (RU-486) in France in 1988 that induces a spontaneous expulsion of a newly implanted embryo without the necessity of any further medical procedure. The Roman Catholic Church in France forced the pharmaceutical firm that produced the pill, Roussel-Uclaf, to withdraw it from the market, but then-President Mitterrand ordered the pill placed back on the market. Faced with a threatened boycott of its other pharmaceutical products organized by the American pro-life forces, the firm was reluctant to introduce the pill into the United States. It was finally persuaded to donate the patent on the pill to the New York–based World Population Council, a contraceptive research group. The FDA has approved the pill as safe and effective and it is now widely available. President George W. Bush angered feminist and abortion rights groups by delaying a decision allowing Medicaid coverage of a morning-after pill known as Plan B that the FDA in 1996 had found "safe and effective" (a pill that prevented the implantation of a fertilized egg in the womb). The pill is currently available. Yet the administration had Medicare cover the costs of anti-impotency pills such as Viagra or Levitra. The Obama administration has reversed some of President Bush's policies on this issue, such as requiring military hospitals and clinics to carry the morning-after pill.

The Supreme Court's *Roe* decision does not require any physician to give an abortion or require any medical personnel to participate in the procedure. Rather, it says in effect that when physicians decide to give abortions to patients who freely seek them at a time when the procedure is safer than childbirth itself, it is none of the state's business. Hence, the agenda of the pro-life forces is to prevent others from violating what they regard as the moral principles of the right to life. Many hospitals, especially religiously sponsored ones, refuse to permit abortions to be performed in their facilities. In some areas, this makes legal abortions unavailable to persons who want them and who are willing and able to pay.

Meanwhile, Pennsylvania enacted a law erecting a number of barriers to the exercise of abortion rights: a mandatory twenty-four-hour waiting period for women seeking abortions, a requirement that a doctor inform the patient of the development of the fetus and of alternatives to abortions, and that minors seeking an abortion obtain the consent of one parent or a judge. The constitutionality of the law was challenged, and both pro-choice and pro-life forces saw the case as providing an instrument for the Supreme Court to issue a definitive reevaluation of the constitutionality of *Roe*. In June 1992, the Supreme Court upheld the Pennsylvania law's abortion restrictions, with several justices citing an "undue burden" standard that Justice Sandra Day O'Connor had urged be adopted in an earlier case. This standard stated that restrictions on abortions were constitutional if they did not place "an undue burden" on women seeking abortions. The Court also, however, explicitly upheld *Roe's* right to abortion.[11]

Of course, abortions are not cheap, and economic considerations limit their availability to the poor. Congress has perpetuated this situation by forbidding the use of Medicaid funds for abortions (which during much of the 1970s were provided under the program) except to save the life of the mother, even in cases of rape or incest. It is important to note, however, that one study showed that the cutoff in Medicaid funds has not substantially reduced the incidence of legal abortions. Apparently, women who want legal abortions will undergo other sacrifices or find other means to pay for them.

Access to abortion is not merely a matter of the legal right to abortion, but of having in fact access to medical personnel and facilities willing and able to perform them. Clinic access has become a contentious political issue. An aggressive pro-life movement has been led by such groups as Operation Rescue, whose tactics include the physical obstruction of clinics performing abortions, and a "Nuremberg Files" website inciting viewers against 225 identified physicians who performed abortions. Two operators of abortion clinics sought injunctive relief from the website-induced harassment under the RICO (antiracketeering statutes) while the demonstrators claimed their right to such activity was protected by the Freedom of Speech Clause of the First Amendment. In *Planned Parenthood of Columbia v. American Coalition of Life Activists,* the Ninth Circuit Court of Appeals upheld the freedom of speech claims against a court injunction prohibiting harassment in the form of mobilizing hatred of abortion providers through the Internet.[12] Congress and some states in the early 1990s enacted laws designed to protect access to abortion facilities by restricting the activities and distances of protesters. The Supreme Court in *Hill v. Colorado* had upheld a state law establishing restrictions on antiabortion protesters within 100 feet of the clinic, commanding an eight-foot space between the protester and the abortion clinic client.[13] The difference between the cases is that the Colorado law involved physical impediments to abortion clinic clients while the Columbia case did not involve physical force, a distinction that the Court has long used.[14]

Pro-life forces have responded in many cases by escalating their tactics, including resorting to violence against medical personnel performing abortions. Since 1993, five people, including two physicians, were murdered at abortion clinics by three individuals who at some point have been associated with the organized harassment of abortion clinics and their patrons. In 1993, Dr. David Gunn was shot and killed by Michael Griffen of Rescue America; in 1994, Dr. John Britton and his escort were murdered by Paul Hill; and in 1995, two receptionists at abortion clinics in Massachusetts were slain by an individual who had been associated with picketing abortion clinics. Pro-choice people were outraged that a number of people in the pro-life movement suggested that these killings were somehow justified in the light of the many unborn children killed by abortion. John Burt of Rescue America said that the shootings were "unfortunate" but a large number of "babies' lives will be saved." Mainstream pro-life groups strongly condemned such killings. Many medical personnel offering abortion services saw these events as an implicit threat to the health and safety of themselves and their families. In some cases, the threats were explicit. This violence continued through 1996 with the bombing of a Planned Parenthood clinic that performed abortions in Spokane, Washington, and a fatal bombing in Birmingham, Alabama, in early 1998. As mentioned earlier, in 2009 Dr. George Tiller, a provider of late-term abortion services, was killed inside his own church in Kansas. As a result of such violence, numerous doctors who were performing abortions are no longer willing to do so. Fewer medical students are electing to learn the procedure, although a couple of states now require that medical residents in obstetrics-gynecology be trained in abortion procedures. It is still true, however, that while abortion may be technically legal, in many parts of the United States it is difficult to find medical personnel willing and able to perform the procedure. This is particularly true in rural areas.

Access to abortion continues to be a source of contention in politics at the national level. The debate over access to abortion became heated in Congress while lawmakers were considering President Obama's health care reform bill in 2010. During the final vote on passage of the health care law, as Democratic Congressman Bart Stupak of Michigan was giving a speech at the podium defending a deal he made with the president to limit the use of federal funds for use in elective abortions, Republican Congressman Randy Neugebauer of Lubbock, Texas, yelled out "Baby Killer," to the shock and astonishment of his colleagues at this breach in etiquette on the House floor. Another issue in access to abortion concerns new state laws requiring doctors who perform abortions at clinics to have admitting privileges at local hospitals, and the imposition of these additional requirements on abortion clinics means that some clinics must shut down.

Contraception.   The same logic that impels concern over the availability of safe, legal abortion applies to the availability of effective contraception. The argument of pro-life forces that abortion should not be used for birth control is strengthened if effective contraception is realistically available. Yet some conservative forces have opposed the promotion of effective contraception.

One example of this is the opposition of such groups to sex education in school on the grounds that it encourages promiscuity. Another is the example of the so-called "squeal rule" established by the Reagan administration and avidly supported by forces of the religious Right. This was the executive order denying federal funds to any clinic that provided contraception aid to minors unless the parents of such minors were notified. Supporters pointed to the value of parental responsibility and control of minors, a quintessential family values position, involving not only parental control but also the protection of middle-class moral principles, especially with regard to extramarital sexual activity. Opponents argued that such a rule would only discourage minors from seeking such aid, not from engaging in sexual activity. The liberal position is that sexual activity is inevitable; therefore, denying access to abortion and birth control will merely produce the spillover effect of unwanted pregnancy. The conservative assumption appears to be that the ability to have illicit sex without the risks of pregnancy encourages promiscuity.

Conservatives are also concerned that some forms of contraception destroy a fetus, thus in effect resulting in an abortion. The politics over contraception policies have become more visible in the wake of the Affordable Care Act. The law mandates that employers (including for-profit companies and most nonprofit corporations such as Catholic hospitals) must provide contraception services such as the morning-after pill to their workers in their health care plans, though churches are exempt from the law. This aspect of the law sparked a lawsuit by Hobby Lobby and a Catholic charity for the elderly called Little Sisters of the Poor. In January 2014, liberal Justice Sonia Sotomayor surprisingly approved an emergency stay to halt the law's implementation against Little Sisters (this case is still working its way through the courts as of this writing). As for Hobby Lobby, the U.S. Supreme Court took up their case, and its details are discussed further below.

The Moral Issue.   Opponents of abortion base their opposition mainly on the premise that the fetus is in fact a human being; therefore, legal abortions are tantamount to the legalization of murder. The point of disagreement is whether life begins at the point of conception. Many aver that human life commences at birth or when the fetus becomes viable outside the womb. Opponents of abortion—led by many New Right conservatives and religious groups—argue that legalized abortions encourage greater use of this procedure, to the point that the procedure becomes a form of birth control. Moral considerations require the state to take a stand against what these opponents see as legalized killing. The data seem to support the claim that the number of abortions has increased considerably since abortion was made legal (though the last two decades have seen a decline in the abortion rate), and it is undeniable that many fetuses are aborted by pregnant women simply because they do not want the child, rather than for reasons of health.

Supporters of legal abortion (i.e., pro-choice groups)—who tend to be liberal and religiously secularized—object to the contentions of pro-life groups on two grounds. First, whether legal or not, women who need abortions will seek them out. Second, pro-choice groups argue that the availability of legal abortions is fundamentally an issue of protecting the civil right of women to make their own decisions about themselves—in this case, that is, the right not to allow the state to dictate what choices they may make about their own bodies.

Pro-choice activists point out that abortion has long been a widespread reality, legal or otherwise. By criminalizing the procedure, the state may reduce the number of abortions, but it cannot prevent many abortions from occurring. Criminalizing abortion may have the impact of driving many pregnant women to incompetent and untrained abortionists, with disastrous effects on the lives and health of the women involved, although pro-life forces dispute these claims. When abortion was against the law, many women died each year, from crudely performed, unsanitary, illegal abortions—women who in many cases would have lived had legal abortions been available. Therefore, supporters of legal abortion emphasize that the number of unborn children saved by criminalizing abortion must be balanced against the number of pregnant women killed or seriously maimed.

To pro-life groups, these considerations pale in the face of their strongly held beliefs that readily available, affordable, and safe abortion (1) constitutes a form of murder, and (2) encourages sexual promiscuity. Here again we find a concern with deterring the promiscuous activity overriding the prevention of unwanted pregnancies, which clearly exacerbates the demand for abortion. The feelings here are so strong that the arguments on this issue are antithetical moral assumptions that cannot be resolved by discussion. What pro-choice groups call choice or freedom, pro-life groups call promiscuity or murder.

Moreover, the issue of legalized abortion is perceived as a matter of equality for women, as the legal availability of abortions gives women greater decision-making power over their lives. They have greater freedom to pursue sexual activity—as men do—without suffering the consequences of childbearing, and they need not retire from economic pursuits to raise children from unwanted pregnancies. Abortion and birth control offer greater alternative possibilities to women beyond their traditional roles of homemaker and raiser of children. On the other hand, many opponents of abortion see it as a fundamental moral issue, a question of human life and dignity and a defense of the family values that defined the United States as a community.

The Continuing Legal Fight over Abortion.   The Supreme Court, as constituted at this writing, does not appear disposed to reject the right to abortion as such but, with a current 5–4 conservative majority, the Court may act to further restrict that right. If *Roe* were to be reconsidered by the Court, however, the decision would be vulnerable on the inferential nature of the right of privacy that underlies it and on the justification of when the fetus acquires life. The Court's justification for allowing states to ban abortion in the third trimester is based on the presumed point at which the fetus becomes independent of the mother in the sense of survival outside the womb. However, since the decision was handed down in 1973, medical technology has enabled fetuses to survive miscarriage in the second trimester, in rare cases as early as twenty-three weeks. The National Abortion Rights Action League (NARAL) estimates as of 2005 that should *Roe* be overturned, pro-life forces in thirty-eight states have the power and determination to again criminalize most or all abortions throughout the gestation period.

As the Supreme Court has chipped away at the right to an abortion in various decisions since *Roe v. Wade*, states have increasingly tested how far they can go in restricting abortions. In 2013, North Dakota passed a couple of antiabortion laws. One law bans abortions after a fetal heartbeat is detected, which can be as early as six weeks after gestation, and the law has been challenged in court. The other North Dakota law requires doctors who perform abortions to have admitting privileges at a local hospital, thus increasing the burdens on abortion clinics in terms of the costs of staying open. Texas passed a similar requirement of admitting privileges and that law was upheld by the U.S. Fifth Circuit Court of Appeals. In 2013, Arkansas passed a law banning all abortions after twelve weeks, but a federal court struck down the law. Arizona tried to ban abortions after twenty weeks in a law passed in 2012, but the law was struck down by the U.S. Ninth Circuit Court of Appeals. A number of other states have made similar attempts in recent years to pass laws designed to curtail abortions or make it more difficult for abortion clinics to operate.

The determination of pro-life forces to criminalize abortion remains unabated despite opinion polls indicating that a majority of Americans support access to legal abortion in some circumstances. The incidence of direct physical impediment to the operation of clinics or medical facilities performing abortions intensified during the 1990s coordinated by Operation Rescue, and employed tactics of sit-ins at abortion facilities. Pro-choice forces have responded by advocating laws and injunctions severely restricting pro-life speech and demonstrations near abortion facilities. The Supreme Court, it will be recalled, upheld such a law in the *Hill* case but also upheld the free speech rights of pro-life activists to mobilize opposition to abortion providers through their website. Pro-life forces argue that this is an assertion of their free speech rights, a right that is asserted on both sides of the morality and family values debate.

End-of-Life Care, Assisted Suicide, and the Preservation of Life

The moral perspective underlying the religious right's position on contraception and abortion, the perspective that elevates the preservation of life, regardless of its quality, to a moral absolute, emerged in the related issue of assisted suicide or euthanasia. Most states do not allow assisted suicide, but currently four states allow physician-assisted suicide (Oregon, Washington, Vermont, and, in a roundabout way, Montana). The debate of what rights people have toward the end of life reached the Supreme Court in 1990 in the case *Cruzan v. Director, Missouri Department of Health*. In that case, Nancy Cruzan suffered injuries in a car accident which caused her to be in a persistent vegetative state, and her family requested that life support be turned off. The state of Missouri objected, however, and the Supreme Court ruled that her family must present "clear and convincing evidence" that Ms. Cruzan would have wanted to refuse medical treatment and have life support turned off in this situation. To satisfy the

Supreme Court's new legal standard clarifying the rights of persons in a coma or a persistent vegetative state, the family then returned to the trial court with more evidence to support their claim that Ms. Cruzan would not have wanted to remain on life support.

Questions about how someone wants to be treated near the end of life or while in a permanent coma can be addressed using a living will. Most people, however, never take the time to draw one up. Thus, questions over the right to terminate life-sustaining treatment (if the person is unable to speak for themselves) often depend on what statements the person in question may have made earlier in life about their intentions. This debate attracted national attention in the case of Terry Schiavo, a Florida woman who had been in a persistent vegetative state for years. Her husband filed legal action to have her feeding tube removed, but Ms. Schiavo's parents fought their son-in-law in court for years to keep their daughter alive. After Ms. Schiavo's feeding tube was removed for a second time by a state judge in 2003, the Florida legislature got involved in an emergency session, passing "Terri's Law," which gave Florida Governor Jeb Bush authority to intervene. The Florida state courts struck down the law, and by January 2005, the parents had taken the case all the way to the U.S. Supreme Court. The Supreme Court refused to hear the appeal, and so a Florida state judge once again ordered Ms. Schiavo's feeding tube to be removed. Shortly thereafter, the U.S. Congress became involved, with conservatives passing a bill that allowed the case to move to federal court—a bill which President Bush promptly signed into law. But the federal courts refused to reinsert the feeding tube, and Ms. Schiavo died. In the wake of this dispute, a number of states have sought to clarify people's rights to life and end-of-life care. More recently, a dispute arose in Texas when a Fort Worth hospital cited a Texas law and refused to end life support for a pregnant woman. In this situation, the question was how to balance the rights of Marlise Munoz versus the rights of the fetus. The husband, with the support of Ms. Munoz's parents, went to court to have her removed from life support. A court agreed that the law had been misinterpreted by the hospital and ordered that Ms. Munoz be removed from life support.

Of a slightly different concern is the issue of whether a conscious person, who is near death and is suffering, can request help in terminating her life early (i.e., assisted suicide). The issue of the right to die and assisted suicide gained wider attention in the 1990s through the efforts of Dr. Jack Kevorkian (otherwise known as "Dr. Death"). Dr. Kevorkian believed in helping terminally ill patients die when they are in pain and express a desire to die. Although Michigan revoked Dr. Kevorkian's medical license, he assisted nearly one hundred presumably terminally ill people in dying during the 1990s. In Oregon in 1994, voters approved an initiative legalizing physician-assisted suicide. The law allows physicians to prescribe drugs to hasten death for patients who have been confirmed to be suffering from a terminal illness and are undergoing considerable pain waiting for their inevitable death. In 2001, the Bush administration challenged the state law, saying it violated the federal government's Controlled Substances Act (CSA). The Supreme Court, in *Gonzales v. Oregon* (2006), upheld the state law, stating that the CSA had to do with drug dealing and that the federal law could not be used to dictate the standards of medical practices in states.[15] As in the cases of abortion and contraception, the religious Right opposes the right to terminate life, while the secular Left supports the Oregon law. Aside from the moral issues involved, some argue that legalizing assisted suicide or euthanasia could result in terminally ill patients being pressured to end their life (or even being involuntarily euthanized) for the purposes of harvesting their organs or cutting down on health costs.

THE FIRST AMENDMENT AND PUBLIC MORALITY: SUPPRESSING OBSCENITY AND OFFENSIVE SPEECH

Freedom of Speech

Socially conservative forces such as the Christian Coalition, in furtherance of so-called family values issues, have also attempted to reverse the liberalization of laws permitting the distribution of literature, films, and other materials with strong sexual content, material they regard as pornographic or obscene. Liberals have also sought to impose their values of tolerance on society by pushing for laws that prohibit speech that they regard as intolerant, hateful, or sexist. Oftentimes, these policies advocated by conservatives or liberals (to regulate obscene or intolerant speech or publications) also implicate First Amendment freedoms of speech and of the press. Thus, the courts often have to step in to provide the boundaries under which these policies can be adopted. First, we take up the issue of obscenity raised by social conservatives.

The concept of obscenity refers to that which offends widely accepted basic values or a sense of decency. In the American context, obscenity has for the most part been applied to sexual content, although more recently liberal forces have been trying to stress the graphic display or depiction of violence as obscene. Of course, the attempt to suppress material on obscenity grounds comes into conflict with the constitutional protection of freedom of speech as well as with the concept of the open society. The extent of that conflict depends on the interpretation that the courts give to the phrase "freedom of speech." Judges have developed a set of principles or criteria by which they may consistently interpret that phrase.

The absolutist position on free speech holds that the Freedom of Speech Clause constitutionally protects all utterances or published material, regardless of their worth. The Supreme Court has rejected the absolutist interpretation. In lieu of such an interpretation, the Court has had to develop criteria or standards by which some categories of speech or expression are deemed unworthy of constitutional protection and are considered outside the bounds of the concept of free speech as contemplated by the Constitution.

Traditionally, in English common law, the concept of freedom of speech merely entailed a restriction on the right of government to suppress what was being said or written in advance of the utterance; in other words, it prohibited

censorship.[16] Legal scholars refer to this as the doctrine of **prior restraint**. The doctrine of prior restraint under English common law equated freedom of speech as the right to publish something without the government prohibiting or restraining you before you even publish. However, even though people are not censored from writing something before it is published, this doctrine leaves open the possibility that government may punish speakers after the material becomes published. Historically, speakers in England might have faced punishment for seditious libel, that is, false criticism of the government.

Freedom of speech now means more than the absence of prior restraint, but the concept has always meant at least that much. In that sense, the absence of prior restraint represents a floor in one's rights to free speech. Thus, when a government moves to shut down a publication or censor material, the government faces a heavy burden to show that such an exercise in prior restraint is justified under the Constitution. Denial of licenses to speak, injunctions not to publish, and the like are strongly presumed to be unconstitutional unless the government can justify their actions based on an extremely compelling interest (and that is usually very difficult to do, unless the publication refers to troop movements during a war or something gravely similar). This is significant because policy to protect public morality has frequently involved censorship of materials thought to be obscene and morally corrupting.

It is, however, especially difficult to reconcile censorship with the concept of an open society presented in these pages. Censorship, after all, pertains to a small elite, often self-designated, telling the general population of presumably rational adults what they are to be permitted to read, hear, or view and to what values or thoughts they may be safely exposed without being morally corrupted. But the concept of an open society entails the assumption that rational adults are the best judges of their own interests, that they are able to choose among the many ideas and values to which they are exposed. Here again we see that the concept of the open society comes into apparent conflict with protection of family values and public morality.

The courts and legal profession have often viewed the Free Speech Clause as primarily protecting political discussion. Beyond that, the courts have defined categories of speech whereby certain expressions are allowed to be regulated by the government. These categories include such expressions as fighting words; commercial speech; libel or slander of private individuals; advocacy of revolution or violence where such advocacy would result in *imminent* lawless action; speech or expression deemed obscene; and speech subject to reasonable time, place, and manner restrictions (such as noise restrictions that would disallow a political protest at 3 a.m. in the morning, or university rules that would prohibit a student from standing up in the middle of astronomy class and begin talking about abortion). The Supreme Court case of *Chaplinsky v. New Hampshire* (1942), a case which has never been reversed, suggests that there are certain categories of speech that are outside the bounds of what people consider to be free speech protected by the Constitution:

> There are certain well defined and limited classes of speech, the prevention and punishment of which has never been thought to raise any

Constitutional problem. These include the lewd and obscene, the profane, the libelous and the insulting or "fighting" words—those that by
their very utterance inflict injury or tend to incite a breach of the peace.
It has been well observed that such utterances are no essential part of
any exposition of ideas and are of such slight value as a step to the truth
that any benefit that may be derived from them is clearly outweighed by
the social interest in order and morality.[17]

The historical trend in behavior by the courts suggest that they are more
likely than not to end up siding with the concept of an open society when interpreting the Constitution, but there is some room for government to engage in
public policy in limiting expression which the majority finds immoral. The courts
often consider the right of expression in terms of democracy and whether the
speech or expression contributes to a free exchange of ideas or infringes on the
rights of others. The next two sections address how two categories of speech—
fighting words and obscene speech—have an impact on the regulation of moral
values within the context of an open society.

Fighting Words and Regulating Insensitive Speech

With the passage of civil rights legislation in the 1960s, the U.S. government
finally began addressing the wrongs committed against racial and ethnic minorities throughout our history. Congress has continued to pass additional civil rights
bills in order to further address issues of inequality. While these laws sought to
outlaw discrimination and provide opportunities for minority groups, an important component for making these laws more effective is changing the hearts and
minds of people and ending a culture of racism. To deal with this concern, some
on the Left have advocated laws which regulate or prohibit insensitive speech or
intolerant expression, including racial or religious slurs. The argument by those
on the Left is that such speech or expression is morally unacceptable in public
discourse and has no value for the free exchange in ideas. To this end, some
communities have enacted laws that specifically banned speech that incites racial
or religious hatred, so-called hate speech laws. Another variant of this effort are
hate crimes legislation. Hate crimes laws provide for additional punishment to
people engaging in a criminal act, if their motives behind the act were based
on ill will toward a specific minority group or religious group or based on a
person's gender or sexual orientation.

Critics claim that the behaviors that such laws are intended to proscribe are
rendered punishable under other existing, conventional statutes such as those
penalizing destruction of property, incitement to violence, and so on. Furthermore, in the context of hate speech, the determiner of whether the speech or
expression is considered "hate" will be the government. Thus, the concern by
critics is that a current majority who controls government will broaden the definition of hate speech and use these laws as an excuse to punish speech with
which the majority ideologically disagrees. For example, would expressing

opposition to affirmative action policies be considered hate speech? In the San Francisco Bay Area in 2010, a high school principal sent several students home for wearing T-shirts showing the American flag on Cinco de Mayo day, a national holiday in the country of Mexico.[18] The principal said that the students could wear the T-shirts on any other day, but not on Cinco de Mayo, because such an action was insensitive to Mexican Americans. Some Mexican American students had said that they were offended that these boys would wear the red, white, and blue on a Mexican holiday. Generally, most advocates of hate speech laws would not consider such expressions hate speech, and it is highly unlikely the courts would uphold such an interpretation under the First Amendment. But, even more generally, it is doubtful the Supreme Court would uphold *any* hate speech law as constitutional, unless it could be shown that such a law falls within the category of unprotected speech known as fighting words.

The problem with using the **fighting words doctrine** to outlaw hate speech is that the Supreme Court has weakened this doctrine over the years, and has permitted a wide array of intolerant speech to occur on the basis that such speech is protected by the Constitution. In the *Chaplinsky* case, the Supreme Court upheld the conviction of Chaplinsky, a Jehovah's Witness, because in essence, he had yelled at a police officer, calling him a "damned fascist" and "a God-damned Racketeer." The state law under which Chaplinsky was tried prohibited "any offensive, derisive, or annoying word to any other person who is lawfully in the street." If this law was upheld, one might assume that laws prohibiting hate speech could also be upheld.

But hate speech laws are unlikely to benefit from the *Chaplinsky* case. The only reason that the U.S. Supreme Court upheld the law was because the state of New Hampshire limited the regulation of the speech in three important ways. First, in order to be prosecuted under this law, the forbidden word had to be directed at a specific person. Second, the word had to "have a direct tendency to cause acts of violence by persons to whom … the remark is addressed." Third, the definition of "offensive" could not be defined simply by whether the "addressee" was offended. In other words, just because someone is offended by a remark does not mean the state could punish the person making the remark. Rather, the Court said that "the test is what men of common intelligence would understand would be words likely to cause an average addressee to fight." Interpreted in this way, the fighting words doctrine would not cover many facets of a hate speech law. For example, publishing a racially intolerant book or having a parade to promote one's intolerance against gays and lesbians, or yelling out racial epithets to oneself on the street could not be prohibited by the government because one is not directing the speech specifically at an individual. On the other hand, one could be prosecuted under the fighting words doctrine for yelling racial epithets specifically at another individual.

The idea that one's offensive statements must be directed at a particular individual was further supported by the Supreme Court in the *Cohen v. California* case (1971). In this case, the Court overturned Cohen's conviction for inciting a disturbance of the peace (Cohen had worn a jacket in the halls of the Los

Angeles County Courthouse bearing the epithet, "Fuck the draft"). In this case, no disturbance actually ever occurred. There was no evidence that Cohen intended to offend anyone or that anyone was actually offended. The Court held that times change and that words that offend at one time and place may not offend elsewhere; in other words, no phrase is inherently and necessarily beyond First Amendment protection.

The problem of prohibiting hate speech was most aptly demonstrated by the 1978 case of the American Nazi Party's request to conduct a parade and rally, complete with swastikas, SS uniforms, and jackboots, down the streets of Skokie, Illinois, a community with a preponderantly Jewish population and numerous survivors of Nazi extermination camps. Clearly, no persuasion was likely to take place in this context. What was being protected was the Nazi Party's right to symbolically and explicitly express its racist and anti-Semitic ideology. The city of Skokie had attempted to prevent the march by several means, including the requirement of a confiscatory bond against potential damage and, perhaps more significantly, an injunction against utterances that castigated any racial or religious group. The U.S. federal district court held that racial slurs are a protected form of speech under the Constitution, and the Illinois Supreme Court held that "... the display of the swastika in Skokie cannot be enjoined under the fighting words exception to free speech, nor can the anticipation of a hostile reaction justify prior restraint."

This case showed that if a parade of anti-Semitic slurs by avowed Nazis through the neighborhood of concentration camp survivors is not fighting words in the Chaplinsky sense of the term, it is hard to imagine any other utterance that would so qualify. In striking down the injunction against racial slurs, the U.S. district court reasoned as follows:

> The question is not whether there are some ideas that are unacceptable
> in a civilized society. Rather the question is which danger is greater: the
> danger that allowing the government to punish "unacceptable" ideas
> will lead to the suppression of ideas that are merely uncomfortable to
> those in power; or the danger that permitting free debate on such
> unacceptable ideas will encourage their acceptance rather than discour-
> aging them by revealing their pernicious quality.

The district court found the former danger to be greater, a decision affirmed by the U.S. Supreme Court.

The Cohen and Skokie cases have very nearly transformed the interpretation of the Freedom of Speech Clause to embrace any politically based form of expressive utterance, and the Supreme Court has continued this libertarian view of free speech rights. In a 1992 case involving the burning of a cross on the lawn of an African American family, the Court struck down a Minnesota hate speech ordinance banning speech that "arouses anger, alarm or resentment in others" as an overly broad infringement on freedom of speech.[19] Obviously, speech that arouses anger or offends is exactly the kind of speech that the First Amendment is designed to protect; one does not need constitutional protection to say what everyone wants to hear.

The Political Correctness Controversy. Still, these court cases have apparently not laid to rest the issue of the constitutional protection of inflammatory speech, especially with regard to the protection of racial slurs. Colleges and universities have taken the lead in the attempt to suppress speech that is regarded as insensitive to targeted racial and ethnic groups. The campaign to suppress speech offensive to some oppressed groups arose from a spate of racial insults on American college campuses. At the University of Michigan, for example, in 1987, a radio talk show host at the university-run station called for listeners to contribute their favorite racial jokes. In 1988, at Yale University, someone painted a swastika and the phrase "white power" on the Afro-American Center.

The University of Michigan took the lead in late 1988 in adopting a rule restricting speech that members of targeted groups found offensive, again raising the question posed earlier with regard to hate speech laws, whether one can, consistent with the concept of freedom of speech, grant anyone the right not to be offended. The policy adopted defined as punishable "any behavior, verbal or physical, that stigmatizes or victimizes an individual on the basis of ethnicity, religion, sex, sexual orientation, creed, national origin, ancestry, age, marital status, handicap, or Vietnam-era veteran status." University officials averred that freedom of speech does not include the right to harass or injure others. Harassment or injury is further described as a situation in which a person perceives that he or she is in "a hostile learning environment." Sanctions may vary from reprimand to expulsion. The significant departure in such policies on "insensitive speech" is to define the offense as how the listeners perceive or react to the speech rather than the content of what is said or the tone and style of the writer or speaker. The punishing of speech because of the way others perceive it or react to it violates an established rule of law called **scienter** (roughly, "knowledge of wrongdoing")—that the distinction between what is permissible and what is sanctioned must be specified in advance of the act in question. One cannot be sure at what others will take offense. Several other schools have adopted policies of speech censorship patterned after the Michigan model, including Middlebury College, Brown University, Pennsylvania State University, Tufts University, Stanford University, and the Universities of California, Connecticut, North Carolina, Pennsylvania, and Wisconsin.[20] Some of these speech codes, however, could be unconstitutional if enforced by a government-run state university. For the state university speech code to be constitutional, it has to be seen as outlawing only fighting words directed at a specific individual.

In some cases, conservative critics of such suppression charge that the leaders in academic communities and the media have imposed a criterion of political correctness on permissible expression. The vagueness of the definition of racial or ethnic insensitivity is seen by some as allowing its use as a tool to limit the expression of positions that contradict a liberal perspective. In some instances it has virtually come to include anything to which the target group members take offense.

For example, Harvard University defined racial harassment as any actions or words "which cause another individual or group to feel demeaned or abused because of their racial or ethnic background." The offense, in this reading, consists not in what the speech in question actually says, but how some people feel about it. In February 1988, Stephan Thernstrom, Winthrop Professor of History at Harvard, was charged with racial insensitivity because he had quoted southern plantation owners on the subject of black character during his lectures. Although his tenure was not threatened, Thernstrom was chastised by university officials and warned to avoid "possible insensitivity in lecturing." He claimed that he was quoting for analytical purposes, not expressing his own views, and that he was unaware of having given offense. A similar event occurred at the University of Maryland when a professor of Latin American History read to his class a description of Native Americans written by Spanish conquistadors. The professor was required to read a formal apology to his class for "racist speech." Such accusations of alleged insensitivity are based upon subjective perceptions of those most easily offended and appear to be impermissibly vague by any interpretation of the First Amendment.

Similarly, an editor of the student newspaper at California State University at Northridge was suspended from school for printing a political cartoon critical of affirmative action, and another student was suspended for writing a letter to the paper criticizing the editor's suspension. There was no suggestion that either the letter or the cartoon was outside the bounds of taste and propriety or unduly inflammatory; rather, the sin seems to be the substance of the position.

Militant Muslims have added their group to the list of people demanding protection from being offended. In 2006, militant Muslims staged violent riots worldwide to protest cartoons published in a Danish newspaper making fun of the prophet Mohammed. Some devout Muslims stated that it brings great offense to their religion to see printed cartoon images of the prophet Mohammed. In Syria, Muslim protesters burned down the Danish and Norwegian embassies.[21] Norway was targeted simply for republishing the cartoons.

In 2010, Comedy Central Network censored portions of an episode of the cartoon *South Park* that showed the prophet Mohammed dressed up in a bear costume. *South Park's* creators Trey Parker and Matt Stone have often poked fun at various organized religions, from Scientology to Buddhism to Christianity. In fact, in one *South Park* cartoon episode, Jesus Christ is depicted defecating on President Bush and the American flag. Previously in 2006, Comedy Central had refused to allow Parker and Stone to include an image of Mohammed in their cartoon. In the 2010 episode, all the previously offended icons (from religious figures to celebrities) file a class action lawsuit against the town of South Park. To get around the problem of displaying Mohammed's image and to call attention to the issue of censorship, Parker and Stone decided to depict Mohammed dressed up in a bear costume throughout the entire cartoon (so that no actual image of the prophet would ever be shown, only the caricature of a bear costume). But ironically, after Comedy Central received threats from a radical Muslim website, they engaged in censorship by bleeping out all references to the prophet before showing the episode. The *L.A. Times* couched the issue as one where "media conglomerates are still struggling to balance free speech with safety concerns and religious sensitivities."[22] UCLA law professor Eugene Volokh told the *L.A. Times*, "The consequence of this position is that the thugs win and people have more incentive to be thugs. There are lots of people out there who would very much like to get certain kind of material removed, whether religious or political. The more they see others winning, the more they will be likely to do the same." In a demonstration of solidarity, *The Simpsons* TV show on the FOX Network showed Bart Simpson writing 100 times on the chalkboard in the opening scene of a 2010 program, "*South Park*—We'd stand beside you if we weren't so scared."

Great effort continues to be made to avoid offending certain groups, as exemplified by the British Broadcasting Company's (BBC) banning the use of the term *terrorists* to refer to the perpetrators of the 2007 London Tube bombings, referring to them instead as "misguided criminals." Dr. Paul Payek, president of the Global Language Monitor, claims "in 2006, the Political Correctness Movement continued to gain momentum...." Clearly, the protection of minorities against being offended by hate speech is taking priority over more rigorous interpretations of freedom of speech. Moreover, the diversity sought by proponents of race-based college admissions (discussed in Chapter 10) apparently does not include diversity of opinion. The political correctness movement is designed to guard against insensitivity to the feelings of affected minority groups. Carrying this goal a step further, a movement known as **multiculturalism** seeks as a goal the protection of the self-esteem of members of these groups, especially through changes in curricula to reflect the contributions of such groups. (Multicultural issues in education are discussed in Chapter 9.)

The campaign to restrain expression is not limited to insensitivity to racial and ethnic groups but has at times required conformity to the values of the intellectual left in general. During the 1991 war in the Persian Gulf, for instance, administrators at the University of Maryland ruled that students may not fly the American flag in support of the war effort because such displays might offend those (including many administrators) who opposed the resort to arms.

Many charge that the nation's universities, heretofore counted on to defend the unfettered exchange of ideas, have now taken the lead in suppressing the expression of ideas that are regarded as politically incorrect. The range of what is considered too insensitive to be permitted is both broad and expanding.

It may be inferred, in light of the Skokie incidents, that the First Amendment protects the right to express pejorative claims about a group in general; therefore, many state university speech codes are carefully drawn to proscribe only insults directed at individuals. Yet the incidents that gave rise to these codes frequently involved insults to groups as a whole. Few people would claim that a Nazi's bigoted speech is worth much of anything, but the Constitution does not allow for the prosecution of one's beliefs, even if those beliefs are intolerant and despicable.

Obscenity and the Marketplace of Ideas

While some liberals tend to promote the idea of censoring offensive hate speech, conservatives tend to advocate censoring what they see as sexually obscene expression. It should be noted that the material in question in obscenity legislation rarely contributes to the free exchange of ideas. Much of it does not even qualify as worthwhile artistic expression by the standards of most critics. Controversial examples include Andres Serrano's photograph of a crucifix in a glass of urine, nude dancer Karen Finley smearing herself with chocolate and moving her hands on her body in a highly suggestive fashion, and performance artist Annie Sprinkle, who invited the audience to closely examine her sexual organs. But a great deal of material that is regarded as artistically valuable has in some places been suppressed on obscenity grounds, some of which are listed in the following discussion. Good literature, attempting to deal with life in a realistic way, does not ignore the reality of human sexuality. The origin of obscenity legislation, however, never rested on critical measures of aesthetic worth; instead, it sought to protect communities from the perceived social evils of sexually explicit material in any context. Essentially, such legislation had two goals: the reduction of sexual stimulation and the perpetuation of the view sometimes found in Christianity that sex for pleasure is an avoidable and undesirable aspect of human personality and interaction. The Puritan tradition in America, once characterized by H. L. Mencken as the nagging fear that somewhere someone may be enjoying himself, was the heir of this view. The suppression of information about sex, however, has been a spillover effect of obscenity legislation.

One source of controversy in this arena is that different individuals have differing levels of tolerance for sexually related material. Some are greatly offended by any four-letter expletive; others are untroubled by graphic depictions of sex acts. Those who are most easily offended tend to be the most active in trying to obtain legislation and ensure its enforcement of their more restrictive moral standards on others. People who are less easily offended are generally less concerned about pornography, and they have left the field to the wishes of the moralists. Moreover, there is an additional pressure that tends to prevent those with a more tolerant attitude from defending pornography too vigorously, for there is a certain stigma attached to taking such a position; one risks being identified as a consumer of pornography and an oversexed deviant. Thus the censor's position seems more legitimate than that of the defenders of freedom of speech and expression.

Censorship, Obscenity, and the Law: The *Roth* Rule

The courts have never taken the position that **obscenity**, defined here as materials of a graphic nature that have the primary purpose to arouse erotic impulses, should itself be granted First Amendment protection. The difficulty is that much material that might otherwise be deserving of such protection contains sexually explicit elements. The constitutional problem has been to devise principles that will allow society to shield its citizens from being unduly sexually stimulated or offended without closing off their access to art, literature, and ideas that are protected by the Free Speech Clause. The common-law interpretation of freedom of speech gave wide latitude to the discretion of government censors in the suppression of sexually relevant material. The nineteenth-century *Hicklin* **test** (1868) judged something to be obscene if any isolated passage in the material has a "tendency to corrupt and deprave those who are open to such immoral influence...."[23] In other words, material may be censored if it contains any passage that is likely to arouse someone who is particularly susceptible to being so aroused. Because it is possible to find some individuals who are offended and aroused by the most innocuous material and because many pieces of serious writing contain some isolated passage that may offend such people, the *Hicklin* test puts freedom of speech on very tenuous grounds. Consequently, there was pressure to liberalize this standard to afford greater protection to art and literature against suppression by the censors.

A more permissive standard was finally handed down in the *Roth* case in 1957. The so-called **Roth rule** has become the standard that subsequent obscenity court decisions either assume or modify. It modified the *Hicklin* test in three important ways: First, the test no longer focused on any isolated passage or words, but rather on whether "the dominant theme of the material, taken as a whole, appeals to prurient [sexual] interests"; second, its standard of measure became whether the material appeals to the prurient interests of the "average" person, not a particularly susceptible segment of society; third, the treatment of sex in the material under question was not to justify censorship unless it was "utterly without redeeming social importance."[24]

Now material can no longer be censored because of some isolated passage or because some individual can find a sexual innuendo where the thought would not occur to most people. Of course, the stipulation that the government can only censor works "utterly without redeeming social importance" opens the door for a wide range of material to be protected from the censors, because even material that most people would find to be predominantly trash may have some small measure of social value. Although *Roth* suggests that a small, peripheral part of sexually relevant material would not condemn a work, it also appears to say that a small, peripheral amount of worthwhile material might save an otherwise worthless piece of sexual exploitation. This part of the *Roth* rule appears inconsistent with its dominant theme.

The *Roth* rule was later modified in two important ways in the *Miller v. California* case (1973).[25] The Supreme Court dropped the key problematic phrase in favor of saying that, in order to be legally censored, material must lack *serious* literary, artistic, political, or scientific values (**LAPS values**). This seems more in line with judging the work as a whole rather than on the basis of some isolated passages. Presumably, under the *Miller* criterion of serious LAPS values, an isolated article in an otherwise provocative and graphic girlie magazine would not, in and of itself, save such material from censorship.

The second way in which the *Miller* case modifies the *Roth* rule is by defining obscenity based in part on local community standards rather than national. The Court explicitly rejected the idea that there can or should be a national standard for what can or cannot be censored. This portion of the ruling appears incongruent with the purpose of the First Amendment to provide some national standards for freedom of speech. The Constitution cannot mean one thing in one state and something else in another state or it would not be law.

Publishing, film, and broadcasting are examples of national commerce, and the legal status of their enormous investments must be predictable throughout the country. Without national standards, the standards for the nation as a whole become the standards of what the most prudish local prosecutors or juries are wont to censor, the lowest common denominator; in effect, this completely negates the average-person criterion of *Roth*. By the *Miller* standard, any community should be able to censor whatever sexually explicit material dominant groups choose to censor without violating the Constitution.

The Court backed off from the implications of the local community standard in *Jenkins v. Georgia* (1974) when it ruled that Georgia could not ban the critically acclaimed film *Carnal Knowledge* on obscenity grounds. The Court rejected a reading of *Miller* "that juries have unbridled discretion to determine what is 'patently offensive.'"[26] Thus a community is not free to censor the mere depiction of sex; the material had to be "patently offensive." The Court even offered a list of the kinds of things that may be censored. But this implies national standards that constrain community discretion. In 1987, the Court backed further away from community standards, substituting a "reasonable man" test, a criterion that would allow the repression of speech that is obscene to ordinary, sane individuals.

There may be a useful distinction between obscenity and pornography. One may accept the concept that the avoidance of sexual stimulation is not a value of sufficient weight to justify the discretion given to censors; yet one may still argue that there remains a category of material that is beyond mere salaciousness: it is "patently offensive." In 1989, the Court further elaborated on the distinction between what may be censored in obscenity cases and what is protected from such challenges by the First Amendment in the dial-a-porn case, *Sable Communications v. Federal Communications Commission*. The Court struck down an amendment to the communications act that banned "indecent" interstate calls. The Court said that while obscene calls may be banned, the denial to adults of access to calls that are merely indecent violates the First Amendment.[27] The same logic was extended in *Reno v. ACLU* to the regulation of the Internet by the Communications Decency Act, signed into law by President Clinton and designed to control children's access to sexually explicit material on that medium. The Court found that the proscribed categories, indecent and patently offensive, were unconstitutionally vague.[28]

There is, of course, a problem in drawing the line between what is obscenity and what is not, but most know intuitively where it is. Justice Stewart put it best in *Jacobellis v. Ohio* (1964):

> I have reached the conclusion that … under the First and Fourteenth Amendments, criminal laws in this area are limited to hard-core pornography. I shall not today attempt to further define the kinds of material I understand to be embraced within that short hand description; and perhaps I shall never succeed in doing so. But I know it when I see it….[29]

Government Subsidies, Sex, and the Arts. The expansion of the concept of protected expression generated controversy over government funding of artistic work with sexual content that was offensive to the moral sensibilities of significant segments of the population. Here the issue was one of government funding, not government suppression. In the one instance, the government funded a photographic exhibition produced by a well-known photographer, Robert Mapplethorpe, including some explicit homoerotica and some photographs involving the genitalia of children. Other funded projects that were offensive to many Americans include the Serrano, Finley, and Sprinkle works mentioned earlier.

The debate over funding such projects demonstrated the absence of any objective criteria over what constitutes artistic merit that would override the public interest in the preservation of public morality. Article I Section 8 of the Constitution says Congress is empowered "To promote the Progress of Science and useful Arts," but of course, what is "useful" is not defined in the document. Those who opposed funding these projects argued that they went beyond the bounds of common perceptions of artistic value and that, in any event, whatever rights may exist to freedom of expression do not extend to a right to public funding, especially when the material in question is deeply offensive to a majority. Those who supported funding of these projects argued that representatives of the artistic community should determine what is art and what deserves to be funded. Because market forces are not presumed to identify and reward genuine artistic merit, the issue of public funding is an important one. A heavy metal rock band will sell many more recordings than a classical violinist. Without public subsidies, many widely respected creators of classical music, dance, drama, and the like could not survive. Congress has debated cutting off funding to the arts through the National Endowment for the Arts (NEA), or at least severely limiting such arts funding. The NEA narrowly escaped fiscal death in 1997. It becomes apparent that as the frontier of what is perceived as having artistic value is expanded further, public tolerance of extending funding or protection to such expression may continue to weaken.

Another form of government subsidy in addition to funding is government providing a forum (or free space) in a public building for artists to showcase their work. Although one's individual right to showcase one's own art on a public sidewalk or park is virtually unlimited, when it comes to public buildings, the government is not required to necessarily display art. Once the government decides to open up space in a public building for art or political messages, however, the Free Speech Clause prevents the government from discriminating based on the content of the art or message being displayed. While the government is not required to showcase obscene material in a building forum it has opened up, the same questions about what is obscene and what is art can sometimes arise just as it has with public funding of art. For example, in Lubbock, Texas, in 2007, just before a planned art event, city officials removed from the city's Buddy Holly Center a Texas Tech University art professor's drawings of a woman breastfeeding because a city official found the drawings "inappropriate for public display."[30] Presumably under this standard, one would gather that many of the great works of art in the Louvre Museum in Paris (a fair amount of which depict women and sometimes men without clothes) would be deemed inappropriate for public display in Lubbock. Lubbock city officials later apologized for their actions and said they made a mistake, but the incident is a perfect illustration of the controversy that continues today about questions over what is considered obscene enough for the government to censor it.

The Conflict between Pornography and Public Morality

A lingering question in the ongoing controversy over obscenity legislation is what social value is preserved by allowing the censorship of patently offensive, hard-core pornography, even assuming that such material can be adequately distinguished. Is the goal of obscenity legislation to protect people from being offended, or is it assumed that certain preventable, harmful behavior and events would be the consequence of the unrestricted dissemination of hard-core pornography? If the former is the value being guarded, government is in the business of controlling thought rather than restricting itself to the control of behavior.

Of course, child pornography, the use of children to produce pornographic books and films, goes beyond thought control, raising issues of the exploitation of those unable to exercise independent judgment. The law has always distinguished the protection needed by children from the needs of adults. Can the law also proscribe computer-generated child pornography? In 2002, the Supreme Court answered this question in *Ashcroft v. Free Speech Coalition* by striking down a ban on computer-generated virtual reality images of children in sexually suggestive depictions. The constitutional basis for banning child pornography concerns the underlying illegal act of exploiting real children in the making of it, whereas in the case of the virtual reality images, the Court claimed the ban "prohibits speech that records no crime and creates no victims by its production."[31] One of the public policy questions raised in the case was whether expression using virtual images of children might increase the tendency of pedophiles to go out and engage in child molestation. But the Court was unpersuaded, responding that "the mere tendency of speech to encourage unlawful acts is not a sufficient reason for banning it."

A principal concern expressed by the Court in the *Ashcroft* case was the fact that the federal law banning virtual images included images of persons who merely appear to be under the age of eighteen, even if they are not. And, there was no exception in the law for work that had a serious literary, political, or scientific value. The Court noted that movies telling the story of William Shakespeare's *Romeo and Juliet,* a literary classic involving a story of a relationship between two teenagers, where Juliet is only thirteen years old, could fall under the scope of this federal ban. As the Court noted, "The work has inspired no less than 40 motion pictures, some of which suggest that the teenagers consummated their relationship."[32]

Some decades ago, Justices Black and Douglas took the position that control of thought is not compatible with an open society. In their dissent from the *Roth* decision, they attacked the central premise of obscenity legislation, that it is permissible to "punish mere speech or publication that the judge or jury thinks has an undesirable impact on thought but is not shown to be part of any unlawful action...." They disagreed with the *Roth* rule because it permits the state to censor material that arouses sexual impulses, whether or not it results in particular forms of behavior. They were suggesting that utterances or ideas that have not been shown to have a likely impact on some unlawful behavior or to cause the physical impeding of some lawful activity are protected by the First Amendment, no matter how much they may offend the moral standards of any particular part of the community. They were essentially rejecting the inferred right not to be offended that we discussed earlier.

The distinction between the impact of material on thought and its impact on action is easier to make in practice than that between hard-core pornography that is patently offensive and soft-core pornography that is mildly offensive. Because these two liberal justices did not believe that material can be censored on the basis of its content, they were the only justices who did not read or review the material at issue in obscenity cases. To them, the material was constitutionally protected, regardless of what it contained.

Some data are available on pornography's impact on behavior. A commission established under President Johnson and reporting years later during the Nixon administration systematically searched for a causal connection between exposure to sexually explicit material and the disposition to engage in antisocial behavior.[33] It failed to find any systematic evidence of such a connection. The presidential commission recommended the abolition of all laws that proscribe the dissemination of sexually explicit material among consenting adults.

Arguments for Censorship. Opponents challenged the commission's findings on several grounds. The commission's studies were carried out on volunteers who were unrepresentative of the population at large. The effects on children were not considered, nor were long-term effects taken into account. Sociological and anthropological research on the long-range effects of sexual permissiveness leans toward the conclusion that such permissiveness is dysfunctional for creative energy and cultural development.[34]

In 1985, Attorney General Edwin Meese of the Reagan administration released a Justice Department–sponsored study purporting to show the harmful effects of pornography. Critics charged that it lumped together a wide range of sex-related material and did not prove the connection it alleged between pornography and criminal actions. A 2009 review of studies on this topic in the *International Journal of Law and Psychiatry* disputed the findings of the Meese report, concluding that the bulk of studies indicate that increased pornography was found to either cause less sex crimes or has no relation at all to the number of sex crimes.[35]

Still, a large segment of the population clings to the belief that pornography leads people to commit sex crimes. A poll taken in 1985, the same year as the attorney general's report was released, showed that 73 percent of those surveyed believed that "explicit sexual magazines, movies and books … lead some people to commit rape or sexual violence."[36] By 1994, while that number had declined to a plurality of 48 percent who believed that sexual materials lead people to rape, it was still higher when compared to 42 percent who did not believe such materials lead to rape.[37] These findings are consistent with the popularity of the solicitor general for the county encompassing Atlanta, Georgia, who defended his concentrating the resources at his disposal on driving pornography out of the city with the bald assertion, "I'm convinced that the use of obscene materials results in many antisocial acts … rape, sodomy, and the molesting of young children."[38] Furthermore, Americans also find pornography morally wrong. A 2012 Gallup survey indicated that 64 percent of Americans believed pornography was morally wrong, while only 31 percent thought it to be morally acceptable.[39] Such persistent beliefs are a political reality that can both affect and undermine whatever legal principles may protect sexually relevant material. Here again, commitment to community moral standards conflicts with belief in an open society.

There is another argument against pornography which stems from quality of life issues in the neighborhoods where sex shops, topless bars, and X-rated movie theaters reside. Neighborhoods that contain such adult businesses are normally associated with increased crime rates and declining property values. Hence, the Supreme Court upheld the constitutionality of municipal zoning restrictions on such industries in a case involving the City of Los Angeles after the city produced a study indicating that high concentrations of adult entertainment establishments are associated with higher crime rates in surrounding communities.[40]

Arguments against Censorship.   Given the weakness of evidence to support an alleged causal effect of pornography on antisocial behavior, liberals argue that what consenting adults read or view is none of the state's business. This concept of the consenting adult implies that people do not have such material involuntarily foisted on them and that the probability is very remote that they could naively or unwittingly place themselves in contact with such material. For example, a theater showing X-rated films should be clearly so identified, and no one should be pressured or even implored to enter. The notion of consenting adults also implies a distinction between what is available to adults and what is available to minors, a distinction the Court clearly upheld when it struck down a law banning the sale "to the general reading public" of any book "tending to incite minors to depraved or immoral acts" or "tending to the corruption of the morals of youth." The Court held that this law reduced the adult population of Michigan to reading only what is fit for children.[41] The argument that individuals must be presumed able to decide for themselves what material is fit for them to read or view does not apply with equal force to minors.

Assuming that the availability of sexually explicit materials is effectively limited to consenting adults and that there is no demonstrated causal connection between adult exposure to pornography and socially disruptive behavior, why not allow rational adults to choose for themselves what materials they can view without becoming morally offended or depraved? The Supreme Court came close to this position in *Stanley v. Georgia* (1969), which involved the seizure of sexually explicit films in a private home. The Court held that "if the First Amendment means anything, it means that a state has no business telling a man, sitting alone in his own house, what books he may read or what films he may see."[42]

But the consenting adults argument was explicitly rejected in *Paris Adult Theater v. Slaton* (1973), in which the Court upheld the right of the state to close down a theater specializing in X-rated films.[43] It was admitted that the theater was so clearly marked that it was impossible to enter it unaware of the sexual nature of the films being shown. It was further admitted that minors were effectively excluded. Nevertheless, the Court still perceived some legitimate state interests in permitting censorship to override any First Amendment values involved. These state interests include "the interest of the public in the quality of life and total community environment, the tone of commerce in the great city centers and, possibly, the public safety itself." The Court further held that even though it had not been shown that there is a causal relationship between exposure to pornography and deviant or objectionable behavior, a state may nevertheless reasonably assume that such a relationship exists in asserting a legitimate interest in regulating what consenting adults may view or read. Why a state may "reasonably assume" something to be true contrary to available evidence was not discussed.

Supporters of censorship correctly point out that much of the material in obscenity cases is obviously pornographic trash and hardly worth protecting. Such material contributes very little if anything to the political purpose of the First Amendment, the free trade in socially relevant ideas. Moreover, although censorship in effect imposes the moral standards of dominant groups on other members of society, such principles may be part of the essence of that society.

Feminist Concerns about Pornography.   A different kind of campaign against pornography has been mounted by a group of feminists, led by law professor Catharine MacKinnon and the late Andrea Dworkin, involving the strategy of obtaining legislation to the effect that such material demeans women, is a form of sex discrimination, and thereby violates their civil rights.[44] The remedy invited by such legislation is civil action against either the producers or the distributors of such material, including the bookseller. Because the criminal process is not involved, the burden of proof is altered from previous strategies of criminalizing the production and distribution of sexually explicit material.

The first example of this was a 1984 law passed by the Minneapolis city council, but vetoed by the mayor. Other such ordinances were introduced in Indianapolis and Los Angeles. These ordinances came under severe criticism on freedom of speech grounds. The critics charged that the standards for determining what may be considered demeaning to the dignity of women are left very imprecise and therefore any bookseller, publisher, or other disseminator of sexually relevant material may find himself or herself the defendant in a lawsuit initiated by any woman who might be so offended. Even if the defendant wins, the costs of being party to such litigation would be great, and so such litigation could cause a severe chilling effect on the willingness of people to handle any sexually relevant material that may offend those most easily offended. The public would then almost be limited to having access only to material inoffensive to the most sensitive women. Laws granting women the right to sue booksellers who distribute salacious material that the plaintiff believes demeans women were tested in

The American Association of Booksellers v. Hudnut (1984), a case challenging the Indianapolis law. The district court judge, a woman, found that the law presented an unconstitutional deterrent to free speech.

It is argued, on the other hand, that pornography does promote and legitimate the image of women merely as sex objects rather than as complete and equal persons. Moreover, some sadomasochistic, hard-core pornography fosters the idea of the physical abuse of women as a manly thing to do. Such material characterized by simulated rape and violence toward women is typical of hard-core pornography today. The dissemination of such sadomasochistic material thus may actually pose a physical danger to women. Pornography in general depicts sex as a conquest, something that men do to women rather than as a mutual expression of affection that men and women do with each other. Studies after the 1970 President's Commission Report discussed earlier do indicate that exposure to the new violent, hard-core pornography does soften attitudes toward rape and the sexual exploitation of women. Indeed, men exposed to such material become more tolerant of sexual violence. Of course, to the extent that it can be shown that the violent forms of pornography make men more tolerant of such violence, the argument is no longer simply one of competing moral perspectives but rather a question of the right of the state to protect the well-being of its female citizens. Whatever the case for censorship on moral grounds, censorship of the kinds of material that can be shown to pose a physical danger to women is another matter.

Censorship and the Open Society.   The problem with censorship on the grounds that material is immoral or offensive is that one has to trust that the censor can selectively stamp out this particular worthless piece of trash or that particular despicable point of view. Censorship is, by definition, delegating the power to one or more persons to decide for everyone else in the jurisdiction which of all future utterances people may see, hear, or read. The adult members of society lose the right to decide for themselves what material is trash and what materials have value, what ideas are legitimate and worthy of consideration, and what ideas are so heinous as to be outside the democratic political arena.

The historical record does not support the idea of government censors using discretion judiciously. Although most Americans can agree that some materials are offensive and worthless, the record is replete with examples of overzealous censors suppressing material that most Americans would find harmless and often of considerable artistic value. The critically acclaimed films *Midnight Cowboy* and *Carnal Knowledge* were censored in some places. Another critically acclaimed film, *Paper Moon*, a comedy involving very little that was even implicitly sexual, was censored because of the use of profane language. The 1960s saw numerous attempts to ban the well-respected novel *Catcher in the Rye* from school libraries. John Steinbeck's *East of Eden*, *The Grapes of Wrath*, *The Red Pony*, and *Of Mice and Men*, and the *Tarzan* series have all been banned in various places in the United States on obscenity grounds, as were several Hemingway novels.

Informal Censorship: Boycotts, Threats, and Public Pressure.   One tactic used to protect society from putatively salacious material is not direct censorship by a public official but rather a boycott of the products of firms that sponsor shows on television allegedly containing such material, a boycott organized and promoted by a nongovernmental source. The chilling effect of the threat of such a boycott has caused sponsorships to be withdrawn in more than one instance. The extent to which the selection and content of shows have been altered because of the boycott threat is unclear. These boycotts are not formally censorship in the traditional sense of a public official banning the dissemination of certain material by law or edict; instead, they constitute a less formal kind of censorship, whereby materials are eliminated from dissemination through the mechanism of socioeconomic pressure. Another informal tactic simply relies on violence and intimidation by those claiming offense. Comedy Central's response to threats from a radical Muslim website by censoring the *South Park* episodes of the prophet Mohammed is not an isolated incident. Fears of violence caused the New York Metropolitan Museum of Art to take down all art in their gallery that depicted Mohammed in any image, and Yale University Press began refusing to print any images of the prophet in any of its books it published.

Another version of these less formal tactics is the pressure to eliminate certain kinds of material from public school textbooks. The testimony at textbook adoption hearings seems to be dominated by those who want material censored from the books; live-and-let-live people who welcome new ideas tend to vacate this field. Some people have become almost fixtures at such hearings in the attempt to make textbooks reflect their view of the world. It is the familiar case of a vocal and passionate minority controlling policy over the more passive majority.

During the 1980s, Norma and Martin Gabler of Texas gained considerable notoriety by devoting their lives and fortunes to the cause of having what they consider to be a liberal view of the world expurgated from schoolbooks. They attacked books containing references to sex, evolution, feminist values, or suggestions that the United States may not always have been right in its foreign affairs. In anticipation of such attacks and public pressure, many publishers self-censor their textbooks in advance. For example, Scott Foresman and Company removed four hundred lines from its high school version of Shakespeare's *Romeo and Juliet* in an effort to eliminate any suggestion of carnal lust between those star-crossed lovers.

The Right wing does not have a monopoly on such attempts to control the content of textbooks. Feminists, for example, show up to complain about demeaning depictions of women. African Americans have caused the censorship of such works as *The Adventures of Huckleberry Finn* and *Gone with the Wind* because they used the "n-word," and Jews have caused the removal of Shakespeare's *The Merchant of Venice* from school districts because of the portrayal of Shylock as a wicked Jew.

Liberal groups, though less concerned with sexual morality, have tried to pressure the networks to reduce the violent content of television shows. There is some circumstantial evidence, mostly of an illustrative variety, that exposure to television violence can result in violent behavior. (A case in point is the man who set fire to his wife in October 1984 after watching *The Burning Bed*.) However, the evidence is inconclusive and the debate continues.

If a major premise of an open society is that reasonable adults are capable of assessing the value of competing ideas, should they also be presumed capable of making moral choices for themselves, provided that such choices do not harm others? When a censor presumes to tell such reasonable, consenting adults what material is too immoral for them to see or read, is that censor not presuming to make moral choices for others? If so, by what criteria can a censor be presumed to be more fit to make moral choices for other people than the people themselves? Thus, the central premise of censorship, that reasonable adults cannot be trusted to make social, political, and moral choices for themselves, is a denial of the essence of an open society. Proponents of censorship argue, however, that an unqualified adherence to the principle of an open society may weaken the commitment to moral and family values that define the essence of America as a community.

CONFLICT OVER THE ROLE OF RELIGION
IN THE UNITED STATES

A general trend toward the **secularization** of society in the Western world has been felt less strongly in the United States than elsewhere. While levels of church attendance and beliefs in God have dropped steadily in Western Europe, the United States is rather unique among industrialized countries in its relatively high levels of religious practice and beliefs in a higher power. The continuing relevance of religiosity in American society is fostered by the prevalence of evangelical and fundamentalist churches in America such as the Southern Baptists, Assemblies of God, and smaller Bible Belt churches, while the salience of religiosity in American political life has been reinforced by the emergence of such religious advocacy groups as Focus on the Family and the Christian Coalition, the latter being the creation of former presidential candidate and televangelist Reverend Pat Robertson. While most secularists in America populate the political Left, conservatives do not have a monopoly on religion, as even some liberals exhibit a religiosity not seen in Europe.

Still, those on the Christian Right feel that their faith and their right to declare it has been under widespread attack by the secular Left. From a ban on the employees of Wal-Mart and other stores from wishing their patrons "Merry Christmas" to an effort to have a large white cross on a hill near San Diego removed, secularists have attacked public expressions of Christian faith. In particular, some public displays of the Ten Commandments have come under attack. For example, in one highly publicized incident, Chief Justice Roy Moore of the Supreme Court of Alabama wheeled a 5,280-pound granite monument of the Ten Commandments into the central rotunda of the state supreme court building. A federal judge ordered Moore to remove the huge monument, but he refused, precipitating his removal from the bench by state authorities for disobeying a federal court order and violating the state's canons of judicial ethics. Meanwhile, leaders on the religious Right have applied pressure on both Congress and the Republican Party platform writers to incorporate the imperatives of fundamental Christian social doctrine into policy proposals. The New Christian Right has focused on the reintroduction of devotional observance in the public sector, especially in public schools.

Freedom of, and from, Religion

Previous sections have shown how the First Amendment protects pluralism, the legitimate coexistence of various points of view and belief systems. The religion clauses of the First Amendment protect the legitimacy of divergent religious orientations, including agnosticism and atheism. If the right to choose one's own views and to evaluate ideas for oneself is a hallmark of the concept of the open society, surely this principle also applies to religion, which touches fundamental and intensely held sets of values and beliefs. It is therefore fitting that the two religion clauses of the Bill of Rights are included in the First Amendment, which is devoted to the protection and legitimacy of pluralism and the open society. Precisely because religious beliefs are so intensely held, however, dominant groups will seek to impose values from those beliefs on their society. Many of the values that the social conservatives and religious Right define as part of the essence of the American community are religiously based. The religious Right therefore seeks to impose conformity to these values through law and social policy, an objective that comes into conflict with the concept of the open society. There are two distinct religion clauses in the First Amendment: the **Establishment Clause** and the **Free Exercise Clause**, which read as follows:

> Congress shall make no law respecting an establishment of religion, or prohibiting the free exercise thereof...

The *Establishment Clause* is concerned with preventing the government from promoting or aiding religion; the *Free Exercise Clause* is concerned with preventing the government from interfering with the practice of religion. To the extent that government implements either of these clauses to its logical extreme, it may be held to violate a conception of the other clause. For example, when government does nothing that may indirectly aid religion, such as not permitting religious practices in public schools even when a decisive majority desires such activity, government may be seen as preventing the dominant forces in the community from practicing their religion as they see fit. In short, these clauses may come into conflict with each other.

The Establishment Clause

Schools.   There is, of course, considerable ambiguity in the phrase "Congress shall make no law respecting an establishment of religion." Reasonable people can and do disagree about precisely what government is prohibited from doing. At a minimum, it is understood that government may not sanction a particular religious sect as the official state religion, a practice common in many European nations. In England, the Anglican Church is the state church; in Scotland, it is the Presbyterian Church; in Spain, the Catholic Church has official status; and in Denmark, the Lutheran Church is the official state religion. A state church or religion means that the head of state normally must be a member of that church, that he or she officially appoints the leading clerics in that church (usually on the advice of political and religious leaders), and that the church and its schools receive overt financial support from the state. In some places, it may mean that the religion's moral views are enacted into law, as exemplified by limitations on divorce, contraception, and abortion in some Catholic countries. Nevertheless, the Western world, on the official level at least, is now generally a model of toleration of religious pluralism, despite the continued existence of established churches.

Beyond this prohibition of an official national church, it is generally agreed that the government in the United States may not legislatively bestow advantages on one or more sects over other religions. That is, any government activities that aid one religious sect must similarly aid all religions. This is known as the **accommodationist** interpretation of the Establishment Clause. If the clause meant no more than this, this interpretation would allow government to promote religion in general as long as one sect was not favored over others.

Another interpretation of the Establishment Clause is sometimes called the **wall of separation** position, using the words of Thomas Jefferson. Not only does this position itself generate controversy, as it is not self-evident that the Establishment Clause forbids government aid to all religions equally; the wall of separation doctrine also generates controversy even among its ostensible adherents concerning precisely what the government may do without breaching the wall. The Supreme Court has seemingly alternated between the wall of separation and accommodationist interpretations of the Establishment Clause. The Court's first Establishment Clause case in 1899 involved the question of whether the federal government could appropriate money toward a Catholic-run hospital in Washington, DC, for the construction of facilities to care for indigent patients. The justices decided that since the money was appropriated for a secular purpose, a hospital, that no violation of the Establishment Clause occurred. Half a century later, in the 1947 *Everson* case, the Court seemed to move toward more of a wall of separation between church and state; although the Court ruled in Everson that it is constitutional to use public money to reimburse parents for bus transportation to both public and parochial schools, Justice Black's opinion explicitly used the wall metaphor in analyzing the case.[45] Four dissenters thought the wall was breached in this instance. The case implicitly established the precedent that the wall of separation doctrine does not prevent some government activities that provide some secondary or spillover benefits to religion if the primary purposes of the policy are secular ones and, in the case of parochial education, if the primary beneficiary is the schoolchild. Thus, the question of where to draw the line went unanswered by the wall of separation position.

The wall of separation interpretation of the Establishment Clause has been used to oppose public aid to private parochial schools. In general, the Court has taken the principle laid down in the *Lemon* case (discussed next) that such aid is permissible if the primary purpose is secular (teaching courses like math, language, or science) and the primary beneficiary is the child rather than the church.[46] More recently, the idea of taking a position of neutrality between government and religion has been gaining a majority of the Court, as *Mitchell v. Helms* upheld the distribution to parochial schools of library and media materials, and computer hardware and software on secular subjects.[47] It is likely that this trend will continue, given the conservatives' 5–4 majority on the Court.

Aid to Parochial Schools.   The *Everson* case (1947), in upholding the reimbursement of public funds to parents for the costs of busing their children to sectarian schools, laid down the **child benefit standard**. This means that if the primary effect of the aid is to benefit the pupil in the attainment of a secular education, a spillover effect of some benefit to a religious institution does not in itself rule that legislation unconstitutional.

The Court applied this principle in the *Allen* case (1968) in holding that it is legal for the state to lend textbooks on secular subjects approved by public school officials to pupils in sectarian schools.[48] Although the Court was willing to approve the loan of textbooks, it drew the line in another case, *Lemon v. Kurtman* (1971), on state reimbursement for the purchase of books and payment of teachers' salaries by sectarian schools.[49] The Court established a three-part test for determining if the laws could survive Establishment Clause scrutiny: (1) The law in question had to have a secular legislative purpose; (2) the law's primary effect could not advance religion, nor could it inhibit religion; and (3) the law could not "foster excessive government entanglement with religion." In the *Lemon* case, the Court found that the law had a secular purpose of enhancing education in all schools. However, the law in question violated the third part of the test because the state set up elaborate systems to ensure that teachers at religious schools which qualified for reimbursement of salaries were not teaching religious instruction. The reality was that the state could not ensure the religious neutrality of sectarian school teachers, whose salaries they would be paying, when they worked under independent religious school administrations. The Court felt that the law created excessive entanglement between government and religion. On the other hand, the Court later upheld a Minnesota law allowing parents a state income tax deduction for certain expenses of a private parochial education as well as for public education.[50] In *Zobrest v. Catalina Foothills School District,* the Court held that the Establishment Clause did not require a school district to deny the services of a sign language interpreter to a hearing-impaired student simply because that student attended a Catholic school.[51]

As it stands, the bulk of the cases indicate that the Court appears willing to allow the state to provide direct aid to parents who then make choices that end up benefiting parochial schools, but the Court draws the line on direct state aid to parochial schools. This point became key to the Court's resolution of whether school vouchers to private schools violated the Establishment Clause. For years, conservatives had been pushing states to adopt voucher programs, where students of public schools could take state money spent on the student and use that money toward tuition costs at a religious school. The Supreme Court addressed the constitutionality of voucher programs in a 2002 case out of Ohio, where the state instituted a voucher program for the Cleveland school system, which had a large population of low-income students, after the school system began failing.[52] Ohio's voucher program offered several options. It allowed parents of the Cleveland school system to receive a scholarship of $2,250 per year to attend an accredited private nonreligious or religious school. Alternatively, students could remain in the Cleveland school district and receive $500 in tutorial assistance. Or, students could move to another public school district willing to accept Cleveland students, and that public school district would then receive the $2,250 in state aid for accepting the Cleveland student. After the program was enacted, 96.7 percent of students who used tuition vouchers chose to attend religious private schools (although there were also nonreligious private schools that participated in the program that were available to parents). The central question for the Court was whether the law impermissibly advanced religion. In a 5–4 decision, the Court upheld the voucher program, in part, because those tuition scholarships that ultimately went to religious schools were the result of the private choices of parents. The Court reiterated the principle that "government programs that neutrally provide benefits to a broad class of citizens defined without reference to religion are not readily subject to an Establishment Clause challenge."[53]

Arguments for Aid.   First, arguments for such aid begin with the fact that sectarian schools do a respectable job in providing a secular education, that is, training pupils in subjects like mathematics, English, science, and geography. In fact, many people feel that, in general, sectarian schools do a better job in that regard than do most public schools. Thus, because sectarian schools perform an important public function, they are said to deserve public support. Moreover, if sectarian schools were to cease to function tomorrow, the existing public school systems would be unable to handle the large population of religious school pupils they would discharge into the public schools. The money not spent on sectarian schools would then have to be spent on a substantial expansion of the public schools.

Second, parents of parochial school pupils carry a double burden: They must pay the property taxes that support public schools and must finance the parochial education of their own children. In effect, they are financially penalized for choosing a religious school education for their children. Therefore, it is argued that the lack of public support for parochial education goes beyond neutrality toward religion. Although it is true that parochial school pupils are free to take advantage of the public school system, if any great number of them did so, that system would collapse if not supported by greatly increased taxation.

Third, arguments for aid to religious schools draw upon the desire to return to the traditional value of strong parental responsibility for the education of their children. Because many evangelical and fundamentalist parents believe that modern, secular education in the public schools undermines traditional Christian teachings, they assert a free exercise right to support for their educational duties.

Arguments against Aid.   Opponents of aid to parochial education see such aid as the first potential break in the symbolic wall that separates church and state, a breach that will make subsequent breaches more likely.

Furthermore, in light of the intense emotion surrounding religion, the danger of parochial school aid is that the benefits will not be allocated equally among all religions, not to mention between organized religion and nonreligion.

Any aid policy will benefit the members and institutions of some religions to the exclusion of those who do not belong to those religions, as different religions have different levels of commitment to parochial education. Perhaps this is one justification for a secularized school system in a society with a variety of religious orientations.

Prayer in School. The problem of parochial schools as an alternative to secularized public schools for parents who want religious content in their child's education remains their affordability for most middle-class families. Hence, many parents continue to press for religious content in the public school curriculum. It would seem, however, that such activity is clearly unconstitutional under the Establishment Clause. Presumably, no devotional activity, no matter how voluntary or nondenominational, may be sponsored by the public schools. But, the concepts of devotional activity and school sponsorship are not unambiguous.

In two separate decisions—the Bible-reading cases, *Schempp* and *Murray* (1963), and the New York regents prayer case, *Engle v. Vitale* (1962)—the Court seemed to take an unequivocal position. In the first case, the Court ruled that devotional reading, without comment, from the New Testament is inconsistent with the Establishment Clause, even when objecting students are excused from class.[54] In the second, it ruled that prayer sponsored by school authorities, regardless of who actually reads it and regardless of how nonsectarian or voluntary the prayer may be, is in violation of the Establishment Clause.[55] In striking down such a prayer, the Court made clear that any prayer sponsored by public school officials is on its face unconstitutional. There is no way that any amount of tinkering with the nature of a school prayer or the mode of its presentation can render that prayer logically consistent with the constraints imposed by the school prayer decision. In the summer of 1985, the Court struck down an Alabama law requiring silent meditation or prayer as an organized activity in its public schools. The Court's opinion did hint, however, that some form of silent meditation might pass constitutional muster. The Court has also ruled that it is unconstitutional to distribute Gideon Bibles in public schools, even though students have the right to refuse to accept one. Meanwhile, militant secularists continue to challenge any mention of God or religion in public school classrooms. The case of *Elk Grove Unified School District v. Newdow* (2004) dealt with a challenge by atheist Michael Newdow to saying the Pledge of Allegiance with words "under God" in a public school attended by his daughter, a challenge dismissed by the Court because Newdow, who brought the case, did not have custody over his daughter in the school and therefore lacked "**standing to sue**" (something personally at stake in the outcome of the case).[56]

The issue of prayer in the schools arose in a different context in *Lee v. Weisman,* this time not inside a classroom, but rather at a school graduation ceremony.[57] Ironically, this case involved a challenge by a Jewish parent to a prayer offered at 1991 graduation ceremonies by a Jewish rabbi. In the overwhelming preponderance of cases, such prayers are offered in the dominant religion of the community. The Supreme Court decided that such graduation prayers are unconstitutional, thereby maintaining exclusion of officially sponsored prayer in public schools, including school-sponsored functions outside the classroom.

More recent attempts to insert prayer into the public schools have involved prayer services initiated by students rather than by school officials and instituted at extracurricular functions. This phenomenon came before the Court in 2000 involving the well-established practice in countless small- to medium-sized communities of holding public prayer at high school football games. In *Santa Fe Independent School District v. Doe,* the Court reviewed a student-led prayer delivered over the public address system prior to each game, a practice approved by a substantial majority of the student body in an annual vote.[58] Community opinion was so strongly supportive of the prayers that the two plaintiffs were permitted by the lower courts to proceed anonymously. The Court struck down the practice by a 6–3 vote as a violation of the Establishment Clause. The Court found that in addition to those who had to attend—players, cheerleaders, band members—there is strong peer pressure on others to attend the high school football game in that small Texas town. Once again, the Court was pointing out that in the area of school-sponsored devotional activities, voluntary is not really voluntary due to peer pressure to conform.

To get around the Establishment Clause rulings, conservatives, such as Texas Republican governor and 2012 presidential candidate Rick Perry, have supported a constitutional amendment to overturn the *Vitale* decision and to establish the right to voluntary prayer in the public schools. In a sense, students still have the right of voluntary prayer. It is important to realize that the courts have in no way limited the right of individuals in school to pray in any private manner they choose. Rather, only organized devotional activity, sponsored by the school, has been banned. Some religious leaders have held that such private prayer is actually more meaningful, as it comes from within an individual by choice rather than being recited by compulsion as part of a group exercise. The advantage of the school-sponsored group prayer that the proposed constitutional amendment would ostensibly protect, according to its supporters, is that it gives official recognition and support to the Judeo-Christian moral values they feel are the core of the American community. This goal assumes greater importance to the more conservative Christians as they perceive those values as increasingly under attack by Islamic militants while liberal secularists strive even harder to take a multicultural approach and thus to avoid offending those who do not share these core American values. More skeptical secular liberals suspect that the dominant group wants the leverage that the amendment would give them to compel others to pray and to do so in a manner determined by the dominant group. As Justice Frankfurter observed in the *McCollum* case, "The law of imitation operates, and non-conformity is not an outstanding characteristic of children."[59] Peer pressure to participate will be strong and accordingly, in the case of organized, school-sponsored religious activities, participation is never really voluntary. Some fundamentalist religious leaders still argue that such organized prayer in the schools is essential to restoring the nation's moral foundations, though other religious leaders contend that prayer must be private and voluntary in order to be meaningful. The Senate has regularly rejected a proposed constitutional amendment to permit such prayer, but the issue is placed back on the agenda by conservative legislators each year.

The prayer and Bible-reading decisions reinforced a tendency for the Court to compel the complete secularization of America's public schools that had previously been apparent in the *McCollum v. Board of Education* case (1948), which had struck down "voluntary" religious training by leaders of the major religions during the school day and on school time. Both the hostile public reaction and noncompliance to this decision and the prayer and Bible-reading cases were extensive in many public school districts throughout the nation. For instance, one national sample of school teachers found that 28 percent continued to recite classroom prayer two years after the *Engle* decision.[60] Noncompliance was heaviest in the Bible Belt South. For example, a survey of 121 of Tennessee's 152 school districts found that only one had eliminated such Bible reading.[61] It has been estimated that almost half of the released time programs continued after *McCollum,* although they were clearly inconsistent with the decision. In the face of such public resistance, the Court backed off somewhat from the implications of *McCollum* and held in a New York case that students could be released for religious instruction during the school day if the instruction took place off the school campus. In doing so, they implicitly rejected much of the logic in the *McCollum* decision.

The trend toward noncompliance with bans on public school religious observances has been a continuous obstacle to the Court-mandated secularization of those schools. In fact, surveys from 2012 show that a majority of Americans still oppose the Supreme Court's ban on prayer in school, with the highest opposition to the Supreme Court's rulings coming from the South. The theoretically simple solution to the degree of religious activity constitutionally allowable (none) has proved more complex than anticipated.

Other Establishment Clause Issues.   The forces that have promoted the secularization of the public schools have broadened their efforts to promote the secularization of other aspects of public life. These efforts came to a head in the lawsuit challenging the right of Pawtucket, Rhode Island, to display a life-size nativity scene at city expense. The Supreme Court continued its tradition of permitting Christmas pageants, Easter celebrations, and the like in public schools (and therefore presumably in public life) on the grounds that these holidays have become so much a part of the American culture that they have significance beyond their sectarian religious meaning. In *Lynch v. Donnelly* (1984), the Court ruled that the Pawtucket Christmas display merely "engenders a friendly community spirit of good will in keeping with the season."[62] However, in a case out of Pittsburgh in 1989, the Court struck down a Christian Nativity scene with the words "Gloria in Excelsis Deo" that was prominently displayed inside the county courthouse, but upheld the public display in another public building of a Jewish menorah (the candleholder commemorating the Chanukah season) because it was accompanied by symbols of the secular aspects of Christmas in "the spirit of religious pluralism."[63] Thus, the Court seemed to create what some legal scholars refer to as the "and Santa too" rule. The Court will permit religious displays on public property at Christmas time, such as a nativity scene or a menorah, if such religious displays are also accompanied or surrounded by more secular objects, such as a Santa Claus, a Christmas tree, candy canes, Frosty the Snow Man, etc. Clearly, unlike the school prayer decisions, which tacked a more "wall of separation" interpretation of the Establishment Clause, these religious display cases evoke the more accommodationist perspective.

A recurring issue in the area of religious material in public places in general and public schools in particular has been the controversy over the display of the Ten Commandments in public school classrooms and other public venues such as courtrooms or parks. The Ten Commandments are, of course, a nonsectarian symbol of the Judeo–Christian tradition that is an important aspect of our culture. In 1980, the Court struck down a Kentucky law that provided for copies of the Decalogue, financed by private funds, to be placed in public school classrooms.[64] The Court held by a narrow majority that no secular purpose was served by the display. Many religious conservatives have refused to accept that decision and continue to fight to have this, among other religious symbols, displayed in classrooms and other public places. In 2005, the Court permitted a large stone monument of the Ten Commandments to remain in a public park located on the grounds of the Texas State Capitol building and the Supreme Court Building in Austin.[65] However, the same Court rejected the right to display the Commandments inside two Kentucky county courthouses.[66] The difference was in the vote of Justice Breyer, who rejected the right to display the Decalogue in the Kentucky case, but who argued in the Texas case that the monument had gone unchallenged for forty years and had historical value. Breyer also noted that the "physical setting of the monument," which was situated among "17 other monuments and 21 historical markers, all designed to illustrate the 'ideals' of those who settled in Texas" suggested to him "little or nothing of the sacred" in that particular Ten Commandments monument.[67] In a 2010 case, the Court faced an issue involving the constitutionality of a seventy-five-year-old National World War I Memorial containing an eight-foot cross located in the Mojave Desert of California on public land that had been conveyed to a private entity in order to avoid an Establishment Clause issue.[68] In a closely divided Supreme Court, the five-member majority upheld the land transfer (which allowed the Cross to stay put), while Breyer, who sided with the dissenters, thought that there was no need to address the Establishment Clause issue and that the Court should instead focus on the legality of the land transfer.

The Free Exercise Clause

The tension between the Establishment Clause and the Free Exercise Clause ("Congress shall make no law … prohibiting the free exercise" of religion) was discussed at the beginning of this section. In light of this tension, the latter clause is most frequently mentioned in conjunction with values threatened by the vigorous enforcement of the former. Thus the effort to secularize the public schools, an effort justified by the Establishment Clause, is frequently opposed in the name of the Free Exercise Clause.

In general, the Free Exercise Clause is most often invoked to protect the religious practices of unconventional groups, as the frequency of Jehovah's Witness cases attests. Previously in free exercise cases going back to the late 1930s, over forty of which from 1938 to 1955 involved the Jehovah's Witnesses because of their aggressive proselytizing, the Court decided in favor of the free exercise claim the majority of the time. The clause had been used to protect the right of Jehovah's Witnesses to proselytize door-to-door and to refuse to pledge allegiance to the flag (many of the Jehovah's Witnesses' cases were interwoven with free speech claims, making it easier for the courts to come down on their side).[69]

But despite some of the successes in Court, particularly by Jehovah's Witnesses, religious groups have had mixed success using the clause to exempt themselves from state laws on the basis of their right to practice their religion. For much of the country's history, it was not uncommon for the Supreme Court and other courts to reject claims by groups asking for protection to engage in religious practices that would be otherwise illegal or would violate strongly held moral imperatives. The courts denied free exercise protection to engage in polygamy, sexual license, and exposure to poisonous snakes as a test of faith.[70] In 1955, the Supreme Court held that the free exercise clause does not give parents the right to withhold vaccinations, essential medical care, or education in the name of religion.[71]

But the Court departed significantly from its previous interpretation of the Free Exercise Clause in the 1963 case of *Sherbert v. Verner,* dealing with the question of whether Sherbert, a Seventh-Day Adventist, could refuse to take work on Saturday and still receive unemployment benefits.[72] The Court decided in favor of Sherbert, creating a new test, which stated that if the government passes a law which burdens the free exercise of religion, the government must justify the law based on a "compelling government interest" and must use the least restrictive means possible to further that interest. This test was later used to excuse the Amish from having to attend high school based on religious reasons.[73] The government could still burden one's free exercise rights if it could show a compelling government interest. For example, in 1984, a faith-healing couple from Albion, Indiana, was sentenced to ten years in prison for withholding medical care from their nine-year-old daughter who had died a "preventable death" from meningitis. The superior court rejected their free exercise claim in finding them guilty of reckless homicide.

In 1990, the Court weakened the free exercise rights of religious groups when it essentially did away with the "compelling interest" test in *Employment Division v. Smith.*[74] In that case, the Court upheld the state of Oregon's refusal to provide unemployment benefits to two Native Americans who were fired from their job for using peyote in Indian religious ceremonies. Oregon had argued that because the two individuals were fired from their job for engaging in an illegal activity—that is, smoking peyote, which Oregon law classified as an illegal drug—the state had a right to deny them unemployment benefits. But, the two Native Americans argued that they should be exempted from the law, because they were using peyote as part of their religious practices. Writing for the majority, Justice Scalia said that the "right of free exercise does not relieve an individual of an obligation to comply with a valid and neutral law of general applicability." Scalia said to rule otherwise would allow a person "to become a law unto himself" in the name of practicing one's religion. In other words, as long as the law was neutral and applied generally to everyone, individuals could not excuse themselves from having to follow the law by claiming that they are exercising their right to practice their religion. Under this new standard, as long as the law in question is a valid and neutral law of general applicability, then the government does not have to demonstrate a compelling interest for that law when it burdens the free exercise rights of certain individuals. But, if such practices like smoking peyote are not protected by the free exercise clause, especially when they seemingly hurt no one else, then what is its point?

Supporters of free exercise, including religious groups across the political and theological spectrum, argued that the principle in the *Smith* case would unduly impede the free exercise of religion, views that led both Republicans and Democrats in Congress to pass the bipartisan 1993 Religious Freedom Restoration Act (RFRA). This Act forbade policies and rules that burden the exercise of religion unless government can show that the burden furthers a "compelling public interest" and that the challenged action is "the least restrictive means of doing so." Essentially, Congress attempted to overrule the Supreme Court by reinstating the *Sherbert v. Verner* test that had been expressly rejected by the Court in the *Smith* case. After RFRA's passage, prison inmates sued, claiming the right to use drugs as part of their "religious experience," and an Amish group won an exemption from posting orange safety triangles on its buggies. In fear of such a flood of claims, sixteen states joined the City of Boerne in challenging RFRA in a 1997 case that represented a constitutional showdown between Congress and the Supreme Court.

In *City of Boerne v. Flores* (1997), the Supreme Court struck the Act down as it related to states, claiming that Congress lacked the authority under the Fourteenth Amendment to require states to accommodate such religious practices, since the Court had already ruled under *Smith* that states were not required to follow the compelling interest test of *Sherbert*.[75] The ruling was somewhat narrow, because the Court allowed for provisions of the Act to stand, which required a compelling interest test for federal government actions. In other words, the Court said that Congress could strengthen the free exercise rights of people above the threshold set by the Court in *Smith,* as long as the new standards only applied to the federal government. Congress, however, lacked the authority to tell states that they had to provide more rights to practice one's religion above and beyond what was required by the Constitution as interpreted by the Court in the *Smith* case. Thus, the *Smith* case represents the bare minimum in terms of our free exercise rights. Congress can pass laws that give us greater free exercise rights, but they cannot compel states to also meet a higher standard than what the Constitution requires.

Still, conservative and religious groups reacted strongly to this decision, arguing that it was an extreme case of judicial activism and an attempt to impose secularization on all aspects of life. Congress reacted to the Court decision by simply repassing a scaled-down version of RFRA, which mostly applied to the rights of prisoners in state prison and the regulations of religious land use, and then justified their authority to pass the law under their power to regulate interstate commerce. After this new law was passed, prisoners of the Satanist and Wicca religions, as well as prisoners belonging to a white supremacist Christian sect, sued the state of Ohio under the new congressional law, claiming that they were not allowed access to religious literature or opportunities to worship. The Court found in favor of the prisoners, upholding this revised version of RFRA in 2005.[76]

POLICY DILEMMAS   The Free Exercise Clause, Contraception, and the Health Care Reform Law

Under President Obama's Affordable Care Act, federal law requires employers to provide health coverage that includes contraceptives. Conservatives view some of these contraceptives, such as the morning-after pill and intrauterine devices, as being tantamount to abortion itself. The law exempts churches from having to provide contraceptive services in their health plans to their workers, but nearly all other employers must provide this coverage. As noted earlier, the Catholic charity group Little Sisters for the Poor was able to get the Supreme Court to temporarily block the law against them. But this aspect of the law was also challenged by for-profit businesses, namely, Hobby Lobby.

The owners of Hobby Lobby are religiously minded people (it is not a publicly traded company). The owners claim that the Free Exercise Clause of the Constitution and the Religious Freedom and Restoration Act protect their religious right to be exempt from having to provide contraceptive services to their employees. Remember that RFRA requires that the federal government has to show a "compelling public interest" before it can burden someone's free exercise rights. Is providing contraceptives to people in their employer health plans a compelling public interest? Furthermore, the government has to use the "least restrictive means" possible when it does burden someone's free exercise rights.

The government argued that Hobby Lobby cannot exempt itself from generally applicable laws that everyone else must follow. Furthermore, supporters of the government's viewpoint note that the Supreme Court has never said that a for-profit company can assert free exercise rights.

Ultimately, the Supreme Court ruled in 2014 that the Obama Administration did not employ the least restrictive means when it mandated that Hobby Lobby cover certain contraceptives for their employees. The Court said that the Administration could have provided Hobby Lobby an exemption to the contraceptive requirement as it had done with churches. This ruling has the potential to allow private corporations that are closely held (whose shares are only owned by a few people) to claim religious exemptions from a host of federal laws and regulations. But, given the flux in precedent over the last few decades, this issue is likely to come back before the Court very soon again in another form.

1. Is contraception a "compelling public interest" that would justify the government burdening the "free exercise" rights of Hobby Lobby?

2. Should for-profit corporations that are privately owned be allowed to claim rights to free exercise of religion as a way to avoid following government laws or regulations like President Obama's health care reform law?

While the *Smith* case foreclosed religious groups exempting themselves from following generally applicable state laws that were neutral in their treatment of religion, the Supreme Court illustrated that it would not allow a state law to stand which targeted and discriminated against a particular religion just because it was unconventional or unpopular. A 1993 case drew a great deal of attention in this regard when adherents to the Santeria religion set up shop in the City of Hialeah, Florida, and began practicing animal sacrifice in their religious ceremonies. City officials and members in the community became alarmed at this development, and the city council passed ordinances banning animal sacrifice in a religious ceremony. However, the law exempted slaughterhouses or the slaughtering of animals for food if "the primary purpose" was for "food consumption." In this case, the *Church of Lukumi Babalu Aye v. City of Hialeah*, a unanimous Court held that the city had singled out that church with the ban on sacrifices; hence, the regulation was not neutral and was a violation of the Free Exercise Clause.[77] But, many of the justices disagreed on exactly why the ordinance was a violation of the Free Exercise Clause. Some wanted to return to the compelling interest test of *Sherbert,* but only a minority of justices wanted to return to that standard.

Finally, the right to free exercise can come into conflict with the Establishment Clause when dealing with government assistance for scholarships. Here, the dual meaning of the religious clauses clashed in one 2004 case in which the Court found that Washington State could exclude "devotional theology" as an acceptable major that could be supported by their scholarship program for gifted students.[78]

SUMMARY

With the exception of some of the obscenity cases, the Supreme Court over the last half-century has oftentimes adopted an interpretation of the Constitution that supports the view of an open society. Efforts mostly by conservatives (but in some instances, liberals as well) to impose their visions of morality on the rest of the country have not been particularly successful, as indicated by some of the religious cases and free speech cases mentioned in this chapter. In considering the Supreme Court's actions, it must be remembered that the point of the concept of civil liberties is that there are some things that a majority cannot do to a minority, no matter how strong that majority may be and no matter how intensely it may want to do so. The efforts by conservatives to reverse the Court on the prayer issue and to circumvent rulings on pornography, as well as liberals' attempts to get around the Free Speech Clause in order to impose regulations that punish offensive speech, suggest that no resolution of issues involving morality or religion can be deemed permanent. Such issues will continue to occupy the public in the decades ahead.

 **RESOURCES**

American Civil Liberties Union: **www.aclu.org**

Americans United for Separation of Church and State: **www.au.org**

Christian Coalition of America: **www.cc.org**

The Institute for Communitarian Policy Studies: **www.gwu.edu/~ccps**

Interfaith Alliance: **www.interfaithalliance.org**

James Madison Center for Free Speech: **www.jamesmadisoncenter.org**

NARAL Pro-Choice America: **www.naral.org**

National Catholic Educational Association (Public Policy Department):
    http://www.ncea.org/data-information/public-policy

National Organization for Women (NOW): **www.now.org**

National Right to Life: **www.nrlc.org**

Glossary

ACA *See* Patient Protection and Affordable Care Act.

accommodationist Interpretation of the establishment clause that would permit even-handed government assistance to religious belief and practice. *See also* wall of separation.

accountable care organizations (ACO) Organizations of physicians, hospitals, and other providers established under PPACA designed to deliver health care more effectively and more efficiently.

ACO *See* accountable care organizations.

ADA *See* Americans with Disabilities Act of 1990.

Adequate Yearly Progress (AYP) Requirement under the No Child Left Behind Act that each state establish clearly defined goals for student and school performance.

AFDC *See* Aid to Families with Dependent Children.

affirmative action Federal policies requiring businesses and educational institutions guilty of past discrimination or in receipt of federal funding to demonstrate by positive action that they attempt to hire and admit minorities and women.

Aid to Families with Dependent Children (AFDC) Primary public assistance entitlement that transferred cash to households with state-determined need; replaced by TANF in 1996.

alternative tax proposals Efforts to supplement or replace the current federal income tax structure with alternatives, especially a flat tax or a value-added tax.

Americans with Disabilities Act of 1990 (ADA) Law that extended to persons with disabilities the kinds of protection granted to minorities and women in the 1964 Civil Rights Act.

amnesty Pardon granted to illegal immigrants for entering the country illegally, including permission to remain in the United States under certain conditions.

appeasement Accommodating grievances of aggressive leaders in hopes that they will abandon their aggressive behavior.

asylee Class of immigrants who claim political persecution in their home country based on their ideas or political activities.

AYP *See* Adequate Yearly Progress.

balance of power Concept that no one power or coalition of powers will be allowed to gain such dominating power as to be able to dictate terms of the relationships among nations.

Bilingual Education Act of 1974 Provided federal funds to meet the language needs of non–English speaking students.

Bill of Rights First ten amendments to the U.S. Constitution.

block grant Money provided by the federal government to state or local units for general purposes instead of specific projects.

***Brown v. Board of Education* (1954)** Landmark decision by the Supreme Court that outlawed "separate but equal" educational facilities.

cap and trade Market-based approach to controlling pollution emissions by granting firms permits for a specified level of emissions (cap) and allowing firms to sell or trade permits for any level they do not use up to their caps.

capitation Physician reimbursement method that pays physicians per patient instead of per procedure as in fee-for-service.

categorical grants Money provided by the federal government to the states for a specific project with stipulations on exactly how the money can be used.

CEA *See* Council of Economic Advisers.

censorship A person or institution with authority to determine to which material society may be safely exposed without endangering public order, morality, or security.

Center for Medicare and Medicaid Innovation (CMMI) Unit of CMS tasked with testing innovative payment and health service delivery models.

Centers for Medicare and Medicaid Services (CMS) U.S. Department of Health and Human Services administrative entity responsible for administering Medicare, Medicaid, SCHIP, and the Patient Protection and Affordable Care Act.

charter school A tuition-free entity that receives funding from the state and provides educational choice to students and parents.

child benefit standard Allows aid to children attending religious schools if the primary effect is to the student in attaining a secular education.

civic conservatism The idea that social rights should be secured by meeting some social obligation; first embodied in the Family Support Act of 1988.

Civil Rights Act of 1964 Law that forbids discrimination on the basis of race, creed, color, national origin, or gender in employment or places of public accommodation.

Civil Rights Act of 1991 Law that forbids racial quotas in hiring; makes statistical disparities in the workforce prima facie evidence of employment discrimination; and places burden of proof on employers to show business necessity for hiring qualifications.

class action suit Case in which one party sues on behalf of all people in a similar situation.

classical diplomacy *See* realism.

CMMI *See* Center for Medicare and Medicaid Innovation.

CMS *See* Centers for Medicare and Medicaid Services.

coinsurance Split insurer and insured pay for any health care claim such as 80%/20%, respectively.

COLA *See* Cost-of-Living Adjustment.

Cold War Post–World War II tension between America and its allies and Soviet Union and its allies.

collective security Agreement by multiple nations to come to each other's assistance if attacked by another nation.

comparable worth Proposed legal guarantee of equal pay between men and women for different jobs requiring equal levels of skill, training, or responsibility.

comparative-effectiveness research Research studies that compare the relative success of medical treatments, tests, and pharmaceuticals in curing or alleviating various medical conditions. Treatments found to be

most effective and least costly should be promoted and covered by public and private insurance.

compelling public interest High standard of proof needed for government to justify in court classifying a group differently from other groups.

competition policy European version of antitrust policy.

conservatism Ideological position favoring individual responsibility, limited government, especially in economic matters, and state responsibility for social programs; usually associated with the Republican Party.

Consumer-driven health plans Free-market-based health insurance products that stress consumer choice and financial incentives for purchase of health insurance and medical care.

containment American Cold War policy of resisting the expansion of communism.

co-payments Amount an insured person has to pay service provider when a medical service is accessed.

Corporate Average Fuel Economy Fuel economy standard requiring that the automobile industry produce a mix of cars with an average fuel efficiency of 26.5 miles per gallon.

Cost-of-Living Adjustment (COLA) A yearly adjustment to benefit levels in many entitlement programs to reflect increases in the cost of living resulting from inflation.

cost-push inflation Cost of goods and services increases even though demand remains constant or decreases.

Council of Economic Advisers (CEA) Panel of respected economists who advise the president on economic policy.

CPS *See* Current Population Survey.

crime index Number of crimes per 100,000 population.

crime rate Usually derived from the FBI *Uniform Crime Report* (issued annually). In that source, it means the number of criminal acts in a category per 100,000 population.

cross-cutting requirements Case in which a condition on one grant is applied to all programs using federal funds.

crossover sanctions Sanctions applied to one program activity for failure to comply with certain conditions in another program.

culture Customs and values of a particular society.

Current Population Survey (CPS) The CPS March Supplement is the annual, nationally representative survey that documents people's income and is also used to derive the national poverty rate by comparing their incomes to the absolute poverty line.

decriminalization The legalization of victimless crimes or substantial reduction of penalties for their violation.

deductibles Amount an insured person pays on a claim before insurance begins to pay.

de facto segregation Educational segregation of races not caused by law or public policy, but by residential choice.

deficit spending Occurs when government expenditures exceed revenues in a given fiscal year.

defined benefit Present form of Medicare and Social Security and pensions in which level of some income or benefits is specified and all recipients meeting specified eligibility criteria are entitled to them.

defined contribution An approach to Social Security and pensions in which a fixed financial contribution for each individual is specified; recipients then receive benefits based on investment return of the funds and any funds they choose to contribute above the specified contribution.

de jure segregation Educational segregation of races caused by state or local law or policy.

demand-pull inflation Prices go up because the demand for goods and services grows faster than available supplies.

demand-side theory Traditional, Keynesian economic theory that the economy is driven primarily by demand for goods and services.

Department of Health and Human Services Principal U.S. agency for protecting the health of Americans and providing essential human services.

depression Prolonged decline in economic activity because of a slump in demand. *See also* recession.

deregulation Removal of rules and restrictions on activities by government organizations.

deterrence Preventing an unwanted act from occurring by the threat of punishment of the potential perpetrator. In foreign policy, the possession of sufficient and varied power to survive the best first strike by a potential foe with enough power and willingness to inflict unacceptable damage on such an attacker.

diplomacy Negotiations among the representatives of governments to resolve differences. Scholars differ as to whether an understood threat of force should be considered part of diplomacy.

direct costs and benefits Those related to the specific allocation of resources and the policy's impact on its intended population.

direct orders Regulations that prohibit or mandate state and local government actions.

discount rate Interest rate charged by the U.S. Federal Reserve Bank on loans to member banks.

disparities Unjustified inequalities in the receipt of benefits such as health care and differences in outcomes according to race and ethnicity, income, education, and occupation.

disposable income Income after taxes and work expenses.

doughnut hole Gap in coverage for prescription drugs under Medicare Part D; patients reaching this level must pay the entire cost of their prescriptions; scheduled to be eliminated under PPACA.

Dreamers Individuals brought to the United States illegally by their parents before age sixteen and who lived here continuously for five years; eligible for a waiver to stay in the country.

dual eligibles Low-income persons covered by both Medicare and Medicaid.

due process of law Second paragraph of the Fourteenth Amendment, referring to the procedures the state must go through in order to take away life, liberty, or property; used to apply the procedural part of the Bill of Rights to state criminal proceedings.

earned income tax credit (EITC) Federal program of cash assistance to low-income working families.

education vouchers Form of education financing that allows public tax dollars to be redeemed at either private or public schools for education services.

EITC *See* earned income tax credit.

elite model Policy process model that focuses on the influence over policy exercised by powerful individuals or groups.

empirical dimension Aspect of policy evaluation referring to the measurable outputs and outcomes of a policy.

enterprise zones Geographic areas designated for economic development where government, private, and nonprofit organizations work together to solve problems with tax incentives and other financial help.

entitlement Government benefit programs to which persons have a legal right because they meet program criteria; for example, Medicare and Social Security.

equality of material well-being Concept of proportional equality; the idea that a social group's percentage in the overall population should be equaled by its share of material benefits.

equality of opportunity Right of all individuals to realize the human potential to become whatever their personal abilities allow, free from barriers imposed by society and its institutions.

equality under law Concept that government must treat people as individuals rather than members of groups; when categorizations are made, the burden of proof rests on government to show they express a valid public purpose.

Establishment Clause Clause in the First Amendment forbidding direct government support of religion and prohibiting granting any one sect special status.

E-Verify System operated by the U.S. government employers must use to determine if applicant is eligible to be employed.

exclusionary rule Constitutional principle that illegally obtained evidence may not be used in court.

externalities Indirect costs or benefits of policies.

fast track authority When president is given authority to negotiate a trade treaty and Congress has to accept or reject it without changes.

Fatah Yasser Arafat's wing of the Palestinian Authority (PA). While the perpetrator of numerous terrorist acts in the past, it occasionally is willing to negotiate with Israel and, hence, is regarded as the comparatively moderate wing of the Palestinian Authority.

Federal Reserve Board (Fed) The central banking authority of the United States and the principal agent of monetary policy.

federalism Political system that distributes powers between a central government (national) and constituent units (states); power relationship cannot be changed except by action of both levels.

fee-for-service (FFS) Health care payment system in which each separate consultation, procedure, or device has a separate and specific price for which the patient or insurance company is billed.

FFS *See* fee-for-service.

fighting words doctrine Supreme Court test in determining whether speech can be punished based on whether words would likely cause an average person to fight.

fiscal cliff Economic challenge faced in 2012 in which Congress had difficulty agreeing on taxing and spending policies posing the threat of the federal government not being able to meet its debt obligations.

fiscal policy Tax policy, spending policy, and debt policy used as tools to stabilize the economy.

Food Stamp Program Provides money to poor families to buy food, originally with a book of stamps but now with debit cards. Name was changed to Supplemental Nutrition Assistance Program.

foreign policy realists Those who see international politics as the struggle among self-interested groups to satisfy their self-interests.

fossil fuel Fuel (coal, oil, or natural gas) formed in the earth from plant or animal remains.

fracking Process in which high pressure water is injected deep into shale rock to release natural gas.

free enterprise Private ownership of the means of production operating through supply and demand.

Free Exercise Clause Clause in the First Amendment that forbids government from impeding the practice of religion.

Gaza Small strip of land on the southern coast of Palestine that fell from Egyptian to Israeli control in the Six Day War. Israel evicted its settlers and turned the land to Palestinian control in spring 2007.

GDP *See* gross domestic product.

general revenue sharing Transfer of money from one level of government to another with little or no restriction on its use.

glass ceiling Unseen barrier that keeps minorities and women from rising to the top levels of employing organizations.

global warming Warming of the earth's atmosphere.

government subsidy Policy that supports a particular group or interest, usually with cash payments.

Great Society Considered the period of 1961–1978 during which substantial expansion of the U.S. welfare state occurred.

gross domestic product (GDP) Measures the value of all goods and services produced in a nation in a single year.

group model Policy process model that emphasizes interest groups that form advocacy coalitions that are active in some policy areas, but not in others.

Hamas Militant wing of the Palestinian Authority (PA) who won control of the PA in a 2007 election and control of Gaza by force. Hamas is explicitly committed to the extermination of Israel and rejects any negotiation with or recognition of that state.

Health Care and Education Reconciliation Act The 2010 budget reconciliation Act that accompanied and made changes in the health care reform legislation (PPACA).

Health Insurance Marketplace (HIM) ACA's web-based location for individuals to shop for health insurance.

health savings accounts (HSA) Individual tax-free savings plans and high deductible insurance used to cover medical expenses.

hegemony A situation in which one nation so dominates other nations that it may dictate the terms of the relationship between them without the need to compromise its interests.

Hicklin **test** Material judged to be obscene if any passage has a tendency to corrupt or degrade.

HIM *See* Health Insurance Marketplace.

historical institutionalism Model of the policy process that stresses how early policy decisions carry large effects through time, so that policies become path dependent.

Home Schooling Parents assume primary responsibility for educating their children instead of relying on public or private schools. Education may be delivered by parents individually or through cooperative efforts with other home schooling parents. Requirements for home schooling vary significantly from state to state.

idealism Principle that there are knowable and universal principles of justice over and above the laws and policies of any particular state. These principles should guide foreign policy.

ideology Ideas and beliefs of a particular people or movement.

imperialism Acquiring of colonies and dependencies.

implementation Steps taken to put a policy into practice to achieve the policymaker's goals.

Independent Payment Advisory Board Organization established by ACA to recommend methods for reducing the rate of growth of health care spending.

independent regulatory commission Agency independent of direct presidential or congressional control, designed to regulate a specific sector of the economy.

indeterminate sentencing Judge specifies a range of time in prison and inmate then becomes eligible for parole after serving the minimum.

indirect costs and benefits Those related to a policy's impact on individuals and groups not intended to be part of the target population.

individual mandate ACA's requirement that most persons purchase health insurance meeting minimum essential standards or pay a tax penalty.

inflation Rise in price of goods and services while the value of goods and services does not increase.

in-kind benefits Public assistance provided in the form of goods, for example, food or housing.

institutional model This model stresses the opportunities and constraints on policy that are part of the very structure of the American constitutional order.

intergovernmental relations Relationships between national government and states and local governments, as well as interactions between and among states and local governments.

interstate compact Formal agreement between or among states to address specific issues.

Intifada Arab term referring to a popular uprising involving recurring use of nonmilitary violence to weaken and ultimately destroy Israel.

iron curtain Divide between eastern and western Europe after World War II symbolized by the Warsaw Pact and North Atlantic Treaty Organization and the Berlin Wall.

Islamism or Islamist Radical and militant aspects of Islam, not the entire Muslim world.

Jihad Muslim concept whose most frequent use in foreign policy means a "holy war" to defend or advance the faith.

laissez-faire Policy allowing business to operate with little interference by government.

LAPS values Supreme Court rule that in order to be censored, material must lack serious literary, artistic, political, or scientific value.

maintenance of effort State and local governments cannot use federal money to replace their own spending on a program.

market capitalism Private ownership of means of production and trade with unrestricted marketplace.

market failure A concept justifying government intervention into a realm of economic activity when the conditions for the effective operation of free markets are absent or imperfect.

Medicaid A state–federal public assistance program to provide health care for low-income persons.

Medicare A federal program of social insurance for the health care needs of elderly and disabled persons.

Medicare Advantage Medicare plans offered by private insurance companies that combine both Parts A and B (and often Part D) into one contract for all covered services.

Medicare Part A Medicare hospital insurance.

Medicare Part B Medicare physician insurance.

Medicare Part C *See* Medicare Advantage.

medigap Federally regulated private insurance policies designed to cover medical expenses not covered by Medicare.

Miranda **rule** Includes (1) the right to remain silent, (2) the right to know that anything said can and will be used against the accused in court, and (3) the right to be represented by counsel, at state expense if necessary.

models of policymaking Pictures of the policy process that summarize the primary forces at work in order to reduce complexity to a degree manageable for policy analysis.

monetary policy A macroeconomic tool that seeks to use the supply of money in circulation to impact interest rates and inflation.

money supply A measure of the amount and value of money in circulation, including currency and deposits in banks, credit unions, and savings institutions.

monopoly Situation in which there is an absence of competition, blocked entry into the market, a single seller, or a few sellers who work together to limit competition.

mother's pension laws State-level cash assistance to widows with children that became a model for the design of federal assistance in the Social Security Act of 1935.

multiculturalism Educational reform movement with objective to change traditional views of the Western European impact on the Americas; emphasis placed on respecting the diverse and disparate ethnic elements in American society.

multilateralism View that serious foreign policies ought to be implemented only in concert with and presumably with the blessing of one's major allies.

national debt Accumulation over time of annual deficits.

national health insurance Health care system in which all citizens have access to health care through guaranteed government-mandated insurance.

nationalism A belief involving an individual identifying with one nation and supporting its actions.

nationalization Government ownership of an enterprise.

natural monopoly Activity so basic to maintenance of society that government monopoly is justified; for example, postal service.

neoclassical economics Free market and probusiness.

neopopulist Part of Republican party that focuses on social issues and conservative view of public morality.

New Right Ideological movement often associated with evangelical Christians; directs most attention to social issues, abortion, same-sex marriage, feminism, pornography, and government interference in religious expression.

No Child Left Behind Act 2002 Reauthorization of the Elementary and Secondary Education Act, which included testing and accountability measures and school choice provisions for parents of children attending low-performing schools. NCLB is subject to reauthorization as of mid 2014.

normative dimension Aspect of policy evaluation referring to values, beliefs, and attitudes of society, of particular groups, and of policy evaluators themselves.

Nuremberg principle Principle that the leadership and population of the sovereign nations of the world are morally obligated to disregard and disobey laws and policies to the extent that these laws and policies violate universal principles of justice.

Obamacare *See* Patient Protection and Affordable Care Act.

obscenity Published material offending fundamental values of a society and containing strong sexual content or egregious violence.

Office of Management and Budget (OMB) Agency in the Executive Office of the President that assists the president in the preparation of the federal budget and oversees budget's execution.

oil depletion allowance Allowed oil companies to deduct part of their gross income from taxable income to allow for the nonrenewability of the oil they produced.

OMB *See* Office of Management and Budget.

OPEC *See* Organization of Petroleum Exporting Countries.

open market operations Tool of monetary policy, used by the Federal Reserve Board, involving the purchase and sale of U.S. Treasury and other federal agency securities.

open society A society in which all perspectives on controversial moral questions are tolerated and may be advocated.

Organization of Petroleum Exporting Countries (OPEC) Organization representing the major oil and natural gas producing nations in the developing world.

outcome evaluation Focuses on impact of a policy or program.

parole Inmate is released from prison before serving full sentence if it is determined that inmate can lead a socially constructive life and reports to parole or probation officer regularly through the end of the original sentence.

partial preemption Situations in which national government requires or permits states to administer policies as long as states meet federal criteria for the program.

path dependency Feature of the historical institutional model that recognizes how actions taken in past policy decisions are difficult to reverse.

patient-centered medical home New form of health care delivery that encourages team-based, multidisciplinary care for persons with chronic conditions.

Patient Protection and Affordable Care Act (PPACA) Health care reform legislation enacted in March 2010.

payment for value Health care delivery system reform that attempts to improve quality of care by rewarding successful patient outcomes.

performance management Ongoing review of program accomplishments and problems, and improving results, through decisions based upon the review, with accountability for performance.

Personal Responsibility and Work Opportunity Reconciliation Act (PRWORA) Public assistance reform legislation passed in 1996.

plea bargaining Offer by prosecutorial forces to reduce criminal charges to those carrying lighter punishment in return for a guilty plea, thus avoiding the costs and uncertainties of a criminal trial.

pluralist model Model of the policy process that stresses that many groups and individuals influence the American democratic system.

policy *See* public policy.

policy adoption Official government action responding to a problem or issue.

policy advocacy Activity by political, interest, or ideological groups or individuals to advance their preferred policy options on the political agenda.

policy analysis Field of political science and public administration principally concerned with describing and investigating how and why policies are proposed, adopted, and implemented.

policy evaluation Process of assessing impacts of a policy, that is, the policy's effects on society compared with the policy's intended goals.

policy impact What actually happens when policy is put into effect.

Poor Law England's 1601 codification of several prior statutes into one law placing responsibility for the poor with local authorities, allowing for harsh treatment of the able-bodied if they refused to work and provided care for the dependent poor.

populism A movement mobilizing less educated persons, placing faith in their common sense wisdom, and expressing distrust of elites in general and intellectuals in particular.

poverty gap Amount of money that is needed to raise all those below the poverty line up to the poverty line.

poverty line An absolute number, computed as three times the U.S. Department of Agriculture's "thrifty food budget"; serves as the income threshold below which a family is considered to be poor.

power Relationship between two or more actors such that the power wielder can get others to do what the power wielder wants them to do and which they otherwise would not have done.

PPACA *See* Patient Protection and Affordable Care Act.

preemption The principle that federal law takes precedence over state law and that the federal government may prohibit state action on an issue.

Preemptive strike/preemptive war Attack on a state or power that poses an imminent threat without waiting for the other state to strike the first blow.

preferential treatment Policy to use membership in a designated group as one positive factor to be taken into account for employment or admission.

prior restraint Right of government to suppress something said or written in advance of the utterance. *See also* censorship.

private goods Goods that can be divided and allocated to some persons, but not others. *See also* public goods.

private rationality Decision-making reasoning that serves individuals but not society as a whole.

privatization (education) Form of education policy in which the operation of either a single school or an entire district may be contracted to a private firm.

process evaluation Assesses activities and structures of policy implementation.

program evaluation Evaluation of the specific programs created by public policies.

progressive *See* liberalism.

Promise Zones Geographic areas targeted for economic development in which government, the private sector, and nonprofits work together for change.

proportional equality *See* equality of material well-being.

prorationing Governmental regulations to impose production quotas on private energy companies in order to reduce supply.

prospective payment system Medical care reimbursement methodology based on fixed payments for certain diagnoses, rather than on the cost of care.

PRWORA *See* Personal Responsibility and Work Opportunity Reconciliation Act.

public choice model A model of the policy process that thinks of those active in policymaking as actors attempting to choose options that maximize their self-interest.

public goods Goods that cannot be divided. *See also* private goods.

public policy An intentional course of action followed by a government institution or official for resolving an issue of public concern.

quotas A specific number or percentage allocated to particular groups in hiring, promotion, or in immigration.

racial preference plan Use of race as one among several factors in selecting from an open applicant pool.

racial profiling Sometime police practice of singling out certain racial groups for more intense scrutiny.

rational–comprehensive model Policy process model that conceives of policymakers taking account of all information and options, then selecting the policy options that best fulfill the policymaker's goals.

realism View that the only legitimate goal of foreign policy is national self-interest.

recession Period where there is a decline in economic activity arising from slump in demand for goods and services. *See also* depression.

recidivism Rate at which people who have been punished for past crimes commit more crimes.

refugee Person displaced from home country because of political instability or persecution.

reserve requirement Amount of money a bank must keep on reserve.

retribution Literally revenge; more generally, punishment to satisfy a sense of justice being served.

risk subsidy Government subsidy that protects businesses or consumers from risks of the marketplace.

rogue state Nation-state that exhibits disregard for accepted rules of international conduct.

Roth **rule** Supreme Court decision that obscenity exists if the dominant theme of the material appeals to the prurient interest and the material has no redeeming social value.

SCHIP *See* State Children's Health Insurance Program.

school choice Allowing parents to send their children to schools outside the school geographic boundary including other public schools, private schools, charter schools, and home schooling.

scienter Knowledge of wrongdoing that must be present to punish speech.

secularization Decline of conventional religion, of regular church attendance, and of belief in traditional religious doctrines, along with restriction of religion to private spheres of life.

sequestration Automatic spending cuts across the board if Congress approves spending levels exceeding targeted budget deficit levels.

service intensity A concept in health care referring to a rising number of procedures per year on the average patient.

settlement houses Residences of highly educated social reformers (usually women) who combined social service work with social reforms.

sexual harassment Legally forbidden situation in which one person, having power over some aspect of another's life uses the power persistently over time to extort sexual favors or create a hostile working environment.

SGR *See* sustainable growth rate.

Sheppard–Towner Act Formally titled The Promotion of the Welfare and Hygiene of Maternity and Infancy Act, was a 1921 act of Congress that is commonly thought to be the Federal government's first foray into social security legislation. The act provided federal assistance to states and became a model for later social assistance efforts.

SHOP *See* Small Business Health Options Program.

single-payer plan Health care access reform proposal that eliminates all private insurance in favor of a national or state-administered single health insurance program.

Small Business Health Options Program (SHOP) Web-based health insurance marketplace for small businesses to obtain insurance for employees.

social assistance programs Means-tested aid programs to minimize economic hardship and alleviate poverty.

social insurance programs Programs of public insurance with mandatory universal or near-universal participation; for example, Social Security and Medicare.

Social Security Act 1935 legislation (amended numerous times since) creating the most important federal programs of social insurance, especially Social Security which provides minimum levels of income for persons aged sixty-five and over, as well as income for disabled workers and surviving spouses and children of deceased workers.

socialism Public or governmental ownership and control of major means of production, distribution, and exchange.

socialized medicine Government-owned and -operated health care system in which all citizens have access to free or very low-cost medical care.

sovereignty Final power of a political unit to make and enforce its own laws.

sphere of influence Territories contiguous to the borders of a major power in which it is assumed the major power will be the dominant influence and hostile systems will not be tolerated.

SSI *See* Supplemental Security Income.

standing to sue Person suing in court must have something personally at stake.

State Children's Health Insurance Program (SCHIP) Federal block grant to states to expand health insurance coverage to children in families with incomes above the Medicaid eligibility level.

street crime Offenses that involve force or threat of force.

subgovernment model Recognizes that different policy areas must be treated differently.

subsidies Money or other support, by government, to entities to promote desired behavior such as increased or decreased production of particular crops by farmers.

sunset laws Statutes requiring a program to be terminated at some specific time unless an evaluation leads to a decision to continue it.

Supplemental Security Income (SSI) Program of cash assistance to aged or disabled persons with incomes below a federal standard.

supply-side economics Macroeconomic approach that emphasizes tax cuts and tax incentives to business in order to promote economic growth.

Supremacy Clause Article VI of the Constitution that makes federal law supreme over state law when exercising a federal government power.

sustainable growth rate (SGR) Medicare's physician reimbursement methodology.

symbolic benefit Policy that has symbolic importance.

tax credit An amount a taxpayer is able to deduct from taxes owed for expenses such as education, energy efficiency, or business investment.

tax cut Reduction in the rate of taxation.

tax efficiency Expanding tax base by reducing impact of laws (for example, depreciation, loopholes).

tax fairness Assigning tax burden to differing income levels and increasing public confidence in the tax system.

tax reform Change in basic type and incidence of taxes.

Tea Party American political movement focusing primarily on reducing spending and taxes active since 2009.

terrorism Random violence against civilian or noncombatant populations to compel another power to change its policies by generating widespread anxiety or fear among its people.

Title IX of the Educational Amendment Acts of 1972 Law forbidding educational institutions receiving federal funds to engage in gender discrimination, especially in athletic programs.

trade promotion authority *See* fast track authority.

Unemployment Insurance Social insurance entitlement program to maintain the income of workers in periods of involuntary unemployment.

unfunded mandates Requirements imposed on state and local governments with no national government funding to implement them.

Uniform Crime Report Official national crime statistics issued by the Federal Bureau of Investigation (FBI).

unilateralism Policies undertaken in foreign policy without first obtaining political and material support from most major allies.

unintended impact Consequence not anticipated as the policy or program was developed.

universal harmony of interests Belief in foreign policy that all people share basic values (health, prosperity, family) that allow them to come to mutual agreement on issues.

victimless crime Crime in which participants are assumed to be consenting or willing adults.

wall of separation Interpretation of the establishment clause that forbids any government support or assistance to religious belief and practice. *See also* accommodationist.

War on Poverty Period of 1964–1972 associated with antipoverty programs' growth and change.

welfare-state capitalism System in which allocation of goods and services is partially planned, but production is in private hands.

West Bank Portion of Palestine that lies between the Jordan River and the 1947 boundaries of Israel. Peace process advocates see this as the major part of the new Palestinian Arab state; however, Israel has not dismantled all the Jewish settlements that sprang up there in the wake of the 1967 war.

white-collar crime Crimes committed by middle-class business executives or professionals within their offices or workplaces, involving financial transactions such as stock fraud, embezzlement, and price fixing.

Wilsonian idealism *See* idealism.

work release Form of alternative sentencing in which inmate is released during his/her work hours and returns to prison afterwards.

work relief Jobs created at government expense that substitute for cash assistance.

Workers' Compensation Social insurance entitlement program to maintain the income and pay medical bills of workers injured on the job.

zero-sum society Sum of gains equal the sum of losses with particular reference to economic activities.

References

Chapter 1

1. James E. Anderson, *Public Policymaking: An Introduction,* 7th ed. (Boston: Cengage, 2011).
2. For example, Kim Quaille Hill, "In Search of Policy Theory," *Policy Currents,* 7 (April 1997): 1–9.
3. James Coleman, *Equality of Educational Opportunity* (EEOC) 1966. Ann Arbor, MI. Inter University Consortium for Political and Social Research.
4. See Jacob S. Hacker, *The Divided Welfare State: The Battle over Public and Private Social Benefits in the United States* (New York: Cambridge Univesity Press, 2002), Chapter 1 for a summary of the model and its application to social policy.
5. C. Wright Mills, *The Power Elite* (New York: Oxford University Press, 1956).
6. For a convenient summary of models and their development, see Joseph Stewart, Jr., David M. Hedge, and James P. Lester, *Public Policy: An Evolutionary Approach,* 3rd ed. (Belmont, CA: Wadsworth, 2008), Chapters 4–9.
7. See Robert A. Heineman et al., *The World of the Policy Analyst: Rationality, Values, and Politics,* 3rd ed. (Chatham, NJ: Chatham House, 2001); Deborah Stone, *Policy Paradox: The Art of Political Decision Making,* 3rd ed. (New York: Norton, 2011); and Henry J. Aaron et al., eds., *Values and Public Policy* (Washington, DC: Brookings Institution, 1994).
8. See the influential work of John W. Kingdon, *Agendas, Alternatives, and Public Policies,* 2nd ed. (New York: Longman, 2010).
9. See Deborah Stone, *Policy Paradox: The Art of Political Decision Making,* 3rd ed. (New York: Norton, 2011); Paul A. Sabatier, "Toward Better Theories of the Policy Process," *PS: Political Science & Politics,* 24 (June 1991): 147–156; and Paul A. Sabatier, ed., *Theories of the Policy Process,* 3rd ed. (Boulder, CO: Westview Press, 2014).
10. More detailed discussion of these stages can be found in Anderson, *Public Policymaking.* See also Charles L. Cochran and Eloise F. Malone, *Public Policy: Perspectives and Choices,* 4th ed. (Boulder, CO: Lynne Rienner Publishers, 2009).
11. See the pioneering study by Jeffrey L. Pressman and Aaron Wildavsky, *Implementation,* 3rd ed. (Berkeley: University of California Press, 1984).
12. Paul A. Sabatier and Daniel Mazmanian, "The Implementation of Public Policy: A Framework for Analysis," in Stella Z. Theodoulou and Matthew A. Cahn, eds., *Public Policy: The Essential Readings* (Englewood Cliffs, NJ: Prentice Hall, 1995), 153–173.

13. Stone, *Policy Paradox,* 261.
14. Jody Fitzpatrick, James Sanders, and Blaine Worthen, *Program Evaluation: Alternative Approaches and Practical Guidelines* (New York: Pearson, 2011).

Chapter 2

1. "Youth Voting," *Circle Fact Sheet,* The Center for Information & Research on Civic Learning & Engagement, July 17, 2013, http://www.civicyouth/quick-facts/youth-voting/, accessed February 14, 2014.
2. E.J. Dionne, Jr., *Why Americans Hate Politics* (New York: Simon & Schuster, 1991).
3. Pew Research Center for the People & the Press, "Trust in Government Nears Record Low, but Most Federal Agencies Are Viewed Favorably," http://www.people-press.org/2013/10/18/Trust-in-government/, accessed February 14, 2014.
4. See Richard Morin, "They Only Know What They Don't Like," *Washington Post National Weekly Edition,* October 3–9, 1994, p. 37; Richard Morin, "Tuned Out, Turned Off," *Washington Post National Weekly Edition,* February 5–11, 1996, 6–8; and Project Vote, "Youth Voting: Registration and Voting among Young Americans," http://projectvote.org/youth-voting-.html, accessed February 27, 2014.
5. *National Federation of Independent Business v. Sebelius,* No. 11-393 (June 28, 2012).
6. Christopher Banks and John C. Blakeman, *The U.S. Supreme Court and New Federalism: From the Rehnquist to the Roberts Court* (Lanham, MD: Rowman & Littlefield, 2012); David H. Rosenbloom, Rosemary O'Leary, and Joshua Chanin, *Public Administration and Law,* 3rd ed. (New York: CRC Press, 2010), Chapter 1; and Charles R. Wise, "The Supreme Court's New Constitutional Federalism: Implications for Public Administration," *Public Administration Review, 61* (3) (May/June 2001): 343–358.
7. Christopher Banks and John Blakeman, "The U.S. Supreme Court and New Federalism"; Paul Posner, "The Supreme Court and the Remaking of Federalism," *Governing,* July 18, 2012, http://www.governing.com/columns/mgmt-insights/col-supreme-court-health-care-ruling-coercion-states-federalism.html, accessed February 14, 2014.
8. U.S. Advisory Commission on Intergovernmental Relations, *Regulatory Federalism: Policy, Process, Impact, and Reform,* vol. 2 (Washington, DC: U.S. Government Printing Office, 1984).
9. Kevin R. Johnson, "Immigration and Civil Rights: State and Local Efforts to Regulate Immigration," *Georgia Law Review, 46* (Spring 2012): 609; and Joseph F. Zimmerman, "The Nature and Political Significance of Preemption," *PS: Political Science & Politics* (July 2005): 360–362.
10. Lawrence D. Brown and Bernard Frieden, "Guidelines and Goals in the Model Cities Program," *Policy Sciences, 7* (December 1976): 488; and Bruce A. Wallin, *From Revenue Sharing to Deficit Sharing: General Revenue Sharing and Cities* (Washington, DC: Georgetown University Press, 1998), Chapter 4.
11. Banks and Blakeman, "The Supreme Court and the Remaking of Federalism."
12. John E. Schwarz, *America's Hidden Success: A Reassessment of Public Policy from Kennedy to Reagan,* rev. ed. (New York: Norton 1988), 116ff.
13. Deborah Stone, *Policy Paradox: The Art of Political Decision Making,* 3rd ed. (New York: Norton, 2011).
14. James Morone, *Hellfire Nation: The Politics of Sin in American History* (New Haven, CT: Yale University Press, 2004).

15. For broad discussion of cultural conflict and of the policy issues directly involved, see James Davison Hunter, *Culture Wars: The Struggle to Define America* (New York: Basic Books, 1991); and Irene Taviss Thomson, *Culture Wars and Enduring American Dilemmas* (Ann Arbor: University of Michigan Press, 2010). Political scientists disagree about how extensive these cultural differences are and about how polarized the electorate is around these differences. See, for example, Morris P. Fiorina, *Culture War? The Myth of a Polarized America* (New York: Pearson, 2005); and Mark D. Brewer and Jeffrey M. Stonecash, *Split: Class and Cultural Divides in American Politics* (Washington: CQ Press, 2007).

Chapter 3

1. John Kenneth Galbraith, *Economics and the Public Purpose* (New York: Signet, 1973), 3–4.
2. This discussion relies heavily on Richard L. Siegel and Leonard B. Weinberg, *Comparing Public Policies* (Homewood, IL: Dorsey Press, 1977), Chapter 4. Also see Richard Lehne, *Industry and Politics: United States in Comparative Perspective* (Englewood Cliffs, NJ: Prentice Hall, 1993), especially Chapters 1 and 2; and Murray I. Weidenbaum, *Business and Government in the Global Marketplace,* 7th ed. (Upper Saddle River, NJ: Prentice Hall, 2004).
3. Milton Friedman, *Capitalism and Freedom* (Chicago: University of Chicago Press, 1962).
4. For an excellent critique of Friedman's position, see Rick Tilman, "Ideology and Utopia in the Political Economy of Milton Friedman," *Polity, 8* (Spring 1996): 422–442.
5. John Kenneth Galbraith explores this and many of the following ideas in three of his books: *The Affluent Society* (Boston: Houghton Mifflin, 1958);

The New Industrial State (Boston: Houghton Mifflin, 1968); and *Economics and the Public Purpose* (Boston: Houghton Mifflin, 1973).
6. The following position is taken by Robert Averitt in *The Dual Economy* (New York: Norton, 1968); and by Robert Seidman, "Contract Law, the Free Market, and State Intervention: A Jurisprudential Perspective," *Journal of Economic Issues, 7* (December 1973): 553–575.
7. Seymour Martin Lipset, *The First New Nation* (New York: Basic Books, 1963), especially Chapters 1 and 2.
8. John Maynard Keynes, *General Theory of Employment, Interest, and Money* (New York: Harcourt Brace, 1936).
9. P. Teske, *Regulation in the States* (Washington, DC: Brookings Institution, 2004).
10. Graham K. Wilson, *Business and Politics: A Comparative Introduction* (New York: Chatham House, 2003).
11. Stephen Labaton, "New View of Antitrust Law: See No Evil, Hear No Evil," *New York Times,* May 8, 2006.
12. G. W. Roster, Jr., *The Status of Class Action Litigation,* American Bar Foundation, Research Contribution No. 4 (Chicago, 1974), examines the development of class action litigation in the United States. See also Deborah R. Hensler, *Class Action Dilemmas: Pursuing Public Goals for Private Gain* (Santa Monica, CA: Rand, 2000).
13. John O. Haley, *Antitrust in Germany and Japan: The First Fifty Years, 1947–1998* (Seattle: University of Washington Press, 2001); and Lehne, *Industry and Politics.*
14. Deborah K. Belasich, *Enterprise Zones: Policy Perspectives of Economic Development* (New York: Garland, 1993); and Peter Hall, "Enterprise Zones: A Justification," *Journal of Urban and Regional Research, 6* (1982): 417–421.
15. The White House, Office of the Press Secretary, "Fact Sheet: President

Obama's Promise Zone Initiative," January 8, 2014, http://www.white house.gov/the-press-office/2014/01/08/fact-sheet-president-obama-s-promise-zones-initiative.

16. Andrew Sissons with Chris Brown, "Do Enterprize Zones Work," February 2011, http://www.thework foundation.com/assets/docs/publica tions/283_enterprise%20zones_24% 20feb_final.pdf.

17. Conrad Weiler, "GATT, NAFTA and State and Local Powers," *Inter-governmental Perspective, 20* (Fall 1993–Winter 1994): 38–41.

18. http://bigstory.ap.org/article/corporate-mergers-start-strong, 2014, accessed March 20, 2014.

19. Richard A. Epstein, *Overdose: How Excessive Government Regulation Stifles Pharmaceutical Innovation* (Institute for Policy Innovation, 2008) and U.S. House of Representatives Committee on Science, Space, and Technology, *Excessive Regulation and High Taxes Stifle Innovation, Job Creation*, March 27, 2012, http://science.house.gov/press-release/excessive-regulation-and-high-taxes-stifle-innovation-job-creation, accessed June 26, 2014.

20. Sam Batkins, "Piling On: The Year in Regulation," January 14, 2013, http//americanactionforum.org/research/piling-on-the-year-in-regulation, accessed March 9, 2014; W. M. Crain, "The Impact of Regulatory Costs on Small Firms," Office of Advocacy, Small Business Administration, 2010, http://www.sba.gov/sites/default/The%20Impact%20%/20Regulatory/%20Costs%20on%20Small%20Firms%/20(Full).pdf, accessed March 9, 2014; and W. M. Capron and R. G. Noll, "Summary and Conclusion," in W. M. Capron, ed., *Technological Change in Regulated Industries* (Washington, DC: Brookings Institution, 1971), 221.

21. Huffington Post, "9 Mergers That Epically Failed," http:// www.huffingtonpost.com/2013/02/23/worst-mergersof-all-time_n_2720121.html.

22. Garry Hull, ed., *The Abolition of Antitrust* (New Brunswick, NJ: Transaction Publishers, 2005); and Martin Fridson, *Unwarranted Intrusion into the Marketplace* (Hoboken, NJ: Wiley, 2006).

23. Raymond J. Ahearn, "CRS Report for Congress: Globalization, Worker Insecurity, and Policy Approaches," February 27, 2012, Congressional Research Service, http://fas.org/sgp/crs/misc/RL34091.pdf, accessed March 11, 2014; Gary Clyde Hufbauer, "Answering the Critics: Why Large American Gains from Globalization Are Plausible," Peterson Institute for International Economics, http://iie.com/publications/papers/paper.cfm?ResearchID-929, accessed June 23, 2010; and Dani Rodrik, *The Globalization Paradox: Democracy and the Future of the World Economy* (New York: Norton, 2012).

24. Raymond J. Ahearn, *CRS Report for Congress;* L. Josh Bivens, *The Gains from Trade: How Big and Who Gets Them?* Economic Policy Institute Working Paper (accessed June 23, 2010); James Petras and Henry Veltmeyer, *Globalization Unmasked: Imperialism in the 21st Century* (Halifax, Nova Scotia: Fernwood Publishing, 2001); Ian Ramsay, "Globalization, the Third Way and Consumer Law: The Case of the U.K," in Jane K. Winn, ed., *Consumer Protection in the Age of the "Information Economy"* (Burlington, VT: Ashgate Publishing, 2006), 59–80; and Dani Rodrik, *Has Globalization Gone Too Far?* (Washington, DC: Institute for International Economics, 1997).

Chapter 4

1. See Timothy Cogley, "What Is the Optimal Rate of Inflation?" *Federal*

Reserve Bank of San Francisco Economic Letter, No. 97–27 (September 19, 1997), for a discussion of the factors the Federal Reserve System can use to determine an optimal rate of inflation; and Roberto Billi, "Optimal Inflation for the U.S. Economy," *American Economic Journal: Macroeconomics* (July 2011), 29–52.

2. W. Arthur Lewis, *Theory of Economic Growth* (New York: Routledge, 2013). Late in 1991, the Commerce Department changed its economic measure from gross national product (GNP) to gross domestic product (GDP). Figures in this book are GDP unless otherwise indicated.

3. See Mary C. Daly, "Assessing the Benefits of Economic Growth," *Federal Reserve Bank of San Francisco Economic Letter,* No. 97–30 (October 17, 1997), for a discussion of various approaches to assess benefits of economic growth.

4. Anthony Solomon, "Economic Ideology and Public Policy," *Challenge* (July/August 1986): 11–17.

5. Edward R. Tufte, *Political Control of the Economy* (Princeton, NJ: Princeton University Press, 1978).

6. For a discussion of some of these issues, see John Faust and Dale W. Henderson, "Is Inflation Targeting Best Practice Monetary Policy?" *Federal Reserve Bank of St. Louis Review* (July/August 2004): 117–143.

7. Congressional Budget Office, "Long-Term Economic Effects of Chronically Large Federal Deficits," Washington, DC, October 2005.

8. Arthur Laffer, "Supply Side Economics," *Financial Analysts Journal* (September/October 1981): 29–43.

9. John K. Galbraith, *Economics and the Public Purpose* (Boston: Houghton Mifflin, 1978).

10. Rick Tilman, "Ideology and Utopia in the Political Economy of Milton Friedman," *Polity, 8* (Spring 1976): 422–442.

11. See the U.S. Treasury Department website, www.financialstability.gov, for current information on TARP and the Emergency Economic Stabilization Act of 2008, accessed June 8, 2010.

12. For a discussion of the origin and impact of subprime mortgages, see Dwight M. Jaffee, "The U.S. Subprime Mortgage Crisis: Issues Raised and Lessons Learned," in Patricia C. Annez, *Urbanization and Growth* (Washington, DC: World Bank, 2009).

13. See www.recovery.gov for current information on the American Recovery and Reinvestment Act; and www.recovery.gov/arra/Pages/default.aspx for information on state by state ARRA spending, accessed February 20, 2014.

14. See the U.S. Internal Revenue Service website, www.eitc.irs.gov, for detailed information on the Earned Income Tax Credit, accessed February 20, 2014.

15. Martin Feldstein and Alan Binder, "Can Tax Reform Save the U.S. Economy?" *International Economy* (2013), http://www.urban.org/UploadedPDF/901479-can-tax-rerorm-save.pdf?RSSFeed=Urban.xml, accessed February 20, 2014.

Chapter 5

1. For a discussion of the coal industry, see Marc Humphries, *Coal: A Primer on the Major Issues* (Hauppauge, NY: Nova Science Publishers, 2004).

2. See Toyin Falola, *The Politics of the Global Oil Industry: An Introduction* (Westport, CT: Prager, 2005).

3. Katherine T. Harris, *Geopolitics of Oil* (Hauppaug, NY: Nova Science Publishers, 2010).

4. Brenda Shaffer, *Energy Politics* (Philadelphia: University of Pennsylvania Press, 2009).

5. See Seymour Warkov, *Energy Policy in the United States* (New York: Macmillan, 1978).

6. U.S. Department of Energy, Energy Information Administration, http://www.eia.gov/dnav/ng/hist/n9010us2A.htm, accessed February 2014.

7. Richard Youngs, *Energy Security: Europe's New Foreign Policy Challenge* (New York: Routledge, 2009).

8. Laurance R. Geri and David E. McNabb, *Energy Policy in the U.S.* (Boca Raton, FL: CRC Press, 2011).

9. Don Kash and Robert Rycroft, *U.S. Energy Policy* (Norman: University of Oklahoma Press, 1984).

10. Julian E. Zelizer, *The Presidency of George W. Bush* (Princeton, NJ: Princeton University Press, 2010).

11. For a discussion of issues related to nuclear energy, see Trevor Findlay, *Nuclear Energy and Global Governance* (New York: Routledge, 2011).

12. Arianna Checchi, Arno Behrens, and Christian Egenhofer, *Long-Term Energy Security Risks for Europe* (Brussels, Belgium: Center for European Policy Studies, 2009).

13. Walter A. Rosenbloom, *Environmental Politics and Policy* (New York: Sage, 2010).

14. Rachel Carson, *Silent Spring* (Boston: Houghton Mifflin, 1962).

15. *Environmental Outlook, 1980* (Washington, DC: U.S. Environmental Protection Agency, 1980).

16. See John Houghton, *Global Warming: The Complete Briefing,* 3rd ed. (Cambridge: Cambridge University Press, 2004) for a discussion of this issue in greater depth. For a skeptical look at claims of global warming and other environmental disasters, see Bjorn Lomborg, *The Skeptical Environmentalist: Measuring the Real State of the World* (New York: Cambridge University Press, 2001).

17. For example, see Joseph A. Ritter, *Water Quality,* 4th ed. (Denver, CO: American Water Works Association, 2010).

18. The Resource Conservation and Recovery Act, PL 94–580, Section 4001 (1976).

19. National Environmental Policy Act, PL 91–190, January 1, 1970.

20. George C. Eads and Michael Fix, eds., *The Reagan Regulatory Strategy: An Assessment* (Washington, DC: Urban Institute Press, 1984).

21. Al Gore, *Earth in the Balance* (New York: Houghton Mifflin, 1992).

22. Alexander Cockburn and Jeffrey St. Clair, "Slime Green," *The Progressive,* May 18, 1996, pp. 18–21.

23. Keith Schneider, "New View Calls Environmental Policy Misguided," *New York Times,* March 21, 1993, p. 1.

24. See Stephen H. Schneider, Armin Rosencranz, Michale D. Mastrandrea, and Kristin Kuntz-Duriseti, eds., *Climate Change: Science and Policy* (Washington, DC: Island Press, 2010) for a discussion of some of these issues.

25. See Guy Benveniste, *Regulation and Planning* (San Francisco: Boyd & Fraser, 1981); and Lester Thurow, *Zero-Sum Society* (New York: Basic Books, 1980).

26. Murray Weidenbaum, Christopher Douglas, and Michael Orlando, *Toward a Healthier Environment and a Stronger Economy: How to Achieve Common Ground* (St. Louis: Washington University, Center for the Study of American Business, 1997).

27. Stephen Huebner and Kenneth Chilton, *EPA's Case for Ozone and Particulate Standards: Would Americans Get Their Money's Worth?* (St. Louis: Washington University, Center for the Study of American Business, 1997).

28. Jacob I. Bregman and Robert D. Edell, *Environmental Compliance Handbook* (Boca Raton, FL: CRC Press, 2002).

29. "Economic Issues Still Dominate Americans' National Worries," *Gallup Economy*, 2012, http://www.gallup.com/poll/153485/economic-issues-dominate-americans-national-worries.aspx, accessed June 2014.

Chapter 6

1. Federal Bureau of Investigation, *Uniform Crime Reports, 2012*, http://www.fbi.gov/about-us/cjis/ucr/crime-in-the-u.s/2012/crime-in-the-u.s.-2012/property-crime/property-crime, accessed February 2014.
2. James Q. Wilson, *Thinking about Crime,* rev. ed. (New York: Basic Books, 1983), especially Chapter 2.
3. U.S. Census Bureau, *Statistical Abstract of the United States,* 100th ed. (Washington, DC: U.S. Government Printing Office, 1978), 177.
4. Federal Bureau of Investigation, *Uniform Crime Reports, 1996* (Washington, DC: U.S. Government Printing Office), 204.
5. Andrew Dugan, 2013, "More Say Crime Is Serious Problem in U.S. Than Locally." *Gallup,* http://www.gallup.com/poll/165677/say-crime-serious-problem-locally.aspx, last accessed February 2014.
6. Mark Green, Beverly Moore, and Bruce Wasserstein, "Criminal Law and Corporate Disorder," in Jerome Skolnick and Elliot Currie, eds., *Crisis in American Institutions,* 4th ed. (Boston: Little Brown, 1979), 527–547.
7. Zachary A. Goldfarb and Jerry Markon, "Justice Probe of Goldman Goes Beyond Deals Cited by SEC," *Washington Post,* May 1, 2010, A1.
8. Elkan Abramowitz and Jonathan Sack, "Why So Few Prosecutions Connected to the Financial Crisis?" *New York Law Journal, 250* (46) (September, 4, 2013).
9. "In Broad Daylight: New Calculator Brings Crime Costs—and the Value of Police—Out of the Shadows," *Rand Review,* Spring 2012, Rand Corporation, http://www.rand.org/pubs/periodicals/rand-review/issues/2012/spring/centerpiece.html.
10. David Hellman, *The Economics of Crime* (New York: St. Martin's Press, 1980), 147.
11. Sponsored by National Institutes of Health, http://monitoringthefuture.org/pubs/monographs/mtf-vol2_2012.pdf and http://monitoringthefuture.org/pubs/monographs/mtf-vol1_2012.pdf, accessed February 2012.
12. National Survey on Drug Use & Health, 2012, http://www.samhsa.gov/data/NSDUH/2012SummNatFindDetTables/NationalFindings/NSDUHresults2012.htm#ch2.
13. National Survey on Drug Use & Health, 2012.
14. FBI's *Uniform Crime Report, 1997,* http://www.fbi.gov/about-us/cjis/ucr/crime-in-the-u.s/1997.
15. Cited in Samuel Walker, *Sense and Nonsense about Crime,* 2nd ed. (Pacific Grove, CA: Brooks/Cole, 1989), 38, 55.
16. Steven D. Levitt, "What Do Declining Abortion Rates Mean for Crime in the Future?" *New York Times* blog, "Freakonomics," January 22, 2008.
17. Levitt, "What Do Declining Abortion Rates Mean for Crime in the Future?"
18. 517 U.S. 456 (1996).
19. U.S. Census Bureau, http://quickfacts.census.gov/qfd/states/00000.html; and Federal Bureau of Investigation, *Uniform Crime Reports, 2012,* http://www.fbi.gov/about-us/cjis/ucr/crime-in-the-u.s/2012/crime-in-the-u.s.-2012/tables/43tabledatadecoverview.pdf.
20. Cited in Stephan Thernstrom and Abigail Thernstrom, *America in Black and White: One Nation, Indivisible* (New York: Touchstone, 1997), 268.

21. *Sourcebook of Criminal Justice Statistics, 2010*, http://www.albany.edu/sourcebook/pdf/t6332010.pdf.

22. Pamela E. Oliver, "Racial Disparities in Imprisonment: Some Basic Information," *Focus, 21* (3) (Spring 2001): 28–31.

23. Oliver, "Racial Disparities in Imprisonment: Some Basic Information."

24. Oliver, "Racial Disparities in Imprisonment: Some Basic Information," 31.

25. "Guidance Regarding the Use of Race by Federal Law Enforcement Agencies," Civil Rights Division, U.S. Department of Justice, June 2003, http://www.justice.gov/crt/split/documents/guidance_on_race.php.

26. "Guidance Regarding the Use of Race by Federal Law Enforcement Agencies," Civil Rights Division, U.S. Department of Justice, June 2003, http://www.justice.gov/crt/split/documents/guidance_on_race.php.

27. *Powell v. Alabama*, 287 U.S. 45 (1932).

28. *Gideon v. Wainwright*, 372 U.S. 335 (1963). This case was made even more famous by the nonfiction book *Gideon's Trumpet* (New York: Vintage Books, 1964) written by *New York Times* reporter Anthony Lewis.

29. The Court has ruled that once a guilty plea has been entered under such a plea bargain, the prosecution's side of the bargain must be kept. Failure by the prosecution to keep its bargain will cause the conviction to be vacated. *Santobello v. New York*, 404 U.S. 257 (1971).

30. For a more detailed discussion of the public policy issues involved in plea bargaining, see Lawrence Baum, *American Courts: Process and Policy*, 6th ed. (New York: Houghton Mifflin, 2008). For an inside look behind the machinations of the plea bargaining process, see Milton Heumann, *Plea Bargaining* (Chicago: University of Chicago Press, 1978).

31. *Escobedo v. Illinois*, 378 U.S. 478 (1964).

32. *Miranda v. Arizona*, 384 U.S. 436 (1966).

33. Lee Epstein and Thomas G. Walker, *Constitutional Law for a Changing America: Rights, Liberties, and Justice* (Washington, DC: CQ Press, 2010).

34. *Mapp v. Ohio*, 367 U.S. 643 (1961).

35. *Chimel v. California*, 394 U.S. 752 (1969).

36. *Terry v. Ohio*, 392 U.S. 1 (1968); *Sibron v. New York*, 392 U.S. 40 (1968).

37. *Katz v. United States*, 389 U.S. 347 (1967).

38. John Shiffman and Kristina Cooke. "Exclusive: U.S. Directs Agents to Cover Up Program Used to Investigate Americans," *Reuters*, August 5, 2013, http://www.reuters.com/article/2013/08/05/us-dea-sod-idUSBRE97409R20130805.

39. *Nix v. Williams*, 467 U.S. 431 (1984); *U.S. v. Leon*, 468 U.S. 897 (1984).

40. See the argument that the criminal justice system must be perceived as "just" in James Q. Wilson and Richard Hernnstein, *Crime and Human Nature* (New York: Simon & Schuster, 1985), 506–507.

41. Thorsten Sellin, *The Penalty of Death* (Beverly Hills, CA: Sage, 1980), 80–81.

42. "Death Penalty," *Gallup*, http://www.gallup.com/poll/1606/death-penalty.aspx, accessed February 2014.

43. Isaac Ehrlich, "The Deterrent Effect of Capital Punishment: A Question of Life and Death," *American Economic Review, 65* (June 1975): 398; Peter Passell and John Taylor, "The Deterrence Controversy: A Reconsideration of the Time Series Evidence," in Chester Pierce and Hugo Bedau, eds., *Capital Punishment in the United States* (New York: AMS Press, 1976), 359; and Sellin, *Penalty of Death*, Chapter 10.

44. Amnesty International, *Death Sentences and Executions in 2012*,

http://www.amnesty.org/en/
library/asset/ACT50/001/2013/
en/bbfea0d6-39b2-4e5f-a1ad-
885a8eb5c607/act500012013en.pdf.

45. These data are from Sellin, *Penalty of Death*, 52.

46. Guy Johnson, "The Negro and Crime," *The Annals of the American Academy of Political and Social Science, 217* (1941): 100. Cited in *Furman v. Georgia,* 408 U.S. 32 (1972).

47. Cited in *Dallas Times Herald,* November 17, 1985; *McClesky v. Kemp,* 481 U.S. 279 (1987).

48. http://www.deathpenaltyinfo.org/
article.php?scid=19&did=246,
accessed October 15, 2007.

49. 408 U.S. 32 (1972).

50. Emily Green, "Forensic Advances Raise New Questions about Old Convictions" *NPR*, March 20, 2013, http://www.npr.org/2013/03/20/
174842256/forensic-advances-raise-
new-questions-about-old-convic
tions, last accessed February 2014.

51. James Whitman "What Happened to Tocqueville's America." *Social Research*, 74(2): 252.

52. Melinda Gann Hall and Paul Brace, "Studying Courts Comparatively: A View from the States," *Political Research Quarterly, 48* (March 1995): 5–29.

53. Brian K. Arbour and Mark J. McKenzie, "Campaign Messages in Lower Court Elections after *Republican Party of Minnesota v. White*," *Justice System Journal*, 32(1): 125–148.

54. James Ridella, "Miranda: One Year Later—The Effects," *Public Management, 49* (July 1967): 183–190. This author found that in data drawn from St. Louis, less than 1 percent of those arrested had been freed on *Miranda* grounds.

55. Gerald N. Rosenberg, *The Hollow Hope: Can Courts Bring About Social Change?* (Chicago: University of Chicago Press, 1991), 324, quoting in part, Welsh S. White, 1986,

"Defending *Miranda:* A Reply to Professor Caplan," *Vanderbilt Law Review, 39*: 20.

56. Rosenberg, *The Hollow Hope*, 329.

57. Richard Medalie, Leonard Zeits, and Paul Alexander, "Custodial Police Interrogation in Our Nation's Capital: The Attempt to Implement *Miranda*," *Michigan Law Review, 66* (May 1968): 1347–1422.

58. Richard Seeburger and Stanley Wetlick, "*Miranda* in Pittsburgh: A Statistical Study," in Theodore Becker and Malcolm Freely, eds., *The Impact of Supreme Court Decisions,* 2nd ed. (New York: Oxford University Press, 1973), 154.

59. Stephen Wasby, *The Impact of the United States Supreme Court: Some Perspectives* (Homewood, IL: Dorsey Press, 1970), 156.

60. Wasby, *Impact,* 162; Stuart Nagel, *The Legal Process from a Behavioral Perspective* (Homewood, IL: Dorsey Press, 1969), 314.

61. Bradley Canon, "Testing the Effectiveness of Civil Liberties Policies at the State and Federal Levels: The Case of the Exclusionary Rule." *American Politics Quarterly, 5* (1977): 75.

62. Donald L. Horowitz, *The Courts and Social Policy* (Washington, DC: Brookings Institution, 1977), 232.

63. *Proffitt v. Florida,* 428 U.S. 242 (1976); *Gregg v. Georgia,* 428 U.S. 153 (1976); and *Jurek v. Texas,* 428 U.S. 262 (1976).

64. Marshall in *Furman,* 408 U.S. 238, at 329; Brennan at 269.

65. *Stanford v. Connecticut,* 492 U.S. 361 (1989); and *Roper v. Simmons,* 543 U.S. 551 (2005).

66. "Death Penalty," *Gallup,* http://
www.gallup.com/poll/1606/death-
penalty.aspx, accessed February 2014.

67. 486 U.S. 356 (1988). See also *Sumnar v. Shuman,* 483 U.S. 66 (1987); *Booth v. Maryland,* 482 U.S. 496 (1987); and *Payne v. Tennessee,* 501 U.S. 808 (1991).

68. *McClesky v. Zant,* 499 U.S. 467 (1991); *Coleman v. Thompson,* 501 U.S. 722 (1991); and *Yost v. Nunnemaker,* 501 U.S. 797 (1991).

69. "Forensic Oversight." The Innocence Project, http://www.innocenceproject.org/fix/Crime-Lab-Oversight.php.

70. Susan Reardon, "Faulty Forensic Science Under Fire," *Nature, 506* (February 6, 2014): 13–14.

71. Justin Peters, "The Unsettling, Underregulated World of Crime Labs," *Slate,* January 14, 2013, http://www.slate.com/blogs/crime/2013/01/14/serrita_mitchell_dna_the_unsettling_underregulated_world_of_crime_labs.html.

72. Christopher Hope, "1000 CCTV Cameras to Solve Just One Crime, Met Police Admits," *U.K. Daily Telegraph,* August 25, 2009, http://www.telegraph.co.uk/news/uknews/crime/6082530/1000-CCTV-cameras-to-solve-just-one-crime-Met-Police-admits.html, last accessed February 2014.

73. Hope, "1000 CCTV Cameras to Solve Just One Crime, Met Police Admits."

74. *United States v. Jones* (2012), 132 S. Ct. 949.

75. "Prisoners in 2011," Bureau of Justice Statistics, http://bjs.gov/content/pub/pdf/p11.pdf.

76. "Obama Drug Policy: Reforming the Criminal Justice System," Office of National Drug Control Policy, www.whitehouse.gov/blog/2011/12/05/obama-drug-policy-reforming-criminal-justice-system, last accessed February 2014.

77. Dan Roberts, "Justice Department Looks to Commute Sentences for Some Drug Offenders," *The Guardian,* January 30, 2014, http://www.theguardian.com/law/2014/jan/30/drug-sentence-reform-senate-justice-department.

78. Andrew Grossman, "Obama to Commute More Drug Sentences,"

Wall Street Journal, January 30, 2014, http://online.wsj.com/news/articles/SB10001424052702303973704579352644100338268, last accessed February 2014.

79. For further reading on this debate among criminologists, see Ilvana Kuziemko and Steven D. Levitt, "An Empirical Analysis of Imprisoning Drug Offenders," *Journal of Public Economics, 8* (2004): 2043–2066; Steven D. Levitt. "The Effect of Prison Population Size on Crime Rates: Evidence from Prison Overcrowding Litigation," *Quarterly Journal of Economics, 111* (1996): 319–351; Thomas B. Marvell and Carlisle E. Moody, "Prison Population Growth and Crime Reduction," *Journal of Quantitative Criminology, 10* (1994): 109–140; Kent Scheidegger and Michael Rushford, "The Social Benefits of Confining Habitual Criminals, *Stanford Law & Policy Review, 11* (1999–2000): 59–64; and Joanna Shepherd, "The Imprisonment Puzzle: Understanding How Prison Growth Affects Crime," *Criminology & Public Policy, 5* (2006): 285–298.

80. Attributed to Norval Morris as reported in Norton Long, "The City as Reservation," *Public Interest, 25* (Fall 1971): 31.

81. Wilson, *Thinking about Crime,* 118.

82. Wayne H. Thomas, *Bail Reform in America* (Berkeley: University of California Press, 1976).

83. Hellman, *Economics of Crime,* 49.

84. Daniel Borunda, "Juarez Nears 5,000 Killings," *El Paso Times,* April 26, 2010, www.elpasotimes.com/ci_14959082?source=most_emailed, accessed June 20, 2010.

85. Alexander Smith and Harriet Pollach, *Some Sins Are Not Crimes* (New York: New Viewpoints, 1975), 100.

86. Susan Brownmiller, *Against Our Will: Men, Women, and Rape* (New York: Simon & Schuster, 1975), 15.

87. Murray Strauss and Richard Gelles, *Intimate Violence: The Causes and Consequences of Abuse in the U.S. Family* (New York: Simon & Schuster, 1989).

88. "Intimate Partner Violence: Consequences," Centers for Disease Control and Prevention, http://www.cdc.gov/ViolencePrevention/intimate partnerviolence/consequences.html, last accessed February 2014.

89. Susan Estrich, *Real Rape: How the Legal System Victimizes Women Who Say No* (Cambridge, MA: Harvard University Press, 1987), 102.

90. "Self-Reported Gun Ownership in U.S. Is Highest Since 1993," *Gallup*, October 26, 2011, http://www.gallup.com/poll/150353/Self-Reported-Gun-Ownership-Highest-1993.aspx

91. *Small Arms Survey 2007: Guns and the City,* http://www.smallarmssurvey.org/files/sas/publications/yearb2007.html.

92. "Now Is the Time: The President's Plan to Protect Our Children and Our Communities by Reducing Gun Violence," January 16, 2013, http://www.whitehouse.gov/sites/default/files/docs/wh_now_is_the_time_full.pdf.

93. "U.S. Remains Divided Over Passing Stricter Gun Laws." *Gallup,* October 25, 2013, http://www.gallup.com/poll/165563/remains-divided-passing-stricter-gun-laws.aspx, last accessed Feburary 2014.

94. Manny Fernandez, "An Entry Reserved for Those with Guns," *New York Times,* March 8, 2013, http://www.nytimes.com/2013/03/09/us/guns-get-a-pass-at-texas-capitol.html?pagewanted=all&_r=0, last accessed February 2014.

95. John Lott, *More Guns, Less Crime* (Chicago: University of Chicago Press, 1998). See also the third edition published in 2010. Lott's book is based on research collected by Lott and his colleague David Mustard.

"Crime, Deterrence, and Right-to-Carry Concealed Handguns," *Journal of Legal Studies, 26*: 1–68.

96. See, for example, Bruce L. Benson and Brent Mast, "Privately Produced General Deterrence," *Journal of Law & Economics, 44* (2001): 1; Stephen G. Bronars and John R. Lott, Jr., "Criminal Deterrence, Geographic Spillovers, and the Right to Carry Concealed Handguns," *American Economic Review, 88* (1998): 475; Carlisle E. Moody, "Testing for the Effects of Concealed Weapons Laws: Specification Errors and Robustness," *Journal of Law & Economics, 44* (2001): 799; David B. Mustard, "The Impact of Gun Laws on Police Deaths," *Journal of Law & Economics, 44* (2001): 635; and Florenz Plassman and John Whitley, "Confirming More Guns, Less Crime," *Stanford Law Review, 55* (2003): 1313.

97. Mark Duggan, "More Guns, More Crime," *Journal of Political Economy, 109* (2001): 1112.

98. David Hemenway, *Private Guns Public Health* (Ann Arbor, MI: University of Michigan Press, 2004).

99. Hashem Dezhbakhsh and Paul H. Rubin, "Lives Saved or Lives Lost? The Effects of Concealed-Handgun Laws on Crime," *American Economic Review, 88* (1998): 468.

100. Ian Ayres and John J. Donohue, III, "Shooting Down the 'More Guns, Less Crime' Hypothesis," *Stanford Law Review, 55* (2003): 1201.

101. See John J. Donohue, III and Steven D. Levitt, "The Impact of Legalized Abortion on Crime," *Quarterly Journal of Economics, 116* (2001): 379. See also John Donahue, III and Steven Levitt, "Further Evidence That Legalized Abortion Lowered Crime: A Reply to Joyce," *Journal of Human Resources, 39*(1) (2004): 29–49; and Steven Levitt, "Understanding Why Crime Fell in the Nineties: Four

Factors That Explain the Decline and Six That Do Not," *Journal of Economic Perspectives, 18*(1) (2004).

102. Don B. Kates and Gary Mauser, "Would Banning Firearms Reduce Murder and Suicide? A Review of International and Some Domestic Evidence." *Harvard Journal of Law and Public Policy, 30*(2) (2007): 673.

103. Kates and Mauser, 2007, 663.

104. *D.C. v. Heller,* 128 S. Ct. 2783 (2008).

105. *Gallup Poll,* February 8–10, 2008, http://www.gallup.com/poll/ 108394/Ameri-cans-Agreement-Supreme-Court-Gun-Rights.aspx.

106. Ben Vollaard and Joseph Hamed, "Why the Police Have an Effect on Violent Crime After All: Evidence from the British Crime Survey," *Journal of Law and Economics, 55*(4) (2012): 920.

107. Joan Petersilia, "California's Correctional Paradox of Excess and Deprivation," *Crime and Justice, 37*(1) (2008): 207–278.

Chapter 7

1. Lawrence R. Jacobs and Theda Skocpol, eds., *Inequality and American Democracy: What We Know and What We Need to Know* (New York: Russell Sage Foundation, 2005).

2. Diane Pearce, "The Feminization of Poverty: Women, Work and Welfare," *Urban and Social Change Review, 11* (1978): 128–136.

3. Research by Kathryn Edin and Laura Lein shows that because cash public assistance benefit levels are well below poverty standards in most states, virtually all women receiving welfare benefits supplement their income with off-the-books work and sporadic contributions from friends and relatives. Kathryn Edin and Laura Lein, *Making Ends Meet: How Single Mothers Survive Welfare and Low-Wage Work*

(New York: Russell Sage Foundation, 1997).

4. Computed from U.S. Bureau of Labor Statistics (2013), "A Profile of the Working Poor," http://www.bls .gov/cps/cpswp2011.pdf, accessed March 2, 2014.

5. Lawrence M. Mead, *Beyond Entitlement: The Social Obligations of Citizenship* (New York: Free Press, 1985).

6. This section uses the Trattner and Patterson histories as main sources: Walter I. Trattner, *From Poor Law to Welfare State: A History of Social Welfare in America,* 6th ed. (New York: Free Press, 1999); and James T. Patterson, *America's Struggle against Poverty in the Twentieth Century* (Cambridge, MA: Harvard University Press, 2000).

7. Trattner, *From Poor Law to Welfare State,* 39.

8. Mead, *Beyond Entitlement.*

9. Ife Floyd and Liz Schott, "TANF Cash Benefits Continued to Lose Value in 2013," Center on Budget and Policy Priorities, http://www .cbpp.org/files/10-21-13tanf.pdf, accessed February 26, 2014.

10. Food and Nutrition Service, "WIC Program Participation and Costs," 2014, http://www.fns.usda.gov/sites/ default/files/pd/wisummary.pdf, accessed March 10, 2014.

11. U.S. Census Bureau, *2012 Statistical Abstract,* Table 473, 312, http:// www.census.gov/compendia/statab/, accessed February 26, 2014.

12. Two accounts of the history of welfare reform are Anne Marie Cammisa, *From Rhetoric to Reform* (Boulder, CO: Westview Press, 1998); and R. Kent Weaver, *Ending Welfare as We Know It* (Washington, DC: Brookings Institution, 2000).

13. *Social Security Annual Statistical Report, 2013* (Washington, DC: Social Security Office of Retirement and Disability Policy, Division of

Research Evaluation and Statistics), SSA Publication No. 13–11827.

14. U.S. Department of Housing and Urban Development, *Volume 1 of the 2012 Annual Homeless Assessment Report* (Washington, DC: U.S. Department of Housing and Urban Development, Office of Community Planning and Development, 2012).

15. Janet Viveiros and Maya Brennan, "An Annual Look at the Housing Affordability Challenges of America's Working Households" (Washington, DC: Center for Housing Policy, 2013).

16. U.S. Government Accountability Office, *Rental Housing Assistance: HUD Data on Self-Sufficiency Should Be Improved*, 2013 (Washington, DC: U.S. Government Accountability Office, Report-GAO 13–581).

17. See *Statistical Abstract,* 2007, Table 468.

18. Martin Gilens, *Why Americans Hate Welfare: Race, Media and the Politics of Antipoverty Policy* (Chicago: University of Chicago Press, 2000).

19. A thorough orientation to Social Security is the *Online Social Security Handbook,* www.ssa.gov/OP_Home/handbook/, accessed March 7, 2014.

20. Congressional Budget Office, *The Outlook for Social Security,* June 2004, Chapter 2.

21. See Richard Morin, "A Welfare Tug of War," *Washington Post National Weekly Edition,* March 14–20, 2001, 34.

22. Center for Budget and Policy Priorities, "Policy Basics: The Earned Income Tax Credit," 2013, http://www.cbpp.org/research/index.cfm?fa=topic&id=27, accessed March 2, 2014.

23. Travis Waldron, "Poverty Rate Would Be Twice as High without Government Programs," http://thinkprogress.org/economy/2014/01/05/3120481/poverty-rate-high-government-programs/.

24. Waldron, "Poverty Rate Would Be Twice as High."

25. See Ellen K. Coughlin, "Experts Add Their Voices to Welfare-Reform Debate," *Chronicle of Higher Education* (August 3, 1994): A6–A7.

26. Government tax and transfer payments have little effect on redistributing income among groups or in reducing inequality. See Patricia Ruggles, "The Impact of Government Tax and Expenditure Programs on the Distribution of Income in the United States," in Lars Osberg, ed., *Economic Inequality and Poverty* (Armonk, NY: M. E. Sharpe, 1991), 220–245.

27. These paragraphs draw upon Ron Haskins, "Welfare Reform, 10 Years Later," *Poverty Research Insights* (Fall 2006): 1–7. See also Ron Haskins, *Work over Welfare: The Inside Story of the 1996 Welfare Reform Law* (Washington: Brookings Institution Press, 2006), especially Chapter 10.

28. Griff Witte, "Off Welfare, but Back in Poverty," *Washington Post National Weekly Edition,* October 4–10, 2004, 29–30; Griff Witte, "The Vanishing Middle Class," *Washington Post National Weekly Edition,* September 27–October 3, 2004, 6–9; Associated Press, "More Than 12 Million Families Went Hungry," *Lubbock Avalanche-Journal,* November 20, 2004, D11; and Stephanie Armour, "What Recovery? Working Poor Struggle to Pay Bills," *USA Today,* June 9, 2004, B1–B2.

29. Christopher Beem, "Work, Parenthood, and the Idea of Reciprocity in American Social Policy," *Focus, 24* (Spring–Summer, 2006): 18–23.

30. Lawrence M. Mead, *The New Paternalism: Supervisory Approaches to Poverty* (Washington, DC: Brookings Institution Press, 1997).

31. Harrell R. Rodgers, Jr., and Lee Payne, "Child Poverty in the American States: The Impact of Welfare Reform,

Economics, and Demographics," *Policy Studies Journal, 35* (February 2007): 1–21.

32. Jeffrey R. Kling, Jens Ludwig, and Lawrence F. Katz, "Neighborhood Effects on Crime for Female and Male Youth: Evidence from a Randomized Housing Voucher Experiment," *Quarterly Journal of Economics* (2005): 87–130.

33. Paul Taylor, "Like Taking Money from a Baby," *Washington Post National Weekly Edition,* March 4–10, 1991, 31.

34. Kristin S. Seefeldt, "After PRWORA: Barriers to Employment, Work, and Well-Being among Current and Former Welfare Recipients," *Poverty Research Insights* (Fall 2004): 1–7.

35. See Mark Rom, "From Welfare State to Opportunity and Responsibility (OAR) Inc.," *Policy Currents, 11* (Summer 2001): 2–7.

Chapter 8

1. Hamilton Moses, III, et al., "The Anatomy of Health Care in the United States," *Journal of the American Medical Association, 310* (November 13, 2013): 1947–1963; quote at 1960.

2. For a summary of these changes, see Moses, "Anatomy of Health Care"; David M. Cutler and Fiona Scott Morton, "Hospitals, Market Share, and Consolidation," *Journal of the American Medical Association, 310* (November 13, 2013): 1964–1970; and Elisabeth Askin and Nathan Moore, *The Health Care Handbook: A Clear and Concise Guide to the United States Health Care System* (St. Louis: Washington University St. Louis, 2012), especially Chapters 1–2.

3. http://www.iom.edu/Reports/2001/Crossing-the-Quality-Chasm-A-New-Health-System-for-the-21st-Century.aspx, accessed July 14, 2014.

4. Barbara Starfield, "Is US Health Really the Best in the World?" *Journal of the American Medical Association, 284* (July 26, 2000): 483–485; Barbara Starfield, "Reinventing Primary Care: Lessons from Canada for the United States," *Health Affairs, 29* (May 2010): 1030–1036; and Cathy Schoen et al., "Access, Affordability, and Insurance Complexity Are Often Worse in the United States Compared to Ten Other Countries," *Health Affairs, 32* (December 2013): 2205–2215.

5. See Robert J. Panzer et al., "Increasing Demands for Quality Measurement," *Journal of the American Medical Association, 310* (November 13, 2013): 1971–1980; and Agency for Healthcare Research and Quality, *National Healthcare Quality Report: 2012,* www.ahrq.gov/research/findings/nhqrdr/nhqr12/index.html, accessed February 24, 2014.

6. Kaiser Family Foundation, http://kff.org/uninsured/fact-sheet/key-facts-about-the-uninsured-population, accessed January 21, 2014.

7. Arthur L. Kellermann et al., "Emergency Care: Then, Now, and Next," *Health Affairs, 32* (December 2013): 2069–2074; and Sara Rosenbaum, "The Enduring Role of the Emergency Medical Treatment and Active Labor Act," *Health Affairs, 32* (December 2013): 2075–2081.

8. Anne B. Martin et al., "National Health Spending in 2012: Rate of Health Spending Growth Remained Low for the Fourth Consecutive Year," *Health Affairs, 33* (January 2014): 67–77.

9. The comparative material in this section is based on Robert H. Blank and Viola Burau, *Comparative Health Policy* (New York: Palgrave Macmillan, 2004); and http://www.iom.edu/reports/2013/US-Health-in-International-Perspective-shorter-lives-poorer-health.aspx, accessed

January 22, 2014. A convenient one-page summary is "US Health Compared with Like Countries," *Journal of the American Medical Association, 310* (November 13, 2013): 1996.

10. Schoen et al., "Access, Affordability, and Insurance Complexity."

11. For a summary of these and other reasons, see Douglas E. Hough, *Irrationality in Health Care: What Behavioral Economics Reveals about What We Do and Why* (Stanford: Stanford University Press, 2013), especially 3–20.

12. Marilyn Moon, *Medicare: A Policy Primer* (Washington, DC: Urban Institute Press, 2006).

13. Kenneth E. Thorpe, "Chronic Conditions Account for Rise in Medicare Spending from 1987 to 2006," *Health Affairs, 29* (April 2010): 718–724.

14. The summary of the ACA depends upon *Landmark: The Inside Story of America's New Health-Care Law and What It Means for Us All* (New York: Public Affairs Report, 2010) and the extensive analysis on the Kaiser Family Foundation website, http://healthreform.kff.org/. See also Askin and Moore, 188–220; John E. McDonough, *Inside National Health Reform* (Berkeley: University of California Press, 2011); and Lawrence R. Jacobs and Theda Skocpol, *Health Care Reform and American Politics: What Everyone Needs to Know*, rev. and updated ed. (New York: Oxford University Press, 2012).

15. *National Federation of Independent Business et al v. Sebelius, Secretary of Health and Human Services, et al.*, 567 U.S. ____ (2012).

16. Kellermann et al., "Emergency Care," and Rosenbaum, "Enduring Role."

17. William P. Brandon and Keith Carnes, "Federal Health Insurance Reform and 'Exchanges'—Recent History," *Journal of Health Care for the Poor and Underserved, 25* (February

2014): xxxii–lvii. This and the next few paragraphs draw on this excellent summary.

18. See William P. Brandon, "Medicaid *Transformed*: Why ACA Opponents Should Keep Expanded Medicaid," *Journal of Health Care for the Poor and Underserved, 23* (2012): 1360–1382.

19. See Panzer et al., "Increasing Demands for Quality Measurement."

20. Mark McClellan et al., "A National Strategy to Put Accountable Care into Practice," *Health Affairs, 29* (May 2010): 982–990; and Timothy Hoff, "Medical Home Implementation: A Sensemaking Taxonomy of Hard and Soft Best Practices," *Milbank Quarterly, 91*(4) (2013): 771–810.

21. Panzer et al., "Increasing Demands for Quality Measurement."

22. Robert A. Cooper, "Unraveling the Physician Supply Dilemma," *Journal of the American Medical Association, 310* (November 13, 2013): 1931–1932; see also Askin and Moore, Chapter 2, and the theme issues on "Reinventing Primary Care," *Health Affairs, 29* (May 2010) and "Redesigning the Health Care Workforce," *Health Affairs, 32* (November 2013).

23. See *Landmark*, Chapter 10, for details.

24. http://www.chrt.org/assets/policy-papers/CHRT_Federally-Qualified-Health-Centers-An-Overview.pdf, accessed January 28, 2014.

25. For a balanced summary of the good and bad of the implementation, see Timothy S. Jost, "Implementing Health Reform: Four Years Later," *Health Affairs, 33* (January 2014): 7–10.

26. Public opinion trends on the ACA are available at www.kff.org.

27. http://kff.org/medicaid/report/the-cost-of-not-expanding-medicaid/, accessed January 30, 2014.

28. For a short summary of these issues, see Jost, "Implementing Health Reform," and Brandon and Carnes, "Federal Health Insurance Reform."

29. John R. Gabel et al., "Small Employer Perspectives on the Affordable Care Act's Premiums, SHOP Exchanges, and Self-Insurance," *Health Affairs, 32* (November 2013): 2032–2039.

30. www.cms.gov/Research-Statistics-Data-and-Systems/Statistics-Trends-and-Reports/DataCompendium/2011_Data_Compendium.html, accessed February 3, 2014.

31. See Brandon, "Medicaid *Transformed*," and www.commonwealthfund.org/~/media/Files/Publications/Issue%20Brief/2013/Dec/1718_Glied_how_states_stand_gain_lose_Medicaid_expansion_ib_v2.pdf, accessed February 3, 2014.

32. See Askin and Moore, *Health Care Handbook*, 108–112.

33. Harold C. Sox, "Resolving the Tension between Population Health and Individual Health Care," *Journal of the American Medical Association, 310* (November 13, 2013): 1933–1934.

34. For a comprehensive review of proposals, see "Medicare and the Federal Budget"; and Kaiser Family Foundation, "Policy Options to Sustain Medicare for the Future," at www.kff.org/medicare/8402.cfm, accessed February 4, 2014.

35. For a balanced summary of premium support proposals, see Kaiser Family Foundation, "Policy Options," 143–149.

36. Paul Ellwood, "Indexed Health Care: An Evolving Health Policy Proposal," http://healthaffairs.org/blog/2013/04/16/indexed-health-care-an-evolving-health-policy-proposal, accessed February 4, 2014.

37. Karen Davis et al., "Medicare Essential: An Option to Promote Better Care and Curb Spending Growth," *Health Affairs, 32* (May 2013): 900–908.

38. http://kaiserfamilyfoundation.files.wordpress.com/2013/07/8457-the-cost-of-not-expanding-medicaid4.pdf, accessed February 4, 2014.

39. See plan by the American Enterprise Institute (www.aei.org/best-of-both-worlds, accessed February 24, 2014). In February 2014, Republican Senators Richard Burr, Tom Coburn, and Orrin Hatch released a blueprint for health reform based on these principles. See http://healthaffairs.org/blog/2014/02/12/a-senate-gop-health-reform-proposal-the-burr-coburn-hatch-plan, accessed February 24, 2014.

40. *Health Care Costs: A Primer* (Menlo Park, CA: Kaiser Family Foundation, 2012); *What Is Driving U.S. Health Care Spending?* (Bipartisan Policy Center, 2012); and David Blumenthal et al., "Health Care Spending—A Giant Slain or Sleeping?" *New England Journal of Medicine, 369* (December 26, 2013): 2551–2557.

41. Gerard F. Anderson et al., "It's the Prices, Stupid: Why the United States Is So Different from Other Countries," *Health Affairs, 22* (May/June 2003): 89–105.

42. Kant Patel and Mark E. Rushefsky, eds., *Health Care Politics and Policy in America*, 4th ed. (Armonk, NY: Sharpe, 2014), Chapter 7.

43. Mark Stabile et al., "Health Care Cost Containment Strategies Used in Four Other High-Income Countries Hold Lessons for the United States," *Health Affairs, 32* (April 2013): 643–650.

44. Steven A. Schroeder and William Frist, "Phasing Out Fee-for-Service Payment," *New England Journal of Medicine, 368* (May 3, 2013): 2029–2032.

45. See the discussion of the political arguments and the provisions of the compromise language in *Landmark,* 31–38 and 179–182.

46. *Landmark,* 3, 26, 132–133.

47. See Joanne Lynn, "Reliable and Sustainable Comprehensive Care for Frail Elderly People," *Journal of the*

American Medical Association, 310 (November 13, 2013): 1935–1936; and Kaiser Family Foundation, "A Short Look at Long-Term Care for Seniors," *Journal of the American Medical Association, 310* (August 28, 2013): 786.

48. Robert H. Brook, "Two Years and Counting: How Will the Effects of the Affordable Care Act Be Monitored?" *Journal of the American Medical Association, 307* (January 4, 2012): 41–42.

Chapter 9

1. Quoted in S. E. Frost, Jr., and Kenneth P. Bailey, *Historical and Philosophical Foundations of Western Education,* 2nd ed. (Columbus, OH: Merrill, 1973), 340.

2. See William Jeynes, *American Educational History: School, Society, and the Common Good* (Thousand Oaks, CA: Sage Publications, 2007) for an expanded discussion.

3. Robert L. Church, *Education in the United States* (New York: Free Press, 1976), 420.

4. National Center for Education Statistics, "Digest of Education Statistics," Table 217, Current Expenditures per Pupil, http://nces.ed.gov/programs/digest/d12/tables/dt12_217.asp, accessed March 2014.

5. U.S. Department of Education, National Center for Education Statistics, *Revenues and Expenditures for Public Elementary and Secondary Schools Districts (Fiscal Year 2010),* Table 2. Total revenues per pupil at the fifth percentile, median, and ninety-fifth percentile, federal range ratio, number of districts, and number of students, by state: School year 2006–2007, fiscal year 2010, http://nces.ed.gov/pubs2013/2013307.pdf, accessed March 2014.

6. See Jared S. Buszin, "Beyond School Finance: Refocusing Education Reform Litigation to Realize the Deferred Dream of Education Equality and Adequacy," *Emory Law Journal, 62*(6) (2013): 1613–1657 for a discussion of critiques of court cases addressing financial disparities.

7. *Serrano v. Priest,* 5 Cal. 3d 584 (1971).

8. *San Antonio Independent School District v. Rodriguez,* 411 U.S. 1 (1973).

9. See Michael Paris, *Framing Equal Opportunity: Law and the Politics of School Finance Reform* (Stanford, CA: Stanford University Press, 2010) for a discussion of some of the factors that affect local district spending.

10. See Dominic J. Brewer and Patrick J. McEwan, eds., *Economics of Education* (San Diego, CA: Elsevier, 2010).

11. See Michale Greenstone, Adam Looney, and Paige Shevling, *Improving Student Outcomes, Restoring America's Education Potential* (Washington, DC: Brookings Institution Press, 2011) for a discussion of student performance in the education funding debate.

12. See William Owings and Leslie Kaplan, *American Public School Finance* (Belmont, CA: Cengage, 2012).

13. The National Commission on Excellence in Education, *A Nation at Risk: The Imperative for Educational Reform* (Washington, DC: U.S. Government Printing Office, 1983), 4.

14. The College Board, *Balancing the SAT Scales* (Princeton, NJ: College Board, 1994).

15. See Shelby J. Haberman and Neil J. Dorans, *Sources of Score Scale Inconsistency* (Princeton, NJ: Educational Testing Service, 2011).

16. See Norman Frederikson, *The Influence of Minimum Competency Tests on Teaching and Learning* (Princeton, NJ: Educational Testing Service, 1994).

17. Diana Pullin, "Minimum Competency Testing: The Denied Diploma and the Pursuit of Educational Opportunity and Educational Adequacy" (ERIC Document

Reproduction Service No. ED 228–279, 1982).

18. J. S. Catterall, "Standards and School Dropouts: A National Study of Tests Required for High School Gradua-tion," *American Journal of Education, 98* (November 1989): 1–34.

19. Danielle B. Kuper, "Reconsidering the Minimum Competency Test Strategy in No Child Left Behind: An Agenda for Reform," *Practical Assess-ment Research and Evaluation, 11*(1) (January 2006), http://pareonline .net/getvn.asp?v=11&n=1.

20. See Dan Goldhabe and M. Hansen, "Race, Gender, and Teacher Testing: How Informative a Tool Is Teacher Licensure Testing?" *American Educa-tional Research Journal, 47*(1) (March 1, 2010): 218–251.

21. See Elvia M. Hernandez, "The Effects of Proper Implementation of Bilingual Programs in Elementary Schools in the United States," in M. S. Plakotnik, S. M. Nielson, and D. M. Pane, eds., *Proceedings of the Eighth Annual College of Education Research Conference* (2009), 62–68, http://education.fiu.edu/research _conference/docs/proceedings/ COERC_2009_Proceedings.pdf, accessed July 18, 2014.

22. Nancy P. Greenman and Ellen B. Kimmel, "The Road to Multicultural Education: Potholes of Resistance," *Journal of Teacher Education, 45*(5) (November–December 1995): 360–368.

23. American Association of Colleges for Teacher Education Commission on Multicultural Education, "No One Model American," *Journal of Teacher Education, 24*(4) (September– October, 1973): 264–265.

24. Jesus Garcia and Sharon L. Pugh, "Multicultural Education in Teacher Preparation Programs: A Political or an Educational Concept?" *Phi Delta Kappan, 74*(4) (November 1992): 214–219.

25. Cecilia Elena Rouse and Lisa Barrow, "School Vouchers and Student Achievement: Recent Evidence, Remaining Questions," *Annual Review of Economics* (2009): 17–42.

26. "45th Annual Phi Delta Kappa/ Gallup Poll of the Public's Attitude Toward Public Schools," *Phi Delta Kappan, 95*(1) (2013); and "Annual Phi Delta Kappa/Gallup Poll of the Public's Attitudes Toward Public Schools," *Phi Delta Kappan, 81*(1) (September 1999): 41–55.

27. See Amy S. Wells and Stuart Biegel, "Public Funds for Private Schools: Political and First Amendment Considerations," *American Journal of Education, 101* (May 1993): 209–233, for a discussion of the legal issues in the voucher debate.

28. The National Commission on Excellence in Education, *A Nation at Risk,* 5.

29. See Alan Vanneman, Linda Hamilton, Janet Anderson, Janet Baldwin, and Taslima Rahman, "Achievement Gaps: How Black and White Students in Public Schools Perform in Mathe-matics and Reading on the National Assessment of Educational Progress, Statistical Analysis Report," National Center for Education Statistics, 2009, for a discussion of educational achievement gaps in the United States.

30. David Lustick, *Certifiable: Teaching, Learning, and National Board Certifica-tion* (Lanham, MD: Rowman and Littlefield, 2011).

31. Thomas Hunt and Monalisa Mullins, *Moral Education in America's Schools: The Continuing Challenge* (Charlotte, NC: Information Age Publishers, 2005).

32. Ellen V. Leininger, "Back to the Basics: Underlying Concepts and Controversy," *Elementary School Jour-nal, 79*(3) (1979): 167–173.

33. *Epperson v. Arkansas,* 393 U.S. 97 (1968).

34. *Edwards v. Aguillard*, 42 U.S. 578 (1987). Additional information for both positions is readily available on the World Wide Web. See the following intelligent design-related websites: Center for Scientific Creation, www.creationscience.com/ onlinebook/; Intelligent Design Network, www.intelligentdesignnetwork .org/.

35. Jeanne M. Powers, *Charter Schools: From Reform Imagery to Reform Reality* (New York: Palgrave MacMillan, 2009).

36. Christopher Green, *The Privatization of State Education: Public Partners, Private Dealings* (New York: Routledge, 2005), 4.

Chapter 10

1. Stephen and Abigail Thernstrom, *America in Black and White: One Nation Indivisible: Race in Modern America* (New York: Simon & Schuster, 1997), 14.

2. Michael Lewis Beck, Charles Tien, and Richard Nadeau, "Obama's Missed Landslide: A Racial Cost," *PS: Political Science & Politics, 43* (January 2010): 69–76.

3. For a detailed account of admissions policies at Harvard, see Alan Dershowitz, *Chutzpah* (Boston: Little Brown, 1991), 66–74.

4. For a full treatment of Berkeley's policies to restrict the admission of Asians, see Dinesh D'Souza, *Illiberal Education* (New York: Free Press, 1991), Chapter 2.

5. Peter Uhlenberg, "Demographic Correlates of Group Achievement: Contrasting Patterns of Mexican Americans and Japanese Americans," in Robert K. Yin, ed., *Race, Creed, Color or National Origin* (Itasca, IL: Peacock Press, 1973), 86.

6. Colin Powell, *My American Journey* (New York: Random House, 1995), 72.

7. Richard Herrnstein and Charles Murray, *The Bell Curve: The Reshaping of American Life by Differences in Intelligence* (New York: Free Press, 1994).

8. Stephen Thernstrom, "The Scandal of the Law Schools," *Commentary, 104* (December 1997): 27–31.

9. *The Civil Rights Cases,* 109 U.S. 3 (1883).

10. *Plessy v. Ferguson,* 163 U.S. 537 (1896).

11. *Brown v. Board of Education of Topeka, Kansas,* 347 U.S. 483(1954). The Court also struck down the constitutionality of government-required segregation in federally controlled territory, in this case Washington, DC, in *Bolling v. Sharpe,* 347 U.S. 497 (1954). Recall that the Fourteenth Amendment only restricts state government; hence, the *Bolling* case was decided under the due process clause of the Fifth Amendment.

12. *Brown v. Board of Education of Topeka, Kansas,* 349 U.S. 294 (1955).

13. *Alexander v. Holmes County Board of Education,* 396 U.S. 19 (1969).

14. James Coleman, *Equality of Educational Opportunity* (Washington, DC: U.S. Government Printing Office, 1966); and U.S. Commission on Civil Rights, *Racial Isolation in Public Schools* (Washington, DC: U.S. Government Printing Office, 1967).

15. *Green v. School Board of New Kent County,* 391 U.S. 430 (1968).

16. *Swann v. Charlotte-Mecklenburg Board of Education,* 402 U.S. 1 (1971).

17. *Heart of Atlanta Motel v. United States,* 379 U.S. 241 (1964); *Katzenbach v. McClung,* 379 U.S. 294 (1964).

18. *Washington v. Davis,* 426 U.S. 229 (1976).

19. Alan Sindler, *Bakke, DeFunis, and Minority Admissions* (New York: Longman, 1978), 59.

20. *Craig v. Boren,* 429 U.S. 190 (1976).

21. *Roe v. Wade,* 410 U.S. 113 (1973).

22. *Lilly Ledbetter v. Goodyear Tire and Rubber Co.,* 550 U.S. 618 (2007).

23. *New York State Club Association v. City of New York,* 108 S. Ct. 2225 (1988).

24. *Christian Legal Society v. Martinez,* 561 U.S. ____ (2010).

25. Feminist Majority Fund, "Gender Equity in Athletics and Sports," http://www.feminist.org/sports/titleIXfactsheet.asp, accessed April 2, 2014.

26. *Gallagher v. C.H. Robinson,* 567 3d 263, 6th Cir. (2009).

27. Katherine Roithe, *The Morning After* (Boston: Little Brown, 1993).

28. http://pollingreport.com/civil.htm, accessed March 23, 2014.

29. *Boy Scouts of America v. Dale,* 530 U.S. 640 (2000).

30. *Bowers v. Hardwick,* 106 S. Ct. 2841 (1986); *Lawrence v. Texas,* 539 U.S. 558 (2003).

31. *U.S. v. Windsor,* 570 U.S. ____ (2013).

32. This discussion of disability is drawn significantly from Ruth Shalit, "Defining Disability Down," *The New Republic* (August 25, 1997): 16–22.

33. *Milliken v. Bradley,* 418 U.S. 717 (1974).

34. *Kaiser Aluminum v. Weber* and *U.S. Steelworkers of America v. Weber,* 443 U.S. 193 (1979).

35. *Ricci v. DeStefano,* 567 US 129 S. Ct. 2658.

36. Carl Cohen, "Justice Debased: The Weber Decision," *Commentary, 68* (September 1979): 43–53.

37. *Richmond v. J. A. Croson Co.,* 488 U.S. 469 (1989); *Wards Cove Packing Co. v. Antonio,* 493 U.S. 802 (1989); and *Adarand Constructors v. Pena,* 515 U.S. 200 (1995).

38. *Hopwood v. Texas,* 78 F.3d 932 (1996) and 116 S. Ct. 2580 (1996).

39. *Grutter v. Bollinger,* 539 U.S. 306 (2003); *Gratz v. Bollinger,* 539 U.S. 244 (2003).

40. *Fisher v. Texas,* 570 U.S. 1 (pending).

41. James Q. Wilson, "Bowling with Others," *Commentary, 124*(3) (October 2007): 34–38.

42. *Parents Involved with Community Schools v. Seattle School District No. 1,* 551 US 701, 127 S. Ct. 2738 (2007).

Chapter 11

1. Kevin R. Johnson, *The Huddled Masses Myth: Immigration and Civil Rights* (Philadelphia: Temple University Press, 2004); and Aristide R. Zolberg, *A Nation by Design: Immigration Policy in the Fashioning of America* (Cambridge, MA: Harvard University Press, 2009).

2. Michael LeMay, *U.S. Immigration* (Santa Barbara, CA: ABC-CLIO, 2003).

3. Michael LeMay, *Guarding the Gates: Immigration and National Security* (New York: Praeger, 2006).

4. Frank D. Bean, Robert G. Cushing, Charles W. Haynes, and Jennifer V. W. Van Hook, "Immigration and the Social Contract," *Social Science Quarterly, 78* (June 1997): 263.

5. Chilton Williamson, Jr., *The Immigration Mystique: America's False Conscience* (New York: Basic Books, 1996), 24–27.

6. Phillip Q. Yang, *Post-1965 Immigration to the United States: Structural Determinants* (Westport, CT: Praeger, 1995), 10.

7. Michael LeMay, *From Open Door to Dutch Door: An Analysis of U.S. Immigration Policy since 1820* (New York: Praeger, 1987), xiii.

8. Barry Edmonston, ed., *Statistics on U.S. Immigration: An Assessment of Data Needs for Future Research* (Washington, DC: National Academy Press, 1996), 10–11.

9. David Bennett, *The Party of Fear: From Nativist Movements to the New Right in American History* (Chapel Hill: University of North Carolina Press, 1988); Vernon M. Briggs, Jr., *Immigration Policy and the American Labor Force* (Baltimore: Johns Hopkins University Press, 1984), 19–22;

Thomas J. Curran, *Xenophobia and Immigration, 1820–1930* (Boston: Twayne Publishers, 1975), 21; James Lincoln Collier, *The Rise of Selfishness in America* (New York: Oxford University Press, 1991); and Cheryl Shanks, *Immigration and the Politics of American Sovereignty, 1890–1990* (Ann Arbor: University of Michigan Press, 2004).

10. U.S. Immigration and Naturalization Service, *An Immigrant Nation: United States Regulation of Immigration, 1798–1991* (Washington, DC: Immigration and Naturalization Service, 1991).

11. Williamson, *The Immigration Mystique,* 47–49.

12. LeMay, *From Open Door to Dutch Door,* 111–112; Michael LeMay, *U.S. Immigration: A Reference Handbook* (Santa Barbara, CA: ABC-CLIO, 2004).

13. Vernon M. Briggs, Jr. and Stephen Moore, *Still an Open Door? U.S Immigration Policy and the American Economy* (Washington, DC: American University Press, 2011).

14. Aviva Chomsky, *"They Take Our Jobs!" and 20 Other Myths about Immigration* (Boston: Beacon Press, 2007); Alfredo Guitierrez, *To Sin against Hope: How America Has Failed Its Immigrants: A Personal History* (London: Verso, 2013); Johnson, *The Huddled Masses Myth;* Armando Navarro, *The Immigration Crisis: Nativism, Armed Vigilantism, and the Rise of a Countervailing Movement* (Lanham, MD: Altamira Press, 2009); Williamson, *The Immigration Mystique,* 47–49; and Zolberg, *A Nation by Design.*

15. Michael Fix and Jeffrey S. Passel, *The Door Remains Open: Recent Immigration to the United States and a Preliminary Analysis of the Immigration Act of 1990* (Washington, DC: Urban Institute, 1991); and Michael Barone, *The New Americans* (Washington, DC: Regnery, 2001).

16. Stephen Moore, "Part Two: The Economic Case for More Immigrants," in Briggs and Moore, *Still an Open Door?,* 84–85; and Julian L. Simon, *The Economic Consequences of Immigration* (Cambridge, MA: Blackwell, 1990).

17. U.S. Bureau of the Census, "The Foreign-Born Population in the United States: 2010," http://www.census.gov/prod/2012pubs/acs-19.pdf, accessed March 26, 2014.

18. http://www.gallup.com/poll/1660/Immigration.aspx, accessed March 26, 2014.

19. Michael Barone, *Shaping Our Nation: How Surges of Migration Transformed America and Its Politics* (New York: Crown Forum, 2013); and LeMay, *Guarding the Gates.*

20. Migration Policy Institute, "Frequently Requested Statistics on Immigrants and Immigration in the United States," http://www.migrationpolicy.org/article/frequently-requested-statistics-immigrants-and-immigration-united-states-0/#2e, accessed March 26, 2014.

21. Pew Research Center, http://www.pewhispanic.org/2013/01/29/statistical-portrait-of-the-foreign-born-population-in-the-united-states-2011/, accessed March 26, 2014.

22. Pew Research Center, Hispanic Trends Project, "Population Decline of Unauthorized Immigrants Stalls, May Have Reversed," http://www.pewhispanic.org/2013/09/23/population-decline-of-unauthorized-immigrants-stalls-may-have-reversed/, accessed March 27, 2014.

23. Office of Immigration Statistics, "Immigration Enforcement Actions: 2012," December 2013 *Annual Report,* http://www.dhs.gov/sites/default/files/publications/ois_enforcement_ar_2012_1.pdf.

24. LeMay, *Guarding the Gates.*

25. Barone, *Shaping Our Nation*; Otis L. Graham, *Unguarded Gates: A History of America's Immigration Crisis* (New York: Rowman & Littlefield, 2004); Otis L. Graham, "The Unfinished Reform: Regulating Immigration in the National Interest," in Roger Daniels and Otis L. Graham, eds., *Debating American Immigration, 1882–Present* (Lanham, MD: Rowman & Littlefield, 2001); and Reclaim American Jobs Caucus, http://www.numbersusa.com/content/news/march-19-2010/reclaim-american-jobs-caucus-introduction.html, accessed June 30, 2010.

26. Randolph Capps, Everett Henderson, John D. Kasarda, James H. Johnson, Jr., Stephen J. Appold, Derek L. Croney, Donald J. Hernandez, and Michael E. Fix, *A Profile of Immigrants in Arkansas* (Washington, DC: The Urban Institute, 2007); Aviva Chomsky, *"They Take Our Jobs!"*; Elzbieta M. Gozdziak and Susan F. Martin, *Beyond the Gateway: Immigrants in a Changing America* (New York: Lexington Books, 2005), Chapter 10; and John R. Logan, Richard D. Alba, and Michael Dill, "Ethnic Segmentation in the American Metropolis: Increasing Divergence in Economic Incorporation, 1980–1990," *International Migration Review,* 34 (Spring 2000): 98–132.

27. George Borjas, *Heaven's Door: Immigration Policy and the American Economy* (Princeton, NJ: Princeton University Press, 2001); and Lawrence E. Harrison, "Immigration Should Be Reduced to Strengthen U.S. Competitiveness," in Scott Barbour, ed., *Immigration Policy* (San Diego: Greenhaven Press, 1995), 34–37.

28. Harrison, "Immigration Should Be Reduced"; and Julie R. Watts, *Immigration Policy and the Challenge of Globalization* (Ithaca, NY: Cornell University Press, 2002).

29. Michael Fix, Demetrious G. Papademetriou, and Melanie Sumption, eds. *Immigration in a Changing Labor Market: Responding to Economic Needs* (Washington, DC: Migration Policy Institute, 2013); Melanie Troutman, Miriam Jordan, and Kris Maher, "Unions Seize on Immigration Debate," *Wall Street Journal,* http://online.wsj.com/news/articles/SB10001424127887324761004578284371137719186, accessed March 14, 2014; "Split in Organized Labor Over Immigration," MSNBC, http://www.nbcnews.com/id/19352537/ns/politics/t/split-organized-labor-over-immigration/#.U8AONe_n_X4; and The Migration Policy Institute, "Immigrant Union Members, Numbers and Trends," http://www.migrationpolicy.org/research/immigrant-union-members-numbers-and-trends, accessed June 30, 2010.

30. Edmonston, ed., *Statistics on U.S. Immigration,* 19–29; Johnson, *The Huddled Masses Myth;* Moore, "Part Two: The Economic Case for More Immigrants," 77–80; and Julian L. Simon, "Immigration to the United States Should Be Increased," in Barbour, ed., *Immigration Policy,* 55–66.

31. Steven A. Camarota and Karen Zeigler, "Trends in Immigrant and Native Employment," Center for Immigration Studies, http://www.cis.org/FirstQuarter2009Unemployment, accessed July 11, 2014; Aviva Chomsky, *"They Take Our Jobs!"*; Chris Isidore, "Jobless Rate Higher for U.S.-born than Immigrants," CNNMoney.com, http://money.cnn.com/2006/04/05/news/economy/jobs_immigrants/index.htm, accessed August 24, 2007; and David M. Kennedy, "Can We Still Afford to Be a Nation of Immigrants?," *The Atlantic Monthly Atlantic Unbound,*

www.theatlantic.com/atlantic/issues/96nov/immigrant/kennedy.htm, accessed January 13, 2005.

32. Marcia Drew Hohn, "Immigrant Entrepreneurs: Creating Jobs and Strengthening the Economy," http://www.cis.org/FirstQuarter 2009Unemployment, accessed March 3, 2014.

33. Elizabeth Corley and Meghna Sabharwal, "Foreign-Born Academic Scientists and Engineers: Producing More and Getting Less Than Their U.S.-Born Peers?" *Research in Higher Education, 48* (December 2007): 909–940; and Vivek Wadhwa, *The Immigrant Exodus: Why America Is Losing the Global Race to Capture Entrepreneurial Talent* (Philadelphia: Wharton Digital Press, 2012).

34. Steven A. Camarota, *Immigrants in the United States* (Washington, DC: Center for Immigration Studies, 2009); Lorraine M. McDowell and Paul T. Hill, *Newcomers in American Schools* (Santa Monica, CA: Rand, 1993).

35. Randy Capps, Michael Fix, Julie Murray, Jason Ost, Jeffrey S. Passel, and Shinta Herwantoro, *The New Demography of America's Schools: Immigration and the No Child Left Behind Act,* http:www.urban.org/UploadedPDF/311230_new_demography.pdf, accessed March 27, 2014; Jorge Ruiz-de-Velasco and Michael Fix with Beatriz Chu Clewell, *Overlooked and Underserved: Immigrant Students in U.S. Secondary Schools* (Washington, DC: Urban Institute, 2000); and Ruben G. Rumbaut, *Immigrant Children in California Public Schools: A Summary of Current Knowledge* (Baltimore: Center for Research on Effective Schooling for Disadvantaged Students, Johns Hopkins University, 1990).

36. Alejandro Portes and Ruben G. Rumbaut, *Immigrant America: A Portrait* (Berkeley: University of California Press, 2006); and Rumbaut, *Immigrant Children.*

37. Steven Camarota, "Immigration's Impact on Public Coffers," http://www.cis.org/articles/2006/sactestimony072606.html, accessed March 27, 2014; Randolph Capps, Michael E. Fix, Everett Henderson, and Jane Reardon-Anderson, "A Profile of Low-Income Immigrant Families," Urban Institute, http://www.urban.org/publications/311206.html, accessed July 1, 2010; and National Immigration Law Center, "Facts About Immigrants' Low Use of Health Services and Public Benefits," http://www.immigrationpolicy.org/just-facts/facts-about-immigrants-low-use-health-services-and-public-benefits, accessed July 1, 2010.

38. Center for Immigration Studies, "Welfare Use by Immigrant Households with Children: A Look at Cash, Medicaid, Housing, and Food Programs," http://www.cis.org/immigrant-welfare-use-2011, accessed March 27, 2014.

39. Camarota, *Immigration's Impact on Public Coffers;* Randy Capps, Michael Fix, Jason Ost, Jane Reardon-Anderson, and Jeffrey S. Passel, *The Health and Well-Being of Young Children of Immigrants,* Urban Institute, http://www.urban.org/UploadedPDF/311139_Childrenimmigrants.pdf, accessed July 11, 2014; and Chomsky, *"They Take Our Jobs!"*

40. Camarota, *Immigration's Impact on Public Coffers.*

41. Patrick J. Buchanan, *Day of Reckoning: How Hubris, Ideology, and Greed Are Tearing America Apart,* reprint ed. (New York: St. Martin's Griffin, 2009); Graham, *Unguarded Gates;* Samuel P. Huntington, *Who Are We? The Challenges to America's National Identity* (New York: Simon & Schuster, 2004); and Arthur Schlesinger, Jr., *The Disuniting of America: Reflections on a Multicultural Society,*

rev. and enlarged ed. (New York: Norton, 1998).

42. Patrick J. Buchanan, *State of Emergency: The Third World Invasion and Conquest of America* (New York: Thomas Dunne Books, 2006); and Graham, *Unguarded Gates.*

43. Federation for American Immigration Reform, "The United States Is Already Overpopulated (2009)," http://www.fairus.org/issue/the-united-states-is-already-overpopulated, accessed March 27, 2014; George F. Kennan, "Immigration to the United States Should Be Reduced," in Barbour, ed., *Immigration Policy,* 17–20; and Dan Stein, "The Federal Government Should Enact a Moratorium on Immigration," in Barbour, ed., *Immigration Policy,* 21–24.

44. Barone, *Shaping Our Nation;* Mark Kirkorian, "The New Case against Immigration, Both Legal and Illegal," http://www.cis.org/newcase, accessed March 27, 2014.

45. Leon F. Bouvier, "Immigration Should Be Restricted for Environmental Reasons," in Barbour, ed., *Immigration Policy,* 38–40; Kirkorian, "The New Case"; and LeMay, *Guarding the Gates.*

46. John Isbister, *The Immigration Debate: Remaking America* (West Hartford, CT: Kumarian Press, 1996), especially Chapter 5.

47. Barone, *Shaping Our Nation;* and William Julius Wilson, *The Truly Disadvantaged: The Inner City, the Underclass, and Public Policy,* 2nd ed. (Chicago: University of Chicago Press, 2012).

48. Elizabeth Bogen, Testimony before the Joint Economic Committee, U.S. Congress, *Hearings on the Economic and Demographic Consequences of Immigration* (Washington, DC: U.S. Government Printing Office, 1986); and Jacob Stowell, *Immigration and Crime: The Effffects of Immigration on Criminal Behavior* (New York: LFB Publishing, 2007).

49. Barone, *Shaping Our Nation;* and Huntington, *Who Are We?*

50. Patrick J. Buchanan, *The Death of the West: How Dying Populations and Immigrant Invasions Imperil Our Country and Civilization* (New York: Thomas Dunne Books, 2001); and Huntington, *Who Are We?*

51. Gutierrez, *To Sin against Hope;* Simon, "Immigration to the United States Should Be Increased"; Elizabeth Martinez, "The U.S. Should Not Make Immigrants Scapegoats," in Barbour, ed., *Immigration Policy,* 17–20; and La Resistencia, "Ethnic Cleansing by Attacks on Immigrants Must Be Stopped," in Barbour, ed., *Immigration Policy,* 108–111.

52. Roy Beck, *The Case against Immigration* (New York: Norton, 1996), Chapter 8.

53. Dirk Chase Eldredge, *Crowded Land of Liberty: Solving America's's Immigration Crisis* (Bridgehampton, NY: Bridge Works, 2001); Federation for American Immigration Reform, "Why America Needs an Immigration Time-Out," http://www.fairus.org/site/PageServer? pagename=iic_immigrationissuecentered1994; and Stein, "The United States Should Enact a Moratorium on Immigration."

54. Camarato, *Immigrant's Impact on Public Coffers;* Kennan, "Immigration to the United States Should Be Reduced"; Lawrence E. Harrison, "Immigration Should Be Reduced to Strengthen U.S. Competitiveness," in Barbour, ed., *Imigration Poicy,* 34–37; Bouvier, "Immigration Should Be Restricted for Environmental Reasons"; and Beck, *The Case against Immigration.*

55. Graham, "The Unfinished Reform"; Harrison, "Immigration Should Be Reduced to Strengthen U.S.

Competitiveness"; and Beck, *The Case against Immigration.*

56. Walter A. Ewing, "From Denial to Acceptance: Effectively Regulating Immigration to the United States" (Washington, DC: The American Immigration Law Foundation, 2004), http://www.ailf.org, accessed January 18, 2005.

57. John Kotkin, "U.S. Immigration Policy Should Be Based on Citizenship," in Barbour, ed., *Immigration Policy,* 84–89.

58. Gregory Auclair and Jeanne Batalova, "Naturalization Trends in the United States," http://www.migrationpolicy.org/article/naturalization-trends-united-states, accessed March 28, 2014.

59. Portes and Rumbaut, *Immigrant America.*

60. Rumbaut, *Immigrant Children.*

61. Peter D. Salins, "U.S. Immigration Policy Should Not Discriminate," in Barbour, ed., *Immigration Policy,* 72–76.

62. Ediberto Roman and Michael A. Olivas, *Those Damned Immigrants: America's Hysteria over Undocumented Immigration* (New York: New York University Press, 2013).

Chapter 12

1. For example, Norman Podhoretz, "World War IV: How It Started, What It Means, and Why We Have to Win," *Commentary, 118*(2) (September 2004): 17–80.

2. Hans Morgenthau, *In Defense of the National Interest (New York: Knopf, 1951); Edward H. Carr, The Twenty Years' Crisis, 1919–1939,* 2nd ed. (New York: St. Martin's Press, 1964); and Kenneth Thompson, *Political Realism and the Crisis of World Politics* (Princeton, NJ: Princeton University Press, 1960).

3. Daniel Jonah Goldhagen, *Hitler's Willing Executioners: Ordinary Germans*

and the Holocaust (New York: Vintage Books, 1997) documents that the Nazi's systematic extermination of the Jews in World War II was not only widely known but enthusiastically supported by millions of ordinary Germans.

4. On the concept of power in political science, see Harold Lasswell and Abraham Kaplan, *Power and Society* (New Haven, CT: Yale University Press, 1950); and Harold Lasswell, *Politics: Who Gets What, When, How* (Cleveland: Meridian Books, 1958).

5. See Hans Morgenthau, *Politics among Nations: The Struggle for Power and Peace,* 3rd ed. (New York: Knopf, 1962), Chapter 12, 178ff.

6. See the discussion of balance and equilibrium in Ernst Haas, "The Balance of Power: Concept, Prescription, or Propaganda," *World Politics, 5* (1953): 459–474.

7. Nicholas J. Spykman, *America's Strategy in World Politics* (New York: Harcourt Brace, 1942), 460.

8. The failure of American policy during this period is the theme of Carr's classic, *Twenty Years' Crisis.*

9. Samuel Huntington, *The Clash of Civilizations* (New York: Simon & Schuster/Touchstone Books, 1997), 209–213.

10. Henry Kissinger, *American Foreign Policy,* expanded ed. (New York: Norton, 1974), 31–32.

11. Thompson, *Political Realism,* 68.

12. Morgenthau, *Politics among Nations,* 414ff; Thompson, *Political Realism,* 189–197.

13. Kenneth Pollock, "Saddam's Useful Idiots," *Wall Street Journal,* March 15, 2004.

14. John Lewis Gaddis, *The United States and the Origins of the Cold War, 1941–1947* (New York: Columbia University Press, 1972).

15. Kennan first stated the doctrine of containment in a now celebrated

"anonymous" article, X, "The Sources of Soviet Conduct," *Foreign Affairs, 25* (July 1957): 566–582; see also George Kennan, "The United States and the Soviet Union, 1917–1976," *Foreign Affairs, 54* (July 1976): 570–590.

16. Reported in Charles Kegley and Eugene Wittkopf, *World Politics: Trend and Transformation*, 4th ed. (New York: St. Martin's Press, 1993), 93.

17. Sir Malcom Kennedy, *A Short History of Communism in Southeast Asia* (London: Wiedenfeld & Nicolson, 1957), 19, argues, "Communism and Nationalism in South and East Asia have become so intertwined as to be almost indistinguishable one from the other."

18. Virginia Thomson and Richard Adloff, *The Left Wing in Southeast Asia* (New York: Sloan for the I.P.R., 1950), 205.

19. For example, Norman Podhoretz, "The Case for Bombing Iran," *Commentary, 123*(6) (June 2007): 17–23.

20. The strongest case for this conclusion is made by Huntington, *The Clash of Civilizations,* 209ff.

21. John Mearsheimer and Stephan Walt, "The Israeli Lobby," *London Review of Books, 28*(9) (May 11, 2006). Compare a more extensive version, John Mearsheimer and Stephan Walt, "The Israeli Lobby and American Foreign Policy," *Middle East Policy, 13*(3) (Fall 2006): 1–59.

22. Joan Peters, *From Time Immemorial: The Origins of the Arab–Jewish Conflict over Palestine* (New York: Harper & Row Perennial Library, 1984), 221.

23. Peters, *From Time Immemorial*, especially Chapters 11–14.

24. Near East Research Inc., *Near East Report*, September 13, 2004, 4.

25. *The International Jerusalem Post*, June 17, 2007, 17.

26. Jerusalem Centre for Public Affairs, "Israel Campus Beat," http://jcpa.org/, accessed October 4, 2004.

27. Yossi Klein Halevi and Michael B. Oren, "Israel's Unexpected Victory over Terrorism," *New Republic* (September 27, 2004): 19–20.

28. Daniel Pipes, *Militant Islam Reaches America* (New York: Norton, 2002), 52–64.

29. Daniel Pipes, "Who Is the Real Enemy?" *Commentary, 113* (January 2002).

30. See the analysis of this trend in Norman Podhoretz, "How to Win World War IV," *Commentary, 113* (February 2002): 19–30.

31. Halevi and Oren, "Israel's Unexpected Victory over Terrorism," 19–23.

32. *The International Jerusalem Post*, June 17, 2007, 17.

33. Christopher Caldwell, "Islamic Europe," *The Weekly Standard* (October 4, 2004): 15–16.

34. Amitai Etzioni, *Security First: For a Muscular, Moral Foreign Policy* (New Haven: Yale University Press, 2007).

35. For example, Norman Podhoretz, "The Case for Bombing Iraq," *Commentary* (June 2007).

36. Whitney Raas and Austin Long, "Osirak Redux: Assessing Israel's Capacity to Destroy Iranian Nuclear Facilities," *International Security, 31*(4) (Spring 2007): 7–33.

Chapter 13

1. "UNC students plan another Tancredo protest," *Raleigh News and Observer* online blog, April 21, 2010.

2. *This minimal definition* may be found expostulated most notably in Joseph Schumpeter's classic, *Capitalism, Socialism and Democracy* (New York: Harper Torchbooks, 1942 and 1962), Chapter 22.

3. Dissenting opinion in *Abrams v. United States,* 250 U.S. 616 (1919), at 630.

4. Benjamin Knoll, "Did Anti-Mormonism Cost Mitt Romney the 2012 Election?" *The Huffington Post,*

Oct 18, 2013, http://www
.huffingtonpost.com/benjamin-
knoll/mitt-romney-mormon_b
_4121217.html, accessed March
2013.

5. Amitai Etzioni, *The Spirit of Community* (New York: Crown Publishers,
1993).

6. For example, Samuel Huntington,
*The Clash of Civilizations: The
Remaking of the World Order* (New
York: Simon and Schuster, 1996),
263–272.

7. Robert D. Putnam, "E Pluribus
Unum: Diversity and Community in
the Twenty-first Century, the 2006
Johan Skytte Prize Lecture," *Scandi-
navian Political Studies, 30*(2) (2007):
137–174.

8. *Roe v. Wade,* 410 U.S. 113 (1973).

9. *Webster v. Reproductive Health Services,*
109 S. Ct. 3040 (1989).

10. *Stenberg v. Carhart,* 530 U.S. 914
(2000); and *Gonzales v. Carhart,* 550
U.S. 124 (2007).

11. *Planned Parenthood of Southeastern
Pennsylvania v. Casey,* 505 U.S. 833
(1992).

12. *Planned Parenthood of Columbia Inc. v.
American Coalition of Life Activists,* 244
F. 3d. 1007 (2001).

13. *Hill v. Colorado,* 530 U.S. 703 (2000).

14. *Adderly v. Florida,* 385 U.S. 39 (1966).

15. *Gonzales v. Oregon,* 546 U.S. 243
(2006).

16. For a scholarly inquiry into the
meaning of the freedom of speech
clause for its authors, a study that
concludes that the authors merely
understood it to embrace this common law definition, see Leonard
Levy, *The Legacy of Suppression*
(Cambridge: Harvard University
Press, 1960).

17. *Chaplinsky v. New Hampshire,* 315
U.S. 568 (1942).

18. Lori Preuitt and George Kiriyama,
"American Flag Clothing Sparks
New Protest," *MSNBC.COM,*

http://www.msnbc.msn.com/id/
36998746/ns/local_news-san_
francisco_bay_area_ca/, accessed
May 6, 2010.

19. *R.A.V. v. City of St. Paul,* 505 U.S.
377 (1992), 379.

20. The discussion of the Michigan policy
is drawn from Dinesh D'Souza, *Illiberal Education* (New York: Free Press,
1991), 140–144.

21. "Embassies Burn in Cartoon Protest,"
BBC News, February 4, 2006, http://
news.bbc.co.uk/2/hi/middle_east/
4681294.stm, accessed May 1, 2010.

22. Scott Collins and Matea Gold, "South
Park Threat No Joke," *Los Angeles
Times,* April 23, 2010, A1.

23. *Regina v. Hicklin,* L.R. 3 Q.B. (1868).

24. *Roth v. United States,* 354 U.S. 476
(1957).

25. *Miller v. California,* 413 U.S. 15 (1973).

26. *Jenkins v. Georgia,* 418 U.S. 153 (1974).

27. *Sable Communications of California v.
Federal Communications Commission,* 49
U.S. 115 (1989).

28. *Reno v. American Civil Liberties Union,*
521 U.S. 844 (1997).

29. *Jacobellis v. Ohio,* 378 U.S. 84 (1974).

30. William Kerns, "Breast-Feeding Art
Ban Spurs Protest Plan," *Lubbock
Avalanche-Journal,* December 20,
2007, http://lubbockonline.com/
stories/122007/loc_227209555.
shtml, last accessed March 2014.

31. *Ashcroft v. Free Speech Coalition,* 535
U.S. 234 (2002).

32. *Ashcroft v. Free Speech Coalition,* 535
U.S. 234 (2002).

33. *The Report of the Commission on
Obscenity and Pornography* (Washing-
ton, DC: U.S. Government Printing
Office, 1970).

34. James Q. Wilson, "Violence,
Pornography and Social Science," *The
Public Interest, 22* (Winter 1971): 45–
61; and J. D. Unwin, *Sex and Culture*
(London: Oxford University Press,
1934). These arguments are well
summarized in Harry M. Clor,

"Commentary on the Report of the Commission on Obscenity and Pornography," in Clor, ed., *Censorship and Freedom of Expression* (Skokie, IL: Rand McNally, 1971): 119–129.

35. Milton Diamond, "Pornography, Public Acceptance, and Sex Related Crime: A Review," *International Journal of Law and Psychiatry, 32* (2009): 304–314.

36. Diana Russell, *Dangerous Relationships: Pornography, Misogyny, and Rape* (Thousand Oaks, CA: Sage, 1998), 158.

37. Russell, *Dangerous Relationships*, 1998.

38. Quoted in *Newsweek,* May 25, 1981, p. 46.

39. *Gallup* May 3–6 Values and Belief Survey (2012), http://www.gallup.com/poll/154799/americans-including-catholics-say-birth-control-morally.aspx, last accessed March 2014.

40. *City of Los Angeles v. Almeda Books,* 535 U.S. 425 (2002).

41. *Butler v. Michigan,* 352 U.S. 380 (1957), at 383–384.

42. *Stanley v. Georgia,* 394 U.S. 557 (1969).

43. *Paris Adult Theater v. Slaton,* 413 U.S. 439 (1973).

44. Catharine MacKinnon, *Only Words* (Cambridge: Harvard University Press, 1993).

45. *Everson v. Board of Education,* 390 U.S. 1 (1947).

46. *Lemon v. Kurtzman,* 403 U.S. 602 (1971).

47. *Mitchell v. Helms,* 530 U.S. 793 (2000).

48. *Board of Education v. Allen,* 392 U.S. 236 (1968).

49. *Lemon v. Kurtzman,* 403 U.S. 602 (1971).

50. *Mueller v. Allen,* 463 U.S. 388 (1983).

51. *Zobrest v. Catalina Foothills School District,* 509 U.S. 1 (1993).

52. *Zelman v. Simmons-Harris,* 536 U.S. 639 (2002).

53. *Zelman v. Simmons-Harris,* 536 U.S. 639 (2002).

54. *School District of Abington Township v. Schempp* and *Murray v. Curlett,* 374 U.S. 203 (1963).

55. *Engle v. Vitale,* 370 U.S. 421 (1962).

56. *Elk Grove School District v. Newdow,* 542 U.S. 1 (2004).

57. *Lee v. Weisman,* 505 U.S. 577 (1992).

58. *Santa Fe Independent School District v. Doe,* 530 U.S. 290 (2000).

59. *Illinois ex. rel. McCollum v. Board of Education,* 33 U.S. 203 (1948), at 227.

60. Frank Way, "Survey Research on Judicial Decisions: The Prayer and Bible Reading Cases," *Western Political Quarterly, 21* (June 1968): 189–205.

61. Cited in Stephen Wasby, *The Impact of the United States Supreme Court: Some Perspectives* (Homewood, IL: Dorsey Press, 1970), 134–135.

62. *Lynch v. Donnelly,* 465 U.S. 668 (1984).

63. *County of Allegheny v. American Civil Liberties Union,* 492 U.S. 573 (1989).

64. *Stone v. Graham,* 499 U.S. 39 (1980).

65. *Van Orden v. Perry,* 545 U.S. 677 (2005).

66. *McCreary County v. ACLU,* 545 U.S. 844 (2005).

67. *Van Orden v. Perry,* 545 U.S. 677 (2005), *Justice Breyer's Concurrence.*

68. *Salazar v. Buono,* 559 U.S. No. 08-472 (2010).

69. *Cantwell v. Connecticut,* 310 U.S. 296 (1940); and *West Virginia State Board of Education v. Barnette,* 319 U.S. 624 (1943).

70. See, among such cases, *Reynolds v. U.S.,* 98 U.S. 145 (1879); and *Hardin v. Tennessee,* 188 Tenn. 17 (1949).

71. For example, *Jacobson v. Massachusetts,* 197 U.S. 11 (1955).

72. 374 U.S. 398 (1963).

73. *Wisconsin v. Yoder,* 406 U.S. 205 (1972).

74. *Employment Division of Oregon v. Smith,* 494 U.S. 872 (1990).

75. *City of Boerne v. Flores,* 521 U.S. 507 (1997).

76. *Cutter v. Wilkinson,* 544 U.S. 709 (2005).

77. *Church of the Lukumi Babalu Aye v. City of Hialeah,* 508 U.S. 520 (1993).

78. *Locke v. Davey,* 540 U.S. 712 (2004).

Index

Note: Page numbers in italic type indicate figures, boxes, or tables.